THE ROUTLEDGE COMPANION TO MIGRATION, COMMUNICATION, AND POLITICS

The Routledge Companion to Migration, Communication, and Politics brings together academics from numerous disciplines to show the legal, political, communicative, theoretical, methodological, and media implications of migration. The collection makes the compelling case that migration does not occur in a vacuum; rather, it is driven by and reacts to various factors, including the political, economic, and cultural worlds in which individuals live.

The 25 chapters reveal the complex nature of migration from various angles, not only looking at how policy affects migrants but also how individuals and marginalized groups are impacted by such acts. In Part I, contributors examine migration law, debating the role of the state in managing migration flows and investigating existing migration policy. Part II offers theories and methods that integrate communication studies, political science, and law into the study of migration, including cultural fusion theory and Gebserian theory. Part III looks at how contemporary perceptions of migration and migrants intersect with media representations across media outlets worldwide. Finally, Part IV offers case studies that present the intricacies of migration within different cultural, national, and political groups.

Migration is the key political, economic, and cultural issue of our time and this companion takes the next step in the debate; namely, the effects of the how, in addition to the how and why. Researchers and students of communication, politics, media, and law will find this an invaluable intervention.

Stephen M. Croucher is Professor and Head of the School of Communication, Journalism and Marketing at Massey University, New Zealand. He researches migration, religion and conflict. He has authored 10 books, numerous book chapters and more than 100 journal articles.

João R. Caetano is Professor of Law and Political Science at Aberta University, Portugal and Pro Rector for International Advancement and Legal Affairs. He researches migration, citizenship and European issues. He has authored more than 100 articles, book chapters and books in several languages.

Elsa A. Campbell is a doctoral candidate in the Department of Music, Art and Culture Studies, University of Jyväskylä, Finland and coordinator of the VIBRAC Skille-Lehikoinen Centre for Vibroacoustic Therapy and Research, Finland. Her research focuses on the use of music and sound vibration in medical rehabilitation settings.

THE ROUTLEDGE COMPANION TO MIGRATION, COMMUNICATION, AND POLITICS

Edited by Stephen M. Croucher, João R. Caetano, and Elsa A. Campbell

Routledge
Taylor & Francis Group
LONDON AND NEW YORK

First published 2019 by Routledge

2 Park Square, Milton Park, Abingdon, Oxon OX14 4RN
605 Third Avenue, New York, NY 10017

Routledge is an imprint of the Taylor & Francis Group, an informa business

First issued in paperback 2022

British Library Cataloguing-in-Publication Data
A catalogue record for this book is available from the British Library

Library of Congress Cataloging-in-Publication Data
A catalog record has been requested for this book

ISBN: 978-1-138-05814-9 (hbk)
ISBN: 978-1-03-233869-9 (pbk)
DOI: 10.4324/9781315164472

Typeset in Bembo
by Swales & Willis Ltd

Visit the eResources: www.routledge.com/9781138058149

CONTENTS

FIGURES

TABLES

CONTRIBUTORS

Olga L. Antineskul is an Associate Professor in the Department of Foreign Languages, National Research University – Higher School of Economics (Perm, Russia). Her research focus, initially primarily on text analysis from a gender perspective, has recently expanded to include psychological aspects of foreign language learning and teaching, with particular reference to Business English, as well as discourse analysis and intercultural communication.

Gina G. Barker teaches at Liberty University in Lynchburg, Virginia, USA. Her research focuses on intercultural adaptation and acculturation processes, intercultural marriage and family communication, cultural influences on news and advertising, as well as on third-culture individuals.

Daniel Bertolucci Torres is a Master's candidate in human rights at Universidade de São Paulo. From 2015 to 2017, he was a lawyer/protection officer at the Refugee Reference Center, Caritas Arquidiocesana de São Paulo.

Pablo Biderbost is Assistant Professor at the Universidad Pontificia Comillas, Spain.

Claudio Bolzman is Professeur Ordinaire at the University of Applied Sciences and Arts of Western Switzerland.

Guillermo Boscán is Associate Professor at the Universidad de Salamanca, Spain.

Elsa A. Campbell is a doctoral candidate in the Department of Music, Art and Culture Studies, University of Jyväskylä, Finland, and coordinator of the VIBRAC Skille-Lehikoinen Centre for Vibroacoustic Therapy and Research, Finland. Her research focuses on the use of music and sound vibration in medical rehabilitation settings.

Pedro Caridade de Freitas has a PhD in Law from the College of Law of Universidade de Lisboa, 2010. He is Associate Professor at the College of Law of Universidade de Lisboa, where he is responsible for lectures on History of Portuguese Law, Roman Law, History of International Relations, and History of International Law. He is also President of the History of Law and Political Thought Society of the College of Law of Universidade de Lisboa.

Janet Colvin is the Associate Dean for the College of Humanities and Social Sciences at Utah Valley University, USA. Dr Colvin has won numerous teaching and research awards including a Board of Trustees award for outstanding contribution to the university. Her main area of research focuses on inclusivity and diversity in the classroom, university, and community.

Stephen M. Croucher is Professor and Head of the School of Communication, Journalism and Marketing at Massey University, New Zealand. He researches migration, religion, and conflict. He has authored 10 books, numerous book chapters, and more than 100 journal articles.

Francisco Javier Donaire Villa is Associate Professor of Constitutional Law at Carlos III University of Madrid, Spain.

Willemijn Dortant is a Lecturer in Media and Communication at Erasmus University Rotterdam (EUR). Her main research interests include minority and social inequality issues.

Debalina Dutta is a Senior Lecturer in the School of Communication, Journalism and Marketing at Massey University, New Zealand. Dr Dutta's research interests are in the areas of gender and culture in science and technology. Her work has been published in outlets such as the *Journal of Intercultural Communication Research* and *Management Communication Quarterly*, among others.

Maria Faraone is a practitioner and academic in the field of resettlement and integration and land use conflict. Her work in resettlement brings together the fields of condition assessments and collaborative engagement to create tailored contextual responses to ease land use conflict. Maria is a Senior Lecturer at Oxford Brookes University in the School of Architecture and teaches in multidisciplinary faculties across scientific, economic, and planning fields. She also researches and has created vision strategies for NGOs in Europe dealing with migration and spatial integration.

Flora Galy-Badenas is a PhD student and Assistant Lecturer at Massey University, New Zealand. Her research interests include intersectionality, gendered/racialized mediation, politics/politicians, (feminist) critical discourse analysis, media studies, cross-cultural/intercultural studies, and communication.

Pedro Góis is a Professor in Sociology and Methodology in the Faculty of Economics, University of Coimbra, and a Researcher at the Centre for Social Studies (CES). He is an expert in sociology of migration and quantitative methodologies. His most recent research-driven publications used quantitative and qualitative methodologies and include papers and books on refugees in Europe; transnational ethnic identity; Portuguese immigration and emigration; Brazilian migration and Eastern European migrants; discrimination practices in the labour market; immigrants' descendants; and diasporic engagement practices and policies.

Eva G. T. Green is Associate Professor of Social Psychology at the University of Lausanne. Her research focuses on intergroup relations (e.g., prejudice, power relations, political identities) in multicultural societies.

Chia-Fang (Sandy) Hsu is Associate Professor of Communication and Journalism at the University of Wyoming, USA. She earned her PhD from Washington State University in 2002. She has taught research methods, nonverbal communication, group communication, and communication and conflict at the undergraduate and graduate levels. Her research interests focus on communication apprehension in various contexts, particularly intercultural interaction.

Liliana Lyra Jubilut has a PhD and a Master's in International Law from the Universidade de São Paulo and a Master's in International Legal Studies (LLM) from the School of Law, New York University School of Law. She is a Professor on the Post-graduate Program in Law at Universidade Católica de Santos, where she coordinates the Research Group "Direitos Humanos e Vulnerabilidades," and has been a part of the coordination of the UNHCR Sérgio Vieira de Mello Chair since 2013.

Eric Mark Kramer is Second Century Presidential Professor of Communication at the University of Oklahoma and Fulbright Scholar to Bulgaria (1992/93). He is also an affiliate faculty of the SIAS Institute and Department of International and Areas Studies and also on the faculty of Film and Media Studies. He is a Senior Editor of the *Oxford Research Encyclopedia of Communication* (2015–present), responsible for the volumes on International Communication. He is Associate Editor of the *Journal of Intercultural Communication Research* (2011–present).

Mingsheng Li is a Senior Lecturer in the School of Communication, Journalism and Marketing, Massey University, New Zealand. He teaches Business Communication and Cross-Cultural Communication at undergraduate and postgraduate levels. His research interests include migrant studies, international education, and issues affecting international students' cultural adaptation.

André de Lima Madureira has a Master's in International Law from Universidade Católica de Santos and an MSc in Human Rights from the London School of Economics. He is a member of the research group "Direitos Humanos e Vulnerabilidades" and of the UNHCR Sérgio Vieira de Mello Chair, both at Universidade Católica de Santos.

Yang Liu received her PhD from the University of Oklahoma, majoring in intercultural communication, and is currently working as an Assistant Professor in the School of English and International Studies, Beijing Foreign Studies University. Dr Liu's research focuses on the *Other*-identity of sojourners and immigrants in host countries, exploring changes brought by intercultural communication to these migrating individuals' cultural identity. Her studies on these topics have been presented and published in three different countries (the United States, China, and South Korea). In addition, Dr Liu has four years' working experience in Journalism, Marketing, and Public Relations.

Elvis Nshom Ngwayuh (PhD, University of Jyväskylä) is a University Teacher in the Department of Language and Communication at the University of Jyväskylä, Finland.

Rachel de Oliveira Lopes is a PhD candidate in International Law at the Universidade de São Paulo. She has a Master's in International Law from Universidade Católica de Santos. She is a Member of the research group "Direitos Humanos e Vulnerabilidades" and of the UNHCR Sergio Vieira de Mello Chair, both at Universidade Católica de Santos.

Tatiana M. Permyakova is a Professor in the Department of Foreign Languages, National Research University – Higher School of Economics (Perm, Russia). Her research interests focus on intercultural communication theories and discourse analysis, with an emphasis on EFL and ELT situations, English for specific purposes, and professional and business communication.

Diyako Rahmani (PhD, University of Jyväskylä) is a Lecturer in the School of Communication, Journalism and Marketing at Massey University, New Zealand.

Julija Sardelić is a Marie Skłodowska-Curie Postdoctoral Fellow at the KU Leuven International and European Studies Institute (LINES). Her research encompasses broader themes of citizenship and migration, but she particularly focuses on the position of marginalized minorities and migrants in Europe (such as Romani minorities, refugees and other forced migrants, legally invisible and stateless persons). Before joining LINES, Julija was a Postdoctoral Researcher in the School of Law and Social Justice (University of Liverpool), a Max Weber Fellow (European University Institute), and a Research Fellow in the School of Law (University of Edinburgh).

Oriane Sarrasin is a Lecturer in the Institute of Psychology, University of Lausanne. In her research, she puts into perspective individual- and contextual-level antecedents of social and political attitudes and behaviors (e.g., toward immigration or environment-related issues).

Shubhra Seth is an Assistant Professor in the Department of Political Science at the Indraprastha College for Women, University of Delhi, India. Her areas of academic interest are in internally displaced persons, forced migration, and disability studies. Her primary research area is conflict-induced internal displacement in South Asia, which she formalised in her PhD (2016) from the School of International Studies, Jawaharlal Nehru University, New Delhi, India.

Mélodine Sommier (PhD) works as an Assistant Professor in Intercultural Communication in the department of Media and Communication at Erasmus University Rotterdam (EUR). She actively publishes about intercultural communication, media representations, migration, and education. Mélodine is particularly interested in the conflation of culture with dimensions such as race and religion, and outcomes regarding the production of difference.

Anthony T. Spencer earned his doctoral degree from the University of Oklahoma (2008) and is currently on the faculty of Universidad Americana in Managua, Nicaragua.

Elira Turdubaeva is Head of the Department of Journalism and Mass Communications at the American University of Central Asia, Bishkek, Kyrgyzstan.

Yi Yang was awarded a Master's Degree in Communication Management by Massey University in 2009. She migrated to Australia in 2012. Her research interests include challenges facing Asian international students. She is currently staying at home looking after her children.

Alena Zelenskaia is an instructor in the Department of Journalism and Mass Communications at the American University of Central Asia, Bishkek, Kyrgyzstan.

Cheng Zeng has a PhD from the University of Jyväskylä and is an Assistant Professor in the Department of Communication at North Dakota State University.

S. D. Zuckerman gained a PhD from the University of Oklahoma in 2003. He is a Fulbright Scholar and Professor of Communication at California, Sacramento and was past president of the International Jean Gebser Society. He is author of a chapter in Volume I of the *Jean Gebser Annual*, a paper presenter and reviewer for the International Jean Gebser Society conferences and publications, and co-author of *Intercultural Communication & Global Integration*, a Gebserian textbook.

INTRODUCTION

Stephen M. Croucher, João R. Caetano, & Elsa A. Campbell

Since human kind began to travel, migration has been an integral human process. How people migrate has changed over time; however, the primary reasons (the why) for migration have remained the same: war, political, economic, social, cultural, and religious. Numerous texts have been written exploring the how and why of migration. Many theories have been posited explaining what happens when migrants arrive in new homelands. In the wake of surging refugee numbers in the European Union, growing rural–urban migration in China, anti-immigrant rhetoric in the US, and changing immigrant/refugee policies in Australia (to name a few), how we approach migration has increasing importance.

In this book, we combine researchers from numerous disciplines to show the legal, political, communicative, theoretical, methodological, and media implications of migration. Collectively, these pieces demonstrate that, to fully understand the complexity of migration, one must look at it from a holistic point of view. As Croucher (2008) stated, migration does not occur in a vacuum; it is driven and a response to various factors including the political, economic, and cultural worlds in which individuals live.

This book has 25 chapters and is divided into four parts: I Migration law, II Migration theories and methods, III The media and migration, and IV Case studies on migration. Within each part, authors cover a host of topics around the intersections of communication, migration, and law. The authors come from a wide range of philosophical and methodological backgrounds, and from various geographic regions.

Part I, Migration law, comprises five chapters. Chapter 1, "Emigration law: does it still make sense?," is by Pedro Caridade de Freitas. Here, de Freitas takes a philosophical approach in asking what an immigrant is and whether the State has an obligation to respond to migration flows.

Chapter 2, "Current challenges to the international protection of refugees and other migrants: the role of and developments from the United Nations 2016 Summit," is by Liliana Lyra Jubilut, André de Lima Madureira, and Daniel Bertolucci Torres. Here, the authors analyze the normative and rhetorical developments of the 2016 UN Summit on Refugees and Migrants and its documents. The chapter presents the current and prospective international landscape of migrants' and refugees' rights and protection.

Chapter 3, "*Quo vadis*? The European Union's migration and asylum policy," is by Francisco Javier Donaire Villa. In this chapter, Donaire Villa reflects on the EU's migration policy. It surveys the most relevant EU legal frameworks, both primary and secondary legislation, distinguishing between those enacted before and since the so-called "refugee crisis." It also addresses the pragmatic programs and solutions devised by the EU. The work concludes with an assessment of the status quo, as well as with tentative considerations on the potential uncertainty of the EU's migration policies.

Chapter 4, "The politics of internally displaced persons," is by Shubhra Seth. This chapter explores the politics surrounding the category of "forced migration" identified by the United Nations as Internally Displaced Persons (IDPs). Millions of people across the globe are displaced due to conflict; they are so vulnerable, yet await recognition by their home states. Living in permanent "relief camps," IDPs struggle to gain their rights as citizens in their own homeland.

Chapter 5, "Refuge and political asylum in Latin America," is by Liliana Lyra Jubilut and Rachel de Oliveira Lopes. This study describes the institutes of political asylum and refuge in Latin America to showcase the peculiarities of each one, as well as the zones of intersection between them. It describes both institutes, then presents the regional aspects of refugee status in Latin America, and turns to the contributions of the Cartagena Declaration and its revisional process and the Inter-American human rights system, which highlights the region's human rights approach towards refugees and political asylees.

Part II, Migration theories and methods, comprises six chapters. Chapter 6, "Method issues and working with newly-arrived women refugees," is by Janet Colvin. This chapter, using interviews with eight newly-arrived refugee women from a variety of circumstances, countries, and cultures, compares the benefits and drawbacks of narrative analysis, small stories, grounded theory, and phenomenological methods to aid in understanding refugee research.

Chapter 7, "Cultural fusion," is by Eric Mark Kramer. This chapter argues that cultural fusion theory (CFT) is an alternative to assimilationist theories. Here, Kramer asserts that CFT and pan-evolution theory argue that foreign ideas and behaviors are integrated by cultural systems, added to already existing repertoires, and made sense of by interlocutors' relative perspectives.

Chapter 8, "Gebserian theory and method," is by S. D. Zuckerman. This chapter introduces the theory and method of Jean Gebser (1905–1973) as it is used in Communication and related disciplines. The chapter covers the five consciousness structures, as well as the ideas of mutation, integrality, and systasis. It advocates using Gebser's method as a holistic and humanizing approach to the study of culture.

Chapter 9, "Immigrant migration and communication apprehension," is by Chia-Fang (Sandy) Hsu. Given the pervasive impact of communication anxiety on immigrants, this chapter reviews literature related to communication anxiety experienced by migrants during the cross-cultural adaptation process. This literature review discusses both the causes of communication anxiety and remedies when adapting to a new culture.

Chapter 10, "Reconstructing the migration communication discourse," is by Pedro Góis and Maria Faraone. It encourages academics to write for the public to balance access to information on critical issues where public sentiment has an important effect, such as the refugee movement. Influencing public sentiment is about using academic research to inspire involvement in debates that seek to find reason and justice. The chapter includes strategies for academics on writing for the general public.

Chapter 11, "Third-culture individuals," is by Gina G. Barker. Here, Barker reviews research on third-culture individuals. While a formal theory of third-culture individuals has yet to emerge, researchers have recently begun testing assertions made in popular and professional literature about their intercultural competence, enhanced adaptability, social sensitivity, open-mindedness, and cultural marginality. This research has produced evidence that their unique intercultural adaptation makes them especially well-equipped to thrive in contexts that require intercultural communication, adaptation, language acquisition, mediation, diplomacy, boundary-spanning, and management of diversity.

Part III, The media and migration, comprises five chapters. Chapter 12, "Migration and migrants within and to Europe," is by Mélodine Sommier, Willemijn Dortant, and Flora Galy-Badenas. This chapter reviews recent academic articles (2001–2016) about media and migration, both within and to Europe. This chapter contributes to understanding how contemporary perceptions of migration and migrants intersect with media representations, while highlighting shortages in academic coverage and providing suggestions for future research. Articles from ten prominent journals dealing with mass media narratives were analyzed using content analysis.

Chapter 13, "Media portrayal of migration from Central Asia," is by Alena Zelenskaia and Elira Turdubaeva. This study reveals how the most visited news websites in Kyrgyzstan depict migration from Central Asia during 2015–2017. The four most popular online news media were selected, whose pages are in both Kyrgyz and Russian. A random sample of approximately 600 articles was analyzed with the help of thematic text analysis and elements of discourse analysis.

Chapter 14, "Kurdish media and immigration policies in the Kurdistan Regional Government," is by Diyako Rahmani. This study compares the approaches of Kurdish mass media and Kurdish social media run by non-professional individuals to the emigration of Kurds to Europe during the 2015 refugee crisis. Textual and visual content analysis of the media showed that, while Kurdish mass media discouraged emigration, Kurdish Facebook administrators encouraged Kurds to emigrate to Europe.

Chapter 15, "Linguistic analysis of the 'immigrant' as represented in the Russian media," is by Tatiana Permyakova and Olga Antineskul. The study addresses the representation of the linguistic and cultural type (LCT) the "immigrant" in the newspaper subcorpus of the Russian National Corpus (RNC), with a sample covering the period from 2000 until the present. The linguistic research methodology involves two stages: first, analysis of the general meanings of "immigrant" in Russian and, second, analysis of its culture-specific meanings. While immigrants in the Russian print media are presented, by and large, as offenders rather than victims, they are also frequently regarded not as a threat but as a benefit to society. The culture-specific concepts that account for this bifurcation are those relating to history, religion, cultural constructs, and ethno-geography.

Chapter 16, "Applications of music for migrants," is by Elsa A. Campbell. The importance of music for health and wellbeing dates back to antiquity. Its role in society as a whole, but also on an individual level, has remained seminal, and its therapeutic efficacy is indisputable whether it is part of larger group-based activities or for personal emotional regulation. This chapter addresses the use of music therapy with migrants, methods and interventions applied in such situations, and its potential for treating symptoms resultant of such physical, emotional, and cultural upheaval.

Part IV, Case studies on migration, has nine chapters. These investigate migration, communication, and politics in various parts of the world. Each demonstrates the intricacies of migration within different groups. Chapter 17, "Patterns of political transnationalism in a non-traditional diaspora," is by Pablo Biderbost, Claudio Bolzman, and Guillermo Boscán. Considering the case of Swiss citizens in Latin America, this chapter is part of a major study aimed at generating empirical evidence in a non-traditional migrant flow. Using online data collection tools, the study population was surveyed to understand its relationship to the Swiss political system. Specifically, information was gleaned on study participants' civic competencies (political knowledge, political efficacy, political attention, and political participation) and levels of ideological continuity/discontinuity.

Chapter 18, "Nicaraguan immigration to Costa Rica," is by Anthony Spencer. While traditional communication research focuses on South to North immigration, much of the world's immigration patterns are South to South. Through observations and in-depth interviews, this chapter examines how "White" Costa Ricans and "Non-White" immigrant Nicaraguans discuss and understand immigration in Costa Rica. The chapter interrogates this data through the lens of language ideology to investigate the phenomenon and hear from both the marginalized Nicaraguan immigrant population as well as the host culture in Costa Rica.

Chapter 19, "Individual and contextual explanations of attitudes towards immigration," is by Eva G. T. Green and Oriane Sarrasin. This chapter introduces multilevel research examining the interplay of individual and contextual accounts of anti-immigration attitudes and radical right-wing voting. This approach allows for examining how the attitudes of individuals are shaped by the socio-structural and normative contexts in which they develop, over and above the individual-level determinants of these attitudes. Research conducted in Switzerland is presented to exemplify this research approach.

Chapter 20, "The politics around Romani migration," is by Julija Sardelić. This chapter traces the political and legal discourse connected to the governance of Romani migration in Europe. First, it shows how State and European Union institutions governed the movement of Roma who are EU citizens living in an EU Member State other than their own country of citizenship. Second, it offers an analysis of the migration of Roma third-country nationals, who sought asylum in different EU Member States. The chapter argues that the notion of Romani migration was used and abused as a symptom within broader political debates on migration governance.

Chapter 21, "Exploring the relationship between acculturation preferences, threat, intergroup contact, and prejudice towards immigrants in Finland," is by Elvis Nshom Ngwayuh and Stephen Croucher. This study had three main aims: first, to examine the relationship between perceived threat (realistic threat and symbolic threat) and acculturation preferences (assimilation and integration) towards immigrants living in Finland; second, to understand the relationship between acculturation preferences (assimilation and integration) and prejudice towards immigrants; and, third, to test the moderating role of intergroup contact on the aforementioned relationships. The sample for this study consisted of 795 Finnish adolescents.

Chapter 22, "(Re)framing cultural intelligence in organizations," is by Debalina Dutta. This chapter interrogates the framework of cultural intelligence by examining the practices of organizational adjustment and barriers faced by minorities. Shifting away from the dominant binaries of inclusion and adjustment by individuals, the role of organizational practices and cultural access is questioned. By qualitatively interviewing 20 women who belong to the North Eastern region of India employed in professional organizations, the chapter articulates new logics of adjustment in the cultural spaces of organizations by organizational entrants.

Chapter 23, "Return migration," is by Mingsheng Li and Yi Yang. This study examines the re-entry acculturative challenges and experiences of foreign-educated Chinese returnees in China. The study found that the receiving countries' push and the origin country's pull factors played a critical role in motivating Chinese students to return to China. The push factors include immigration policy changes, difficulties finding employment, the glass-ceiling effect, White privilege, and discrimination. Chinese students were lured back to China by these pull factors: rapid economic development, career opportunities, attractive government policies, family ties, and a sense of belonging.

Chapter 24, "Communication with non-host-nationals in migration," is by Yang Liu. The role of interaction with host-nationals in promoting sojourners' intercultural adjustment has been discussed in depth. However, two other types of communication have been neglected in intercultural communication studies. One is sojourners' communication with their co-ethnics and the other is with their international fellows (international students from other countries). This chapter focuses on these two aspects and argues that these two types of communication can contribute to sojourning students' acculturation in host cultures by providing social support.

Chapter 25, "Internal migrants and their left-behind families in China," is by Cheng Zeng. Rural migration in China has a profound impact on the demographics and ways of life in both receiving and sending areas. Migrant workers are needed for economic growth, but they are not welcomed by the locals and are generally living marginalized lives in host cities. This is particularly true in China, where the largest labor migration in human history has taken place: 270 million rural citizens have moved to urban cities for a better future. In addition to everyday discrimination, rural migrants experience institutional discrimination based on the household registration system (*hukou*) in China. This chapter adds to the migrant literature by reviewing previous research on domestic migrants and their left-behind families in China.

This compilation displays the complex nature of migration from various angles, not only looking at how policy affects migrants but also taking a closer look at how individuals and marginalized groups are impacted by such acts. These chapters take the next step in the migration discussion; namely, the *effects* of the how, in addition to the how and why. Migration is essentially a story about humans. The *human* in migration processes and outcomes is integral in understanding how policy and law-makers can manage situations such as the so-called "refugee crisis" without losing sight of the people at the focal point of the situation. Migration research should not be isolated from the realities of migration experiences and both the human rights (Fiddian-Qasmiyeh, Loescher, Long, & Sigona, 2014) and emotional and psychological implications thereof. These chapters – addressing both forced and non-forced migration – show that discrimination of and prejudice towards the "other" is a human reaction to migration regardless of the context.

The intricacies of dealing with mass migration are evident in the misunderstanding associated with migrants' and refugees' rights within this difficult issue and how multi-level attitudes shape this understanding. Bringing these concepts to the fore is an increasingly pertinent act and we hope this companion to migration, communication, and politics will provide greater insight into the complex, multi-layered, and intensely human experience that is migration.

References

Croucher, S. M. (2008). *Looking beyond the hijab*. Cresskill, NJ: Hampton Press.

Fiddian-Qasmiyeh, E., Loescher, G., Long, K., & Sigona, N. (Eds.). (2014). *The Oxford handbook of refugee and forced migration studies*. New York: Oxford University Press.

PART I

Migration law

1
EMIGRATION LAW

Does it still make sense? Some short historical and legal reflections

Pedro Caridade de Freitas

Introduction

We cannot address migration flows without making a prior delimitation of the topic. Nowadays, there are several migration flows. In developed countries, we witness a globalization movement with highly qualified professionals moving from one country to another to develop their professional activity, either because they work in multinational companies and integrate the internal mobility of the company or because they seek better working conditions in another country. These migrants are highly educated people with expert knowledge.

These sorts of migration flow have been understood as part of the process of development of modern economies according to a 2010 United Nations document on international migration and development. We also witness migration flows from underdeveloped countries to developed countries by those in pursuit of a better quality of life. These people run away from unemployment, hunger, and thirst. These sort of migrants are often referred to as economic displaced people or economic migrants.

Finally, and related to the latter, we find the migration flows that followed the "Arab Spring" of 2011. In this case, we are looking at movements prompted by war, political instability, and hunger; that is, refugees seeking the elementary conditions for survival. It is not easy to delimit the various categories, since a war refugee is also an economic refugee and may also be a political refugee. I will focus on the latter in this text.

Since 2011, conflicts have emerged in several Arab countries on the shores of the Mediterranean. Tunisia, Egypt, Libya, and Syria have witnessed and still witness popular uprisings aiming at the deposition of authoritarian regimes existing in each country. Syria is still experiencing a bloody civil war that is killing thousands of people and prompting an unprecedented wave of refugees.

The European Union has expressed its views on these events in the Middle East and established political guidelines and priorities for its future action in its Extraordinary European Council Statement of March 11, 2011, published in the *Official Gazette* on 20 April 2011. The purpose of the European Union is to safeguard the human rights of people in conflict and to assist those Member States more directly affected by the resulting migration flows. The

United Nations has taken a similar position. The uprisings give rise to civil wars involving several factions, which increased the flow of migrants.

With the conflicts in Libya and Syria, after 2011, which are bloodier, and the establishment of the self-named Islamic State, the flow of migrants heading for Europe has increased exponentially, the main destinations being Italy, namely, the island of Lampedusa, and Greece as a result of geographic proximity. The European Union and its Member States have been facing a massive influx of refugees at their borders and feel the need to provide a timely response to these flows of people. Europe is seen as the "safe haven" by thousands of families who, by land and by sea, risking their lives in overcrowded vehicles and rubber rafts, seize their chance to gain freedom and better life conditions. During the first five months of 2015, more than 1,800 people perished when crossing into Europe and about 51,000 reached Europe, fleeing war, hunger and the economic, social, and political conditions of countries in the Middle East, Africa, and Asia. The devastating global economic crisis and, the flow of migrants from countries involved in conflict and refugees from sub-Saharan Africa require specific and solid positions from those countries most directly affected by the immigration flows.

The challenges are enormous. We need to save lives, both because thousands of people perish in those long crossings and because many others are involved in human trafficking networks that condemn migrants to slavery; we have to welcome them and provide them with decent living conditions. But the challenge is even greater than that and requires direct intervention in the various countries in conflict to promote peace and foster their sustainable development. Only in this way is it possible to start reducing the migration flows.

The states, for economic and social reasons, tend to impose restrictions and immigration quotas. However, and despite the importance of those criteria, humanitarian issues must be taken into consideration. The emergence of migration flows, as well as the position of southern European countries, leads us to consider that cooperation between the home countries of refugees and those countries through which they transit should constitute a corollary of modern international law. The drama of the refugees is not an issue of our times and, as such, in order to understand the reasons behind the migration flows and the political and economic situations of the various countries of origin, it is necessary to know both the history of international law and the history of international relations. Historical, political, economic, and social factors are paramount in explaining these movements. We are not dealing with the first migration flow to have occurred during the last two centuries and, as such, lessons from history must be learnt. The principles that should guide the migration flows were thoroughly investigated and established by the Peninsular School of Natural Law, namely, by Francisco Vitoria; therefore, it is urgent that we revisit his thinking.

The social contract

The modern state, created with the establishment of the Westphalian Peace (Freitas, 2015), is anchored in the social contract, according to which there is a legal link between the citizen and the state. The social contract idea was developed according to different premises by Hobbes and Locke and culminated in the thoughts of Rousseau. For Hobbes, the social contract takes the form of *pactum subjectionis* (the agreement to submit), whereby the only legitimate will, in the civil society, is that of the monarch, who is called upon to safeguard his subjects from arbitrariness. Locke and Rousseau argue that law is in the hands of the people, who adjust it according to their free will. Although the people waive some rights to create a national community, that community does hold on to some natural rights (Maltez, 1998).

The contractarian doctrine advocates the existence of two moments in the establishment of political power:

1. The first moment is the civil association pact, by means of which people give up their natural freedom and agree to create a new society under the protection of a power and subject to common laws.
2. The second moment is the definition of the form of government, by which the society, previously connected by the civil link, chooses the constitution, appoints the person or persons to whom the supreme power should belong, and establishes the fundamental laws which govern that republic (Merêa, 1943).

This pact establishes both the public law, which guides relations between individuals and the state, and the civil law, which regulates private relations among community members.

The subject of emigration and immigration rights

The topic of refugees as members of a national political community can be assessed on the basis of the contractarian conception. All citizens of a state have a link with it. In a situation of war, which prompts a massive flow of refugees or in the case of political refugees, the legal link connecting the citizen to the state is disrupted. In this sequence, it is important to understand if it is possible to create a new legal link with another host state. The topic of emigration thus always involves two issues: the first one refers to knowing if a given individual may abandon his or her territory of origin against the will of the state; the second one concerns whether a state is obligated to welcome a citizen of another state into its territory and to establish with him or her a new legal link. In principle and over time, legal thought began to recognize the obligation of one state to accept the citizens of another whilst nonetheless imposing some eligibility requirements.

Frédéric Martens considered, in 1886, that emigration is an imprescriptible right that belongs to each individual and therefore each citizen is free to change his or her nationality (Nys, n.d.). I cannot overlook the fact that we are facing not only a legal but also a political, economic and social issue, which, in many cases, justifies the adoption by states of measures that both restrict the right of national citizens to exit them and the right of citizens of other states to enter them (ibid).

The people's law in the Peninsular School of Natural Law

The Peninsular School of Natural Law (Silva, 1991; Wieacker, 1993), of juris naturalist nature, is consistent with second scholasticism and is marked by the metaphysical reasoning of international law. The jurist theologians turn to natural law to justify international law and restate the theocentric conception of the state and the law (Almeida Costa, 2002; Freitas, 2012). In the fields of philosophy and law, the Peninsular School draws inspiration from Aristotelian and Thomistic thinking, which sees man as by nature a rational and social being. Based on these premises, the Peninsular School concludes that states are, by nature, social beings that need one another and which, together, constitute a universal community (Verdross, 1963). Until voyages of discovery, the world was considered to be a very small place, reduced to Europe and a few other territories. In the tradition of Roman law, the maritime space is considered to be a public domain, its jurisdiction being exercised by a city, a state, or an empire.

Among the topics addressed by this school, we should mention the establishment of a new international law that tried to respond to issues emerging from discoveries; namely, the occupation of discovered or conquered territories, the freedom of the seas and trade, and the lawful condition of the inhabitants of new lands. The ruling powers in Portugal and Spain treated the Native Americans as being outside the law by denying them legal protection and viewing them as barbarians (Scott, 1928). Some of the Peninsular School jurists, such as Vitoria and Luis de Molina, warned about this legal treatment in their studies, thereby contributing to the development of relations between peoples.

Francisco Vitoria's thinking

The first great creator of modern international law was Francisco Vitoria, Dominican and professor at the University of Salamanca. Of his works, it is worth remembering *Relectiones*, namely, *De Indis* (*The Native Americans*) and *De iure belli hispanorum in barbaros* (*The Spanish War with Native Americans*). An analysis of Vitoria's internationalist thinking, despite its brevity, highlights its importance in terms of understanding the application of international law beyond the limits of European time and space. We are aware that Vitoria's thinking did not set the trend in the seventeenth, eighteenth, and nineteenth centuries, which were marked instead by Hugo Grotius's thinking. Vitoria wrote his lessons in Latin, considering it the elegant and educational language of that time and, before the hegemony of the modern state in international relations as a result of the Thirty Years War and the Westphalian Peace. Vitoria is also a product of *Respublica Christiana* (*The Christian Republic*) and of a thinking focused on the papal hegemony and international law focused on the relations among men.

In contrast, Grotius is a contemporary of the religious wars and the wars between the Holy Roman German Empire and several independent territories that defended their independence and international supremacy; in other words, Grotius is an advocate of the state as a sovereign entity with no rival in the external, independent, and equal order. The state defines modern international relations, not the individual or the people; therefore, we cannot be surprised that it is the work of Grotius – *De Iure Belli ac Pacis* (*The Law of War and Peace*) – that marks the establishment of international relations because it was written not in Latin but in contemporary language, which enabled direct access to all those who served the state. But, returning to Vitoria, he had the capacity to adapt the medieval jus naturalism and the Aristotelian and Thomist theories to the "law" and the "society." As stressed by António Truyol y Serra (1984, p. 23), Vitoria is a great internationalist because "he is a great theoretician of the political society." Francisco Vitoria considers humankind as part of a "community of the peoples of all the earth" (Truyol y Serra, 1990, p. 77). All people are called upon by natural law to become "republics" or states and to build their own societies. Each community should constitute a perfect community, not dependent on another republic, approve its own laws, and have its own government and magistrates. With this idea of the perfect community, Vitoria theorizes, in my opinion, the concept of sovereignty (Freitas, 2012; Truyol y Serra, 1946).

According to Vitoria, the people who organize themselves in states are joined together by means of human nature, constituting an *orbe*, characterized by being "a family of states linked by man's natural sociability" (Truyol y Serra, 1990, p. 77). According to this conception, Vitoria is accused of desecularization international law, replacing the idea of Christianity by that of the *orbe* (Truyol y Serra, 1990). The *orbe* "is not a super-state, but a family of peoples" (Truyol y Serra, 1958, p. 118). *Communitas orbis* is Vitoria's major contribution to international thinking. Vitoria bases his thinking on a community and not on an individualistic dimension, so that it is possible to speak about the rights of people and not of the individual in his work (Homem, 2003). The *orbe* does not originate from a contract, therefore the connection between communities is made through *ius gentium* (international law), which is conceived, according to the Roman tradition, as the universal law of humanity and as the law of peoples in their reciprocal relations; in other words, an *ius inter gente* (law among the peoples) (Truyol y Serra, 1990), which becomes a positive law through the signature of treaties and conventions among men.

For Vitoria, the people's law "is the one established by the natural reason among all peoples" (1998, III, §2, p. 130). The *orbe*, which results from the idea of *totus orbis* (the whole world), is not a creation of the human will but, rather, the result of the rational nature of man. The international community constitutes the corollary of the principle of states' interdependence, which, as duly stressed by Truyol y Serra (1958), personifies, at the universal level, the interdependence of individuals before the state. Vitoria follows closely Gaius's definition of the people's law – "*quod naturalis ratio inter omnes homines constituit, vocatur ius gentium* (international law is a natural law between the peoples)" – which conveys the idea of a "universal common law" based on the "unity of rational human nature" and comprises public and private elements (Truyol y Serra, 1946, p. 51). Despite Gaius's influence, Vitoria changes the sense of the Roman definition, replacing the expression *homines* with *peoples*. With this change, Vitoria integrates the *ius gentium* (international law) concept of all peoples and nations, as he considers them *ius inter gentes* (law among the peoples) (Marín López, 1984), giving rise to the modern concept of international law.

According to this definition, Vitoria acknowledges a positive people's law created by, and for, the *orbe*. Vitoria's theorizing of *ius gentium* set him apart from his contemporaries. The legal unit defended by Vitoria comprises rules inferred from the universal principles of natural law that were used in the new historical reality, positive rules derived from the tacit consent of most men and rules resulting from mandatory agreements signed between states. Vitoria's *ius inter gentes* is wider in scope than a law between states, since it confers the *people's* category on more rudimentary political organizations such as those of the Native Americans. Once created by the authority of the *orbe, ius gentium* becomes mandatory for all states. Humankind's natural rights, which constitute the people's law, should be adhered to by all peoples included in the *communitas orbis*. Those who commit unlawful deeds must be addressed by acts of retaliation or fair wars.

Legitimate and illegitimate titles

As a corollary to this definition, Vitoria acknowledges, in *De Indis* e *De Indis prior* (*The Native Americans and the Previous Native Americans*), the international legal personality of non-Christian political communities and considers them legally equal to Christian communities according to natural law (Truyol y Serra, 1990). In *De Potestate Civili* (*The Civil Authorities*), Vitoria, following Aristotle, considers that verbal communication enables one to distinguish men from animals. The Native Americans, having a language and communicating with one another, "have power over themselves, their property and their institutions" (Marques, 2015, p. 198). Vitoria describes the legitimate and illegitimate titles of acquisition applied by the Spanish to conquer the Native Americans in two lessons: the first on the more recently discovered Native Americans (international law in times of peace) and the second on the Spaniards' fight against the Native Americans (international law in times of war). According to Vitoria, legitimate titles of acquisition are: (1) natural society and communication; (2) spreading of the Christian religion; (3) avoiding the return to idolatry of converted people; (4) assigning of a Christian prince to converted people; (5) avoiding tyranny and the application of humiliating laws; (6) true and voluntary acceptance of the Spanish king; and (7) fellowship and friendship (1967, I, 1).

Vitoria considers the following titles of acquisition of territories belonging to the Native Americans by the Spaniards as non-legitimate: (1) the emperor as the owner of the world; (2) the authority of the Pontiff; (3) the right to discover; (4) refusal to accept the Christian faith; (5) the barbarians' sins; (6) true and voluntary election of the Spanish king; and (7) special acceptance of God (I, 2). According to Vitoria, the peoples of the Americas own their property, therefore the Christians "cannot occupy their properties" simply because the Native Americans are barbarians (I, 1,§ 1, p. 14), since the "mortal sin [barbarism] does not prevent the civil power nor the true power" (I, 1, § 3, pp. 17–19; 1998, I, §§ 5,6, pp. 68–70). To treat the Native Americans as enemies is a violation of natural law.

Power constitutes one of the principles of natural law for Vitoria, since nothing exists outside the divine authority, God being the creator of all things. Vitoria argues, as such, that the Native Americans' territories cannot be considered *res nullius* (no matter) and that, with their discovery, comes awareness of their existence but not a right to occupy them (Scott, 1928, p. 96). For Vitoria, the right to discover is a sufficient title for things which have no right to be occupied according to the people's law and natural law, as mentioned in *Instituciones*, II, I, 12 and *Digestum* 41, 2. This title may only be applied when the thing is *res nullius*, in other words, does not belong to anyone. This is not the situation of the Native Americans, who are the true public and private owners of the discovered territories (Vitoria, 1967, I, 2 § 10, p. 54). Vitoria questioned the Spanish colonization of the new world, namely, when it occurred in a violent manner (Vitoria, 1998, III, § 2, pp. 129–132) and taking without justification the property of Native Americans. However, he acknowledges that sublimation can take place on the basis of Native Americans' incapacity to govern themselves, but such incapacity must be proven, a protectorate created, and the Native Americans treated in a humane manner (Truyol y Serra, 1946). Colonization should constitute an authority over peoples who have neither social nor political capacity to govern themselves. Therefore, the Spaniards have the right to travel through Native Americans' territories "to settle in them, to trade, either by importing products and/or by exporting gold, silver and other materials" (Vitoria, 1967, I, 3, § 2, pp. 80–81). Luís de Molina, in turn, challenged Vitoria's thesis, advocating that each sovereign state could limit international trade and forbid other states to engage in it (Pereña Vicente, 1957).

The *ius communicationis*

Among the titles mentioned by Vitoria as means to legitimize the occupation of the American continent by the Spanish, the first is the right to free movement and communication – *ius communicationis* (the right to free movement and communication). Man is a sociable being and human sociability enables all men to get in touch with one another. For that reason, *ius communicationis* is the basis of the community. From *ius communicationis*, or the right of people to get in touch with one another, emerge many other rights, such as: *ius peregrinandi et degendi*, the right to travel and to settle; *ius commercii*, the right to trade; *ius occupationis*, the right to occupy; and *ius migrandi*, the right to migrate (Veloso, 2009). The natural rights identified by Vitoria are common to all people, peoples, and even states. The theorization of *ius communicationis* results from the fact that Vitoria understands the world as an organism within which men live in a situation of total brotherhood and, as such, the right of communication among them should exist. As a corollary, one who is born in a place should acquire citizenship of that place or state.

For Vitoria, natural law gives rise to the duty to welcome foreigners traveling in a given territory and, consequently, it is inhumane to mistreat them without proper justification (1967, I, 3, § 1, pp. 77–80). Based on *ius peregrinandi* and referring to the time when Vitoria writes, the Spanish have the right to travel and settle in American lands and should not be prevented from doing so. On these grounds, Vitoria concludes that it is legitimate for any person to go to a given independent territory and travel through it without trouble, since according to *Instituciones*, the air, rivers, sea, ports, and public roads, which enable the terrestrial movement of people and goods, derive from natural law and are common to all men. Therefore, the movement of people may not be prohibited (I, 3, § 1). The possibility of man's wandering may not be questioned by the existence of states and borders, since the right to movement is inherent to man's condition. Based on this premise, any human law that prohibits the movement of foreigners within states is considered unfair, as it violates both natural and divine rights (ibid).

Vitoria goes further and argues that not only is the right of movement or *ius peregrinandi* a natural right but also that men have the right to settle peacefully in foreign territories. In *Relectio de Indis*, Vitoria describes this thesis using the example of the proximity of Spain and France. He states that it is not legal for the French to prohibit the Spanish (and vice versa) from traveling through France and settling there because such a prohibition would constitute damage and an injustice (ibid). Foreigners are not only entitled to settle in the territory of another state but can also engage in trading (ibid), in compliance with the laws and rules of that state. *Ius commercii* is, therefore, a corollary of *ius communicationis*.

Another corollary of *ius communicationis* is the establishment of domicile. Everyone who travels to and decides to settle in another territory is entitled to establish his or her domicile in the host location, as well as enjoy the rights of and fulfil their duties toward the host territory. In this way, those who migrate shall not feel strangers in lands inhabited by "brothers." This thesis establishes Vitoria as a precursor of the idea of the free movement of people and of the advocacy of migration flows as emerging from human nature and, as such, arising from natural right.

The *ius soli*

Working on the idea of *ius communicationis*, Vitoria goes even further when defending the *ius soli* in the acquisition of nationality, since, according to the people's law, one who is born in a given city should be considered its citizen. Foreigners living in another territory should be entitled to the same right of acquisition of citizenship provided they abide by the rules imposed by the host state (Vitoria, 1967, I, 3, § 4). This is the principle of *ius migrandi*. Advocacy of the *ius soli* criteria for the acquisition of nationality relates to the constant concern of Vitoria's thinking, which is to establish that people with no legal affiliation regarding a territory nonetheless live within the international community; in other words, to prevent the existence of stateless people (Barcia Trelles, 1928).

Limitation of people's free movement

Emigration has been understood as a personal right of man, resulting from each person's individual freedom. Therefore no state may prevent its citizens from abandoning it and developing their professional activities in another country. At the beginning of the twentieth century, Fiore (1911) considered that the citizen should undertake, at the very least, compulsory military service as an obligation of their citizenship status. Notwithstanding the fact that emigration constitutes a human right, the host state may restrict it when it is deemed excessive to prevent possible political, economic, and social disruptions. There should be a weighting between the interests of the host state and those of the immigrants and the native people.

Migration flows should not cause any damage to the host state, which is why Vitoria argues that it is legal for the state to prevent people who originate from a country with which it is at war from crossing its borders (Vitoria, 1967, I, 3, § 1). With this thesis, Vitoria argues that the Native Americans cannot prevent Spaniards from traveling through and settling in their territories unless they are at war with Spain or the Spanish presence harms or causes damage to the native people. Finally, if the emigrants travel, trade, and live in a peaceful way and without causing damage to their "host" – in other words, act always without misconduct or fraud – the host state should do nothing against them (I, 3, § 7). Also, should the Native Americans, the host state, use violence to expel the Spanish, with no justification, they commit an injustice and this conduct may legitimate the declaration of war (I, 3, § 5). In a state of war, it is legal to dispossess and capture enemies (I, 3, § 7). Therefore, war aims at providing safety and peace for migrant populations.

Ius communicationis corollary

Francisco Vitoria's thinking, as well as the subsequently created doctrine, reverberates still today, namely, in Article 13 of the Universal Declaration of Human Rights, adopted and proclaimed by the General Assembly of the United Nations on December 10, 1948, which provides that:

1. Everyone has the right to freedom of movement and residence within the borders of each State.
2. Everyone has the right to leave any country including his own, and to return to his country.

Emigration is, therefore, a universal human right or, in other words, the natural right of each person and, rather than oppose waves of migration, states should host them unless they have negative impacts on their political, economic, and social life. In that case, host states should work out the best policy for managing migration flows and should not abandon protection of the human rights of migrants.

States should balance their own interests and the rights of migrants in order to create legislation regulating migration flows and the rights and duties of immigrants. In recognition of these principles, the United Nations Conference of Plenipotentiaries approved the Status of Refugees and Stateless people in 1951, which duly came into force on April 22, 1954. This status defines the refugee and his or her general obligations; in particular, compliance with the legal framework of the host state. It also acknowledges, on the other hand, the rights awarded to foreigners in general, as well as to its national citizens, regarding paid work, accommodation, education, and health care. The legal status of refugees, according to Article 12, is governed by the law of the country of domicile or, in its absence, by the law of the country of residence.

Conclusion

Francisco Vitoria is considered by some as the founder of modern international law and as the precursor to a universalistic and humanistic vision of the people's law, through his advocacy of the right of Native Americans to their lands, governments, and organizations and also to humane treatment, which, if not based on human laws, which tend to exclude it, should at least be based on the divine right to such. The idea of international community created by Vitoria is not limited to the traditional vision of Christian states, but extends this idea to other non-Christian communities, namely, those of Native Americans. Vitoria does not advocate, as such, a "European International Law," an "International Law of the Christian States," or an "International Law of the Civilized States," but an "International Law of the Peoples" (Scott, 1928, p. 127).

Time proved him right, but it was necessary to get to the twentieth century. During this time gap, international law was considered the law of civilized peoples, of the European peoples and, later on, around the beginning of the nineteenth century, there was an opening up to the American states that were being created. If the defense of the universalization of the international community is one of Vitoria's legacies, considering that nations are linked by natural law is another characteristic of his thinking. If the state is subject to natural law, as mentioned by Kleffens, "then sovereignty shall not be unlimited, but, due to the very nature of things, it will be subject to the rules and restrictions which are part of or derive from or are permitted by the natural law" (1956, p. 62).

Considering the premises described here, I understand that the host states should integrate refugees and grant them the rights provided for in the various conventions approved by the United Nations. However, it is necessary to go further and consider that current international law, which is still linked to the ties of Westphalia, should not, within the context of humanitarian law, forego the principle of non-intervention and intervene in the states in conflict, with the purpose of preserving human rights. In my opinion, it is incumbent on states to protect their citizens' rights and when it does not do so, namely, in situations of war, the international community should hold the state accountable, so as to defend and protect, even if turning to military intervention carried out always within the scope of the United Nations, the rights of refugees. To respond to the challenges posed by the movement of refugees in the world of today, international law should focus more and more on the defence and protection of the human person. Therefore, it makes sense to keep on talking about migration rights, especially the rights of refugees.

References

Almeida Costa, M. J. (2002). *História do direito português* (3rd ed.). Coimbra: Almedina.

Barcia Trelles, C. (1928). *Francisco de Vitoria fundador del Derecho Internacional Moderno*. Valladolid: Universidad de Valladolid.

Fiore, P. (1911). *Le droit international codifié et sa sanction juridique*. Paris: A. Pedone.

Freitas, P. C. (2012). *Portugal e a comunidade internacional na segunda metade do século XIX*. Lisbon: Quid Juris.

Freitas, P. C. (2015). *História do direito internacional público*. Cascais: Principia.

Homem, A. P. B. (2003). *História das relações internacionais. O direito e as concepções políticas na idade moderna*. Coimbra: Almedina.

Kleffens, E. & Van, N. (1956). A Soberania em Direito Internacional. In *Lições proferidas na Academia de Direito Internacional da Haia*. Coimbra: Coimbra Editora.

Maltez, J. A. (1998). *Princípios de ciência política – O problema do direito*. Lisbon: Instituto Superior de Ciências Sociais e Políticas.

Marín López, A. (1984). Francisco de Vitoria y la Escuela Española de Derecho Internacional. *Revista Española de Derecho Internacional, XXXVI*(1), 9–20.

Marques, M. R. (2015). Do direito natural aos direitos naturais. In A. P. B. Homem & C. Brandão (Eds.), *O Itinerário jusnaturalista dos direitos humanos da "primeira geração"* (pp. 187–229). Coimbra: Almedina.

Merêa, P. (1943). O problema da origem do poder civil em Suaréz e em Pufendorf. In Faculdade de Direito (Ed.), *Boletim da Faculdade de Direito da Universidade de Coimbra, XIX*, 289–306.

Nys, E. (n.d.). *Le Droit International. Les Principes, Les Théories, Les Faits*, Vol. II. Paris: Marcel Rivière.

Pereña Vicente, L. (1957). Circunstancia histórica y derecho de gentes en Luis Molina. *Revista Española de Derecho Internacional*, *X*(1–2), 137–153.

Scott, J. B. (1928). *El origen español del derecho internacional moderno*. Valladolid: Universidad de Valladolid.

Silva, N. E. G. (1991). *História do direito português* (2nd ed.). Lisbon: Fundação Calouste Gulbenkian.

Truyol, Y. & Serra, A. (1946). *Los principios del derecho público en Francisco de Vitoria*. Madrid: Ediciones Cultura Hispánica.

Truyol, Y. & Serra, A. (1958). *Genèse et fondements spirituels de l'idée d"une communauté universelle. De la civitas máxima stoïcienne à la civitas gentium moderne*. Lisbon: Faculdade de Direito.

Truyol, Y. & Serra, A. (1984). Vitoria y su lugar en la historia del pensamiento. *Revista Española de Derecho Internacional*, *XXXVI*(1), 21–28.

Truyol, Y. & Serra, A. (1990). *História da filosofia do direito e do estado*. Lisbon: Instituto de Novas Profissões.

United Nations (2010, August 2). *Use of mercenaries as a means of violating human rights impeding the exercise of the right of peoples to self-determination*. A/65/203. Retrieved from http://dag.un.org/handle/11176/154618

Veloso, P. P. A. (2009). Os Fundamentos Pré-Modernos do Direito Internacional e a Legitimação dos Atos Estatais. *Revista Ius Gentium. Teoria e Comércio no Direito Internacional*, 2(1), 11–36.

Verdross, A. (1963). *Derecho internacional público*. Madrid: Aguilar.

Vitoria, F. (1967). *Relectio de indis, o libertad de los indios*. Madrid: Consejo Superior de Investigaciones Científicas.

Vitoria, F. (1998). *Sobre el poder civil, sobre los índios, sobre el derecho de guerra*. Madrid: Tecnos.

Wieacker, F. (1993). *História do Direito Privado Moderno* (2nd ed.). Lisbon: Fundação Calouste Gulbenkian.

2

CURRENT CHALLENGES TO THE INTERNATIONAL PROTECTION OF REFUGEES AND OTHER MIGRANTS

The role of and developments from the United Nations 2016 Summit

Liliana Lyra Jubilut, André de Lima Madureira, & Daniel Bertolucci Torres

Humankind is "facing the biggest refugee and displacement crisis of our time" (UNHCR, 2016a, p. 5). From 1996 to 2012, the number of forced displaced persons around the world was maintained at a range of between 40 and 50 million; however, mostly driven by the Syrian conflict, since 2013 onwards the figures have consistently increased (ibid, p. 6). By the end of 2017 there were 25.4 million refugees, 3.1 million asylum seekers, and 40 million internally-displaced persons (IDPs) (UNHCR, 2018). The number of "voluntary" migrants has also been increasing; 258 million persons were living abroad in 2017 (United Nations, 2017).

Even if a "human-rights-oriented approach has progressively informed the state-sovereignty focused perspective over the years following the atrocities of the Second World War" (Barbour, 2008, p. 3) and has been tied up with the global political agenda, international commitments towards the protection of migrants have either been lacking and/or biased by individual states' own agendas, given that "international law has been dominated by a 'state-sovereignty-oriented approach', where states are the primary subjects of the international legal order and are bound only through consent" (ibid). One of the main gaps in the governance of migration and the protection of migrants is still the lack of international norms on the topic.

To try to make progress in closing this gap, the United Nations Summit for Refugees and Migrants (UN Summit) took place on September 19, 2016 and aimed to engage the international community in "changing gear"[1] in relation to the protection of forced displaced persons (UNHCR, 2016b) and other migrants. Focusing on addressing large movements of persons, it resulted in the New York Declaration and the commitment to adopt two global compacts – one led by the United Nations High Commissioner for Refugees (UNHCR) on refugees and another on migrants led by states – by late 2018.[2] The UN Summit was the first initiative of this type and in a world of increased migration and closure of borders it is relevant to assess its outcomes to establish what has already been secured and what needs to be addressed in terms of the normative aspects of the governance of migration. Thus, this chapter aims to analyze, mainly through dialog with current events and document analysis, the normative developments resulting from the UN Summit and the NY Declaration and to present the current and prospective international landscape of migrants' and refugees' rights and protection.

Current challenges to the international protection of refugees and other migrants

To be able to assess the developments resulting from the NY Declaration, it is necessary to begin by describing the current scenario of challenges in global migration to consider if the document has tackled and is able to deal with the real landscape of obstacles faced by refugees and other migrants. Nowadays, the governance of migration faces several challenges from a normative standpoint, among which the following five need to be highlighted.

The first challenge relates to the existing (or non existing) regimes of protection of migrants. To date, of all migrants only refugees can count on an international regime of protection.[3,4] IDPs have international norms on their behalf but those are either principles,[5] not hard international commitments, or regional frameworks with limited scope.[6] Migrant workers rely on an international treaty,[7] but one that is poorly ratified.[8] In this sense, being a refugee may be the only way to ascertain protection, if you are a migrant. This is complicated, given that the definition of refugee enshrined in the 1951 Convention Relating to the Status of Refugees (1951 Refugee Convention) is both limiting and deemed outdated. In regard to the former, only a person with a well-founded fear of being persecuted as a result of his or her nationality, race, religion, political opinion, or membership of a social group that is outside his or her country of origin and both needs and deserves international protection (i.e., is subjected to neither cessation nor exclusion clauses)[9] can be recognized as a refugee. In relation to the latter, the 1951 Refugee Convention was influenced by the post-Second World War historical context (Koser, 2015). As a result, the definition seems to be incapable of dealing with other current causes of forced migration, such as environmental displacement,[10] other humanitarian causes, or voluntary migration.

Legally speaking, the universal definition of refugee features two main shortcomings that hinder the protection of those forced migrants. First, it lacks a better integration with the three dimensions of human rights (Jubilut & Madureira, 2014), considering only violations of civil and political rights for the purpose of refugee status determination, which makes the protection of, for instance, economic migrants and environmental displaced persons difficult. Second, the above-mentioned five grounds of persecution listed by the 1951 Refugee Convention restrict its scope (ibid). As only individuals who have a well-founded fear of persecution on account of race, nationality, religion, political opinion, and membership of a particular social group can be recognized as refugees, persons who, for instance, flee settings of gross and generalized violations of human rights or civil unrest often need to be protected either by complementary forms of protection[11] or regional responses, such as those encountered in Africa[12] and Latin America.[13]

A second normative challenge in the governance of migration, related to the first one, exists in the labeling of migrants. As only refugees are legally entitled to protection, labeling migrants to separate them from refugees has become a common practice. If, on the one hand, this practice can assist in determining specific causes of displacement and needs of protection, on the other hand, it can also undermine even refugees' access to international protection. The purpose of labeling migrants has changed in recent decades (Zetter, 2007). If, in the late 1980s, non-governmental organizations (NGOs) were labeling refugees for humanitarian purposes, states in the global north are currently responsible for instrumentalizing the label "refugee" to manage new globalized flows (ibid). By creating labels such as "illegal migrants," "economic refugees," "temporary protection" and so on, states obscure the label "refugee" rather than clarify it (ibid, pp. 188–189). In doing so, they create a scenario in which claiming asylum becomes a challenge even for those who fall under the 1951 Refugee Convention definition (ibid). Moreover, in a scenario involving mixed migration flows and in which being considered a refugee may be, as aforementioned, the only avenue for protection, cheapening legal classifications might overburden the refugees' regime and "underplay the status of 'refugees' in international law" (Gilbert, 2016) or "minimize the refugee character" (Durieux, 2017) (thus, jeopardizing refugees' protection) and, at the same time, reinforce the continuous lack of protection for other migrants (Ceriani, 2016), in a lose–lose situation.[14] Mixing refugees and other migrants in the governance of migration can suit states' agendas (ibid) and reinforce the need for global governance of all aspects of migration, but the challenges in doing so need to be dealt with and particularities respected so as to avoid negative consequences in the protection of human beings in situations of displacement.

A third relevant normative challenge is the existence of obstacles to migrants in accessing international protection. States are closing their borders, restricting access to refuge protection, and criminalizing both the act of claiming asylum and the act of migrating. They are also in some cases violating their obligations under international law – both in terms of international refugee law (with the norm of *non-refoulement*[15]) and international human rights law.[16] An outcome of this scenario is the current lack of secure channels for refugees and other migrants to access safe territories and, once inside them, to access protection in safe places. This, in turn, fuels the market for smuggling migrants[17] and makes refugees and other migrants risk their lives on dangerous routes and pushes persons into hazardous situations.[18]

A fourth challenge in the governance of migration from a legal standpoint also refers to international human rights law and relates to securing specific protection in relation to specific vulnerabilities that may exist among migrants. International migrants may be seen as vulnerable in light of their lack of international protection and the constant violations of their (human) rights. Also, migration in itself can exacerbate this situation: "Migration in the context of globalization brings opportunities but also important challenges of vulnerability and discrimination" (Office of the High Commissioner for Human Rights (OHCHR), 2011, p. 8). Moreover, in some cases vulnerabilities can be present in more than one way. The elderly, women, persons with disabilities, LGBTI persons, persons with health (physical or mental) issues, and children are, for example, more vulnerable in the context of migration and this needs to be taken into consideration in the creation of norms to protect them.[19]

A fifth normative challenge in the governance of migration relates to finding durable solutions for migrants and refugees (Madureira & Jubilut, 2016). This challenge encompasses at least three topics: (1) international cooperation, (2) the securitization of migration, and (3) finding durable solutions. In terms of international cooperation, one sees that there is a crisis in this regard both in relation to migration and within the refugee regime.[20] According to Türk and Garlick (2016):

> There is a pressing need in today's context to reinforce international cooperation in order for protection, assistance, and solutions, in ways that reflect States' commitments to the principles of solidarity and responsibility-sharing. Predictability and equity are also intrinsic features of any functioning international cooperative framework. . . .
>
> *(pp. 657–658)*

Also, there is an imperative need to focus on the "centrality of [the] 1951 Geneva Convention and its 1957 Protocol," on the 2030 sustainable agenda paradigm and, most importantly, migration governance must be built on the idea of a global partnership and shared responsibility (EEAS, 2016a). However, this does not seem to be the case, given that, as mentioned, the only international treaty on migrants is poorly ratified; also, responsibility for refugee protection is very poorly balanced due to the fact that 85 percent of refugees are being hosted in developing countries (UNHCR, 2018) and "[o]ver four out of every five refugees [are] located in a neighbouring country to the one from which they fled" (ibid). This highlights the fact that currently neither burden-sharing nor responsibility-sharing mechanisms are being adequately implemented. In terms of the securitization of migration, countries have been adopting restrictive measures and criminalizing actions against migrants, as mentioned earlier. Moreover, following 9/11 there has been a notable increase in the relating of themes such as terrorism, international security, and refugees (Gibney, 2002, p. 40). Additionally, countries often ignore "the reality of push and pull factors" and end up using repressive policies, notably in terms of the tightening of border controls and of fighting undocumented frontier crossing by using detention and extraterritorial border control (Crépeau, 2017b).

Lastly, in terms of access to (human) rights and effective protection after migration, translated in durable solutions, there are complex challenges. Integration of migrants remains a key topic and a multifaceted task. In particular for refugees there is a paradox: although they are the single group of migrants with a specific protection regime, data points out that this advantage is not translated into durable solutions even for them. By the end of 2016, approximately two-thirds of all refugees (i.e., 11.6 million people) were in protracted situations (UNHCR, 2017, p. 22); 4.1 million refugees had been in these situations for more than 20 years (ibid), thus suffering human rights abuses (Bakewell, 2014, p. 136), with no prospect of an end to their refugee status. Moreover, many refugees still cannot benefit from any of the three existing durable solutions used by UNHCR (integration, resettlement, or voluntary repatriation). All these normative challenges in the governance of migration are intertwined and need to be addressed in order for refugees and other migrants to actually have international protection. Thus, it is relevant to describe what the NY Declaration of the UN Summit put forward in this regard.

Background, legal perspective, and legal structure of the 2016 UN Summit and the NY Declaration

Efforts have been made in recent years in respect of improving the international governance of migration (OHCHR, 2011). In 2005, Kofi Annan, then UN Secretary-General, was unable to bring states together in an international conference to discuss the issue of migration (Guild & Grant, 2017). Thus, his solution was to invite a Global Commission on International Migration outside the UN (ibid). In 2006, the UN's General Assembly held its first High-Level Panel Meeting on Migration and, as a result, in 2007 an inter-governmental Global Forum on Migration and Development[21] was established outside the UN, and the Global

Migration Group was developed to gather together migration-related UN entities to exchange information and knowledge on the matter (ibid). Following these efforts, Annan's successor, Ban Ki-moon, continued to place the challenges of the protection of refugees and other migrants on the international agenda. In 2013, the UN convened the High-Level Dialogue on Migration and Development, which resulted in a declaration on the part of the General Assembly[22] (Martin, 2015).

In April 2016, Ban Ki-moon presented his report – "In safety and dignity: Addressing large movements of refugees and migrants"[23] – in which, and among several relevant points, he highlighted the necessity of creating international plans of action based both on burden-sharing and on the dignity of refugees and other migrants (United Nations General Assembly, 2016a). For him, "if one lesson can be drawn from the past few years, it is that individual countries cannot solve these issues on their own. International cooperation and action to address large movements of refugees and other migrants must be strengthened" (p. 2). He stated that, even though the international refugee and other migrant crisis is serious, solutions can be found once Member States "act together and share responsibility more equitably" (p. 2) and that the consequences of inaction can be a cause of "greater loss of life and heightened tensions among Member States and within communities" (p. 3).

The report stressed that, although humanitarian actions are needed, they are "not a viable long-term response to large movements of people" (p. 10), and that efforts are "imperative in order to include both refugees and migrants who stay in national and local development plans to ensure their livelihood opportunities while strengthening the resilience of and development opportunities for host communities" (p. 10). Following this report, in September of the same year state delegates gathered in New York to attend the UN summit to address the refugee and migrant issue, on which occasion the NY Declaration[24] was adopted.

Like the Secretary-General's report, the NY Declaration is an instrument of soft law, but one that has been adopted by the affirmative votes of states displaying the agreements that they accepted on the topic of protecting refugees and other migrants. The NY Declaration was adopted by the 193 states that are members of the UN (UNHCR, 2016c, p. 1), an impressive feat as the "global governance of international migration has been much more controversial than has been the case regarding most other transnational issues" (Martin, 2015, p. 64). This document will be guiding the global initiative on the topic of migration governance. In general, the document focuses on giving a global meaning to the phenomenon of large movements of refugees and other migrants, and tries to create a uniform and global response to the situation of both (even though the causes, labels, and normative architecture for refugees and other migrants are distinct). In paragraph 6, the NY Declaration explains that the definition of *large movements* takes into account "a number of considerations, including: the number of people arriving, the economic, social and geographical context, the capacity of a receiving State to respond, and the impact of a movement that is sudden or prolonged" (United Nations General Assembly, 2016b, p. 2, para. 6). The NY Declaration is divided into four sections and has two annexes. In its introduction, the text highlights that, to protect persons amidst large movements, which "may involve mixed flows of people, whether refugees or migrants, who move for different reasons but who may use similar routes" (p. 2, para. 6), it is necessary to fully face it as a "global phenomena that call for global approaches and global solutions" (p. 2, para. 7).

In addition, it recalls existing general documents that should guide the debate on the topic, such as the 2030 Agenda for Sustainable Development (pp. 1–4, paras. 4, 16, 17), the Charter of the United Nations, the Universal Declaration of Human Rights, and the core of international human rights treaties (p. 2, para. 7). It also evokes specific frameworks such as the Sendai Framework for Disaster Risk Reduction 2015–2030, the Paris Agreement on Climate Change, the Addis Ababa Action Agenda of the Third International Conference on Financing for Development (p. 4, para. 19), and the Brazil Declaration and Plan of Action (p. 2, para. 7). The NY Declaration stresses the commitment to international law and highlights that agreed-upon commitments are taking "into account different national realities, capacities and levels of development and respecting national policies and priorities" (p. 5). The NY Declaration brings three types of commitment: (1) commitments to be applied to both refugees and migrants, (2) commitments towards migrants, and (3) commitments towards refugees.

The commitments of the NY Declaration

Commitments towards the protection of both refugees and migrants

The first main commitment brought by the NY Declaration concerning both refugees and other migrants is the need to regulate migration from a "people-centered" perspective (United Nations General Assembly, 2016b, p. 5). Second, it highlights the obligation to offer adequate responses to vulnerable persons. Whether they are refugees or other migrants, persons with special needs and vulnerabilities need to be subject to special approaches amidst large movements of persons and the development of global commitments to protect them. These include

> women at risk, children, especially those who are unaccompanied or separated from their families, members of ethnic and religious minorities, victims of violence, older persons, persons with disabilities, persons who are discriminated against on any basis, indigenous peoples, victims of human trafficking, and victims of exploitation and abuse in the context of the smuggling of migrants.
>
> *(p. 5, para. 23)*

This approach can be said to be based on human rights as the protection of persons and of their specific needs is at its core. Implementing such an approach would call for a framework of migration governance based on international human rights law as a way of diminishing political and ideological national differences and approaches to human rights that are in place in the world today as well as strengthening commitment to protection based on agreed-upon and universal standards that have been set into law. International human rights law contains a set of core rights that cannot be violated and that are (from an international law perspective) consensually universal. These rights should constitute the minimum standards for the protection of refugees and other migrants, both those that apply to all human beings and those for specific groups.

The NY Declaration continues to stress the need to protect vulnerable groups of persons from "discrimination and exploitation ... [and] sexual, physical and psychological abuse, violence, human trafficking and contemporary forms of slavery" (p. 6, para. 29). The health care needs of persons with HIV are also highlighted (p. 6). The need to apply a gender-specific approach to protecting women and girls is also present (p. 6). Concerning children, the NY Declaration stresses the need to "comply with our obligations under the Convention on the Rights of the Child" (pp. 6–7, para. 32) and emphasizes the need to give primary consideration to the "best interest of the child" (p. 7, para. 33), notably when addressing unaccompanied and separated children.

Another commitment concerning both refugees and other migrants is the need to bring a sense of humanity to border control and to avoid the criminalization of the act of crossing borders. Although recognizing that "States are entitled to take measures to prevent irregular border crossings" (p. 5, para. 24), the NY Declaration takes note of the need to create alternatives based on dignity when it concerns "the human rights of all persons crossing, or seeking to cross, international borders" (p. 6, para. 24). However, and in apparent contrast to this approach, the NY Declaration also demonstrates some degree of tolerance to detention based on migratory reasons, once it affirms that states will be pursing alternatives to detention but "will use it [detention] only as a measure of last resort" (p. 7, para. 33).

The NY Declaration's concern regarding human trafficking is clear. Recalling that refugees and other migrants in the context of large movements of persons are "at greater risk of being trafficked and of being subjected to forced labour" (p. 7, para. 35), the NY Declaration recommends the ratification and implementation of the United Nations Convention against Transnational Organized Crime and its two relevant protocols (p. 7, para. 34) and affirms states' commitment to review national legislation on this matter as well as to implement the United Nations Global Plan of Action to Combat Trafficking in Persons (p. 7, para. 36). As a constant, the NY Declaration places emphasis on the need to avoid, and to criminalize, smuggling and human trafficking. However, it has been defended that the only way to actually reduce smuggling and unethical recruiting is to undercut the smugglers and exploitative recruiters by offering regular, safe, accessible, and affordable mobility solutions, in the form of visas or visa-free travel opportunities, with all the identity and security checks that efficient visa regimes can provide. In effect, one must take over the mobility market. Migrants do not want to be undocumented. They would rather pay a visa officer than a smuggler, rather arrive by plane than on a leaky boat, and rather work above the table than below it (Crépeau, 2017a). There is, thus, a need for expanding the possibilities of visas but in the NY Declaration the issue of new visas only appears in the section on commitments towards refugees (United Nations General Assembly, 2016b, p. 14). Commitments to work on the root causes of large movements of persons, inclusive of forced displacement and protracted refugee situations, and adequate humanitarian financing to host countries and communities are also pointed out (p. 8). Actions on avoiding xenophobia and discrimination, access to social rights, justice, and language training are presented as measures to reduce marginalization and radicalization (p. 8). Finally, the need to collect data is established as a commitment to be taken seriously, "particularly by national authorities" (p. 8, para. 40).

Commitments towards the protection of migrants

On the commitments towards migrants, the NY Declaration repeatedly brings forward the need to consider the 2030 Agenda for Sustainable Development[25] as the basis for creating a world where migration is a choice and not a necessity (United Nations General Assembly, 2016b, p. 9, para. 43), placing emphasis on the need to strengthen the capacities of countries of origin (p. 9). It highlights that the act of migrating is a human right, as "everyone has the right to leave any country, including his or her own, and to return to his or her country" (p. 9, para. 42). In terms of normative architecture, on the one hand, states that adopted the NY Declaration declared that they "will consider reviewing [their] migration policies with a view to examining their possible unintended negative consequences" (p. 9, para. 45). On the other hand, the NY Declaration encourages the ratification of the International Convention on the Protection of the Rights of All Migrant Workers and Members of Their Families (p. 10) and making the International Organization for Migration (IOM) the "global lead agency on migration" (p. 10, para. 49). It also encourages other bilateral, regional, and global initiatives that could help the implementation of the 2030 Agenda (p. 10) and briefly considers the return of migrants to their countries of origin or nationality (p. 11, para. 58).

Concerning migrants who were forced to move due to "natural disaster", the NY Declaration refers to the need to improve states' participation in the Agenda for the Protection of Cross-Border Displaced Persons in the Context of Disasters and Climate Change resulting from the Nansen Initiative (p. 10). It also highlights the need to build cooperation among countries of origin, in transit and as destinations, to ensure that unauthorized migrants are able to return to their countries of origin, and to consider the principle of *non-refoulement* (p. 11). Furthermore, repeating a topic presented on the commitments to both refugees and migrants, the NY Declaration demonstrates concern for the protection of vulnerable groups such as children, especially unaccompanied and separated minors, as well as the need to create special forms of protection for women and girls (p. 11). This section finishes with the commitment to set up intergovernmental negotiation with the purpose of creating "a global compact for safe, orderly and regular migration at an intergovernmental conference to be held in 2018" (p. 12, para. 63), the groundwork for which is established in Annex II of the NY Declaration.[26] In this annex the NY Declaration provides directions on the content of a future compact on migration, requiring that it should "promote holistic approaches that take into account the causes and consequences of the phenomenon" and acknowledge "that poverty, underdevelopment, lack of opportunities, poor governance and environmental factors are among the drivers of migration" (p. 22). It also establishes that "an intergovernmental conference on international migration" is to take place in 2018 at which a global compact on migration "will be presented for adoption" (p. 23, para. 9).

Commitments towards the protection of refugees

Regarding the commitments towards refugees, the NY Declaration's first consideration is the need to work on the root causes of forced displacement (United Nations General Assembly, 2016b, p. 12). In terms of the existing legal structure, the NY Declaration encourages states that have not signed the international treaties on refugees to do so, and also requests that those states that have made reservations to them to withdraw such limitations (p. 12). The NY Declaration also points out that the international law framework relating to refugees should be strengthened (p. 12), while reaffirming the right of asylum and the principle of *non-refoulement* (p. 13), and highlighting the need for, and importance of, international cooperation and burden and responsibility sharing (p. 13) and the role of UNHCR in coordinating a comprehensive framework for refugees. All of these are relevant issues in a world where "[r]efugee movements have unfortunately become a politically toxic issue" (Crisp, 2017), and highlight the importance of a declaration that "[upholds] the basic principles of refugee protection and committed states to address refugee issues in a more cooperative and coordinated manner" (ibid).

The NY Declaration mentions the need to ensure fast procedures and easing of administrative barriers to process refugee status determination (United Nations General Assembly, 2016b, p. 13). A controversial provision in this regard, however, is that the "ability of refugees to lodge asylum claims in the country of their choice may be regulated, subject to the safeguard that they will have access to, and enjoyment of, protection elsewhere" (p. 13, para. 70). This is controversial insofar as the NY Declaration seems to be admitting the possibility that refugees cannot choose where they can deposit their asylum claim, which can be understood as an obstacle in the need to ensure burden-sharing and international cooperation. The section dedicated to commitments towards refugees also places emphasis on the need to create instruments for the effective protection of vulnerable persons in the context of large movements of persons. Besides pointing out the promotion of appropriate mechanisms to process the request for refugee status of children (p. 13), the NY Declaration recognizes statelessness as one of the causes of forced displacement and encourages states that have not yet committed to the two main treaties on statelessness (i.e., the 1954 Convention relating to the Status of Stateless Persons and the 1961 Convention on the Reduction of Statelessness) to consider doing so (p. 13).

In terms of durable solutions, the NY Declaration also stresses that refugee camps should be an exception (p. 13–14); that the international community should work on supporting countries that host large refugee populations (p. 14); and that states should work toward durable solutions, especially in response to protracted refugee situations (p. 14). Notably, concerning resettlement, the NY Declaration encourages countries to make use of resettlement and to considering doing so as early as possible (p. 14, paras. 77–78). The NY Declaration also briefly addresses the issue of complementary pathways for admission of migrants (p. 19, para. 9).[27]

Regarding humanitarian aid, the NY Declaration reaffirms the already existing framework in terms of providing assistance in urgent situations and also supporting countries and communities affected by large movements of persons (p. 14). Educational rights, especially in the context of childhood, basic health rights, notably for women and girls, and labor rights, encouraging the opening of labor markets to refugees, are also emphasized (p. 15, paras. 81–84).

The last three paragraphs of this section focus on the need for coordinated action to protect refugees on the part of host countries and communities and other stakeholders, such as international, private, and local institutions, with the support of the United Nations and the help of civil society. Furthermore, there is recognition of the "gap between the needs of refugees and the available resources," in light of which the NY Declaration encourages donors' support by making "humanitarian financing more flexible and predictable" (p. 15, para. 86). It also welcomes efforts by the World Bank and other multilateral actors to make financing more effective. As is the case for migrants, the NY Declaration establishes the groundwork for a Global Compact on Refugees in 2018, which aims to create hard international commitments towards refugees. In its Annex I, the NY Declaration establishes that said compact should entail the following elements: (i) reception and admission of refugees; (ii) support for immediate and ongoing needs; (iii) support for host countries and communities; (iv) durable solutions; and (v) ways forward, with respect to the near future regarding the creation of a more comprehensive refugee response framework.

The NY Declaration in the face of the normative challenges

The NY Declaration is undoubtedly a positive step in the international protection of refugees and other migrants given that it is the first comprehensive document on the topic and that it sets forward a pathway for the adoption of legally binding documents in 2018. Furthermore, the NY Declaration clearly highlights important issues in the governance of migration and the protection of refugees and other migrants, such as emphasizing the already existing human rights regime and strengthening the need for states to ratify all related treaties.

In terms of the normative challenges presented above, the NY Declaration can be subject to mixed reviews or give "reasons for both disappointment and hope" (Papademetriou & Fratzke, 2016). On the one hand, the NY Declaration (i) explicitly mentions the need to consider the specific protection of vulnerable groups; (ii) establishes that refugees and other migrants "have the same universal rights and fundamental freedoms" (United Nations General Assembly, 2016b, p. 2), thus aiding in mitigating the protection concerns associated with "labeling migrants"; (iii) alludes to the need for protection of migrants who lack an international regime of protection (such as environmentally displaced persons) and the need to strengthen the existing structures of protection; and (iv) recalls the need to re-examine the implementation of durable solutions. On the other hand, the proposed commitments of the document are not fully attached to any practical proposals for solutions to "people-centered" policies and regimes in situations of displacement, leaving the NY Declaration with a lack of implementation tools[28] in several areas and a feeling that the document's rhetoric is far from the migrants' reality (Howden, 2016).

Furthermore, and creating another set of implementation challenges, is the fact that even though the NY Declaration opts for combining the governance of refugees and other migrants in one document, albeit separating them once deemed needed, it does not define any of the categories that might impose difficulties in enhancing protection for both groups in a scenario of mixed migration flows. This search for "a common reaction to the 'massification' of a cross-border flow" might lead to "the contamination of the qualitative by the quantitative. And, in any event, a state enjoys a fair amount of discretion in deciding that, while the people concerned may be refugees, they are not 'its' refugees" (Durieux, 2017).

In addition to these issues relating to normative challenges, it is relevant to point out that, as the NY Declaration sets the tone for the Global Compacts, at least four trends might be of concern. All of these seem to stem from the deeply-rooted migration myth of opposing interests of the state and the needs of human beings, when, in fact, migration is a phenomenon that has individuals as its subjects and constituents (Jubilut & Lopes, 2017) and also benefits states (ibid, p. 53). It is true that there has been recognition of such a view, for instance the High Representative of the Union for Foreign Affairs and Security Policy and Vice-President of the European Commission, Federica Mogherini, affirmed that solutions for migration should be centered on human beings and highlighted migration's relevance to host societies and that Europeans "should understand that we need migration for our economies and for our welfare systems, with the current demographic trend we have to be sustainable."[29] However, it appears that such points of view are not predominant within the NY Declaration even though they could guide a new (European and global) approach to migration and be present in the Global Compacts and that an adversarial position of states versus human beings is still behind migration governance leading to the four trends of concern in the NY Declaration.

The first trend relates to the rhetoric used by the NY Declaration, as it seems to paint a scenario that is not true to reality and at times is too idealistic. Recently, the world has seen severe violations of the human rights of refugees and other migrants, especially after 2015 following the "massive" arrivals in Europe, which were highlighted by the death of thousands of migrants in the Mediterranean Sea and the inhumane border control used by some countries in the form of pushbacks, detentions and relocations. These situations are not, however, expressly addressed by the NY Declaration, albeit that the emphasis of the document is on the need to "save lives" or to address the "moral and humanitarian" challenges in the governance of migration.[30]

Moreover, even though the NY Declaration seems to bring elements of "people-centered" guidelines to responses to migration, most proposals seem to be focused on states' concerns rather than on seeing the human side of migration. Examples in this regard are noted in paragraphs 24 and 33 of the NY Declaration (as described above), which respectively allow for a considerable degree of discretion on the issues of border control and detention, thus favoring a state-centric perspective rather than a human rights approach. In the sense of how much the actual global regime for the protection of migrants and refugees is contaminated by an evasive and reluctant state-view approach, "it is ironic that 50 years ago nations were able to see the broader picture, while some today seem unable or unwilling to think and act internationally in the face of challenge that requires international and cooperative responses" (Goodwin-Gill, 2017). Another trend of concern is that, as in many international documents, the NY Declaration seems to bring more promises and ideas than actual means to implement its principles and guidelines, which seem extremely relevant in the complex scenario of migration. The lack of implementation mechanisms as well as of binding international norms and obligations regarding the governance of migration is not only a current problem but also a concern for any future endeavors in this area.

Lastly, it seems that the NY Declaration prefers to emphasize the convincing of states that it is good for them to receive migrants, rather than to make a stronger case for the respect of human rights in migration and in migration governance. The NY Declaration highlights, for example, that receiving migrants would be a good way to implement the 2030 Agenda (United Nations General Assembly, 2016b, p. 9, para. 46) and tries to demonstrate how migration can be positive for the countries of reception (ibid). It seems, then, that the NY Declaration could have done more to dilute the opposition between states' interests and human beings' needs when addressing migration. This shortcoming should be avoided in the Global Compacts of 2018.

Conclusion

The governance of migration is currently a significant global challenge and the lack of strong normative structures makes it even more difficult. In trying to advance in creating ways to address this issue, the UN held the 2016 Summit and adopted the New York Declaration on Refugees and Migrants. The document is historical in its efforts to address large movements of persons and to pave the way for two Global Compacts – one on refugees and another on migrants in general. It has shortcomings, mainly in relation to its success in dealing with the perceived opposition between the interests of states and the needs of human beings to migrate, which ought to be corrected following the adoption of the Global Compacts so that refugees and other migrants will have actual regimes of protection that are respected and implemented by states. However, the NY Declaration does make advances in terms of stating long fought after ideas in adding a human rights or "people-centered" perspective to migration. This is to be commended, as human beings are not only the subjects and regulators of migration but also the ones who actually create the phenomenon (Jubilut & Lopes, 2017).

Notes

1 An expression used by Filippo Grandi at the opening of the UN 2016 Summit on Refugees and Migrants.
2 United Nations, main page of the New York Declaration (http://refugeesmigrants.un.org/declaration).
3 Encompassing the 1951 Convention relating to the Status of Refugees (www.refworld.org/docid/3be01b964.html), the 1967 Protocol relating to the Status of Refugees (www.refworld.org/docid/3ae6b3ae4.html and UNHCR (www.unhcr.org).
4 Migrans can, however, count on the International Organization for Migration (www.iom.int).
5 See, for instance, the Guiding Principles on Internal Displacement. www.unhcr.org/protection/idps/43ce1cff2/guiding-principles-internal-displacement.html.
6 See the African Union Convention for the Protection and Assistance of Internally Displaced Persons in Africa (also known as the Kampala Convention). www.unhcr.org/about-us/background/4ae9bede9/african-union-convention-protection-assistance-internally-displaced-persons.html.
7 The International Convention on the Protection of the Rights of All Migrant Workers and Members of their Families is available at: www.ohchr.org/EN/ProfessionalInterest/Pages/CMW.aspx.

8 As of May 29, 2017 the Convention has been subject to 51 ratifications and 15 states are party to it, with the vast majority being states from the Global South. http://indicators.ohchr.org/

9 Article 1 of the 1951 Refugee Convention.

10 In 2013, an estimated 22 million were environmentally displaced, according to UNHCR. www.unhcr.org/pages/49c3646c10a.html

The most cited estimative figure for 2050 is 200 million environmental migrants (Laczko & Aghazarm, 2009, p. 5).

11 In legal terms, "complementary protection" describes protection granted by States on the basis of an international protection need outside the 1951 Convention framework (McAdam, 2005, p. 4).

12 According to Article I (2) of the OAU Convention Governing the Specific Aspects of Refugee Problems in Africa, a refugee is also any person compelled to leave his or her country owing to external aggression, occupation, foreign domination or events seriously disturbing public order in either part or the whole of his or her country of origin or nationality.

13 In accordance with the third conclusion of the 1984 Cartagena Declaration on Refugees, the term "refugee" should also apply to those persons who flee their countries because their lives, safety or freedom have been threatened by generalized violence, foreign aggression, internal conflicts, massive violation of human rights, or other circumstances that have seriously disturbe public order.

14 "[..T]he categorical classification and separation between migrants and refugees or between economic migration and forced migration, together with other concepts, has led, on one hand, to a situation where the rights of migrants are increasingly being left unprotected. On the other hand, paradoxically, it brings the human right to asylum and one of the principle (sic) ways in which it is realised – refugee status – into question" (Ceriani, 2016, p. 99).

15 Initially established by Article 33 of the 1951 Refugee Convention, *non-refoulement* prevents the sending/return of a person to a place where his or her life, security and liberty might be at risk

16 An example can be seen within the context of forcibly displaced children from Central America seeking international protection in the US. Recent reports have shown that, since January 2014, many US deportees from Central America have been killed shortly after being returned to their countries of origin, including children. See, for instance, www.theguardian.com/us-news/2015/oct/12/obama-immigration-deportations-central-america. Other examples of violations of migrants' rights to access safe territories are the occurrence of "push-backs," transfers and returns at borders. See, as examples of these instances: http://reliefweb.int/report/world/dangerous-game-pushback-migrants-including-refugees-europe-s-borders, www.unhcr.org/news/press/2017/4/58eb7e454/unhcr-urges-suspension-transfers-asylum-seekers-hungary-under-dublin.html, and www.newsdeeply.com/refugees/community/2017/04/13/a-troubling-trend-of-u-s-turning-away-asylum-seekers-at-mexico-border.

17 For more on this, see www.unodc.org/toc/en/crimes/migrant-smuggling.html.

18 The deaths of migrants in the Mediterranean Sea while trying to reach Europe in the past three years can be seen as examples of these facts. In 2014, 3,283 migrants died while crossing the Mediterranean due to the lack of secure channels, with figures jumping to 3,784 in 2015 and 5,089 in 2016. https://missingmigrants.iom.int/latest-global-figures. Another example is the fact that migrants are being sold as slaves in Libya (www.theguardian.com/world/2017/apr/10/libya-public-slave-auctions-un-migration).

19 For instance, it is well acknowledged that asylum-seeking unaccompanied children face several threats during their displacement: as "many abandon home to avoid forced recruitment, only to find that being in flight still places them at risk of recruitment, especially if they have no documentation" (United Nation General Assembly, 1996, para 68).

20 See, for instance, Alexander Betts' interview on Al Jazeera's *Inside Story*, June 19, 2015, in which he states that, "It is not just a crisis of numbers, it is a crisis of politics and a crisis of the failure of international cooperation." (www.rsc.ox.ac.uk/news/its-not-just-a-crisis-of-numbers-its-a-crisis-of-politics-and-a-crisis-of-failure-of-international-cooperation-alexander-betts).

21 "It is an annual States-led, voluntary, informal and non-binding ... platform for States to conduct informal dialogue and cooperation on migration and development issues" (United Nations Office of the High Commissioner for Human Rights, 2011, p. 24).

22 Declaration of the High-level Dialogue on International Migration and Development. A/68/L.5.

23 Retrieved from www.refworld.org/docid/5732e34e4.html.

24 Retrieved from www.un.org/ga/search/view_doc.asp?symbol=A/71/L.1.

25 The link between migration and development is a common assertion nowadays, and it has been posited that even though the act of migrating may stem from a great variety of circumstances, there

is still a strong and actual link between the act of living outside one's home country and development, both at an individual level and to the country of origin or destination: "International migration is one of the main transformation factors of the world we live in. It is also a consequence as it maintains complex relations with the changing of societies and economies of a world in movement with more and more vast distances and that nurture among them multiple interdependences. It has always been a part of economic and political evolution, being an engine of change in the societies of departure and destination" (our translation from the original in French (De Wenden, 2009, p. 40).

26 The process of adopting the Global Compact on safe, orderly, and regular migration is underway, and has been regulated by the Modalities Resolution A/71/L.58 of January 2017.

27 For more on complementary pathways for admission, especially in Latin America, see Jubilut. (2017).

28 An example of this is the criticism that "the Declaration misses the opportunity to give proper weight to the need for more pragmatic and attainable commitments to expand legal pathways of migration (encompassing resettlement, humanitarian visas, student and work permits, etc.), which could result in a considerable blow to the smuggling business" (Almeida & Bamberg, 2016).

29 https://eeas.europa.eu/headquarters/headquarters-homepage/20176/remarks-federica-mogherini-valletta-joint-action-plan-2017-senior-officials-meeting_ru.

30 In relation to the EU's response to migration, it has been defended, for instance by Federica Mogherini, on the grounds that its work with partners should "flow into the new Global Compact" (European External Action Service (EEAS), 2016b), which could be an improvement on international cooperation on migration governance, especially if the foundation of said collaboration is the protection of migrants and refugees.

References

Almeida, G. & Bamberg, K. (2016, November 24). *The UN Summit for refugees and migrants: A mirror of the current EU migration policy?* Odysseus Network. Retrieved from http://eumigrationlawblog.eu/the-un-summit-for-refugees/

Bakewell, O. (2014). Encampment and self-settlement. In E. Fiddian-Qasmiyeh, G. Loescher, K. Long, & N. Sigona (Eds.), *The Oxford handbook of refugee and forced migration studies* (pp. 127–138). Oxford: Oxford University Press.

Barbour, B. (2008). *Embracing the "responsibility to protect": A repertoire of measures including asylum for potential victims.* New Issues of Refugee Research: UNHCR. Retrieved from www.refworld.org/docid/4c23256a0.html

Ceriani, P. (2016). Language as a migration policy tool. *SUR Revista Internacional de Direitos Humanos, 23,* 97–111.

Crépeau, F. (2017a, March 24). *A new agenda for facilitating human mobility after the UN Summits on refugees and migrants.* Open Democracy. Retrieved from www.opendemocracy.net/beyondslavery/safepassages/fran-ois-cr-peau/new-agenda-for-facilitating-human-mobility-after-un-summits-on-refuge

Crépeau, F. (2017b, June 8). *UN Rapporteur: We need a long-term strategy for human migration.* Retrieved from www.newsdeeply.com/refugees/community/2017/06/08/u-n-rapporteur-we-need-a-long-term-strategy-for-human-migration

Crisp, J. (2017, September 18). *New York Declaration on refugees: A one-year report card.* Retrieved from www.newsdeeply.com/refugees/community/2017/09/18/new-york-declaration-on-refugees-a-one-year-report-card

De Wenden, C. W. (2009). *La globalisation humaine* [*The human globalization*]. Paris: Presses Universitaires de France – PUF.

Durieux, J.-F. (2017, April 3). *Too many migrants, or too many concepts?* Refugee Law Initiative blog. https://rli.blogs.sas.ac.uk/2017/04/03/too-many-migrants-or-too-many-concepts/

European Council on Refugees and Exile. (2017). *Protection in Europe.* Retrieved from www.ecre.org/topics/areas-of-work/protection-in-europe.html

European External Action Service (EEAS). (2016a, 20 September). *Mogherini calls for global compact to meet challenge of migration.* Retrieved from https://eeas.europa.eu/topics/nuclear-safety/10090/mogherini-calls-for-global-compact-to-meet-challenge-of-migration-_en

European External Action Service (EEAS). (2016b, September 20). *Speech by Federica Mogherini at the roundtable 5 on global compact at the United Nations.* Retrieved from https://eeas.europa.eu/headquarters/

headquarters-homepage/10081/speech-by-federica-mogherini-at-the-roundtable-5-on-global-compact-at-the-united-nations-_en

Gibney, M. J. (2002). Security and the ethics of asylum after 11 September. *Forced Migration Review, 13*, 40–42.

Gilbert, G. (2016, September 19). *Glimmers of hope*. Kaldor Center for International Refugee Law. Retrieved from www.kaldorcentre.unsw.edu.au/publication/glimmers-hope

Goodwin-Gill, G. (2017, October 7). *A half-century of universal refugee protection under threat*. Retrieved from www.newsdeeply.com/refugees/community/2017/10/04/a-half-century-of-universal-refugee-protection-under-threat

Guild, E. & Grant, S. (2017, January 8). *Migration governance in the UN: What is the global compact and what does it mean?* Queen Mary School of Law Legal Studies Research Paper No. 252/2017. Retrieved from https://ssrn.com/abstract=2895636

Howden, D. (2016, September 22). *Mismatch between rhetoric and reality at refugee summits*. Refugees Deeply. Retrieved from www.newsdeeply.com/refugees/articles/2016/09/22/mismatch-between-rhetoric-and-reality-at-refugee-summits

Jubilut, L. L. (2017). Humanitarian alternative pathways for protection for forced migrants in Latin America. In M. McAuliffe & M. K. Solomon (Conveners), *Migration research leaders' syndicate: Ideas to inform international cooperation on safe, orderly and regular migration* (pp. 117–122). Geneva: IOM.

Jubilut, L. L. & Lopes, R. O. (2017). Strategies for the protection of migrants through international law. *Groningen Journal of International Law, 5*, 34–56.

Jubilut, L. L. & Madureira, A. L. (2014). Os desafios de proteção aos refugiados e migrantes forçados no Marco de Cartagena + 30 [The challenges of protection for refugees and forced migrants in the Cartagena + 30 framework]. *REMHU – Revista Interdisciplinar da Mobilidade Humana, 22*, 11–33.

Koser, K. (2015, September 21). *Time to reform the international refugee regime*. Oxford University Press blog. Retrieved from http://blog.oup.com/2015/09/international-refugee-regime-reform/

Laczko, F. & Aghazarm, C. (Eds.). (2009). *Migration, environment and climate change: Assessing the evidence*. Geneva: IOM.

Madureira, A. L. & Jubilut, L. L. (2016). *Durable solutions – 5 implementation challenges and possible pathways for improvement*. Melbourne: Refugee Research Blog.

Martin, S. (2015). International migration and global governance. *Global Summitry, 1*, 64–83.

McAdam, J. (2005). *Complementary protection and beyond: How states deal with human rights protection*. New Issues in Refugee Research: UNHCR. Retrieved from www.unhcr.org/research/working/42fb1f045/complementary-protection-beyond-states-deal-human-rights-protection-jane.html

Office of the High Commissioner for Human Rights (OHCHR). (2011). *Migration and human rights: Improving human rights based governance of international migration*. Retrieved from www.ohchr.org/Documents/Issues/Migration/MigrationHR_improvingHR_Report.pdf

Papademetriou, D. G. & Fratzke, S. (2016). *Global refugee summits offer reasons for both disappointment and hope*. Migration Policy Institute. Retrieved from www.migrationpolicy.org/news/global-refugee-summits-offer-reasons-both-disappointment-and-hope

Türk, V. & Garlick, M. (2016). From burdens and responsibilities to opportunities: The comprehensive refugee response framework and a global compact on refugees. *International Journal of Refugee Law, 28*, 656–678.

United Nations Department of Economic and Social Affairs. (2017). *International migration report 2017*. Retrieved from www.un.org/en/development/desa/population/migration/publications/migrationreport/docs/MigrationReport2017_Highlights.pdf

United Nations High Commissioner for Refugees (UNHCR). (2016a). *Global trends: Forced displacement in 2015*. Retrieved from www.refworld.org/docid/57678f3d4.

United Nations High Commissioner for Refugees (UNHCR). (2016b). *Opening of the high-level meeting to address large movements of refugees and migrants*. Remarks by Filippo Grandi, United Nations High Commissioner for Refugees. Retrieved from www.unhcr.org/admin/hcspeeches/57dfe7ee4/opening-high-level-meeting-address-large-movements-refugees-migrants-remarks.html

United Nations High Commissioner for Refugees (UNHCR). (2016c). *New York Declaration for refugees and migrants: Quick guide*. Retrieved from www.unhcr.org/57e4f6504.pdf

United Nations High Commissioner for Refugees (UNHCR). (2017). *Global trends: Forced displacement in 2016*. Retrieved from www.unhcr.org/5943e8a34.pdf.

United Nations High Commissioner for Refugees (UNHCR). (2018). *Global trends: Forced displacement in 2017*. Retrieved from www.unhcr.org/globaltrends2017/

United Nations General Assembly. (2016a). *Safety and dignity: Addressing large movements of refugees and migrants.* Retrieved from www.refworld.org/docid/5732e34e4.html

United Nations General Assembly. (2016b). *New York Declaration for refugees and migrants: Resolution adopted by the General Assembly.* A/RES/71/1. Retrieved from www.refworld.org/docid/57ceb74a4.html

Zetter, R. (2007). More labels, fewer refugees: Making and remaking the refugee label in an era of globalization. *Journal of Refugee Studies, 20*, 172–192.

3

QUO VADIS? THE EUROPEAN UNION'S MIGRATION AND ASYLUM POLICY

Legal basis, legal challenges, and legal possibilities

Francisco Javier Donaire Villa

Does a European Union migration and asylum policy actually exist? If so, is it in crisis following the massive arrival of migrants from 2013 onwards (the so-called "Refugee Crisis")? This chapter intends to deal with these questions through a review of the most relevant EU legal frameworks, distinguishing between legislation enacted before and since the Refugee Crisis. It will also address the pragmatic programs and solutions devised thus far by the EU in the face of this complex scenario. Finally, this chapter will outline some conclusions and lines of reflection on the present and future of the EU migration policy.

Causes and origins of the EU migration and asylum policy: the internal market

Clearly, the internal market had the greatest effect on the EU's competences regarding migration. The initial draft of the Treaty establishing the European Economic Community (EEC Treaty) laid down a principle of free movement of persons as a constituting element of the common market. The resulting freedoms of movement (of workers, establishment, and services) were conferred on European Community (EC) nationals, with an extension only to their non-EC national family members.

The 1960s and 1970s EC Regulations and Directives based on the EEC Treaty, as well as a broad understanding of these personal freedoms construed by the EC Court of Justice's case law, reduced border controls for EC nationals to the mere presentation of a passport or an identity card in order to gain access to a Member State other than that of origin. Non-EC nationals, by contrast, had no general freedom of movement within the EC.

In the mid-1980s, the Single European Act reframed the common market into the internal market as an area without internal borders where the free movement of persons would be ensured. However, it did not introduce legal bases for the lifting of controls at these borders, nor for enacting the accompanying measures (including immigration issues). This was mainly due to the opposition of the UK, with unanimity being required for the amendment of the EEC Treaty. Subsidiary EC competences deriving from former Article 235 of the Treaty also required unanimity, which led to a deadlock.

This gave rise to the intergovernmental cooperation outside the EC among the other Member States, with the Schengen acquis (the rules regulating abolishment of border controls) standing out. The Maastricht Treaty maintained that approach, although it incorporated in the newborn European Union (EU) a non-communitarian pillar on justice and home affairs (a mechanism of intergovernmental cooperation among Member States within the EU, but without transfer of national competences to the EU institutions and based on the unanimous vote of ministerial representatives of all Member States meeting in the EU Council), which included the treatment of immigration issues.

The Treaty of Amsterdam 1999 was a landmark in the communitarian dealing with immigration matters. In exchange for the opting-out of the United Kingdom (UK) and Republic of Ireland, this treaty confirmed the lifting of intra-communitarian border controls as a legal consequence of the EEC Treaty's general principle of free movement of persons within the internal market. A new general objective of the EU, the completion of an area of freedom, security and justice, encompassed both the lifting of internal border controls and the adoption of the accompanying measures. New legal bases were provided to that effect, including in particular EU actions on migration and asylum of third-country nationals. An ad hoc protocol integrated the Schengen acquis into the EU as a form of reinforced cooperation among Member States others than UK and Ireland, with a special non-communitarian status for Denmark.

The Treaty of Nice 2003 introduced only minor amendments, whereas the Treaty of Lisbon, the last one redrafting EC and EU treaties for the time being, and in force since December 2009, communitarized all the EU policies in the area of freedom, security, and justice by eliminating the EU's former third intergovernmental pillar. Focusing on our particular interest here, this treaty widened the pre-existing legal bases of the EU's migration policy.

EU general legislation on migration policy: overview

Article 79 of the Treaty on the Functioning of the European Union (TFEU; also referred to as the Treaty of Rome), the former EEC Treaty, empowers the EU to establish a common immigration policy. Essentially, it covers legal immigration (entry and residence conditions, visas and permits, family reunification, rights including conditions for residence in other Member States, and the supporting of Member States' actions on integration) and illegal immigration (repatriation and expulsion, fight against trafficking of human beings, and agreements with non-Member States regarding their readmission of non-EU nationals).

Member States have themselves reserved the exclusive competence to establish volumes of admission of third-country nationals in their respective territories for the purpose of seeking work. They have also established a sense of solidarity in relation to an equitable sharing of responsibility among Member States (Article 80 of the TFEU) as common principles in migration issues, including the financial aspect.

Developments in secondary legislation essentially encompassed setting out rules on the uniform format for residence permits, the establishment of a single procedure to apply for a single permit allowing third-country nationals to reside and work, the rights of third-country nationals legally residing in a Member State, and the fight against illegal immigration, including expulsion and repatriation. Council Regulation 1030/2002 (Council of the EU, 2002a) established a uniform format for third-country nationals' residence permits to be used by all Member States, according to highly developed technical standards to prevent imitation and counterfeiting, and allowing the inclusion in the permits of relevant information from the perspective of combating illegal immigration. However, Directive 2011/98 (European Parliament & Council of the EU, 1998), on the single permit, does not determine the material conditions to be fulfilled by applicants in order to have the legitimate expectation of obtaining such a permit, leaving this issue to the law of the respective Member States, in correspondence with the fact that this is a field of shared competence between Member States and the EU, as provided for by Article 4 (2) (j) TFEU.

Both the procedure and the resulting permit refer to situations other than long-term legal residents. These have their legal framework in Council Directive 2003/109 (Council of the EU, 2003b). However, this directive only addresses the essential features of the procedure: application, issuance, refusal, or modification of the Single Residence Permit regulated therein, referring its format to Regulation 1030/2002 (Council of the EU, 2002a). In particular, Directive 2003/109 (Council of the EU, 2003b) establishes the minimum set of rights linked to the granting of the permit. This implies the recognition of a principle of non-discrimination on grounds of nationality with respect to nationals from the Member State that issues the permit (Article 12 of the directive).

Perhaps the most "productive" area in terms of translation into secondary legislation is that concerning the fight against illegal immigration. Part of it was enacted by the former EU third pillar, like the Council Framework Decision 2002/946/JHA (Council of the EU, 2002b), aimed at strengthening the national criminal legislation for the suppression of aid to irregular entry, movement, and residence. However, the EU's third pillar acquis was often complemented by EC legal instruments, such as Directive 2002/90 defining the facilitation of unauthorized entry, transit, and residence (Council of the EU, 2002c).

Two legal instruments of secondary law are outstanding in this area because of their general dimension and relevance. These are Directive 2008/115 (Council of the EU, 2002c), also known as the Return Directive, and Directive 2001/40 (Council of the EU, 2001) on mutual recognition of decisions to expel third-country nationals. Of particular importance, Directive 2008/115 (European Parliament & Council of the EU, 2008) established common rules on return, expulsion, use of coercive measures, detention, and prohibition of entry of third-country nationals.

Directive 2011/36 (European Parliament & Council of the EU, 2011a), combating trafficking in human beings, is also important here. Its content provides for strong protection of victims' rights, in particular for, but not limited to, minors, and especially if they are unaccompanied minors. Relatedly, Directive 2004/81 (Council of the EU, 2004a) regulates the issuing of a residence permit to third-country nationals who are victims of human trafficking.

The common European asylum system: the treaty, Dublin regulations and related acts

The EU asylum policy, as set out in Article 78 of the TFEU, essentially means that a single Member State examines and subsequently grants or denies the status of refugee or that of subsidiary protection (both legal notions lately recast under the single concept of "international protection"), the contents and procedures of which are likewise established or harmonized by the EU. As a general implementing secondary law measure, Regulation 604/2013/EU (European Parliament & Council of the EU, 2013b), also known as the Dublin Regulation, relies on the principle of the Member State of first entry as the only one responsible for the examination and resolution of all applications for international protection lodged by each third-country national in any, several, or all Member States. In addition, Eurodac Regulation (European Parliament & Council of the EU, 2013a) establishes the procedure for the computer registration of each applicant's fingerprints in order to help enforce the Dublin Regulation.

Applicants' reception conditions are provided for in Directive 2013/33 (European Parliament & Council of the EU, 2013d), whereas requirements for recognition as beneficiaries of international protection, and what such uniform status refers to, are currently laid out in Directive 2011/95 (European Parliament & Council of the EU, 2011b), also known as the Qualification Directive. The need for protection is a key element of that recognition. It is defined by this directive as the applicant's well-founded fears of being persecuted, or the actual risk of suffering serious harm. The directive also envisages the denial of the application if the risk of persecution was created by the applicant after leaving the country of origin.

Likewise, the Qualification Directive establishes the eligibility requirements for subsidiary protection: being the subject of serious damage, such as being sentenced to the death penalty; suffering torture or inhuman or degrading treatment or penalty in the country of origin; or serious and individual threats to life or physical integrity in situations of armed conflict. As regards the content of the international protection offered by this directive, it essentially equals refugee status and that of persons requiring subsidiary protection, both structured as a set of rights. Among these rights are access to employment and related training, remuneration, social security, working conditions in accordance with national legislation, education (full access for minors and, for adults, the same access as that offered to third-country nationals legally residing in the relevant Member State), social assistance, health care, housing on the same basis as third-country nationals legally residing, and integration programs.

Procedural aspects, and the corresponding applicants' rights, are laid down by Directive 2013/32, also known as the Asylum Procedures Directive (European Parliament & Council of the EU, 2013c). Applicants have the right to see their applications and resolutions carried out individually, objectively, impartially, and within a reasonable time in language they understand, to receive all relevant information thereof, to contact the Office of the United Nations High Commissioner for Refugees (UNHCR) or other organizations, and to get legal assistance and free legal representation upon appeal. Specific guarantees are established for unaccompanied minors.

Applications may be refused if the Member State lacks competence for their examination, or be inadmissible if another Member State has granted international protection, or if a third state is considered safe for the applicant or his or her first country of asylum. Definitions thereof are provided. Applicants are allowed to remain temporarily in the Member State until a decision of first instance (or resolving appeal) is made, although not giving rise to the right to obtain a residence permit.

(Soft-law) measures on migrants' integration

The EU's competence to integrate legally resident immigrants is of a complementary and coordinative nature, and consists of the supporting of Member States' actions without harmonization of their respective national legislations, as provided for by Article 79.4 of the TFEU. Accordingly, the implementing measures adopted are essentially soft-law in nature. They are either measures to finance European and national programs fitting into the framework of principles set by the EU's non-binding instruments, or recommendations and similar documents aimed at promoting and supporting actions by Member States.

The Council endorsed the common basic principles for the integration of immigrants in 2004 (Council of the EU, 2004b, p. 19). Based on this, the Commission adopted a Common Agenda on Integration in 2005 (European Commission, 2005) and a new European Agenda for the Integration of Third-Country Nationals in July 2011 (European Commission, 2011a), highlighting challenges and exploring the role of countries of origin in the integration process. An annexed Commission Staff Working Paper (European Commission, 2011b) contained a list of EU initiatives supporting the integration of third-country nationals. In 2016, the Council adopted its Conclusions on the Integration of Third-Country Nationals Legally Residing in the EU (Council of the EU, 2016).

Immediate and long-term EU actions in the face of the migrant crisis: the Commission's agenda on migration

In the aftermath of the shipwrecks off the coast of the Italian island Lampedusa, where hundreds of migrants lost their lives, the EU began to address what, at that time (2013), was first considered a maritime crisis, with the primary aim of saving immigrants' lives in the Central and Eastern Mediterranean. In April 2015, the Dublin ordinary system collapsed under the weight of the huge influx of migrants and refugees to the external borders of Italy and Greece. These had been unable to follow the principle of the Member State of first entry being responsible for the examination of third-country nationals' protection applications. This gave way to a "wave-out" policy of migrants and refugees to the northern Member States, opening new paths such as the Western Balkans migratory route. In response, internal border controls in the Schengen Area were reintroduced among several Member States, even by means of new physical barriers such as walls and fences that were hastily erected (European Commission, 2016a, p. 2).

As far as the EU's response to the migration crisis is concerned, a special meeting of the European Council in April 2015 (European Council, 2015a), the Commission's European Agenda on Migration (European Commission, 2015a), and a Eurochamber's Resolution of April 12, 2016 (European Parliament, 2016) coincided on the necessary reinforcement of the principle of internal solidarity among Member States. This was to provide support to Italy and Greece as frontline countries facing the migratory challenge. All Member States agreed to organize an emergency relocation scheme on a voluntary basis, triggering the emergency clause enshrined in Article 78(3) of the Treaty. The European Council special meeting of April 2015 also agreed to tackle the core structural causes of "illegal migration," to enhance cooperation with States of origin and transit of the flows, and to prevent irregular migration (European Council, 2015a).

The Commission's European Agenda on Migration simultaneously addressed the migration crisis and developed the political priorities on migration set out by President Jean-Claude Juncker in his investiture speech at the European Parliament (Juncker, 2014, pp. 10–11). This agenda, on the one hand, outlined immediate measures to respond to the crisis situation in the Mediterranean and, on the other, the medium- and long-term initiatives to provide structural solutions for a better or more robust managing of all aspects of migration. On this basis, the European Commission issued a set of initiatives in 2015 that included:

1) A relocation scheme aimed at third-country nationals in need of international protection within the EU (for the first time within the EU's migration policy) from Member States under extreme migratory pressure (European Commission, 2015b).
2) A proposal for a common list of safe third countries of origin (European Commission, 2015c).

3) The establishment of "hotspots," defined by the Commission as "a section of the EU external border or a region with extraordinary migratory pressure which calls for reinforced and concerted support by EU Agencies" (European Commission, 2015d).
4) A proposal for the establishment of a European Border and Coast Guard (EBCG) (European Commission, 2015f).

Immediate measures: the successive relocation and resettlement schemes

As part of the immediate measures to address the migration crisis, the Agenda on Migration announced that the Commission would propose a mechanism to trigger the emergency response system envisaged under Article 78(3) of the Treaty by the end of May. It would be a temporary distribution scheme for persons in clear need of international protection, with fair and balanced participation of Member States according to criteria such as GDP, population size, unemployment rate, and past numbers of asylum seekers and resettled refugees.

Soon afterwards, the European Council of June 25 and 26, 2015 agreed on the relocation from Italy and Greece to other Member States of 40,000 persons in clear need of international protection, over a two-year period. However, as this voluntary scheme soon revealed itself to be insufficient, the Council, at the proposal of Commission President Jean-Claude Juncker, adopted two legally binding decisions in September 2015, which established a temporary and exceptional relocation mechanism for 160,000 applicants from Greece and Italy that were in clear need of international protection: Decision 2015/1523 (Council of the EU, 2015b) and Decision 2015/1601 (Council of the EU, 2015c). These were accepted by Member States, with the exception of the Visegrad Group (Hungary, Czech Republic, Poland, and Slovakia).

In a nutshell, both decisions entailed a (temporary) derogation of the Dublin system, as Member States (or "Member States of relocation") other than those of first entry (in this case, Greece or Italy) became responsible for examining the application of the person to be relocated. Their purpose seems to have been partially achieved in June 2017, according to the thirteenth Commission report on relocation and resettlement (European Commission, 2017e). Despite that fact, the Commission decided to launch infringement procedures against the Czech Republic, Hungary, and Poland in June 2017 for not fulfilling their obligations under both Council decisions (ibid, p. 9).

In July, besides the aforementioned measures, Member States agreed on an EU-wide Resettlement Scheme to Europe for 20,000 displaced persons in clear need of international protection from the Middle East, North Africa, and the Horn of Africa (Council of the EU, 2015a). This two-year scheme was supported by the EU budget. Finally, on July 13, 2016, the Commission proposed a permanent EU Resettlement Framework (European Commission, 2016i) to establish a common set of standard procedures for the selection of resettlement candidates and a common protection status. This initiative was intended to provide a better focus for European resettlement efforts in the future.

Recasting of the common European asylum system

In the wake of the 2015 European Agenda on Migration, on April 6, 2016 the Commission proposed a reform of the Common European Asylum System to render it a more humane, fair, and efficient policy, as well as a better managed legal migration policy (European Commission, 2016b). On May 4, 2016, the Commission presented the first set of proposals:

1) Recasting Dublin III Regulation in search of a sustainable and fair system to determine the Member State responsible for examining asylum applications (European Commission, 2016c).
2) Creating a genuine European Union Agency for Asylum to ensure the efficiency of the European asylum system (European Commission, 2016d).
3) Reinforcing the Eurodac system to better monitor secondary movements and facilitate the fight against irregular migration (European Commission, 2016e).

The first package was followed by a second one on July 2016 for the Common European Asylum System's reform. It consisted of the following proposals:

1) Recasting the Reception Conditions Directive (European Commission, 2016f).
2) Replacing the Qualification Directive (European Commission, 2016g) with regulations affording deeper harmonization among Member States and the Asylum Procedures Directive (European Commission, 2016h).

The proposal to recast the Qualifications Directive aims at better preparation on the part of Member States to enable them to tackle massive arrivals of international protection seekers while safeguarding their fundamental rights in general and of children in particular. To avoid pressure on internal border controls and asylum-shopping, this proposal establishes new targeted restrictions and negative legal consequences for applicants' secondary movement to any other Member State from that responsible for examining the application if those restrictions are not abided by. In a similar vein, reform of the Dublin III Regulation would result in a reduction of benefits for applicants who leave the Member State where they are required to be present. In turn, integration possibilities for well-grounded applicants would, for example, improve through easier access to employment and remuneration.

The European Parliament articulated a completely different focus for the reform of the Dublin system. Its Resolution of April 12, 2016 (European Parliament, 2016) goes further than the Commission's proposals and suggests the centralization of applications at the EU level, as well as the allocation of responsibility for any non-EU national asylum-seeker. The draft report of the Eurochamber's Committee on Civil Liberties, Justice, and Home Affairs criticizes the stress placed on sanctions and possible abuse of the Dublin system, and identifies the need for enhancing the integration of asylum and protection-seekers (European Parliament, 2017).

Enhancing the Agencies: EASO and Frontex (reframed as the European Border and Coast Guard Agency)

In 2016, the Commission suggested the revision of the Common European Asylum System (CEAS) and the Dublin distribution mechanism to facilitate and improve their functioning (European Commission, 2016c). One of its proposals was amendment of the mandate of the European Support Asylum Office (EASO) to strengthen its operational profile "on the ground" and allow it to play an active new policy-implementing role.

This functional enhancement is even reflected in its new name, the European Asylum Agency, rather than the former Support Agency. Its general mission would be to ensure the efficient and uniform application of EU asylum law by and in Member States, and its tasks would mainly involve the following:

1) Operating as the reference point for the fair and sustainable distribution of asylum and international protection applications among Member States according to the recasting of the Dublin legal system.
2) Monitoring Member States' implementation of the CEAS.
3) Providing operational assistance through the deployment of teams in hotspots experiencing extraordinary migratory pressure.
4) Organizing and coordinating operational and technical measures on its own initiative or by request of the corresponding Member State.

The proposal allows the Commission to adopt an implementing act choosing technical and operational measures to be executed by the Agency in support of a Member State whenever the CEAS may be in risk of collapsing. This Member State would in turn have the legal duty to cooperate with the Agency. Such an initiative (as of the end of June 2017) is still pending approval by the European Parliament and has raised reservations on the part of several Member States regarding the Agency's operational and implementation powers conferred by the Commission.

By contrast, the European Parliament and the Council adopted – in a record time of just nine months – Regulation 2016/1624 on the new European Border and Coast Guard Agency (European Parliament & Council of the EU, 2016b) from the Commission's proposal (European Commission, 2015f). It now brings together the recast and renamed Frontex and Member States' national border control services. The new Agency is endowed with a monitoring and risk analysis center, a pool of border guards and technical equipment, as well as the competences and resources to:

1) Conduct mandatory assessments on Member States' vulnerabilities or operational capacity.
2) Deploy supporting teams for joint operations and rapid border intervention even in the case of unwillingness on the part of the concerned Member State.
3) Mobilize European return intervention teams to return illegally-remaining third-country nationals, who must be provided with a Standard European Travel Document for Return envisaged by Regulation 2016/1953 (European Parliament & Council of the EU, 2016c).
4) Send liaison officers to launch joint operations with neighboring third countries, even on their own territory.

The European Border and Coast Guard became operational on 6 October 2016 (European Commission, 2017d).

The EU's international outsourcing of migration and asylum

Another cornerstone of the EU's migration and asylum actions lies in the "outsourcing" of both policies. The seminal Conclusions of the 1999 European Council of Tampere invited Member States to conclude readmission agreements, to include standard clauses in other European Community international treaties, and to establish partnerships with third countries concerned as key elements for the success of the migration and asylum policy (European Council, 1999).

The EU's Readmission Agreements (EURAs) impose reciprocal obligations on the contracting parties to readmit their respective nationals and also, more significantly, third-country nationals and stateless persons. To date, 17 EURAs have been signed, with Hong

Kong, Macao, Sri Lanka, Albania, Russia, Ukraine, Macedonia, Bosnia and Herzegovina, Montenegro, Serbia, Moldova, Pakistan, Georgia, Armenia, Azerbaijan, Turkey, and Cape Verde. Likewise, the inclusion of readmission commitments in general collaboration, cooperation, or association agreements of the EU with third countries is common (Díaz Morgado, 2015, p. 159).

By contrast, Mobility Partnerships (MPs) are not international treaties, but take the shape of joint declarations between the partner country, the EU, and Member States wishing to take part in the deal. In exchange for its promise to fight and prevent illegal migration to the EU, the signing third country benefits from technical and economic assistance to develop migration management capacities and legal paths for migration of its nationals to the EU.

This legal structure was chosen by Member States because of their rejection of legally-binding instruments, and also because an international treaty might find it difficult to be ratified by national parliaments (Reslow, 2012, p. 231). As non-desirable consequences, the European Parliament lacks participation, and the EU Court of Justice has no clear means of control (Carrera & Hernández, 2009, p. 30). MPs were initially signed with Cape Verde (June 5, 2008), Moldova (June 5, 2008), Georgia (November 13, 2009), Armenia (October 27, 2011), and Azerbaijan (December 5, 2013). Significantly, coinciding with the start of the migration crisis, a second wave of MPs has been agreed, with Morocco (June 3, 2013), Tunisia (March 3, 2014), and Jordan (October 9, 2014). More recently, an MP has been reached with Belarus (13 October, 2016).

The European Neighbourhood Policy (ENP) is a similar outsourcing initiative. Its purpose (European Commission, 2016j) is to ensure the economic and political stability of the EU's surrounding non-Member States. The ENP resulted from the initial Barcelona Process created in Spring 1995, and became the Union for the Mediterranean in Autumn 2008 in conjunction with the Eastern Partnership initiated in Spring 2009 (Gylfason & Wijkman, 2012, p. 4). It was formally launched in 2003 (European Commission, 2016i), first reviewed in 2011 (European Commission & EU High Representative for Foreign Affairs and Security Policy, 2011), and then again in 2015 (European Commission & EU High Representative for Foreign Affairs and Security Policy, 2015).

The ENP includes measures to promote legal mobility and migration, diminish irregular migration, and conduct effective border management (European Commission, 2017c). Priorities are established in tailored soft-law action plans (APs) with every partner country, the legal basis of which lies in a previously bilateral association agreement between the EU and the corresponding Member State (Maggi, 2016, p. 85). ENP projects are funded by the European Neighbourhood Instrument (ENI) created by Regulation 232/2014 (European Parliament & Council of the EU, 2014); €15.4 billion was provided for the period 2014–2020.

The November 2015 Valletta Summit of the EU and African heads of state or government agreed upon the Africa–EU Partnership (European Council, 2015b), encompassing the 23 countries of Sahel/Lake Chad, Horn of Africa, and North Africa, and created an EU Emergency Trust Fund of over €2.5 billion to contribute to better migration management and address root causes of destabilization, forced displacement, and irregular migration in the area (European Commission, 2017b). November 2015 also witnessed, as an urgent measure at the height of the migration crisis at the South Eastern external border, the activation of an EU–Turkey Joint Action Plan (JAP) previously agreed upon in October. It offered EU support to maintain Syrian refugees in Turkish territory and set out a commitment to strengthen cooperation to prevent irregular migratory flows to the EU (European Commission, 2015e). As a result of this commitment, it would subsequently be agreed upon in the EU–Turkey Joint Statement (European Council, 2016), active from March 18, 2016, that for every Syrian national returned from the Greek islands, another would be resettled to the EU directly from Turkey (the so-called "1:1 mechanism"). Following this Statement, the Commission identified that irregular arrivals dropped by 97 percent, and that lives lost at sea also decreased substantially (European Commission, 2017a).

Concluding remarks

Returning to the questions raised at the beginning of this chapter, we can now claim that no real or complete EU migration and asylum policy exists. First, this is because it is a matter of the EU's shared competence. Second, it is because Member States, as masters of the EU Treaties, have individually reserved the exclusive competence to establish the volume of admission to third-country nationals that intend to seek work in the respective State territory, as provided for in Article 79(5) TFEU. This means, as Mistri and Orcally (2015, p. 243) point out, that "undoubtedly the EU has no jurisdiction in determining immigration flows, nor their composition." Such limits simply lead us to conclude that there is no general, comprehensive European Union migration policy, because the core of such a policy, the decision on the admission of third-country nationals, and how many of them, as well as the foundations of their very admission or exclusion, legally rests with the national competence of Member States.

Member States fashion their national migration policies according to varying models, with heterogeneous requirements for the access of immigrants to the respective national labour markets (Lahav, 2004, p. 8). This is further confirmed by the fact that the EU derivative legislation refers only to the admission of very specific groups of third-country nationals. Also, this legislation has been enacted in the form of directives, a source of EU law that does not result in the same legal harmonizing effect as that provided by regulations. These include the Students Directive 2004/114 (Council of the EU, 2004c), Researchers Directive 2005/71 (Council of the EU, 2005), Highly Skilled Workers (Blue Card) Directive 2009/50 (Council of the EU, 2009), and Family Reunification Directive 2003/86 (Council of the EU, 2003a), the latter repealed and recast by Directive 2016/801 (European Parliament & Council of the EU, 2016a).

Indeed, this national competence on the access of third-country nationals to each Member State's labour market could be transferred to the EU. This would even allow the EU to carry out a policy that would avoid spill-over across Member States as a result of divergence among national legislation on this matter and, at the same time, to use the same integration patterns that have successfully performed in the completion and functioning of the internal market. That would also mean the abandonment of the security logic with which the Treaty regulates migration policy, allowing it to become an EU policy in itself, with its own regulating Title within the Treaty, at the same level as other EU policies (such as those on the Internal Market, on the Area of Freedom, Security and Justice, on Transport, and so on). But, for that to occur legally and politically, an amendment of the treaties is required. So it is ultimately a question of political (democratic) will.

This chapter concludes by answering the second question posed at the beginning: Is the EU migration policy currently in crisis? On a more general level, this specific issue leads to the more generic matter of the EU in crisis itself (financial crisis, Brexit). However, in a more specific context, that of the current migration crisis (mitigated lately, as already seen in terms of the number of arrivals, although not in terms of the dramatic root causes such as the Syrian conflict and others), it has been said that it is not really a crisis of numbers but a crisis of solidarity (UN Secretary General, 2016). This also implies, in particular, that we are not witnessing a legal crisis, although legal amendment to the EU's secondary law is under way and may be necessary. However, certain aspects to be modified in the migration and asylum policy – for example, centralized implementation of the Dublin system or management of external borders on the part of EU institutions or agencies – would require an amendment of the TFEU, since Articles 4(2) and 72 set out "the constitutional principle that member states are responsible for their own internal security" (Den Heijer, Rijpma, & Spijkerboer 2016, pp. 638–641) .

In turn, other amendments require a change of politics without changing the policy, because the TFEU already provides suitable legal bases and procedures. That being the case, it is again a matter of political will. Such a thing may happen as a result of reverting the current restrictive rationales that underlie the Dublin recasting packages or by getting past the logic of mere containment of migratory fluxes inspiring the more than dubious EU outsourcing of migration and asylum described *supra*. In sum, it is about a refinement or change of these concrete politics into others. This is not only a serious and responsible response but is also in accordance with the EU's demographic needs (an aging population) and would be more sensitive to fundamental rights.

References

Carrera, S. & Hernández, R. (2009). The externalisation of the EU's labour immigration policy: Towards mobility or insecurity partnerships? CEPS Working Document, 321. Retrieved from www.ceps.eu/system/files/book/2009/10/WD321%20Carrera%20and%20Sagrera%20e-version%20final.pdf

Council of the EU. (2001). Council Directive 2001/40/EC of 28 May 2001 on the mutual recognition of decisions on the expulsion of third country nationals. *Official Journal of the European Communities, 149*, 34–36.

Council of the EU. (2002a). Council Regulation (EC) No 1030/2002 of June 13, 2002 laying down a uniform format for residence permits for third-country nationals. *Official Journal of the European Communities, 157*, 1–7.

Council of the EU. (2002b). Council Framework Decision 2002/946/JHA of 28 November 2002 on the strengthening of the penal framework to prevent the facilitation of unauthorised entry, transit and residence. *Official Journal of the European Communities, 328*, 1–3.

Council of the EU. (2002c). Council Directive 2002/90/EC of 28 November 2002 defining the facilitation of unauthorized entry, transit and residence. *Official Journal of the European Communities, 328*, 17–18.

Council of the EU. (2003a). Council Directive 2003/86/EC of 22 September 2003 on the right to family reunification. *Official Journal of the European Union, 251*, 12–18.

Council of the EU. (2003b). Council Directive 2003/109/EC of 25 November 2003 concerning the status of third-country nationals who are long-term residents. *Official Journal of the European Union, 16*, 44–53.

Council of the EU. (2004a). Council Directive 2004/81/EC of 29 April 2004 on the residence permit issued to third-country nationals who are victims of trafficking in human beings or who have been the subject of an action to facilitate illegal immigration, who cooperate with the competent authorities. *Official Journal of the European Union, 261*, 19–23.

Council of the EU. (2004b, November 19). Common basic principles for the integration policy of immigrants. 14615/04.Press release of the 2618th Council Meeting (Justice and Home Affairs). Retrieved from www.consilium.europa.eu/ueDocs/cms_Data/docs/pressData/en/jha/82745.pdf.

Council of the EU. (2004c). Council Directive 2004/114/EC of 13 December 2004 on the conditions of admission of third-country nationals for the purposes of studies, pupil exchange, unremunerated training or voluntary service. *Official Journal of the European Union, 357*, 12–18.

Council of the EU. (2005). Council Directive 2005/71/EC of 12 October 2005 on a specific procedure for admitting third-country nationals for the purposes of scientific research. *Official Journal of the European Union, 289*, 15–22.

Council of the EU. (2009). Council Directive 2009/50/EC of 25 May 2009 on the conditions of entry and residence of third-country nationals for the purposes of highly qualified employment. *Official Journal of the European Union, 155*, 17–29.

Council of the EU. (2015a, July 22). Conclusions of the representatives of the governments of the member states meeting within the Council on resettling through multilateral and national schemes 20,000 persons in clear need of international protection. Retrieved from http://data.consilium.europa.eu/doc/document/ST-11130-2015-INIT/en/pdf

Council of the EU. (2015b). Council Decision (EU) 2015/1523 of 14 September 2015 establishing provisional measures in the area of international protection for the benefit of Italy and of Greece. *Official Journal of the European Union*, *239*, 146–156.

Council of the EU. (2015c). Council Decision (EU) 2015/1601 of 22 September 2015 establishing provisional measures in the area of international protection from the benefit of Italy and Greece. *Official Journal of the European Union*, *248*, 80–94.

Council of the EU. (2016). Conclusions on the integration of third-country nationals legally residing in the EU. Retrieved from http://data.consilium.europa.eu/doc/document/ST-15312-2016-INIT/en/pdf

Den Heijer, M., Rijpma, J., & Spijkerboer, T. (2016). Coercion, prohibition, and great expectations: The continuing failure of the common European asylum system. *Common Market Law Review*, *53*, 607–642.

Díaz Morgado, C. (2015). La lucha contra la inmigración irregular. In F. J. Donaire Villa & A. Olesti Rayo (Eds.), *Técnicas y ámbitos de coordinación en el Espacio de Libertad, Seguridad y Justicia* (pp. 141–161). Madrid: Marcial Pons.

European Commission. (2005, September 1). A common agenda for an integration framework for the integration of third-country nationals in the European Union. COM(2005) 389 final. Retrieved from http://eur-lex.europa.eu/LexUriServ/LexUriServ.do?uri=COM:2005:0389:FIN:EN:PDF

European Commission. (2011a, July 20). European Agenda for the integration of third-country nationals. COM(2011) 455 final. Retrieved from http://ec.europa.eu/transparency/regdoc/rep/1/2011/EN/1-2011-455-EN-F1-1.pdf

European Commission. (2011b). EU initiatives supporting the integration of third-country nationals. SEC (2011) 957. http://data.consilium.europa.eu/doc/document/ST-15312-2016-INIT/en/pdf.

European Commission. (2015a, May 13). Communication on a European agenda on migration. COM (2015) 240 final. Retrieved from http://eur-lex.europa.eu/legal-content/EN/TXT/PDF/?uri=CELEX:52015DC0240&from=en

European Commission. (2015b). Recommendation to the member states, of 8 June, on a European resettlement scheme. Retrieved from https://ec.europa.eu/home-affairs/sites/homeaffairs/files/e-library/documents/policies/asylum/general/docs/recommendation_on_a_european_resettlement_scheme_en.pdf

European Commission. (2015c, September 9). Proposal for a regulation of the European Parliament and of the Council establishing an EU common list of safe countries of origin for the purposes of directive 2013/32/EU of the European Parliament and of the Council on common procedures for granting and withdrawing international protection, and amending directive 2013/32/EU. COM(2015) 452 final. Retrieved from http://eur-lex.europa.eu/resource.html?uri=cellar:a5874209-56cc-11e5-afbf-01aa75ed71a1.0009.02/DOC_1&format=PDF

European Commission. (2015d, October 14). Managing the refugee crisis: State of play of the implementation of the priority actions under the European Agenda on Migration. COM(2015) 510 final. Retrieved from http://eur-lex.europa.eu/legal-content/EN/TXT/?qid=1498557230171&uri=CELEX:52015DC

European Commission. (2015e, December 15). EU–Turkey joint action plan. Press release. Retrieved from http://europa.eu/rapid/press-release_MEMO-15-5860_en.htm

European Commission. (2015f, December 15). Proposal for the establishment of a European Border and Coast Guard (EBCG). COM(2015) 671 final. Retrieved from http://eur-lex.europa.eu/resource.html?uri=cellar:3086c6c9-a3e7-11e5-b528-01aa75ed71a1.0023.02/DOC_1&format=PDF

European Commission. (2016a, March 4). Back to Schenge – a road map. COM(2016) 120 final. Retrieved from https://ec.europa.eu/home-affairs/sites/homeaffairs/files/what-we-do/policies/borders-and-visas/schengen/docs/communication-back-to-schengen-roadmap_en.pdf

European Commission. (2016b, April 6). Towards a reform of the Common European asylum system and enhancing legal avenues to Europe. COM(2016) 197 final. Retrieved https://ec.europa.eu/home-affairs/sites/homeaffairs/files/what-we-do/policies/european-agenda-migration/proposal-implementation-package/docs/20160406/towards_a_reform_of_the_common_european_asylum_system_and_enhancing_legal_avenues_to_europe_-_20160406_en.pdf

European Commission. (2016c, May 4). Proposal for a regulation of the European Parliament and of the Council establishing the criteria and mechanisms for determining the member state responsible for examining an application for international protection lodged in one of the member states by a third-country national or a stateless person (recast). COM(2016) 270. Retrieved from https://ec.europa.eu/transparency/regdoc/rep/1/2016/EN/1-2016-270-EN-F1-1.PDF

European Commission (2016d, May 4). Proposal for a regulation of the European Parliament and of the Council on the European Union Agency for Asylum and repealing Regulation (EU) No 439/2010. COM(2016) 271 final. Retrieved from https://ec.europa.eu/home-affairs/sites/homeaffairs/files/what-we-do/policies/european-agenda-migration/proposal-implementation-package/docs/20160504/easo_proposal_en.pdf

European Commission. (2016e, May 4). Proposal for a regulation of the European Parliament and of the Council on the establishment of "Eurodac" for the comparison of fingerprints for the effective application of Regulation (EU) No 604/2013 (Recast). COM(2016) 272 final. Retrieved from https://ec.europa.eu/transparency/regdoc/rep/1/2016/EN/1-2016-272-EN-F1-1.PDF

European Commission. (2016f, July 13). Proposal for a Directive of the European Parliament and of the Council laying down standards for the reception of applicants for international protection (Recast). COM (2016) 465 final. Retrieved from https://ec.europa.eu/home-affairs/sites/homeaffairs/files/what-we-do/policies/european-agenda-migration/proposal-implementation-package/docs/20160713/proposal_on_standards_for_the_reception_of_applicants_for_international_protection_en.pdf

European Commission. (2016g, July 13). Proposal for a directive on standards for the qualification of third-country nationals or stateless persons as beneficiaries of international protection, for a uniform status for refugees or for persons eligible for subsidiary protection and for the content of the protection granted and amending Council Directive 2003/109/EC. COM(2016) 466. Retrieved from https://ec.europa.eu/home-affairs/sites/homeaffairs/files/what-we-do/policies/european-agenda-migration/proposal-implementation-package/docs/20160713/proposal_on_beneficiaries_of_international_protection_-_subsidiary_protection_eligibility_-_protection_granted_en.pdf

European Commission. (2016h, July 13). Proposal for a regulation of the European Parliament and of the Council establishing a common procedure for international protection in the Union and repealing Directive 2013/32/EU. COM(2016) 467. Retrieved from http://eur-lex.europa.eu/resource.html?uri=cellar:2c404d27-4a96-11e6-9c64-01aa75ed71a1.0001.02/DOC_1&format=PDF

European Commission. (2016i, July 13). Proposal for a regulation of the European Parliament and of the Council Establishing a Union Resettlement Framework and Amending Regulation (EU) No 516/2014 of the European Parliament and the Council. COM(2016) 468. Retrieved from www.europarl.europa.eu/RegData/docs_autres_institutions/commission_europeenne/com/2016/0468/COM_COM%282016%290468_EN.pdf

European Commission. (2016j, December 6). European neighbourhood policy. Retrieved from https://ec.europa.eu/neighbourhood-enlargement/neighbourhood/overview_en

European Commission. (2017a, March 17). Factsheet: EU–Turkey statement: One year on. Retrieved from https://ec.europa.eu/home-affairs/sites/homeaffairs/files/what-we-do/policies/european-agenda-migration/background-information/eu_turkey_statement_17032017_en.pdf

European Commission (2017b, May 11). Factsheet: EU emergency trust fund for Africa. Retrieved from https://ec.europa.eu/europeaid/sites/devco/files/factsheet-emergency-trust-fund-africa-2017_en.pdf

European Commission. (2017c, May 18). Revised European Neighbourhood policy: Supporting stabilisation, resilience, security. European Commission press release. Retrieved from http://europa.eu/rapid/press-release_IP-17-1334_en.htm

European Commission. (2017d, June 13). Factsheet: A European Border and Coast Guard. Securing Europe's external borders. https://ec.europa.eu/home-affairs/sites/homeaffairs/files/what-we-do/policies/european-agenda-security/20170613_ebcg_en.pdf

European Commission. (2017e, June 13). Thirteenth Commission's report on relocation and resettlement. COM(2017) 330. Retrieved from http://eur-lex.europa.eu/resource.html?uri=cellar:3688a7a5-50fe-11e7-a5ca-01aa75ed71a1.0001.02/DOC_1&format=PDF

European Commission & EU High Representative for Foreign Affairs and Security Policy. (2011, June 8). A partnership for democracy and shared prosperity with the Southern Mediterranean. COM(2011) 200. Retrieved from http://eur-lex.europa.eu/legal-content/EN/TXT/PDF/?uri=CELEX:52011DC0200&from=EN

European Commission & EU High Representative for Foreign Affairs and Security Policy. (2015, November 18). Review of the European Neighbourhood Policy. JOIN(2015) 50 final. Retrieved from http://eeas.europa.eu/archives/docs/enp/documents/2015/151118_joint-communication_review-of-the-enp_en.pdf

European Council. (1999). Tampere European Council 15 and 16 October: Presidency conclusions. Retrieved from www.consilium.europa.eu/en/european-council/conclusions/pdf-1993-2003/TAMPERE-EUROPEAN-COUNCIL–PRESIDENCY-CONCLUSIONS-15-16-OCTOBER-1999/

European Council. (2015a, April 23). Special meeting of the European Council.. Statement. Retrieved from www.consilium.europa.eu/en/press/press-releases/2015/04/23-special-euco-statement/

European Council. (2015b, 11–12 November). Valletta Summit on migration. Political declaration. Retrieved from www.consilium.europa.eu/en/meetings/international-summit/2015/11/11-12/

European Council. (2016, March 18). EU–Turkey joint statement. Retrieved from www.consilium.europa.eu/en/press/press-releases/2016/03/18-eu-turkey-statement/

European Parliament. (2016). Resolution of 12 April on the situation in the Mediterranean and the need for a holistic EU approach to migration. P8_TA(2016)0102. Retrieved from www.europarl.europa.eu/sides/getDoc.do?pubRef=-//EP//NONSGML+REPORT+A8-2016-0066+0+DOC+PDF+V0//EN

European Parliament. (2017). Draft report of the Committee on Civil Liberties, Justice and Home Affairs on the Commission proposal of the regulation to substitute the Qualification Directive. 2016/0223 (COD). PR/1118879/EN, PE599.799v02-00. Retrieved from www.europarl.europa.eu/sides/getDoc.do?type=COMPARL&mode=XML&language=EN&reference=PE599.799

European Parliament & Council of the EU. (1998). Directive 2011/98/EU of the European Parliament and of the Council of 13 December 2011, on a single application procedure for a single permit for third-country nationals to reside and work in the territory of a member state and on a common set of rights for third-country workers legally residing in a member state. *Official Journal of the European Communities, L343*, 1–9.

European Parliament & Council of the EU. (2008). Directive 2008/115/EC of the European Parliament and of the Council of 16 December 2008 on common standards and procedures in member states for returning illegally staying third-country nationals. *Official Journal of the European Union, L348*, 98–107.

European Parliament & Council of the EU. (2011a). Directive 2011/36/EU of the European Parliament and of the Council of 5 April 2011 on preventing and combating trafficking in human beings and protecting its victims, and replacing Council framework decision 2002/629/JHA. *Official Journal of the European Union, L101*, 1–11.

European Parliament & Council of the EU. (2011b). Directive 2011/95/EU of the European Parliament and of the Council of 13 December 2011 on standards for the qualification of third-country nationals or stateless persons as beneficiaries of international protection, for a uniform status for refugees or for persons eligible for subsidiary protection, and for the content of the protection granted (recast). *Official Journal of the European Union, L337*, 9–25.

European Parliament & Council of the EU. (2013a). Regulation (EU) No 603/2013 of the European Parliament and of the Council of 26 June 2013 on the establishment of "Eurodac" for the comparison of fingerprints for the effective application of regulation (EU) No 604/2013 establishing the criteria and mechanisms for determining the member state responsible for examining an application for international protection lodged in one of the member states by a third-country national or a stateless person and on requests for the comparison with Eurodac data by member states' law enforcement authorities and Europol for law enforcement purposes, and amending Regulation (EU) No 1077/2011 establishing a European Agency for the operational management of large-scale IT systems in the area of freedom, security and justice (recast). *Official Journal of the European Union, L180*, 11–30.

European Parliament & Council of the EU. (2013b). Regulation (EU) No 604/2013 of the European Parliament and of the Council of June 2013 establishing the criteria and mechanisms for determining the member state responsible for examining an application for international protection lodged in one of the member states by a third-country national or a stateless person (recast). *Official Journal of the European Union, L180*, 31–59.

European Parliament & Council of the EU. (2013c). Directive 2013/32/EU of the European Parliament and of the Council of 26 June 2013 on common procedures for granting and withdrawing international protection (recast). *Official Journal of the European Union, L180*, 60–95.

European Parliament & Council of the EU. (2013d). Directive 2013/33/EU of the European Parliament and of the Council of 26 June 2013 laying down standards for the reception of applicants for international protection (recast). *Official Journal of the European Union, L180*, 96–116.

European Parliament & Council of the EU. (2014). Regulation (EU) No 232/2014 of the European Parliament and of the Council of 11 March 2014 establishing a European Neighbourhood Instrument. *2014 Official Journal of the European Union, L77*, 27–43.

European Parliament & Council of the EU. (2016a). Directive (EU) 2016/801 of the European Parliament and of the Council of 11 May 2016 on the conditions of entry and residence of third-country nationals for the purposes of research, studies, training, voluntary service, pupil exchange schemes or educational projects and au pairing. *Official Journal of the European Union, L132*, 21–57.

European Parliament & Council of the EU. (2016b). Regulation (EU) No 2016/1624 of the European Parliament and of the Council of 14 September 2016 on the European Border and Coast Guard and amending Regulation (EU) 2016/399 of the European Parliament and of the Council and repealing Regulation (EC) No 863/2007 of the European Parliament and of the Council, Council Regulation (EC) No 2007/2004 and Council Decision 2005/267/EC. *Official Journal of the European Union, L251*, 1–76.

European Parliament & Council of the EU. (2016c). Regulation (EU) 2016/1953 of the European Parliament and of the Council of 26 October 2016 on the establishment of a European travel document for the return of illegally staying third-country nationals, and repealing the Council recommendation of 30 November 1994. *Official Journal of the European Union, L311*, 13–19.

Gylfason, T. & Wijkman, P. M. (2012). Which conflicts can the European Neighbourhood Policy help resolve? CESIFO Working Paper, 3861. Retrieved from https://ideas.repec.org/p/ces/ceswps/_3861.html

Juncker, J. C. (2014, July 15). Political guidelines for the next European Commission, opening statement in the European Parliament plenary session, Strasbourg. Retrieved from https://ec.europa.eu/commission/sites/beta-political/files/juncker-political-guidelines-speech_en_0.pdf

Lahav, G. (2004). *Immigration and politics in the new Europe: Reinventing borders*. Cambridge: Cambridge University Press

Maggi, E. M. (2016). *The will of change: European neighborhood policy, domestic actors and institutional change in Morocco*. Wiesbaden: Springer.

Mistri, M. & Orcally, G. (2015). The European Union's immigration policy: A stalled form of the strategy of conflict? *International Economics and Economic Policy*, *12*, 230–256.

Reslow, N. (2012). Deciding on EU external migration policy: The member states and the mobility partnerships. *Journal of European Integration*, *34*, 223–239.

UN Secretary General. (2016, April 21). Safety and dignity: Addressing large movements of refugees and migrants. Report of the Secretary General. United Nations General Assembly. Seventieth session. Retrieved from http://documents-dds-ny.un.org/doc/UNDOC/GEN/N16/112/62/pdf/N1611262.pdf?OpenElement

4
THE POLITICS OF INTERNALLY DISPLACED PERSONS

Shubhra Seth

The word 'home' in the lexicon reads as the place where one lives permanently, especially as a member of a family or household. The phrase 'I am home' provides a sense of comfort at the end of a day's work to many once they get back to their destination. That lifeless structure of brick, cement, bamboo, or mud becomes the station of our lives and our habitation.

House, habitation, dwelling, abode, residence – these are all myriad meanings of the word home. If we replace these synonyms with words like uprooted, flee and homeless and simultaneously juxtapose these words with home as a noun, it presents us with a dilemma. This dilemma creates the category of internally displaced persons (IDPs); they are homeless at home and uprooted in their own habitat.

Introducing the category: internally displaced persons

A home or place of habitation is a necessity and a basic human right for all individuals. The recent challenge the international community is trying to effectively manage is that of the masses in flight or those uprooted in their own home states. In the last decade of the twentieth century, with the end of the Cold War, the world witnessed an explosion of civil wars erupting on all continents. Stricter immigration policies in the Western world along with the growing scale of the refugee problem in the changing international and political order brought about a new approach emphasising preventive protection of the vulnerable population in the countries of their origin. This was a result of the host states showing signs of fatigue in response to the number of refugees seeking asylum and crossing international borders (Barutciski, 1999). Forced migration as a result of internal strife or conflict while being contained within their national borders – this was a strange oxymoron for the Member States and the United Nations (UN) and its various agencies. It brought the new crisis of IDPs to the international arena and initiated a heated debate about the notions of sovereignty and responsibility when faced with this vulnerable category who were homeless at home.

The internally displaced share a common feature of being coerced to move or forced to flee from their homes, yet what posed a unique challenge for the international community was that, unlike refugees, these IDPs remained within their national borders. After the end of the Second World War, the United Nations worked towards outlining a mechanism and framework to combat the refugee problem with the 1951 Convention Relating to the Status of Refugees and the United Nations High Commissioner for Refugees (UNHCR). However, the same agency could not be applied to IDPs since they remained within the borders of their own countries and under the jurisdiction of their own governments. Ironically, those were also the same governments that bore the blame for their displacement and were often unwilling to provide for their well-being and security.

The need to recognise IDPs as a category became more pressing because of the rapidly swelling numbers within their own countries due to armed conflict, ethnic strife, and human rights abuse. When first counted in 1982, only 1.2 million people could be found forcibly displaced in 11 countries. By 1995, there were an estimated 20 to 25 million in more than 40 countries, almost twice as many as refugees (Cohen & Deng, 1998a). The international community had established a minimum safety framework for refugees who were either coerced into moving from their place of habitation or forced into exile and the UNHCR coming to their rescue. The absence of any convention or UN recognised framework for the protection of IDPs made their situation more vulnerable as they continued to suffer within their own borders.

In March 1992, a Commission Resolution called on the Secretary-General to appoint a representative for IDPs with their main task being to examine the applicability of international human rights conventions, humanitarian laws and refugee laws for the protection of the IDPs (see United Nations Commission on Human Rights (UNCHR), 1992). After the UNCHR approved the resolution, the then Secretary-General, Boutros Boutros-Ghali, designated Francis M. Deng, a distinguished diplomat from Sudan, to serve as the Representative of the Secretary-General on Internally Displaced Persons. Deng's position was voluntary and similar to that of other representatives and rapporteurs emanating from the UNCHR. Roberta Cohen, a human rights specialist and former US deputy assistant Secretary of State for Human Rights, served as co-director and senior adviser to Deng in this project until his 12-year mandate expired in 2004.

The development of a comprehensive global approach, effective assistance and protection of IDPs has been independently formulated and financed under the guidance of the Project on Internal Displacement (PID). The project was born of necessity, given the miserably inadequate resources to deal with displaced persons. The mandate and PID cannot be considered in isolation from one another. The primary institute associated with PID from the time of its inception has been the Brookings Institution, and over the years this institution has conducted several collaborative studies on the internally displaced. The Guiding Principles on Internal Displacement, adopted in a resolution by the United Nations in 1998, were a remarkable achievement and provided recognition of the millions of IDPs by the international community, thus acknowledging the tireless efforts of the PID.

Central idea of the project on internal displacement

The central idea behind the efforts to assist and protect IDPs was 'sovereignty as responsibility'. In their study, 'Masses in Flight', Cohen and Deng (1998a) recommended, 'recasting sovereignty as a concept of responsibility, that is, as an instrument for ensuring the protection and welfare of those under a state's jurisdiction' (p. 275). They suggested, furthermore, that a balance must be created 'between the principle of non-intervention in internal affairs and the equally compelling obligation to provide humanitarian assistance and promote observance of human rights' (ibid). The authors laid out both the international legal basis for providing physical and legal protection to the internally displaced and strategies for implementing protection as well as providing emergency aid. The Guiding Principles on Internal Displacement set out specific rules for protection during and following displacement. In other words, in the kitchen called Project on Internal Displacement, the recipe that was being worked on was that of a comprehensive approach to the problems of IDPs.

This idea has two essential parts: (1) governments are responsible for the human rights of their citizens as part of the essence of statehood; (2) when they are unwilling or unable to provide security and wellbeing for their citizens, an international responsibility arises to protect vulnerable individuals (Weiss & Korn, 2006). Hence, sovereignty is conceived as a conditional right dependent upon respect for a minimum standard of human rights and upon each state honouring an obligation to protect its citizens. If governments are unwilling or unable to protect them, the responsibility to protect such vulnerable individuals should be borne by the international community of states.

Broadly, it was the responsibility to protect that was reflected in the paraphrasing of sovereignty as a form of responsibility, often pointed as the philosophical foundation of the principles. The two crucial characteristic features of IDPs were that they were coerced into moving or fleeing but nonetheless had to remain within their own national borders. The traditionally accepted understanding of IDPs was persons being uprooted as a result of conflict and human rights violations. Since this problem of IDPs was viewed by and juxtaposed with that of refugees but within one's own border, conflict became a main variable through which to understand the needs of IDPs. During debates and brainstorming discussions, however, it was felt that persons uprooted by natural and human-made disasters or development projects are also displaced and can be neglected or discriminated against by their own government on political or ethnic grounds or there can be other forms of human rights violations.

The road taken for the formulation of the Guiding Principles on Internal Displacement was the adoption of a 'needs-based approach' as opposed to a 'rights-based approach'. This approach was almost like reading the subject backwards; in other words, it aimed to identify the needs of the internally displaced and then to examine the extent to which existing international humanitarian law and human rights conventions could be tailored in one document to address their specific needs. Walter Kalin, Representative of the Secretary-General on the Human Rights of Internally Displaced Persons, took the baton from Francis Deng and continued to steer the Project on Internal Displacement forward. Kalin and Robert Goldman, another principal team member of the same project, pointed out that displacement,

> breaks up the immediate family, cuts off important social and cultural community ties; terminates stable employment relationships; precludes or forecloses formal educational opportunities; deprives infants, expectant mothers, and the sick of access to food, adequate shelter or vital health services; and makes the displaced population especially vulnerable to acts of violence, such as attacks on camps, disappearances or rape.
>
> *(Cohen & Deng, 1998b, pp. 74)*

The Guiding Principles reflected in the Bill of Rights for IDPs sought to address each of the aforementioned issues under the headings of prevention, assistance and protection, and remains similar in content to the Bill of Rights for Refugees as outlined in the 1951 Refugee Convention. Roberta Cohen aptly summarised how this approach was taken to develop the Guiding Principles for the internally displaced and, once adopted, how they represented a sensible step forward. First, there was no government support for the development of a legally binding treaty on a subject as sensitive as internal displacement. Second, treaty-making could take decades whereas there was an urgent need for an immediate document to address the emergency needs of IDPs. Third, sufficient international laws existed to make it possible to weave the multiple provisions, otherwise dispersed in a large number of instruments, together in one document, which would be adapted to the needs of the internally displaced (Cohen, 2004).

Further, Cohen opines that these principles, 30 in number, provided guidance to all actors and institutions that deal with the internally displaced, be it governments, international organisations or non-governmental organisations (NGOs). These principles offered standards of protection during displacement, combining the spectrum of civil, economic, political, social and cultural rights with the specific needs of IDPs. Most importantly, they provided needed protection during return, resettlement and reintegration. To summarise, they provided the common minimum standard for the treatment of the IDPs, the latest challenge of masses in flight that the international community was faced with in the final decade of the twentieth century. The purpose of the PID was not to create a privileged category or a special status group for IDPs; rather, it was to ensure that, in a given situation of crisis and conflict, they, like others, would be protected and their unique needs acknowledged and addressed.

Throughout the process of debate on and formulation of the Guiding Principles, one basic notion remained constant: primary responsibility for the displaced rests with their own governments. Though the Guiding Principles would prove to be a powerful tool for assisting millions of displaced persons in the world, there were serious objections and concerns regarding the question of sovereignty of the state in a matter that primarily remained within its domestic jurisdiction. Also, these Guiding Principles were non-binding instruments, which – if seen in another light – could also wield greater influence since they were based on the already existing obligations of the state, be it providing food, shelter or protection to IDPs. However, the think tank labouring behind developing these Guiding Principles remained sceptical regarding whether worldwide usage and implementation of these principles would result in broader acceptance of a document developed outside the traditional intergovernmental process through which instruments such as conventions and resolutions of the UN are developed.

Definition of internally displaced persons

Against the backdrop of reservations and concerns discussed in the above section, the Guiding Principles on Internal Displacement, covering important ground in terms of combating the challenge of internal displacement, were presented to the UN Commission on Human Rights and defined IDPs thus:

> [P]ersons who have been forced or obliged to flee or to leave their homes or places of habitual residence in particular as a result of or in order to avoid the effects of armed conflict, situations of generalized violence, violations of human rights or natural or human-made disaster, and who have not crossed an internationally recognized state border.
>
> *(Deng, 1998)*

Deconstructing internal displacement

This section shall attempt to understand the three primary types of displacement in which most of the literature is classified, thus enabling us to understand the characteristic features of each separately. The Guiding Principles spell out situations leading to displacement in the definition of IDPs, which are: armed conflict, episodes of generalised violence, violations of human rights, or natural and man-made disasters. Displacement can be studied through a different lens; it can be classified as different types with reference to the trigger points or causes of internal displacement. Principle 6 of the Guiding Principles (United Nations, 1998, p. 7) covers the following:

1. Every human being shall have the right to be protected against being arbitrarily displaced from his or her home or place of habitual residence.
2. The prohibition of arbitrary displacement includes displacement:

   a) When it is based on policies of apartheid, 'ethnic cleansing' or similar practices aimed at/or resulting in altering the ethnic, religious or racial composition of the affected population.
   b) In situations of armed conflict, unless the security of the civilians involved or imperative military reasons so demand.
   c) In cases of large-scale development projects, which are not justified by compelling and overriding public interests.
   d) In cases of disasters, unless the safety and health of those affected requires their evacuation.
   e) When it is used as a collective punishment.
   f) Disaster-induced displacement, development-induced displacement and conflict-induced displacement are the three most studied and discussed nodes in the literature on the study of internal displacement as a concept. A brief outline of each of the three shall enable us to understand the characteristic features of each of the above-mentioned classifications.
   g) Disaster-induced displacement.

The United Nations has defined a disaster as 'a serious disruption of the functioning of a society, causing widespread human, material, or environmental losses which exceed the ability of the affected society to cope using its own resources' (United Nations Disaster Relief Organization, 1992, pp. 13–15). Disaster is mostly classified into two types, natural and man-made. Natural disasters can further be studied under three sub-categories, namely, sudden impact, slow-onset and epidemic disasters; while man-made disasters include the categories of industrial/technological disasters and complex emergencies. Thus:

a) Sudden impact disasters include earthquakes, floods, tidal waves, tropical storms, volcanic eruptions and landslides. Floods are associated with sudden migrations of large populations while earthquakes take a heavy toll on human life and may cause overwhelming infrastructural damage.
b) Slow-onset disasters include droughts, famine, environmental degradation, deforestation or conversion of arable lands to deserts. These disasters are the result of adverse weather conditions along with poor land use.
c) Epidemic disasters are triggered by diseases like cholera, measles, respiratory infection, malaria and, increasingly, HIV. These generally do not cause large-scale displacement but threaten displaced populations who stay clustered in overcrowded and unsanitary conditions following a major disaster.
d) Industrial/technological disasters result from industrial and technological activities that lead to pollution, spillage of hazardous materials, explosions and fires. They may

occur from poor planning and construction of facilities or from neglect of safety procedures.

e) Complex emergencies are understood as human-made with multiple contributing factors (which may include war, internal conflict and even natural disaster). Such emergencies are marked by large-scale displacement, food insecurity, human rights violations and elevated mortality (Holtermann, Gaull, & Lucas, 1998, cited in Robinson, 2003, p. 9).

Development-induced displacement

> Forced population displacement is always crisis-prone, even when necessary as part of broad and beneficial development programmes. It is a profound socio-economic and cultural disruption for those affected. Dislocation breaks up living patterns and social continuity. It dismantles existing modes of production, disrupts social networks, causes impoverishment of many of those uprooted, threatens their cultural identity, and increases the risks of epidemics and health problems
>
> *(Cernea, 1995, p. 94).*

In the 1950s and 1960s, with newly independent states emerging on all continents across the globe, the dominant view in development was informed by modernisation theory. This theory, if put crudely, viewed development as transforming traditional, simple, Third World societies into modern, complex, Westernised ones. Thus, capital-intensive, large-scale development projects were steps taken towards a better future. If people were uprooted during the process of development it was deemed a necessary evil or even an actual good, since it made them more susceptible to change (see Voutira & Harrell-Bond, 2000).

All forced displacement is prone to major socio-economic problems and risks. The Impoverishment Risks and Reconstruction model (IRR; Cernea, 1988, 2006) explores the different risks that await the internally displaced person. These risks can also be used as different components or variables to deconstruct displacement and understand the intensity of complications that surround this category of IDP. According to Cernea, the IRR is synchronic or an amalgamation of several interlinked applications, as it captures the processes that are parallel and simultaneously reflect the movement in time from destitution in displacement to recovery in resettlement. A common pattern of eight interlinked variables was formulated using this model, which defined the impoverished position and socio-economic effects of an individual's displacement. At the core of this model are three primary concepts: risk, impoverishment and reconstruction. Cernea uses the sociological concept of risk to identify the possibility that a certain course of action will trigger future injurious effects – losses and destruction, as described by Giddens (1990), and the concept of risk posited as a counter-concept to security as examined by Luhman (1993).

This also exposes the vulnerability of IDPs, particularly when faced with conflict- induced displacement. In recent decades, a 'new development paradigm' has been articulated, which aims to reduce poverty and to promote environmental protection, social justice and human rights. Within this new paradigm, development has been seen as simultaneously bestowing benefits and imposing costs. Amongst its greatest costs has been the involuntary displacement of millions of vulnerable people (Robinson, 2003, p. 10).

Eight variables/common processes were identified using the IRR and cumulatively studied to construct a general risk pattern for the displaced. Cernea, after researching for almost two decades, notes that, before displacement actually begins, these eight components are only impending social and economic risks (Cernea & Dowell, 2000). However, if timely and effective counteraction is not initiated when faced with the crisis of displacement, these potential hazards convert into actual impoverishment disasters. The eight components deconstructing the syncretic process of displacement as listed appear under the sub-heading 'development-induced displacement' but the variables and interlinked risks are common in situations of conflict-induced displacement as well. The eight risks are:

1) *Landlessness.* Expropriation of land removes the productive system, commercial activities and basis of constructing livelihoods. It is one of the principal forms of de-capitalisation, as they lose both natural and man-made capital. According to the IRR model, unless these productive systems are created elsewhere or replaced with alternative steady income-generating employment, the affected families remain impoverished and gradually over the years landlessness sets in, thereby making it increasingly difficult to break this mould of impoverishment.
2) *Joblessness.* The risk of losing employment is very high for both urban and rural displacement. Since creating new jobs requires substantial investment, unemployment or underemployment among resettlers often endures long after physical relocation has been completed. The previously employed may lose in three ways. In urban areas, workers lose jobs in industry and services. In rural areas, landless labourers lose access to work on land owned by others and also lose the use of assets under common property regimes. Self-employed small producers, craftsmen, shopkeepers and others lose their small businesses too.
3) *Homelessness.* Loss of shelter is intrinsic in the definition of the displaced. Most often, shelters or relief homes are provided sooner or later thus making it a temporary problem. However, the continuing situation of worsening housing standards and the feeling of homelessness due to the loss of original habitat remains a crisis for the displaced. Also, in a broader cultural sense, loss of the family's individual home and loss of a group's cultural space both result in alienation and status deprivation.
4) *Marginalisation.* Marginalisation refers to the feeling of being utterly neglected or side-lined, either over the duration of time or suddenly, as in the case of conflict-induced displacement. Marginalisation occurs when the cultural status of displaced persons is belittled in the place of relocation, where they are regarded as 'strangers' and denied entitlements and opportunities. Marginalisation occurs as the affected families lose their economic power and spiral downwards in terms of mobility, incurring severe livelihood problems as a result. The middle-income farm households become small landholders and small shopkeepers and craftsmen downsize and slip below poverty levels. Many displacees cannot use their earlier acquired skills at the new location and their human capital is thus rendered inactive or obsolete. Economic marginalisation is often accompanied by social and psychological marginalisation, as the social status of affected families declines, accompanied by a loss of confidence in themselves and society and feelings of injustice and deepened vulnerability. The IRR model clearly identifies that the coerciveness of displacement and the victimisation of resettlers tend to depreciate resettlers' self-image. Indeed, they are often perceived by the host communities as a socially degrading stigma. The facets of marginalization are multiple yet corrective measures are few and far between for IDPs.
5) *Food insecurity.* Food insecurity and undernourishment are both results of forced uprooting. It increases the risk of people becoming temporarily or chronically undernourished. During relocation or resettlement, the availability of food crops declines and sources of income generation diminish. For affected families, the rebuilding of regular food

production capacity or sufficient means of economic resource generation in most cases take years, so hunger and undernourishment tend to become lingering long-term effects.

6) *Increased morbidity and mortality*. Displacement induced social stress and trauma have sometimes been found to be accompanied by the outbreak of, in Cernea's terms, relocation-related diseases or illnesses. Unsafe water supplies and improvised sewage systems also increase vulnerability to epidemics. Infants, children and the elderly are the worst affected in such situations.
7) *Loss of access to common property resources*. Loss of access to common property assets, particularly for poor landless people, is a major blow when displacement happens. Loss of access to common property assets like pastures, forested land, burial grounds and so on leads to significant deterioration in income and livelihood resources. Hardly any of these common property assets are compensated for by state governments.
8) *Social disarticulation*. This includes dismantled social networks, dilution of common interests and the severing of prior ties with neighbours. In other words, displacement manifests as social disarticulation within the kinship system, whereby intimate bonds weaken and give way to growing alienation and lower cohesion within family structures. Forced displacement tears apart the decades-old existing social fabric, fragments the community and scatters kinship groups. As a result, local voluntary associations and self-organised, mutual service patterns are damaged. All of these factors together involve long-term consequences because they add up to a loss of 'social capital', which cannot be compensated for by government documents and policies because they develop over years of cohabiting in a particular neighbourhood and cement with time.

Two more risks intrinsic to development have been added to those described above by Robinson (2003). These additional risks are drawn from the work of Muggah (2000) and Downing (2002):

a) *Loss of access to community services*. Health care facilities and education opportunities for the children are the most costly impoverishment risks in the situation of displacement because delayed opportunity for the education of children impacts an entire generation waiting to build and carve their future.
b) *Violation of human rights*. Displacement from habitual residence followed by loss of property and absence of fair compensation together constitute a human rights violation. Robinson adds that arbitrary displacement can lead to violation of civil and political rights, which may include degrading treatment, arbitrary arrest, temporary and permanent disenfranchisement and the loss of one's political voice. Displacement not only carries the risk of human rights violations at the hands of state authorities and security forces but also the risk of spreading ethnic violence when new settlers move in amongst existing populations.

The IRR model puts forward a valuable tool for understanding and assessing many risks inherent in situations of not only development-induced displacement but also conflict-induced displacement. Though the normative bedrock of development-induced displacement rests on a given 'eminent domain' of the state, which consists of the state's right to expropriate property in certain circumstances, mostly citing the overall advantage of the nation or the state as the rallying point (Muggah, 2003), almost all of the variables are found in equal measure posing similar risks for those displaced due to conflict as well.

Conflict-induced displacement

Reflecting on the available literature on displacement and forced migration, it may be useful to read them as three points situated along a continuum: disaster-induced displacement, development-induced displacement and conflict-induced displacement. Robinson (2003) opines that both disaster-induced displacement and conflict-induced displacement are situated on two sides or extremes of the spectrum of displacement with regard to the response from the state. In the context of disaster-induced displacement, states are keenly interested in seeking outside aid and attention for victims of flood, famine or earthquake. However, at the opposite end is conflict-induced displacement, when such episodes of displacement take place when people are forced to flee; here, states tend to take a restrictive and highly selective view regarding who is to gain access to which displaced populations and for what purpose. On this spectrum, then, development-induced displacement occupies a middle ground where states encourage and accept technical assistance and funding but seldom make public details of the arbitrary treatment, impoverishment or denial of rights of those displaced as a result of such development projects (ibid).

The archetypical, long understood example of forced migration is that of the refugee. The 1951 Refugee Convention spells out that a refugee is someone who,

> owing to a well-founded fear of being persecuted for reasons of race, religion, nationality, membership of a particular social group or political opinion, is outside the country of his nationality, and is unable to, or owing to such fear, is unwilling to avail himself of the protection of that country.
>
> *(United Nations General Assembly, 1951)*

This definition guides the work of the United Nations High Commissioner for Refugees (UNHCR).

Conflict-induced displacement has similar 'push factors', the major point of difference being that IDPs remain within the confines of their state while refugees cross internationally recognised borders to seek protection in such situations. 'Displacement' occurs where coercion is employed – choices are restricted, the affected population faces more risks than opportunities and is vulnerable as a result of staying in their 'place' of residence. This distinguishes conflict-induced displacement from 'voluntary' and 'economic' migration. Thus, displacement by its very definition is forced and involuntary, involving some form of de-territorialisation (Hyndman, 2000).Though the policies designed and formulated for IDPs are distinct from those designed for refugees, as Kalin (2000) observed, the discourse on internal displacement and resettlement draws heavily on the instruments for refugee protection and related conventions developed over the years. The movements triggered under conflict-induced displacement are spontaneous, unpredictable and considered illegal under international humanitarian and human rights laws. Resettlement after such episodes of displacement is usually an un-coordinated exercise arising from the need of the hour and is regarded by many donors and policy makers as temporary. In contrast to this, development-induced displacement is planned. In some cases, detailed resettlement and compensation procedures are worked out because the assets expropriated, under legal sanction and obligations on the part of the acquiring agency, are obvious. In such situations, resettlement is perceived by donors and policy makers to be a process leading to a permanent relocation (Muggah, 2003).

Conflict-induced displacement has long-term and lasting consequences because continued social and economic exclusion intensifies the deprivation of such IDPs. Michael Cernea (2000) points out that forced displacement epitomises the social exclusion of certain groups of people as it culminates in not only physical exclusion from a geographic territory but also economic and social exclusion from a set of functioning networks. This is a more significant problems for conflict-induced IDPs. Mishra (2004) observes that the breakdown of some multinational states, proliferation of conflict involving 'ethnic cleansing', civil war, insurgency, guerrilla warfare, primarily within borders of the state but having international ramifications, were the pertinent features of the post-Cold War world. According to Mishra, 'This has changed the very nature of conflict – from conventional wars between nation states to inter-communal conflict within states' (p. 6).

This change in the nature and definition of conflict is thus seen as a major catalyst, leading to a new category of domestic refugees who, in the decades following the Cold War, swelled in numbers and surpassed the number of refugees. It is this category of person, displaced and de-territorialised by conflict, who came to be internationally covered under the term internally displaced persons. Figure 4.1 shows the numbers of conflict-induced IDPs and refugees worldwide. The figures, spanning across a decade and a half (15 years), show that conflict-induced IDPs now almost double refugees worldwide and numbers are still growing. Hence, conflict-induced displacement has gained much attention in UN initiatives and discussions in recent years on account of its deep political, social and economic ramifications.

Figure 4.1 compares the number of IDPs resulting from conflict and the number of refugees in the years following 1998, the same year in which the Guiding Principles on Internal Displacement entered into the lexicon of the United Nations and its Member States took notice of the 'internal refugees' existing within their own borders. It is important to note the alarming rate at which millions of people are being displaced due to conflict every year. Figure 4.1 shows that 28–33 million people became conflict-induced IDPs during the 1998–2013 period in comparison to the almost 16 million who became refugees. Conflict remains an essential variable for understanding and studying displacement, whether armed conflict, situations

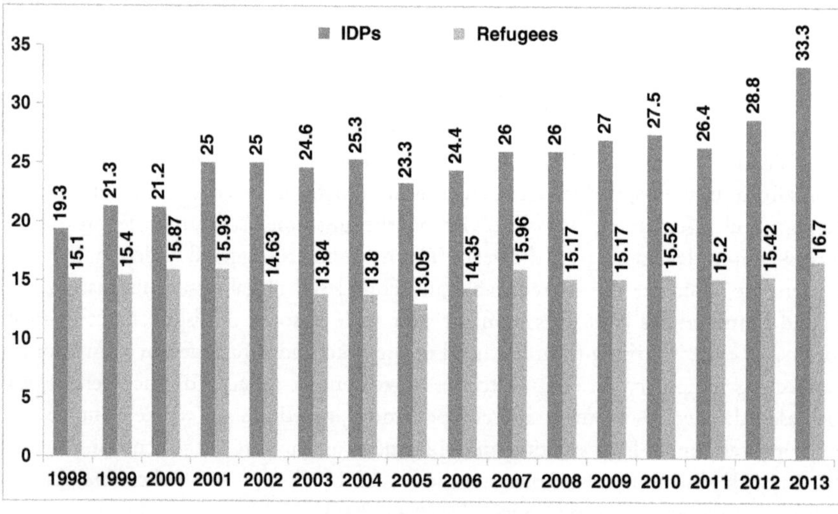

Figure 4.1 Comparison of total number of estimated IDPs due to conflict and refugees worldwide (number of people in million, 1998–2013)

Source: www.internal-displacement.org/global-figures

of generalised violence or violation of human rights. It is possibly this catalyst of conflict that led the United Nations to consider IDPs as internal refugees and subsequently to draw up the Guiding Principles using existing conventions on refugees as the reference point.

The gap between Guiding Principles and laws

This bridge from Guiding Principles to hard laws has now been under construction for decades. This gap may possibly be understood as the 'politics of internally displaced persons'. The *Oxford Dictionary* defines politics thus: 'The activities associated with the governance of a country or area, especially the debate between parties having power' (https://en.oxforddictionaries.com/definition/politics). Since the internally displaced remain the responsibility of their own governments, they form primary subjects in matters of governance. As politics is defined as a debate between parties, we may fix the debate for the purpose of this chapter as negotiations between international organisations and state machinery, the reference point of which is the marginalised IDP.

The 'politics' surrounding the category of IDPs is two-fold. First, as discussed in the previous section, state or government responses to disaster-induced displacement and development-induced displacement are overtly different to responses for conflict-induced displacement. In most cases there exists a reluctance by the state to even recognise people displaced due to conflict. The covert reason for the reluctance of successive governments to identify and enact legal instruments for the protection of conflict-induced displaced persons is that doing so would reflect badly on the domestic law and order situation. More accurately, it would reflect the ability of political parties in power to negotiate such episodes of civil war, communal conflicts, generalised violence and gross human rights violations. Also, although IDPs currently more than double the number of refugees, unlike the United Nations High Commissioner for Refugees (UNHCR), no independent international organisation exists that is mandated to protect them and to draw up plans for their rehabilitation. The Internal Displacement Monitoring Centre (IDMC) is the lone unique source of information on and analysis of internal displacement – every year this centre provides estimated figures and data on the global scale and pattern of internal displacement (Birkeland and Jennings, 2011). Established in 1998 by the Norwegian Refugee Council, the IDMC, at the request of the United Nations, maintains an online database of comprehensive information on internal displacement spanning more than 50 countries.

The second layer of 'politics' involving IDPs due to conflict is the use of the instrument of soft law as a means of constructing a coherent framework for governments dealing with IDPs. The generic term 'soft law' covers several instruments and is negotiated as a quasi source of international law. Soft laws may be defined as 'normative provisions contained in non-binding texts' (Global Protection Cluster (GPC), 2010; Shelton, 2000, p. 292; United Nations Office for the Coordination of Humanitarian Affairs (OCHA), 1999). In spite of the ongoing international IDP crisis, states continue to avoid recognising and rehabilitating them, take refuge within the non-binding and voluntary resolutions/recommendations set out in the Guiding Principles of the United Nations.

Non-binding to binding: Africa paves the way

Even after two decades and an ever-growing number of IDPs there exists a deep reluctance on the part of states and their governments to establish the Guiding Principles on Internal Displacement as hard laws. Amidst continuing apathy by the states, only two such initiatives

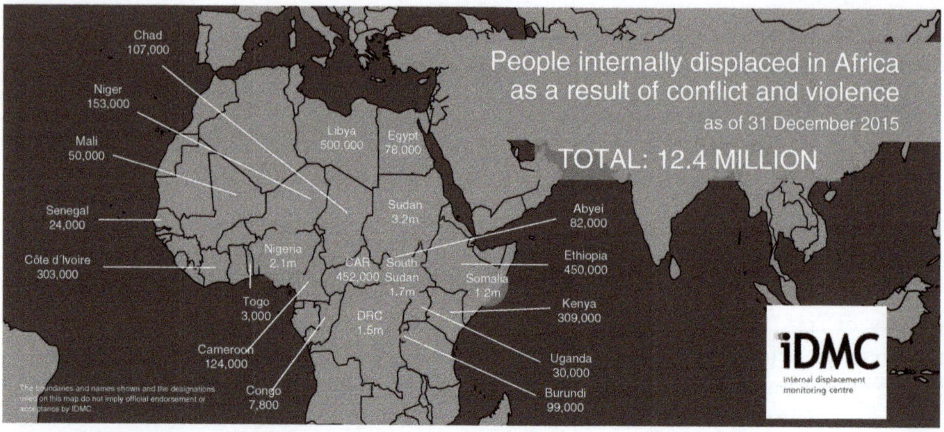

Figure 4.2 People internally displaced in Africa due to conflict and violence

Source: Norwegian Refugee Council/Internal Displacement Monitoring Centre (NRC/IDMC) (2016)

have been taken whereby the charter of the Guiding Principles has undergone legal metamorphosis and taken the shape of hard laws – both in Africa. These legal instruments – the Protocol on the Protection and Assistance to Internally Displaced Persons and the Kampala Convention – are in agreement that it is the primary duty of the state to provide protection and humanitarian assistance to IDPs within its territory. However, here displacement has been measured in relation to the variable of conflict. The reason behind the committed concern shown by the African Union to frame legal instruments protecting conflict-induced displacement can be found in the numbers shown in Figure 4.2.

Initiative one

The Protocol on the Protection and Assistance to Internally Displaced Persons, otherwise known as the Great Lakes Protocol, was adopted under the auspices of the International Conference on the Great Lakes Region on December 14, 2006. This protocol was initiated within a political process concurrent with the post-conflict reconstitution in the Great Lakes Region (see Dailey, 2006).This region is located in the heart of Africa, stretching from Sudan in the North-East to Angola and Zambia in the South and from Central African Republic in the West to Kenya and Tanzania in the East. The Protocol was formulated to provide a legal framework for the holistic understanding, adoption and implementation of the Guiding Principles (Beyani, 2008). Emphasis was given to the fact that states signing up to the Protocol would assume legal obligations to implement the Guiding Principles, affirming the idea of political ownership of the responsibility to protect displaced persons.

Initiative two

The second instrument is the Kampala Convention (African Union, 2009), one step ahead of the Great Lakes Protocol. One of the encouraging signs of international acceptance of the

Guiding Principles is the gradual adoption and implementation of numerous national laws and policies addressing internal displacement in all regions of the world (Brookings Institute & LSE Project on Internal Displacement, n.d.). The Kampala Convention is seen as a landmark step in addressing conflict-induced displacement. A joint effort by the member states of the African Union, it has been widely appreciated by the Project on Internal Displacement. Dr Chaloka Beyani, Special Rapporteur on the Human Rights of Internally Displaced Persons (2010–2016), participated in the negotiation with member states and assisted in drafting this important international instrument. The Kampala Convention can be used to guide policy frameworks initiated at the national level, a novel effort in the move to recognise conflict-induced displacement.

The Kampala Convention is an attempt on the part of member states of the African Union to protect and assist IDPs in Africa. It was adopted in Kampala, Uganda, on October 23, 2009 and enforced on December 6, 2012. In the preamble to the Convention the states recognised that persistent and recurrent conflict is are the primary factor leading to displacement, followed by natural disasters and, lastly, development. This Convention affirms the basic understanding that armed conflict, ethnic strife and situations of generalised violence are recognised by the governments as causes of displacement. Subsequently, these governments adhere to the Guiding Principles on Internal Displacement and adopt them in their own national laws to uphold the rights and dignity of those displaced.

Merits of the Kampala Convention: a leap forward

The Kampala Convention (henceforth Convention) is recognised by the Project on Internal Displacement, which monitors displacement issues worldwide and promotes the dissemination and application of the UN Guiding Principles on Internal Displacement, as a remarkable initiative on the part of the African Union. Some of the noteworthy objectives of the Convention are:

1) To establish a legal framework for preventing internal displacement and protecting and assisting IDPs in Africa.
2) To prevent the political, social, cultural and economic exclusion and marginalisation that causes displacement of populations or groups of persons by virtue of their social identity, religion or political opinion.
3) To respect and ensure protection of the human rights of IDPs, including the provision of humane treatment, non-discrimination, equality and equal protection of law.
4) To incorporate in domestic law the obligations of the Convention, either by enacting new laws or amending existing legislation for protecting and assisting IDPs.
5) To support collaboration with international organisations, humanitarian agencies and civil society organisations in accordance with their mandates for assisting IDPs.
6) To prevent discrimination on the basis of a person's internal displacement and to ensure they are afforded relevant rights and freedoms.
7) To recognise sexual and gender-based violence in all its forms and to take steps to prevent IDPs experiencing it.
8) To take necessary measures to ensure that IDPs, who are citizens in their country of nationality, enjoy their civic and political rights. (Go to www.au.int/en/Convention.pdf for the full document.)

The eighth point above underlines the pertinent point that IDPs continue to remain citizens of their respective countries and, unlike refugees, neither cross the borders of their home countries nor seek asylum in other countries. To summarise, the 'politics' surrounding IDPs will continue as a game of pass the parcel until every state understands that a stable population is a quintessential feature of statehood and, as a corollary, that a stable population is a vital element of a stable state. The answer to the conundrum of millions of homeless and uprooted IDPs is to accept and respect the concept of sovereignty as responsibility.

Epilogue

Internally displaced persons resemble a meandering river, which continuously changes its course as a result of the terrain. Those displaced by conflict remain forever displaced because the few proactive national laws and policies that do exist are unable to address this global crisis and home is becoming an elusive truth for IDPs. The foremost task for states is to recognise that the global refugee crisis has its roots in the internal violence, civil wars and gross human rights violations that exist within their borders. Citizens displaced as a result of conflict suffer due to the lack of responsible state initiatives, reconciliation, rehabilitation and responsibility. Worse, they feel threatened in their homes and thus begins the mass exodus across borders: this journey marks the transformation of IDPs into refugees. The everyday life of IDPs involves finding a definition for themselves, identifying laws, policies and conventions that can protect and uphold their human rights, struggling to exist in relief camps and competing for limited resources. They experience the agony of losing family members in episodes of violence and the sense of helplessness that results from being unable to provide a secure future for their progeny (Benhabib and Resnik, 2009). Internal displacement is a global crisis of the past, the present and the future – all three tenses apply to IDPs who lack defence (protection from the state and government) and remain homeless for generations.

The ongoing crisis in the Rakhine State of Myanmar drew the attention of the world with a fresh spate of violence that resulted in the mass exodus of the ethnic minority Rohingya population. Persistent attempts by this minority community to cross the border to neighbouring Bangladesh indicates that many are internally displaced in Myanmar and continue to face violence. The United Nations Secretary-General has described the continuing crisis in Rakhine against the minority group as a 'textbook example of ethnic cleansing' (Rushing, 2017).

The world can read this 'textbook' and many more descriptions can be added to these pages of episodes of violence against minority groups who face displacement across different parts of both the northern and southern hemispheres. The rising number of IDPs warrants attention by all Member States. The hour has come when recognising this global humanitarian crisis is mandatory and every state should take steps towards respecting the concept of sovereignty as responsibility.

References

African Union. (2009). *African Union convention for the protection and assistance of internally displaced persons in Africa (Kampala convention), adopted by the special summit of the union held In Kampala, Uganda, 23 October.* Retrieved from www.au.int/en/sites/default/files/AFRICAN_UNION_CONVENTION_FOR_THE_PROTECTION_AND_ASSISTANCE_OF_INTERNALLY_DISPLACED_PERSONS_IN_AFRICA_(KAMPALA_CONVENTION).pdf

Barutciski, M. (1999). Questioning the tensions between the refugee and IDP concepts: A rebuttal. *Forced Migration Review, 4*, 35.

Benhabib, S. & Resnik, J. (2009). *Migrations and mobilities: Citizenship, borders and gender.* New York: New York University Press.

Beyani, C. (2008). The politics of international law: Transformation of the guiding principles on internal displacement from soft law into hard law. *Proceedings of the Annual Meeting (American Society of International Law), 102*, 194–198.

Birkeland, N. M. & Jennings, E. (Eds.) (2011). *Internal displacement: Global overview of trends and developments in 2010*. Internal Displacement Monitoring Centre, Norwegian Refugee Council. Retrieved from www.internal-displacement.org/publications/global-overview-2010.pdf

Brookings Institute & LSE Project on Internal Displacement. (n.d.). *Compilation of national laws and policies on internal displacement*. Retrieved from www.brookings.edu/about/projects/idp/resources/idp-policies-index

Cernea, M. M. (1988). *Involuntary resettlement in development projects*. Technical Paper, No.80. Retrieved from http://hvtc.edu.vn/Portals/0/files/6357013323426329920-8213-1036-4.pdf

Cernea, M. M. (1995). Social integration and population displacement. *International Social Science Journal, 143*, 91–112.

Cernea, M. M. (2000). Risks, safeguards and reconstruction: A model for population displacement and resettlement. *Economic and Political Weekly, 35*, 3659–3678.

Cernea, M. M. (2006). Re-examining 'displacement': A redefinition of concepts in development and conservation policies. *Social Change, 36*, 8–35.

Cohen, R. (2004). The guiding principles on internal displacement: An innovation in international standard setting. *Global Governance, 10*, 459–480.

Cohen, R. & Deng, F. M. (Eds.). (1998a). *The forsaken people: Case studies of the internally displaced*. Washington, DC: Brookings Institution.

Cohen, R. & Deng, F. M. (1998b). *Masses in flight: The global crisis of internal displacement*. Washington, DC: Brookings Institution.

Daley, P. (2006). Challenges to peace: Conflict resolution in the Great Lakes region of Africa. *Third World Quarterly, 27*, 303–319.

Deng, F. (1998, February 11). *UN Guiding Principles on Internal Displacement*. E/CN.4/1998/53/Add.2. Retrieved from www.un-documents.net/gpid.htm

Downing, T. E. (2002). *Avoiding new poverty: Mining-induced displacement and resettlement*. International Institute for Environment and Development, 3. Retrieved from http://pubs.iied.org/pdfs/G00549.pdf

Giddens, A. (1990). *The consequences of modernity*. Stanford, CA: Stanford University Press.

Global Protection Cluster (GPC). (2010). *Handbook for the protection of internally displaced persons*. Retrieved from www.refworld.org/docid/4790cbc02.html http://www.unhcr.org/1951-refugee-convention.html

Holtermann, K., Gaull, E., & Lucas, R. (1998). Disaster dimension. In S. Abdallah & G. Burnham (Eds.), *The Johns Hopkins and Red Cross/Red Crescent public health guide for emergencies*. Baltimore, MD: Johns Hopkins University Press.

Hyndman, J. (2000). *Managing displacement: Refugees and the politics of humanitarianism*. Minneapolis, MN: University of Minnesota.

Kalin, W. (2000). *Guiding Principles on Internal Displacement: Annotations*. American Society of International Law and the Brookings Institution Project on Internal Displacement. Retrieved from www.Brookings.Edu/~/Media/Research/Files/Reports/2008/5/Spring-Guiding-Principles/Spring_Guiding_Principles.pdf

Luhmann, N. (1993). *Risk: A sociological theory (communication and social order)*. (B. Rhodes, Trans.). Berlin: De Gruyter.

Mishra, O. (Ed.). (2004). *Forced migration in the South Asian Region: Displacement, human rights and conflict resolution*. Kolkata: Jadavpur University, Brookings Institution and Manak Publications.

Muggah, R. (2000). Through the developmentalist's looking glass: Conflict-induced displacement and involuntary resettlement in Colombia. *Journal of Refugee Studies, 13*, 133–164.

Muggah, R. (2003). A tale of two solitudes: Comparing conflict and development-induced displacement and involuntary resettlement. *International Migration, 41*(5). doi:10.1111/j.0020-7985.2003.00259.x

Norwegian Refugee Council/Internal Displacement Monitoring Centre (NRC/IDMC). (2016). *Internal displacement, Africa: Internal displacement as of December 2015*. Retrieved from www.internal-displacement.org/Africa-Report/20161209-IDMC-Africa-report-web-en.pdf

Omprakash, M. (Ed.). (2004). *Forced migration in the South Asian Region: Displacement human rights and conflict resolution*. Kolkata: Jadavpur University, Brookings Institution and Manak Publications.

Robinson, W. C. (2003). *Risks and rights: The causes, consequences, and challenges of development-induced displacement*. Occasional paper. Washington, DC: Brookings Institution–SAIS Project on Internal Displacement, p. 9.

Rushing, E. (2017). *How many internally displaced Rohingya are trapped inside Myanmar?* Internal Displacement Monitoring Centre, Norwegian Refugee Council. Retrieved from www.internal-displacement.org/library/expert-opinion/2017/how-many-internally-displaced-rohingya-are-trapped-inside-myanmar

Shelton, D. (Ed.). (2000). *Commitment and compliance: The role of non-binding norms in the international legal system*. Oxford: Oxford University Press.

United Nations. (1998, 11 February). *Guiding principles on internal displacement*. Doc. E/CN.4/1998/53/Add.2. Retrieved from www.un-documents.net/gpid.htm

United Nations Commission on Human Rights (UNCHR). (1992). Resolution 1992/73, 5 March. Retrieved from www.refworld.org/docid/3b00f0e71c.html

United Nations Disaster Relief Organization. (UNDRO). (1992). *An overview of disaster management*. New York: UNDRO, pp. 13–15

United Nations General Assembly. (1951, 28 July). *Convention relating to the status of refugees*. United Nations, Treaty Series, vol. 189, p. 137. Retrieved from https://treaties.un.org/pages/ViewDetailsII.aspx?src=TREATY&mtdsg_no=V-2&chapter=5&Temp=mtdsg2&clang=_en

United Nations Office for the Coordination of Humanitarian Affairs (OCHA). (1999). *Handbook for applying the guiding principles on internal displacement*. Retrieved from www.refworld.org/docid/3d52a6432.html

Voutira, E. & Harrell-Bond, B. (2000). "Successful" refugee resettlement: Are past experiences relevant? In M. Cernea & C. McDowell (Eds.), *Risks and reconstruction: Experiences of resettlers and refugees*. Washington, DC: World Bank.

Weiss, T. G. & Korn, D. A. (2006). *Internal displacement: Conceptualization and its consequences*. New York: Routledge.

5

REFUGE AND POLITICAL ASYLUM IN LATIN AMERICA

Relevance, characteristics, and normative structure

Liliana Lyra Jubilut & Rachel de Oliveira Lopes[1]

Since the ratification of the 1951 Convention Relating to the Status of Refugees (1951 Refugee Convention) by most Latin American states,[2] the institutes of political asylum and refuge coexist in the region as forms of implementation of the right of asylum (Piovesan & Jubilut, 2011, p. 213). Political asylum has been in force in Latin America since the nineteenth century (with the Treaty on International Penal Law of 1889[3]),[4] and still persists, now existing in parallel to the provisions of the 1951 Refugee Convention, which has a broader scope and is intended to protect those persecuted not only due to political opinion, but also by virtue of race, religion, nationality, and membership of a particular social group (1951 Refugee Convention, Article 1) . This extension of the protective scope to the victims of persecution is characteristic of Latin America (Freier, 2015; Piovesan & Jubilut, 2011). Historical processes concerning the alteration of the grounds and peculiarities of persecution have been accompanied by changes in mechanisms of victim protection used in the region.

If, before the 1970s, there were no reports of any kind of persecution other than political – for which individual political asylum prevailed – thereafter, the outbreak of migratory crises caused by other sorts of persecution[5] highlighted the need for the 1951 Refugee Convention and its additional 1967 Protocol Relating to the Status of Refugees,[6] which, in turn, have also proved to be insufficient in meeting the specific protection needs of the region and have required an even broader definition of refugee status criteria (Arboleda, 2001), consummated by the 1984 Cartagena Declaration on Refugees (Cartagena Declaration),[7] that also recognizes as refugees:

> persons who have fled their country because their lives, safety or freedom have been threatened by generalized violence, foreign aggression, internal conflicts, massive violation of human rights or other circumstances which have seriously disturbed public order.[8]

The protection expansions, however, did not remove the importance of the international, even if more restricted, paramenters, in that certain zones of exclusive application of this remain, while, at the same time, more protection is also in play with the Cartagena Declaration definition. The right of asylum finds its best implementation in the region in the combination of the coexistence of political asylum and refugee status, both in its international and regional standards.

Considering the areas of intersection and exclusiveness of the scope of political asylum and refuge, and the importance of both in Latin America, this chapter aims to describe the two institutes in order to showcase the peculiarities of each one, as well as the zones of intersection between them. It begins by describing the institutes of political asylum and refuge in general, then presents the regional aspects of refugee status in Latin America, and, in this sense, turns to the contributions of the Cartagena Declaration and its revisional process and of the Inter-American human rights system, which highlights the region's human rights approach towards refugee and political asylees. This chapter stems from an interest in describing the enlargement of the protection space in Latin America to forced migrants who suffer persecution through political asylum and refuge, and adopts a descriptive tone so as to present this still relatively unknown landscape.

The institutes of refuge and asylum and their coexistence

The right of asylum (generally considered) has a long-standing position in history and is a human right that has been enshrined in the contemporary architecture of the protection of human beings in Article XIV of the Universal Declaration of Human Rights, which determines that, "Everyone has the right to seek and to enjoy in other countries asylum from persecution." One sees that the right is protected but that the instruments for its implementation are open to determination, as can be seen in Figure 5.1. Most states have, since the 1951 Refugee Convention, opted to implement the right of asylum through refugee status, but as seen in Latin America, said right relies on the concession of political asylum (through territorial asylum or diplomatic asylum), or on the recognition of refugee

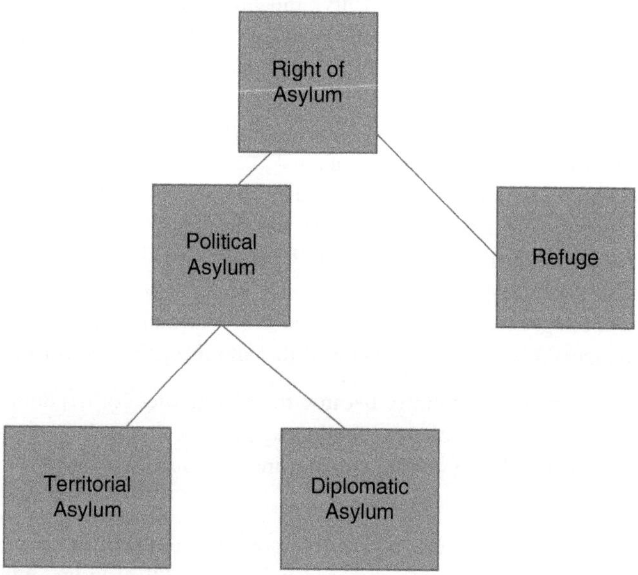

Figure 5.1 Instruments of the right of asylum

status, or on both, depending on the political options and cultural characteristics of each country.

Asylum has its origin in classical antiquity, being present in Egypt and Greece for instance (Jubilut, 2007), and was related to religious standards (Barreto, n.d.). It was elevated to a legal institution by the Roman Empire, and later, with the rise of liberalism and the French Revolution, assumed political outlines. It was then denied to common criminals (Fischel de Andrade, 1996). From then on it became known as *political* asylum (ibid).

Political asylum can be defined as the protection that a state grants to an individual who is suffering political persecution. This granting of protection can occur "in its [a state's] *territory* (*territorial asylum*) or in *some other place* under the control of certain of its [the state's] organs (such as diplomatic premises and warships [*diplomatic asylum*])" (Gil-Bazo, 2015, p. 7). The granting of political asylum is an act of sovereignty and therefore is *discretionary*. Also, the decision to grant asylum is *constitutive* of the right and *not limited* to requirements other than *actual* political persecution (Jubilut, 2006).

From this, one sees that, although limited in its contours, political asylum leaves ample leeway to states to determine when and to whom they want to grant this form of protection. This is even more true as there is *no institutional body* responsible for the effectiveness and/or the supervision of the application of political asylum (ibid) and the main obligation arising from its granting is the right of *legal residence* in the state of asylum (ibid).

Refugee status, on the other hand, has a broader scope in terms of the motives and the degree of persecution that might generate its need, and is regulated by international norms. International norms relating to refugee status date back to the beginning of the twentieth century, stemming from the massive flows generated by the Russian Revolution and the two world wars (Fischel de Andrade, 1996), and their universal cornerstones reside in the 1951 Refugee Convention and its 1967 Protocol.

Refugee status has the nature of a conventional *obligation* consisting of the protection of those who, being *outside* the state of origin, have a *well-founded fear* of persecution based on *race, nationality, religion, membership of a particular social group, or political opinion* and, for such reasons, cannot or do not want to return to his or her usual place of residence and therefore remain without any state protection (1951 Refugee Convention, Article 1). Being a right, if a person meets these requirements she or he ought to be recognized as a refugee, while conversely if she or he does not meet the provisions of the 1951 Refugee Convention, the person ought not to be recognized as a refugee. States are bound by the international delimitations of refugee status, which is the instrument of the right of asylum with the contours of a legal obligation.

The norms of refugee status also determine the existence of *exclusion clauses*[9]: circumstances in which – due to the person's acts – she or he is undeserving of international protection through refugee status. In the cases of exclusion clauses, a person might meet the requirements set out in the definition of refugee status by the 1951 Refugee Convention, but might also meet the threshold that avoids its implementation, such as the committing of genocide,[10] crimes against humanity,[11] and acts contrary to the principles and purposes of the United Nations (UN).[12]

In the determination of recognition of refugee status, the well-founded fear of persecution has paramount importance (Goodwin-Gill & McAdam, 2011; Hathaway & Foster, 2014). It is to determine its existence that one looks into the objective situation of the country of origin (or residence) of the person asking to be recognized as a refugee. This practice, combined with the nature of refugee status as a legal obligation, allows one to say that it is the objective situation of the country of origin that "makes" a person a refugee (Goodwin-Gill & McAdam, 2011, pp. 63–64) and not the formal recognition of this status by a state. In this sense, the recognition of refugee status is *declaratory* and does not constitute the right itself (Jubilut, 2006).

It is due to the relevance of the objective situation of the country of origin for refugee status that the 1951 Refugee Convention allows for *cessation clauses*[13] to the extent that the cause of an individual's refugee status ceases to exist and international protection is no longer necessary. Even though refugee status is a right in itself and its recognition is declaratory, the importance of states applying it correctly is vital for refugees' protection, so much so that the United Nations High Commissioner for Refugees (UNHCR) was created as an organ of the UN vested with the responsibility of supervising the implementation of International Refugee Law, and thus the recognition of refugee status and, consequently, this manner of implementation of the right of asylum.

The instruments of the right of asylum share some similarities, apart from this common universal legal basis. A first resemblance between political asylum and refuge is the purpose of "granting protection to individuals who fear persecution in their country of origin or habitual residence" (ibid, p. 28). In this sense, they are both humanitarian institutes, and are based on solidarity and international cooperation. Another important shared characteristic derives from the understanding of the principle of *non-refoulement*[14] – that arises from international refugee law and that prohibits the returning of individuals to territories where their lives, security, or integrity may be threatened – as a principle of *jus cogens*[15] (Allain, 2001) and, therefore, as an international obligation, being applicable also to political asylum. This argument reinforces the understanding of political asylum as a humanitarian institute, for the preservation of human dignity, and provides the base for "the qualified obligation of states to grant asylum" (Gil-Bazo, 2015, p. 11). Tables 5.1 and 5.2 synthetized the above-mentioned similarities and differences of political asylum and refugee status.

Apart from these common grounds for political asylum and refuge, and the already mentioned specific characteristics of each that highlight their differences, it is important to mention other topics on which there is still debate.

The first one relates to the bond established by each institute (Barreto, n. d.): while in political asylum, the bond of protection of the individual is established exclusively with the host state, which may dispose of such a relationship by its sole discretion; in refuge, the bond is established with the international community, which is obliged to protect the refugee for as

Table 5.1 Similarities between political asylum and refuge

Similarities	
General goal	Both institutes aim to protect individuals outside their state of origin
Specific goal	Protect individuals from persecution
Legal basis	Article XIV of the Universal Declaration of Human Rights
Legal contexts	Based on respect of human rights
International context	Based on international cooperation and solidarity
Nature	Humanitarian character
Basic protection	Mandatory removal of persons protected by the institutes is limited by international law, through *non-refoulement*

Source: Jubilut (2006, 2007)

Table 5.2 Differences between political asylum and refuge

Differences	*Political asylum*	*Refuge*
Origins	Antiquity	Beginning of the twentieth century
Legal basis	Regional treaties	International treaties (1951 Convention and 1967 Protocol); regional treaties (OUA Convention of 1969); documents (Cartagena Declaration of 1984 and the Directives of the Common European Asylum System)
Legal nature	States have discretion in applying (i.e., it is a discretionary act)	States do not have discretion in applying. If the conditions established by international law are met, the person should be recognized as a refugee
Legal nature of the decision	Constitutive act (i.e., it is the granting of asylum that constitutes the rights of the asylee)	Declaratory act (i.e., the recognition of refugee status merely declares a situation that was already in existence and establishes that the rights of refugee status should be respected)
Current geographical application	Mainly in Latin America	Universal
Basis of application	*De facto* persecution (i.e., the persecution has to have occurred)	Well-founded fear of persecution (i.e., there has to be evidence that persecution may occur)
Basis of persecution	Political acts	Race, religion, nationality, political opinion and membership of a particular social group
Limits in granting	No limits on whom asylum is granted by a state	Exclusion clauses establish who cannot be recognized as refugees
International regime	Non-existent	The United Nations High Commissioner for Refugees is vested with the responsibility to oversee that the norms of the international regime and the rights of refugees are respected by states
Extraterritoriality	Does not need to be in place (in the modality of diplomatic asylum)	Needs to be in place
Duration	There are no previsions covering time limits or ending	Cessation clauses mean that the regime envisions an end to the refugee status

Source: Jubilut (2006, 2007)

long as the fear of persecution lasts. In political asylum, there is no previous relation with the host state, which only establishes itself with the reception of the asylee, and in accordance with the will of the host state; in refuge, there is a previous obligation of the international community to preserve the human dignity of the persecuted human being (ibid). In this sense, solidarity, in the refuge regime, is pre-existing, in the sense that it is established before the facts by the conventional bonding; while in political asylum, solidarity is only an expectation (ibid).

The second debate relates to the human rights nature of political asylum,[16] given that, to the extent that human rights are characterized as *erga omnes*[17] obligations (Meron, 2003), it is still controversial. Even though political asylum is currently universally based on the right of asylum enshrined in Article XIV of the Universal Declaration of Human Rights, as it is a question of a state's power, insofar as it is at the state's discretion, there is still some questions surrounding its nature as a human right (Medeiros, 2017). An example of this lingering debate was Ecuador's request to the Inter-American Court of Human Rights for an advisory opinion titled the "institution of asylum in its different forms and to the legality of its recognition as a human right of every individual in accordance with the principle of equality and non-discrimination" (Government of the Republic of Ecuador, 2016), which resulted in Advisory Opinion 25 of the Court stating that, even though the right of asylum is a human right, as well as refuge and territorial asylum, diplomatic asylum is not protected as such in the Inter-American Human Rights Regime (IACHR, 2018).[18] A third debate refers to the continued importance of the coexistence of both refugee and political asylum, especially in relation to whether the latter can still be seen as a relevant institute. An answer to this question needs to be in the affirmative sense.

In relation to Latin America, one sees that the region's history is rife with political instabilities ranging from *coups d'état* by military agents to the establishment of dictatorships by individuals who ascended to power through an initial democratic process. These events "often victimized important political figures (e.g. presidents or prime ministers) whose continued presence in the country in question could mean either death to the individual or instability to the country" (Jubilut, 2006, p. 29). Finding a way of protecting them was relevant both politically and through a humanitarian lens. As some of these persons could not be protected by international refugee law, political asylum was a relevant alternative.

Moreover, it is quite possible that the importance of political asylum is also related to the pattern of regional solidarity. Regional solidarity is one of the most invoked principles by the regional documents on the matter, and has been applied since the struggle for emancipation by the countries in the region from the European metropolises (Menezes, 2011, p. 249). In many regional conferences, the principle of solidarity is referred to by states as the foundation for the establishment of regional institutions, as well as for alliances against external aggression (ibid).

Despite the democratic wave identified in the region since the end of the 1980s, the need of protection has not been extinguished. In this sense, and recalling that political asylum is – in its contemporary form – an institution of liberalism, as aforementioned, for protection against arbitrary political persecution, it seems that the institution's persistence in most of the Latin American constitutions is positive.

In practice, political asylum was not abandoned, and still remains a legal institution in most Latin American states, and a part of the legal and historical regional tradition (Barreto, n.d.). In addition, both the Convention on Diplomatic Asylum (1954)[19] and the Convention on Territorial Asylum (1954),[20] signed within the framework of the Organization of American States (OAS), remain in force.[21]

It should also be noted that, despite some considerations on the overriding nature of the distinction between political asylum and refuge, especially outside Latin America (Lambert, Messineo, & Tiedemann, 2008, p. 17) – where the same treatment is usually given to both institutes (with, for instance, asylum seekers being granted refugee status) – this subject is still of interest to the world (Gil-Bazo, 2015). This has been seen in the episodes involving Julian Assange, who was granted political asylum by Ecuador in its Embassy in London, as well as Edward Snowden,[22] who was given protection in Russia. The relevance of this subject is not only of a practical nature but also normative when considering "asylum as a general principle of international law" (ibid) and applicable to the protection of human dignity, and that,

> [f]ar from being obsolete, despite the establishment of the refugee protection regime as a matter of international law, this provision constitutes a reference on which constitutions around the world still formulate asylum in their bill of rights as an essential element of liberal-democratic states.
>
> *(Gil-Bazo, 2015, p. 23)*

Political asylum still being a relevant instrument for the protection of persecuted persons and the need of refuge being unquestionable (for instance, in light of the 25.4 million refugees by the end of 2017) (UNHCR, 2018), the coexistence of the institutes is positive (Medeiros, 2017) and allows for the expansion of the humanitarian space, thus benefiting those in need of international protection. This coexistence should take into consideration, on the one hand, that political asylum can benefit those persecuted in situations not covered by the conventional regime of refuge and, on the other hand, that "refuge has a deeper sense of normativity and hence assists many more people" (Jubilut, 2014, p. 251). In all three debates, however, it should be noted that, despite the historical and cultural affinity between Latin American states, there are at play issues of interest and power that guide international relations. One such question is that of reciprocity: bonds for political asylum concessions or for refugee status recognitions are also conditioned by the expectation of retribution, by reputation, and by interdependence (Guzman, 2008). In this sense, the Latin American multilateral scenario for refuge highlights the relevance of responsibility-sharing, especially when one considers that the region is the scene of several migratory crises,[23] as well as a route for migrants and a reception space. At the same time, unilateral decisions on political asylum consider the need to preserve political relations and depend on the interests at stake, as the shadow of political instability has never totally disappeared.

These perspectives may determine how a human rights nature can be attributed to each of the institutes. The need for responsibility-sharing establishes a more constructivist[24] orientation to the treatment of the institute of refuge in the region, by valuing the social meaning of practices so that universality is more naturally established. This would allow refuge to be seen not only as a right but as a human right, due to its foundations, goal, and universality. At the same time, questions of sovereignty prevail in political asylum. Even though political asylum becomes a fundamental right, that must be respected as such by the states that enshrine it in their constitutions or national legislation, and, due to its basis and goal, needs to always be applied with a human rights approach that allows for the manifestation of international human rights courts in response to violations of this right, there is no way to disregard the discretion of its insertion in internal systems and as a political-cultural option.

From the above, one can see that both institutes, therefore, bring positive aspects to the table, but it is relevant to describe the region's main trends in refugees' protection (i.e., its regional definition and the regional system of human rights protection) for several reasons, such as the fact that refuge "can be said to have been the preferred method in the region [Latin America] for advancing protection for people suffering or that may suffer persecution" (Jubilut, 2017, p. 251), and that Latin America is considered both as a refugee-producing (with reports of massive displacement, including on a long-term basis, of people with a well-founded fear of persecution and affected by serious and widespread violations of human rights) and a refugee-welcoming region (Jubilut, 2016).

Regional refugee law in Latin America

The Cartagena Declaration on Refugees and the documents by its revisional process

Despite the regional importance of political asylum and the fact that it allows for expanded protection, refuge is, as mentioned, the main form of humanitarian protection for forced migrants in Latin America. If Latin American history entailed the coexistence of political asylum and refuge, in a sense of "maintain[ing] their tradition of granting protection to persecuted people who either lay outside the definition of a refugee according to the 1951 Convention or to whom granting refuge was not a wise political move" (Jubilut, 2006, p. 30), on the other hand, and for that very reason, it also accommodated more comprehensive criteria for refugee status determination (RSD).

The first initiative for creating regional refugee law was launched by the 1969 Organisation of African Unity Convention Governing the Specific Aspects of Refugee Problems in Africa (OAU Convention) to address the massive flows generated by the struggles for independence in that continent. In addition to the universal concept, the OUA Convention also understands as a refugee a person who is obliged to leave her or his country of origin by virtue of external aggression, occupation, foreign domination, or events seriously disturbing public order in either part of or the whole of the country.[25] As it turns out, proof is not required that the life or safety of the individual is threatened (Arboleda, 2001).

Latin America followed suit in creating regional refugee law. The aforementioned instabilities, including totalitarianism, abuse of power, and the establishment of dictatorships in the 1970s and 1980s, led to the need to expand the refugee definition in the region. The concept of the 1951 Refugee Convention – which mentions neither economic and social rights or gender issues, nor internally displaced or environmentally displaced persons – did not address the situations of all forced migrants (Jubilut & Madureira, 2014), including the massive flows of persons in need of protection in Central America in the early 1980s (ibid). In light of this, the Latin American and Caribbean academic community and civil society, and the international community – represented by the United Nations High Commissioner for Refugees and the United Nations Development Programme – met at the Colloquium on the International Protection of Refugees in Central America, Mexico and Panama (*Colloquio sobre la Protección Internacional de los Refugiados en América Central, México y Panamá – Problemas Jurídicos y Humanitários*), in Cartagena das Índias, Colombia, and adopted the 1984 Cartagena Declaration on Refugees (Cartagena Declaration).

This was the first international document to "recognize that victims of widespread violence, internal conflicts and massive violations of human rights deserved refugee status" (Arboleda, 2001, p. 86). Although inspired by the OUA Convention, the drafters of the Cartagena Declaration were also influenced by the normative tradition of political asylum, and maintained the need for an existing threat so that refugee status might apply; but "[i]n practice, this wording has not been rigidly interpreted and the definition is not limited by it" (ibid, p. 87). Moreover, the threat has gained ampler contours as it encompasses cases in which persons are fleeing as, their "lives, safety or freedom have been threatened by generalized violence, foreign aggression, internal conflicts, massive violation of human rights or other circumstances which have seriously disturbed public order" (Cartagena Declaration, third conclusion).

The regional practice since then has been to grant refugee status by either applying the 1951 Refugee Convention definition or to persons fleeing "gross and generalized violation of human rights" (ibid), or even combining both sets of criteria. Despite its non-binding nature, the Cartagena Declaration was widely accepted, conceived as a "document consolidating the principles of regional and customary international law" (Arboleda, 2001, p. 91), and was supported by the OAS and the UN General Assembly, as well as having its force recognized by UNHCR (Jubilut, 2007). The document also called on the states of the region to insert the most favorable criterion for the recognition of refugee status into their national legal systems. This call has so far been accepted by Argentina, Belize, Bolivia, Brazil, Chile, Colombia, Ecuador, El Salvador, Guatemala, Haiti, Honduras, Mexico, Nicaragua, Paraguay, Peru, and Uruguay,[26] which have also incorporated gross and generalized violation of human rights as a criterion for refugee status in their national legislations.

In recognizing as refugees those fleeing "gross and generalized violation of human rights," the Cartagena Declaration, in addition to creating a new recognition criterion for refugee status, expressly aligns international refugee law with international human rights law and international humanitarian law, reinforcing the complementarity criterion among the regimes, and placing the human rights approach to refugee issues at the center of protection (Esthimer, 2016).

The Latin American normative structure on refuge thus assumes the 1951 Refugee Convention as a minimum standard of protection, which can be amplified by the Cartagena Declaration, and interpreted in light of the international and regional human rights regimes. The Cartagena Declaration gave rise to the *spirit of Cartagena*, that is, a vocation to reinforce and revise the mechanisms of refugee protection in Latin America according to evolving needs. For this purpose, an on-going revisional process, with the support of UNHCR, exists, meetings being held every ten years since the adoption of the Cartagena Declaration, or in the context of commemorations of other relevant dates for refugee protection (Jubilut, 2014), to discuss the current protection needs of refugees and other forcibly displaced persons and to adopt new documents that add to regional refugee law in Latin America. In contrast to the original document, the instruments of regional refugee law established by the revisional process of the Cartagena Declaration have all been drafted and adopted by states.

So far, states in the region have adopted the 1994 San José Declaration on Refugees and Displaced Persons, the 2004 Mexico Declaration and Plan of Action, the 2011 Brasilia Declaration on the Protection of Refugees and Stateless Persons in the Americas, and the 2014 Brazil Declaration and Plan of Action. These documents tackle challenges involving, *inter alia*, complementary protection, internally displaced persons, quality of asylum, statelessness, and mixed flows. The 1994 San José Declaration on Refugees and Displaced Persons[27] reaffirmed the principles contained in the Cartagena Declaration, while emphasizing the convergence of refugees and human rights regimes, and called upon states to harmonize their actions in a coordinated framework. It also highlighted gender issues by emphasizing the importance of considering the needs of female refugees.

The 2004 Mexico Declaration and Plan of Action[28] "is a different sort of document; it goes beyond legal definitions and lofty pronouncements, and it identifies specific steps that states can take to cooperate more effectively ... for the protection of refugees and internally displaced persons" (Costa, 2010, p. 357). Its main concern was for the refugees and internally displaced persons (IDPs) resulting from the civil conflicts in Colombia that had been ongoing since the 1960s. The two main purposes of the Mexico Declaration were: (a) to improve international protection, through the training of humanitarian actors and the development of research on the theme of the refugee; and (b) to implement durable solutions that would guarantee the quality of refuge in the region, through three different programs: *borders of solidarity*, based on secure access; *cities of solidarity*, based on local integration and self-sufficiency;

and *resettlement in solidarity*, based on responsibility sharing, through the resettlement of refugees to a third state in the region (Barichello, 2012; Jubilut, 2017).

The Brasilia Declaration on the Protection of Refugees and Stateless Persons in the Americas[29] is a memorial to the regional agreement "to continue developing a regional framework of cooperation for responding to forced and mixed migration" (Costa, 2010, p. 359). It recalls that the situation of forced migration in Latin America did not recede, and that the normative framework for refuge in the region still had protective vacuums (Jubilut, 2014). It is the only document understood as part of the revisional process of the Cartagena Declaration that stems from the celebration of a document other than the Declaration, as it also celebrates the 1951 Refugee Convention and the 1961 Convention on the Reduction of Statelessness.

The 2014 Brazil Declaration and Plan of Action[30] recalls the regional commitment to the protection of forced migrants. It was the result of a more democratic process (Jubilut & Madureira, 2014), in that it had the effective participation of civil society, non-governmental organizations and, above all, refugees, including women and young people. It reaffirms respect for diversity (gender–age–diversity) and highlights concerns regarding the trafficking of persons, migration, and the detention of unaccompanied children and, above all, the quality of life in refuge. It reinforces the importance of durable solutions while, at the same time, assumes the importance of complementary actions. From the above, it is evident that the Cartagena Declaration and all of the documents created by its revisional process have a strong tie to and involve dialogue with human rights, reinforcing the need for refugee rights and human rights for the integral protection of refugees (Jubilut & Madureira, 2016) as the tenor of regional refugee law established in Latin America.

The dialogue with human rights and the role of the Inter-American Human Rights System

The relevance of the human rights approach highlighted by the Cartagena Declaration and its derivative documents is strengthened in Latin America due to the coexistence of the specific regime of refugee protection with the Inter-American Human Rights System (IAHRS), in a pattern of complementarity regarding the protection of refugees. In so far as "the broad framework of human rights . . . [is], in principle, applicable to aliens, including those who are seeking asylum" (Cantor & Barichello, 2013, p. 692), the IAHRS has the mandate to also assist in the protection of refugees.

The IAHRS comprises the set of rules and institutions that together form the structure of the OAS with respect to human rights (which has Canada and the United States as member states, together with the majority of the countries in Latin America). The main organs of the IAHRS are: the Inter-American Commission on Human Rights (IACHR), which, being part of the institutional framework of the OAS, is able to review the practices of all member states of the organization; and the Inter-American Court of Human Rights (IACtHR), established by the American Convention on Human Rights (ACHR), and binding only those states that have ratified the ACHR and accept its jurisdiction.

The IACHR has the power to examine petitions on human rights violations and to issue recommendations on them, besides presenting country reports on human rights and submitting its annual report to the OAS General Assembly. The IACtHR, for its part, may offer advisory opinions to the states, upon request, as well as decide on judicial matters after the case has already been presented to and assessed by the Commission and after all domestic remedies have been exhausted. The main documents are the ACHR, the American

Declaration on the Rights and Duties of Men (ADHR), and the Protocol of San Salvador, which provides for economic, social, and cultural rights.

Both the ACHR[31] and the ADHR[32] provide for the right of asylum. It is said, though, that the provisions still have a historical restrictive pattern, insofar as they limit said right to political motivation, under domestic legislation (Cantor & Barichello, 2012), and without reference to refuge. Nevertheless, in the IAHRS, the right of asylum is dually protected: if there is a right to *seek* asylum in general, the IAHRS also provides for the right to *receive* asylum, thus reinforcing protection. Moreover, Article 22(8) of the ACHR is explicit regarding *non-refoulement*, which broadens the protective spectrum insofar as, given that it is a general legal principle that respects the universality of human rights, there is no margin for subjectivity in its application (Cantor & Barichello, 2013). Respect for *non-refoulement* has been a cornerstone of the IAHRS as,

> both the Commission and the Court have made use of their powers to order precautionary or provisional measures in order to prevent the imminent violation of human rights of asylum-seekers and refugees, *inter alia*, through prohibiting their deportation or expulsion.
>
> *(ibid, p. 23)*

Besides the application of *non-refoulement*, the IACHR and the IACtHR have developed actions on the subject of migration with a view to defending the human rights of (forced or irregular) migrants, including refugees, which can be seen in decisions that have ensured the right to non-discrimination, equal treatment, due process of law, and minimum guarantees in cases of detention and expulsion (Cantor & Barichello, 2013).

More specifically, four initiatives need to be highlighted. The first initiative is demonstrated in the IACHR document entitled, "Human Rights of Migrants, Refugees, Stateless Persons, Victims of Human Trafficking and Internally Displaced Persons: Norms and Standards of the Inter-American Human Rights System,"[33] in which the standards applied in the region for migrants are summarized, tackling the issues of the prohibition of slavery, servitude and human trafficking, freedom of movement and residence, the right to a fair trial in deportation or extradition hearings, the right to family life, the prohibition of torture or other inhumane or degrading treatments, the right to personal liberty and procedural guarantees in immigrants' detentions, the right to seek and receive asylum, the right of nationality, the right to nationality, the right to property, and the principle of *non-refoulement*.

The second initiative is the set of advisory opinions given by the IACtHR on the rights of migrants, that should logically also apply to refugees. In this set, it is relevant to highlight Advisory Opinion 16 of October 1, 1999, requested by Mexico in relation to the "right to information on consular assistance in the framework of the guarantees of the due process of law" (IACtHR, OC 16/1999); Advisory Opinion 18 of September 17, 2003, also requested by Mexico, on the "juridical condition and rights of undocumented migrants" (IACtHR, OC 18/2003); and Advisory Opinion 21 of August 19, 2014, requested by Argentina, Brazil, Paraguay, and Uruguay on the "rights and guarantees of children in the context of migration and/or in need of international protection" (IACtHR, OC 21/14), all of which led to the expansion of the humanitarian space of protection in Latin America, and show a proactive attitude on the part of the IACtHR (Gilberto, 2016), as well as the progressive and expansive character of human rights (ibid) that also apply to migrants.

The third initiative is the judgment by the IACtHR on the Pacheco Tineo case of November 25, 2013.[34] This was the first case of the IACtHR that focused on refugees and refugees' rights, and it chose to deal with conceptual and procedural standards for refugee status determination (RSD) in the region (ibid). In conceptual terms, the Pacheco Tineo judgment does not innovate, but recalls and applies the regional definitions of refugees (ibid). However, in terms of procedural standards, the IACtHR establishes the following as refugees' rights: the right to adequate time and means to present one's case; the right to be informed about the procedures; the right to be heard by the competent authority to present one's case; the right to have one's case examined and decided objectively; the right to a motivated decision; the right to be informed of the decision in one's case so as to be able to present an appeal if necessary; the right to appeal that will suspend the effects of the first decision until being decided; and the right to confidentiality (Sijniensky, 2016).

The fourth initiative is the abovementioned Advisory Opinion 25, which dealt with the assessment of the human rights nature of the right to asylum in the Inter-American regime, and found both refuge and territorial asylum protected as such as parts of the right to seek and be granted asylum (IACHR, 2018).

These initiatives demonstrate that the IAHRS is completing the process of expanding the humanitarian space in Latin America in terms of protection from persecution, which started with political asylum and evolved into a regional refugee law regime that combines universal protection with regional concepts and applies a human rights-based approach to the protection of refugees.

Conclusion

The right of asylum has a strong normative basis in Latin America. On the one hand, political asylum is a possible alternative in the region for the protection of persons fleeing political persecution. On the other hand, regarding the protection of refugees in the region, almost all Latin American and Caribbean states (with the exception of Cuba and Guyana, and of Venezuela, which is only party to the 1967 Protocol) are parties to the 1951 Refugee Convention[35] and most of them have incorporated the right of asylum at the constitutional level.[36]

Nevertheless, the conventional concept of refugee was insufficient, as it did not meet all of the possible needs for protection of the forced migrants in the region. This situation demanded a more comprehensive criteria for refugee status determination, which was promoted by the Cartagena Declaration, and reinforced by the subsequent documents adopted in its revisional process. These have all reinforced a human rights approach to refugee protection and the protection of other forced migrants in the region.

This dialogue between refugee law and human rights is strengthened in Latin America by the actions of the IAHRS, which has developed both standards of protection specific to migrants and applied *erga omnes* obligations, such as the principle of *non-refoulement*, to migrants in general and, therefore, also to refugees. Even though the multiple levels of institute, process and instrument might, at first, be confusing, the coexistence of political asylum, international norms on refugee status, and regional norms (stemming from the Cartagena Declaration and its revisional process and from the IAHRS) allows for a pattern of protective expansion against persecution in the region, with each aspect reinforcing and dialoguing with the others, and strengthening, rather than undermining, the protection of refugees and the implementation of the right of asylum in Latin America.

Notes

1 This chapter is dedicated to the memory of Stefania Eugenia Barichello, who was meant to co-author it.
2 These states are: Antigua and Barbuda, Argentina, Bahamas, Belize, Bolivia, Brazil, Chile, Colombia, Costa Rica, Dominican Republic, Ecuador, El Salvador, Guatemala, Haiti, Honduras, Jamaica, Mexico, Nicaragua, Panama, Paraguay, Peru, St. Kitts and Neves, Saint Vincent and the Grenadines, Suriname, Trinidad and Tobago, and Uruguay (www.unhcr.org/protection/basic/3b73b0d63/states-parties-1951-convention-its-1967-protocol.html.
3 www.refworld.org/docid/3ae6b3781c.html.
4 See Article 16. This provision was maintained by several subsequent documents. Full list in United Nations High Commissioner for Refugees. *El Asilo en Los Instrumentos Internacionales y las Constituciones Políticas Iberoamericanas*, 30 June 2011.
5 The need for reconfiguration of asylum, in order to reach other situations, not only political, of persecution that arose with the establishment of the dictatorships of the 1960s and 1970s. Until then there were no reports of migratory flows or asylum applications for other than political reasons (Arboleda, 2001, p. 83).
6 "Ecuador was the first Latin American country to ratify the Convention in 1955 and its Protocol in 1969. Another group of South American countries followed to ratify the Convention in the early 1960s and the Protocol in the mid 1970s. Most Central American countries ratified the Convention and its Protocol in the late seventies and early eighties. Mexico was the last country in the region to ratify both in 2000" (Freier, 2015, p. 123).
7 www.oas.org/dil/1984_cartagena_declaration_on_refugees.pdf. .
8 Cartagena Declaration, Third Conclusion.
9 See 1951 Refugee Convention, Article 1(D, E, and F).
10 According to the Convention on the Prevention and Punishment of the Crime of Genocide, "genocide means any of the following acts committed with intent to destroy, in whole or in part, a national, ethnical, racial or religious group, as such: (a) Killing members of the group; (b) Causing serious bodily or mental harm to members of the group; (c) Deliberately inflicting on the group conditions of life calculated to bring about its physical destruction in whole or in part; (d) Imposing measures intended to prevent births within the group; (e) Forcibly transferring children of the group to another group" (Article II). See also Article 5 of the Rome Statute of the International Criminal Court.
11 According to the Rome Statute of the International Criminal Court, "'crime against humanity' means any of the following acts when committed as part of a widespread or systematic attack directed against any civilian population, with knowledge of the attack: a) Murder; b) Extermination; c) Enslavement; d) Deportation or forcible transfer of population; e) Imprisonment or other severe deprivation of physical liberty in violation of fundamental rules of international law; f) Torture; g) Rape, sexual slavery, forced pregnancy, enforced sterilization, or any other form of sexual violence of comparable gravity; h) Persecution against any identifiable group or collectively on political, racial, national, ethic, cultural religious, gender as defined in paragraph 3, or other grounds that are universally recognized as impermissible under international law, in connection with any act referred to in this paragraph or any crime within the jurisdiction of the Court; i) Enforced disappearance of persons; j) The crime of apartheid; l) Other inhumane acts of a similar character intentionally causing great suffering, or serious injury to body or to mental or physical health" (Article 6).
12 The objectives and principles of the United Nations are set out in the first chapter of the UN Charter, Articles 1 and 2.
13 See 1951 Refugee Convention, Article 1(C).
14 See 1951 Refugee Convention, Article 33.
15 The expression "*jus cogens*" comes from Latin and means a peremptory/cogent right. In international law, according to Article 53 of the Vienna Convention on the Law of Treaties, it means the norms that cannot be derogated (i.e., limited or suspended) by any other norm.
16 The links between international human rights law and international refugee law have long been established and accepted (see, for instance, Hathaway (1991), Chetail (2014), and Burson and Cantor (2016)).
17 The expression "*erga omnes*" come from Latin and means "towards all," and legally means an obligation or duty which is imputed to all persons.
18 More information on the request can be found at: www.corteidh.or.cr/docs/solicitudoc/solicitud_18_08_16_eng.pdf.

19 Available at www.refworld.org/docid/3ae6b3823c.html.
20 Available at www.refworld.org/docid/3ae6b36614.html.
21 See www.oas.org/dil/treaties_year_text.htm#1954.
22 For more information on these cases, see OAS, Resolution of the Twenty-Seventh Meeting of Consultation of Ministers of Foreign Affairs, August 24, 2012 (www.oas.org/en/media_center/press_release.asp?sCodigo=E-67) and European Parliament, Draft Report Claude Moraes (PE526.085v02-00) on the US NSA surveillance programme, surveillance bodies in various Member States and their impact on EU citizens' fundamental rights and on transatlantic cooperation in Justice and Home Affairs, Doc 2013/2188(INI), January 24, 2014, Motion for a resolution para 76 (amendment 354), 48.
23 There are, for instance, reports of conflicts and displacements in Colombia, the Northern Triangle of Central America (El Salvador, Guatemala, and Honduras), Venezuela, Haiti, the Dominican Republic, and Cuba.
24 For the constructivist theory of international relations, the relations between actors of international regimes or their behavior towards certain objects are justified by the meaning that other actors or objects possess, taking into account their own identities, their shared beliefs, and the practices they participate in (Hurd, 2008).
25 According to Article 1(2) of the AU Convention Governing Specific Aspects of Refugee Problems in Africa, "The term 'refugee' shall also apply to every person who, owing to external aggression, occupation, foreign domination or events seriously disturbing public order in either part or the whole of his country of origin or nationality, is compelled to leave his place of habitual residence in order to seek refuge in another place outside his country of origin or nationality."
26 According to UNHCR and as of May 2015. www.acnur.org/index.php?id=bdl&no_cache=1&tx_news_pi1%5BoverwriteDemand%5D%5Bcategories%5D=1458&selectedCat=1458&fmenu=0&cHash=f9d1e796c7a95fa6962b88f837e9dfb5.
27 Available at www.refworld.org/docid/4a54bc3fd.html.
28 Available at www.refworld.org/docid/424bf6914.html.
29 Available at www.unhcr.org/4cdd3fac6.pdf.
30 Available at www.refworld.org/docid/5487065b4.html.
31 Article 22(7) ACHR establishes that, "Every person has the right to seek and be granted asylum in a foreign territory, in accordance with the legislation of the state and international conventions, in the event he is being pursued for political offenses or related common crimes."
32 Article XXVII ADHR establishes that, "Every person has the right, in case of pursuit not resulting from ordinary crimes, to seek and receive asylum in foreign territory, in accordance with the laws of each country and with international agreements."
33 Available at www.oas.org/en/iachr/reports/pdfs/HumanMobility.pdf.
34 Available at www.corteidh.or.cr/docs/casos/articulos/seriec_272_ing.pdf.
35 According to UNHCR, these states are: Antigua and Barbuda, Argentina, Bahamas, Belize, Bolivia, Brazil, Chile, Colombia, Costa Rica, Dominica, Dominican Republic, Ecuador, El Salvador, Guatemala, Haiti, Honduras, Jamaica, Mexico, Nicaragua, Panama, Paraguay, Peru, Saint Vincent and the Grenadines, Suriname, Trinidad and Tobago, and Uruguay (www.unhcr.org/protection/basic/3b73b0d63/states-parties-1951-convention-its-1967-protocol.html).
36 According to UNHCR: Bolivia, Brazil, Colombia, Costa Rica, Cuba, Dominican Republic, Ecuador, El Salvador, Guatemala, Honduras, Mexico, Nicaragua, Paraguay, Peru, and Venezuela (www.acnur.org/fileadmin/scripts/doc.php?file=fileadmin/Documentos/BDL/2004/2542; www.acnur.org/index.php?id=bdl&no_cache=1&tx_news_pi1%5BoverwriteDemand%5D%5Bcategories%5D=1458&selectedCat=1458&fmenu=0&cHash=f9d1e796c7a95fa6962b88f837e9dfb5).

References

Allain, J. (2001). The *jus cogens* nature of *non-refoulement*. *International Journal of Refugee Law*, *13*, 533–558.

Arboleda, E. (2001). La Declaración de Cartagena de 1984 y sus semejanzas com la Convención de La Organización de la unidade Africana de 1969: Uma perspectiva comparativa [The 1984 Cartagena Declaration and its similarities with the Convention of the Organization of African Unity of 1969: A comparative perspective]. In S. Namihas (Ed.), *Derecho Internacional de Los Refugiados* [*International refugee law*] (pp. 81–91). Peru: Pontificia Universidad Católica del Perú: Instituto de Estudios Internacionales, Fondo Editorial.

Barichello, S. E. (2012). A evolução dos instrumentos de proteção do direito internacional dos refugiados na América Latina: Da Convenção de 1951 ao Plano de Ação do México [The evolution of the international refugee law in Latin America: From the 1951 Convention to the Mexico Plan of Action]. *Universitas Relações Internacionais, 10*, 33–51.

Barreto, L. P. T. (n.d.) *Das diferenças entre os institutos jurídicos do asilo e do refúgio* [*The differences between the legal institutes of asylum and refuge*]. Retrieved from www.mj.gov.br/snj/artigorefugio.htm

Burson, B. & Cantor, D. J. (Eds.). (2016). *Human rights and the refugee definition – Comparative legal practice and theory*. Leiden: Brill Nijhoff.

Cantor, D. J. & Barichello, E. B. (2012). *Protection of asylum-seekers under the inter-American Human Rights System*. Retrieved from https://papers.ssrn.com/sol3/papers.cfm?abstract_id=2306126

Cantor, D. J. C. & Barichello, S. E. (2013). The Inter-American Human Rights System: A new model for integrating refugee and complementary protection. *The International Journal of Human Rights, 17*, 689–706.

Chetail, V. (2014). Are refugee rights human rights? An unorthodox questioning of the relations between refugee law and human rights law. In R. Rubio-Marín (Ed.), *Human rights and immigration* (pp. 19–72). Oxford: Oxford University Press.

Costa, D. (2010). Introductory note to the Brasilia Declaration on the Protection of Refugees and Stateless Persons in the Americas. *International Legal Materials, 50*, 358–360.

Esthimer, M. (2016). *Protecting the forcibly displaced: Latin America's evolving refugee and asylum framework*. Retrieved from www.migrationpolicy.org/article/protecting-forcibly-displaced-latin-america%E2%80%99s-evolving-refugee-and-asylum-framework

Fischel de Andrade, J. H. (1996). *Direito internacional dos refugiados – Evolução Histórica (1921–1952)* [*International refugee law – Historical evolution (1921–1952)*]. Rio de Janeiro: Renovar.

Freier, L. F. (2015). A liberal paradigm shift? A critical appraisal of recent trends in Latin American asylum legislation. In J. P. Gauci, M. Giuffré, & E. L. Tsourdi (Eds.), *Exploring the boundaries of refugee law: Current protection challenges* (pp. 118–148). Leiden: Brill Nijhoff.

Gil-Bazo, M. T. (2015). Asylum as a general principle of international law. *International Journal of Refugee Law, 27*, 3 28.

Gilberto, C. M. (2016). *A proteção aos refugiados no Sistema Interamericano de Direitos Humanos: Reflexões a partir do Caso Pacheco Tineo* [*Protection of refugees in the Inter-American Human Rights System: Reflections from the Pacheco Tineo case*]. Master's dissertation. Retrieved from http://biblioteca.unisantos.br:8181/handle/tede/3301

Goodwin-Gill, G. S. & McAdam, J. (2011). *The refugee in international law*. New York: Oxford University Press.

Government of the Republic of Ecuador. (2016). Request for an advisory opinion presented by the government of the republic of ecuador to the Inter-American Court of Human Rights concerning the scope and purpose of the right of asylum in light of international human rights law, inter-American law and international law. Note No. MREMH-GM-2016/18974. Retrieved from www.corteidh.or.cr/docs/solicitudoc/solicitud_18_08_16_eng.pdf

Guzman, A. T. (2008). *How international law works: A rational choice theory*. Oxford: Oxford University Press.

Hathaway, J. C. (1991). Reconceiving refugee law as human rights protection. *Journal of Refugee Studies, 4*, 113–131.

Hathaway, J. C. & Foster, M. (2014). *The law of refugee status*. Cambridge: Cambridge University Press.

Hurd, I. (2008). Constructivism. In C. Reus-Smit & D. Snidal (Eds.), *The Oxford handbook of international relations* (pp. 317–326). Oxford: Oxford University Press.

Inter-American Court of Human Rights (IACHR). (2018). *Opinión Consultiva 25 de 30 de mayo de 2018 solicitada por la República de Ecuador*. Retrieved from www.corteidh.or.cr/docs/opiniones/seriea_25_esp.pdf

Jubilut, L. L. (2006). Refugee law and protection in Brazil. *Journal of Refugee Studies, 19*, 22–43.

Jubilut, L. L. (2007). *O direito internacional dos refugiados e sua aplicação no ordenamento jurídico brasileiro* [*International refugee law and its application in the Brazilian legal system*]. São Paulo: Método.

Jubilut, L. L. (2014). Fora and programmes for refugees in Latin America. In A. Abass & F. Ippolito (Eds.), *Regional approaches to the protection of asylum seekers: An international legal perspective* (pp. 245–266). Farnham: Ashgate.

Jubilut, L. L. (2016, 21 November). *Latin America and Refugees: A panoramic view*. Retrieved from https://voelkerrechtsblog.org/latin-america-and-refugees-a-panoramic-view/

Jubilut, L. L. & Madureira, A. D. L. (2014). Os desafios de proteção aos refugiados e migrantes forçados no marco de cartagena + 30 [The challenges of protection for refugees and forced migrants in the Cartagena + 30 framework]. *Revista Intedisciplinar de Mobilidade Humana, 43*, 11–33.

Jubilut, L. L. & Madureira, A. D. L. (2016). *Thinking long-term: A foundational framework for durable solutions for refugees*. Oxford Human Rights Hub blog Retrieved from http://ohrh.law.ox.ac.uk/thinking-long-term-afoundational-framework-for-durable-solutions-for-refugees

Lambert, H., Messineo, F., & Tiedemann, P. (2008). Comparative perspectives of constitutional asylum in France, Italy and Germany: Requiescat in pace. *Refugee Survey Quarterly*, *27*, 16–32.

Medeiros, F. A. (2017). *Asilo e refúgio: Semelhanças e diferenças entre dois institutos de proteção humanitária* [*Asylum and refuge: Similarities and differences between two institutes of humanitarian protection*]. Rio de Janeiro: Lumen Juris.

Menezes, W. (2011). *Direito Internacional na América Latina* [*International law in Latin America*]. Curitiba: Juruá.

Meron, T. (2003). *International law in the age of human rights: General course of public international law*. Boston, MA: Martinus Nijhoff.

Piovesan, F. & Jubilut, L. L. (2011). Regional developments: Americas. In A. Zimmermann (Ed.), *Commentary on the 1951 Convention Relating to the Status of Refugees and its 1967 Protocol* (pp. 205–224). Oxford: Oxford University Press.

Sijniensky, R. I. (2016). *El acceso y el debido proceso en los procedimientos de determinación de la condición de refugiado – Jurisprudencia de la Corte IDH* [*Access and due process in refugee determination procedures – Jurisprudence of the Inter-American Court of Human Rights*]. Ponencia en la Mesa de Alto Nivel Una respuesta latinoamericana a la crisis global de refugiados: De compromisos a resultados.

United Nations High Commissioner for Refugees (UNHCR). (2017). *Global trends: Forced displacement in 2016*. Retrieved from www.unhcr.org/5943e8a34

United Nations High Commissioner for Refugees (UNHCR). (2018). *Global trends: Forced displacement in 2017*. Retrieved from www.unhcr.org/globaltrends2017/

PART II

Migration theories and methods

6

METHOD ISSUES AND WORKING WITH NEWLY-ARRIVED WOMEN REFUGEES

Janet Colvin

The number of international refugees across the world is the highest to date (United Nations, 2014). The US Committee for Refugees and Immigrants (2017) indicates that over 60 million people worldwide have been forcibly displaced. While the numbers of resettled refugees are relatively small compared to the total number of displaced people, about 67 percent were resettled in the United States, with the majority being women and children (United Nations High Commissioner for Refugees (UNHCR), 2017).

Most of the research on refugees to date has been dominated by a medical perspective, including both the physical (e.g., Baird & Boyle, 2012; Johnson, Thompson, & Downs, 2009; Krupar, 2016; Murray, 2014; Seu, 2003; Straus, McEwen, & Hussein, 2009) and mental (e.g., De Haene, Dalgaard, Montgomery, Grietens, & Verschueren, 2013; Johnson et al., 2009; Keselman, Cederborg, Lamb, & Dahlström, 2010; Lenette, 2015; Liu, Meeuwesen, van Wesel, & Ingleby, 2015; O'Neil, 2008; Slobodin & de Jong, 2015) health of the refugees. Baird and Boyle (2012) note that this medical perspective is understandable given that most host countries are trying to manage problems relating to infectious diseases, malnourishment, and psychological trauma. Many of these studies are also conducted from what is seen as a deficit paradigm, whereby problems and weaknesses are emphasized rather than contributions or successes (Berger, 2004).

While trauma- and health-related issues may be critical, there are also a limited number of emerging studies that examine not only the way in which refugees manage such issues but also how they use resilience to help them cope with resettlement in general (Goodman, Vesely, Letiecq, & Cleaveland, 2017; Gozdziak & Long, 2005; Pieloch, McCullough, & Marks, 2016). However, overall, very little is understood about the actual experiences and understandings of the relocation process of refugee women and children. In fact, the majority of the research about women refugees comes from a dominant culture perspective to create an understanding of how immigrants are absorbed into a culture. Berger (2004) argued that this perspective excludes women who experience immigration and focuses more on the situation than the identity of the women. She suggests that research allowing for identification of the meaning and experience of women who emmigrate allows them to express their viewpoints and values their perceptions.

This topic is important for studying women's refugee experiences, but equally important is the method employed. Many of the medical studies conducted have utilized quantitative surveys as a method (e.g., Bastin et al., 2013; Berthold et al., 2014; Nelson-Peterman, Toof, Liang, & Grigg-Saito, 2015; Ruiz-Casares, Cleveland, Oulhote, Dunkley-Hickin, & Rousseau, 2016). While quantitative researchers approach the world from a fundamental belief in an independent, objective, material reality, qualitative researchers look for multiple meanings and interpretations of those meanings. For those using qualitative methods to get at the meaning of the refugee experience, narrative has been the most utilized (e.g., Berger, 2004; Chamberlain & Leydesdorff, 2004; Crezee, Jülich, & Hayward, 2011; De Haene et al., 2013; Murray, 2014; Schweitzer, Greenslade, & Kagee, 2007).

Qualitative methods allow for description, sharing of personal experiences, reflection and in-depth understanding. Qualitative researchers look for ways to portray social action, describe behaviors in everyday life, and understand the meaning perspectives of those involved (Erickson, 2013). Anderson (2012) asserts that, with interpretive methods we learn "how other people make sense of the world in which they live and that they help create. It's not about cataloguing behaviors; it's about achieving insight into the lives of others" (p. 361). To promote a better understanding of women's lives and experiences through sharing, qualitative approaches are better able to approach deeper understanding and awareness. However, even if one focuses on a qualitative paradigm, how might changing methods alter the perspective of women and their experience?

Background

There are two contexts that are important for this study. The first is the role the State of Utah plays in refugee resettlement. The second is the viewpoint of refugee women. Each year, the White House submits a memorandum to the Secretary of State and Congress authorizing whether or not refugees will be allowed into the US, including a determination of the number of refugees to be admitted. The Office of Refugee Resettlement (2017) is responsible for services after arrival in the US and coordinates domestic resettlement with the states. Over the past 30 years, Utah has averaged approximately 1,100 refugees a year (Utah Refugee Services Office, 2017). The Utah Department of Workforce Services, Utah State Refugee Services Office, International Rescue Committee and Catholic Community Services all partner to provide services to refugees for the first two years of resettlement in Utah. Similar to what UNHCR notes, Utah's refugee population has more women and children and the majority come from Southeast Asia (Myanmar, Bhutan, Karen and Hmong), Africa (Somalia, South Sudan, Burundi, DR Congo, Ethiopia and Eritrea) and the Middle East (Iraq, Iran and Syria) (G. Brown, personal communication, October 17, 2016).

If women are a large majority of the refugee population, how do they experience resettlement? Berger (2004) notes, "less attention has been paid to understanding the meaning and experience of those who go through the process of immigration, especially women" (p. 26). Jacoby Boxer (1998) suggests that not only is it important to understand women's experiences but that the best way to get at such understanding is through sharing experiences so as to learn the meaning of them in their lives. This chapter is based on a series of interviews with refugee women in an attempt to understand and share experiences through the perspectives different methods afford.

Researcher background

After developing an intercultural communication class six years ago and wanting to find a way for students to participate in interacting with, and learning from, those whom students might identify as different from themselves, I contacted the state refugee agency to develop a service-learning program for my course. Since the inception of this course and the service-learning component, I have worked with local refugee groups, had students conduct service-learning projects with refugees, and interacted with local and state government refugee agencies. In the process, I have become very familiar with a number of refugee families, caseworkers, volunteers, and government representatives. This is important because qualitative researchers "are required to sensitize and familiarize themselves with the culture to be studied" (Berger, 2004, p. 32). Repeatedly in my interactions with refugee agencies, the phrase "international refugee" is heard. These words are used to describe individuals, groups and communities of refugees and yet differences are very apparent when working with individuals. I sought to understand how these differences might (or might not) affect the way in which agencies work with refugee groups, and, more specifically, with women. I thus interviewed eight women from different countries and regions who had been resettled from international refugee camps within the previous six months.

Participants were selected through a convenience process. An email was sent to the coordinators of three different refugee agencies. Coordinators then contacted newly-arrived refugee women to determine who would be willing to be interviewed and receive a $50 gift card for their participation. After 12 women were identified, eight were chosen because of their variety in age, family status, and country of origin. Two were from two different regions of Burundi (one, age 42, husband, 11 children; one, age 30, husband not in US, six children); one from DR Congo (age 44, husband, mother, 12 children); one from Somalia (age 35, husband not in US, six children); one from Syria (age 37, husband, five children), one from Iran (age 38, husband, two children); and two from Iraq (one, age 42, husband, mother-in-law, two children; one age 40, widowed, one son). Additionally, because only two of the women spoke limited English, an interpreter was used for the African women (Swahili) and for those from the Middle East (Arabic). The interpreters were identified by the community coordinators and were familiar to the interviewees. Each interview consisted of nine open-ended questions:

- Can you tell me about yourself and your family?
- Can you describe what it is like to be a refugee?
- What was your life like before you came to the US?
- What has it been like since you have been in the US?
- How would you define home?
- Can you tell me a story that describes what it is like to be a refugee?
- What were your ideas about the US before you came here?
- Where did you get those ideas from?
- Do you have anything else you would like to tell me/talk about?

Interviews ranged from 20 to 45 minutes. Before and during the interviews, I had to consider my own positionality. It was important for me to recognize my position and privileges when conducting interviews with the women. I came in as a white woman, a citizen of the US, and a university professor who had the power to request the interviews. I hoped to minimize some of this difference by making the women more comfortable and conducting the interviews in their homes and using a translator with whom they were familiar. Interestingly enough, in every case, the interviews ended up being with not just the women but also with their children (and in one case her husband), sitting in the room and discussing each question and answer communally.

What is the best way to analyze interviews, and especially interviews with women who are refugees? In this study, the research questions were left broad enough to enable a variety of approaches to analysis. There are multiple qualitative methods that utilize the use of interviews, such as discourse analysis (e.g., Bakhtin, 1981; Baxter, 2002), practitioner action research (e.g. Kemmis & McTaggart, 1988; Schon, 1983), autoethnography (e.g., Denzin, 1989; Manning & Kunkel, 2015), ethnography (e.g., Geertz, 1978; Lindsley, 1999), narrative (e.g., Connelly & Clandinin, 1990; Scharp & Thomas, 2016), grounded theory (e.g., Charmaz, 2011; Glaser & Strauss, 1967), and phenomenology (e.g., Creswell, 2013; Moustakas, 1994). However, because of their strong focus on stories, making sense of reality and inductivity, narrative, small stories, grounded theory, and phenomenological methods were selected to deduct meaning from the women's interviews. The remainder of this chapter explores how these methods could be used to analyze the interview data, identifies how each has strengths and weaknesses and offers varying insights into the experiences of refugee women.

Methods

Narrative

Narrative approaches are perhaps the most frequently used methods for studying refugees. Berger (2004) examined how immigrant (mostly refugee) women tell their stories. Others have looked at how people who migrate create space for their preferred identities (Blackburn, 2010); how transnational people use and understand memories (Chamberlain & Leydesdorff, 2004); and how migration affects children's narratives about attachment and security (De Haene et al., 2013). Narrative research takes the stance that everyone has stories that connect events. Della Pollock says, "a story is not a story until it is told; it is not told until it is heard; once it is heard, it changes . . . a story is not a story until it changes" (2015, p. 81). It can be said, then, that stories do not exist until they are told. In the telling, narrators not only constitute experience but also make sense of the past (Brockmeier, 2000). Clandinin (2006) suggests that narrative combines the dimensions of continuity (past, present and future), situation (place), and interaction (personal and social). Personal narratives allow one to look at life events with a temporal and logical order and in the process demystify them and establish coherence across past, present, and future (Ochs & Capps, 1996). Narratives construct, deconstruct and reconstruct stories (Josselson, 2006) and should always be considered in context with an eye toward understanding for whom the story is told and what it accomplishes. Narratives are especially useful in addressing complexity and diversity in the intersection of culture, person, and change (Daiute & Lightfoot, 2004). However, Munz (2016) notes that women's experiences are not usually viewed as an important aspect of grand narratives and are, in fact, a group of people who "are often underrepresented or muted in history" (p. 56).

In examining the refugee women's interviews using a narrative method, the focus is on questions of an autobiographical nature, connecting events in a sequence that reflects on later action, and for meanings that the women want the listener to take away from the story told. In particular, I was looking for stories about being a refugee and how the women situated themselves; that is, the significance of social positioning as it relates to identity in their stories (Riessman, 2003), and how these stories situate refugee women in the negotiation of their new life or "lived experience" (Clandinin, 2006). To gain an understanding of how refugee women situate themselves and create meaning in their lives, the following questions were asked: "What can you tell me about yourself and your family?", "Can you describe for me what it means to be a refugee?", "How would you define home?", and "Can you tell me a story about what it is like to be a refugee?"

One of the main ways in which utilizing a narrative method helped create meaning and coherence from the interview data was its identification of the overwhelming theme of *family*. In what follows, I give examples of how these women composed their lives as family narratives:

> So back there, life was not good. Food, they didn't get enough food, water was a problem, schooling for the children was a problem. But here, now, life is good.
>
> *(Interviewee 2)*

> Here is very good, since they [her children] can get enough food, they can get clothes . . . they can get water which was scarce over there, so life here is very good because they can get the things they were lacking back there, they come and they can get it here.
>
> *(Interviewee 1)*

> So, because our family is here, here is home.
>
> *(Interviewee 6)*

Utilizing a narrative method allows one to analyze the interviews to look for connections between events and overarching themes to determine how stories connect and create meaning(s) for the women. An overarching theme in this case is *food*, and how food denotes a good life.

While this is a helpful method in terms of looking for connections, it was not as helpful as I had anticipated. Specifically, there were three issues that made it difficult to see narrative as perhaps the best method. First, these women were newly arrived in the US and, as such, their stories were made up of discrete events rather than strong or threaded together connections among the events. Second, their stories were punctuated by examples of wanting to know what I, as the researcher, was looking for, as seen in this statement by the translator after I asked what one woman and her daughter had discussed for so long: "they wanted to know what answer you were looking for." This became a moment of recognition for me about my own identity and privilege and how it impacted not only the interview but also the women's stories. Finally, all of these women were happy to be in the US after an arduous process of gaining refugee status and their subsequent immigration. Their stories indicated not just what their experiences were but were punctuated with examples of being grateful to be here, whereas someone who had been here longer might see arrival as part of an overarching story, not a moment in time. Narrative as a method might be particularly helpful and relevant for examining these same women's stories through the process of recursive interviewing in order to build deeper research–participant rapport and develop larger narratives.

Small stories

One way in which narrative might be of more benefit is a fairly new focus; that is, a focus not on large-scale narratives encompassing significant life events but, rather, on what

Georgakopoulou and Bamberg identify as small stories (Bamberg & Georgakopoulou, 2008; Georgakopoulou, 2006). They see small stories as brief, short, transient, and sometimes insignificant moments, as well as "allusions to [previous] tellings, deferrals of tellings, and refusals to tell" (Bamberg & Georgakopoulou, 2008, p. 381). Parker and Craig (2017) used small stories in a study of high-poverty urban schools to look for examples in which educators and students "live and tell on the edges, in small moments unseen, unheard, and unaccounted for in grand narratives" (pp. 120–121). In a study of a health promotion study, Sools (2013) used small stories to study on-going conversations in everyday interactions. Even more applicable to the stories of newly-arrived refugee women, Bamberg (2004) documents how analyzing small stories allows study of identities that are "in-the-making" or "coming-into-being."

One of the women expressed concern about her children regarding the change in their behavior since leaving the refugee camp and settling in the US. She said,

> In Africa … you can spank your children, you can, your children belong to the community back there, but now here you don't have, you know, it's only talking to your children about behavior, you can't do anything. You can't touch.
>
> *(Interviewee 2)*

Another woman spoke about feeling as though her identity had changed from being someone's who was intelligent and employed to someone who was starting over:

> I feel when I was in Iraq like I am a good education, like I have a good education, good job, now I feel like I am, I am just like ah uh I have no degree or nothing to start with because everything is just different than how I used to live. I just think, I have [long pause] I know nothing here.
>
> *(Interviewee 8)*

Analyzing small stories such as these could help one focus understanding on how the women make and remake themselves and their family relationships (i.e., not spanking) or on how their identity has changed. Pauses and moments of silence can also "speak volumes"; for example, in the case of interviewee 8 above, the long pause lasted about 20 seconds, which emphasized the final statement of realization: "I know nothing here." Such small story analysis could be helpful in looking at underrepresented narratives and fleeting moments of narrative that might otherwise be easily missed. However, ultimately, they must be placed back into some larger narrative to see where and how they create overall coherence.

Grounded theory

While grounded theory may be used in prescriptive technical procedures (Strauss & Corbin, 1998), others view it as either induction or emergence (Glaser, 1965), or as a constructivist quest for interpretive understanding (Charmaz, 2011) and see grounded theory strategies as flexible guidelines rather than rigid rules. Grounded theory is seen as a guideline (rigid or flexible), and provides a tool for analyzing interviews, narratives, case studies, and field observations. The positionality of this approach differs from that of the other methods included thus far in this chapter. Grounded theory is a technique for engaging content, and for looking for patterns of behavior that focus on a main concern, but does not focus necessarily on the context of that content. It is included here on account of its frequent use in qualitative analysis and because of its ability to develop themes in areas where prior applicable theoretical frameworks may not exist.

Data analysis using grounded theory typically begins with a question rather than a theoretical framework and, as various ideas and concepts are repeated, repetitions can be grouped, ultimately leading to the development of new theory. Grounded theory does not test theory, content, or word count. Rather, it presents new modes of interaction and organization through a series of steps that is attentive to issues of interpretation (Suddaby, 2006).

This method moves across data, typically actual discourse of informants, and "compares fragments of data with each other, then data with codes, codes with categories, and categories with categories. Each comparative step successively raises the level of abstraction of the analysis" (Charmaz, 2011, p. 172). Through this process, the researcher seeks out links between analytical categories and explores concepts and theories as they emerge from the data (Daymon & Holloway, 2002). As links are made, inductive constructs appear guided by the overarching research questions that help to explicate the data and allow for discovery of emerging patterns (Glaser & Strauss, 1967; Strauss & Corbin, 1998). One of the main strengths of grounded theory is seen to be the "engagement with those living the phenomenon" (Corley, 2015, p. 602). However, Corley, supporting Charmaz's interpretivist argument, argues that such engagement calls for letting the informants guide the sequence rather than following Glaser's exact steps. Such an engagement may be more messy but Corley suggests it will ultimately allow for better understanding of what is happening as categories and themes emerge.

Regardless of perspective, in grounded theory validity occurs through constant comparison to arrive at "an approximate certainty of the truth of an inference or knowledge claim" (Lund, 2005, p. 121). Reliability occurs as various stakeholders read through the codes to assure that they reflect an accurate interpretation of the context and participants. Various programs such as NVivo and ATLAS.ti software aid in comparing codes and themes.

Grounded theory is an effective way to study topics such as self, identity, and meaning (Charmaz, 2011), which are integral to refugee women's stories. This might be especially true in the case of such stories. Two criticisms of narrative methods are that the in-depth telling of stories may be too traumatic or the teller may have forgotten events (Lapan, Quartaroli, & Riemer, 2012). In the case of this research, women have assuredly witnessed trauma and been traumatized themselves, but they did not know me personally and may have been unwilling to trust me with a retelling of events and/or been too traumatized to speak of them. Grounded theory may allow for more reconstructions of smaller reconstructions, which are "renderings of the shared experience, not the experience itself" (ibid, p. 44).

In approaching this topic with grounded theory, after interviews and field notes were transcribed line-by-line coding was employed (Glaser, 1978), as each fragment of data was given a code. Codes arose from my interaction with the data rather than applied. Some of the initial codes that developed related to the women being scared they couldn't speak the language, being worried about their children, leaving family behind when they came to the US, and demographics. However, this was just a starting point. As I read and re-read the codes, I deconstructed them and made comparisons between the data, which Lapan and colleagues suggest "expedites constructing a strong fit between data and codes" (2012, p. 46). For example, the categories of difficult adjustments, family welfare, and how the US is different for the women became centered around a larger category of "concerns." Comments relating to "What is home?" and "What is a refugee?" became part of a "demographics" code. Ultimately, the final codes were (1) demographics, (2) concerns, (3) situations before entering the US, (4) situations after entering the US, and (5) definitions.

Using grounded theory allowed me to understand the themes expressed by all eight women and to view their identity, not as I understood it to be, but how they wanted to portray it. One of the surprising findings from coding data in this way was the repeated theme of *family* in every code. While this can be seen as a narrative as mentioned earlier, it can also demonstrate how codes are expressed and realized. In this research, women talked about reasons for leaving their homeland and referred to family. They talked about concerns about their relocation and referred to family. They talked about what it meant to be a refugee and referred to family. They talked about definitions of home and referred to family. When asked to talk about what it means to be a refugee, they did not talk about traumatic experiences or themselves; rather, they spoke about the children being refugees and how they had adapted to being in refugee camps and then coming to the US. By viewing themes and codes, it became apparent that the women understood themselves not through their own experiences, but through the experiences of their children.

Repeated interviews or application of coding to various data collection points would lead to what Glaser (1978) calls theoretical sampling or identification of codes that would lead to an integrated theoretical framework. Glaser and Strauss (1967) define this as "the process of data collection for generating theory whereby the analyst jointly collects, codes and analyzes his data and decides what data to collect next and where to find them" (p. 45). In the case of refugee women, development of such a framework could lead to understanding the refugee women's identity (especially that of those newly arrived in the US) and what it means for both the women and those who work with them.

Interestingly enough, there are some (e.g. Lal, Suto, & Ungar, 2012; Thornberg & Charmaz, 2012) who suggest that a combination of narrative inquiry and grounded theory could yield even richer data and understanding of meaning. Lal and colleagues argue that the strengths of one approach can offset the limitations of the other. For example, if grounded theory is seen as being too fragmented and decontextualized, narrative can help in understanding overarching participant stories. On the other hand, if narrative inquiry is seen as being too personal and situated, grounded theory can help in understanding the "dynamic nature of core categories that emerge in a grounded theory analysis" (Lal et al., 2012, p. 14). Ruppel and Mey (2015) also see the combination of these two approaches as being helpful in a parallel process of shaping of development of codes and categories, and integrating narrative elements as a presentation of results.

Phenomenology

Phenomenology research is based on living (Dowling, 2007; Manen, 2007) and an attempt to define the characteristics of experiences (Moustakas, 1994). Researchers using this method look for a phenomenon and then both the uniqueness and the commonalities in this phenomenon that can be applied across individuals (Husserl, 1931). It is a philosophical structure that attempts to make sense of interpretation and move beyond the observable to the intentionality of actions. Use of this method focuses "less on the interpretations of the researcher and more on a description of the experiences of participants" (Creswell, 2013, p. 59), asking about the what-ness of an experience (Manen, 1997a).

Researchers using this method try to gain an understanding of, and imagine, the informant's experience. The purpose is to capture the essence of a certain phenomenon (Lindseth & Norberg, 2004). For example, Gish and colleagues (2017) looked at how older people driving cars with advanced vehicle technologies refashion embodied relationships with driving rather than how such technologies could aid older drivers. Lindseth and Norberg (2004) questioned nurses and physicians about their ethics by conducting interviews on their lived experiences of ethically difficult situations in healthcare. In another study, dialogic moments from interpersonal relationships were analyzed to understand how participants experience profound connections with another person (Montague, 2012).

A phenomenological approach can be used to study the refugee women's experiences because interviews attempt to capture how each understands and creates meaning from their subjective realities (Manen, 1997a). It helps us understand the women's stories through their intentions rather than based on details of what actually happened (Dalib, 2011). Indeed, regardless of the possible trauma experienced by these women, by focusing their stories on their children it became apparent that their intention was to keep their families safe and intact rather than to elicit sympathy.

To use a phenomenological method, the researcher needs to explain and express their social positioning, experiences, and identity, and how these might provide insight into both the interview process and how the data are shaped (Berger, 2015; Finlay, 2002). Manen (1997b) suggests that the researcher's interests and commitments should be deeply connected to both the context and the participants of the study. After working with refugees for the last five years and hearing refugees described as a coherent group – for example, "What do the refugees need?" – I wanted to understand if newly-arrived women refugees from different countries had different points of view regarding their lived experience to really understand the meaning of being a woman refugee. From this perspective, I sought to know the meaning of the phenomenon of being a refugee woman, not necessarily each person in her own complexity.

The interview questions were intended to elicit detailed descriptions of a situation, for example "What is it like to be a refugee?" and "Can you tell me about the idea of home?" Once the interviews were conducted, coding took place by using a preliminary code (Creswell, 2013) on which the literature has focused (e.g., Kirk, 2010; Ochs & Capps, 1996; Reynolds, Wetherell, & Taylor, 2007; Riessman, 2003) such as identity. This code entailed such things as how the women position themselves and others, and how they exercise agency while also being defined by the availability and accessibility of discourses (Gillies, 1999). In the interviews I conducted, over and over again, women positioned themselves as the caretakers of their family, not as refugees themselves. One woman said, "When I came, the children were able to go to school, they can get water, they can get food" (Interviewee 4). Another said, "Anywhere my kids are safe, that is where I will be home" (Interviewee 2).

The next step in coding a phenomenological approach is to look for descriptive coding to summarize topics (Creswell, 2013). Such summarization identifies significant themes or ideas that are shared in common across all eight women. In this study, themes included *family, demographics,* and *safety*, as these were the dominant themes shared across all of the women's stories. Within these themes, codes are summarized and major ideas are grouped into smaller constructs (ibid). For example, the theme of *family* aids in understanding how the women related all their comments to the idea of family in some way, regardless of whether they were from Africa or the Middle East, were aged 25 or 45 or had many or few children. Not only did they talk about family in answer to questions, but they all included family as they talked and discussed the answers that they were going to share. Their personal identity actually became secondary to their identity as mothers.

Because of the complexity of the refugee experience, future studies with women who have been in the US longer than six months may reveal that those who have recently arrived are not yet trusting enough to reveal trauma and instead focus on discrete stories about family. It may be, as described in the Royal Women's Hospital pamphlet (2001), that women are "often reluctant to speak about such horrendous crimes because of the pain of remembering and the fear of reprisal." Or it may be that the phenomenon of being a woman refugee may be less about trauma and more about resiliency and focus on family.

Phenomenology enables one to look beyond just the words of refugee women and to interpret the narrative formed by their words. As each of the interview questions was answered, the words were interpreted as understanding that family is an identity to which each of these women adhered. This approach enables one to look beyond words for overarching meaning. However, it can be difficult to prevent researcher-induced bias and ensure that the understanding of the researcher is coherent with the participants' intended meaning. Do refugee women really see their words as creating a coherent narrative of family? Are the experiences of these eight women typical of other refugee women? Did the difficulty of expressing themselves through an interpreter or their desire to please me as the researcher create obstacles that affected my understanding of the experience? These are problems that must be considered and accounted for when using a phenomenological approach.

Conclusion and future research

To help understand how newly-arrived international refugee women are making or remaking themselves into either someone who wants to be seen as a refugee (they receive assistance) or not seen as a refugee (they may be this temporarily but that is not how they want to be identified) and to make meaning of their stories, numerous qualitative methods could be employed. The methods described in this chapter, allow for description, sharing of personal experiences, reflection, and in-depth understanding. Each method offers insights into refugee women's experiences in different ways.

A narrative method allows researchers to connect events and discover overarching themes to determine how stories connect and create meaning. Using narratives in interviewing refugee women brought out consistent stories about how they were each grateful to be in the US and how they both came to help their families and how they were also concerned about their families. In this study, it was difficult to find overarching themes perhaps because the women were not completely trusting yet. What they did offer were a series of smaller events, stories, and even silences that the use of small stories helped in creating a more coherent narrative. Small stories need to eventually be placed back into a larger narrative at some point through the use of more interviews. Use of grounded theory allowed for the discovery and development of themes from the women themselves such as concerns about relocation, what it means to be a refugee, and how family becomes an issue throughout every theme. This methodology also requires repeated interviews to eventually develop an integrated theoretical framework. Phenomenology enables me to go beyond the personal identities of the women to look for ways in which all the women interviewed positioned themselves. In this study, the women identified themeslves not as individuals but as mothers concerned about their families. I was able to look beyond individual words for the overarching meaning of family. However, this method also required me to critically examine researcher-induced bias to determine if I was understanding what the participants really meant. Additionally, having an interpreter added another obstacle or layer to determining meaning. Overall, each method enabled me to hear the story of family but hear it in small moments, in themes, in social action, in behaviors, and in overarching meaning.

As Pollock (2005) identified, "A story is not a story until it changes; it is also not a story until it somehow changes us, listener and teller alike" (p. 83). At each stage, the researcher influences the direction and meaning of the research. Each method has strengths and weaknesses that must be thoughtfully considered before it is utilized. Each is effective at providing insight into either individual stories or the overall experience of being a woman refugee. Ultimately, however, the goal is to get beneath the surface and find meaning in the experience of women refugees and what we can learn from their stories.

References

Anderson, J. A. (2012). *Media research methods: Understanding metric and interpretive approaches.* Thousand Oaks, CA: Sage.

Baird, M. B., & Boyle, J. S. (2012). Well-being in Dinka refugee women of Southern Sudan. *Journal of Transcultural Nursing, 23*, 14–21.

Bakhtin, M. M. (1981). Discourse in the novel (C. Emerson & M. Holquist, Trans). In M. Holquist (Ed.), *The dialogic imagination: Four essays by M. M. Bakhtin* (pp. 259–422). Austin, TX: University of Texas Press.

Bamberg, M. (2004). Talk, small stories, and adolescent identities. *Human Development, 47*, 366–369.

Bamberg, M. & Georgakopoulou, A. (2008). Small stories as a new perspective in narrative and identity analysis. *Text & Talk, 28*, 377–396.

Bastin, P., Bastard, M., Rossel, L., Melgar, P., Jones, A., & Antierens, A. (2013). Description and predictive factors of individual outcomes in a refugee camp based mental health intervention (Beirut, Lebanon). *PLOS One, 8*, e54107–e54107.

Baxter, J. (2002). Competing discourses in the classroom: A post-structuralist discourse analysis of girls' and boys' speech in public contexts. *Discourse & Society, 6*, 827.

Berger, R. (2004). *Immigrant women tell their stories.* New York: Haworth Press.

Berger, R. (2015). Now I see it, now I don't: Researcher's position and reflexivity in qualitative research. *Qualitative Research, 15*, 219–234.

Berthold, S., Kong, S., Mollica, R., Kuoch, T., Scully, M., & Franke, T. (2014). Comorbid mental and physical health and health access in Cambodian refugees in the US. *Journal of Community Health, 39*, 1045–1052.

Blackburn, P. J. (2010). Creating space for preferred identities: Narrative practice conversations about gender and culture in the context of trauma. *Journal of Family Therapy, 32*, 4–26.

Brockmeier, J. (2000). Autobiographical time. *Narrative Inquiry, 10*, 51–73.

Chamberlain, M. & Leydesdorff, S. (2004). Transnational families: Memories and narratives. *Global Networks, 4*, 227–241.

Charmaz, K. (2011). A constructivist grounded theory analysis of losing and regaining a valued self. In J. W. Wertz, K. Charmaz, L. M. McMullen, R. Josselson, R. Anderson, & E. McSpadden (Eds.), *Five ways of doing qualitative analysis: Phenomenological psychology, grounded theory, discourse analysis, narrative research, and intuitive inquiry* (pp. 165–204). New York: Guilford Press.

Clandinin, D. J. (2006). Narrative inquiry: A method for studying lived experience. *Research Studies in Music Education, 27*, 44–54.

Connelly, F. M. & Clandinin, D. J. (1990). Stories of experience and narrative inquiry. *Educational Researcher, 19*(5), 2–14.

Corley, K. G. (2015). A commentary on 'what grounded theory is. . .'. *Organizational Research Methods, 18*, 600–605.

Creswell, J. W. (2013). *Qualitative inquiry and research design: Choosing among five approaches.* Los Angeles, CA: Sage.

Crezee, I., Jülich, S., & Hayward, M. (2011). Issues for interpreters and professionals working in refugee settings. *Journal of Applied Linguistics & Professional Practice, 8*, 253–273.

Daiute, C. & Lightfoot, C. (2004). Theory and craft in narrative inquiry. In C. Daiute & C. Lightfoot (Eds.), *Narrative analysis: Studying the development of individuals in society.* Thousand Oaks, CA: Sage.

Dalib, S. (2011). What it takes to interact with 'the other': A phenomenology of interethnic communication competence among students in an American university. *Human Communication, 14*, 221–239.

Daymon, C. & Holloway, I. (2002). *Qualitative research methods in public relations and marketing communications.* London: Routledge.

De Haene, L., Dalgaard, N. T., Montgomery, E., Grietens, H., & Verschueren, K. (2013). Attachment narratives in refugee children: Interrater reliability and qualitative analysis in pilot findings from a two-site study. *Journal of Traumatic Stress, 26*, 413–417.

Denzin, N. K. (1989). *Interpretive biography.* Thousand Oaks, CA: Sage.

Dowling, M. (2007). From Husserl to van Manen: A review of different phenomenological approaches. *International Journal of Nursing Studies, 44*, 131–142.

Erickson, F. (2013). A history of qualitative inquiry in social and educational research. In N. K. Denzin & Y. S. Lincoln (Eds.), *The landscape of qualitative research* (pp. 89–124). Thousand Oaks, CA: Sage.

Finlay, L. (2002). Negotiating the swamp: The opportunity and challenge of reflexivity in research practice. *Qualitative Research, 2*, 209–230.

Geertz, C. (1978). *The interpretation of culture.* New York: Basic Books.

Georgakopoulou, A. (2006). Thinking big with small stories in narrative and identity analysis. *Narrative Inquiry, 16*, 122–130.

Gillies, V. (1999). An analysis of the discursive positions of women smokers. In C. Willig (Ed.), *Applied discourse analysis: Social and psychological interventions* (pp. 66–86). Buckingham: Open University Press.

Gish, J. A., Grenier, A., Vrkljan, B., & Van Miltenburg, B. (2017). Older people driving a high-tech automobile: Emergent driving routines and new relationships with driving. *Canadian Journal of Communication, 42*, 235–252.

Glaser, B. G. (1965). The constant comparative method of qualitative analysis. *Social Problems, 4*, 436.

Glaser, B. G. (1978). *Theoretical sensitivity*. Mill Valley, CA: Sociology Press.

Glaser, B. G. & Strauss, A. L. (1967). *The discovery of grounded theory: Strategies for qualitative research.* Chicago, IL: Aldine.

Goodman, R. D., Vesely, C. K., Letiecq, B., & Cleaveland, C. L. (2017). Trauma and resilience among refugee and undocumented immigrant women. *Journal of Counseling & Development, 95*, 309–321.

Gozdziak, E. & Long, K. C. (2005). *Suffering and resiliency of refugee women: An annotated bibliography 1980–2005.* Washington, DC: Institute for the Study of International Migration, Georgetown University.

Husserl, E. (1931). *Ideas: General introduction to pure phenomenology*. New York: Humanities Press.

Jacoby Boxer, M. (1998). *When women ask the questions; Creating women's studies in America.* Baltimore, MD: Johns Hopkins University Press.

Johnson, H., Thompson, A., & Downs, M. (2009). Non-Western interpreters' experiences of trauma: The protective role of culture following exposure to oppression. *Ethnicity & Health, 14*, 407–418.

Josselson, R. (2006). Narrative research and the challenge of accumulating knowledge. *Narrative Inquiry, 16*, 3–10.

Kemmis, S. & McTaggart, R. (Eds.). (1988). *The action research planner.* Geelong, VA: Deakin University Press.

Keselman, O., Cederborg, A., Lamb, M. E., & Dahlström, Ö. (2010). Asylum-seeking minors in interpreter-mediated interviews: What do they say and what happens to their responses? *Child & Family Social Work, 15*, 325–334.

Kirk, J. (2010). Gender, forced migration and education: Identities and experiences of refugee women teachers. *Gender & Education, 22*, 161–176.

Krupar, A. (2016). Being untaught: How NGO field workers empower parents of children with disabilities in Dadaab. *Global Education Review, 3*, 105–121.

Lal, S., Suto, M., & Ungar, M. (2012). Examining the potential of combining the methods of grounded theory and narrative inquiry: A comparative analysis. *Qualitative Report, 17*, 1–22.

Lapan, S. D., Quartaroli, M. T., & Riemer, F. J. (2012). *Qualitative research: An introduction to methods and designs.* San Francisco, CA: Jossey-Bass.

Lenette, C. (2015). Mistrust and refugee women who are lone parents in resettlement contexts. *Qualitative Social Work: Research and Practice, 14*, 119–134.

Lindseth, A. & Norberg, A. (2004). A phenomenological hermeneutical method for researching lived experience. *Scandinavian Journal of Caring Sciences, 18*, 145–153.

Lindsley, S. L. (1999). A layered model of problematic intercultural communication in U.S.-owned Maquiladoras in Mexico. *Communication Monographs, 66*, 145–167.

Liu, C.-H., Meeuwesen, L., van Wesel, F., & Ingleby, D. (2015). Why do ethnic Chinese in the Netherlands underutilize mental health care services? Evidence from a qualitative study. *Transcultural Psychiatry, 52*, 331.

Lund, T. (2005). The qualitative–quantitative distinction: Some comments. *Scandinavian Journal of Educational Research, 49*, 115–132.

Manen, M. van(1997a). *Researching lived experience: Human science for an action sensitive pedagogy*. London: State University of New York.

Manen, M. van(1997b). *Researching lived experiences: Human science for action sensitive pedagogy*. London: Althouse Press.

Manen, M. van(2007). Phenomenology of practice. *Phenomology and Practice, 1*, 11–30.

Manning, J. & Kunkel, A. (2015). Qualitative approaches to dyadic data analyses in family communication research: An invited essay. *Journal of Family Communication, 15*, 185.

Montague, R. R. (2012). Genuine dialogue: Relational accounts of moments of meeting. *Western Journal of Communication, 76*, 397–416.

Moustakas, C. (1994). *Phenomenological research methods.* Thousand Oaks, CA: Sage.

Munz, S. (2016). *The farmer's wife: An oral history project.* Athens, OH: University of Ohio Press.
Murray, D. A. B. (2014). The (not so) straight story: Queering migration narratives of sexual orientation and gendered identity refugee claimants. *Sexualities, 17*, 451–471.
Nelson-Peterman, J. L., Toof, R., Liang, S. L., & Grigg-Saito, D. C. (2015). Long-term refugee health: Health behaviors and outcomes of Cambodian refugee and immigrant women. *Health Education & Behavior, 42*, 814–823.
O'Neil, M. (2008). Theorizing narratives of exile and belonging: The importance of biography and ethno-mimesis in 'understanding' asylum. *Qualitative Sociology Review, 2*, 22–38.
Ochs, E. & Capps, L. (1996). Narrating the self. *Annual Review of Anthropology, 25*, 19–43.
Office of Refugee Resettlement. (2017). Retrieved from www.acf.hhs.gov/orr
Parker, D. C. & Craig, C. J. (2017). An international inquiry: Stories of poverty–poverty stories. *Urban Education, 52*, 120–151.
Pieloch, K. A., McCullough, M. B., & Marks, A. K. (2016). Resilience of children with refugee statuses: A research review. *Canadian Psychology/Psychologie canadienne, 57*, 330–339.
Pollock, D. (2005). *Remembering: Oral history performance.* New York: Palgrave Macmillan.
Pollock, M. S. (2015). *Storytelling apes: Primatology narratives past and future.* Pittsburg, PA: Pennsylvania State University Press.
Reynolds, J., Wetherell, M., & Taylor, S. (2007). Choice and chance: Negotiating agency in narratives of singleness. *Sociological Review, 55*, 331–351.
Riessman, C. K. (2003). Performing identities in illness narrative: Masculinity and multiple sclerosis. *Qualitative Research, 3*, 5–32.
Royal Women's Hospital. (2001). *Working women's health: The journey through: Newly arrived immigrants and refugees.* Melbourne, VA: Royal Women's Hospital.
Ruiz-Casares, M., Cleveland, J., Oulhote, Y., Dunkley-Hickin, C., & Rousseau, C. (2016). Knowledge of healthcare coverage for refugee claimants: Results from a survey of health service providers in Montreal. *PLOS One, 11*, e0146798-e0146798.
Ruppel, P. S. & Mey, G. (2015). Grounded theory methodology: Narrativity revisited. *Integrative Psychological & Behavioral Science, 49*, 174–186.
Scharp, K. M. & Thomas, L. J. (2016). Family 'bonds': Making meaning of parent–child relationships in estrangement narratives. *Journal of Family Communication, 16*, 32–50.
Schon, D. C. (1983). *The reflective practitioner: How professionals think in action.* New York: Basic Books.
Schweitzer, R., Greenslade, J., & Kagee, A. (2007). Coping and resilience in refugees from the Sudan: A narrative account. *Australian & New Zealand Journal of Psychiatry, 41*, 282–288.
Seu, B. I. (2003). The woman with the baby: Exploring narratives of female refugees. *Feminist Review, 73*, 158–165.
Slobodin, O. & de Jong, J. T. V. M. (2015). Mental health interventions for traumatized asylum seekers and refugees: What do we know about their efficacy? *International Journal of Social Psychiatry, 61*, 17.
Sools, A. (2013). Narrative health research: Exploring big and small stories as analytical tools. *Health: An Interdisciplinary Journal for the Social Study of Health, Illness and Medicine, 17*, 93–110.
Straus, L., McEwen, A., & Hussein, F. M. (2009). Somali women's experience of childbirth in the UK: Perspectives from Somali health workers. *Midwifery, 25*, 181–186.
Strauss, A. L. & Corbin, J. (1998). *Basics of qualitative research: Techniques and procedures for developing grounded theory* (2nd ed.). Thousand Oaks, CA: Sage.
Suddaby, R. (2006). From the editors: What grounded theory is not. *Academy of Management Journal, 4*, 633.
Thornberg, R. & Charmaz, K. (2012). Grounded theory. In S. D. Lapan, M. T. Quartaroli, & F. J. Riemer (Eds.), *Qualitative research: An introduction to methods and designs* (pp. 41–68). San Francisco, CA: Jossey-Bass.
U.S. Committee for Refugees and Immigrants. (2017). *Exploring the issues.* Retrieved from http://refugees.org/explore-the-issues/refugees-facts/
United Nations. (2014). *2014 Syria regional response plan: Strategic overview.* New York: United Nations.
United Nations High Commissioner for Refugees (UNHCR). (2017). *UNHCR refugee resettlement trends 2017.* Retrieved from www.unhcr.org/en-us/resettlement-data.html
Utah Refugee Services Office. (2017). Retrieved from http://jobs.utah.gov/refugee/

7

CULTURAL FUSION

An alternative to assimilation

Eric Mark Kramer

This chapter reviews cultural fusion theory (CFT) as an explanation for the process of intercultural communication. This chapter first addresses limitations and inconsistencies in current theories of intercultural communication, including those in the theory of cross-cultural adaptation and the diffusion of innovations theory. This chapter then proceeds to compare and contrast these with CFT as an alternative approach. Concepts essential to CFT, such as a critique of the metaphysics of dualism, and discussions of co-evolution, pan-evolution, assimilation, integration, systems theory, entry valence, and entry trajectory are discussed. According to CFT, communication is conceived as a polysemic conversational process with countless messages and origins. Other theories tend to be dualistic.

Cultural fusion theory was first introduced by Eric Mark Kramer (1992). Subsequently, several master's theses, dissertations, books, book chapters, and journal articles have appeared testing the theory in several countries and contexts. Ongoing research by major intercultural experts such as Todd Sandel and his colleagues in Asia and Stephen Croucher and his colleagues in Europe and beyond have demonstrated the value of CFT, especially as compared to cross-cultural adaptation theory (Croucher, 2008; Croucher & Cronn-Mills, 2011; Croucher & Harris, 2012; Croucher & Kramer, 2017; Sandel & Chung-Hui, 2010). The paradigm is shifting from a predominantly Parsonian 1960s mechanistic structural functionalism that postulates teleological final solutions to human evolution that do not exist, to a systems approach that stresses reciprocity of influences and co- and pan-evolutionary dynamics within a globalized communication ecology. The difference is fundamental, and while some claim that their structural functionalist approach is the same as systems theory, this will be debunked below as the difference is clarified.

Fusion presumes a multiplicity of resources, including competencies that can be combined. Fusion is integration. Integration means both mixing and addition. Assimilation is not integration despite how the words have been misused. Assimilation is the elimination of differences and therefore identities and meanings. Assimilation can end. Assimilation is complete when there is nothing left to mix. Assimilation means the termination of integration. Homogeneity leads to high context communication because everything can presumably be assumed. There is little new left to talk about. Energy levels are low. Mindfulness and vigilance are reduced. This may appear soothing, but it is not only nihilistically monotonous but ultimately makes individuals and systems inflexible and as such unable to respond to unforeseen challenges.

Monocultures have few responses to unexpected threats. Their repertoire for success is limited. By comparison, multicultural systems are adaptable and robust, offering multiple channels for expression (different forms of music and dance, genre of literature, fashion, and so forth), and answers for challenges such as multiple pharmacological cures, architectural solutions, philosophical traditions, and multiple strategies for innovation. Multicultural systems not only have choices but internal exchange (competitive and complimentary) among options also offers fusional innovations. Unexpected combinations can provide solutions when monocultures cannot. In short, two heads are better than one.

Multicultural systems have thriving internal dialogs that are fertile grounds for fusional improvisation and invention. For instance, during the Second World War the fact that the United States Marine Corps could call on Navajo Indians to develop codes based on their language proved extremely valuable during the struggle for survival in the South Pacific theater. A system comprised of many cultures, including minority worldviews, harbors multiple options to handle challenges. Only one, or a single fusional combination, such as combining Navajo with modern military operations and technical apparatuses (radios), need succeed for the overall system to endure.

We cannot know when, or which option, or fusional combination of options will be effective until and unless a need arises to test the person or system. It is dangerous to eliminate options or narrow solutions without being able to foresee what the future may bring. What we do know is that the fewer resources, strategies or options a person or system has the less agile their responses and thus the more vulnerable they are. A lack of options is boring and inflexible. A multilingual individual has more resources (competencies) than a monolingual individual. Despite the fact that some lifeforms such as single-celled protozoa have proven very successful, enduring unchanged for millions of years, life continues to proliferate forms. Evolving variance does not stop. Life does not put all its eggs in one basket. Systems with complex and varied responses to challenges are the most successful.

The duality (dialectic) of sender–receiver leads to an us/them dichotomy, which often takes the form of my intent, my voice and my agenda–your compliance. It is linear and often literally portrayed in books as an arrow from a sender to a receiver, and in cybernetics, a feedback arrow is added from the receiver back to the sender. This is highly reductionistic and so simplistic as to be misleading in terms of explaining actual human interaction. Nevertheless, most communication theories are linear and sequential, with intent implied. Concepts of hybridization and third-culture syntheses also presume a model of communication involving only two interlocutors.

Cultural fusion theory builds on a different model, one that proposes that humans live within a semantic field filled with information from multiple sources, varying salience, interpretive-based understandings and participatory/reciprocal converse expressions. This approach is based in hermeneutics and systems theory. This principle of endless variance and interpretation without a transcendental authority (including a single coercive majority culture) that is presumed by CFT is a basic tenet of hermeneutic systems theory as first articulated by Nicolai Hartmann ([1938] 2013) and Alfred North Whitehead (1929), later adopted by Hans-Georg Gadamer, Niklas Luhmann, Anthony Giddens and others. Structure itself is a process – structuration. Established senses are knowable as such if, and only if, there are alternative senses present.

According to CFT, we live in semantic fields with countless messages and information flows. As we make sense of them, they interact in unpredictable ways, sometimes leading to true innovation and insight. Someone watching a movie about plants may get an idea they apply to architecture or clothing design. Contact, exposure to difference, involves risking one's sense of the lifeworld, including one's sense of self-identity and, more basically, how one will receive future information. The risk is not of elimination but of reinterpretation. The process of reinterpretation cannot be avoided so long as lifetime is operant. Only in death do we stop changing.

The linear model is deeply rooted in a Western modality traceable to Plato. It is dialectical, postulating two resolute positions – for/against, us/them, defense/prosecution. One might say that the older linear model is axiomatically (definitively) Euclidian, while the newer fusional field theory is more elastically Gaussian. The linear model was conceived by Plato as a method for adjudicating the exclusive and singular truth-value of claims. After Aristotle, this model came to be seen as depicting all communication, not just argumentation. But human interaction (participatory ecology) involves much more than simply seeking a final solution, a last definitive word. It is a self-sustaining generative source of meaning, a churning plenum – our semantic habitus. Efforts to vitiate voices and restrict participation need to be interrogated.

The need for conceptual precision

When I originally read the theory of cross-cultural "adaptation," several things struck me. First, the use of terms such as adaptation, integration, assimilation, evolution, and equilibrium were inconsistent internally and inconsistent with their usage in the scientific literature with which I was familiar. For instance, Gudykunst and Kim (2003) state: "the cross-cultural adaptation process involves a continuous interplay of deculturation and acculturation that brings about change in strangers in the direction of assimilation, the highest degree of adaptation theoretically conceivable" (p. 360). But adaptation is not the same thing as assimilation, which is not the same thing exactly as conformity (as assimilative blending can affect all ingredients). Because of the confusion, the word adaptation has been put into quotation marks herein as it pertains to the theory of cross-cultural adaptation.

As one reads the theory of cross-cultural "adaptation," it is made abundantly clear and reinforced by Gudykunst and Kim that what they mean by adaptation is an "upward-forward progress" (p. 382)

> toward assimilation, that is, a state of a high degree of acculturation into the host milieu and a high degree of deculturation of the original culture. It is a state that reflects a maximum convergence of [a] stranger's internal conditions with those of the natives and of a minimum maintenance of the original cultural habits theoretically conceivable.
>
> *(p. 360)*

Manifesting classic dualistic metaphysics, Gudykunst and Kim set up a conflict between internal subjective and external objective poles of reality, stating that culture is "internal to the individual" (p. 272) but that "objective" reality is "external" (p. 378). The primitive spatial metaphysics is self-evident. In this way of conceptualizing communication, the minority, the newcomer is separated from the semantic field. They are not part of the system. In order to avoid "mental disturbance" (disequilibrium; p. 377) there needs to be a "balance" of inside with outside the immigrant's head. The goal is convergence to a single worldview. The cross-cultural adaptation model encourages the elimination of diversity.

Furthermore, the fundamental conceptual confusion is that adaptation and conformity to an already extant culture are *two completely different processes*. Gudykunst and Kim use the word adaptation but describe a process of conformity. Mutation, the formation of a new successful lifestyle or form, does not mean repetition of the same or a blending away of all ethnic and cultural differences. It is in fact *the opposite of conformity*. To avoid competition with itself, life endlessly diversifies forms and in the process *the environment changes – diversifies*. Strategies for success continually emerge and multiply. Life flourishes in an abundance of solutions. Healthy systems keep writing new songs, using new instruments, and devising new architectures, arts, sciences, literatures, and lifestyles.

Evolution presents diversity and diversity enhances survival

In communication, diversity of positions generates dialog and meaning and alters the discourse. This process, including brainstorming, generates alternative solutions. This is more than diffusion, dissemination, or grafting (Derrida, [1972] 1981; Rogers, 1962). Positions and genres proliferate. Art and science require originality. *Originality, not repetition of the same, is the motor of progress of all cultural forms from farming to art to medicine.* Dialog and diversity constitute the artistic and scientific environment, the ecology of these living discursive traditions.

New art and new research do not fit pre-established reality but rather change reality. Change, evolutionary, progressive, whatever form, manifests the contribution that is divergence. Science evolves because new and different theories are proposed, new instruments are devised, new perspectives are created. We play in the invisible, in the dark, pushing perception outward by creating ways to see frequencies that we presume are there but cannot yet detect (Merleau-Ponty, [1964] 1968). There is no final goal that would signal "the end" because the unknown stretches endlessly before us. Each scientific research finding **is science** *sui generis*. This is the gift of uncertainty. It is the playground of curiosity and creativity. The Other is not always repulsive but often beckoning us to look, listen, taste, touch, and smell something enticingly unfamiliar. But it does take a bit of courage to try the new. Conservatism lacks courage. It fears what it does not already know. It seeks permanence, equilibrium, death.

The newness newcomers bring to a society changes it and as such they are active participants in it. Their difference is their contribution. This is what integrality means. Innovation defines the direction of the future, not past successes. This is the fundamental law of communication – identity and meaning (be it appreciated or shunned) depends on and is a measure of difference. Progress and regress are difference. The final and utterly ironic contradiction to the theory of cross-cultural adaptation is that, after the making of mainstream culture, a monolith of conformity pressure to which submission is the very definition of realism and rationality, the Gudykunst and Kim (2003)conclude with a call to change the culture and offer one "by design" (p. 395). This new culture will be comprised of a new kind of psychically evolved "universal person" with a "special kind of personal orientation" (p. 383) and attributes. All of us are encouraged to be passively malleable and to conform while creative vision and audacious, even prescriptive, ambition is reserved for the authors of the theory of cross-cultural adaptation.

Instrumental talk and effective communication

The dialectically-based models of communication, including intercultural communication, tend to presuppose the purpose of talk to be instrumental – argumentation and compliance-gaining. Compliance in different theories presumes this dualistic modality, described in various ways such as a spiraling toward final conformity/agreement, to describe a good, correct sort of person who exhibits "appropriate" ways of thinking, feeling, and behaving (Gudykunst & Kim, 2003; Kim, 2017). Conformity is equated with competence so that often cross-cultural adaptation is also referred to as intercultural competence. You are competent, right, healthy, in line with the natural order, when you agree with me, the person seeking compliance. The model of cross-cultural adaptation theory reduces communication to a unidirectional, narrow intention.

Power and ego-agency are fundamental. The new kind of "virtuous person" (Gudykunst & Kim, 2003, p. 385) who is pious and loyal (p. 396) will be carefully programmed by major institutions of socialization controlled presumably by those who follow the list of transcultural, universal, moral, and ethical precepts supplied by Gudykunst and Kim. They call for "a monumental task of projecting and cultivating a new direction for human character formation" (p. 388). By contrast, CFT does not aspire to moralize, but the context for its formation includes reflection on other theories that in fact do seek to engineer a world with no anxiety or tension, no inefficiencies or "incompetence." To gain such a utopia one must acknowledge that much would be lost – namely, innovative adaptability itself. According to the theory of cross-cultural "adaptation," the contribution of difference that is defined by the newcomer is *a priori* denied as unhealthy. Only conformity is good.

However, one source of difference is not only allowed but promoted by Gudykunst and Kim (2003), and that is their plan for engineering a new type of person and society. The contradiction is stark, especially given that one of them is an immigrant. On one hand, the theory of cross-cultural adaptation calls for complete conformity. Those who do not completely conform, such as the authors themselves, who call for a major overhaul of our culture, are "maladapted." On the other hand, the overhaul in culture so prescribed is intended to generate a whole new post-human being. The confusion, born of metaphysical thinking (dualism), is sorted out here.

Stage 1: the goal of cross-cultural adaptation theory is total conformity

According to the theory of cross-cultural "adaptation," "psychological health" is a measure of conformity. The major prescription for a newcomer, such as any minority in an unequal power relationship, including an immigrant, to maintain "psychological health" and avoid anxiety and "maladaptation" (Gudykunst & Kim, 2003, p. 372), is to encourage the subaltern to do everything they can to "unlearn" their indigenous "ethnic identity" (p. 372). As stated, "psychological health, reflected in the Newcomers' smooth and effective dealings with the host environment . . . a healthy personality is able to perceive the world and himself *correctly*" (p. 373). What is "correct" perception? It is the host society's "expectations that strangers conform to its existing cultural norms and values" (p. 371). This is further clarified by Gudykunst and Kim:

> Differences in physical appearance, language, verbal and nonverbal behaviors, rules and norms of social engagement, and economic and political ideology, as well as religious beliefs, ceremonies, and rituals, are some of the major ethnicity gaps to be overcome in the adaptation process.
>
> *(p. 368)*

"Ethnicity gaps" and difference must be eliminated and overcome for society and its members to achieve "psychic equilibrium" and for minorities to "be fit to live in the company of others" (p. 358). The minority is fit to live only insofar as they cease to be as a minority. Total transformation in the direction of mainstream ways is the only path to salvation. "Communication competence" is equated with compliance behaviorally, emotionally, and cognitively. The theory of cross-cultural adaptation never suggests that a contrary view may be very competently communicated. "Competence" itself is reduced to conformity to all forms of socio-cultural life in the goal of eliminating "ethnic gaps." The value is "functional fitness" and efficiency of replicating and maintaining the status quo. Failing to agree substantively or using an innovative message-form is defined by the theory of cross-cultural adaptation as incompetence and "miscommunication" (p. 361) at best and as irrational hostility at worst. When applied to intercultural communication, the cross-cultural adaptation model describes that what is appropriate is to be identical with what is dictated by a dominant mainstream culture. Meaning/intent, reality, is transmitted from a dominant pole, an active speaker, to a passive hearer. One teaches while the other "learns." Anything other than reception and agreement on the part of the subaltern receiver is seen from the dominant position as problematic, as a failure to communicate or, worse, as overt insubordination. Strategic intent is presumed in the old linear model and compliance equated with "learning" is the goal. So, according to the linear model, to become a member of the club, so to speak, the immigrant must not merely mimic the behaviors of the "mainstream" but also somehow "unlearn" (p. 360) and "disintegrate" (p. 381) themselves while internalizing the sense (the feelings and meanings) presented by the dominant members. Consequently, co-existence is not merely confounded and must be abandoned, but the newcomer's or minority reality is deemed by this metaphysical scheme to be "unrealistic" and as such mentally "unbalanced" (p. 383). External objective reality cannot be unjust or in any other way wrong. The ways, norms, and values of the dominant class are the only real ones.

According to Gudykunst and Kim, the old adage of when in Rome, do as the Romans do, is not enough. According to cross-cultural adaptation theory, acting like the locals does not equate with the fundamental "need to conform" (p. 373), to undergo basic "psychic transformation" (p. 376) to become a different person, which requires "reprogramming" (p. 358) of one's "operational skills together with cognitive and affective orientations" (p. 364). The prescription offered by cross-cultural adaptation theory is that the newcomer erase her mind, as it were, and reprogram it "cognitively, affectively, and behaviourally" (p. 367). The moral justification is efficiency, efficiency to the point of no longer needing to communicate at all once the singularity of total identification with the mainstream enables "telepathic and intuition sensitivity" (p. 273).

Exactly how one allows the mainstream beliefs, values, norms, and habits to displace one's self is unanswered except through disintegration of the original self and unlearning the past. How this is to be accomplished is not explained. We are told that so long as unlearning does not occur, then the adoption of a new self in consonance with the dominant mainstream culture cannot occur. Beyond this, if we cede to Gudykunst and Kim that one can somehow willfully unlearn and deculturize oneself by avoiding ethnic media and association with other expatriates, friends and family, and increasingly come to inhabit the worldview of the dominant culture, other issues arise that would not enhance mental stability but actually threaten it. Such erasure and reprogramming of the internal self presents a special challenge which W. E. B. Dubois (1995) already recognized in 1903 as the problem of double-consciousness. What is one to do if the more one successfully internalizes the dominant "objective" reality, the more one should hate oneself? This occurs when the majority worldview perceives your race, gender or status as an immigrant to be inherently inferior, even malevolent. As stated in the theory of cross-cultural "adaptation," "ethnicity gaps," and ethnic markers need to be eliminated. So, the more one internalizes the mainstream perspective, the more one must see one's self as the essential problem for stability and balance. Or what if the more a newcomer acts like locals, the more they find her to be bizarre, as when Japanese call foreigners who think they are Japanese *henna gaijin* (strange strangers)? Typically, and especially in multicultural environments such as cosmopolitan "world cities," people expect foreigners to be different, and *that* is what is okay.

According to the assimilationist model, the path to "successful assimilation" ironically requires that one accept not equality but a subaltern status to an absolute degree thus manifesting the complete erasure of one's original self. Assimilation thus is not to become the same as the dominant group, or equal with them, but quite the contrary, to erase oneself in ways they never do. The effort to become the same constitutes a process that they will never comprehend. The immigrant experience can never be "the same" as the local indigenous experience. This is not a problem, however, unless becoming the same (total assimilation) via deculturation and unlearning the self is the one and only goal, which is precisely the prescription of many advocates for social engineering a monoculture, including cross-cultural adaptation theory (Gudykunst & Kim, 2003).[1] Nevertheless, countless examples exist in everyday life that prove "success" is not identical to simple repetition of the same, of assimilation. According to cross-cultural adaptation theory, however, being different can never lead to success. But being "original" is often the key to satisfaction, recognition and reward.

Paradigmatic shift away from metaphysics (dualism)

Metaphysical dualism that separates components from identification with the system is a fundamental misunderstanding. It is vital to understand that everything is *always already* communicating, as Gadamer ([1960] 2004) put it. To misunderstand this aspect of a systemic process is to fail to grasp the fundamental principle of systems theory; namely, interconnectivity and the fact that one "cannot not communicate" (Watzlawick, Beavin, & Jackson, 1967, p. 49). Such changes that are beyond anyone's control (the blind watchmaker hypothesis), such as the famed "butterfly effect," are viewed with fear and trepidation only from the perspective of the status quo. According to CFT, there is no right or wrong.

One does not "enter" a finished and fixed culture. This is object bias. Rather, one begins to participate in culturing. For "better" or "worse," even tourism affects economies, healthcare systems, transportation systems, and legal systems; in short: culture. Participation includes unavoidable involvement in the ongoing authorship of norms, rules, beliefs, expectations, motivations, behavior patterns, values, and laws. Immigrants and newcomers do not merely conform or fail. They also change the society they join, and this fact fuels much of the xenophobia we see in the world. According to Gudykunst and Kim's (2003) prescriptive ideology, only one type of person need be flexible – the newcomer. Apparently, once assimilated, they should cease to be open-minded or mindful at all and expect subsequent newcomers to get with the plan. All responsibility for smooth, efficient communication is placed on the minority while the indigenous or dominant mainstream person can run on autopilot, presuming a style of naturalness and rightness of the system. Gudykunst and Kim exclude minorities (immigrants, refugees, visitors ... all newcomers) from the act of cultural production because, as they very "clearly" state, the

> reason for the essentially one-sided change is the difference between the size of the population sharing a given stranger's original culture and that of the population sharing the host culture . . . the dominant power presents . . . a coercive pressure on them to adapt.
>
> *(p. 360)*

There is no doubt that power inequality exists, but CFT is not an ideology critique. It also recognizes that power is not measured simply by numbers in a group. As for the reduction of influence to sheer numbers, a single foreign family moving into a neighborhood or school district has a greater impact on the culture than the simple addition of more of the same. It is important to remember that numeric quantity does not necessarily correlate with influence. Minorities often have an impact greater than their numbers as they often serve as the change agents of a presumably stable, static host society. Terrorists understand this all too well. One or two attacks that actually kill and injure far fewer people than car accidents on the same day provoke all sorts of reactions.

The power of one

At the end of summer 1911, on 29 August to be exact, local folk in Oroville, California noticed a malnourished old man walking down the middle of Main Street. The sheriff took the starving man into custody. All that he carried with him was a bow, five arrows, a basket of acorn meal, some shell bead money, and a few obsidian flakes. His name was Ishi. He was the last of the Yahi group of the Yana Indians. His story diffused through the telegraph wires and newspapers. Across the US and then around the world he was proclaimed the last "wild Indian" in America. After smallpox and measles, massacres, attacks by cattlemen and surveyors, Ishi was the last survivor, and starving he gave up and walked into "another world." He was a boon to anthropology. He was taken to the University of California, Berkeley, where Alfred Kroeber and Edward Sapir worked with him and made their careers off him. In "captivity," Ishi succumbed to tuberculosis just five years later.

One of Kroeber's students, and eventually his wife, Theodora wrote a famous account of Ishi, *Ishi in Two Worlds* ([1961] 2002). Ishi, a lone figure, walking into an American town when he did, changed social science and the popular sentiment about centuries of cultural expansion, diffusion, and destruction. He raised consciousness about culture and its fragility, especially in the face of racist hubris, powerful ambition, and greed. One person, without intent or understanding, affected the world.

In 1980, German missionaries moved to a remote area in Papua New Guinea. Intrepid, one might say, they took their five-year-old daughter Sabine (Kuegler, 2005). For the next 12 years, she lived "among" an "untouched," "lost" tribe, the Fayu, who were "discovered" in the 1970s. When her Fayu "brother" died, she decided to leave. At age 17 she enrolled in a boarding school in Switzerland. She was never able to totally acculturate to Europe, and in her autobiography, she writes that she learned fear in the modern world. Despite intertribal violence and other hardships, she was happy in the "lost tribe," but lost herself in the modern world. The Fayu had more time and were more welcoming. Kuegler's lesson for us is the experience of transformation that she has never forgotten and which continues. Neither she nor Ishi could "unlearn" who they were and who they became and the profound difference that made their journey memorable, even of interest, to millions. Nor perhaps should they. They had much to teach us. Lessons forgotten or unlearned are missed opportunities.

Difference as community

When immigrants first come to new countries they tend to enclave, to not abandon their communities but establish small outposts that enable them to become functional. For example, a newcomer arrives and looks for a job. They go to the local Eastern Orthodox Church or Asian community center where they find other immigrants who can help them to integrate. The continued association with one's original culture can greatly improve integration. Today, people do this with social media. The social support enables newcomers to succeed. Much of what they already know, such as how to drive, how to parent, how to cook, how to program computers or weld or do landscaping, is still operant. In fact, they may have things to teach the locals. They just need help with local interpretations and norms. They may always have accents – phonetically, behaviorally, and affectively – but those can make them interesting.

Stage 2: the end of the spiral toward total assimilation is "intercultural personhood" – the transcending of all culture via assimilation

Much writing about human immigration and migration presents a mechanistic structural functional model reducing explanations for human behavior to trait psychology (Kim, 2008; Kim & McKay-Semmler, 2012). Under such metaphysical biases, culture does not exist except, and this is absurd, as a "parochial" hindrance to "effective," "competent" communication. Indeed, being human, all too human, meaning perspectival, is the ultimate problem according to the theory of cross-cultural adaptation. Culture too is held as a "defilement" (Gudykunst & Kim, 2003, p. 385). But this calamity can be overcome with designed reprogramming on a mass scale in accordance with cross-cultural adaptation prescriptions, which will produce the "universal person," achieving "intercultural personhood." However, there is confusion as to whether this victory over culture will result from natural "evolution" among those with the appropriate personality traits or if it must be engineered. In any case, change in a very specific direction is valuated, with planning to avoid free communication and random innovation. The goal, the final solution, is to dehumanize mortal human beings, for to be human is to have a point of view, to be an enculturated person.

To assimilate or to "rise above" all culture?

A basic contradiction and a major self-privileging irony common to engineers

The entire argument made by Gudykunst and Kim (2003) is that the more a person deculturizes and unlearns their home culture and the more they internalize the host culture's ways of thinking, feeling, and behaving, the better will be their overall psychological health and wellbeing. But then, Gudykunst and Kim veer off on a contradictory tangent and argue that, as this process of sinking deeper and deeper into a single culture progresses, the person will suddenly become enlightened and achieve "intercultural personhood" so becoming a "universal person," a status so virtuous that they argue:

> If intercultural personhood is deemed a valid educational goal, and we believe that it is[,] an extensive search for ways to articulate and implement intercultural human development must be undertaken. The propagation of the goal must go beyond the educational process directly to the political processes and the mass media. Media, in

> particular, can play a pivotal role in the spread of interculturalness as a human social value and thus produce a gradual change in the mindset of the general public.
>
> *(p. 389)*

The theory of cross-cultural adaptation sees misunderstandings and resistance to coercion in intercultural communication and intercultural settings as a problem in need of a solution. The solution is the elimination of culture and communication as "intercultural personhood" aspires to "rise above the hidden forces of culture," the "defilements" that are culture (p. 385). The goal is to help immigrants rise beyond the "limits of many [curious to know which ones are not limited] cultures and ultimately of humanity itself" (p. 385). So we are to rise above culture but, if possible, how is this a good thing? The engineered "by design" new "universal person" and monoculture will reprogram us all and redefine through enculturation and acculturation "what is real, what is true, what is right, what is beautiful, and what is good," and how to "think, feel, and behave" (p. 376). What exactly is the true, beautiful, and good is never defined. But we are assured that the authors know the best direction of 'internal growth' for everyone (p. 380) and what we will need to respond to future challenges.

Gudykunst and Kim present no lack of confidence as they launch their proposed overhaul of culture itself and engineer a new kind of "virtuous" (p. 385) person. The intensely negative evaluation of cultural difference as "defilement" and the universal scope of the culture critique that is cross-cultural adaptation theory is extraordinary. It inflates to a critique of humanness itself proposing a new post-human being that exists without culture. How do we solve problems of miscommunication based on cultural differences? We eliminate culture entirely. No more defilements of cultural parochialism, no more chances for intercultural communication at all. Problem solved. But this is not realistic or even desirable (Kramer, 1992, 1993, 2000a, 2000b, 2000c, 2003a, 2003b, 2003c, 2011, 2014, 2016a, 2016b; Kramer & Ikeda, 2001; Kramer, Callahan, & Zuckerman, 2012).

Very differently, CFT accepts the tenet that communication always includes miscommunication (Budick & Iser, 1996; Fish, 1982). This is a fact of life and to deny that is to deny life. The desire to eliminate "parochial" worldviews because they engender inefficiency and uncertainty involves what Nietzsche ([1887] 1974) called the great exhaustion that can no longer handle the mundane vagueness or the "mosquito bites" of reality, namely, the reality of negotiating reality, *qua* relationships. Life struggles.

We find a fundamental contradiction here for the minority person trying to understand the prescription offered by the theory of cross-cultural adaptation. Literally from one page to the next the minority person suffering from poor "functional fitness" (p. 376) and "psychological health" (p. 376) due to "conformity pressure" (p. 371) is told that the solution, the "need to conform" may be "blocked" (p. 373) by their own personalities, by innate "predispositional factors" (p. 368) such as "physical appearance" and personality traits and attributes that determine one's "adaptive potential" (p. 369). But a few pages later we are told that "programming," – that is, the "cultural imprinting [that] governs our personalities and behavior" (p. 376) – can be changed, producing via socialization a different kind of person. But what kind? A totally assimilated perspectival human or a post-human being beyond all culture?

That question is not answered by the theory that proposes the contradictory path of correct evolution. So we will focus on the more mundane argument of assimilation. If our "adaptive potential" is based on innate pre-dispositional factors including "basic personality dispositions" (p. 368), attributes and traits such as "gregariousness" and "extroversion," as

Gudykunst and Kim (p. 369) claim, then the only solution to the problem of "'maladaptation" is to eliminate those personalities that may resist being "emancipated" from their indigenous cultures and identities, who may be "unrealistic" and "counterproductive" (p. 380), who fail to exhibit "upward-forward progression accompanying an increased level of functional fitness (greater adaptation) and psychological health" (p. 382). Ironically, social critique from the minority is characterized by Gudykunst and Kim as a form of maladaptive mental illness and possibly worthy of criminalization as they characterize "dissatisfaction with life in the host society" as "hostility and aggression toward the host environment" (p. 372).

According to the theory of cross-cultural "adaptation," ethnic pride, recognition, or even simple continuance of contact with one's community manifest incompetence and immaturity. It is "aggressive self-assertion and promotion of identity," marked by "ethnolinguistic vitality and intergroup behavior [and] strong ethnic group" relations. Though this attitude of having some residual ethnic identification is "not necessarily a disease for which adaptation is the cure, it is at the very heart" of the need to deculturize and unlearn the self. Unlearning the self and deculturization, in a zero-sum sense, is necessary, according to Gudykunst and Kim (2003), to make room for "self-understanding" and personal evolution toward assimilation that promises mental health and peace. "Human development" (p. 376), then, is to not grow a repertoire of competencies and understandings but to unlearn one set to make room for another, correct, set that is the dominant mainstream culture, no matter where or when.

CFT: a more consistent and conceptually precise explanation

Domination versus choice

In their discussion of power and coercion, what Gudykunst and Kim (2003) are clearly describing is not adaptation, which would be the emergence of a new lifeform/lifestyle, but rather pressure to conform to a pre-existing culture, conceived as something finished and something one enters like a stone edifice. The theory of cross-cultural adaptation rejects the ability to evaluate the status quo (except for their own claim for a need to re-engineer everyone) because all such evaluation must assume a position outside the dominant way of thinking in order to judge it, a position, ironically defined as mental illness by them. According to this model, suggested improvements from "outsiders" can never be entertained. Enrichment from intercultural interaction is discouraged. But clearly, the concern about immigrants is precisely that they do bring change. Yet, in reality, many corporations, universities and other organizations seek out and hire minorities, including immigrants, precisely because they hope that they will bring innovative ideas and differing perspectives to the organizational culture. The point here is that everyone is always already part of the system no matter their influence. Boundary conditions for a system are also in flux with exogenous as well as endogenous forces of change.

We clarify points: first, in terms of survival and power, the dominant culture is not necessarily the majority culture. In fact, it almost never is. Either an economic elite tends to dictate cultural trends, or an even smaller minority of rulers, such as a political party or a royal establishment, controls resources and institutions from courts to police and military operations. Second, might literally makes right for the theory of cross-cultural adaptation. Anyone who resists conformity or offers alternatives is deemed "maladjusted" and in "need of psychotherapy" (p. 382). Beyond being simple-minded (lacking "cognitive complexity" according to Gudykunst and Kim; pp. 382–383), the nonconformist is "unbalanced"

(p. 383), "immature" (p. 381), "self-deceiving," "cynical" (p. 380), "hostile" (p. 380), and, worst of all, "counterproductive" to the effort to maintain the status quo, which Gudykunst and Kim call "the accepted modes of experience" that constitute "external, objective circumstances" (p. 378).

The old structural functional dualistic mode of thinking emerges once again. According to cross-cultural "adaptation," the newcomer's perspective is subjective and unrealistic while the dominant ideology is objective and realistic. This is the basic "violence of metaphysics," as Derrida ([1967] 1978) put it. According to Gudykunst and Kim (2003), the majority is literally right because they are the majority. Everyone but a handful of people say the Earth is flat, therefore it is "objectively" flat and you best memorize and repeat this for your own good. Hence, my identification of this theory with Confucianism.

While the rhetoric about "personality traits" being the source of adaptable or unadaptable people would suggest an immutable genetic source, reminiscent of Victorian ideas, as a scientific theory, CFT harbors no such valuations or human engineering ambitions. Such ambitions are hardly new, however, as they repeat Herbert Spencer's nineteenth-century essays in Victorian England, exploiting even the same rhetoric that he used about social adaptation and evolution to convince new subjects of the British Empire to accept their colonial "reality."

According to CFT, social systems cannot avoid change as their memberships change. This can be an endogenous process; for instance, in Japan the fertility rate continues to drop and so Japanese society is undergoing some dramatic changes. Systems also change due to exogenous forces. The influx of immigrants in many societies (welcomed or not) is changing the atmospherics, the semantic field of many nations. The direction of change is not "essentially one-sided." The immigrant community and the host society share a common skin. Semantic and cultural "spaces," like physical space, are functions of structure. A single wall creates two rooms and, as it changes, the shape and size of the rooms also change. This is integral, as understood in CFT.

Cultural fusion theory makes a different assumption about communication and about the multicultural world. First, there is no final goal to be engineered, no singular utopian society or particularly ideal-type person. Second, without a final goal there is no intent (to be thwarted) manifested in the agency of a sender targeting a receiver. I encounter countless "messages" daily and most are not intended for me as a target. I may listen to music (read literature, play games, watch movies, read news…) from around the world and either I choose to repeatedly attend to it and perhaps incorporate some sounds and phrases into my own compositions or I do not. They remain in the world as semantic field. Influence and effect is a matter of exposure (intentional or not) as well as perceived use and gratification as much as any strategic intent of the sender. What the music I listen to means to me is not dictated by the source. Indeed, the source may have no clue I even exist. Much of the semantic field is anonymous. Meaning and sense are produced via interaction (random and planned). Even in a master/slave relationship, the master cannot control what things mean to the slave or how the slave feels. Behavioral compliance is not the same as attitudinal change. It has been well established and repeatedly replicated since the work of Leon Festinger and James Carlsmith (1959) that forced compliance, such as mainstream coercion, leads to psychological instability in the form of cognitive dissonance and often behavioral resistance along with negative opinion formation.

Change, including "progress," requires deviance

The consequence of exposure to huge amounts of information is a semi-coherent lifeworld that is not a noun but a verb. Meanings come in and out of focus, relationships fluctuate, new information constantly arises as sense mutates. The human lifeworld is a communicative process without a teleological resolution or an omniscient and omnipotent authority – no ultimate plan or design. It is a constantly changing assortment, a massive bricolage of shared and divergent meanings with no final goal or end that would bring monolithic structure (an end to entropy), and absolute silence (a final solution, a final equilibrium). From memory to imagination, current observation to logical conjecture, the world is not just a mixture of meanings but of media, which media theorists, at least since Lewis Mumford (1934), have noted, have semantic import. Even the way in which meanings may be "negotiated" varies. The marginal voice is the origin of progress. Even intrapersonal doubt is the origin of modified thinking. Redundancy, including isolation, is uninformative and static. Consequently, communication may confirm our biases and beliefs, that our way is the "best" way, our cuisine and music is the "best," or we may find alternatives challenging and even appealing, that is, having value. Either way, exposure has consequences and that is a fusional process that changes the meaning of "our way" and "their way," and as judged as "better," "worse," or simply different.

The limits of diffusion theory

Diffusion is unilinear and does not incorporate feedback or integration of information by means of interpretation. According to the notion of communication as diffusion, information moves as a finished objective message from source to receiver like transferring packets of information (informatics as opposed to communication). The impact is on the receiver as a target audience. Diffusion of innovations theory (Rogers, 1962) was born of the same academic context as direct effects media theory. Diffusion of innovations theory spawned the notion of development communication and the neo-Hegelian model of economic evolution, with the "take-off stage" in cultural and economic history promoted by Walter Rostow in his *Non-Communist Manifesto* (1960).

With the help of US foreign aid funding, telecommunication infrastructures were built in developing countries to facilitate the diffusion of innovations that it was presumed would naturally, logically, lead to the goal of re-engineering entire societies en masse from agrarian and possibly socialistic cultures into the better industrialized consumer-based capitalist variety. Other means were also implemented, such as the establishment of US institutions such as the East-West Center in Hawaii, peculiarly founded by Congressional mandate in 1960, to combat the spread of socialist and communist ideologies in Asia. The School of the Americas had a similar origin and purpose, but with a more military academy approach, for the development of Central and South America. To that end, handpicked students from authoritarian nations such as Suharto's Indonesia, Marco's Philippines, Generalissimo Chek's Republic of China, Generalissimo Park's South Korea, Generalissimo Nhu's Republic of Vietnam, and so forth, were brought to the United States to learn the doctrine of inevitable progress via neo-Hegelian social Darwinian imposed "evolution" upward and forward toward Westernization. Rostow's philosophy of imposed economic development and the "New Man" fused well with Confucianism, an ideology Confucius himself might well have disliked as it imposed rote memorization and staunch conservatism that hampered intellectual growth and innovation across cultural, economic, and political forms for centuries. Authority to determine the "correct" future was thus instituted.

While diffusion of innovations and nation-building went hand-in-hand, history has shown that people are not blank slates or robots to be reprogrammed at will. It is a common view that intercultural interaction leads to cultural imperialism and/or cultural appropriation, but diffusion as a simple transfer and holistic adoption did not occur. One cannot mistake Japan or Vietnam for California or France. Centuries of cultural inertia imbedded in language and ritual itself has proved quite resilient. Instead, we see pockets of tradition and fusion.

According to diffusion, transactional processing is not considered. No doubt the quantity of unequal flow can lead to an asymmetrical conversation. But even powerful empires, such as the Roman and British Empires, were profoundly influenced by the cultures they invaded and imported. CFT recognizes the diffusional aspect of communication but also recognizes the reciprocal aspect of communication. Even initiating and interrogating another still poses risks to the interrogator's worldview. The process itself influences all involved. Conversation is not a private property. Even in relationships with great power disparities, no one is immune to change. Slavery is corrosive to a master's humanity, and history has not interpreted that powerful position kindly. No meta-authority controls the interpretation of things. Even Michel Foucault (1964) had to concede to Sartre that he was able to somehow escape his own all-encompassing episteme to describe and critique it. The freedom of the world is in our open horizon toward it. Freedom is manifested in how we respond to what has happened to us, including colonizing forces and assimilative coercion.

The iron clamps of historical reason (including "natural" economic forces and genetically predisposed biological traits) hold only so long as people fail to see the power of assembly and resistance. Authority does not fear history but people. No one person, as the Martinique-born Francophone poet/philosopher Aimé Césaire (1957) wrote in his resignation letter to the French Communist Party, has the right to claim the sole interpretation of history, or as Nietzsche ([1887] 1974) put it, the right to deny all other interpretations but the one from one's own little corner. Elites present their worldview as objective truth and cast the subaltern worldview as nothing but subjective fallacy – uninformed or even childish nonsense. Imperialism typically justifies itself with its own metaphysical, meaning "objective" and "self-evident," version of natural superiority and historical rationality. However, this is self-serving rhetoric. It is not self-evident that just because a group may tend to dominate some aspects of a society that, therefore, economic success, cognitive complexity, and even sanity correlate with how much one attempts to identify with them, as argued in the theory of cross-cultural adaptation. This is a sort of meta-justification or handmaiden to ideological coercion as such academic writing itself is not the words of a privileged elite but, rather, supports and justifies their inherent right to impose their worldview regardless of time, place, or content. This justifies efforts to generate and maintain false consciousness, the internalization of the ideology privileged elites promote whereby they dominate because they innately deserve to. Rhetorical essays and handbooks arguing for institutionalized propaganda to justify and promote efforts in social engineering to protect the status quo manifest such ideological efforts. Imbedded within the rhetoric is sanitized tribalism; the justification for coercion as being natural, inevitable, rational, because this is my land and other humans who move onto it do not belong until and unless they become me, until they fit my criteria of humanhood (think, feel and behave as I say). It is very spatial, very ethnocentric, ultimately demanding of human beings to agree to become "deculturized," to "unlearn" themselves.

Evolution properly understood as non-teleological, non-ideological

Though one cannot erase oneself, perspective is mutable. However, to use the current metaphysical lingo, the "direction of change" is not toward some final "evolutionary" goal of perfect assimilative conformity as life has no final absolute ideal form, nor does change occur on only one side of an encounter. Life does not converge on one perfect form. Rather – and despite of the existence of very successful forms – life continually proliferates new forms, experimenting and expanding. Cultural life is the same; only through total isolation could one avoid all change (and, even then, sheer boredom would motivate deviation). The notion that life and culture are evolving in a particular direction implicating particular values is not Darwinian but rather the product of Charles Darwin's half-cousin and founder of eugenics, Francis Galton (along with his protégé Carl, but later spelled with a K, as he changed the spelling to be more Germanic-like, Pearson). Only Galton's ideology of social Darwinism, a moniker Charles disliked profoundly, suggests that evolution could and should be guided in ways that would reinforce the imperial power and wealth of England. Galton's version of evolution is Hegelian not Darwinian and it cynically exploited scientific terms and statistical methods to appear as mainstream science.

Cultural fusion theory is based on the observation that cultures are changed by the introduction of new elements and that even arrogant empires expend great effort to access foreign things and ways because they perceive them as desirable, even "precious" (such as gems, minerals, food stuffs, including coffee, tea, spices, and also philosophies); all manner of things that end up fundamentally enriching and changing the very cultures (beliefs, values, expectations, motivations, and behaviors) of imperial power centers such as London. With today's globalized communications, the old spatial metaphysics of center versus periphery has become even more outdated. The richer countries are in some ways measurable by their ability to access the Internet and thus to expose themselves to alternative styles, arts, and ways of living. But, as demonstrated by the International Telecommunication Union's technology and connectivity (ICT) measures, access to the Internet is expanding rapidly, skipping wired delivery entirely in much of the world (ITU, 2018). Reciprocity is increasing. On a global scale, the "periphery" is increasingly gaining the "floor" and talking back. It has taken what the West has given it – electricity, harmonic music and instruments, telecommunications technologies, and so forth – and is now responding so that we are seeing exciting new cinemas emerging, new musical forms, new forms of sport and comedy, pedagogy and healthcare, attitudes toward aging, family, friendship, time, space, and so forth.

Multicultural environments – human ecologies with multiple cultural dimensions constituting most modern societies, especially with increasing globalization – are deemed by Gudykunst and Kim (2003) to be a form of social failure. Those who personify multi-cultural and co-cultural complexities (persons who are multilingual and multicultural) fair little better according to Gudykunst and Kim's judgments, as they state: "co-ethnics are themselves poorly adapted" (p. 366).

Dualistic co-evolution compared to the pan-evolutionary lifeword field

Cultural fusion theory differs. Co-evolution is a major component of CFT, but CFT also expands the principle to recognize the complexity of the global semantic field we inhabit. This is the recognition of the pan-evolutionary multi-directional process that is the semantic field. In today's information environment, we observe a pan-evolutionary churning involving far more than just one centralized (alternative) source of information diffusing into virgin fields of scarce ideas and cultural practices, uncivilized types in need of "development" into civilized mainstream people, as it has been described in development communication and diffusion of innovation literatures.

Time presents an open horizon. The attempt to control human evolution itself has proven to be enormously arrogant and dangerous. The inclusion of the concept of evolution generally and co-evolution more specifically within CFT has been expanded to what is called pan-evolution. Co-evolution is similar to the notion of hybridity. It limits our understanding of cultural interchange to only two cultures synthesizing into a third culture. According to cultural fusion however, this does not adequately recognize the fact that, within the semantic field of human experience, especially in today's world with so many channels of information available from all over the globe, each human has become a node of convergence of far more than just two cultures.

Pan-evolution involves the sometimes, but not always, reciprocal nature of direct and indirect communication from multiple sources. Intent is not necessary for influence to occur. Also, messaging often passes through several nodes and relays before a person receives the information that has been thusly modified. Channels of cultural inspiration and influence have exploded in quantity. Origin has become less privileged. As messages are conveyed and shared, they change. Noise in the signal and interpretation are inevitable. How something is received is a function of interpretation that is the sum-total of one's prejudices, both enabling and limiting (Gadamer, [1960] 2004). Importantly, such change includes how individuals and societies perceive and handle difference (en-counters) in the future. Societies and individuals change their receptivity of newcomers based on many factors, including past experience with newcomers, economic and political contingencies, perceived motive for migration, and so forth. For instance, a host society may change policies and practices based on past waves of migrants so that future waves encounter a different set of boundary conditions and receptivity valences.

Cultural fusion theory recognizes that integration is a temporal phenomenon and involves archival processing (accrual of experience) as a compiling memorial activity. Integration is not a zero-sum process, as Gudykunst and Kim (2003) argue, which requires that a person must first unlearn and deculturize themselves in order to learn anything new. This is demonstrably false. The mind is not a finite container. Rather, experience accrues and with each new experience, old experiences are reinterpreted. This is a fundamental law of hermeneutic definition of interpretation/integration. Integration is a pan-evolutionary process. Furthermore, integration is a continually churning process whereby my next experience will alter how I understand my past experiences. I read a novel as a teen, a college student, then as an adult. With each reading the novel changes because I have changed, and I reflect on my previous readings and can see how limited they were. With experience, life becomes more complex.

We communicate; we talk in order to do something other than to exchange programmed information like computers. We talk to maintain community – to participate – in a shared process. Alterity, including slight differences in perspective (accent), is the essence of dialog and the ever-present source of the human lifeworld (Gebser, [1949] 1986; Levinas, [1947] 1987). Community is not always easy but it has been found by countless versions and generations to be "worth it." Worth it to engage in, tolerate, negotiate, and take on obligations of reciprocity (Buber, [1937] 1971). Community demands attention and effort, but it gives much back in return. One of the things it gives back is ourselves as meaningful members (Levinas, [1968] 2005). Hence, the point of Derrida's ([2009], 2011) and Ben-Tovim's (2008) analyses of *Robinson Crusoe*. A world of permanent sameness would be completely predictable and utterly unbearable (Deleuze, [1968] 1994). The Other saves me from the solitary confinement of total equilibrium, a zero energy state. Psychological "balance" is a dangerous metaphor. I get up in the morning because I don't know what will happen today.

The gift of uncertainty and a healthy system

The gift of uncertainty is not only "anxiety" but hope. It is the open horizon where our projects and agency, invention and innovation thrive. Ishi, tragically, was certain he was the last one.

For a *system* to be healthy it must be able to truly evolve – change – not just repeat "the same" (Deleuze, [1968] 1994). This is not a prescription but an observation. Moreover, this claim is applicable to, and can be demonstrably verified by, cases of large organizations and even nation-states. According to CFT, systems are permeable and living. Otherwise, they are history. Even the global system relies on energy from the sun and has been changed by extraterrestrial forces such as meteor strikes. Compared to natural history, social systems change very rapidly and they are very permeable.

Forces of change are both endogenous and exogenous. A major volcanic eruption in Asia may well have caused a "mini ice age" that affected the wheat harvest in Europe leading to the "Age of Revolution" and massive social changes. But a major endogenous force also helped propel this great cultural change. A rebirth had been building so that the decade of bad harvests were the final straw. Indeed, as Galileo was put on trial for claiming the Earth moves and is not the center of all, his simple observation about the geometry of a revolving object in space would change the meaning of the word "revolution" itself to connote reversals of power structures all over the (ironically named) globe, a tidal wave of change that evolved into the Western European "Enlightenment," an identifiable movement that continues to expand, inspiring many actions and reactions. The cultural precursor to the European Enlightenment involved the Renaissance rehabilitation of the pagan Greco-Romans. Change can come from history. Heroes are often selected to legitimize movements.

Attempts to close systems and force them to reproduce without access to innovation and deviance renders systems stagnant, without options to respond to ecological changes from within and without. The "Great Hunger," the Irish famine, was not a natural but a human-produced disaster. It demonstrated that rigid conformity to a pre-established and single scheme; to one set of beliefs about human nature, agriculture, centralized imperial control, and ethnicity; to one type of potato that presented only one solution to disease – all this established reality rendered an entire population profoundly vulnerable. Everything was interconnected with the humble potato. The real problem was that the logic, the schema of interconnections, was inflexible. It imposed itself with "coercive force," compelling the population to conform to an artificial, ideal ideology. The potato is not indigenous to Europe. It was imported to Ireland as part of a larger centralized plan. This arrogance (to utterly fail to appreciate the complexity of natural and social systems such as food production and reproduction) produced the problem because the Irish were literally forced to abandon other crops they had cultivated for hundreds of years. The fact that only one type of potato was instituted is the problem of monoculture.

The point here is that, when a single culture is enforced, solutions to unforeseen threats become drastically limited. The one type of potato could resist some diseases but not all. It presented a limited set of traits, limited defenses. In a more complex and divergent agriculture with several kinds of potato, the famine would have been averted. But only one was used. Monoculture is inherently weak, un-adaptive, static, limited in its responses. This is the argument against cross-cultural adaptation theory, which claims that the solution to all problems is conformity to a single mainstream culture. Encouraging monoculture actually subverts adaptability. When a system is stressed, what at other times may be recessive qualities may become operational and dominant. We may not like people who are capable of violence or who are "class clowns," unless and until we need warriors and we crave comedians. There is a season for all things, but we don't know how many seasons there can be. As the old adage goes, "it [life] takes all kinds." Artificially eliminating diversity by design can prove fatal. Some vision is shortsighted.

Entry valence and entry trajectory

Cultural fusion theory also introduces the notion of entry valence, which takes into account how a person fuses with a social environment – the interplay of prejudices. The process, in hermeneutic terms, involves more than the level of receptivity or "interaction potential" of a host environment. Different people manifest differing valences or trajectories of fusion not in terms of "adaptive predisposition", which for Gudykunst and Kim (2003, p. 370) means how willing and able a newcomer is to conform to a host culture and which they argue is largely a matter of innate personality traits "internal" to the newcomer. Rather, entry valence has to do with the process of fusion and typical factors such as cultural proximity and linguistic commonality but also the identity of the Newcomer as a social construct at the moment of entry. A "well"-educated and "wealthy" physician coming to the United States will have an experience different to that of an illiterate farmer or laborer. They may even have differing legal statuses. The French physician may be very comfortable with US urban environments while a Maung refugee from the deep mountain forests of Burma may not.

Given variation in hermeneutic horizons, individuals adjust differently. There is no single way to be "successful," "adaptable," or even "psychologically healthy," "mature," "competent," and "open minded" (values and judgments Gudykunst and Kim use to describe the "well-adjusted" sojourner). Assimilative conformity suggests only one right way, but this belies the fantastic variety of solutions readily observable that people present to the process of cultural fusion and adjustment. The *wonder* of biology and social systems is the diversity of forms and solutions life presents. Uncertainty provokes much more than just anxiety. Uncertainty, which is essential to curiosity, motivates experimentation.

Entry valence also involves the motivation for migration/immigration. Am I entering the country under my own free will? Am I entering as a tourist for a short stay with the expectation of fun, or am I a refugee who has been assigned a country that is willing to take me as I am forced to flee my home and as such am an unwilling sojourner? Or is this a trip that is ambivalent in terms of duration? As an exchange student, I enter expecting to stay only long enough to complete my college degree, but I realize I may also stay longer if career opportunities present themselves. Am I compelled by my career trajectory to come to your country as a multi-year transfer salaried employee of a multinational corporation or non-governmental organization? Am I a diplomat or soldier, a missionary, or seeking to extract resources?

The point here is that the experience of my entry valence will involve my *motives, expectations* and *willingness* to migrate or immigrate as well as various and sundry reception factors. Why I am moving is vital to how the experience will be understood by both indigenous persons and me, the newcomer. Attributions will also differ as to understanding my behaviors. As per hermeneutic principles, as I gain experience and information, attributions shift along with my understanding of things.

Entry trajectory is like the splash of me diving into water. The splash does not belong to me and I do not entirely control it but partially. The splash does not belong to the pool. The splash is an integral phenomenon that does not exist independent of the host society or the newcomer but only happens as a common moment in time when they come together. The newcomer may enter a nation that has policies hostile to immigrants but yet find individuals who are very welcoming. Entry trajectory is a complex combination of factors, many of which cannot be preplanned or controlled. We may also be aware of them or unconscious of their influences. Entry trajectory affects how I will feel about *joining* a new environment. There is no single set of communication strategies and tactics or appropriate attitudes that fit all newcomer experiences.

Fusional accrual and horizonal complexity

Growing a repertoire of cultural skills

Fusion is not an object or behavior. Rather, it is a process of churning experience involving a constant integration of incoming information that has profound consequences for understanding, sense-making and behavior. Sense and meaning are two different things. Meaning is specific and involves disambiguation. Meaning tends to be intimately associated with linguistic articulation and cultural norms. Sense is more amorphous – atmospheric. I may have a feeling or mood about a room, person, city, and so on that is hard to define and specify and which I may not share with others. Sense often impacts expectations, motivations, and behaviors. It can influence communication but, unlike the effort to share meanings, sense is often unshared.

Fusion involves both sense and meaning. Fusion has the reflexive nature that, with experience, future perception, including sense and meaning, is altered. For example, initially I may not be able to recognize a pattern in chess that constitutes a coordinated attack, but with experience, I become familiar with various patterns and can readily recognize a particular pattern as willful, purposeful, and threatening. The pattern can be recognized by many as an "attack." It has that meaning. It is a gambit for assaulting my positions. Differently, the sense of being threatened may not be reducible to my pattern acuity. I was in peril all along and did not even see it. Or I think I am "in trouble" when no one else "sees" it. Sense can coalesce into focused meaning. Seeing is not recognition. I may be fully capable of seeing the chessboard and pieces but be unable to recognize a pattern. Recognizing relationships is essential to understanding. Cultural variance is often experienced as having differing senses about a place, event, prospect, opportunity, person, risk. Different cultures see different patterns. We have the stars but many zodiacs and sharing the different patterns can be enriching.

Fusion is the process of synthesizing perceptions into shifting patterns. Patterns are often transitory. Fusion is a process of learning and appropriation. It involves integration, which means interpretation and modification in the act of appropriation. When I "take in" some new knowledge and "make it mine," I am changed. The same occurs when newcomers join a community. Newcomers enrich communities. Vital communities "learn" and increase in complexity; "grow." Their vitality attracts energy-giving change. Dying, stagnant communities are not attractive. Equilibrium is an inert state. Conservatives fear movement lest the "balance" is lost and things change. Demonstrably, the world's populations are on the move and seeking vitality and stimulation: "development" (Skeldon, 2018; UN Population Division, 2018). "International migration is a global phenomenon that is growing in scope, complexity and impact" (UN Population Division, 2018, p. 1). Because there are more migrants in the world today than ever before, more than 230 million international immigrants according to the United Nations (2013), the twenty-first century has been called "the age of migration" (Castles & Miller, 2009). While the "goodness" of this, and opinions about the "best" direction can be debated, the fact that it is happening cannot. Thus, the need and impetus for improved theories to help us understand our existential condition.

Expansion of horizon through encountering differences

Horizon is something like a measure of perspective. Heidegger ([1949] 2005) discussed the nature of horizon as a process of *Gestell*, enframing (and well before framing theory in journalism). It has to do with how my horizon constitutes my attitude. Attitude here is used in the phenomenological sense that encompasses what determines the relationship of contact, as for example when an airplane is approaching contact with the ground and how its axis references the horizon. I may take "to hand" a baseball bat as a weapon, as equipment for play, as an heirloom to be autographed and displayed, as a source of wood for a fire, as a gift to bestow. What a thing "is," what it means and its sense depends on the attitude of its appropriation; the nature of how it relates to context. This is contingent. Difference is always available.[2]

Other cultures teach us our limitations and open us to new vistas. They even teach us to reconsider what communication itself is. John Carrington (1949), a Christian missionary who arrived in the Belgian Congo in 1938, personifies an example of "the West" discovering the intricacies, sophistication, and elegance of other ways of communicating. He had assumed only Europeans had accomplished the ability to communicate nearly instantly beyond the horizon with wired and wireless telegraphy and telephony. Messenger pigeons and chains of fire towers built by ancients conveyed information only so far and fast as they could carry physical media or by line-of-sight. But he discovered that sans wired and wireless electromagnetic devices, African villagers knew of his travel plans and arrival times well before he had physically started. He learned that Africans, often across tribal boundaries and transcending spoken language, shared at least two distinct and complex codes of drumming and could relay information beyond horizons and through the night, bad weather and densest forests with little effort. Carrington published an account of Lokele tribe drumming in 1944 and later published his famous work, *The Talking Drums of Africa*, in 1949, in which he fully introduced to non-Africans the astounding complexity of these codes and their ability to translate spoken languages even as encroaching modernity was silencing them. He himself dedicated much time to becoming a drum speaker and this willingness to take seriously and respect the drum led Africans to claim that he was actually a black person reincarnated as a white man. Carrington becoming a drum speaker, even a "black man," is an example of cultural fusion. It highlights one of the ways in which colonialism affected not just the colonized but also the colonizer in a pan-evolutionary (not merely co-evolutionary) process of fusion. While Europeans primitively used the drum primarily to keep a monotonous beat to music, Africans and others around the globe, such as the layered simultaneous multi-rhythmic and "breakneck speed" of Papua New Guinea tribal drums first described by Arthur Wichmann in 1890 and later by the ornithologist Jared Diamond (1992), had been conveying complex messages in "real time" for centuries.

As the number of cultures dwindles, the chance for encountering dramatic difference also dwindles. Convergence on a similar world culture may prove efficient in some ways but is profoundly impoverishing in others as the opportunity of growth through difference fades. However, it seems that the human craving for stimulation is such that the rather spontaneous emergence of subcultural trends will continue and perhaps even accelerate, as we see in places like Tokyo. This endless source of innovation and deviation is what Kramer (1997) means by the "Jazziness" of human cultural formation. Experimentation and improvisation are what humans do. We are never threatened by the "prison-house" of language because here, too, we are constantly inventing new phrases, ways of using old words, and new words to express new experiences; difference is liberating.

To be adaptable, alternative perspectives are necessary and should be valued. This is what Kramer means by "appreciating validities" (p. 183). A nurse writes a description of the First World War, a soldier does "the same," a general, a child living near the front, even a horse. All may be very valid, empirically verifiable, but all are different. Each adds to my understanding of the phenomenon, the "First World War." The mosaic expands. Avoiding complexity is de-meaning.

Beyond duality: the parts are the system

Let us look at an example of the newcomer not merely fitting in to the establishment but altering it fundamentally, integrally. In the biological world, life expands by means of diversification of forms. Such forms do not fit pre-established niches or a pre-given environment. They do not so much fit in as they alter the game. They are the niche. If they become extinct no "empty niche" exists. The universe is not a huge parking lot waiting for forms to fit into pre-established spaces. This divine-like plan is an unnecessary metaphysical speculation. Organizations may present "slots" to be filled but the dynamic organization has members who invent new activities calling for new skills, new competencies. Life forms and their connectivity constitute the ecology and as they change so too does "the" environment, which is the entanglement of all participants exhibiting multidirectional causes and effects – direct and indirect interdependent changes. An example is the Great Oxygenation Event (GOE, also called the Oxygen Catastrophe, Oxygen Holocaust, the Great Oxidation, and so forth), about 2.2 billion years ago, which saw the appearance of a build-up of free oxygen (dioxygen O_2) in the Earth's atmosphere causing a mass extinction of obligate anaerobic organisms. The global event was generated by oceanic cyanobacteria and other terrestrial photosynthetic organisms such as multicellular plants that produced oxygen as a metabolic by-product while also fixing nitrogen. The point is that life does not fit into an ecology. *It is the ecology*. When new forms arise, they change the environment. The change then creates opportunities for life to do what it does – diversify. The movements of people change neighborhoods, cities, countries, the overall geographic pattern and distributions of the human world.

In this example, thanks to the rise of anaerobic organisms producing oxygen, aerobic organisms that consume oxygen emerged. With a new ecology, new relationships of symbiosis, parasitism, mutualism, competition, and so forth emerged. This is a pan-evolutionary, dynamic process whereby every form has direct or indirect consequences for every other form. While free oxygen formed a "toxin" to much life, it also created an opportunity for a whole new class of life to emerge and a stunning diversity of new forms and relationships – a new world.

Co-evolution theory is now regarded as state-of-the art in biology. It is a primitive form of integration theory. It attempts to explain a set of observed facts (as any decent theory should); in this case, symbiosis – the inter-activity between species such as ectosymbiosis (mistletoe is a popular example) and endosymbiosis (where one species lives within another). The quality of the relationships varies and has been broadly categorized. Some are parasitic in quality, some mutualistic, others commensalistic. The most interesting and thriving communities are complex ones exhibiting great variation of forms (i.e. New York City, the Great Barrier Reef). Redundancy is uninteresting (literally uninformative in information theory) – pure quantity. Symbiosis is what biologists call an obligate relationship. It is a quality of relationship.

The key is mutualism. It is not a matter of psychological health or satisfaction or being civil with one another. It is a matter of non- or pre-cognitive ordination and structuration on a complex scale. A cognitive approach would be artificial selection as opposed to natural selection. Such an approach presumes one knows what is best (usually presuming all sorts of unstated criteria such as sin, wealth attainment, longevity or other amorphous ideas of "the good in itself" or "success"). But, in fact, molecules do not reason that since flowering plants do not exist they should reorganize themselves to become the first flowering plants. Rather, randomness happens. However, in the human habitat, which is largely artificial by definition, the issues of randomness and purpose interact, and stress and conflict occur not just as an instinct but as a matter of taste. Most basically, styles emerge and are either efficient (reproduce themselves) or deficient (fail to endure). A form of efficiency can be to endure by being integrated into another form (endosymbiosis) such as using a banjo in world jazz via adoption by a Japanese artist to contrast with the sound of the Japanese shamisen. This involves culture in terms of expectations, beliefs (appropriate goals), taste, willful experimentation, randomness (accident), and so forth. Fear of altering traditional forms (be it ways of doing finance, playing basketball, worship practices, funerary practices, whatever) is quite common but almost never prevails. Change will not be denied. Conservatives almost always end up on the "wrong side of history" because they have no history; they prefer permanence (Whitehead, 1929). But, even ways of exhibiting conservatism evolve.

Conclusion

This chapter presented a summation of the theory of cultural fusion. Fusion is not simple hybridity or other dualistic notions of co-cultural mixing. It is far more complex. World music, cuisine, even ways of educating the young, manufacturing things, providing health care, making war and peace – everything has multiple channels of semiosis (in the communicative realm). Human relationships, even those involving unequal power distribution, present multiple qualities such as symbiotic, communalistic, mutualistic, and so forth. Many who are parasitic are at the same time hosts. Influences and dependencies shift and reciprocate.

Fusion, the entanglement of individuals and communities, and the consequences of entanglement are expanding rapidly. Due to international and intercultural communication, isolated, monolithic "mainstream" cultures have not existed for decades. The US, arguably the greatest colony and the origin of the post-colonial movement, has never presented a "mainstream culture" but instead a churning multicultural plenum with permeable borders. It has always exhibited turbulence (even among the myriad of Native Nations), which conservatives, who prefer "equilibrium," find disturbing. What is turbulence? It is difference. It results from movement. As one component moves, others react.

Fusion has many qualities, including mutuality, a form of co-evolution. But, today, this churning ecology is characterized by pan-evolution, meaning that influences are more than two cultures bridged by a third. In this global communication ecology, 'appropriateness' is transient given that multiple frames of reference do not host a single cultural dominance. When I watch music videos from Nigeria or Siberia, I am hosting cultural forms that may well influence my own musical compositions and/or video production practices. Fusion is a form of entanglement at the personal and organizational level. We are increasingly colonizing each other. Globalization has reciprocity. We are experiencing cultural echoes across the globe. There is no avoiding the fact that one's perspective, one's "hermeneutic horizon" is threatened each time one communicates with another. This may cause anxiety, conflict, and dissonance and there are theories that exploit fear of these things to win converts, but communication is also the opening of ourselves to others, and without this we cannot grow and enjoy the novelty of alternative ideas, cuisines, arts, legal systems, entertainments, philosophies, literatures, sciences, histories, and so forth.

Notes

1 Cross-cultural adaptation theory is also occasionally, and less commonly, called intercultural adaptation theory by the same authors. While I will stick with the most common moniker used by Young Yun Kim, cross-cultural adaptation, this is actually problematic. Cross-cultural communication does not occur. There is theorizing about commonalities 'across' cultures presented as scholarly compilations of literatures, surveys of cultural artifacts and practices found in social scientific, historic and comparative compendia. Cross-cultural analyses are comparative and presume knowledge of categories of activities and artifacts (such as tools), such as commonly observed propensities toward supernatural beliefs, ritual behavior, artistic expression, economic activity, and so forth; forms of expression identified in two or more cultures. Cross-culturalness is comparative, and in order to do meaningful comparisons such work must first establish common categorical bases so that one is comparing art with art and not art with craft, for instance. But even the process of categorizing phenomena involves a cultural bias. Intercultural communication is different from the study of common categories of phenomena across cultures. Intercultural communication occurs when two people from two different cultural backgrounds meet and talk. It is a subset of interpersonal communication. This is what we seek to understand with CFT. In short, not many people spend their time, often in solitary study, compiling and comparing philosophies, religions, arts, economic systems, psychological predispositions, styles of talking (high versus low context for instance), child-rearing practices... This level of abstraction is not pursued by many outside Western-style academe.

2 It is essential to note that, while there may be many perspectives about a person or event, validity is still important. Relativism is limited by the fact that if I too face a burglar in the night and seize upon a baseball bat for protection, under those same circumstances it is a weapon for me too. This is demonstrable and replicable. A court of law would understand the categorical claim that the baseball bat constituted a weapon even as it was removed from its display case where it lay at hand, as Heidegger would say, as an heirloom.

References

Ben-Tovim, R. (2008). Robinson Crusoe, Wittgenstein, and the return to society. *Philosophy and Literature, 32*, 278–292.

Buber, M. ([1937] 1971). *I and Thou* (W. Kaufmann, Trans.). New York: Charles Scribner's Sons.

Budick, S., & Iser, W. (Eds.). (1996). *The translatability of cultures: Fiburations of the space between*. Palo Alto, CA: Stanford University Press.

Carrington, J. (1949). *Talking drums of Africa*. London: Carey Kingsgate Press.

Castles, S., & Miller, M. (2009). *The age of migration* (4th ed.). Basingstoke: Palgrave Macmillan.

Césaire, A. (1957). *Letter to Maurice Thorez*. Paris: Presence Africaine.

Croucher, S. (2008). *Looking beyond the hijab*. New York: Hampton Press.

Croucher, S., & Cronn-Mills, D. (2011). *Religious misperceptions: The case of Muslims and Christians in France and Britain*. New York: Hampton Press.

Croucher, S., & Harris, T. (2012). *Religion and communication: An anthology of theory, research, and methods*. New York: Peter Lang.

Croucher, S. M., & Kramer, E. M. (2017). Cultural fusion theory: An alternative to acculturation. *Journal of International and Intercultural Communication, 10*, 97–114.

Deleuze, G. ([1968] 1994). *Difference and repetition* (P. Patton, Trans.). New York: Columbia University Press.

Derrida, J. ([1967] 1978). *Writing and difference* (A. Bass, Trans.). Chicago, IL: University of Chicago Press.

Derrida, J. ([1972] 1981). *Dissemination* (B. Johnson, Trans.). Chicago, IL: University of Chicago Press.

Derrida, J. ([2009] 2011). *The beast and the sovereign*, Vol. 2 (J. Bennington, Trans.). Chicago, IL: University of Chicago Press.

Diamond, J. (1992). *The third chimpanzee: The evolution and future of the human animal*. New York: Hutchinson Radius.

Dubois, W. E. B. (1995). *The souls of Black folk*. New York: Penguin Putnam.

Eldridge, N., & Gould, S. (1972). Punctuated equilibria: An alternative to phyletic gradualism. In T. Shoopf (Ed.), *Models of paleobiology* (pp. 82–115). San Francisco, CA: Freeman Cooper.

Elkind, D. (2006). *The hurried child*. New York: Perseus Books.

Fish, S. (1982). *Is there a text in this class?* Cambridge, MA: Harvard University Press.

Foucault, M. (1964). Débat sur la poésie. *Tel Quel, 17*, 77.

Friedman, M. (1996). *Type A behavior*. New York: Plenum Press.

Gadamer, H.-G. ([1960] 2004). *Truth and method* (4th revised ed.) (W. Glen-Doepel, J. Cumming & G. Barden, Trans.). London: Continuum.

Festinger, L., & Carlsmith, J. (1959). Cognitive consequences of forced compliance. *Journal of Abnormal and Social Psychology, 58*, 203–210.

Gebser, J. ([1949] 1986). *The ever-present origin*, Vol. 2 (N. Barstad & A. Mickunas, Trans.). Athens, OH: Ohio University Press.

Gudykunst, W., & Kim, Y. Y. (2003). *Communicating with strangers*. New York: McGraw-Hill.

Hartmann, N. ([1938] 2013). *Possibility and actuality*. Berlin: De Gruyter.

International Telecommunications Union. (2018). *ICT statistics*. Retrieved from www.itu.int/en/ITU-D/Statistics/Pages/default.aspx

Heidegger, M. ([1949] 2005). *The question concerning technology*. (W. Levitt, Trans.). New York: Harper Collins.

Kandel, E., Dudai, Y., & Mayford, M. (Eds.). (2016). *Learning and memory*. New York: Cold Spring Harbor Laboratory Press.

Kim, Y. Y. (2006). From ethnic to interethnic: The case for identity adaptation and transformation. *Journal of Language and Social Psychology, 25*, 283–300.

Kim, Y. Y. (2008). Toward intercultural personhood: Globalization and a way of being. *Globalization and Diversity* [Special Issue]. *International Journal of Intercultural Relations, 32*, 359–368.

Kim, Y. Y. (2017). Cross-cultural adaptation. *Oxford Encyclopedia of Communication*. doi: 10.1093/acrefore/9780190228613.013.21.

Kim, Y. Y., & McKay-Semmler, K. (2012). Social engagement and cross-cultural adaptation: An examination of direct and mediated interpersonal communication activities of educated non-natives in the United States. *International Journal of Intercultural Relations, 37*, 99–112.

Kramer, E. M. (Ed.). (1992). *Consciousness and culture: An introduction to the thought of Jean Gebser*. Westport, CT: Greenwood.

Kramer, E. M. (1993). Understanding co-constitutional genesis. *Integrative Explorations: Journal of Culture and Consciousness, 1*, 40–46.

Kramer, E. M. (1995). A brief hermeneutic of the co-constitution of nature and culture in the West including some contemporary consequences. *History of European Ideas, 20*, 649–659.

Kramer, E. M. (1997). *Modern/postmodern: Off the beaten path of antimodernism*. Westport, CT: Praeger.

Kramer, E. M. (2000a). Contemptus mundi: Reality as disease. In V. Berdayes & J. W. Murphy (Eds.), *Computers, human interaction, and organizations: Critical issues* (pp. 31–54). Westport, CT: Praeger.

Kramer, E. M. (2000b). Cultural fusion and the defense of difference. In M. K. Asante & J. E. Min (Eds.), *Socio-cultural conflict between African and Korean Americans* (pp. 183–230). New York: University Press of America.

Kramer, E. M. (2000c). Ressentiment and racism. In M. K. Asante & E. Min (Eds.), *Socio-cultural conflict between African and Korean Americans* (pp. 35–70). New York: University Press of America.

Kramer, E. M. (2003a). Introduction: Assimilation and the model minority ideology. In E. M. Kramer (Ed.), *The emerging monoculture: Assimilation and the "model minority"* (pp. xi–xxi). Westport, CT: Praeger.

Kramer, E. M. (Ed.). (2003b). *The emerging monoculture: Assimilation and the "model minority."* Westport, CT: Praeger.

Kramer, E. M. (2003c). Introduction: Assimilation and the model minority ideology. In E. M. Kramer (Ed.), *The emerging monoculture: Assimilation and the "model minority"* (pp. xi–xxi). Westport, CT: Praeger.

Kramer, E. M. (2008). Theoretical reflections on intercultural studies: Preface. In S. M. Croucher (Ed.), *Looking beyond the hijab* (pp. ix–xxxix). Cresskill, NJ: Hampton.

Kramer, E. M. (2011). Preface. In S. Croucher & D. Cronn-Mills (Eds.), *Religious misperceptions: The case of Muslims and Christians in France and Britain* (pp. vii–xxxii). New York: Hampton Press.

Kramer, E. M. (2012). Addressing the grand omission: A brief explanation of the pragmatics of intercultural communication in terms of spiritual systems: A taxonomic approach. In S. M. Croucher & T. M. Harris (Eds.), *Religion and communication: An anthology of extensions in theory, research, and methods* (pp. 189–221). New York: Peter Lang.

Kramer, E. M. (2014). Innovative communication needs versus the ideology of conformity. In M. Iwakuma (Ed.), *The struggle to belong: Stepping into the world of the disabled* (pp. ix–xix). Hampton: New York.

Kramer, E. M. (2016a). Immigrant identity: Part I. *Social Inquiry into Well-Being, 2*, 1–11.

Kramer, E. M. (2016b). Immigrant identity: Part II. *Social Inquiry into Well-Being, 2*, 12–23.

Kramer, E. M., & Ikeda, R. (2001). Japanese clocks: Semiotic evidence of the perspectival mutation. *American Journal of Semiotics, 17*, 71–137.

Kramer, E. M., Callahan, L. C., & Zuckerman, S. D. (2012). *Intercultural communication and global integration*. Dubuque, IA: Kendall Hunt.

Kroeber, T. ([1961] 2002). *Ishi in two worlds: A biography of the last wild Indian in North America*. Berkeley, CA: University of California Press.

Kuegler, S. (2005). *Jungle child and child of the jungle: The true story of a girl caught between two worlds*. New York: Warner Books.

Levinas, E. ([1947] 1987). *Time and the other* (R. Cohen, Trans.). Pittsburgh, PA: Duquesne University Press.

Levinas, E. ([1968] 2005). *Humanism of the other* (N. Poller, Trans.). Urbana-Champaign, IL: University of Illinois Press.

Levine, R. (1998). *The geography of time*. New York: Basic Books.

McKay-Semmler, K., & Kim, Y. Y. (2014). Cross-cultural adaptation of Hispanic youth: A study of communication patterns, functional fitness, and psychological health. *Communication Monographs, 81*, 133–156.

Merleau-Ponty, M. ([1964] 1968). *The visible and the invisible* (A. Lingis, Trans.). Evanston, IL: Northwestern University Press.

Merton, T. (1976). *Ishi means man*. London: Unicorn Press.

Mumford, L. (1934). *Techniques and civilization*. New York: Harcourt.

Nietzsche, F. ([1887] 1974). *The gay science* (W. Kaufmann, Trans.). New York: Vintage.

Rogers, E. (1962). *Diffusion of innovations*. New York: Free Press.

Rostow, W. (1960). *The stages of economic growth: A non-Communist manifesto*. Cambridge: Cambridge University Press.

Sandel, T. (2015). *Brides on sale: Taiwanese cross-border marriages in a globalizing Asia*. New York: Peter Lang.

Sandel, T., & Chung-Hui, L. (2010). Taiwan's fifth group: A study of the acculturation and cultural fusion of women who have married into families in Taiwan. *Journal of International and Intercultural Communication, 2*, 249–275.

Skeldon, R. (2018). *Global migration: Demographic aspects and its relevance for development*. Technical paper No. 2013/6. Retrieved from www.un.org/esa/population/migration/documents/EGM.Skeldon_17.12.2013.pdf

United Nations. (2013). *Trends in international migrant stock: The 2013 revision – Migrants by age and sex*. Retrieved from www.un.org/en/development/desa/population/publications/pdf/migration/migrant-stock-age-2013.pdf

United Nations Population Division. (2018). *International migration*. Retrieved from www.un.org/en/development/desa/population/theme/international-migration/

Watzlawick, P., Beavin, J., & Jackson, D. (1967). *Pragmatics of human communication: Pathologies and paradoxes*. New York: W. W. Norton.

Whitehead, A. (1929). *Process and reality*. New York: Macmillan.

Wilson, E. (1986). *Biophilia*. Cambridge, MA: Harvard University Press.

Wilson, E. (2016). *Half-earth*. New York: Liveright Publishing.

8

GEBSERIAN THEORY AND METHOD

S. D. Zuckerman

Of all the methodological approaches used in the communication discipline, none is more complex or more inherently rich than that commonly referred to as "Gebserian." This approach, which is both theoretical and methodological, emanates from the work of Jean Gebser (1905–1973). Gebser was a polymath who is claimed by philosophers, linguists, philologists, historians, art historians, literary critics, education scholars, and communication scholars among others. While his "collected works" are published in an eight-volume German-language set, his writings include many other manuscripts, large and small. His major work *Ursprung und Gegenwart* (1949) was translated by Barstad and Mickunas (1984) as *The Ever-Present Origin*. Mickunas has translated and circulated parts of other works, notably *The Transformation of the Occident*. More recently, some of his other works have been translated and prepared for publication by an independent researcher Cheak (2015, 2017) and two of Gebser's monographs were translated and presented at the Gebser Society annual conference by Zuckerman (2016). Two of Mickunas' students helped to cultivate Gebser scholarship: at the University of Oklahoma, Eric Kramer has supervised many Gebserian doctoral dissertations in addition to his own prolific standard-setting scholarship, and Michael Purdy edited *Integral Explorations* a peer-reviewed journal. Kramer's (1992) *Culture and Consciousness: An Introduction to the thought of Jean Gebser* took Gebser to a circle wider than his students and protégés (this author included). Kramer also served as series editor of a series of edited volumes of Gebser scholarship and was instrumental in obtaining the Jean Gebser Special Collection in the History of Science Library at the University of Oklahoma. Running in parallel, Feuerstein's scholarship informed many, including Allan Combs and Ken Wilber, whose work has attracted a tremendous following. Combs has supervised many students at the California Institute of Integral Studies, and Wilber has written more than 20 books, many informed directly by Gebser. While the Mickunas–Kramer–Purdy branch tends to produce social science and humanities scholarship, the Feuerstein–Wilber–Combs branch tends to take a more metaphysical approach. Cheak (2017) calls the former a "political-philosophical" approach and the latter a "spiritual-philosophical" approach. In Australia, Neville cultivated a community of scholars who followed his lead in applying Gebser to education. The English-speaking Gebser community thus comes from one of these three approaches. North American Gebserians tend to come from one of the first two. Until a few years ago, those two communities operated separately; now, however, they are coming together.

There is no singular Gebserian methodology per se. Gebser scholars come from a variety of fields as diverse as philosophy, fine arts, social science, humanities, and even from the hard sciences. Given the obvious differences between the subjects and orientations across so many different fields, that which connects Gebserian scholarship is the presupposition of Gebser's phenomenology of consciousness expressed in his consciousness structures, and the ways in which humans and our cultural and material creations are reflections of the internal states of humanity. A brief introduction of Gebser's research and worldview is hence necessary.

Gebser's life's work was a thorough study of the scope of human culture, including our art, philosophy, language, myth, religion, architecture, and sociology. Unlike many of his European contemporaries, Gebser did not confine his investigations to European culture, nor did he fall into the trap of orientalizing Asia, Africa, pre-European Australia, and pre-Columbian America. What resulted was a thorough phenomenology of human consciousness. Though it shares similarities with developmental models, Gebser's presentation of what he called his five *consciousness structures* is much deeper, holistic, and more comprehensive. It is important to note that Gebser's structures are macro-level, to be applied to culture groups. He did not intend this to be a psychological model.

Gebser's consciousness structures are collectively a framework through which we, on the macro-level, interact with the world. Consciousness structures denote distinct ways of thinking and organizing ourselves and our societies, and expressing human thought. These structures govern everything from the degree of dimensionality (e.g., flat/two-dimensional/three-dimensional) we see and reproduce to how we understand our relationship to nature and Earth to our metaphysical orientation to how abstract our thoughts are. Gebser meticulously supported his conceptualizations of these specific consciousness structures with a great deal of historical evidence from fields including (but not limited to) art, language, urban planning, philosophy, religious studies, archaeology, and linguistics. In a basic sense, consciousness structures may be likened to similar ideas such as *Habitus, Horizons*, or *Lifeworld*. That said, consciousness structures are more thoroughly developed and their manifestations more specifically mapped out by Gebser than these related ideas.

Another aspect that separates Gebser's consciousness structures from similar ideas is that they are *additive*, not *sequential*. That is, we do not cease to be one when we advance to the next. Rather, we retain and remain the former as we progress to the next. The prior structures remain part of our being, though the additional structures may obscure the presence of the prior ones. The process of advancing from one structure to the next is what Gebser calls *mutation*. Gebserian mutations are not absolute, not always apparent at the time, not always smooth, not instantaneous, and not irreversible. Mutations often come with shock and pain that one may liken to those of birth.

Consciousness structures and mutations

Archaic Consciousness

The earliest consciousness structure is the *Archaic*. It is the timeless state of early humanity reflected in our earliest myths. The idea of Eden, a perfect garden in which time is as meaningless as pain, is *Archaic Consciousness*. Creation myths such as the emanation from a great pond reflect this just as much. Archaic consciousness contains no sense of the passage of time; everything is now. There is no "then," no "today," because those moments depend on a division of time into a when that is not happening now. We often refer to Archaic Consciousness as dreamlike, because our dreams occur in the present, often jumping back and forth between scenes that cannot happen simultaneously, even as they do. This sensation is disconcerting because we do not live in a timeless state. Our everyday existence is chronological. Another way in which Archaic Consciousness differs from our interaction with the world is that Gebser describes Archaic Consciousness as non-dimensional or having zero dimensions.

The first mutation

An important part of Gebser's model is that there is an *efficient* and a *deficient* version of each consciousness structure. In the efficient mode, the consciousness structure works, people live in a harmonious way, and human consciousness can grow. When the structure begins to fall short, and human growth is stunted, the consciousness takes on what Gebser calls a deficient mode. In short, it stops working, and triggers what Gebser calls a *mutation*. Through this mutation, humans move to the next consciousness structure.

Magical Consciousness

About the time that early humans organized ourselves into societies, we see the emergence of *Magical Consciousness*. According to Gebser, our early ancestors saw the world as a one-dimensional relationship of interaction. Early humans organized themselves into tribes, basing membership on blood. Rivers flooded their banks because the river or its gods were either happy enough to reward us with water for thirsty soil or angry enough to destroy our villages. Volcano eruptions, eclipses, and weather were all functions of our interaction with them. The magic world required chants, incantations, and – in another blood/magic tie – sacrifices to directly appeal to the powerful gods and spirits. This is the point in time when we first see shamans who exhibit the ability to enter into the dreamlike trances needed to understand and interact with the spirits. This is the first instance of a key concept that makes Gebserian theory different from every other evolutionary or stage theory: *integrality*.

Integrality

Gebser believed that we do not leave consciousness structures behind when we mutate out of them. Rather, the former structure remains part of our consciousness, usually in a latent or unexpressed way. Gebser believed that our humanity would be enhanced if we activate multiple consciousness structures at once. In this case, the shamans were able to achieve integrality when their rituals allowed them to express both their Archaic Consciousness and Magical Consciousness structures simultaneously.

The second mutation

While efficient Magical Consciousness created human cohesiveness and a set of practices that allowed shamans integrality and gave the rest of the tribe a way to understand and interact with their world, deficient Magical Consciousness was a violent, tribal world based on blood membership and blood rite. This led to the second mutation and the genesis of Mythical Consciousness.

Mythical Consciousness

Mythical Consciousness is a two-dimensional understanding of the world, in which the direct relationship between humans and the flooding river are replaced with indirect and symbolic relationships. It is at this point in time when humanity starts to move toward monotheism, and we see nameless, faceless deities appear in human consciousness alongside, or instead of, the anthropomorphic gods of earlier times. Religions embrace symbols that replace the totems of earlier times. In India, stone deities are seen as manifestations of omnipotent gods instead of the *only* manifestation that could be taken or destroyed by rivals. Mythical peoples still valued membership, even tribal membership, but found ways for people to join the tribes. Again, the earlier consciousness structures remained in the background, so we see the example of Judaism allowing even male converts, provided they undergo an actual or symbolic circumcision.

The third mutation

The *deficient mythic* appears in the mutation that happens when the mythical systems fail to provide a way for people to hold or express the different perspectives that become apparent to them. Even within tribal or religious communities, people begin to assert that they see things differently; even our art reflects it. As the medieval gives rise to the Renaissance, Florentine painters begin to experiment with three-dimensional perspective on canvas. Such words, some of which seem crude to us today, demonstrate that each of us, including the artist, see the world from our particular vantage points. Of course, even a three-dimensional painting of the interior of a cathedral or of a religious scene is still, at heart, a depiction of a mythical subject. Still, by putting it into a third dimension, the artist states boldly that the individual has a distinct and singular point of view. While we take this idea for granted today, and the individual is the basic building block of society, declaration of particularistic perspective threatened the mythical order.

Mental-Rational Consciousness

Mental-Rational Consciousness, which some call *perspectival*, is the dominant structure of our contemporary age. Our current age has been one of discovery and creativity made possible because reason and rationality have replaced dogma and superstition as the main apparatus of political and social power. Today's version of Galileo must draft an argument and muster evidence to compel a peer review committee to accept his conclusions; he does not face a church inquisitor. For several hundred years, this has been the dominant paradigm in much of the world. In this arena, ideas are accepted or rejected based on their logic and evidence rather than the degree to which they acquiesce with spiritual dogma. Government, too, has followed suit. The Mental-Rational era produced democratic institutions, challenged heredity authority, and even declared the death of God. Mental-Rational Consciousness created the modern nation-state and replaced subject-hood with the concept of citizenship, which could be earned or discarded through legally-defined procedures.

The fourth mutation

Yet, the self-same *perspectivalism* that appeared in art at the beginning of the Renaissance had a deficiency built into it; deficient Mental-Rational Consciousness becomes so perspectival as to shatter any cohesion. One can see the splintering of the Roman Church, first into two, and now into the many hundreds of denominations of the Christian faith. This is perspectivalism writ large; despite what the maxim says, each man has become an island as we have fragmented ourselves further and further. A popular question on American social media at this moment is whether the United States has disintegrated into two or more nations. This is nothing new, of course, for a nation that fought a Civil War in the 1860s experienced the culture wars of the 1960s–1990s and gave the world the Me Generation. But, Gebser would not be surprised if what we see now were not simple factionalism but extreme sociopolitical fragmentation. Gebser understood that a dangerous drawback of perspective is that it can be literally self-limiting and can inhibit the empathy we need to be compassionate beings in caring societies. For this reason, he saw perspective as deficient Mental-Rational Consciousness.

Integral consciousness

Having lived through the Second World War, Gebser believed that the postwar years were the beginning of the mutation toward an *aperspectival consciousness structure* called integrality. This is the last of Gebser's consciousness structures, though Wilber (1981) adds several more in relation to time. Integrality is a fourth-dimension (time) consciousness in which we engage the world with all five structures simultaneously. When we do this, we move beyond our positionality to interact with the world through our own perspectives and those of others. That is, integrality is a state in which we are both bound by and free from our own perspectives. In the efficient mode of this structure of consciousness, we will be able to see transactions from all perspectives, including our own and those of others. Integrality will allow us to engage with others in a way that transcends tolerance to achieve a sense of deep understanding.

Integrality, systasis, and diapheneity

The degree to which one can integrate all five consciousness structures is a point of disagreement in Gebser circles. Scholars from the Mickunas–Kramer–Purdy branch tend to argue that Gebser's focus is macro-level, and that the mutation that results in aperspectival consciousness will affect humanity as a whole, though some may achieve it sooner than others (Purdy, 2017). Scholars from the Feuerstein–Wilber–Combs branch tend to be more comfortable saying that individuals can achieve this state on their own. Many of Wilber's writings contain instructions to achieve this state. Despite this significant difference, Gebserians tend to agree that integrality activates through *systasis*, which is best thought of as a blending of all consciousness structures, of all awareness, of all ideas, of all internal systems. Systasis connects the complete parts of our selves, but also the incomplete parts. Though this seems illogical (how can we blend *all* systems, even those that contradict, or *all* parts, even incomplete ones?), it is extra-logical or consistent with the idea of aperspectival as linguistically analogous to amoral (that is, outside of the moral/immoral binary system), systasis is *alogical*. Breaking free of – yet preserving – mental-rational systems is indeed the mutation that leads to efficient integrality. In order to fully understand Integral Consciousness, Gebser believed that humans need *diaphaneity*, or transparency; we must recognize ourselves and our place within the natural world. Living through diaphaneity can be difficult because it requires humanity to engage with the non-mental-rational parts of being human. In the contemporary era, we use highly abstract terms to describe equally highly abstract thoughts (this chapter in this book is an example), but diaphaneity demands that we engage, in equal parts, the archaic, the magical, and the mythical in ourselves. That it is difficult to do so in these times when we describe ourselves in mental-rational terms (e.g., sex, nationality, age, etc.) is evidence of a deficient mental-rational consciousness that categorizes, separates, and atomizes us. As such, a Gebserian would view neo-positivist worldviews and methodologies as deficient mental-rational consciousness and would eschew them for a more holistic approach that takes not just sense data but the *sensory experience* as more real. Likewise, the Gebserian would not merely categorize research participants by race, sex, or nationality but would interrogate what those terms mean in historical and experiential ways, and how even they are an incomplete assessment of who we are.

Applications

Given the inherent complexity of Gebserian theory and the significant differences in the two North American branches, Gebserian research tends to use phenomenological methods to study culture, language, and interaction. This makes Gebserian theory an indispensable approach to the study of the dynamics of migration and intercultural communication. Indeed, it would be difficult to understand the complexity of human migration without a clear view of the myth and magic of the relative cultures, the differences in perspective, and the ways in which the cultures are in efficient or deficient modes. Researchers interested in conflict can examine utterances, norms, artifacts, or architecture to see how consciousness structures are manifested.

An example of such a study is Zuckerman's (2005) semiotic study of murals in Belfast, Northern Ireland. This study showed how murals are magical territory markers that tell all who pass by that they have entered a particular group's territory. These markers often depict blood, especially in the Loyalist (extreme pro-UK) and Unionist (pro-UK) murals. One example that Zuckerman discussed is the murals that depict the bloody, severed Red Hand of Ulster from an ancient myth of a prince who beat his brother in a race to claim the land by chopping off his own hand and throwing it on to the beach in order to be the first to touch it. Blood is part of magical culture, but the use of the Bloody Hand as a territory marker and warning of violent consequences for those who enter in contemporary Belfast is an extreme example of deficient magic. As clear as this marker is in Gebserian terms, its significance cannot be understood without knowledge of group identity and history. Thus, the model can help identify, clarify, and explain the significance of the item in the mural. While other semiotic methods can interrogate the historical significance of the Red Hand of Ulster, Gebserian scholarship can unpack it without denaturing it by removing it from its current context and usage.

Another application of Gebserian theory is Kramer's dimensional accrual and dissociation (DAD) theory (2013), which links Gebser's consciousness structures to communication behaviors. Kramer argues that human communication has become more abstract – that is, less literal – as we have moved from Archaic Consciousness all the way to Mental-Rational Consciousness. This is not limited to the ways in which we use language, but is also about the information we share with that language. In other words, we have become higher-order thinkers who use higher-order language to express higher-order thoughts. As a guiding approach, DAD theory is illuminating to situations of migration and conflict because it accepts – as does all Gebserian theory – the ever-presence of the consciousness structures prior to the mental-Rational dominance of the present-day. As Kramer says, "Pride and prejudice cannot be socially engineered out of existence" (p. 138). Our attitudes and behaviors, especially the unpleasant ones, are real, even if they are irrational, or even pre-rational. DAD theory does not make judgments about the type of communication (e.g., magical, mythical, etc.) used, because people will rely on the message they feel to be most effective. Moreover, the type of communication can be examined to see the consciousness structures at work. After all, most people are not self-aware enough to articulate,

> I am uncertain about my cultural and financial stability in the face of an influx of well-educated immigrants who look and pray differently than I do, and thus I must reassert some type of ownership over my nation-state, and I must emphasize the primacy of my religious faith.

Such a statement would be accurate but unrealistic to expect in the lived experience of many who may be unable to collect, let alone articulate, such thoughts. We would not expect that mental-rational people would be able to do the very thing we know they cannot. DAD theory recognizes that profane or bigoted utterances (e.g., racial, ethnic, or gender slurs), the adoption of nationalistic symbols or slogans, or even styles of dress, are communicative acts impregnated with great meaning.

Communication approaches from semiotics to the coordinated management of meaning theory can substantiate similar observations, but few deliver the explanatory power that DAD can; the slogans, the signs, the uniforms are all outward expressions of deficient Magical Consciousness, and thus the theory gives us not just a clear lens through which to observe and describe the phenomenon we can call "nationalistic reaction to immigration," it gives us a matrix for analysis and even a path for conflict resolution in such situations. Gebser can be used analytically, explaining why a mutation occurred, why one did not, or ways in which a culture exhibits either the deficient or efficient version of a given consciousness structure. For example, Zuckerman (2017) argues that the US and several other countries are experiencing what he calls a "retro-mutation" that uses deficient magic to create "deficient tribalisms" that manifest a "deficient nationalism." Zuckerman uses cultural artifacts such as politicans' quotes, legislation, election results, and even works of public art to support his point. Current political trends include the rise of Donald Trump, whose campaign and time in office have included implied and overt threats of violence against protesters, a description of the press as "the lying media," condemnation of Mexican immigrants as criminals and rapists, and the delay or failure to condemn overt neo-Nazis. President of the Philippines, Rodrigo Duterte, uses similar rhetoric and has encouraged his people to enact vigilante justice against suspected drug dealers. A non-violent version of this retribalizing has posed a significant challenge to the European Union in the forms of the adoption of Brexit to election successes of the far right in France, Germany, Austria, Hungary, and Poland. Zuckerman believes that these macro-level contemporary changes reflect a "change of course" from the neoliberalist globalism of the postwar years and represents a potentially hazardous re-emergence of pernicious types of separatism in the political and social spheres.

These three examples illustrate how Gebserian theory and method are one and the same, in that the consciousness structures model, complete with its mutations and efficient and deficient modes, provides ample opportunity for the study of the cultural and political impact of migration or of culture in general. Scholars can use Gebser for description, tracing how a culture fits within a particular (e.g., mythical) consciousness structure, or how/when a mutation occurred. The model does not require value judgment. Rather, it presupposes a profound respect for the cultural forms and their resultant expression.

References

Cheak, A. (2015). Rendering darkness and light present: Jean Gebser and the principle of diaphany. In A. Cheak & S. Dalla Valle (Eds.), *Diaphany: A journal and nocturne* (p. 1). Auckland: Rubedo Press.

Cheak, A. (2017). *The angel of winter: Gebser's wintergedicht and the inspiration for the ever-present origin.* Presented at the 47th International Jean Gebser Society Conference, October 6–8, New York.

Gebser, J. ([1944] 2017). *Rilke und Spanien.* (A. Cheak, Trans.). Auckland: Rubeido Press.

Gebser, J. ([1949] 1985). *Ever-present origin.* (N. Barstad & A. Mickunas, Trans.). Athens, OH: University of Ohio Press.

Kramer, E. M. (1992). *Consciousness and culture: An introduction to the thought of Jean Gebser.* Westport, CT: Praeger.

Kramer, E. M. (2013). Dimensional accrual and dissociation: An introduction. In J. Grace & E. M. Kramer (Eds.), *Communication, comparative cultures, and civilizations* (Vol. 3, pp. 123–184). New York: Hampton Press.

Purdy, M. (2017). *Efficient mental, integral mutation and listening.* Paper presented at the International Jean Gebser Society, Seattle, WA.

Wilber, K. (1981). *Up from Eden: A transpersonal view of human evolution.* Garden City, NY: Anchor/ Doubleday.

Zuckerman, S. D. (2005). To argue you have no opinion is to insult people: Gebserian analysis of identity in Northern Ireland. *Communication, comparative cultures, and civilization annual*, Vol. 1. Creskill, NJ: Hampton Press.

Zuckerman, S. D. (2016). *Humanity and technology in Gebser's later works.* Paper presented at the International Jean Gebser Society, Seattle, WA.

Zuckerman, S. D. (2017). *Nationalism and the politics of transparency.* Paper presented at the International Jean Gebser Society, New York.

9

IMMIGRANT COMMUNICATION APPREHENSION

Chia-Fang (Sandy) Hsu

Regardless of the reasons for migrating to a foreign country, it may be an intimidating or a scary moment for a migrant to talk to the local people when he or she first arrives in the new country. Migrants may feel awkward and tense when interacting with host nationals, partly because of communication obstacles. For example, they may fear being embarrassed or ridiculed by others while trying to speak in a foreign language. Higher degrees of communication anxiety often lead to decreased willingness to communicate (Lu & Hsu, 2008). Anxiety is one of the major obstacles to intercultural communication effectiveness and intergroup relations (Gudykunst, 1993; Neuliep & Ryan, 1998; Stephan & Stephan, 1985). Anxiety not only negatively influences communication satisfaction and effectiveness in cross-cultural interaction (Gudykunst, 2005), but also impedes acquiring adequate socio-cultural skills and psychological wellbeing while adapting to a new culture (Hsu & Chen, 2011).

Despite the negative and pervasive impact of anxiety, most of the literature on immigrants' migration has focused on cross-cultural adaptation outcomes, including psychological adjustment (e.g., life satisfaction) and socio-cultural functions (e.g., befriending local people [Kim, 2001]). Relatively little attention has been paid to examining the causes of communication anxiety and remedies when adapting to a new culture. In the United States, communication anxiety has been found to negatively impact the quality of a person's life, including personal, social, and professional aspects thereof (Daly, Caughlin, & Stafford, 2009). For immigrants, the negative consequences associated with communication anxiety could be even worse. About two-thirds of migrants worldwide speak a native language different than host nationals, and their employment opportunities decrease and work difficulties increase as a result of language barriers (OECD, 2015). Interaction with people from cultures other than our own tends to involve the highest degree of strangeness and the lowest degree of familiarity (Gudykunst & Kim, 2003). Consequentially, immigrants may even experience much higher uncertainty and anxiety levels than host country people.

Moreover, previous studies on cross-cultural adaptation (e.g., Rui & Wang, 2015) relied on an intergroup anxiety scale (Stephan & Stephan, 1985) that measured anxiety experienced with out-group members rather than in specific communication situations. Given that what occurs mostly in intercultural interaction involves communication, it is important to examine the factors explaining immigrants' communication anxiety. Thus, this chapter reviews literature related to communication anxiety experienced by migrants during cross-cultural adaptation. This literature review includes both trait and situational explanations for communication anxiety, with a focus on the application of Ayres' (1997) component theory of communication apprehension. This chapter also reviews and recommends intervention techniques for reducing immigrants' communication apprehension.

Intercultural communication apprehension

Communication apprehension (CA) was defined by McCroskey (1977) as fear or anxiety associated with either real or anticipated interaction with others. Neuliep and McCroskey (1997) further defined intercultural communication apprehension (ICA) as fear or anxiety associated with communication with people from different cultural groups. Spielberger (1966) made a distinction between the concepts of state and trait anxiety. A state refers to a transitory condition varying over time, while a trait is seen as a more stable individual difference or personality characteristic. As a trait, ICA refers to generalized context or person-group CA – a relatively enduring personality type orientation toward communication in a given type of context or a given person or group of people (McCroskey, 1984). The trait perspective emphasizes the roles of heredity and environment in the development of CA (Hsu, 2010), while the state perspective emphasizes the influence of situational factors on anxiety, such as novelty, unfamiliarity, and dissimilarity (Buss, 1980). Personality traits, such as extroversion, openness to experience, and agreeableness, are positively related to ICA, which supports the trait perspective (Cavanaugh, 2015).

Although ICA has not been examined using experimental designs with the manipulation of situational factors from the state perspective, Ayres (1997) developed a component theory of CA, postulating that an individual's CA is a product of the interaction between his or her self-perceptions of motivation, negative evaluation, and communication competence in a given situation. Motivation refers to "one's subjective desire to accomplish instrumental, affiliative, and/or identity goals in communication settings" (p. 53); evaluation refers to "a person's subjective appraisal of how others are reacting to him or her" (p. 55); and communication competence refers to "one's subjective assessment of his or her communication ability in a given circumstance" (p. 59). Ayres' theory predicted that an individual will experience extremely high CA when he or she is highly motivated to accomplish a goal, thinks he or she will be or is being negatively evaluated, and doubts his or her ability to communicate competently in the situation. To date, Ayres' component theory has been found to predict both trait and state CA in public speaking, a job interview, and an organizational setting (Ayres, Hsu, Schmidt, & Sonandre, 2009) but has not been applied to explain intercultural interaction. The one and only cross-cultural study (Hsu, 2004) found that Chinese people in Taiwan experienced higher levels of trait CA than Americans and the differences can be explained by higher levels of fear of negative evaluation and lower levels of self-perceived communication competence among Taiwanese people. Given that little research has tested this theory in intercultural settings, the following sections apply the three components of this theory to explain ICA.

Motivation

Immigrants' motivation can be defined as the desire to accomplish a goal through communication with the host people. The goals can be instrumental (e.g., to secure a job), affiliative (e.g., to make a friend), or identity-related (e.g., to fit into a group). A newcomer's level of cultural adaptation is significantly influenced by their overall motivation to adapt to the surrounding environment (Berry, 1997; Kim, 2001). Those newcomers who are more motivated to adapt are more likely to adopt the behaviors, values, traits, and norms of the host culture. However, such desire might increase ICA levels. As Ayres, Hsu et al. (2009) pointed out, "if you are motivated to accomplish something and communication is necessary to that accomplishment, then the potential for communication apprehension exists" (p. 70). Higher levels of motivation have been found to increase state CA in public speaking and employment interviews (Ayres, 1997; Ayres, Hsu et al., 2009).

Migrants face a complex set of physical, psychological, and social challenges in daily life. Prior meta-analyses (Cantor-Graae & Selten, 2005) identified migration as one of the best-established environmental risk factors for psychiatric disorders across countries, particularly in individuals who appear to be different from their social environment (e.g., on the basis of skin color or foreign accent). Fitting in to the host cultural environment is a challenge for many migrants. The more motivated immigrants are to be successful in the host country, the more pressure they will feel to conform to the host culture and the higher their anxiety levels will be. For example, students with English as a second language who held more performance-oriented goals (e.g., the desire to appear competent in front of others) and identification-oriented goals (e.g., to talk like a native-English speaker) experienced higher levels of fear in relation to failing English class, fear of negative evaluation, and speech anxiety in English (Koul, Roy, Kaewkuekool, & Ploisawaschai, 2009). In contrast, students with xenophilic orientation (i.e., learning English to make friends with foreigners) and cultural orientation (i.e., learning English to expand understanding of foreign countries and cultures) experienced lower levels of fear of negative evaluation and speech anxiety.

Fear of negative evaluation

Immigrants' fear of negative evaluation can result from their expectation that host people will react negatively to them. One reason for negative expectations is uncertainty. For example, based on personal observation, some Japanese exchange students who studied at American universities for a semester or two tended to have a hard time conversing with domestic students because they were uncertain about what to expect and worried about making mistakes. Once the students got used to the language and the new environment, they were willing to leave their comfort zone and began exploring by building relationships with host nationals. Research has confirmed that, when the uncertainty associated with an intercultural communication increases, and the interaction partner is viewed as less predictable, anxiety also increases (Duronto, Nishida, & Nakayama, 2005). Intolerance of uncertainty, where ambiguous situations are perceived as threatening, was further regarded as a significant risk factor for generalized anxiety disorder (Boswell, Thompson-Hollands, Farchione, & Barlow, 2013).

Host nationals' negative reactions may threaten an immigrant's self-concept. In any context, people tend to avoid differences between their performances and others' appraisals of those performances by seeking reassurance or reinforcement of their behaviors (Joiner, 1999; Schmaling & Becker, 1991). They seek others' appraisals that confirm their self-concept, and feel comfortable when others' evaluations of them and their self-concept are consistent (Jung & Hecht, 2008). Higher CA people perceived larger differences between their own self-image and others' perceptions of them (Jung, 2011).

Fear of negative evaluation could differ among different ethnic groups. For example, Asian Americans have higher levels of social anxiety and more concerns regarding losing face than other groups. Face loss concerns make one highly sensitive to the expectations of others and motivated to prevent negative evaluations by others (Lau, Fung, Wang, & Kang, 2009). The collectivistic values of East Asia may increase self-consciousness and social-evaluative concerns. Although Latino immigrants emphasize social harmony and interdependence like East Asians, they also value sociability and avoidance of rejecting others, which may reduce anxiety in stressful social situations (Schreier et al., 2010).

According to intergroup anxiety theory (Stephan & Stephan, 1985), ICA may also arise from perceptions of threat or fear of negative appraisal, such as being embarrassed, ridiculed, or rejected by host nationals. For example, socially outgoing international students faced difficulties in establishing relationships in America because prejudice and interpersonal relationships were negatively correlated (Mustafa, Hamid, Ahmad, & Siarap, 2012). The feeling of rejection among Muslims in France also made them feel less comfortable communicating with French people (Croucher & Rahmani, 2017). People with foreign accents were perceived as less competent, trustworthy, and socially attractive (Dovidio & Gluszek, 2012). As a result, host nationals were less willing to communicate with them (Montgomery & Zhang, 2017). For example, an interview study (Ojima, 2017) found that foreigners' unclear pronunciation made it hard for some domestic students to understand the main points, creating an impression of non-native speakers' incapability of conveying their opinions.

Further, biological evidence indicates that neural processing of social-evaluative stress is associated with perceived discrimination related to minority status (Akdeniz et al., 2014). Ethnic minority immigrants experience significantly higher perceived social-evaluative stress levels than those in the dominant group (ibid). This finding cannot be explained by language and cognitive capability because the study's participants were highly educated immigrants who were fluent in the host language. Thus, even if an immigrant speaks the host language fluently, perceived discrimination may still lead to fear of negative evaluations.

Self-perceived communication competence

Migrants' self-perceived communication competence may be influenced by their language confidence, cultural knowledge, and cultural sensitivity. There is no doubt that language abilities are required to successfully connect immigrants to their peers and wider communities (Cole, 1998). However, many immigrants' native language is different from the host language. As a result, immigrants with higher education degrees often struggle in the host country's labor market to a greater degree than their native peers because of poor language skills (OECD, 2015). Language abilities not only affect career development, but also social relationships with host nationals. For example, many international students have a hard time initiating a conversation with American students. A lack of confidence when speaking English increases anxiety among international students (Kudo & Simkin, 2003). The low level of language confidence also impedes international students' self-disclosure. Revealing personal stories or thoughts is important for developing personal relationships with host nationals. International students are afraid to initiate conversation with native speakers because they worry their audience will not be able to understand them. The lack of self-disclosure caused by their poor language skills creates a barrier for students in terms of trying to engage in high-quality message exchanges (Kudo & Simkin, 2003). Based on personal experience, international faculty members also worry that their listeners may ask them questions that they will be unable to answer, not as a result of lack of knowledge but because of a fear of misunderstanding the questions. For instance, a newly-hired Japanese faculty member said that she felt worried when the students spoke in class because her listening comprehension skills were not sufficient. Even as a professional in her field, understanding questions was a completely different problem for her.

Intercultural sensitivity refers to the ability to develop an emotional response to understanding and appreciating cultural differences in communication (Chen & Starosta, 1997). It contains five dimensions: interaction engagement, respect for cultural differences, intercultural confidence, interaction enjoyment, and intercultural attentiveness (Chen & Starosta, 2000). People with a higher degree of intercultural sensitivity are less communicatively apprehensive in intercultural interaction (Chen, 2010). Particularly, respect for cultural differences and intercultural enjoyment help people to better adjust to an uncertain or ambiguous situation caused by the unpredictable nature of intercultural interaction (ibid).

In sum, based on Ayres' (1997) component theory, an immigrant will experience extremely high CA when he or she is highly motivated to accomplish a goal, such as having a successful career, thinks he or she will be or is being negatively evaluated, and doubts his or her ability to communicate competently with host nationals. Given these possible causes of ICA, it is important to review the interventions or programs that could help reduce ICA among immigrants.

Interventions for ICA

During recent decades, much effort has been put into the development of intervention techniques in CA (see Hsu, 2009, for a comprehensive review), but few studies have been conducted into reducing ICA directly. In addition, considerable interest has been devoted to examining how to reduce the majority members' intergroup anxiety and improve their attitudes toward stigmatized minority groups (Miles & Crisp, 2014; Tropp & Pettigrew, 2005). Relatively less attention has been paid to developing ways to help newcomers or immigrants adapt to host culture. Thus, this section reviews the available approaches or methods developed in the areas of intergroup anxiety and communication apprehension, and discusses how they can be used to reduce immigrants' ICA.

In intervention research, the most common approach used to reduce intergroup anxiety is through intercultural contact. The methods used to increase intercultural contact include semester-long courses, short intercultural interactions, independent self-construal priming, and imagined interaction and visualization. The central idea of these methods is that increasing exposure to intercultural interaction leads to lower anxiety levels and better attitudes toward people of diverse backgrounds (Allport, 1954). For semester-long courses, for example, domestic undergraduate students experienced intercultural interactions in an online elective course called "Global Understanding," which is implemented via an international network of instructors at partnered universities around the globe. The course connects students with peers from other countries and cultures via online video conferencing, instant messaging platforms, and email, which allow students to learn directly from one another about their respective countries and cultures. Students reported a stronger desire to interact with culturally different others and to decrease xenophobia after taking the course (Chia, Poe, & Wuensch, 2009).

Similar courses targeting learning about the host culture should be offered to international students. Newcomers experience anxiety because they are unfamiliar with the norms, rules, values, and communication patterns of the host culture (Gudykunst & Kim, 2003). Moreover, they may be frustrated when they experience prejudice or discrimination in their interactions with domestic students. If they learn about the background of the host country or factors that may lead to prejudice or discrimination, maybe they will be able to understand why some domestic students are not comfortable interacting with them; such understanding might lead to more tolerance and forgiveness. For example, an interview study (Ojima, 2017) revealed that domestic students may feel hesitant about having a conversation with international students because they have little knowledge of what might be culturally offensive in such students' own countries and thus fear offending them. This discomfort induced feelings of avoidance or wishing to leave the interaction as soon as possible. If an international student understands the reasons for avoidance, perhaps he or she will be less offended by the unwelcome manners of a domestic student. The ability to empathize or take another's perspective – imagining how someone else perceives things – is an important factor in a person's desire to engage in intercultural communication (Cavanaugh, 2015).

Another approach incorporates group work between domestic and international students. For example, in one Australian university, Cruickshank, Chen, and Warren (2012) organized the "Teaching English to Speakers of Other Languages" course around structured group work throughout the semester. Students were organized into out-of-class work groups, each group consisting of a maximum of two native English speakers with international students from different language backgrounds. Local students were not placed with friends. The findings indicate greater class interaction, higher satisfaction ratings, and better learning outcomes as a result of using these strategies. This study identified three key features underpinning the pedagogy: international students working from a position of power equality in class; both groups of students enacting the role of "expert," and support in language and learning how to learn being embedded in assessment and outcomes.

While the above semester-long courses might help reduce ICA, they may not be feasible for universities that are unable to incorporate such courses into the curriculum. Heuett and Westerman (2014) demonstrated that even a brief intercultural interaction reduces both US and Middle Eastern students' state CA and improves attitudes towards each other. In an experiment designed to reduce CA, each student was assigned to a group of six participants (three participants from the Middle East and three participants from the United States). The brief interaction involved three conversation topics (gender roles, education, or stereotypes) to discuss for 15 minutes. Participants reported lower state CA levels and improved attitudes toward each other from pre-test to post-test.

Newcomers to a host country are also recommended to undergo speech therapy. Neiman and Rubin (1991) reported that foreign dialect clients displayed significantly lower levels of communication apprehension, higher levels of communication competence, and communication satisfaction after three months of their respective therapies. The procedures focused on the ability to discriminate between and correctly use American English phonemes; discriminate and produce words with minimal phonemic pairs; correctly use other linguistic elements (such as tense, plurals, pronouns, articles, stress, intonation, etc.); and increase comprehension of and ability to express common terms used in daily communication.

Semester courses and speech therapy improve self-perceived communication competence and decrease CA (Cruickshank et al., 2012; Neiman & Rubin, 1991). However, they may be limited in reducing fear of negative evaluation. According to the component theory of CA, immigrants' CA can be aroused by negative expectations of intercultural interaction with host nationals. The following techniques involving priming, imagined intergroup contact, and visualization can be used to reduce immigrants' negative thoughts and enhance their positive thoughts toward host nationals.

As reviewed earlier, the collectivistic values of East Asia may increase social-evaluative concerns. People from collectivistic cultures tend to subscribe to interdependent self-construals – an individual's behavior is mostly motivated by maintaining harmony in relationships, while the independent self-construal in western cultures involves the view that the self is a unique, distinct, and autonomous entity (Markus & Kitayama, 1991). Independent self-construal has been found to be associated with lower trait CA (Hsu, 2004). Independent self-construal priming involves writing down as many examples as one can think of from personal experiences representing this situation: "I enjoy being unique and different from others in many respects." Japanese students who underwent independent self-construal priming reported lower levels of social anxiety and fear than those who did not receive such treatment (Norasakkunkit & Kalick, 2009).

Another technique, imagined intergroup contact (Crisp & Turner, 2009), is a cognitive intervention designed to improve intergroup relations. Vezzali, Crisp, Stathi, and Giovannini (2015) found that imagined intergroup contact facilitates intercultural communication among international students and host country natives engaging in a university exchange program. International students who had recently arrived in Italy were asked to imagine having a relaxed and comfortable interaction with an Italian stranger, and to think about what they would learn and how they would feel. The students reported more frequent self-disclosure, more positive evaluation of host natives, and lower intergroup anxiety than those students who did not undergo this intervention.

Another cognitive intervention technique, visualization (Ayres & Hopf, 1985), has been used extensively to treat anxiety associated with public speaking and job interviews (see Ayres, Hopf et al., 2009). Visualization involves imagining oneself on the day one is to give a speech while listening to a script (about 20 minutes). Participants are asked to remain relaxed using positive thoughts and feelings (ibid). Ayres, Hopf and colleagues (2009) argued that, if one can imagine the situation vividly enough, the act of positive visualization can override one's emotional connections to negative past experiences. Thus, the script can be modified to help newcomers prepare for a positive social interaction when encountering a new, unfamiliar host national. For instance, some excerpts of the script can be adapted to the following:

> When your encounter is finished, you have the feeling that it could not have gone better . . . The introduction went well, the conversation was relaxed, and you came away feeling as though you gained a new perspective on the topic you discussed . . . On top of that, you were full of confidence and energy equal to that of your new friend.

Visualization could be effective for reducing ICA because it replaces possible negative expectations on the part of immigrants with positive thinking about host country people. Another advantage of visualization is that it can be used as a self-help treatment via audio and videotape (Ayres, Hopf et al., 2009).

Summary and conclusion

Given the pervasive impact of communication anxiety on immigrants, this chapter reviewed literature related to communication anxiety experienced by migrants during the cross-cultural adaptation process. The literature review discussed both the causes of communication anxiety and remedies that can be used when adapting to a new culture. Based on Ayres' (1997) component theory of communication apprehension, an immigrant's ICA is a product of the interaction between his or her self-perception of motivation, negative evaluation, and communication competence during an intercultural encounter with host country nationals. Several intervention techniques are recommended to reduce ICA, including semester-long courses, short intercultural interactions, speech therapy, independent self-construal priming, imagined intergroup contact, and visualization. All of these methods might help reduce uncertainty and fear of negative evaluation and improve self-perceived communication competence. However, none of the interventions specifically addresses one component of CA – motivation. An immigrant's desire to fit in to the host cultural environment (e.g., appear competent like a native speaker) might increase his or her ICA (Koul et al., 2009). The anxiety aroused by fear of not meeting performance-oriented goals has been widely discussed in the fields of music and sport (Beckmann & Elbe, 2015; Wilson & Roland, 2002). Musicians and athletes were instructed to manage anxiety through goal setting, cognitive restructuring (changing thinking through self-talk), and vivid imagery in mental rehearsals (Clark & Williamon, 2011). Thus, besides learning important skills and applying positive thinking, more interventions should be developed to help immigrants set more reasonable goals for integrating with the host culture and its nationals.

References

Akdeniz, C., Tost, H., Streit, F., Haddad, L., Wüst, S., Schäfer, A., ... Meyer-Lindenberg, A. (2014). Neuroimaging evidence for a role of neural social stress processing in ethnic minority-associated environmental risk. *JAMA Psychiatry*, *71*, 672–680.

Allport, G. W. (1954). *The nature of prejudice*. Reading, MA: Addison-Wesley.

Ayres, J. (1997). *A component theory of communication apprehension*. Ruston, WA: Communication Ventures.

Ayres, J. & Hopf, T. (1985). Visualization: A means of reducing speech anxiety. *Communication Education*, *34*, 289–296.

Ayres, J., Hopf, T., Hazel, M. T., Sonandre, D. M., & Wongprasert, T. K. (2009). Visualization and performance visualization. In J. A. Daly, J. C. McCroskey, J. Ayres, T. Hopf, D. M. Sonandr, & T. K. Wongprasert (Eds.), *Avoiding communication: Shyness, reticence, and communication apprehension* (3rd ed., pp. 375–394). Cresskill, NJ: Hampton Press.

Ayres, J., Hsu, C.-F., Schmidt, N. L., & Ayres-Sonandre, D. M. (2009). A component theory of communication apprehension: Nervous system sensitivity, motivation, negative evaluation, and communication competence as predictors of state communication apprehension. In J. A. Daly, J. C. McCroskey, J. Ayres, T. Hopf, D. M. Sonandr, & T. K. Wongprasert (Eds.), *Avoiding communication: Shyness, reticence, and communication apprehension* (3rd ed., pp. 67–83). Cresskill, NJ: Hampton Press.

Beckmann, J. & Elbe, A.-M. (2015). *Sport psychological interventions in competitive sports*. Newcastle upon Tyne: Cambridge Scholars.

Berry, J. W. (1997). Immigration, acculturation, and adaptation. *Applied Psychology*, *46*, 5–34.

Boswell, J. F., Thompson-Hollands, J., Farchione, T. J., & Barlow, D. H. (2013). Intolerance of uncertainty: A common factor in the treatment of emotional disorders. *Journal of Clinical Psychology*, *69*, 630–645.

Buss, A. (1980). *Self-consciousness and social anxiety*. San Francisco, CA: Freeman.

Cantor-Graae, E. & Selten, J. P. (2005). Schizophrenia and migration: A meta-analysis and review. *American Journal of Psychiatry*, *162*, 12–24.

Cavanaugh, S. A. (2015). Intercultural contact, communication apprehension, and social perspective. *Working Papers on Language and Diversity in Education*, *1*, 1–25.

Chen, G. M. (2010). The impact of intercultural sensitivity on ethnocentrism and intercultural communication apprehension. *Intercultural Communication Studies*, *19*, 1–9.

Chen, G. M. & Starosta, W. J. (1997). A review of the concept of intercultural sensitivity. *Human Communication*, *1*, 1–16.

Chen, G. M. & Starosta, W. J. (2000). The development and validation of the intercultural sensitivity scale. *Human Communication*, *3*, 1–15.

Chia, R. C., Poe, E., & Wuensch, K. L. (2009). Attitude change after taking a virtual global understanding course. *International Journal of Social Sciences*, *4*, 75–79.

Clark, T. & Williamon, A. (2011). Evaluation of a mental skills training program for musicians. *Journal of Applied Sport Psychology*, *23*, 342–359.

Cole, E. (1998). Immigrant and refugee children: Challenges and opportunities for education and mental health services. *Canadian Journal of School Psychology*, *14*, 36–50.

Crisp, R. J. & Turner, R. N. (2009). Can imagined interactions produce positive perceptions? Reducing prejudice through simulated social contact. *American Psychology*, *64*, 231–240.

Croucher, S. & Rahmani, M. R. (2017). A longitudinal analysis of communication traits between immigrants and non-immigrants. Paper presented at the annual convention of the National Communication Association, Dallas.

Cruickshank, K., Chen, H., & Warren, S. (2012). Increasing international and domestic student interaction through group work: A case study from the humanities. *Higher Education Research & Development, 31*, 797–810.

Daly, J. A., Caughlin, J., & Stafford, L. (2009). Correlates and consequences of social communicative anxiety. In J. A. Daly, J. C. McCroskey, J. Ayres, T. Hopf, D. M. Sonandre, & T. K. Wongprasert (Eds.), *Avoiding communication: Shyness, reticence, and communication apprehension* (3rd ed., pp. 23–50). Cresskill, NJ: Hampton Press.

Dovidio, J. F. & Gluszek, A. (2012). Accents, nonverbal behavior, and intergroup bias. In H. Giles (Ed.), *The handbook of intergroup communication* (pp. 87–99). New York: Routledge.

Duronto, P. M., Nishida, T., & Nakayama, S. (2005). Uncertainty, anxiety, and avoidance in communication with strangers. *International Journal of Intercultural Relations, 29*, 549–560.

Gudykunst, W. B. (1993). Toward a theory of effective interpersonal and intergroup communication: An anxiety/uncertainty management perspective. In R. L. Wiseman & J. Koester (Eds.), *Intercultural communication competence* (pp. 33–71). Newbury Park, CA: Sage.

Gudykunst, W. B. (2005). An anxiety/uncertainty management (AUM) theory of effective communication: Making the mesh of the net finer. In W. B. Gudykunst (Ed.), *Theorizing about intercultural communication* (pp. 281–322). Thousand Oaks, CA: Sage.

Gudykunst, W. B. & Kim, Y. Y. (2003). *Communicating with strangers: An approach to intercultural communication* (4th ed.). Boston, MA: McGraw-Hill.

Heuett, K. B. & Westerman, C. Y. K. (2014). Reducing negative affect about intercultural interactions through inoculation. *Journal of International Communication, 20*, 42–51.

Hsu, C.-F. (2004). Sources of differences in communication apprehension between Taiwanese and Americans. *Communication Quarterly, 52*, 370–389.

Hsu, C.-F. (2009). Treatment assessment of communication apprehension: A meta-analytic review. In J. A. Daly, J. C. McCroskey, J. Ayres, T. Hopf, D. M. Ayres, & T. K. Wongprasert (Eds.), *Avoiding communication: Shyness, reticence, and communication apprehension* (3rd ed., pp. 257–273). Cresskill, NJ: Hampton Press.

Hsu, C.-F. (2010). Acculturation and communication traits: A study of cross-cultural adaptation among Chinese in America. *Communication Monographs, 77*, 414–425.

Hsu, C.-F. & Chen, J. (2011). The influences of host and ethnic internet use on socio- cultural and psychological adaptation among Chinese international students in the United States: Communication anxiety and uncertainty reduction as mediators. Paper presented at the annual convention of the International Communication Association, Puerto Rico.

Joiner, T. E. (1999). A test of interpersonal theory of depression in youth psychiatric inpatients. *Journal of Abnormal Child Psychology, 27*, 77–85.

Jung, E. (2011). Identity gap: Mediator between communication input and outcome variables. *Communication Quarterly, 59*, 315–338.

Jung, E. & Hecht, M. L. (2008). Identity gaps and level of depression among Korean American immigrants. *Health Communication, 23*, 313–325.

Kim, Y. Y. (2001). *Becoming intercultural: An integrative theory of communication and cross-cultural adaptation.* Thousand Oaks, CA: Sage.

Koul, R., Roy, L., Kaewkuekool, S., & Ploisawaschai, S. (2009). Multiple goal orientations and foreign language anxiety. *System, 37*, 676–688.

Kudo, K. & Simkin, K. (2003). Intercultural friendship formation: The case of Japanese students at an Australian university. *Journal of Intercultural Studies, 24*, 91–114.

Lau, A. S., Fung, J., Wang, S. W., & Kang, S. M. (2009). Explaining elevated social anxiety among Asian Americans: Emotional attunement and a cultural double bind. *Cultural Diversity and Ethnic Minority Psychology, 15*, 77–85.

Lu, Y. & Hsu, C.-F. (2008). Willingness to communicate in intercultural interactions between Chinese and Americans. *Journal of Intercultural Communication Research, 37*, 75–88.

Markus, H. R. & Kitayama, S. (1991). Culture and the self: Implications for cognition, emotion, and motivation. *Psychological Review, 98*, 224–253.

McCroskey, J. C. (1977). Oral communication apprehension: A summary of recent theory and research. *Human Communication Research, 4*, 78–96.

McCroskey, J. C. (Ed.). (1984). *Avoiding communication: Shyness, reticence, and communication apprehension* (Vol. 1). Beverly Hills, CA: Sage.

Miles, E. & Crisp, R. J. (2014). A meta-analytic test of the imagined contact hypothesis. *Group Processes & Intergroup Relations, 17*, 3–26.

Montgomery, G. & Zhang, Y. B. (2017). Intergroup anxiety and willingness to accommodate: Exploring the effects of accent stereotyping and social attraction. Paper presented at the annual convention of the International Communication Association, San Diego, CA.

Mustafa, H., Hamid, H. A., Ahmad, J., & Siarap, K. (2012). Intercultural relationship, prejudice, and ethnocentrism in a computer-mediated communication (CMC): A time-series experiment. *Asian Social Science, 8*, 34–48.

Neiman, G. S. & Rubin, R. B. (1991). Changes in communication apprehension, satisfaction, and competence in foreign dialect and stuttering clients. *Journal of Communication Disorders, 24*, 353–366.

Neuliep, J. W. & McCroskey, J. C. (1997). The development of intercultural and interethnic communication apprehension scales. *Communication Research Reports, 14*, 385–398.

Neuliep, J. W. & Ryan, D. J. (1998). The influence of intercultural communication apprehension and socio-communicative orientation on uncertainty reduction during initial cross-cultural interaction. *Communication Quarterly, 46*, 88–99.

Norasakkunkit, V. & Kalick, S. M. (2009). Experimentally detecting how cultural differences on social anxiety measures misrepresent cultural differences in emotional well-being. *Journal of Happiness Studies, 10*, 313–327.

Ojima, Y. (2017). *Communication apprehension between American students and international students*. Unpublished manuscript. Laramie, WY: Department of Communication & Journalism, University of Wyoming.

Organisation for Economic Co-operation and Development (OECD). (2015). *Indicators of immigrant integration 2015: Settling in*. Paris: OECD. Retrieved from https://data.oecd.org/migration/foreign-born-unemployment.htm

Rui, J. R. & Wang, H. (2015). Social network sites and international students' cross-cultural adaptation. *Computers in Human Behavior, 49*, 400–411.

Schmaling, K. & Becker, J. (1991). Empirical studies of the interpersonal relations of adult depressives. In J. Becker & A. Kleinman (Eds.), *Psychological aspects of depression* (pp. 169–185). Hillsdale, NJ: Lawrence Erlbaum.

Schreier, S. S., Heinrichs, N., Alden, L., Rapee, R. M., Hofmann, S. G., Chen, J., . . . Bögels, S. (2010). Social anxiety and social norms in individualistic and collectivistic countries. *Depression and Anxiety, 27*, 1128–1134.

Spielberger, C. D. (1966). Theory and research on anxiety. In C. D. Spielberger (Ed.), *Anxiety and behavior* (pp. 3–19). New York: Academic Press.

Stephan, W. G. & Stephan, C. W. (1985). Intergroup anxiety. *Journal of Social Issues, 41*, 157–176.

Tropp, L. R. & Pettigrew, T. F. (2005). Relationships between intergroup contact and prejudice among minority and majority status groups. *Psychological Science, 16*, 951–957.

Vezzali, L., Crisp, R. J., Stathi, S., & Giovannini, D. (2015). Imagined intergroup contact facilitates intercultural communication for college students on academic exchange programs. *Group Processes & Intergroup Relations, 18*, 66–75.

Wilson, G. D. & Roland, D. (2002). Performance anxiety. In R. Parncutt & G. E. McPherson (Eds.), *The science and psychology of music performance* (pp. 47–61). New York: Oxford University Press.

10

RECONSTRUCTING THE MIGRATION COMMUNICATION DISCOURSE

The call for contextual and narrative-based evidence in the deconstruction of fear

Pedro Góis & Maria Faraone

The following figure (10.1) illustrates the range of news media being analysed and compared. This also shows the separation between popular and informed news outlets, and academic data in order to gauge the shifts being referred to in the chapter. The refugee sources range across this spectrum.

This chapter considers the impact of the general migration message for social cohesion. It is important to site our position as authors. We believe migration and the latest refugee movement into Europe beginning in 2015 to be a normal human response; a virtuous, inevitable, and necessary phenomenon, one through which people move towards a society that has a safer location, more resources, and affords greater opportunities. But, as new people in these societies, the outsider, the foreigner, the alien, is always susceptible to suspicion and ill-treatment. We see this primarily and immediately in reporting about these newcomers, their movements, interests, values, and intentions; this reporting is often opinion based. Migrants portrayed in this way are represented as a threat because they do not fit the conservative criteria of who we imagine to be part of our society; partly because they are unknown and partly because people from Arab cultures and Islamic faiths, which comprise the majority of the recent refugees/migrants, have been publicly and consistently problematised. The Pew Research Center (2017) estimated that 78 per cent of the refugees arriving in Europe from 2010 to 2016 were Muslim.

Journalists' reporting, in tabloids and broadsheets alike, frequently sensationalises and entertains, exploiting receiving societies' fears and ignorance in search of audiences and profit. Inclusion of the independent non-profit motivated individual voice would at least offer greater balance, even if that individual (refugee) voice is motivated by desire for a better life. Freedom of the press, as underpinned by most legal systems, calls journalists to account through the criminal justice system. This is a constraint aimed at only limited situations. In

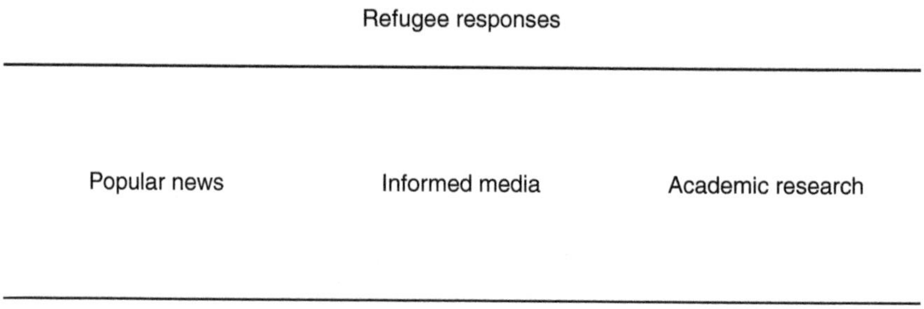

Figure 10.1 Refugee responses

the UK, for example, unless reporting promotes hatred or the aims of terrorist organisations, the state and state funding for legal redress for the victims is absent; mere skewed data, or clever and emotive use of language, however damaging, requires the defenceless to defend themselves by bringing action in civil courts, which is costly, slow and may in turn afford little effective remedy. Migrants become easy targets and the implications for two-way integration and quality of life for society as a whole are profound. How do we find a way to respect the freedom of the press (a near-sacred component of a liberal democracy) while still defending the rights of vulnerable and oppressed groups and offering reliable information to society as a whole? Can we disseminate empirically-based evidence and knowledge with the possibility of gathering new and informed opinions?

The movement of people into and out of societies is a situation that is not likely to change. It is, and has always been, a structural component of evolving societies. The key difference today is that, while refugees have usually represented a relatively small percentage of the population and one which has been able to disappear relatively quickly, 2015 saw a marked increase when the largest annual flow of refugees arrived into Europe since 1985 (Pew Research Center, 2016). Coupled with exponential growth in the use of information technology, the response to this increase has resonated across other European countries. Far-right and conservative nationalist parties have grown in response to these demographic changes (for example, the popularity of leaders such as Nigel Farage in the UK, Marine Le Pen in France, Golden Dawn in Greece, and Jorg Meuthen in Germany) (Tartar, 2017). The rise of the far right has been accompanied by the use of specific words; the shift in description of the migration phenomenon as a "refugee movement" to the "refugee crisis" is enormous (Erder, 2016). The former refers to a chain reaction forming part of historic activity across the world while the latter foreshortens this view and softens the question of other causes and effects, leaving the refugees themselves as key perpetrators. What has been eliminated from the "refugee crisis" descriptor is any possible reference to Europe's imperialist and colonial past and the continuity of the Western legacy, and, indeed, the profitability of firearms trading, which has contributed to the very conditions from which people flee today. The idea of "crisis" has been promoted by political elites and propagated by mainstream media, which significantly stimulates fears associated with financial burdens, cultural and religious differences, and the need for security from terrorists. "Crisis" has been an extremely powerful word in Europe, particularly since 2008 given the social consequences of the "global economic crisis" (Otker-Robe & Podpiera, 2013).

In parallel with social media and popular journalism reflecting the fears and anxieties of the established population of receiving countries, the most informed members of the academic community have not contributed to the public dissemination of more accurate information. Academia has, for the most part, failed to create a large enough space within which to disseminate data on the long-term impacts of this "crisis" and in which informed public opinion can form. We argue here that this very communication is what allows society to exist, for without it we neither know nor understand each other and we cannot work towards shared objectives with a unified vision. Without communication, only individuals remain; without cohesion, society is built under duress rather than organically.

Academics, as scientists, are people who gather and analyse evidence that is tested for reliability and validity. In this context, they can review history to find repeating patterns so that we can learn and develop better and more adaptive solutions to promote quality of life and shape the future. We maintain that advocating for migration as a human right is a consequence of knowledge attainment and moral progression. No human being should be condemned to unwanted and artificial inertia.

We must also be aware that, even when we have it, information from evidence-based and scientific sources is often beset by cognitive dissonance (Festinger, 1957); that is, the feeling of uncomfortable tension that comes from holding two conflicting thoughts in mind at the same time. To resolve this conflict, humans invent stories. In very simple terms, it may be uncomfortable to witness human suffering but if we can persuade ourselves that the sufferers somehow deserve it, we feel better. In the case of the refugee movement, we can extend Festinger's (1957) theory to the societal scale.

Methodology

We aim to show how media interpretations with skewed evidence and context are sold to the general public as an easy fix to resolve the cognitive dissonance that the plight of the refugees evokes. We will do this by highlighting the viewpoint of refugee newspapers such as *Daily Resistance* emerging from European refugee groups. Needless to say, the priorities notable in the refugee newspapers are the drivers that inspired hope for a better life in Europe, with respect for human rights, security, education, personal liberty, employment, and self-determination.

Daily Resistance is a publication that opposes oppression and the subsequent criminalisation of those who flee from oppressive conditions. It is rooted in political and social activism. The newspaper upholds and reiterates the demands of the refugee movement: to abolish all *lagers* (refugee camps), end the German policy of *Residenzpflicht* (which requires refugees to stay within certain boundaries), stop all deportations, and allow refugees to work and study. The paper is printed in different languages that cater to its readership, including Farsi, Arabic, Turkish, German, French, and English (Sultan, 2016). Articles are written by refugees living in the camps, as well as by members of activist groups around Europe, including Women in Exile, The Voice Refugee Forum, and Street Roots; in many ways, it is a coming together of networks.

Based in Berlin, *Daily Resistance* is described by its editors as follows:

> [We are] people who are fighting against being dehumanized by law, criminalized by politicians, capitalized by the lager industry and instrumentalized by the media; [it is] . . . with the support of very few citizens and friends in solidarity who are actively fighting with us to overcome this unjust and unhuman [inhumane] condition which is the reality and waste of our lifetime.
>
> *(Ulu, 2016, p. 1)*

Comparing reporting and voices

We will look at three events that have so far taken centre stage for the refugee movement. The first is the death by drowning of the young boy Alan Kurdi in September 2015; the second is the New Year's Eve Cologne attacks in the same year; and the third is the reporting on the EU–Turkey deal in March 2016.

These events illustrate shifting sentiment regarding migrants and refugees since 2015. This shift went from refugees being described in the British media as "cockroaches" (*ITV News, 2015*) to a temporary refugee sympathy after Alan's death, which made international headlines. The subsequent re-criminalisation of refugees was aided by the reporting of events such as the New Year's Eve attacks in Cologne. Reporting has gone full circle with the EU–Turkey deal touted as the only way to protect EU citizens as well as refugees.

Alan Kurdi

One of the most resounding events for the refugee movement into Europe, which caused a global reaction, was the death of the young boy Alan Kurdi on September 2, 2015. He was attempting to reach Turkey from the Greek island of Kos. The very poignant image of his body washed up on shore brought the reality of the life-threatening crossing of the Aegean into sharp focus in the Western world. In some ways, he served as a martyr for the Syrian refugees, at the time catalysing governments and communities into action in support of those in need. He brought a human face to the plight of those refugees on the move who, as noted above, in earlier accounts in the UK press had been described as "cockroaches" (*ITV News*, 2015) but who were now considered to deserve a safe place. Government and EU action followed.

The *Daily Resistance* newspaper article provided a completely different perspective. It described responses to the photograph as a competition among those countries that contributed to the conditions from which refugees are fleeing "over how humanist they are by crying over him" (Ulu, 2016). There is little focus on Alan's death but there are many references to the murdered, tortured, and persecuted people who form part of the refugee groups. The death of Alan appeared to be a common and expected event given the stories being recounted therein. A key and quite significant reference came in the form of highlighting "humanitarian theatre" (ibid. p. 1):

> Hypocritical policies have been made over the image of the Kurdish child – photographed like lying on the beach. He died trying to escape the war and massacre in Kobane. The governments, who caused people to flee the countries where they lived, have started a competition over how humanist they are by crying over him. Germany, the leader of the EU countries, was on the front line as the leading actor of this "humanitarian theatre." However, this humanism theatre had to cede its place to reality without lasting very long. Politicians, who so recently were giving speeches about humanism, started trying to pass new laws about restricting [refugees'] ability to leave the province [to which they were assigned]; the coupon system, bringing back the food packages, stopping cash payments to refugees, and quickening deportation.

While bias in reporting may be inevitable, it is the extent to which context is embedded that allows some degree of balance or, at least, choice for the reader and wider society. While we can try to police media outlets, we could also create new and support existing parallel reporting sources such as these refugee papers and encourage more accessible academic reporting to add wider and more complete context.

New Year's Eve incidents in Cologne

A dramatic turn in sentiment followed the reporting of the Cologne New Year's Eve attacks in 2015–2016. This change pitted the rights of asylum seekers in general and their degree of status deservedness against asylum-seeking perpetrators of male violence, in fact common to both source and receiving societies alike. In an article titled "RAPE GANG," *The Sun* (Crouch, 2016) reported: "Chilling new footage of Cologne New Year's Eve attacks reveals how migrants demonically outnumbered cops . . . amid fears of more violence this year." The article piqued the public interest by suggesting the reporters had footage of sex attacks, thus eroding public sentiment towards refugees. The report claimed that, "Specially trained police were present to record the 'harrowing cries of women'" (ibid). Another paper (Noack, 2016) reprinted the story more than six months later in an article titled "2,000 men 'sexually assaulted 1,200 women' at Cologne New Year's Eve party." It was thus reported, as if for the first time, six months after the event itself. This reporting sensationalised the already popular media reports of refugees as rapists and terrorists, thus distracting the reader from the reasons behind their forced displacement.

From another perspective, the *Financial Times* (Wagstyl, 2016) in an article titled "Taboos shattered as Germany agonises over Cologne attacks: Mass sexual assault raises issues of immigration, religion and crime." While the account is outlined to include a range of issues, the focus of cultural differences and expectations to explain the behaviour could also serve to increase cognitive dissonance in that it justifies rejection of an unknown group. In contrast, a *Daily Resistance* report by the Women in Exile group focuses on the idea that creating tighter asylum laws, in the name of women's rights, in fact makes the situation more difficult for women refugees and increases their vulnerability to these kind of atrocities (Women in Exile, 2016, p. 5).

The *Guardian* article titled "Let's not shy away from asking hard questions about the Cologne attacks" (Hinsliff, 2016) presents a balanced debate that is respectful to the victims of the attacks as much as it encourages debate regarding long-standing issues related to poverty and the failures on the part of the state to address them:

> Too often anti-immigrant feeling stems from what's really a long-running failure of the state – to protect children at risk, to provide enough social housing or school places, to police what has reportedly been a rough area of Cologne for years – which becomes more visible as the population grows. And since that growth can't be turned on and off like a tap, whatever some politicians say, the answer is for governments to do what we elect them to do: rise to the challenge, calm the fear that breeds extremism by demonstrating they can cope.
>
> *(ibid)*

Academics could contribute to this debate with empirical evidence on the shifts over time and make this publicly accessible.

The attacks on women in Cologne were unacceptable in any context, regardless of religion, race, or other classifying trait. They were mainly reported as a singular incident, reigniting the issue of quicker deportation in order to "protect women." In contrast, an article by Women in Exile, titled "Stop justifying the tightening of your racist (sic) asylum-laws and deportations in the name of women*rights!" (2016, pp. 6–7), outlines that the vast number of sexual and violent attacks on women in the camps had not been reported until recently and that women and children in desperate and vulnerable situations have been housed with men. From these publicly undocumented stories there are also many European men within and outside camps taking advantage of the vulnerable and weaker refugee women and children. From the refugee perspective, creating more vulnerability within their population through deportation will not solve these problems but increase them.

Refugees' perspectives and grievous conditions and experiences are secondary to the media's focus shifting away from initial welcome to coping and number management. On one hand, refugees are offered food and translated legal advice. However, on the other, they are also described as invaders of Europe (*Investor's Business Daily*, 2015). The position of the media, whether one of support or of resistance, in relation to migrant refugees frames a need for them to adjust to receiving societies with full responsibility for the migration instead of a situation of two-way integration that is more conducive to harmonious integration (Ager & Strang, 2008). As Aikins and Bendix (2016) write: "There is an apparent need on both ends of the spectrum to have refugees conform to expectations" (p. 3).

The EU–Turkey deal

The EU–Turkey agreement was made on March 18, 2016 by the 28 EU Member States. The idea was that all new irregular migrants who crossed the Aegean into Greece after March 20, 2016 would be returned to Turkey. For Turkey, this meant that the EU would resettle Syrian refugees residing in Turkey in EU Member States. A further incentive for Turkey was visa liberalisation for Turkish nationals entering the EU, along with financial support for Turkey's refugee population (Batalla Adam, 2017). Populist pressure across the EU meant this agreement brought relief across the board and was a surprisingly efficient solution given the range of attitudes across the Member States. To put this in place, policy makers would deal with a legal grey area on EU laws concerning detention and the right to appeal.

Two years on, the result was a growing number of refugees stuck on the islands of Greece, with reports of increasing self-harm and suicide by Amnesty International and Médecins Sans Frontières (Doctors Without Borders) (Dearden, 2017). On September 23, 2017, a state of emergency was announced by Councillor Kokkalis (2017) of the Piraeus Municipality. The 7,000 who arrived each day in 2015 were expeditiously setting out across Europe; the EU–Turkey deal, which was intended to be a deterrent to further arrivals, slowed the count to 1,000 per week. The difference seems large, but considering that the refugees now cannot leave the island of Lesvos, caring for the recent and stranded new arrivals is a daunting task and one that has been taken up by civic society.

The goodwill stories reported are mostly about the work of grassroots groups, which have been attributed to national efforts (Theodorou, 2018). As highlighted by the Weisekiez Initiative (2016), a split between the "good" (deserving) and the "bad" (undeserving) refugee was created by discerning between the economic migrant and the more legitimate, in this case, Syrian refugee. In reality, these are never clearly demarcated boundaries because there is a difficulty in outlining classifications. A victim of terror cannot self-determine and a person in poverty comes from a society where it is onerous to support development, which could thus lead to desperation. It is not clear how anyone could take on the daunting task of classifying people in this way, especially when there is immense overlap in terms of causes and consequences.

A sample of the various reported perspectives on the deal as outlined below shows the varying support for and rejection of refugees. It is important to note that the samples chosen come from available English language media given the accessibility of such reporting for the authors, which in itself highlights a limitation to the chapter and further limitation to the dissemination of knowledge to the general public of Europe, the Middle East, and North Africa. This is especially relevant given that the geography of the refugee movement as a whole encompasses the departure and arrival points of refugees. As reported by the *Irish Times* (Lynch, 2016) in an article titled "Turks in line for visa-free EU travel by May; Hundreds of migrants may have drowned in Mediterranean this week, UNHCR says," the writer conflates the question of the EU–Turkey deal by suggesting that it includes visa-free travel for Turkish citizens, which was one interpretation and not based on policy evidence.

A separate opinion piece published by the *Irish Times* (Mustafa, 2016) titled "Lesbos centre is a prison posing as a refugee camp; Moria is proof the EU and Turkey put politics and economics ahead of the right of people" gives a narrative account of the experiences at sea, the deaths, and the orphaned children. The online news outlet called *allAfrica*, with *Al Jazeera* and *COMTEX*, published an article titled "The year the world stopped caring about refugees" (Safdar & Strickland, 2016). Preethi Nallu, editor of *Refugees Deeply*, interviewed in this article, suggests:

> The year 2016 proved that militarising the Mediterranean and fortifying borders are not tenable solutions. With mutating smuggling networks that extend from the Logar villages of Afghanistan to the depths of the Sahara, combating the illicit migrant "trade" is not as simple as shooting smugglers on sight or erecting new barriers.
>
> While the EU–Turkey deal has thwarted arrivals to Greece for one season, it is merely a bandage on an infection. Italy's new record this year, with more than 171,000 arrivals by sea, is proof that such deals simply shift the routes.

Irregular, illegal, clandestine, migrant, refugee, asylum seeker – barring reductive definitions, the media must explore and connect the conditions that are driving millions of people across the globe to cross borders and embark on life-risking journeys. The article links the political changes, the policies aiming to resist refugee arrivals in Europe, with the actual impact on the ground. It describes three failed tactics: exporting control to rich countries; the deporting of refugees who return after deportations; and monetisation, where corrupt regimes take European (Western) money to cooperate with control policies but actually only strengthen their own power and corruption. Nallu suggests that it is the role of the media to examine and make public these issues for the general public (ibid). The general public has the power to lobby governments and they are the groups who lead the real grassroots efforts that have been making a difference, from shoreline reception to resettlement and two-way integration.

A *Guardian* article titled "Surge in migration to Greece fuels misery in refugee camps" (Smith, 2017) describes the already over-subscribed camps receiving more people who are stuck in place, with 200 people arriving each day. The migration movement has not subsided but continues to ebb and flow. A report by the publication *New Europe* (2017), titled "UNHCR migrant arrivals falls, while the likelihood of death persists," suggests that fewer migrants are arriving but the risk of death is still very high.

In contrast, a *Daily Resistance* article by the political group Weisekiez Initiative (2016) highlights the conditions of containment from within the camps, the fact that the media is not interested in the violence within the camps and that Western society is missing two critical points: first, that the "welcome culture" is mainly provided by volunteer grassroots groups even if credit is being given a more nationalist tone; and second, that the distinction between asylum seeker and economic migrant is causing "people made asylum seekers" that bring suspicion to all but, most importantly, that this distinction is irrelevant. That is, those fleeing fled "the devastating consequences of capitalism, the effects of (neo)colonial exploitation and imperialist wars." The refugee perspective is that the German government is also the cause of the conditions that forced people to flee, be it because of war or economic desperation.

From a cognitive dissonance perspective

Festinger's (1957) theory of cognitive dissonance suggests that we seek consistency in our beliefs and attitudes in any situation where two cognitions are inconsistent. The theory stems from the idea that the drive to maintain cognitive consistency, that we are empathic for instance, can give rise to behaviour that is not in alignment with this, for instance not wanting to support migrants. Thus, to balance this argument we either ignore the evidence where it is available or we make and look for evidence based on more irrational judgments, for instance that the migrants are a threat.

The response to our own dissonance holds even stronger sway when with others and we are communicating and connecting within a society (ibid). It is a systematic method of creating a comforting truth regardless of the evidence and mainstream media or social media can serve to both exploit and concretise these positions. Use of cognitive dissonance is useful where people are thinking, and are perhaps in denial, about the situation and conditions faced by migrants; for example, those who believe migrants in the camp in Calais would fare better back in their home country, as they do not consider the truth about the reality they face there. Readers of *The Sun* and the "tabloid" press really do not feel that they have to construct another version of reality (Reeves, Mckee, & Stuckler, 2015). They have merely consumed the version of reality fed to them by the "tabloid" press and feel no need to question it. This version of reality being fed by the "tabloids" is important, though, because it feeds into the prejudice that many migrants face when they arrive in a new country, breeding hostility and justifying discrimination and even acts of violence. With all the wealth, security, resources, healthcare, and freedom available in receiving countries, how can it be that so many others do not have this? How is it that we deserve it and they do not? How do we make sure we do not become them? Unable to answer, we hold more strongly to the capacities within our world and see the "needy outsider" as a threat to our own security and well-being. For this reason, it is essential that academia is able to challenge the tabloid version of the "truth" using the range of mainstream and social media.

In addition to this, Kolbert (2017) outlines how the human capacity for cooperation is our basic advantage over other species. Kolbert suggests that reason evolved as a tool to better enable cooperation. Mercier and Sperber, in the *Enigma of Reason* (2017), explained that the modern man has evolved reason to suit his ultra-social, elitist lifestyle. This means the reasoning that appears to be irrational and unintelligent can actually be perceived as astute from the perspective of a social interaction and cooperative position. So, when people corroborate with each other, there is a kind of confirmation bias and they accept only information that suits the beliefs they already hold (ibid.). So we can say that bias in reporting encourages a social form of cognitive dissonance, a collective version. Mercier and Sperber (2017, p. 121) suggest that the main role of reason is not to debate or guide toward truths and considered conclusions but rather to aid us in coming to terms with and justifying the conclusions we have already reached after the facts are revealed.

From the perspective of cognitive dissonance, this means that people will more readily accept evidence that placates the discords between their beliefs and their behaviour. For instance, believing that migrants are bad or a threat allows them to continue behaving in ways that are anti-immigration, such as perpetuating a belief of the threat of migrants to employment and the welfare state.

The limitations in the current discourse, and a lack of understanding of the context it is set within, has given momentum to movements like Brexit,[1] the election of President Trump in the United States, and the rise of nationalistic and fascist movements in various European countries (Lewis & Sumit, 2017). All these cases manipulated particular aspects of migration to establish the need for the culturally protective positions that these movements represent. But how do we overcome this? Using evidence-based information in context and communicating to a wider audience is not a new concept, but this has remained ineffective at countering the spread of a kind of decided ignorance (Reeves, Mckee, & Stuckler, 2015). Of course, there are other issues magnetising a desire to remain convinced, such as cognitive dissonance, but we need to find new ways to bring the message forward. Keeping with the legitimacy of academia in evidence-based writing is mandatory, but also writing in a way that brings empirical data to the foreground. The comparison of reports on the same events shows differences in style, objectives, and positions. What becomes evident in this comparison is that, when complex ideas are simplified, and there is no context, then there is a danger that the message becomes diluted. On the one hand, this can lead to confusion in the message. On the other hand, it can professionally compromise the reputation of the writer. Although this is a danger, we must recognise that there are many ways to present objective data in a way that is understood at different levels of complexity by different audiences. Table 10.1 compares reporting on the most polarising and commonly misunderstood of the three events, the Cologne rapes. The table shows that there is a need for academic input. The empirical data is uncompromising but it can be communicated in a simpler way by academics who, even though they themselves are not unbiased, rely on referencing and may take a longer time to report than do daily news outlets.

In each article we can see a gap between knowledge and perception, which could, given a widening of the research findings of academics, be more effectively challenged, at least to the audience of the more objective mainstream news and social media outlets.

The value of addressing cognitive dissonance is significant and far reaching. The attitudes of larger receiving societies can have an important impact on quality of life for newcomers. For example, we know from evidence-based research that legal rights and access to citizenship prevent marginalisation and social conflict (Castles, 2014). Following this, we also know that cultural integration only becomes relevant where there is economic and legal security and that the character of future ethnic groups will be influenced most by state actions that occur in the early stages of resettlement (Ager & Strang, 2008).

The extent to which historical context informs the reading of contemporary evidence-based information is critical to achieving more objective and balanced reporting. The extent to which history informs the way contemporary evidence is received also undermines the real crisis occurring in Europe today: the racialisation of difference. National identity and the welfare state are a result of the legacy of colonialism and the trend towards greater inequality led by globalisation, deregulation, and privatisation. This has led to a racialisation of difference and a shift towards assimilationist thinking and watered down multicultural principles (Portes & Rumbaut, 2006). Reporting on refugees deepens this pre-existing crisis.

Communicating science-based migration information to the general public (public dissemination)

Migration is globally increasing in absolute terms but has remained stable relative to the global population. According to the 2015 UNFPA Annual Report, *For People, Planet, and Prosperity* (cited in Wagstyl, 2016), the number of international migrants worldwide reached 244 million people in 2015, representing a 44 per cent increase since 2000 and a

Table 10.1 How the 2016 German incidents were communicated (messages) and received (responses)

	Populist news: *The Sun* (Crouch, 2016)	**Broadsheet news:** *Financial Times* (Wagstyl, 2016)	**Broadsheet news:** *The Guardian* Hinsliff (2016)	**Refugee perspective:** *Daily Resistance*/ Women in Exile (2016)
How it was reported	Rapists on the loose	Presents a range of issues, including the potential limitations of multiculturalism	Balanced debate considering both victims and long-standing issues related to state failures	Threat to refugee women's rights
How it was received by audience	Promotes bigotry and racism	Potentially reinforces cognitive dissonance in response to refugee issues even though attempting to separate the identity of criminal from that of refugee	Expands range of considerations from individual incident to generic issues of poverty in society	Expands public perception from a homogenous refugee group to a broadly heterogenous one including but also beyond gender
Impact of academics engaging	Highly limited due to reluctance of audience/ media to engage	Fact/context could be more effectively used by researchers and academics within the field to challenge the public debate	Extend the debate by detailing the history of state failures with factual information related to a longer timescale	Fact/context could be more effectively used by researchers and academics within the field to challenge the public debate

5 per cent increase since 2013. Although the number of international migrants has grown in absolute terms, the share of international migrants in the world population has stayed constant at around 3 per cent of the global population. In other words, just 3 out of 100 individuals are migrants. Some of the main drivers of international migration around the world include escape from conflict and persecution, and the search for economic or career opportunities.

How to communicate

Communicating migration information to the general public can be complicated because of low levels of science or statistics literacy. For example, "The assumed annual increase in population [due to the 2015–2016 refugee surge in the EU] is of 0.15 percent of the EU total population (or 0.8 million) in 2015–2017 and 0.1 percent in later years" (International Monetary Fund, 2016). Even societies with high levels of overall literacy can have low science or statistics literacy with regard to interpreting these kind of statistics. Information from academic sources would need to be translated in order to more effectively impact on wider audiences.

Research is under-represented within public debates (Boswell, 2009) and that is because the work of academics is generally not accessible to the larger public outside academia or the knowledge communities, either in terms of writing style or due to limited dissemination in subscription-only journals. Vocabulary forms part of the writing style and the distinct academic style serves to resonate within academic circles. The public at large lack comprehension of academic writing within specific fields that could provide information on the objective of particular research. This is especially the case with regard to the debates on migration (ibid).

Furthermore, there is a discord between the definitions used in public discourse versus the looser definitions established by the media. For instance, refugees, migrants, and terrorists are not part of the same family with clear delineating distinctions. The media conflates these to follow public thinking, conjoining these titles and contributing to a growing and generalised bias against broader communities (Bachelet, 2017). A study by Blinder and Allen (2016) also noted that the comparative evidencing tool of the British Social Attitudes Survey used a definition of immigration that conflicted with that of the United Nations and the UK government.

Apart from issues of definition, academics write for academia and this presents another kind of communication discord. There are significant structural reasons why academics write for other academics and this is true across most fields, not just in the migration discourse. These relate to the currency of academics and the constant validating that is required in terms of publications in peer-reviewed journals. The problem is that this immensely useful analysis does not serve the public, except often in small part and indirectly, but it also does not surface to inform the policy debates or is "dumbed down" by policy makers (Boswell, 2009).

Providing scientists and scientific institutions with the resources they need to have meaningful conversations with policy or decision makers and other stakeholders is very different from communicating with the general public. Both approaches are needed. So, how can this be facilitated?

One approach is the inclusion of expanded voices – that is, of the refugees/migrants themselves. The alternative narrative is missing, the reality that provides a landing ground for academic thinking. In this case, academia as an industry must find ways to create currency for these kinds of dialogue, which have perhaps equal validity for their impact on society.

As a twist on this perspective, in an interview with Afghan politician and activist, Malalai Joya, in speaking about Farkhunda, the 27-year-old woman beaten and killed by a mob in Kabul, she asks:

> I wonder if Farkhunda was the daughter of this Angela Merkel and many other Merkels, if people could put their feet in the shoes of this victim's family, then maybe they would understand a little bit of what is going on in Afghanistan.
>
> *(Joya, 2016, p. 12)*

So long as these are children of other families, she argues, political and material wars will continue to be waged and innocents killed in Afghanistan, Syria, Yemen, Libya, and Somalia.

Camilla Gibb (2016) suggests that there is a way to encourage empathy through narrative and witness storytelling. It creates associations and parallels our own attempts to create meaning and it also provides a platform for cohesion between communities and inter-personal relationships. Migrants in Europe bring evidence of global conflicts with them that are disconnected in every sense from our own European experience. Reconstructing and sharing traumatic events, be they poverty or more perilous life circumstances, can be a source of restorative power for the migrants themselves. We can extend Gibb's thinking to suggest that cognitive dissonance is also applied to migrants and the issue of survivor guilt. Migrants also need to deal with the question of why others have not been as lucky as them. Gibb's work is focused on the restorative power of storytelling and the narrative voice and this could potentially also hold the key to resolving cognitive dissonance. It is inside these commonalities that empathy can be encouraged for both migrants and receiving societies.

The use of information

Scientists' societal role changes fundamentally according to whether they are considered guardians of indisputable certainties or are "simply" just one minor contributor to a politicised picture of reality (Boswell, 2009). In recent years, a great deal of top-quality research worldwide has been produced concerning the nature versus nurture of migration and its influence upon our modern economies and societies. In a parallel knowledge-providing system (the media and social media), facts about migration are emerging (ibid). Typically, these facts are based on the simplification of a complex reality but are much more efficient in the delivery of information than academic literature on the topic. These two distinctive systems produce different information. This difference is shown in the way that the information is acquired and in the dissimilar consequences in the way it is used, communicated, or integrated in our common memory through the traditional social process of learning and sharing knowledge. We are not suggesting that this knowledge, in both mainstream and social media, is produced in a strategic or politically-induced way; however, we are stressing the long-term, unintended consequences of fact oversimplification versus communication on the full complexity of the reality (for example, we can refer to Table 10.1 whereby the more biased news outlets actually present less information).

The limitations of evidence-based knowledge on migration

Our very evidence-based collection mechanisms are themselves distanced from the ground level. The Migrant Integration Policy Index (MIPEX; CIDOB, 2015), for instance, is a way to measure integration-related policies for migrants in the EU. The impact of these policies on a range of issues, from education, employment, and health, together with aspects of inclusivity, is demonstrated over time, and the data this index provides is evidence based because it links demographic changes, development indicators and shifts in public perceptions over time. The focus is on policy and what seems to be working as opposed to an analysis of the gaps. The impact of communication on the broader public would mean exploring these gaps. The irony of the MIPEX on inclusivity is that it does not include feedback from real people at the ground level; those who are the focus of such data. What do we really know, for instance, about the desires of migrants and refugees? We have not asked what they want, where they want to live, who they are, and, if they had a choice, where and why they would choose a certain destination. While the MIPEX provides a policy impact analysis of integration indices, the real test is about questioning the impact at the everyday, ground level.

Oxford University has used the contemporary evidence base IPSOS/Mori, recording the shift in sentiment of attitudes to migration in the UK. Blinder and Allen (2016) examined public attitudes towards immigration in the UK, including levels of concern. The evidence shows that, from 2009 to 2013, the British public has shifted opinion towards the idea of positive impact on the economy and quality of life. However, the research suggests that there are gaps in terms of describing, as well as explaining, these responses. The level of real information that the public holds is also missing. For instance, the foreign-born population amounts to 11 per cent, but respondents to the survey overestimated this figure, assuming an average of 25 per cent. In general, it outlines that the public overestimated more recent migration trends when compared to data from 2013, which is not surprising given that media campaigns including the story behind the Brexit campaign focused on the need to have better control over migration (Lewis & Sumit, 2017).

The specific ways in which data and information are gathered and whether they are believed remains unclear. What is clear, however, is that where the public gets it wrong is also in keeping with trends across Europe. Making academic findings accessible is required, but a comparative analysis across Europe is still lacking. Some argue that the resurgence of nationalism has used the mechanism of migration as a catalyst (Lewis & Sumit, 2017). The Brexit campaign took an anti-migration stance and focused on the threat to employment that contradicted evidence (Petrongolo, 2016). For instance, data related to demographics and impacts suggests that there are no threats posed in terms of employment except at the very basic level of unskilled labour (ibid). Data also indicated economic growth, which impacts positively on all of society (OECD, 2015). This then begins to create a split whereby the media chooses to differentiate between the "useful" refugee and the "useless" one. This split happened in Germany's push for compulsory EU quotas by highlighting which refugees are useful for the labour market (Traynor, 2015). While considering it a Europe-wide crisis, it is a way in which the neoliberal capitalist system is using the migration movement by blocking and filtering it (Ziga, 2016, p. 5), and again distracting attention away from the global and historic causes of this migration. Three years on from 2015, we can see the impact has been to separate those countries willing to respond to the request to accommodate asylum seekers and refugees. Sweden has shown immense solidarity to the refugees, as has Greece, despite its financial crisis and despite pressure to do so, given its specific geography. The media, however, continues to dramatise particularly criminal or dangerous situations and there is less balanced reporting on the capacity of humanity in the activist and everyday type of response to housing, education, legal support, and integration projects; for example, the Dirty Girls of Lesvos, a network of women who wash the materials given to migrants by humanitarian organisations to be reused rather than leaving them to be trashed (Theodorou, 2018), and the Newly Arrived Architects in Sweden (NAAIS) group, a network to support architects and engineers by offering advice and training to increase their employability.

Conclusion

In the past few years, expanded platforms to access knowledge in the EU and in academia specifically have led us to believe that we are in touch with evidence-based knowledge and the full landscape of truths that are subjective and emerging from a variety of viewpoints. All sources will hold their particular bias but what is important is their contribution to ongoing debates that are in search of resolutions as opposed to any universal truths. Instead, we are witnessing a growing gap between belief and evidence. Across some EU countries there are signs of shifting positions towards the far right for which these weaknesses have been catalysts from as early as 2008 and which have been exacerbated by more recent anti-migration discourse from 2015 to 2017 (Bachelet, 2017; Davies & Jackson, 2008). We are seeing shifts towards ideals that have been manufactured from a lack of evidence-based knowledge, in line with preconceived ideas as opposed to questioning and critical thinking about what is available and what might be missing; this is representative of a cultured and legitimised ignorance.

Scientific evidence is not informing political debate at large, which leaves ground for politicians to use *migration* as a base for fear mongering and to bolster a leadership position in order to take charge of such issues. The academic silo has not challenged society in general with communication discourse so as to be able to transfer critical thinking or create hope, and has distanced itself from the public media domain. There is a schism between scientific evidence and public debate, which may be encouraging the negative shift away from tolerance. Reporting from the Kara Tepe camp on the Greek island of Lesvos, Bowman made a link between the dire situation of refugees and our reporting standards: "As media, communicators, and humanitarians, it is time to stop pandering to a discourse that obscures the real story of migration" (cited in Bowman, 2017, p. 2). The impact of this has begun to challenge the premise of multiculturalism and to create more profound, long-lasting damage.

Our work now as academic researchers is about addressing the link between core belief and evidence-based knowledge. Communication channels with larger society will be more about the type and methods of collecting and presenting evidence, thus communication is in itself a political endeavour. Methods and sources are important, as are the final channels of communication and dissemination. It is apparent that communication and media related to migration that reaches a wider audience significantly affects political directions and the extent to which solutions and eventually cohesion are possible. We are seeing the emergence of online platforms such as the European Journalism Observatory (EJO) where research into the media is analysed and shared with partner websites across Europe (Lees, 2016).

If we are successful in presenting a balanced account of evidence on the catalysts and impacts of migration, this will mean that we are creating a more inclusive debate and making the case for getting on with it. We will be shifting public sentiment towards achieving the more beneficial condition of two-way integration instead. Inclusion of the narrative voice is a critical aspect of this.

There is so much at stake in the way we report on and respond to migrants and the idea of migration. In EU terms, it is the influx of young people that will ease the demographic shift to an otherwise ageing and shrinking Europe. Apart from this more measurable economic interest, it is appealing on the basis of our common humanity and this is far more profound, impactful, and long-lasting. While media is the mechanism to deliver such connectivity, we cannot count on the self-interest of these privately-owned communication vehicles, as migration is not the only news topic they seek to sensationalise. We, as researchers, have access to another, more historically linked and critically analysed, evidence-based knowledge base and can create parallel lines of dissemination, particularly where public debate is not being influenced by research. It is not a skill or endeavour to be taken lightly. It carries the daunting burden of overcoming our own cognitive dissonance but, most importantly, of reflecting continuously on the matter so that we report publicly and link history to changing circumstances and recent and ongoing developments. We, as an academic community, must also share our research through intellectually, freely available means, which are captivating and inclusive of the narrative perspective. This is vital to establishing the right and just inclusion of newcomers to Europe.

Note

1 Brexit is an abbreviation for "British exit," referring to the UK's decision in the June 23, 2016 referendum to leave the European Union (EU).

Bibliography

Ager, A. & Strang, A. (2008). Understanding integration: A conceptual framework. *Journal of Refugee Studies, 21*, 166.

Aikins, J. K. & Bendix, D. (2016). Beyond #refugeeswelcome: The spectre of racist violence and lessons from refugee resistance in Germany. *Daily Resistance*.Retrieved from https://asylstrikeberlin.files.wordpress.com/2016/03/daily-resistance-feb16-web-version.pdf

Bachelet, S. (2017). Trumps, pirates, refugees and terrorists. *PoLAR Series*. Retrieved from https://politicalandlegalanthro.org/2017/02/14/trumps-pirates-refugees-and-terrorists-a-view-from-the-mediterranean/

Batalla Adam, L. (2017). The EU–Turkey deal one year on: A delicate balancing act. *International Spectator, 52*(4), 44–58.

BBC News. (2016, March 8). Migrant crisis: EU–Turkey plan one-in, one-out deal. Retrieved from www.bbc.co.uk/news/world-europe-35749837

Berger, P. L. & Luckmann, T. (1967). *The social construction of reality*. Garden City, NJ: Doubleday.

Blinder, S. & Allen, W. L. (2016). Constructing immigrants: Portrayals of migrant groups in British national newspapers, 2010–2012. *International Migration Review, 50*, 3–40.

Boswell, C. (2009). Knowledge, legitimation and the politics of risk: The functions of research in public debates on migration. *Political Studies, 57*, 165–186.

Bowman, H. (2017, October 18). Opinion: The European refugee crisis is a communications disaster. Here's why. Retrieved from www.devex.com/news/91215

Carlyle, T. (1841). *On heroes, hero-worship, & the heroic in history: Six lectures; reported, with emendations and additions*. London: James Fraser.

Castles, S. (2014). International migration at a crossroads. *Citizenship Studies, 18*, 190–207.

Chomsky, N. (2016, May 5). Noam Chomsky for refugee crisis. Retrieved from https://chomsky.info/05052016/

CIDOB & Migration Policy Group. (2015). MIPEX migration integration policy index. Retrieved from www.mipex.eu

Collett, E. (2016). The paradox of the EU–Turkey deal. Retrieved from www.migrationpolicy.org/news/paradox-eu-turkey-refugee-deal

Crouch, H. (2016, December 15). You cannot touch me. *The Sun*. Retrieved from www.thesun.co.uk/news/2407734/cologne-new-years-eve-sex-attacks/

Dabashi, H. (2017, July 10). Freewheeling journalism and the "monopoly of truth". Retrieved from www.aljazeera.com/indepth/opinion/2017/07/freewheeling-journalism-monopoly-truth-170710091857520.html

Davies, P. & Jackson, P. (2008). *The far right in Europe: An encyclopedia*. Oxford: Greenwood World Press.

Dearden, L. (2017, July 14). EU–Turkey deal "driving suicide and self-harm" among refugees trapped in Greek camps. *The Independent*. Retrieved from www.independent.co.uk/news/world/europe/refugee-crisis-latest-asylum-seekers-greece-camps-lesbos-suicide-self-harm-children-human-rights-a7836196.html#gallery

Investor's Business Daily. (2015, September 9). Editorial. Migrants: "Refugees" or invaders?, p. A12.

Daily Resistance. (2016). Editorial. Retrieved from https://dailyresistance.oplatz.net/the-first-issue-of-the-newspaper-daily-resistance-is-now-out/

Erder, S. (2016). Preliminary thoughts on the Syrian refugee movement. New perspectives on Turkey. *Istanbul, 54*, 119.

Festinger, L. (1957). *A theory of cognitive dissonance*. Stanford, CA: Stanford University Press.

Fuchs, C. (2004). *Christian Science as a self-organizing meta-information system*. Social Science Research Network, Working Paper Series.

Gerard, L. (2016, September 3). Reporting the news or fanning the flames of hatred? SubScribe blog: Notes on the best and worst of British journalism. Retrieved from www.sub-scribe.co.uk/2016/09/the-press-and-immigration-reporting.html

Gerard, L. (2017a). A year of migration in the white tops. Retrieved from www.sub-scribe2015.co.uk/whitetops-immigration.html#.WeHoMGO9rOg

Gerard, L. (2017b, February 28). The press and immigration part II: The inside story. Retrieved from www.sub-scribe.co.uk/2017/02/the-press-and-immigration-part-ii.html

Gibb, C. (2016). *The stories we tell: Imposing order on experience*. VIC Report (Winter edition). Toronto: University of Toronto

Giddens, A. (1984). *The constitution of society*. Berkeley, CA: University of California Press.

Greenslade, R. (2016, September 5). Newspapers publish anti-immigration stories but what is to be done. *The Guardian*. Retrieved from www.theguardian.com/media/greenslade/2016/sep/05/newspapers-publish-anti-immigration-stories-but-what-is-to-be-done

Herman, E. S. & Chomsky, N. (2002). *Manufacturing consent: The political economy of the mass media*. New York: Pantheon.

Hinsliff, G. (2016). Let's not shy away from asking hard questions about the Cologne attacks. *The Guardian*. Retrieved from www.theguardian.com/commentisfree/2016/jan/08/cologne-attacks-hard-questions-new-years-eve

Holý, L. (1996). *The little Czech and the Great Czech nation: National identity and the post-communist transformation of society*. Cambridge: Cambridge University Press.

Hutton, W. (2017, January 22). Interview. Amartya Sen: "Referendums are like opinion polls. Sometimes they're very wrong". *The Guardian*. Retrieved from www.theguardian.com/books/2017/jan/22/amartya-sen-brexit-trump-press-freedom

International Monetary Fund. (2016). The refugee surge in Europe. Retrieved from https://www.imf.org/external/pubs/ft/sdn/2016/sdn1602.pdf

Joya, M. (2016, 12 April). My Country Looks Like a Sick Cow. *Daily Resistance*. https://oplatz.net/wp-content/uploads/2016/06/Daily-Resistance-Issue-2-Web.pdf

Kingsley, P. (2016, March 7). One in, one out: The EU's simplistic answer to the refugee crisis. *The Guardian*. Retrieved from www.theguardian.com/world/2016/mar/07/one-in-one-out-the-eus-sim plistic-answer-to-the-refugee-crisis

Knorr-Cetina, K. (1988). The micro social order. Towards a reconceptualization. In N. G. Field (Ed.), *The micro-social order, actions and structure: Research methods and social theory* (pp. 21–53). London: Sage.

Kokkalis, P. (2017, September 23). LATRA innovation summit, Athens. Retrieved from www.design4-peace.org/athens

Kolbert, E. (2017, February 27). Why facts don't change our minds: New facts about the human mind show the limitations of reason. *The New Yorker*. Retrieved from www.newyorker.com/magazine/2017/02/27/why-facts-dont-change-our-minds

Lees, C. (2016). How Europe's media covered the migration crisis. English EJO (European Journalism Observatory). Retrieved from www.ox.ac.uk/research/how-europe%E2%80%99s-media-covered-migration-crisis

Lewis, D. & Sumit, D. (2017). Immigration and the rise of the far-right parties in Europe. Dice report. *ProQuest, 15*(4), 10–15. Winter.

Leydesdorff, L. (1994). The evolution of communication systems. *International Journal of Systems Research and Information Science, 6*, 219–230.

Luhmann, N. (1988). Familiarity, confidence, trust: Problems and alternatives. In D. Gambetta (Ed.), *Trust: Making and breaking of cooperative relations* (pp. 94–107). Oxford: Blackwell.

Luhmann, N. (1990). *Essays on self-reference*. New York: Columbia University Press.

Luhmann, N. (1995). *Social systems*. Stanford: Stanford University Press.

Luhmann, N. (1999). *Die Gesellschaft der Gesellschaft* [*The society of society*]. Frankfurt am Main: Suhrkamp taschenbuch wissenschaft.

Luhmann, N. (2000). *The reality of the mass media*. Cambridge: Polity Press.

Lynch, S. (2016, May 5). Turks in line for visa-free EU travel by May. *Irish Times*. Retrieved from www.irishtimes.com/news/world/europe/visa-free-eu-travel-for-turkish-citizens-has-hard-road-ahead-1.2635000

McLuhan, M. (1967). *Understanding media: The extensions of man*. New York: McGraw-Hill.

Mercier, H. & Sperber, D. (2017). *The enigma of reason*. Cambridge, MA: Harvard University Press.

Merrill, J. (2015, October 24). Lesbos mayor Spyridon Galinos: "How I am coping with up to 7,000 new refugees each day". *The Independent*. Retrieved from www.independent.co.uk/news/world/europe/lesbos-mayor-spyridon-galinos-how-i-am-coping-with-up-to-7000-new-refugees-each-day-a6707696.html#gallery

Meyrowitz, J. (1985). *No sense of place: The impact of electronic media on social behavior*. Oxford: Oxford University Press.

Mustafa (2016, December 31). Lesbos centre is a prison posing as a refugee camp. *Irish Times*. Retrieved from www.irishtimes.com/opinion/out-of-syria-lesbos-centre-is-a-prison-dressed-up-as-a-refugee-camp-1.2919297

Nallu, P. (2016, December 29). 2016: The year the world stopped caring for refugees. Retrieved from www.aljazeera.com/indepth/features/2016/12/2016-year-world-stopped-caring-refugees-161227090243522.html

New Europe Report. (2017, August 24). UNHCR migrant arrivals falls, while the likelihood of death persists. *New Europe Online*. Retrieved from www.unhcr.org/uk/news/press/2017/8/599ec5024/europe-refugee-migrant-arrivals-fall-reports-abuses-deaths-persist.html

Noack, R. (2016, July 11). 2,000 men "sexually assaulted 1,200 women" at Cologne New Year's Eve party. *Independent Online*. Retrieved from www.independent.co.uk/news/world/europe/cologne-new-years-eve-mass-sex-attacks-leaked-document-a7130476.html

Organisation for Economic Co-operation and Development (OECD). (2015). International migration statistics. Retrieved from www.oecd-ilibrary.org/social-issues-migration-health/data/oecd-international-migration-statistics_mig-data-en

Otker-Robe, I. & Podpiera, A. M. (2013). The social impact of financial crises: Evidence from the global financial crisis (English). Policy Research working paper, no. WPS 6703. Retrieved from http://documents.worldbank.org/curated/en/498911468180867209/The-social-impact-of-financial-crises-evidence-from-the-global-financial-crisis

Petrongolo, B. (2016). Do immigrants harm the job prospects of UK-born workers? London School of Economics and Political Science blog. Retrieved from http://blogs.lse.ac.uk/brexit/2016/10/19/do-immigrants-harm-the-job-prospects-of-uk-born-workers/

Pew Research Center. (2016). Number of refugees to Europe surges to record 1.3 million in 2015. Retrieved from www.pewglobal.org/2016/08/02/number-of-refugees-to-europe-surges-to-record-1-3-million-in-2015/

Pew Research Center. (2017). Majority of recent refugees are Muslim. Retrieved from www.pewforum.org/2017/11/29/europes-growing-muslim-population/pf_11-29-17_muslims-update-06/

Popper, K. (2002). *Conjectures and refutations*. London: Routledge.

Portes, A. & Rumbaut, R. (2006). *Immigrant America: A portrait*. Berkeley, CA: University of California Press.

Reeves, A., Mckee, M., & Stuckler, D. (2015). "'It's The Sun wot won it": Evidence of media influence on political attitudes and voting from a UK quasi-natural experiment. *Social Science Research*, *56*(3), 44–57.

Safdar, A. & Strickland, P. (2016, December 29). 2016: The year the world stopped caring for refugees. Retrieved from www.aljazeera.com/indepth/features/2016/12/2016-year-world-stopped-caring-refugees-161227090243522.html.

Schutz, A. (1962). *Collected papers I: The problem of social reality*. (M. Natanson, Ed.). The Hague: Martinus Nijhoff.

Sen, A. (1970). *Collective choice and social welfare*. Detroit, MI: Holden-Day.

Sloman, S. & Fernbach, P. (2017). *The knowledge illusion: Why we never think alone*. New York: Riverhead Books.

Smith, H. (2017, September 29). Surge in migration to Greece fuels misery in refugee camps. *The Guardian*. Retrieved from www.theguardian.com/world/2017/sep/29/surge-in-migration-to-greece-fuels-misery-in-refugee-camps.

Squires, N. (2017, March 14). A year on from the EU–Turkey deal, refugees and migrants in limbo commit suicide and suffer from trauma. *The Telegraph*. Retrieved from www.telegraph.co.uk/news/2017/03/14/year-eu-turkey-deal-refugees-migrants-limbo-commit-suicide-suffer/

Stiglitz, J. E. (2012). *The price of inequality: How today's divided society endangers our future*. New York: W.W. Norton.

Stiglitz, J. E. (2015, June 29). Joseph Stiglitz: How I would vote in the Greek referendum. *The Guardian*. Retrieved from www.theguardian.com/business/2015/jun/29/joseph-stiglitz-how-i-would-vote-in-the-greek-referendum

Sultan, N. (2016, August 20). This newspaper is written for refugees, by refugees. *Vice magazine*. Retrieved from www.vice.com/en_uk/article/nnknbg/this-newspaper-is-written-by-refugees-for-refugees-daily-resistance

Tartar, A. (2017). *How the populist right is redrawing the map of Europe*. Bloomberg. Retrieved from www.bloomberg.com/graphics/2017-europe-populist-right/

Theodorou, J. (2018). What grassroots groups can teach us about smart aid. *Refugees Deeply*. Retrieved from www.newsdeeply.com/refugees/community/2018/02/21/what-grassroots-groups-can-teach-us-about-smart-aid

Traynor, I. (2015, October 23). Germany to push for compulsory EU quotas to tackle refugee crisis. *The Guardian*. Retrieved from www.theguardian.com/world/2015/oct/23/refugee-crisis-germany-push-compulsory-eu-quotas

Ulu, T. (Ed.) (2016, March 9). *Daily Resistance*. Retrieved from https://dailyresistance.oplatz.net/the-first-issue-of-the-newspaper-daily-resistance-is-now-out/

Ulu, T. (Ed.). (2016b, June 13). *Editorial. Daily Resistance*. Retrieved from https://oplatz.net/wp-content/uploads/2016/06/Daily-Resistance-Issue-2-Web.pdf

Wagstyl, S. (2016). Taboos shattered as Germany agonises over Cologne attacks: Mass sexual assault raises issues of immigration, religion and crime. *Financial Times*. Retrieved from www.ft.com/content/386ed934-bb94-11e5-bf7e-8a339b6f2164

Weisekiez Initiative. (2016). Permanent "emergency" [illegible] the lagers at THF. *Daily Resistance*. Retrieved from https://oplatz.net/wp-content/uploads/2016/06/Daily-Resistance-Issue-2-Web.pdf

Women in Exile. (2016). Stop justifying the tightening of your racists asylum-laws and deportations in the name of women*rights! *Daily resistance*. Retrieved from https://asylstrikeberlin.files.wordpress.com/2016/03/daily-resistance-feb16-web-version.pdf

Ziga. (2016). The construction of the European Union's immigration system. *Daily Resistance*. Retrieved from https://asylstrikeberlin.files.wordpress.com/2016/03/daily-resistance-feb16-web-version.pdf

11

THIRD-CULTURE INDIVIDUALS

Gina G. Barker

Third-culture individuals

Migration is no small phenomenon. In 2015, an estimated 244 million people – 3.3 percent of the world's population – lived outside their country of origin (United Nations Population Fund, 2017). Many of these migrants were refugees forced from their homes by war, while others emigrated for economic or social reasons. People also move abroad short term to study or work. Sometimes families stay behind. Other times, children are raised abroad. These are third-culture individuals. Exposed to a foreign culture or cultures during their developmental years, they remain culturally different from other migrants as well as from other co-nationals as adults. This group of multicultural individuals has been recognized in popular and professional writing since the 1990s and has recently gained attention in the scholarly literature. Since their cultural identity is derived largely from an atypical childhood involving intercultural transition and adaptation experiences, people with this particular background generally refer to themselves as third-culture kids or TCKs, even as adults. For this reason, some researchers prefer to use the term adult third-culture kids.

Drawing upon research originating in a variety of academic fields, this chapter will first define and conceptualize third-culture individuals (TCIs) and their third culture. Next, it will review common challenges TCIs face. The last section identifies and discusses benefits emerging from their unique experiences and specialized skills. Cultural marginality will serve as the organizing theme. Schaetti (1996) noted that TCIs "do not tend to fit perfectly into any one of the cultures in which they have lived, but may fit comfortably on the edge, in the margins of each" (p. 178). This experience carries the potential to develop into encapsulated marginality where they feel trapped in perpetual cultural homelessness, or evolve into constructive marginality, where a strong multicultural identity emerges and specialized skills are put to use.

The nature of cultural marginality

Third-culture individuals (TCIs) are men and women who lived in a country other than that of their nationality during their developmental years, generally as children of corporate employees, military or government personnel, missionaries, or aid workers. What makes them different from people who emigrate as adults is that they become socialized into their home and host cultures simultaneously and develop their individual identity while influenced by several different cultural frameworks, where acculturating adults already have a cultural identity and a more or less established worldview. The field of developmental psychology has identified middle childhood, i.e., ages 6–12, as the stage in which children form a rudimentary identity, grasp interpersonal dependence, and learn basic social skills and early adolescence, i.e., ages 12–18, as a period of meta-development, which includes comprehension of social norms and subgroups, increased cognitive complexity, and further establishment of an individual identity.

What makes TCIs different from second-generation immigrants or refugees is that they have every intention of returning to the countries of their respective passports at some point, where the former typically settle into the host country their parents brought them into, even if they end up moving between two cultural frameworks in a bicultural environment. By contrast, expatriate families are often quite mobile and do not necessarily stay connected to the different cultural contexts once lived in, but they do maintain a strong affiliation to their home culture. However, one of the frequently documented experiences of TCIs is that once they return to the country of their passport – which often coincides with starting college – they expect to feel at home but quickly realize they do not fit in and have little in common with their co-national peers. Not only may they lack knowledge of popular culture, speak with an accent, and feel disconnected from core cultural features but, more importantly, they often hold a different set of values, subscribe to a different worldview, and are profoundly shaped by intercultural experiences to which their peers cannot relate (Eakin, 1996; Hervey, 2009; Klemens & Bikos, 2009; Purnell & Hoban, 2014; Yoshida et al., 2009).

From the above conceptualization, it becomes evident that there is great variety within the TCI phenomenon, depending on the number of countries lived in, age while abroad, fluency in foreign languages, and level of host-culture immersion. Since a young person may become linguistically and culturally fluent in as little as a year, the number of years outside one's country matters mostly in terms of corresponding lack of home-culture exposure. The experience of cultural marginality is not exclusive to TCIs; however, it is a core feature of the third culture.

The term third culture was originally coined to describe the blend of home and host cultures that forms within expatriate communities (Useem, Donoghue, & Useem, 1963). Later, the meaning of the term shifted to signify the unique and shared experience of TCIs, who grow up between cultures and adopt aspects of the various cultures immersed in without gaining full ownership in any one of them (Pollock & Van Reken, 2009). The third culture is understood and defined as a culture exclusively made up of all TCIs worldwide, who possess the ability to blend and bridge existing cultures and reaffirm this third culture whenever they interact with each other. It is arguable whether the term culture is used appropriately in this context, since this third culture is not self-sustained and cannot reproduce itself, which are two criteria that are central to mainstream conceptualizations of culture. On the other hand, there is overwhelming evidence that TCIs thrive in culturally diverse environments and experience a stronger cultural bond with other TCIs than with monocultural co-nationals (Greenholtz & Kim, 2009; Moore & Barker, 2012; Peterson & Plamondon, 2009; Walters & Auton-Cuff, 2009; Westropp, Cathro, & Everett, 2016; Yoshida et al., 2009).

Challenges of encapsulated marginality

The early literature on TCIs was produced mainly by international organizations and schools in an attempt to assist and educate parents living abroad. This literature, which includes survey research findings and numerous accounts of TCIs' life experiences (Dixon & Hayden, 2008; Eidse & Sichel, 2004; Langford, 1998; Pascoe, 2006; Pollock & Van Reken, 2009; Smith, 1996), highlights many of the negative effects of an internationally mobile and culturally diverse lifestyle on children. When their marginality is encapsulated, TCIs feel alienated, disoriented, and isolated, unable to reconcile their fragmented, cultural selves. Lacking a sense of belonging to any one country, TCIs feel at home everywhere and nowhere, and answering the simple question "Where are you from?" is highly problematic. One TCI aptly described this tension of being able to blend into a cultural setting with little conscious effort but without feeling a part of it as follows:

> I don't feel like I belong, I feel like a tourist when I go to my home country. Yet, I feel like I can fit in and adapt easily without having that sense of belonging or attachment to that culture. That's what's incredible about this lifestyle.
>
> *(cited in Moore & Barker, 2012, p. 558)*

The experience of cultural homelessness is not unique to TCIs; it may also affect multi-racial, multi-ethnic, and other multicultural individuals. Navarrete and Jenkins (2011) theorized that people who are culturally homeless are rejected by multiple groups, feel like they do not belong to any group, struggle to attain membership within the desired group(s), and strive to find a cultural home. Often having more than one language or culture present within the family, they may also view themselves as culturally different from their own family members as well as their social surroundings. Walters and Auton-Cuff's (2009) qualitative study detailed how frequent transitions and the pervasiveness of being different profoundly complicate the identity development of TCIs. One of the interviewees explained,

> I would feel empty ... cause maybe I was getting more accepted, getting more culturally accepted by others, but because that's not the real me, I would come home empty ... I think I felt empty because people accepted me for not being myself ... it was a fake me.
>
> *(p. 766)*

TCIs' development is also characterized by multilingual identity constructs (Tannenbaum & Tseng, 2015).

When TCIs first realize that the home-culture schema they acquired abroad and during occasional home-country visits does not match reality, they often experience severe reverse culture shock. Their acculturative stress and inner conflict do not arise from an inability to adapt and blend in, but from realizing that they are profoundly different. They are sometimes referred to as hidden immigrants. American TCIs reported having trouble accepting home-culture perspectives, worldviews, and values (Klemens & Bikos, 2009). Negative experiences in earlier transitions also make adjustment more difficult (Hervey, 2009). TCIs returning to Japan reported that greater difficulty was associated with feeling less accepted, being less positive about their experiences abroad, trying harder to conform, and having fewer people accepting them as TCIs (Yoshida et al., 2009). Drawing upon third-culture and culture shock literature as well as interviews, Purnell and Hoban (2014) proposed a four-stage transition model of this critical time in a TCI's life. The four stages are *preparation for transition, initial transition, adaptation*, and *stabilization*. Feelings of not being understood and not fitting in were associated with the initial transition stage. During the adaptation stage, which occurred 6–24 months after re-entry, TCIs were found to limit their interaction with other university students in favor of other TCIs, family, friends, or colleagues. A few participants struggled with depression and anxiety caused by isolation or grief as a result of being separated from family or friends.

A mobile lifestyle involving multiple transitions during childhood and adolescence often leads to experiences of loss. Along with the somewhat obvious losses of people and places, constant change and unpredictability may translate to an existential loss of trust and security that leads to an inability to perceive the world as a safe place (Gilbert, 2008). Another recurring theme in the accounts provided by TCIs is that their grief is often disenfranchised because it is ill-fitted with their parents' international pursuits and may, therefore, remain hidden. One TCI shared, "It was clear to me at an early age that my parents' work was more important than I. I felt abandoned and insignificant my entire childhood" (cited in Wrobbel & Plueddemann, 1990, p. 372). Pollock and Van Reken (2009) noted that many TCIs have a systems identity, stemming from the cause or venture their parents work for. They said,

> Members of specific third culture communities may be more directly conscious than their peers at home of representing something greater than themselves – be it their government, their company, or God. Jobs can hinge on how well the adults' behavior, or that of their children, positively reflects the values and standards of the sponsoring agency.
>
> *(p. 18)*

For many TCIs, the only stable relationships are those within the immediate family, which tends to result in strong ties to parents and siblings (Eakin, 1996; Langford, 1998; Lijadi & van Schalkwyk, 2014). Many TCIs continue their international, mobile lifestyle as adults. Reluctant to settle down in one place and put down roots, they sometimes refer to themselves as global nomads. One TCI framed his reticence to settle down and commit to one location and one set of social relationships as not wanting to miss the excitement of new beginnings, as

> like an amusement ride, they keep swinging you around. At first it is exciting, but after several rounds it feels the same, you become numb. But it is addictive; you want to do it again, to go for the ride, to feel the excitement of the first round followed by swinging in the air.
>
> *(cited in Lijadi & van Schalkwyk, 2014, p. 15)*

As this quote suggests, this may lead to difficulty establishing long-term relationships and to make long-term commitments (Westropp et al., 2016). Although third-culture children's general problem-solving skills have been found to exceed those of monocultural children (Lee, Bain, & McCallum, 2007), TCIs' social problem-solving abilities may be under-developed because they are accustomed to move rather than resolve interpersonal conflicts (Eakin, 1996).

If unresolved, the issues resulting from TCIs' grief over losses, lack of stability and a sense of belonging, and inability to form deep relationships may remain. Literature emerging from the counseling field explains the potential long-term effects of developmental intercultural transitions and traumatic intercultural experiences, and several treatment models tailored to TCIs have been proposed. For example, Melles and Frey (2014) proposed a relational-cultural therapy model to address parental issues, emotional disengagement, role-playing to please or fit in, and inability to settle down. Davis, Edwards, and Watson (2015) advocated for process-experiential/emotion-focused therapy to address TCIs' identity conflicts, confusion, and lack of self-integration. The authors explained,

> In any given context, there are parts of their personal identity that are foreign to those of the local peer groups. Such experiences can generate internal conflicts between the different cultural parts of the self with accompanying feelings of self-consciousness, shame, fear, and frustration.
>
> *(p. 173)*

McDonald (2010) stressed the importance of using culturally sensitive counseling models and a person-centered, strength-based approach to assess TCIs' health and wellness views and multicultural/third-culture identity.

Some researchers have proposed that a postmodern theoretical framework might be useful when analyzing the complex, transitional, and multifaceted social reality of TCIs (Grimshaw & Sears, 2008). Lacking conventional prescriptions for how to develop their life trajectories, they are faced with a seemingly limitless range of lifestyles to choose from.

Benefits of constructive marginality

Third-culture individuals who are able to embrace the third culture as part of their identity and get comfortable in the margins of different cultural groups may find opportunities to use their intercultural experiences in constructive ways. Intercultural scholars, who have taken an interest in TCIs since the early 2000s, have begun to examine TCIs and produce evidence that the unique background of TCIs has allowed them to acquire specialized skills, enhanced intercultural competence, and interpersonal sensitivity.

The research seems to suggest that constructive marginality emerges as the result of a deliberate choice to focus on the benefits – rather than the detriments – of being multi-cultural. Hoersting and Jenkins (2011) examined the relationships among perceptions of cultural homelessness, a multicultural identity, and self-esteem among TCIs. The results of their study showed that a low cultural homelessness score was associated with an emotional attachment to a multicultural identity and that affirming this identity buffered the negative association between cultural homelessness and low self-esteem. However, the authors did not find significant correlations between perceived cultural homelessness and merely self-identifying oneself as a third-culture or multicultural individual or having a culturally diverse social network.

Moore and Barker's (2012) qualitative study involving interviews with TCIs provided insights into how TCIs' multiculturalism is experienced and managed. Participants in this study described themselves as having a blended cultural identity or multiple cultural identities that they shift between, but not both. Although the difference between the two identity constructs is subtle, those with a blended identity described how they had integrated elements from different cultures into one multicultural identity to which they adhere consistently regardless of their context. One participant explained, "I have one identity, but I understand both cultures. I know how to put them together in one piece which is me. I know how to mix both of them in a way that I can adapt wherever I'm at" (p. 557). By contrast, those with multiple cultural identities described alternating among these seamlessly and with little conscious effort. One TCI said,

> I'm like a hybrid, right? I can function in both cultures. So, I can go to Brazil and nobody would ever notice that I've been living in the U.S. for my whole life, and a lot of times here in the U.S. people are surprised when I tell them that I was born and raised in Brazil.
>
> *(p. 557)*

Because of this enhanced ability to adapt to new situations and to easily blend in, TCIs are sometimes referred to as cultural chameleons; a construct that involves both cognitive differentiation and enhanced interpersonal communication competence. Westropp et al. (2016) identified TCIs as "more sophisticated in their reading of context and with their approaches to creating relationships" (p. 342). This notion was supported in Lyttle, Barker, and Cornwell's (2011) study, in which TCIs scored higher on social sensitivity than monocultural people. One TCI described using this ability as follows:

> I've become very, very aware of everything that I say or do. I can't change my accent but I can change my dress, I can change how I physically present myself. It's come to a point where I am very aware of my physical surroundings and even how I use my gestures; it's not random, it's very deliberate . . . It's about making them feel catered to. If you want people to accept you or if you want people to open up to you.
>
> *(cited in Westropp et al., 2016, p. 343)*

The social ability of TCIs has also been examined in two different studies in terms of social initiative and extroversion, respectively, but in neither case was it found to be significantly enhanced. Social initiative is one of five dimensions on the Multicultural Personality Questionnaire (van der Zee & van Oudenhoven, 2000), which has been validated across various cultures and ages for assessment of intercultural competence. However, third-culture teens did not score higher on social initiative than monocultural teens when using this instrument (Dewaele & Van Oudenhoven, 2009). Conceptually similar, extroversion did not predict intercultural competence among TCIs in the second study (Tarique & Weisbord, 2013) either. The reason may be TCIs' tendency to observe, to make sure they understand a particular social context accurately before they initiate. Several researchers have also tested the claim of TCIs' enhanced adaptability. Tarique and Weisbord (ibid) reported that the intercultural experiences of TCIs predicted both flexibility and tolerance of ambiguity. Lam and Selmer (2004) found higher levels of flexibility among third-culture adolescents, whereas the third-culture teens in Dewaele and Van Oudenhoven's (2009) study did not emerge as being more flexible than their monocultural peers.

TCIs' intercultural communication competence is acquired during development and the associated abilities are, therefore, deeply embedded in their frames of reference. As a result, they are believed to be well-equipped for acquiring competence in new cultures. However, although various psychological attributes of TCIs have been examined to determine what makes them unique in this regard, the empirical evidence is inconclusive. Examining the adjustment resulting from intercultural adaptation, Selmer and Lauring (2014) compared TCIs with people who acculturated as adults in a sample of expatriates residing in Hong Kong. While the TCIs scored higher on general adjustment to the host society, there was no difference between the two groups in level of interaction adjustment. The researchers reasoned that the multi-lingual abilities of the TCIs may not be of much help in mastering a complex language such as Cantonese. Testing the assumption of TCIs' enhanced ability to transition among cultures, the study showed that time in the host location and previous experience as an adult expatriate predicted interaction adjustment among non-TCIs but not among TCIs, because the former would rely on experiences from their current and previous assignments, whereas TCIs would rely on their experiences living abroad as children. Similar results were reported by Hanek, Lee, and Brannen (2014). TCIs in their study were less adaptive to foreign cultures than other multicultural individuals. The authors reasoned that TCIs may be overconfident in their cultural skills and, therefore, less motivated to attend to cultural differences. Alternatively, they may be disinterested in assimilating into a foreign culture, instead remaining superficially engaged, detached, or disengaged. Taken together, research to date seems to indicate that TCIs benefit from their background when adapting to an unfamiliar culture, but that it is not yet clear exactly what their advantage is.

Another benefit associated with a multicultural identity is open-mindedness. Having experienced cultural differences first-hand during their formative years and internalized features from various cultures, TCIs may be considered cultural hybrids. As such, they tend to exhibit openness to and appreciation for different people and diverse perspectives. This disposition has been conceptually linked to high levels of ethno-relativism and low levels of ethno-centrism and prejudice, but the results of several studies are somewhat contradictory. Third-culture adolescents in Lam and Selmer's (2004) study scored higher on dimensions of open-mindedness, neutrality, respect for others, tolerance of others' behaviors and views, and a positive attitude toward other cultures. In addition to being more open-minded, third-culture teens are also more culturally empathetic than their monocultural peers, according to Dewaele and Van Oudenhoven's (2009) research. Melles and Schwartz (2013) found that a positive attitude toward racial diversity could be predicted from the number of different countries TCIs have lived in. A similar correlation seems to exist with reduced authoritarianism. Linked to prejudice, discrimination, ethno-centrism, and lack of openness, Peterson and Plamondon (2009) conceptualized authoritarianism as a possible reactive response to uncertainty caused by multiple transitions. Interestingly, the number of home-country visits seemed to also play a role. Finally, a psychometric case study analysis of a TCI's intercultural sensitivity revealed a worldview that is simultaneously ethno-relative and ethno-centric – a paradox that the researchers (Greenholtz & Kim, 2009) interpreted as a trait unique to TCIs. The ethno-relative tendency is a result of early exposure to different cultures, while the ethno-centric tendency stems from a strong home-country affiliation that is instilled in TCIs by parents – who often act as formal or informal ambassadors – and nurtured through strong familial ties.

The internationally mobile tendencies of TCIs have not gone unnoticed, and their acceptance of cultural differences, foreign languages, and future orientation appears to be higher than among monocultural youth (Gerner, Perry, Moselle, & Archbold, 1992). Their participation in higher education is above average, but their educational paths are unconventional, with about half of them attending three or more colleges. They are drawn to international careers in which they can exercise expertise, leadership, and independence, which many find in the human services field (Bikos et al., 2014; Bonebright, 2010). When comparing British third-culture adolescents living in Hong Kong with both British monocultural adolescents in the UK and Chinese monocultural adolescents in Hong Kong, higher scores on perceptions of being international and a stronger focus on international careers were reported by the TCIs (Lam & Selmer, 2004).

Because of TCIs' enhanced interpersonal, group, and intercultural communication skills, they are recognized as diplomatic negotiators and mediators who are equipped with an invaluable ability to suspend judgment while examining both sides of an issue or situation (McCaig, 1996; Westropp et al., 2016). Their cultural hybridity and expanded worldview give them the capacity for boundary-spanning and management of diversity beyond national borders. Brimm (2010) explained

> They develop the ability to look at issues from an outsider's perspective. Their experience across cultures gives them multiple lenses and perspectives for seeing and understanding the world around them ... They can develop chameleon-like

> behavior to fit quickly into new environments and learn a range of flexible thinking skills to cope with the demands of change.
>
> *(p. 38)*

However, the way in which TCIs' specialized skills play out in different contexts needs more attention from researchers in order to clarify of what TCIs specialized skills and attributes actually consist.

In closing, this chapter described men and women who share a third culture that they acquired outside of their home culture sometime between the ages of 6 and 18 as children of corporate employees, military or government personnel, missionaries, or aid workers. Because of their atypical, mobile upbringing involving multiple transitions and unique experiences of intercultural adaptation, many of them find themselves in the margins of and between different cultures. This chapter reviewed research and emerging theories about the challenges of encapsulated marginality and the serious implications of cultural homelessness, loss, grief, acculturative stress, reverse culture shock, and an inability to form deep interpersonal relationships that many TCIs face. This chapter also reviewed research and theory-building on the benefits and opportunities associated with constructive marginality, such as enhanced adaptability, social sensitivity, and intercultural communication competence; open-mindedness; a positive attitude toward cultural differences and diversity; and a quest for international adventures.

> The one thing [being a TCI has] helped me the most with is relating to different people. It makes it a lot easier to adapt to new situations and environments, and just a lot easier to get to know somebody because you're not just used to this one thing, you have multiple experiences.
>
> *(cited in Moore & Barker, 2012, p. 560)*

References

Bikos, L. H., Haney, D., Edwards, R. W., North, M. A., Quint, M., McLellan, J., & Ecker, D. L. (2014). Missionary kid career development: A consensual qualitative research investigation through a social cognitive lens. *Career Development Quarterly*, *62*, 156–174.

Bonebright, D. A. (2010). Adult third culture kids: HRD challenges and opportunities. *Human Resource Development International*, *13*, 351–359.

Brimm, L. (2010). *Global cosmopolitans: The creative edge of difference*. New York: Palgrave Macmillan.

Davis, P. S., Edwards, K. J., & Watson, T. S. (2015). Using process-experiential/emotion-focused therapy techniques for identity integration and resolution of grief among third culture kids. *Journal of Humanistic Counseling*, *54*, 170–186.

Dewaele, J. M. & Van Oudenhoven, J. P. (2009). The effect of multilingualism/multiculturalism on personality: No gain without pain for third culture kids? *International Journal of Multilingualism*, *6*, 443–459.

Dixon, P. & Hayden, M. (2008). "On the move": Primary age children in transition. *Cambridge Journal of Education*, *38*, 483–496.

Eakin, K. B. (1996). You can't go "home" again. In C. D. Smith (Ed.), *Strangers at home: Essays on the effects of living overseas and coming "home" to a strange land* (pp. 57–80). Bayside, NY: Aletheia Publications.

Eidse, F. & Sichel, N. (2004). *Unrooted childhood*. Yarmouth, ME: Intercultural Press.

Gerner, M. E., Perry, F., Moselle, M. A., & Archbold, M. (1992). Characteristics of internationally mobile adolescents. *Journal of School Psychology*, *30*, 197–214.

Gilbert, K. R. (2008). Loss and grief between and among cultures: The experience of third culture kids. *Illness, Crisis and Loss*, *16*, 93–109.

Greenholtz, J. & Kim, J. (2009). The cultural hybridity of Lena: A multi-method case study of a third culture kid. *International Journal of Intercultural Relations*, *33*, 391–398.

Grimshaw, T. & Sears, C. (2008). "Where am I from?" "Where do I belong?" The negotiation and maintenance of identity by international school students. *Journal of Research in International Education, 7*, 259–278.

Hanek, K. J., Lee, F., & Brannen, M. Y. (2014). Individual differences among global/multicultural individuals: Cultural experiences, identity, and adaptation. *International Studies of Management and Organization, 44*, 75–89.

Hervey, E. (2009). Cultural transitions during childhood and adjustment to college. *Journal of Psychology and Christianity, 28*, 3–12.

Hoersting, R. C. & Jenkins, S. R. (2011). No place to call home: Cultural homelessness, self-esteem and cross-cultural identities. *International Journal of Intercultural Relations, 35*, 17–30.

Klemens, M. J. & Bikos, L. H. (2009). Psychological well-being and sociocultural adaptation in college-aged, repatriated, missionary kids. *Mental Health, Religion and Culture, 12*, 721–733.

Lam, H. & Selmer, J. (2004). Are former "third culture kids" the ideal business expatriates? *Career Development International, 9*, 109–122.

Langford, M. (1998). Global nomads, third culture kids, and international schools. In M. C. Hayden & J. J. Thompson (Eds.), *International education: Principles and practice* (pp. 28–43). London: Kogan Page.

Lee, Y. J., Bain, S. K., & McCallum, R. S. (2007). Improving creative problem-solving in a sample of third culture kids. *School Psychology International, 28*, 449–463.

Lijadi, A. A. & van Schalkwyk, G. J. (2014). Narratives of third culture kids: Commitment and reticence in social relationships. *The Qualitative Report, 19*, 1–18.

Lyttle, A., Barker, G. G., & Cornwell, T. (2011). Adept through adaptation: Third culture individuals' interpersonal sensitivity. *International Journal of Intercultural Relations, 35*, 686–694.

McCaig, N. M. (1996). Understanding global nomads. In C. D. Smith (Ed.), *Strangers at home: Essays on the effects of living overseas and coming "home" to a strange land* (pp. 99–120). Bayside, NY: Aletheia Publications.

McDonald, K. E. (2010). Transculturals: Identifying the invisible minority. *Journal of Multicultural Counseling and Development, 38*, 39–50.

Melles, E. A. & Frey, L. L. (2014). "Here, everybody moves": Using relational cultural therapy with adult third-culture kids. *International Journal for the Advancement of Counselling, 36*, 348–358.

Melles, E. A. & Schwartz, J. (2013). Does the third culture kid experience predict levels of prejudice? *International Journal of Intercultural Relations, 37*, 260–267.

Moore, A. M. & Barker, G. G. (2012). Confused or multicultural: Third culture individuals' cultural identity. *International Journal of Intercultural Relations, 36*, 553–562.

Navarrete, V. & Jenkins, S. R. (2011). Cultural homelessness, multiminority status, ethnic identity development, and self esteem. *International Journal of Intercultural Relations, 35*, 791–804.

Pascoe, R. (2006). *Raising global nomads: Parenting in an on-demand world*. Vancouver, BC: Expatriate Press.

Peterson, B. E. & Plamondon, L. T. (2009). Third culture kids and the consequences of international sojourns on authoritarianism, acculturative balance, and positive affect. *Journal of Research and Personality, 43*, 755–763.

Pollock, D. C. & Van Reken, R. E. (2009). *Third culture kids: Growing up among worlds*. Boston, MA: Nicholas Brealey.

Purnell, L. & Hoban, E. (2014). The lived experiences of third culture kids transitioning into university life in Australia. *International Journal of Intercultural Relations, 41*, 80–90.

Schaetti, B. (1996). Phoenix rising: A question of cultural identity. In C. D. Smith (Ed.), *Strangers at home: Essays on the effects of living overseas and coming "home" to a strange land* (pp. 177–188). Bayside, NY: Aletheia Publications.

Selmer, J. & Lauring, J. (2014). Self-initiated expatriates: An exploratory study of adjustment of adult third-culture kids vs. adult mono-culture kids. *Cross Cultural Management, 21*, 422–436.

Smith, C. D. (1996). *Strangers at home: Essays on the effects of living overseas and coming "home" to a strange land*. Bayside, NY: Aletheia Publications.

Tannenbaum, M. & Tseng, J. (2015). Which one is Ithaca? Multilingualism and sense of identity among third culture kids. *International Journal of Multilingualism, 12*, 276–297.

Tarique, I. & Weisbord, E. (2013). Antecedents of dynamic cross-cultural competence in adult third culture kids (ATCKs). *Journal of Global Mobility, 1*, 139–160.

United Nations Population Fund. (2017). *Migration*. Retrieved from www.unfpa.org/migration

Useem, J., Donoghue, J. D., & Useem, R. H. (1963). Men in the middle of the third culture: The roles of American and non-western people in cross-cultural administration. *Human Organization, 22*, 169–179.

Walters, K. A. & Auton-Cuff, F. P. (2009). A story to tell: The identity development of women growing up as third culture kids. *Mental Health, Religion and Culture*, *12*, 755–772.
Westropp, S., Cathro, V., & Everett, A. M. (2016). Adult third culture kids' suitability as expatriates. *Review of International Business and Strategy*, *26*, 334–348.
Wrobbel, K. A. & Plueddemann, J. E. (1990). Psychosocial development in adult missionary kids. *Journal of Psychology and Theology*, *18*, 363–374.
Yoshida, T., Matsumoto, D., Akashi, S., Akiyama, T., Furuiye, A., Ishii, C., & Moriyoshi, N. (2009). Contrasting experiences in Japanese returnee adjustment: Those who adjust easily and those who do not. *International Journal of Intercultural Relations*, *33*, 265–276.
Zee, K. I. van der & van Oudenhoven, J. P. (2000). The Multicultural Personality Questionnaire: A multidimensional instrument of multicultural effectiveness. *European Journal of Personality*, *14*, 291–309.

PART III

The media and migration

12

MIGRATION AND MIGRANTS WITHIN AND TO EUROPE

Reviewing media studies of the past decade (2001–2016)

Mélodine Sommier, Willemijn Dortant, & Flora Galy-Badenas

This chapter will provide a review of media studies on migration both *within* and *to* Europe published since the turn of the century. By doing so, the limited notion of migration as a one-time geographical movement may be enriched by a consideration of migrants, their mobility, and their representations in the media after settlement on the European continent. The primary goal of this study is to define if and how migration features in recent scholarly articles that consider the development and transmission of mass media narratives. Therefore, the exploration is confined to a narrowed-down set of sub-disciplines within the broad field of media studies, i.e., journal articles related to media sociology, mass communication, and critical discourse analysis. Using quantitative content analysis to summarize the state of the literature on the topic, the current study points out gaps and emerging topics in studies on media and migration. It thereby delineates future research directions that are relevant to both the fields of media and migration studies.

On a practical level, a review study is extremely relevant to define how present-day understandings of migration and migrants intersect with media representations. As debates on migration are nowadays increasingly politicized (Brug, D'Amato, Ruedin, & Berkhout, 2015), it is worthwhile considering to what extent and how media researchers have taken upon this increase. The timeframe of the study indeed covers many significant events connected to public discourse on migration in Europe, such as terrorist attacks within and beyond the European borders, the Greek financial crisis, and expansion of the Schengen borders in 2007–2008. The most recent events, such as Brexit and the so-called "refugee crisis," underline an even stronger urgency to study how, on the one hand, mediatized articulations of migratory movements and, on the other hand, public discourses are mutually related.

This chapter first elaborates on the methods used while selecting and analyzing scholarly articles for the current review. Second, a quantitative description of the data facilitates a cross-sectional identification of focal points in media journals. Articles are defined in terms of the media outlet, geographical location, type of migrants, and topics they tend to focus on, as well as their methodological frameworks. Following this quantitative overview, the chapter provides a detailed discussion of the main themes identified in the data. This section is divided into a discussion of strongly- and moderately-related topics and the central theme of European migration. In the conclusion, key methodological and conceptual limitations are summarized, creating a platform for discussion about the future of media research on the topic of migration within and to Europe.

Method

For the current study, 100 articles (see the Appendix for the full list of references) from ten prominent academic journals dealing with mass media narratives were reviewed, focusing on their negotiation of migration within and to Europe. These journals (see full list in Table 12.1) were selected based on a cross-comparison of results from three main metric systems (i.e., Google Scholar Metrics, Scimago, and Citesore). The tools used by metric systems to rank academic journals are often criticized for being too partial or biased (Pendlebury, 2008). For this reason, the authors decided to combine results from three metric systems in order to gain a more balanced overview of the top journals on mass media since 2001. Within the selected journals, original articles (i.e., commentaries and book reviews were excluded) published in English between 2001 and 2016 were selected using the following keywords: immigration, migration, migrant, refugee, asylum-seeker, and Europe. These search terms were chosen to include research about both the process (i.e., immigration, migration) and individuals (i.e., migrant, refugee, asylum-seeker). The keyword "Europe" was added after realizing that many articles were focusing on migration within and to non-European countries, particularly on the United States of America, Australia, and New Zealand. After applying these keywords, three journals (*Discourse Studies, Human Communication Research*, and *Communication Research*) were eventually left out due to the absence and/or scarcity of hits.

Following data collection, all articles ($N = 100$) were divided among the three authors and coded to evaluate their degree of relatedness to the topic of migration in Europe. Throughout the coding and organizing of the data, all three authors worked together by interchanging articles, and comparing and negotiating coded parts of each other's data to ensure a good level of intercoder reliability. First, articles that were off-topic (e.g., migration as journalist practice, migration due to climate change) were excluded. After that, the authors organized the articles by relevance. Criteria for defining the relevance of articles were as follows:

1. Articles considered very relevant ($n = 51$) dealt directly with immigration, migration, immigrants, and migrants (i.e., representation/framing of immigrants in the media, immigrants' media use, stereotypes in the media, ethnic and minority media, discourse about migration issues, and visual representations of refugees/asylum-seekers).
2. Articles considered moderately relevant ($n = 38$) referred to migration and/or migrants as a background to the primary topic being discussed (e.g., the phenomenon studied was relevant to migration but only indirectly linked to migration/migrants; the articles questioned how journalism dealt with race/ethnicity/national identity/religion, therefore hinting at migrants on few occasions).
3. Articles ($n = 11$) that mentioned migrants/migration once or twice but not in relation to the main topic of the study were considered irrelevant and excluded from the dataset. Following data reduction, 89 articles (89 percent) were kept for in-depth analysis, out of which 51 (57.3 percent) were identified as closely related to the topic of migration in Europe and 38 (42.7 percent) as moderately related. The detailed overview of data reduction and classification of articles per journal is presented in Table 12.1.

Table 12.1 Overview of the dataset composition per journal prior to and following data reduction

Journal name	*Article collected*	*Articles kept for analysis*	*Closely-related articles*	*Moderately-related articles*
Journal of Communication	3	2	1	1
Media, Culture & Society	35	31	20	11
New Media and Society	12	11	5	6
Journalism Studies	16	13	3	10
International Communication Gazette	13	13	9	4
Journalism	6	4	3	1
European Journal of Communication	8	8	5	3
Journalism and Mass Communication Quarterly	2	2	1	1
Mass Communication and Society	3	3	3	0
International Journal of Press/Politics	2	-	1	1
TOTAL	100	89	51	38

Quantitative overview of the data

Of all the articles we analyzed ($N = 89$), 35 (39.32 percent) collected data from newspapers. With the exception of one article that analyzed cartoons, the other articles did not systematically specify what content was examined within newspapers. It is worth pointing out that 17 out of these 35 articles (48.57 percent) collected data from British newspapers, including both broadsheets and tabloids. In addition to printed media, 23 (25.84 percent) of all the analyzed articles collected data from TV. Among them, 12 did not further specify the type of data being used. The 11 other articles focused on transnational TV channels, commercials, documentaries, soap operas, and news. Third, 20 (22.47 percent) of the articles dealt with data from online sources (websites, blogs, social media, forums, official documents). Lastly, 11 articles (12.36 percent) reported data from various sources, including radio, the BBC (as a general broadcast source), ethnic media, magazines, mobile phones, and information and communication technologies (ICTs).

Within the dataset, seven articles focused on migration in/to Europe without specifying a national and/or regional focus. When, alternatively, considering migration at the national level, many studies focused on the UK ($n = 28$), with Scotland studied as a separate area in one article. Although to a lesser extent, The Netherlands ($n = 12$), France ($n = 9$), Germany ($n = 7$), the Nordic countries – Finland, Denmark, Norway, and Sweden – ($n = 17$), and Belgium ($n = 11$) were fairly well-researched too. Among articles focusing on Belgium, six looked at the country as a whole, and five focused on Flanders. While most research focused on just one single country, 13 articles compared European countries to one another, and European countries to non-European ones (e.g., Cameroon, Turkey, and the United States).

Among articles investigating migration as a process, 14 researched immigration, three studied migration, and one looked at processes of refuge. In those articles, immigration and migration were looked at as general issues, and thus were not linked to individuals per se. In addition, 16 articles did not specify the direction of migration and explored the topic from a theoretical perspective. Other than looking at migration as a process or concept, 55 studies

(61.79 percent) focused on migrants as individuals. Out of these articles, 54 focused on *im*migrants and only one looked at *e*migrants. While some authors used the term immigrant as a collective concept, others focused on specific sub-communities, including Muslim, African, Black, Turkish, Roma, Arab, Moroccan, and Irish immigrants. Beyond references to *im*migrants, some authors particularly spoke about migrants (n = 11), asylum-seekers (n = 9), and refugees (n = 7), though using these terms as generic categories without associating them with any nationality. Asylum-seekers were identified as "boat people" on two occasions in the context of the recent Mediterranean/refugee crisis.

Regarding methodological frameworks, 50 (56.18 percent) of all the articles we analyzed used a qualitative approach. Among those qualitative studies, discourse analysis (n = 6), critical discourse analysis (n = 5), content analysis (n = 5), framing (n = 5), and textual analysis (n = 4) were the most commonly used methods. Only 18 articles (20.22 percent) within the entire dataset used quantitative methods, predominantly content analysis (n = 9). While most articles used a single method, eight articles (8.98 percent) used a mixed-method approach. Those articles, for the most part, conducted qualitative and quantitative content analysis (n = 5). Finally, two articles were theoretical, and 11 (12.36 percent) did not specify their methodological approach at all.

Lastly, despite a great variety of topics, four main lines of research appeared across the whole dataset. The first topical line captured the media coverage, portrayal, and representation of various minority groups. Within this research domain, attention was focused on the potential effects of media coverage on perceptions of and attitudes towards migrants. A second line of research dealt with the interplay between media and audiences using two main approaches. On the one hand, the role of different media was studied with regard to migrants' integration processes, the reinforcement of stereotypes, diversity and migration promotion, the production and circulation of feared Islamization, and the construction of national multicultural consensus. On the other hand, studies explored the role of migrants in producing and participating in alternative media, their use of media to maintain relationships and to feel at home in the new environment, differences of media usage between migrants and natives, and migrants' self-initiated seeking of media attention. The third important line of research tackled discourse related to migration and concomitant issues. Such studies explored media discourse of integration, interculturality, discrimination, marginalization, terrorism, and national identity. In addition, the construction of national identity, national-selves, and racism in public discourses were significant themes within this research domain. Finally, the fourth line of research included studies exploring media framing from various perspectives, including the framing of asylum-seekers, multiculturalism, and human trafficking in the media. Additionally, the degree of influence media framing holds over political agenda-setting was explored, oftentimes related to generated public sentiment towards migrants. Lastly, articles within this research area looked at framing in regard to its effect on migrants. These four overarching themes were present throughout the data among closely- and moderately-related articles alike. A more detailed account of the topics identified in the data will be presented hereafter, starting with the themes identified as closely related.

Discussion of the closely-related themes

Studies that dealt primarily with (im)migration and (im)migrants were grouped together as "closely related" and read through thoroughly to identify the themes they covered. Table 12.2 provides an overview of the main research areas and their salience.

Table 12.2 Identified themes among the closely-related articles (n = 51) in the dataset

Closely–related themes	*n*	%
Immigrants' representation/framing in the media	13	14.61
Discourses about migration issues	12	13.48
Immigrants' media use for specific purposes	8	8.99
Ethnic/minority media	8	8.99
Stereotypes in the media	7	7.86
Visual representations of refugees/asylum-seekers	3	3.37
Total	**51**	**57.30**

Note. For each article, the most prominently present theme was coded. As a result, the total number of themes identified (N = 89; n "closely related" = 51, n "moderately related" = 38) equals the number of articles analyzed.

As expected, many articles (n = 13) dealt with the frames used to represent (im)migrants in the media. Most articles within this theme investigated newspapers (n = 9) while one article focused on the radio and three on television. Overall, three main areas of research were identified within this theme: representations of (1) immigrants (n = 5), (2) asylum-seekers (n = 4), and (3) potential effects of migrants' representations in public debates (n = 4). Few studies investigating the framing of immigrants focused on specific groups (e.g., Thorbjørnsrud and Ustad Figenschou's (2016) study of unauthorized migrants), while most studies took a broad approach with no clear immigrant target groups. Studies measuring the effects of frames were divided among two main lines of research by either exploring political agendas (i.e., to what extent does media discourse on migrants affect political decisions and/elections) or public perceptions of migrants (i.e., to what extent does media discourse on migrants affect people's attitudes towards migrants).

Articles focusing on asylum-seekers presented different frames utilized by the media and how they were constructed. Horsti (2013), for instance, discussed the construction of asylum-seekers as victims through a concomitant process of both de-religionizing and de-racializing them. Overall, findings from studies on asylum-seekers presented traditionally dominant frames (i.e., ambivalence between asylum-seekers as *threats* and *victims*) (Long, 2013; Nyers, 2013), and sometimes discussed these in relation to media genre. Matthews and Brown (2011), for instance, drew attention to the overtly negative tone of tabloid discourse on asylum-seekers. A few studies (n = 3) also tackled the topic of forced migration by investigating visual representations of refugees and asylum-seekers. Out of these, two articles explored visual depictions of "boat people" during the recent Mediterranean/refugee crisis (e.g., Musarò, 2016).

Among articles looking at immigrants' representations in the media, few (n = 7) specifically focused on stereotypical discourses and portrayals. These studies tackled the processes of essentialization and homogenization through which stereotypes and monolithic views of cultures and communities were constructed (e.g., Schneider, 2001). Some of the studies within this theme also explored ways in which the media could challenge reified perceptions of cultures (e.g., Zambon, 2016). Out of these seven articles, six were based on textual or discursive analysis of media texts and only one on interviews with media practitioners (i.e., Klein, 2011). This imbalance is recurrent throughout the dataset and underlines the tendency of the media studies reviewed for this chapter to focus on content and reception rather than on processes preceding and accompanying production.

Many articles (*n* = 12) also explored media discourse on migration. Within this topic, attention was drawn to multilingualism, multiculturalism, and/or cultural diversity (*n* = 7). For instance, Signer, Puppis, and Piga (2011) investigated linguistic practices and policies within the multilingual Swiss media landscape. Their findings suggested that linguistic minorities and migrants are underserved by media content fitting their lingua-cultural backgrounds. Besides addressing multilingualism, studies tackled discourses of migration in relation to integration policies. Two articles considered multiculturalism in British media discourse during the London 2012 Olympic Games. These studies paid attention to this media event and its national resonance by investigating how discourses of multiculturalism were intertwined with positive national narratives and representations of Britishness (e.g., Black, 2016).

Another prominent area of research dealt with immigrants' media use (*n* = 8). Within this theme, four articles focused on the interplay between identity formation and ICT. These articles showed the importance of ICT as a medium for immigrants to maintain contact with relatives and friends back home (e.g., Bonini, 2011) while highlighting the different facets involved in this process. Burrell and Anderson's (2008) ethnographic study underlined the plurality of immigrants' ethnic identities and homes due to multiple migration experiences or relations to diasporic communities. In the same study, the authors showed that media use is not only a tool for immigrants to look back but also an instrument for them to look forward. Through their media uses, participants in Burrell and Anderson study were able to build their social capital as immigrants by developing a varied international network and making empowering choices regarding their present and future migratory experiences. Overall, the topic of media use was often studied in relation to power structures and whether those tended to be reproduced or challenged. Some studies discussed the ambivalent influence of media on migrants' social status. Kim (2016), for example, explored how mobile phones may, on the one hand, facilitate migrants' employment but, on the other hand, re-emphasize their subjection to workplace power imbalances. In another study, Kang (2012) explored the intersection between gender roles, digital skills, and power structures among transnational families. Kang's (2012) study showed that digitally competent men tend to take the lead while communicating with their offspring living abroad. Remarkably, silencing of and restrictions imposed on older women were found to modify the traditional feminine roles of looking after and bringing together families in this study.

In a few articles, the topic of media use was tightly connected to the theme of ethnic and minority media (*n* = 8). Two articles within that theme focused on the relation between ethnic media and immigrants' adaptation paths (e.g., Arnold & Schneider, 2007). All other articles (*n* = 6) paid attention to the type of content produced (e.g., overlaps between national and transnational products) and its importance in giving immigrants a voice to position themselves within host societies (e.g., Macgilchrist & Böhmig, 2012; Ogunyemi, 2007). Overall, articles exploring ethnic/minority media emphasized the active role played by immigrants in Europe as both media users and producers. These articles also underlined migrants' presence as engaged nationals who endeavor to make their voices heard in the public sphere. These studies therefore contrasted with most other themes in the data, which often examined what was said about migrants rather than what they said themselves. Though it is a fundamental necessity to tackle issues of (mis)representation, their dominance within media studies may contribute to the construction of migration as a phenomenon of importance for hosts and media users rather than for migrants themselves.

Discussion of the moderately-related themes

Of all the articles we analyzed, 38 (42.7 percent) were coded as being only moderately related to the topic of migration within and to Europe. Although these articles discussed phenomena relevant to the research topic, they remained quite implicit in their references to migration and/or migrants. Articles were grouped into three main categories that illustrated how these articles indirectly dealt with migration and migrants within and to Europe (see Table 12.3: (1) articles using migration as a background and/or discussing a related phenomenon, (2) articles describing migration in political discourse, and (3) articles discussing journalistic approaches to minority culture.

First, 13 out of the 38 moderately-related articles (14.60 percent of the whole dataset) dealt with migration and/or migrants to briefly embed the topic of primary focus. For example, Marchionni (2012) referred to asylum-seekers and refugees while providing a background to the phenomenon of human trafficking as discussed by elite press, i.e., within leading newspapers such as the *Washington Post*, the *New York Times, The Guardian*, and *The Times*. However, the outcomes of her study limitedly focused on the politics of sex trafficking, lacking clear reference to the migrant background of the victims of human trafficking. In an article by Hoops, Thomas, and Drzewiecka (2016), the manifestation of the migrant subject seemed more articulated. Still, media representations of Polish immigrants in the UK press were analyzed only instrumentally, i.e., to address the broader issue of neoliberalism and nationalist discourse in the British media. These two examples illustrate how a variety of research topics investigated by media scientists over the past decade did indeed loosely relate to the phenomenon of migration in Europe. This is not surprising, as in our globalizing world, migrants co-feature in multiple transnational processes with which the media have had to deal. Remarkably, though, the saliency of migration as a related topic of interest oftentimes lacked explicit recognition in the scholarly articles we analyzed. We conclude that, in multiple cases, immigration discourse has failed to be holistically addressed in the broader contexts of transnational media research.

Second, 11 of the moderately related articles (representing 12.36 percent of the whole dataset) were concerned with migration as something political programs and/or politicians take on. Instead of questioning the direct influences of media discourse on political processes (something discussed as a theme closely related to the topic of migration in Europe), these articles dealt rather implicitly with the intersections between media and political discourse in two distinct ways. First, some of the articles questioned how media venues covered or dealt with migration debates in the political sphere. Still, the primary goal of these articles was to explore how media logics facilitated political messaging and party popularity. Migration and migrants were only referred to as being part of the political agendas prone to media

Table 12.3 Identified themes among moderately-related articles (n = 38) in the dataset

Moderately-related themes	*n*	*%*
On the topic of race/ethnicity and hinting at migrants on few occasions	14	15.73
Phenomenon relevant to migration but not studied directly in relation to migration or migrants	13	14.61
Migration/migrants as something politics talks about	11	12.36
Total	**38**	**42.70**

influences. In another article, Sevenans and Vliegenthart (2016) explored the extent to which conflict framing of immigration in the media moderated agenda-setting in the political sphere. They concluded that the media had played a significant part in determining the primacy of migration questions in the Dutch and Belgian parliaments. As another example, Herkman (2017) explored how the life cycle of Nordic populist parties developed according to the media attention they received. As expected, in both of these articles, some (right-wing) parties' outspoken criticism of immigration was touched upon. However, describing changes in migration rhetoric was rather subordinate to the investigation of media influences on political viability.

Contrasting this focus on persuasive media logic, some articles approached the mediatization of migration issues from a political perspective. Within this strand of research, articles, for instance, explored to what extent politicians deliberately used media to communicate their opinions on immigration and migrant communities. In those cases, the political usage of media logic was the main topic of interest. Yet, as we observed in the previous examples as well, migration issues nevertheless received considerable attention. Atton (2006), for example, analyzed how the British National Party (BNP) utilized its website to socialize supportive audiences into accepting racial policies. Since immigration rhetoric predominantly defined the BNP's agenda, the scientific analysis of statements online transmitted primarily targeted the mediatization of migration politics. Similarly, analyzing the development of the French Front National's online platform, Bratten (2005) primarily aimed to explore transitions in mediatized immigration discourse rather than focus on the migration debate itself.

These examples illustrate how migration politics were not the primary focus in 11 studies regarding political discourse in the data, though migration was nonetheless touched upon. Interpreting this finding, we might argue that the attention given to anti-immigrant politics in media research over the past two decades concerned a rather latent consequence of shifts in Western European political landscapes, which are described by Rydgren (2007). The increased popularity of radical right-wing parties, thriving on anti-migration politics, has directed the study of mediatized politics towards an analysis of migration-related content. Still, the attention given to migration and migrants in these articles has often just been of instrumental value to the broader topic of right-wing political mediatization. For this reason, these articles were categorized as being only moderately related to the topic of migration and migrants within and to Europe.

Lastly, 14 out of the 38 moderately-related articles (15.73 percent of the whole dataset) dealt with the way journalists handled topics related to minorities. Even though migrants were mentioned occasionally, migration as a journalistic theme was not saliently present. Instead, the authors focused on how the press approached tensions and questions arising in European multicultural societies. Specifically, these studies examined representations of ethnic, racial, and religious/extremist themes in the press, overlooking the category "migrant" as the primary definer of their background. The following two examples illustrate how migrant-related topics were framed as religious or racial discourse studies in many of the retrieved articles. First, an article written by Triandafyllidou (2009) dealt with the framing of the religious cartoon crisis in media artifacts stemming from the UK and Greece, two countries identified in her study as hosting migrant communities from Islamic countries. This article focused on European values in a transnational discursive space, a topic that can inherently be traced back to the process of (Muslim) migration to the European continent. However, the emphasis on migrant communities in this article was replaced by a focus on Europe's struggle with *religious* identity claims. In another article, by Darling-Wolf (2008), the author chose to explore how in France (and in the United States) *racial* relations are negotiated in reportage on hurricane Katrina (the US) and riots (France). Despite the relation between the sensitivity of racial reportage in France and the multi-colored composition of its migratory population, only a few references were made to the migration background of the country's racially diverse population. Acknowledging the remarkable discursive shifts in migrant-related referencing, the concluding discussion will explicitly touch upon its implications for future research.

Concluding remarks

The present literature review allows us to draw some conclusions regarding (1) methodological issues and (2) the scope of topics characterizing journal articles on migration in Europe over the past two decades as ascertained by studies. First, we found that 11 studies (12.36 percent) did not clearly specify which methodological approaches they used. This draws attention to a larger issue underlying the observed lack of transparency in scientific publications (Morse, Barrett, Mayan, Olson, & Spiers, 2002) and the need to further insist on sharing how data are dealt with and how findings are obtained. The importance of ensuring methodological transparency is further emphasized by the dominance of qualitative research in our sample (i.e., 56.18 percent of all articles reviewed). This echoes a common criticism of qualitative research that does not account for the subjectivities entailed in this methodology (Noble & Smith, 2015), even though transparency has been elevated as a central tool to ensure credible and reliable research (Silverman, 2011).

Second, we found that a vast majority of studies analyzed media content and very few studies investigated processes associated with the production thereof. The attention paid to processes of media creation mostly came from studies looking at ethnic and minority media (n = 8), which, however, represented only 8.98 percent of the overall dataset. The scarcity of studies looking at how media practitioners make decisions and reflect on their professional choices urges for future research that connects media discourse to concrete editorial and journalistic practices. An important direction for future studies is to challenge understandings of media discourses as floating and pre-existing entities.

Overall, we collected 100 articles, out of which 89 were connected to the topic of migrants and migration within and to Europe. Considering the substantive coverage of the Mediterranean/refugee crisis in the media over recent years (Hoyer, 2016), we expected a noticeable number of journal articles to reflect on this media coverage. However, in total, only three articles focused on the recent arrival of refugees in Europe. The timeframe used for data collection might explain this small number and we expect many more studies to be published on this topic in coming years.

The dataset used for this study turned out to be very small, at least in comparison to the vast number of studies focusing on migration beyond the European context. First, it could be that the discussion of migration within and to Europe in the media has not primarily taken place in publications from the field of Media Studies, but rather in publications related to sociology and migration. Despite our aim of studying the topic of migration within and to Europe as a dynamic, multi-directional process, binary understandings of migration oftentimes predominated in journal articles. Within the topic of migration to Europe, most articles focused on non-European immigrants while migration within Europe was hardly tackled. This could mean that migration within European countries is understudied or categorized using different terms (e.g., expatriates, international students, transboundary commuting), and therefore not identified by the scope of this literature review. Future studies should therefore reconsider the use of different and/or truncated search terms that may account for the limited number of migration references found without researchers being aware of it. Nevertheless, the overt attention paid to migration from outside of Europe that was noticed in the current study already supports the idea that media studies, in anticipation of (mass-)media patterns, contribute to constructing migration as a phenomenon experienced by European *hosts* and non-European *migrants*. Associated with this issue is the lack of research looking at emigration. The construction of immigration as predominantly a non-European experience also relates to the terms used to describe immigrants. This literature review indeed draws attention to the relation between the notions of race, ethnicity, and religion and the topic of migration.

Assessing the literature from the past two decades gives us opportunities to reflect on the evolution of the dichotomous separation between migrants and hosts. Specifically, discourse (in academia and the media) seems to have evolved from migrant/non-migrant denominations to racial/non-racial and religious/non-religious categories. It has been interesting to observe that migration-related topics were framed either ethno-racially or religiously within a considerable number of articles. Since the studies we analyzed themselves reflected on journalist artifacts, this observation could point to a more general journalistic shift of framing. In their study of the Dutch press, Roggeband and Vliegenthart (2007) observed that migrants (or their offspring) are recurrently framed as belonging to the Islamic denomination post 9/11. Especially the Muslim identity, as a fixed and visible minority label, has nowadays become a salient social category that outweighs the importance of its members' additional identities and backgrounds (Modood, 2003; Sommier, 2017). Building on these observations in the Dutch media context, we could expect that the binary opposition of migrants versus non-migrants has become outdated and been replaced by a focus on more specific cultural identifiers across the European press. The suggested shift from the migrant category to religious, cultural, and racial denominations hints at the construction of immigrants as *others* and positions them outside of the European imagined community. Such a substitution of migration terminology might explain the limited relatedness of many articles to the topic of migration to Europe. Moreover, we might have to consider implications of racial and religious references as proxies for the migrant category in future research. It would be interesting to explore whether media scientists increasingly endorse religious identity, ethno-racial frames as well. That is, future research should explore whether the racialization of Islamic religion in the media is further reified and stabilized in both academic and public discourse.

References

Arnold, A. K. & Schneider, B. (2007). Communicating separation? Ethnic media and ethnic journalists as institutions of integration in Germany. *Journalism, 8*, 115–136.

Atton, C. (2006). Far-right media on the internet: Culture, discourse and power. *New Media and Society, 8*, 573–587.

Black, J. (2016). "As British as fish and chips": British newspaper representations of Mo Farah during the 2012 London Olympic Games. *Media, Culture & Society, 38*, 979–996.

Bonini, T. (2011). The media as "home-making" tools: Life story of a Filipino migrant in Milan. *Media, Culture & Society, 33*, 869–883.

Bratten, L. C. (2005). Online zealotry: La France du peuple virtuel. *New Media and Society*, 7, 517–532.

Brug, W. van der, D'Amato, G., Ruedin, D., & Berkhout, J. (Eds.). (2015). *The politicisation of migration*. London: Routledge.

Burrell, J. & Anderson, K. (2008). I have great desires to look beyond my world: Trajectories of information and communication technology use among Ghanaians living abroad. *New Media & Society, 10*, 203–224.

Darling-Wolf, F. (2008). Holier than thou. *Journalism Studies, 9*, 357–373.

Herkman, J. (2017). The life cycle model and press coverage of Nordic populist parties. *Journalism Studies, 18*, 430–448.

Hoops, J. F., Thomas, R. J., & Drzewiecka, J. A. (2016). Polish "pawns" between nationalism and neoliberalism in British newspaper coverage of post-European Union enlargement Polish immigration. *Journalism, 17*, 727–743.

Horsti, K. (2013). De-ethnicized victims: Mediatized advocacy for asylum seekers. *Journalism, 14*, 78–95.

Hoyer, A. (2016). *Spanish news framing of the Syrian refugee crisis*. WWU Honors Program Senior Projects, 26. Retrieved from http://cedar.wwu.edu/wwu_honors/26.

Kang, T. (2012). Gendered media, changing intimacy: Internet-mediated transnational communication in the family sphere. *Media, Culture & Society, 34*, 146–161.

Kim, Y. (2016). Mobile phone for empowerment? Global nannies in Paris. *Media, Culture & Society, 38*, 525–539.

Klein, B. (2011). Entertaining ideas: Social issues in entertainment television. *Media, Culture & Society, 33*, 905–921.

Long, K. (2013). When refugees stopped being migrants: Movement, labour and humanitarian protection. *Migration Studies, 1*, 4–26.

Macgilchrist, F. & Böhmig, I. (2012). Blogs, genes and immigration: Online media and minimal politics. *Media, Culture & Society, 34*, 83–100.

Marchionni, D. M. (2012). International human trafficking: An agenda-building analysis of the US and British press. *International Communication Gazette, 74*, 145–158.

Matthews, J. & Brown, A. R. (2011). Negatively shaping the asylum agenda? The representational strategy and impact of a tabloid news campaign. *Journalism, 13*, 802–817.

Modood, T. (2003). Muslims and the politics of difference. *Political Quarterly, 74*, 100–115.

Morse, J. M., Barrett, M., Mayan, M., Olson, K., & Spiers, J. (2002). Verification strategies for establishing reliability and validity in qualitative research. *International Journal of Qualitative Methods, 1*, 13–22.

Musarò, P. (2016). Mare Nostrum: The visual politics of a military-humanitarian operation in the Mediterranean Sea. *Media, Culture & Society, 39*, 11–28.

Noble, H. & Smith, J. (2015). Issues of validity and reliability in qualitative research. *Evidence-Based Nursing, 18*, 34–35.

Nyers, P. (2013). *Rethinking refugees: Beyond state of emergency*. New York: Routledge.

Ogunyemi, O. (2007). The black popular press. *Journalism Studies, 8*, 13–27.

Pendlebury, D. A. (2008). The use and misuse of journal metrics and other citation indicators. *Archivum Immunologiae et Therapiae Experimentalis, 57*, 1–11.

Roggeband, C. & Vliegenthart, R. (2007). Divergent framing: The public debate on migration in the Dutch parliament and media, 1995–2004. *Western European Politics, 30*, 524–548.

Rydgren, J. (2007). The sociology of the radical right. *Annual Review of Sociology, 33*, 241–262.

Schneider, J. (2001). Talking German: Othering strategies in public and everyday discourses. *International Communication Gazette, 63*, 351–363.

Sevenans, J. & Vliegenthart, R. (2016). Political agenda-setting in Belgium and the Netherlands: The moderating role of conflict framing. *Journalism & Mass Communication Quarterly, 93*, 187–203.

Signer, S., Puppis, M., & Piga, A. (2011). Minorities, integration and the media: Media regulation and media performance in multicultural and multilingual Switzerland. *International Communication Gazette, 73*, 419–439.

Silverman, D. (2011). *Interpreting qualitative data. A guide to the principles of qualitative research* (4th ed.). London: Sage.

Sommier, M. (2017). Representations of individuals in discourses of laïcité from *Le Monde*: Confirming or challenging the republican framework of identity? *Social Identities, 23*, 232–247.

Thorbjørnsrud, K. & Ustad Figenschou, T. (2016). Do marginalized sources matter? *Journalism Studies, 17*, 337–355.

Triandafyllidou, A. (2009). The Mohammed cartoon crisis in the British and Greek press. *Journalism Studies, 10*, 36–53.

Zambon, K. (2016). Negotiating new German identities: Transcultural comedy and the construction of pluralistic unity. *Media, Culture & Society, 39*, 1–16.

Appendix: Articles (*N* = 89) used for data analysis

Closely-related articles

Abadi, D., d'Haenens, L., Roe, K., & Koeman, J. (2016). Leitkultur and discourse hegemonies: German mainstream media coverage on the integration debate between 2009 and 2014. *International Communication Gazette, 78*, 557–584.

Arnold, A. K. & Schneider, B. (2007). Communicating separation? Ethnic media and ethnic journalists as institutions of integration in Germany. *Journalism, 8*, 115–136.

Balch, A. & Balabanova, E. (2011). A system in chaos? Knowledge and sense-making on immigration policy in public debates. *Media, Culture & Society, 33*, 885–904.

Black, J. (2016). "As British as fish and chips": British newspaper representations of Mo Farah during the 2012 London Olympic Games. *Media, Culture & Society, 38*, 979–996.

Bonini, T. (2011). The media as "home-making" tools: Life story of a Filipino migrant in Milan. *Media, Culture & Society, 33*, 869–883.

Burrell, J. (2008). "I have great desires to look beyond my world": Trajectories of information and communication technology use among Ghanaians living abroad. *New Media & Society, 10*, 203–224.

Castelló, E., Dobson, N., & O'Donnell, H. (2009). Telling it like it is? Social and linguistic realism in Scottish and Catalan soaps. *Media, Culture & Society, 31*, 467–484.

Chalaby, J. K. (2005). Deconstructing the transnational: A typology of cross-border television channels in Europe. *New Media & Society*, 7, 155–175.

Croucher, S. M., Oommen, D., Borton, I., Anarbaeva, S., & Turner, J. S. (2010). The influence of religiosity and ethnic identification on media use among Muslims and non-Muslims in France and Britain. *Mass Communication and Society, 13*, 314–334.

Dekavalla, M. (2016). Framing referendum campaigns: The 2014 Scottish independence referendum in the press. *Media, Culture & Society, 38*, 793–810.

Dolan, P. (2014). Cultural cosmopolitanization and the politics of television in 1960s Ireland. *Media, Culture & Society, 36*, 952–965.

Domínguez, M., Pineda, F., & Mateu, A. (2014). Life in a nutshell: Evolution of a migratory metaphor in Spanish cartoons. *Media, Culture & Society, 36*, 810–825.

Dzięglewski, M. (2016). The economic, social and ontological security of Polish post-accession migrants in popular media narratives. *Media, Culture & Society, 38*, 827–843.

Echchaibi, N. (2001). We are French too, but different: Radio, music and the articulation of difference among young North Africans in France. *International Communication Gazette, 63*, 295–310.

Eckert, S. & Chadha, K. (2013). Muslim bloggers in Germany: An emerging counter public. *Media, Culture & Society, 35*, 926–942.

Giglou, I. R., Ogan, O., & D'Haenens, L. (2016). The ties that bind the diaspora to Turkey and Europe during the Gezi protests. *New Media & Society*, 1–19.

Gorp, B. van (2005). Where is the frame? Victims and intruders in the Belgian press coverage of the asylum issue. *European Journal of Communication, 20*, 484–507.

Horsti, K. (2013). De-ethnicized victims: Mediatized advocacy for asylum seekers. *Journalism, 14*, 78–95.

Igartua, J.-J. & Cheng, L. (2009). Moderating effect of group cue while processing news on immigration: Is the framing effect a heuristic process? *Journal of Communication, 59*, 726–749.

Ihlen, O. & Thorbjornsrud, K. (2014). Making news and influencing decisions: Three threshold cases concerning forced return of immigrants. *European Journal of Communication, 29*, 139–152.

Jacobs, L., Claes, E., & Hooghe, M. (2015). The occupational roles of women and ethnic minorities on primetime television in Belgium: An analysis of occupational status measurements. *Mass Communication and Society, 18*, 498–521.

Jacobs, L., Meeusen, C., & d'Haenens, L. (2016). News coverage and attitudes on immigration: Public and commercial television news compared. *European Journal of Communication, 31*, 642–660.

Kang, T. (2012). Gendered media, changing intimacy: Internet-mediated transnational communication in the family sphere. *Media, Culture & Society, 34*, 146–161.

Kim, Y. (2016). Mobile phone for empowerment? Global nannies in Paris. *Media, Culture & Society, 38*, 525–539.

Klein, B. (2011). Entertaining ideas: Social issues in entertainment television. *Media, Culture & Society, 33*, 905–921.
Kroon, A., Kluknavská, A., Vliegenthart, R., & Boomgaarden, H. (2016). Victims or perpetrators? Explaining media framing of Roma across Europe. *European Journal of Communication, 31*, 375–392.
Lecheler, S., Bos, L., & Vliegenthart, R. (2015). The mediating role of emotions: News framing effects on opinions about immigration. *Journalism & Mass Communication Quarterly, 92*, 812–838.
Macdonald, M. (2007). Television debate, interactivity and public opinion: The case of the BBC's "Asylum Day". *Media, Culture & Society, 29*, 679–689.
Macgilchrist, F. & Böhmig, I. (2012). Blogs, genes and immigration: Online media and minimal politics. *Media, Culture & Society, 34*, 83–100.
Matthews, J. & Brown, A. R. (2011). Negatively shaping the asylum agenda? The representational strategy and impact of a tabloid news campaign. *Journalism, 13*, 802–817.
Meeusen, C. & Jacobs, L. (2016). Television news content of minority groups as an intergroup context indicator of differences between target-specific prejudices. *Mass Communication and Society, 20*, 1–28.
Moore, K. (2013). "Asylum shopping" in the neoliberal social imaginary. *Media, Culture & Society, 35*, 348–365.
Musarò, P. (2016). Mare Nostrum: The visual politics of a military-humanitarian operation in the Mediterranean Sea. *Media, Culture & Society, 39*, 11–28.
Ndangam, L. N. (2008). Free lunch? Cameroon's diaspora and online news publishing. *New Media & Society, 10*, 585–604.
Ogunyemi, O. (2007). The black popular press. *Journalism Studies, 8*, 13–27.
Pas, D. van der (2014). Making hay while the sun shines: Do parties only respond to media attention when the framing is right? *International Journal of Press/Politics, 19*, 42–65.
Philo, G. (2002). Television news and audience understanding of war, conflict and disaster. *Journalism Studies, 3*, 173–186.
Pineda, A., Garcia-Jimenez, L., & Rodrigo-Alsina, M. (2016). I believe they felt attacked. Discursive representation and construction of interculturality in Spanish news television. *International Communication Gazette, 78*, 585–605.
Polson, E. & Kahle, S. (2010). Limits of national discourse on a transnational phenomenon: A case study of immigration framing on the BBC Online. *International Communication Gazette, 72*, 251–268.
Rogers, J., O'Boyle, N., Preston, P., & Fehr, F. (2014). The significance of small differences: Cultural diversity and broadcasting in Ireland. *European Journal of Communication, 29*, 399–415.
Ross, K. (2004). Political talk radio and democratic participation: Caller perspectives on Election Call. *Media, Culture & Society, 26*, 785–801.
Schneeweis, A. (2012). If they really wanted to, they would: The press discourse of integration of the European Roma, 1990–2006. *International Communication Gazette, 74*, 673–689.
Schneider, J. (2001). Talking German: Othering strategies in public and everyday discourses. *International Communication Gazette, 63*, 351–363.
Shaw, I. S. (2012). Stereotypical representations of Muslims and Islam following the 7/7 London terror attacks: Implications for intercultural communication and terrorism prevention. *International Communication Gazette, 74*, 509–524.
Signer, S., Puppis, M., & Piga, A. (2011). Minorities, integration and the media: Media regulation and media performance in multicultural and multilingual Switzerland. *International Communication Gazette, 73*, 419–439.
Silk, M. (2014). "Isles of wonder": Performing the mythopoeia of utopic multi-ethnic Britain. *Media, Culture & Society, 37*, 68–84.
Smets, K. (2016). Ethnic media, conflict, and the nation-state: Kurdish broadcasting in Turkey and Europe and mediated nationhood. *Media, Culture & Society, 38*, 738–754.
Thorbjørnsrud, K. & Ustad Figenschou, T. (2016). Do marginalized sources matter? *Journalism Studies, 17*, 337–355.
Vliegenthart, R. & Roggeband, C. (2007). Framing immigration and integration: Relationships between press and parliament in the Netherlands. *International Communication Gazette, 69*, 295–319.
Wakeford, N. (2003). The embedding of local culture in global communication: Independent internet cafés in London. *New Media & Society, 5*, 379–399.
Zambon, K. (2016). Negotiating new German identities: Transcultural comedy and the construction of pluralistic unity. *Media, Culture & Society, 39*, 552–567.

Moderately-related articles

Ashuri, T. (2007). Television tension: National versus cosmopolitan memory in a co-produced television documentary. *Media, Culture & Society*, *29*, 31–51.

Atton, C. (2006). Far-right media on the internet: Culture, discourse and power. *New Media & Society*, *8*, 573–587.

Awad, I. (2012). Desperately constructing ethnic audiences: Anti-immigration discourses and minority audience research in the Netherlands. *European Journal of Communication*, *28*, 168–182.

Banaji, S. & Cammaerts, B. (2015). Citizens of nowhere land. *Journalism Studies*, *16*, 115–132.

Berkowitz, D. & Eko, L. (2007). Blasphemy as sacred right/rite. *Journalism Studies*, *8*, 779–797.

Bratten, L. C. (2005). Online zealotry: La France du peuple virtuel. *New Media & Society*, *7*, 517–532.

D' Haenes, L., Koeman, J., & Saeys, F. (2007). Digital citizenship among ethnic minority youths in the Netherlands and Flanders. *New Media & Society*, *9*, 278–299.

Darling-Wolf, F. (2008). Holier than thou. *Journalism Studies*, *9*, 357–373.

Driessens, O., Joye, S., & Biltereyst, D. (2012). The X-factor of charity: A critical analysis of celebrities' involvement in the 2010 Flemish and Dutch Haiti relief shows. *Media, Culture & Society*, *34*, 709–725.

Ekström, M. & Johansson, B. (2008). Talk scandals. *Media, Culture & Society*, *30*, 61–79.

Eriksson, M. (2015). Managing collective trauma on social media: The role of Twitter after the 2011 Norway attacks. *Media, Culture & Society*, *38*, 365–380.

Figenschou, T. U. & Beyer, A. (2014). The limits of the debate: How the Oslo terror shook the Norwegian immigration debate. *International Journal of Press/Politics*, *19*, 430–452.

Hatakka, N. (2016). When logics of party politics and online activism collide: The populist Finns Party's identity under negotiation. *New Media & Society*, 1–17.

Herkman, J. (2015). The life cycle model and press coverage of Nordic populist parties. *Journalism Studies*, *18*, 430–448.

Hoops, J. F., Thomas, R. J., & Drzewiecka, J. A. (2016). Polish "pawns" between nationalism and neoliberalism in British newspaper coverage of post-European Union enlargement Polish immigration. *Journalism*, *17*, 727–743.

Horsti, K. (2016). Digital Islamophobia: The Swedish woman as a figure of pure and dangerous whiteness. *New Media & Society*, *19*, 1–18.

Jansson, A. (2002). Spatial phantasmagoria: The mediatization of tourism experience. *European Journal of Communication*, *17*, 429–443.

Kuppens, A. & Mast, J. (2012). Ticket to the Tribes: Culture shock and the "exotic" in intercultural reality television. *Media, Culture & Society*, *34*, 799–814.

Marchionni, D. M. (2012). International human trafficking: An agenda-building analysis of the US and British press. *International Communication Gazette*, *74*, 145–158.

Meer, N. (2006). "Get off your knees." *Journalism Studies*, *7*, 35–59.

Men, J. (2016). Chinese media in Brussels and EU–China relations. *International Communication Gazette*, *78*, 9–25.

Nickels, H., Thomas, L., Hickman, M., & Silvestri, S. (2012). Constructing "suspect" communities and Britishness: Mapping British press coverage of Irish and Muslim communities, 1974–2007. *European Journal of Communication*, *27*, 135–151.

Nickels, H. C., Thomas, L., Hickman, M. J., & Silvestri, S. (2012). De/constructing "suspect" communities: A critical discourse analysis of British newspaper coverage of Irish and Muslim communities, 1974–2007. *Journalism Studies*, *13*, 340–355.

Ogan, C., Willnat, L., Pennington, R., & Bashir, M. (2014). The rise of anti-Muslim prejudice: Media and Islamophobia in Europe and the United States. *International Communication Gazette*, *76*, 27–46.

Pantti, M. & Wieten, J. (2005). Mourning becomes the nation: Television coverage of the murder of Pim Fortuyn. *Journalism Studies*, *6*, 301–313.

Parry, K. (2011). Images of liberation? Visual framing, humanitarianism and British press photography during the 2003 Iraq invasion. *Media, Culture & Society*, *33*, 1185–1201.

Połońska-Kimunguyi, E. & Gillespie, M. (2016). European international broadcasting and Islamist terrorism in Africa: The case of Boko Haram on *France 24* and *Deutsche Welle*. *International Communication Gazette*, *9*, 1–31.

Poole, E. (2016). Constructing "British values" within a radicalisation narrative. *Journalism Studies*, *19*(3), 1–16.

Reijnders, S. (2005). The people's detective: True crime in Dutch folklore and popular television. *Media, Culture & Society*, *27*, 635–651.
Saha, A. (2012). "Beards, scarves, halal meat, terrorists, forced marriage": Television industries and the production of "race." *Media, Culture & Society*, *34*, 424–438.
Schemer, C. (2012). The influence of news media on stereotypic attitudes toward immigrants in a political campaign. *Journal of Communication*, *62*, 739–757.
Scott, M. (2009). Marginalized, negative or trivial? Coverage of Africa in the UK press. *Media, Culture & Society*, *31*, 533–557.
Sevenans, J. & Vliegenthart, R. (2016). Political agenda-setting in Belgium and the Netherlands: The moderating role of conflict framing. *Journalism & Mass Communication Quarterly*, *93*, 187–203.
Thomas, R. J. & Antony, M. G. (2015). Competing constructions of British national identity: British newspaper comment on the 2012 Olympics opening ceremony. *Media, Culture & Society*, *37*, 493–503.
Triandafyllidou, A. (2009). The Mohammed cartoon crisis in the British and Greek press. *Journalism Studies*, *10*, 36–53.
Van Sterkenburg, J., Knoppers, A., & De Leeuw, S. (2010). Race, ethnicity, and content analysis of the sports media: A critical reflection. *Media, Culture & Society*, *32*, 819–839.
Williams, A. E. & Toula, C. M. (2016). Solidarity framing at the union of national and transnational public spheres. *Journalism Studies*, 1–17. doi.org/10.1080/1461670X.2015.1134274.
Zoonen, L. van, Vis, F., & Mihely, S. (2011). YouTube interactions between agonism, antagonism and dialogue: Video responses to the anti-Islam film *Fitna*. *New Media & Society*, *13*, 1283–1300.

13

MEDIA PORTRAYAL OF MIGRATION FROM CENTRAL ASIA

Thematic analysis of Kyrgyz and Russian language online news media

Alena Zelenskaia & Elira Turdubaeva

Migrants overcome social isolation through the use of media. They communicate with their immediate family members and friends by means of social networks, and monitor home-based websites or press to stay tuned to events at home (see Ibraeva, 2016). On the other hand, the media outlets in their home countries never lose sight of their countrymen abroad, as is revealed by a quick search for articles on migration on news media sites. They follow the changes in migrants' legal and economic statuses in the host countries and collect stories about the everyday lives of compatriots, and do so with a certain degree of empathy. By presenting certain news stories, journalists form images about the migrants and migrant life for the citizens of the country of origin and among candidates for migration. According to King and Wood (2001), "media originating from the migration sending country . . . are playing a dynamic role in cultural identities and politics of diasporic communities" (p. 2).

The focus of this chapter is on how the mass media in Kyrgyzstan construct the phenomenon of migration from Central Asia to Russia and any other countries outside the region. When those from Central Asian republics are highly motivated to move for socio-economic reasons, the picture conveyed by journalists may communicate certain meanings and influence decision making. In recent years, numerous studies have been conducted on the news discourse on migration and images of Central Asian migrants in the Russian mass media (e.g., Khismatullina, Garaeva, & Akhmetzyanov, 2017; Nam et al., 2017; Saraeva, 2011), but there seems to be little research dealing with the images of the Central Asian migrants in their homelands. This chapter seeks to fill this gap and contribute to the body of work on mass media techniques for framing news stories on migration, in particular those from Central Asia. Embedded in the context of media effects research, this study also aims to reveal the key inputs of Kyrgyzstan news outlets in terms of the subsequent decision making (to migrate or not to migrate) and perception of countrymen participating "in migration."

After the collapse of the USSR, the Central Asian region was on the move, with part of its Slavic population migrating in the first flow in the 1990s and the successive migration of the so-called "aboriginal" population taking place in the early 2000s. Nowadays, the number of international migrants from five Central Asian republics – Kazakhstan, Kyrgyzstan, Tajikistan, Turkmenistan, and Uzbekistan – comprises around 5.5 million people (International Migration Report 2017, p. 26). This includes those who resettled permanently and acquired citizenship of the receiving countries as well as those who represent the group of seasonal or circular workers. Kyrgyzstan is deeply affected by this modern trend of migration from Central Asia. Along with Uzbek and Tajik, Kyrgyz migrants constitute a flow of up to 4.2 million people, working mainly in the Russian Federation, Kazakhstan, and other countries of the Commonwealth of Independent States (CIS) (Ryazantsev, 2016). Of these Central Asian countries, Kyrgyzstan has one of the largest migrant communities living outside the country, side by side with other Central Asian expatriates. Experts estimate that the number of Kyrgyz migrants working abroad ranges from 620,000 in 2010 to 1 million people in 2012 (Vinokurov, 2013, p. 2). According to unofficial estimates, about 1 million Kyrgyz migrants live in Russia alone, as the main receiving country. As a result, Central Asian migration remains high on the agenda of Kyrgyzstan's news media.

In comparison to other Central Asian migrants, Kyrgyz migrants are in a special position. In contrast to Uzbeks and Tajiks, Kyrgyz migrants find themselves in favorable circumstances after the accession to the Eurasian Economic Union (EAEU) in August 2015. The EAEU is a supranational organization, which covers five economies (Armenia, Belarus, Kazakhstan, Kyrgyzstan, and Russia), and "in the long term can be similar to the European Union" (Kubayeva, 2015, p. 3). This economic union, although often regarded as an ambitious geopolitical project of Russia, has the primary purposes of "providing legal framework for energy markets and free movement of labor" (ibid, p. 4). In line with the official goals of the union, one of the main pledges of the Kyrgyzstani government was that Kyrgyz migrants' lives within the borders of the EAEU would become easier in terms of regulation (i.e., President of the Kyrgyz Republic, 2015). It was impossible to respond negatively to such a promise because Kyrgyzstan is widely dependent on remittances and migration has a positive impact on the economy. Integration into the EAEU became "a solution to the problem of illegal migration [to Russia and Kazakhstan] by providing better conditions for migrants such as equal rights, healthcare and income" (Kubayeva, 2015, p. 11).

The accession of Kyrgyzstan to the EAEU set the sampling frame for this study. The data collected are taken from news media between January 2015 and May 2017 so as to include both the period before and after the accession. This was to ascertain (a) expectations regarding migration and (b) its perceived short- and long-term effects. The aim of our study is to reveal how the most visited news websites in Kyrgyzstan depict migration from Central Asia during the period of 2015–2017. It raises the following questions: What are the main themes to which journalists pay attention? Which sending and receiving countries are the focus of news stories and how are they portrayed? Are there differences in the coverage among selected online news resources? Are there differences between news coverage in Kyrgyz and Russian?

Theoretical framework

This study uses Entman's (1993) framing theory to analyze online news coverage of migration from Central Asia. According to Entman, framing involves "selecting some aspects of a perceived reality and mak[ing] them more salient in a communicating text, in such a way as to promote a particular problem definition, causal interpretation, moral evaluation, and/or treatment recommendation" (p. 52). Frames are constructed through the strategic use or omission of certain words and phrases (ibid). Certain frames are pertinent only to specific topics or events and may be labeled issue-specific frames. An issue-specific approach to the study of news frames allows for a profound level of specificity regarding details relevant to the event or issue under investigation.

Entman noted that frames have several locations, including the communicator, the text, the receiver, and the culture. These components are integral to a process of framing that consists of distinct stages: frame-building, frame-setting and investigating the individual- and societal-level consequences of framing. Frame-building refers to the factors that influence the structural qualities of news frames. Factors internal to journalism determine how journalists and news organizations frame issues. Equally important, however, are factors external to journalism. The frame-building process takes place in a continuous interaction between journalists and elites and social movements. The outcomes of the frame-building process are the frames manifest in the text.

Entman (p. 52) suggested that frames in the news can be examined and identified by "the presence or absence of certain keywords, stock phrases, stereotyped images, sources of information and sentences that provide thematically reinforcing clusters of facts or judgments." We also paid attention to other applicable operationalizations and took into account the four elements of frame analysis identified by Pan and Kosicki (1993): thematic structure, syntactical structure, script structure, and rhetorical structure. These were applied to define the frames and underlying messages that accompany certain topics in the news. In this case, "migrant," "migration," and related contextual synonyms were used as the words around which the frame is constructed.

It is important to mention that framing theory has several typologies, and the proposed approach defines media frames "as an independent variable having an impact on attitudes, opinions, or individual frames" (Scheufele, 1999, p. 110). That means they lack a link "between media frames as inputs . . . and audience frames, as outcomes" (p. 111). To put it another way, we cannot predict what media effects the studied frames have. This is not a shortcoming but a first step towards news discourse analysis on migration from Central Asia as a whole.

A note on the media landscape in Kyrgyzstan

In the Soviet period, since Kyrgyzstan belonged to one of the 15 Soviet republics, Kyrgyz mass media were a part of the Communist Party of the Soviet Union. They were subjected to strict governmental control and distinguished by a lack of pluralism. Upon the devolution of the USSR, a swift proliferation of private newspapers, television channels, and radio stations marked the 1990s and 2000s. Although most of the urban centers, with their highly literate and educated population, have had access to newspapers and television coverage, the capital of Kyrgyzstan, Bishkek, remains the most competitive media market. According to the Ministry of Culture, Information and Tourism (cited in *Vesti*, 2014), the three newspapers with the largest circulations appear in Bishkek: the daily Super Info (99,000) and Vecherniy Bishkek (51,000) and the weekly Delo No. (16,000). Many other newspapers have a limited circulation, of approximately fewer than 16,000 copies per issue. In this media landscape, print media are the most various: 159 titles, including three main dailies and four other major papers. Overall, active media outlets in Kyrgyzstan number more than 1,500, including 26 radio stations, 25 terrestrial television stations, 3 local cable networks and 3 Internet television providers (ibid).

In the post-Soviet period, significant changes in ownership occurred and some of the media outlets became privately owned. Nowadays public, state-run, private, and international broadcasters coexist in Kyrgyzstan. State sovereignty led not just to the development of independent from the state media outlets but also to the new language policy in the media sphere. Kyrgyzstan, as a multi-ethnic country with large Russian and Uzbek minorities, adopted a bilingual system of Kyrgyz and Russian. As Russian was the dominant language during the Soviet era, the position of the Kyrgyz language was enhanced through a special law that required transmitting at least 50 percent of all programming in Kyrgyz (the Kyrgyz Public Television and Radio Corporation Law). It aimed mostly at the regulation of television and radio broadcasting, having left out internet-based media. Still, news agencies and websites in their majority accept the bilingual approach by default and publish materials in both Kyrgyz and Russian. Taking into consideration that 85 percent of the population (5.1 million citizens) of Kyrgyzstan in 2016 were Internet users (National Sustainable Development Strategy for the Kyrgyz Republic for the period 2013–2017), we may conclude that news websites or their information reproduced through social networks have appeal among a wide readership.

Method

Data

In conceptualizing this study, we decided to analyze the popular online news media, whose articles are in both Kyrgyz and Russian. The rationale for the analysis of online media was two-fold: the data are available electronically and can be investigated more easily, and some of the online media in Kyrgyzstan have considerably wider readership than their printed counterparts. However, the main motivation for using online media in our analysis was that almost every online news outlet shows the number of views per article and comments related to them. That was helpful during the sampling stage. Realizing that the number of people following the pages on social networks may not reflect the number of actual readers, we nevertheless considered it one of the most reliable instruments for measuring readership and popularity of online media. This is supported by a growing body of academic work on the measurement of the spread of news on social media (i.e., Bandari, Asur, & Huberman, 2012; Lerman & Ghosh, 2010). For the purposes of analysis, four media outlets were chosen with Facebook followers in excess of 35,000 people. The following online bilingual news media from January 2015 to May 2017 were examined: (1) *Вечерний Бишкек* (*Vecherniy Bishkek*, VB), (2) Азаттык Үналгысы (Azattyk), (3) Спутник Кыргызстан (Sputnik), and (4) Kloop.

Vb.kg is the electronic version of the daily newspaper *Vecherniy Bishkek*, which is known as the leading and most read Bishkek city newspaper (Ministry of Justice, 2013). The website Azattyk.org is the online medium of the radio station of the same name, which belongs to the Radio Free Europe/Radio Liberty group, funded by the United States Congress. Similarly, the website Sputnik.kg represents the radio station Sputnik Kyrgyzstan, which is part of the media group Rossiya segodnya, financed by the Russian government. Finally, Kloop.kg is the newest outlet, created and sponsored by different grants, mainly of Dutch origin. All four online resources are directed at the same wide audience and convey more or less the same information. However, they may display different ideological emphases due to the history of their development and the financial support provided by internal and external actors. To sum up, the four news websites were chosen based on: (1) their wide readership and (2) their supposedly different political stances.

Procedure

To compile data for this project, we implemented keyword searches on the selected websites. The related terms were "migrant" and "migration" in both Kyrgyz and Russian. We bolstered the search by finding all materials tagged "Migration" even if they did not contain the word in the texts. After that, we scanned the news items for general content and filtered out those that had no connection to migration from Central Asia. We pooled 941 observations in Russian that emerged from the Azattyk searches, 460 from VB, 386 from Sputnik, and 36 from Kloop into one data set. In Kyrgyz, these numbers are: Azattyk – 930, VB – 430, Sputnik – 350, and Kloop – 25.

The analysis of Russian and Kyrgyz language news pieces was carried out by the authors independently from each other in two stages. The method we used is a modification of the thematic qualitative text analysis described by Udo Kuckartz (2014, pp. 69–88). The basic cycle of thematic analysis offered by Kuckartz presupposes seven phases, which constitute two coding processes (pp. 70–80). The first process ends at the point at which the main categories are developed and the passages assigned to each of the main categories are compiled. Then, an investigator has to determine sub-categories inductively and code all of the data again using the elaborated category system. We modified the research cycle by substituting the second coding process with in-depth interpretation of selected cases; hence, we followed only one coding process, separately. During this phase, we exchanged information about the discovered topics, negotiated them, and recoded the data if it was required. Figure 13.1 is a schematic representation of the study process.

During the first steps of our analysis, designated "topic analysis," we focused primarily on reading of the headlines and, if necessary, lead paragraphs of the whole data set to reveal categories for further analysis. We proceeded based on the traditional insight within Van Dijk's (1988) discourse-analytic framework that the "headline and lead summarize the news text and express the semantic macrostructure" (p. 53). In other words, placement in the headline reflects the emphasis of the main topic and this topic functions as the central organizing idea of a news piece.

Topic analysis is primarily a quantitative procedure to measure the frequency with which topics (categories) are presented in headlines. The 77 topical categories that emerged inductively from this process fell within nine broad domains: (1) intergovernmental and international relationships, (2) anti-migrant statements by politicians, (3) life of migration, (4) bureaucracy, (5) consequences of migration, (6) crimes and accidents, (7) Kyrgyzstan's domestic affairs, (8) economy, and (9) miscellaneous.

Alongside these topics, we classified the news items for each language separately under the following categories: year of publication, number of views, comments or shares, and countries of origin and destination. The subsequent cluster sampling was carried out randomly based on two variables: (1) number of views, shares, or comments and (2) frequency of topics. With the help of Excel tools the most popular articles and topics were identified. In each case, the ten most viewed/commented on/shared news pieces were selected for further analysis. In addition, the ten most popular topics for each of the websites were catalogued and cross-listed. After the lists of common and distinctive topics were compiled – 24 in Russian and 22 in Kyrgyz – a random sample of articles was chosen. The total number of sampled observations constituted 10 percent of the universe of every website.

The second stage of analysis involved reading the chosen articles carefully. Furthermore, we analyzed the texts employing qualitative techniques such as frame analysis. After that, we compared our independent results.

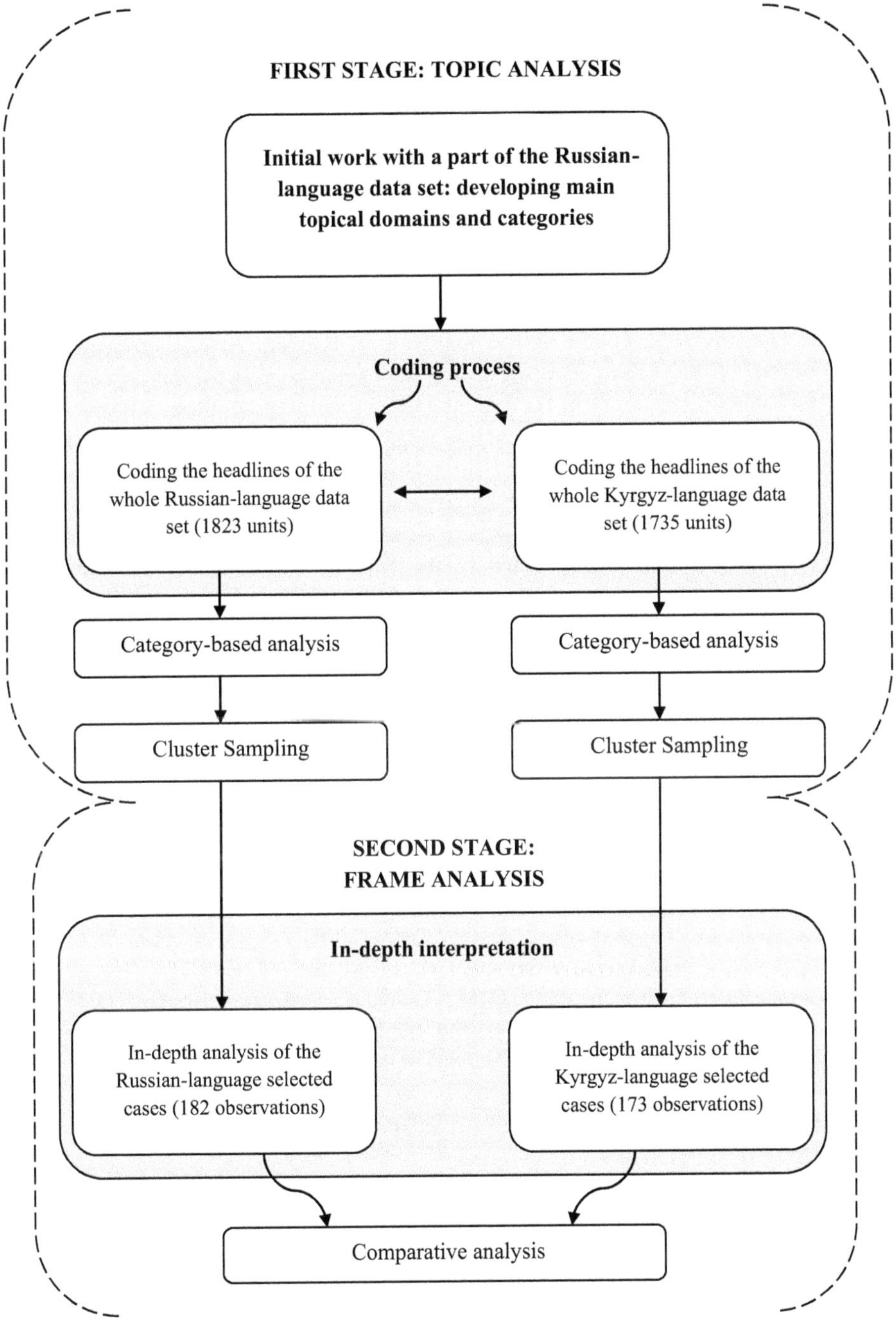

Figure 13.1 Schematic representation of the research process

Results

This section is organized according to the stages of analysis. Primarily the results of our quantitative analysis will be presented, then we will proceed with the findings of our qualitative and comparative analyses.

Topic analysis of the Russian language news media

Preliminary analysis revealed that the same number of articles on migration were published in Russian and Kyrgyz. From January 2015 to May 2017, the range of topics on the Russian versions of the four news websites displayed significant differences (see Table 13.1). Being a website that regularly publishes articles on migration in Russian, Azattyk covers almost all topics (73 out of 77) that were identified during the coding process. Kloop, in contrast, has the most modest scope of topics in our sample (18). In absolute numbers, VB and Sputnik demonstrate similar results – 54 and 55 topics, respectively. However, considering that VB has a smaller universe, Sputnik has a more diverse palette of topics on migration. In Kyrgyz, the patterns are similar. The first ten topics are encountered in one third (35 percent) of news during the period. Azattyk focuses mainly on the topics that have negative connotations. Seven of the first ten topics are devoted to the difficulties of migration, such as police misconduct, religious extremism among Central Asians living abroad, and the hardship

Table 13.1 The ten most frequently-mentioned topics in regard to migration across four Russian language news websites, January 2015–May 2017

Azattyk	*Kloop*	*Sputnik*	*Vecherniy Bishkek*
Crimes (11%)	Blacklists (17%)	EAEU (11%)	Illegal migration (8%)
Employment opportunities (5%)	New regulations (11%)	Remittances (11%)	EAEU (7%)
Children as victims of migration (4%)	Migrants' new values (6%)	Blacklists (8%)	Accidents (6%)
New regulations (3%)	Sobyanin's saying (6%)	Discussion and debate (7%)	Blacklists (5%)
ISIS/extremism (3%)	Pensions in EAEU (6%)	Accidents (5%)	Discussion and debate (5%)
Detentions and deportations (2%)	Health care in EAEU (6%)	Intergovernmental relations (4%)	Statistics (5%)
Leisure time of migrants (2%)	Remittances (5%)	New regulations (3%)	New regulations (5%)
Difficulties of migration (2%)	Crimes (5%)	Employment opportunities (3%)	Intergovernmental relations (4%)
Women and migration (2%)	Detentions and deportations (5%)	Everyday life of migrants (3%)	Crimes (4%)
Police arbitrariness (1%)	Leisure time of migrants (5%)	Crimes (2%)	Detentions and deportations (4%)
Other (65%)	Other (28%)	Other (43%)	Other (47%)

women and children experience during – or because of – migration. News related to the sixth thematic domain – "crimes and accidents" – appears in 28 percent of all publications. The most popular categories Azattyk journalists write about are: (1) crimes (11 percent, sixth domain); (2) employment opportunities (5 percent, third domain); and (3) children as victims of migration (4 percent, fifth domain). The topic of crimes stands out, occupying more than a tenth of all materials about migration, and is constantly present in the top five topics of each year. The publications on crimes are almost equally distributed among the crimes committed against migrants and by them. Special attention is given to the crimes perpetrated by Kyrgyz against their fellow countrymen in Russia. When we compare the presentation of different topics across the three years, the greatest degree of change appeared to occur with an increase in the number of articles on detentions and deportations; the largest decrease occurred in relation to the number of articles about the Eurasian Economic Union (EAEU) and Kyrgyzstan's upcoming accession to it.

In contrast to the Russian version of Azattyk, the Russian version of Sputnik during the research period concentrates primarily on the discussion of the accession to EAEU (11 percent), remittances of migrants (8 percent) and inclusion in the "blacklists" of the Russian Federal Migration Office (8 percent). The ten most frequently encountered topics constitute 57 percent of all publications and the majority are neutral. The patterns in topic representation in 2015 are representative of the topic pattern throughout the studied period; in 2016 the largest number of news articles was dedicated to remittances and accidents. It is the first year after accession of Kyrgyzstan to the EAEU and the topic of EAEU membership has been given less attention, completely disappearing from the top five ranking of topics in 2017. It is replaced by a new theme, that of "discussion and debate". In general, 28 percent of the general population of the news at Sputnik is devoted to intergovernmental and international relationships.

Similar findings were revealed during analysis of the *Vecherniy Bishkek* website, whereby the ten most popular topics represent 53 percent of all observations. More than a quarter of the universe (26 percent) falls under the "intergovernmental and international relationships" thematic domain. Interest in the EAEU shows the same pattern as that of Sputnik: it is in the top ten in 2015, fades in 2016 and disappears in 2017. That said, the topic of accession to the EAEU was ranked second in the most popular themes during the whole period (7 percent). The topic of "illegal migration" received the most news space and accounts for 8 percent of articles, while 6 percent of all articles concerned accidents occurring during the process of migration or in the receiving country. *Vecherniy Bishkek* demonstrates an equal distribution of negative and neutral topics among the most covered themes. Analysis of the website's news items also revealed that the third year (2017) is distinguished by an almost even number of new pieces on each of the presented topics. *Vecherny Bishkek* is also the only website that writes about the return migration from Kyrgyzstan to Russia, using the term "compatriots" to refer to resettling Russians or other ethnic groups whose descendants came to Kyrgyzstan during the Soviet period or earlier. Finally, a series of interviews with migrants living in different countries of the world (in most cases in Western or economically more developed countries than Kyrgyzstan) stands out in the website's universe. These interviews fall under the "life of migration" thematic domain, making it the second largest.

The smallest corpus of the articles at Kloop written in Russian does not reveal any statistically significant trends. The top ten topics are presented in 72 percent of publications, and only two of them stand out – inclusion of migrants in "blacklists" (17 percent) and the new laws applied to migrants (11 percent). This means that, during the three-year period, the reader might have encountered six articles on the first topic and four on the second. This sporadic addressing of the topic of migration demonstrates the little interest journalists have in it. Moreover, six publications were reprints of Azattyk texts, and another one was from the TV channel Current Time, which belongs to the same group as Azattyk. This explains why, at the second stage of analysis, Kloop was less present.

Media coverage in Russian varied according to whether articles concerned receiving countries or countries of origin. Migrants from Kyrgyzstan to Russia received the most attention from all four outlets. Kazakhstan is considered a country of destination rather than origin, although several publications were about Kazakhstan citizens living in Russia. Central Asia as a whole region of origin appears mostly in publications dedicated to extremism and crime. This may be due to the fact that Russian media outlets are mostly sources for the articles on the aforementioned topics, and in Russia it is not customary to specify the nationality of the criminals or extremists in order to not "foment inter-ethnic discord." Uzbekistan and Tajikistan appear in news on remittances, general statistics on migration, and frequently on crimes and accidents. Turkmenistan was mentioned only once by VB. Among the destination countries besides Russia and the EAEU countries, Turkey, South Korea, the US and Syria/Iraq received the most attention. Table 13.2 summarizes the distribution of countries discussed by the media outlets.

Table 13.2 Distribution of countries of origin and destination by Kyrgyz websites in Russian

Azattyk	*Kloop*	*Sputnik*	*Vecherniy Bishkek*
Country of origin			
Kyrgyzstan (761)	Kyrgyzstan (34)	Kyrgyzstan (341)	Kyrgyzstan (398)
Tajikistan (93)	Central Asia (4)	Central Asia (24)	Central Asia (17)
Central Asia (67)	Uzbekistan (2)	Uzbekistan (16)	Uzbekistan (12)
Uzbekistan (67)	EAEU (1)	Tajikistan (14)	Tajikistan (9)
Kazakhstan (7)		CSTO (1)	CIS (7)
EAEU (2)		CIS (1)	EAEU (3)
CIS (2)			CSTO (2)
			Turkmenistan (1)
Country of destination			
Russia (759)	Russia (32)	Russia (265)	Russia (348)
Abroad: not specified (88)	EAEU (1)	EAEU (56)	EAEU (44)
Kazakhstan (48)	Crimea (1)	Kazakhstan (30)	Abroad: not specified (22)
Turkey (37)	Turkey (1)	Abroad: not specified (25)	Kazakhstan (22)
EAEU (19)	Abroad: not specified (1)	USA (8)	South Korea (12)
Syria (11)		Turkey (6)	CIS (6)
USA (11)		South Korea (6)	Turkey (4)
South Korea (9)		Syria (5)	UAE (2)
Iraq (7)		CSTO* (4)	Japan (2)
Japan (4)		Belorussia (2)	USA (2)
Other (22)		Other (18)	Other (10)

Note. The total number of references to a country is usually higher than the number of articles analyzed because many articles referred to multiple countries
* CSTO – Collective Security Treaty Organisation

Topic analysis of Kyrgyz language news media

Analysis of topics referred to in Kyrgyz language news media revealed the following new categories: death of migrants, slavery, and human trafficking.

Vecherniy Bishkek covered migration from the stance of its having mostly negative consequences, such as labor migrants' deaths as the result of fire, car accidents, and accidents at work (ten news stories). The second major topic was the blacklisting of labor migrants (eight news stories). Kyrgyzstan's accession to the EAEU and its positive consequences for Kyrgyz migrants in Russia were covered in three news stories and the same number of news stories covered the issue of registration of migrants in Russia. Two news stories were about deportations of Kyrgyz labor migrants from Russia.

Vecherniy Bishkek covered mostly the Kyrgyz government's position on migration by referring to the official statements of President Atambaev and prime ministerial official statements on problems of labor migrants in Russia. It also covered problems of Kyrgyz labor migrants in Korea, Dubai, and the UAE in three news stories.

Sputnik dedicated the majority of its news stories to the deaths of Kyrgyz labor migrants in Russia in fires at the workplace, such as sewing and printing factories, and other accidents (31 news stories). The major accidents were two big fires in the same year, one in a printing house in which 17 Kyrgyz women died, one of whom was pregnant, and another in a sewing factory in which eight Kyrgyz women died.

Some of the other victims were killed by Russian police. The second major topic covered by Sputnik was violence against Kyrgyz labor migrant women in Russia (18 news stories) in the form of sexual violence, human trafficking, and slavery. One of the victims of sexual violence was a young Kyrgyz girl who was raped by the owner of a house where she was employed as a cleaner

Human trafficking and slavery stories were not only about Kyrgyz labor migrants in Russia but also concerned Turkey and Kazakhstan. For example, one story covered the enslaving of 14 women in a sewing factory in Russia and how they were rescued. Another detailed slavery of Kyrgyz labor migrants in the farms of Kazakhstan. Several stories concerned Kyrgyz girls enslaved and forced to work as prostitutes in Antalya and other Turkish cities. For example, one described 11 Kyrgyz girls who were rescued from sex slavery in Turkey. The third major topic covered by Sputnik focused on the amount of money transferred by Kyrgyz labor migrants in Russia and abroad (13 news stories).

Another topic was newborn babies who were left by Kyrgyz labor migrant women in Russia. For example, five newborn babies who were left by their mothers in Russia were brought to Kyrgyzstan. These stories also dealt with homelessness among Kyrgyz labor migrants in Russia; for example, one described a mother who was living with her newborn baby on a train in Moscow and another concerned a girl who gave birth to her baby in a public toilet and had nowhere to live.

Overall, Sputnik's coverage of labor migration from Kyrgyzstan highlighted the negative consequences of migration, such as violation of migrants' rights, death of migrants, discrimination against migrant women and girls, problems gaining permission to work, being blacklisted, and leaving Russia because of registration issues.

The news stories on migration in the Kyrgyz language version of *Azattyk* are similar to its Russian language counterpart; they focus mainly on topics that have negative connotations. Nine of the top ten articles are devoted to the difficulties of migration, such as blacklists, deportations of migrants, registration of migrants, new regulations controlling migrants' permission to stay in Russia, controls of migrants by police, arrests of migrants in a temporary jail run by Russia's migration service, police misconduct, violation of migrants' rights by employers and police in Russia, and the hardship experienced by women and children during or because of migration. News related to the sixth thematic domain – "crimes and accidents" – appears in 38 percent of all publications. The seven most popular categories covered by Azattyk journalists are *blacklists* (38 percent) and *children as victims of migration* (30 percent). The topic of migrants' children who are left in Kyrgyzstan is divided into three sub-themes: children as victims of domestic violence by their relatives; early marriages among migrants' children; school dropouts among migrants' children, and newborns who are left by their mothers in Russia and then taken back to Kyrgyzstan. For example, one news story tells about 48 newborns left by migrant women in Russia and later brought back to Kyrgyzstan.

The topic of *crimes* stands out, occupying more than a quarter of all materials about migration, and is constantly present in the top five topics of each year. The publications on crimes describe those committed against migrants. For example, news stories covered the approximately 500 dead bodies – "Cargo 200" – that were brought to Kyrgyzstan from Russia in one year. Most migrants' deaths are the result of killings, and fire and road accidents.

The topic of *migrant women's rights and the consequences of migration on their health* was the fourth main topic on Azattyk's agenda, covering sexual harassment of migrant women, sex slavery and women as victims of domestic violence or who contract HIV from their husbands who work in Russia, abortions among migrant girls, and migrant mothers who leave their children. Early marriage and maternal mortality are also covered in many news stories. For example, one news article states that every sixth woman who dies during childbirth is a migrant.

Migrants' rights are the fifth main topic covered by Azattyk. This subject covered: migrants in custody in the Russian migration service temporary jail as the result of illegal migration, migrants who were victims of employers not paying their salaries, migrants' medical insurance, dual citizenship problems in Kyrgyzstan and Russia, and police control of migrants. The sixth main topic is *new law on migration* in Russia, which means that migrants require work permits. *Slavery and human trafficking of migrants* was covered by Azattyk in seven news stories from January 2015 to May 2017. These detailed: sex slavery and human trafficking of migrant women from Central Asia to Russia, Turkey, and the UAE, and slavery of migrant workers in Kazakhstan. Overall, Azattyk's coverage of migration has negative connotations.

The Kyrgyz version of Kloop covered migration issues in 36 news stories, and about a quarter (eight stories) were reprints of Azattyk articles. The top ten topics are covered in 75 percent of publications, and six of them concerned inclusion of migrants on "blacklists" and the new rules applied to migrants. The issue of violence against migrants' children who were left in Kyrgyzstan was covered in six articles. The fire in a printing house in Moscow in which 14 Kyrgyz women and young girls died was covered in four news stories.

Frame analysis of the Russian language outlets

The frame analysis of the body of articles in Russian provides interesting evidence about the different types of framing on the same topics.

Eurasian Economic Union

The Kyrgyz accession to the EAEU received a great deal of attention from all news outlets analyzed. Sputnik and *Vecherniy Bischkek* repeatedly reported that the Union will grant preference to Kyrgyz migrants and serve as a body for their civil rights. The new EAEU rules regarding the terms of entering the labor markets of countries in the Union and the conditions of stay in the receiving countries are the primary elements of the Eurasian Economic Union theme. Providing information about the new rules appeared to be the purpose of many articles on VB and Sputnik. *Vecherny Bishkek* did it often in a dry, formal manner. Sometimes the VB news contained just a list of new rules, as if it were an extraction from the official documents, with the expected readership being migrants themselves or their family members. Reporters frequently asked high-ranking officials from Kyrgyzstan or Russia to comment on the upcoming membership. The range of respondents was confined to officials or experts taking part in conferences, round tables or meetings; migrants' voices were absent.

The reporting pattern at Sputnik was similar to that at VB, although the articles were less lackluster in the sense of generic syntactic structures and scripts. Sputnik reports relied on the opinions of experts and officials as well, and Kyrgyz President Atambaev's point of view seemed to be the most valuable among these. According to him, first and foremost, hundreds of thousands of Kyrgyz migrants living in Russia would benefit from EAEU membership. The leitmotif of the Sputnik observations on the EAEU was that migrants need and are being properly informed about the new rules, and that there is a great deal of work ahead for the Kyrgyz and Russian governments, especially in terms of synchronizing legal frameworks. Both Sputnik and VB were cautious in stating the effects of the EAEU accession, although some positive results were highlighted. When the remittance flows from Russia to Kyrgyzstan grew at the end of 2016 after more than a year of decline, they were linked to the newly-acquired membership of the EAEU. Similarly, the fact that Tajiks and Uzbeks were forging Kyrgyz passports was attributed to the attractiveness of membership of the Union. These two websites largely expressed a pro-government point of view, presenting the EAEU as the right choice, especially with regard to migration.

Azattyk's framing of the topic was different. The journalists paid very little attention to explicit explaining of the new rules and regulations and tended to see only negative aspects of the changes or expressed doubts regarding whether Moscow will implement the agreements and Kyrgyzstan will receive the promised benefits. In the few months after the accession, journalists reported on the on-going difficulties of migrants' lives that were not relieved by Union membership. For example, when the remittances from Russia shrank, the Azattyk journalists talked about violated expectations. Laypeople were one of the major sources of information; however, Azattyk journalists also cited comments made by officials. The migrants' comments were usually negative in nature, intended to suggest that life in the EAEU does not bring preferential treatment or positive changes. Azattyk quoted in full the comments of Moscow's mayor, Sergey Sobyanin, on Kyrgyz migrants being a problem for Moscow. The full quotation concerned the accession of Kyrgyzstan to the EAEU and the subsequent huge influx of Kyrgyz migrants to Moscow. In contrast to Azzatyk, Sputnik and VB did not emphasize this part of the mayor's statement. In quoting Sobyanin, Azattyk could have tried to stress that membership of the EAEU did not actually alleviate the difficulties of migrants' lives as had been promised and that they are not really welcome in Russia.

Bureaucracy in Russia: "blacklists" and Sakharovo

The data reveal that the topics of "blacklists" and a multifunctional center for provision of services for migrants in the Moscow region called Sakharovo were highlighted differently by the four websites. All online media acknowledged that these topics were problematic. VB and

Sputnik frequently emphasized that there is some work going on to solve the problems. After just a few articles, Sputnik closed the theme of a disorder at Sakharovo center. The journalists published news describing migrants' complaints about the long queues, then addressed the resolution of the problem: the Russian authorities had established a round-the-clock service at the center. Azattyk, in contrast, tried to persuade its readers that the long queues in which migrants had to wait were an extraordinary and destructive experience. This rhetoric highlights that the website exaggerated these hardships (e.g., "standing in queues half of one's life"), added additional clarifications (e.g., the queue that has already been called long in the same sentence is then described as "the queue where people stand in a serpentine fashion"), and used derogatory language.

The rules of the Sakharovo center are described by Azattyk as complicating the life of migrants rather than making it easier. The migrants are depicted as people who will "have to" or "must" obey the rules, and the rules are hard to follow. Several articles (going beyond the topic of Sakharovo) argue that acknowledging the Kyrgyz driving license in Russia will be expensive for migrants in terms of both effort and money. As usual, only interlocutors expressing negative opinions were visible. This creates the impression that Russia would not provide better facilities and intentionally complicated migrants' lives. In a similar manner, the situation with the Russian blacklists has been aggravated. Azattyk reported that, in spite of all promises, Kyrgyz migrants will not be excluded from these lists. Lawyers' opinions on the whole system of blacklisting were quoted, which suggested that removing migrants names would be ill-conceived and unworkable. Migrants who falsified their documents and illegally crossed borders were justified in their actions because of the unworkable system. The new rules outlining that migrants should cross the border only once was not a solution, because those migrants interviewed were of the opinion that return tickets were too expensive. Azattyk also gave voice to migrants whose strategy was to keep quiet and wait in Russia until their time on blacklists expired. Kloop followed a similar approach in describing the system as ineffective.

VB and Sputnik chose a supportive frame and tried to embrace the issue of constant cooperation between Kyrgyz and the governments of the EAEU members, mainly Russia. Both websites reported on the legal ways in which migrants can remove their names from blacklists. In the case of VB and Sputnik, officials and representatives of the Kyrgyz diaspora in Russia delivered information on the best ways to get removed from blacklists. Sputnik frequently published infographics to illustrate these options. Physical addresses were provided to inform migrants where they could get help. As in the case of the EAEU rules, Sputnik and VB aimed to inform and clarify rather than criticize or disparage the existing system of migration controls.

Arbitrariness of the police

The prevalence of the "crimes and accidents" thematic domain emphasizes that Azattyk is generally inclined to present migration as a traumatic and dangerous experience. The website frequently reported on arrests, detentions, and deportations of migrants. News on individual cases of arrests or detentions is usually supported by statistics or estimations on the total number of arrested migrants. The reports usually lack officials' comments, and the utterances of migrants give the impression that they were arrested or detained unlawfully and without reason. The topic of arrests and detentions work in conjunction with the topic of the arbitrariness of the Russian or – rarely – Turkish police. Azattyk gave a lot of attention to the story of a five-month-old baby from Tajikistan who was seized from a migrant's family by the police and died under unclear circumstances. The story unfolded as a drama and was placed within the field of the Russian police's arbitrary actions. The name of the baby – Umarali – even became a kind of metaphor, and Azattyk journalists used it in the headline of another story, thus alluding to this emotive case. *Vecherny Bishkek* depicted the topic in the same way, although on a less dramatic scale. On the Sputnik website, the theme of police arbitrariness was barely present, and, if it was mentioned, the coverage was not particularly critical. For example, Sputnik covered the story of policemen in Russia accepting a bribe so they could buy themselves a cake.

Women as migrants and children as victims of migration

Azattyk covered another story demonstrating the unlawful and unprofessional conduct of Russian police. It concerned a Kyrgyz woman who wished to obtain Russian citizenship and had prepared all the necessary documentation. Instead of accepting the documents, however, the Russian authorities accused her of forging the papers and handed her over to the police, who then beat and tortured her. Azattyk covers numerous cases of women suffering during migration. It even published a story of a Kyrgyz wife whose husband left her in favor of another woman in Moscow. In this story, which was reprinted on Kloop, the root of the misfortune was the migration itself, which changes people and their values. Azattyk is the only one of the four websites that highlights the dangers of female migration.

Another frequently covered topic is children as victims of migration. Azattyk journalists focus primarily on children who are left in the care of their relatives in Kyrgyzstan while their parents work abroad. Some of these children do not attend school and are beaten by their relatives. The stories covered by Azattyk frame migration as having a negative impact on migrants' families. Kloop reprinted several stories published by Azattyk, following the negative framing of the topic of women's migration. Sputnik and VB devote considerably less attention to these topics and focus instead on positive aspects of migration and depict women in a more positive light, providing stories of success. ==Sputnik is inclined to write about families that do not leave their children in the countries of origin, but bring them to the destination countries. Admitting the difficulties of upbringing children in migration, Sputnik reports on cases of finding solutions to the problems – like translation of the school textbooks into Kyrgyz language or establishing private nurseries for migrants' children.

Analysis of the Kyrgyz language content of the websites

The frame analysis of the body of articles in the Kyrgyz language revealed additional themes and frames on migration.

"Blacklists"

Analysis reveals that all of the media outlets in our sample covered the issue of "blacklists." This was the number one topic of Azattyk and Kloop, the second of VB, and the fourth of Sputnik.

Azattyk reported on the difficulties encountered by labor migrants in Russia, frequent unjustified police controls, and arrests. Deportations of migrants and requirements to register were also main issues. Without registration, migrants face huge difficulties in terms of getting jobs, sending their children to schools and kindergarten, accessing medical care, and even being in public places. One story concerns a mother who was deported to Kyrgyzstan and had to leave her newborn baby in Russia. According to some news reports, thousands of migrants have had to change their names on their passports in order to enter Russia and circumvent blacklists, and Russian authorities add Central Asian migrants' names to these lists for minor things. Sputnik covered this issue only in a few reports, denying its importance. It also reported on money sent by migrants from Russia to their home country. It was the third most significant topic covered by Sputnik (13 stories).

Children as victims of migration

Migrants' children as victims of migration was the second most significant topic covered by Azattyk and Kloop; Sputnik covered this issue in only three news reports, and VB simply ignored it. Azattyk published 28 news stories on children of migrants who are left with their relatives in Kyrgyzstan, violence against them by their relatives, school dropouts, people who had recently married, and newborn babies left by migrant mothers in Russia. One news story concerns 48 newborns who were left by migrant women in Russia and taken to Kyrgyzstan. A similar story was published by Sputnik on five newborns who were left by migrant mothers in Moscow and were brought to Kyrgyzstan. Kloop dedicated five news stories to the problems of migrants' children.

Death of migrants

The theme of accidents in the Kyrgyz language media, especially in Azattyk, focused on the death of migrants in Russia. The death of migrants was Sputnik's number one topic and it dedicated 31 news reports to this issue; Azattyk published 27, VB ten, and Kloop four. The number of articles on the aforementioned topic has increased because of some tragic major accidents that happened in 2015–2017. The major topic of all media outlets in our sample was the death of Kyrgyz migrant women and girls in a printing house fire in Moscow.

Azattyk used the term "200 kilogram luggage" to describe the number of dead Kyrgyz migrants in Russia. VB also reported on the number of migrant deaths in Russia; according to its story, 430 Kyrgyz citizens had died within seven months in Russia. The deaths of the women and girls in the printing house was given huge coverage by Azattyk and prompted an equally huge response from readers, whose letters were featured on the website. Azattyk criticized the Kyrgyz government for not caring about its citizens who are working in Russia, for not creating job opportunities in Kyrgyzstan for them, and for not protecting their rights in Russia. Azattyk used very emotional comments, feedback, and readers' reactions to criticize the Kyrgyz government, and hold it responsible for the death of young girls and women. Migrants' murders and attacks were the second major topic, after fires and car accidents. "Do not leave. It is bad there" was the main frame of news focusing on the death of migrants and various accidents.

Violence against migrant women

The majority of news stories about the difficulties migrant women face, and violence against them, were covered by Azattyk (22 news stories), followed closely by Sputnik (18 news stories). Physical and sexual violence against migrant women, sex trafficking, slavery of migrant women, and women migrants' health consequences, such as maternal mortality, abortions among migrant girls and HIV, were the main topics. Domestic violence in migrants' families in Russia and violence against migrant women by their Kyrgyz compatriots in Russia were also main issues covered by Azattyk. Sex trafficking of women to Turkey and the UAE was also a main topic reported by Azattyk. One news story described 11 girls being rescued from sex slavery in Turkey, and another 11 women who were rescued from labor slavery in a sewing factory in Russia. Another news story was on secret abortions among migrant girls in Russia. Difficulties migrant girls face in giving birth was covered in one news story, reporting that a girl delivered a baby in a public toilet in Russia and had no place to stay with her newborn baby. Several stories report on migrant mothers leaving their newborns in Russia. Sexual harassment of migrant women was another sub-category within main topics. One news story reported on a girl who was raped by a house owner who had employed her as a house cleaner in Moscow.

Slavery and human trafficking

Slavery and human trafficking stories were present in almost all of our sample media outlets. Migrants kept in slavery in a Moscow sewing factory, in the fields and farms of Kazakhstan, and the sex slavery of migrant women in Turkey were the main issues of all media outlets.

Conclusion

In sum, how the EAEU, female migration, children of migrants, and bureaucratic steps and constraints were represented provide rich examples of how differently the four websites frame migration. Migration is constructed within very narrow frames; for example, coverage of low-skilled labor migration surpasses the coverage of high-skilled labor migration or student migration. As soon as the main destination country is Russia, labor migration is synonymous with migration to Russia.

Sputnik and Azattyk represent two extremes of the framing divide. Sputnik (and to a lesser degree VB) frames migration as an unavoidable, omnipresent phenomenon. Although all of the web portals admit the connection between Kyrgyzstan, Tajikistan, and Uzbekistan through remittances and labor markets to Russia and Kazakhstan, Sputnik and VB stress these countries' cooperation with Russia and Kazakhstan more than Azattyk and Kloop. Overall, Sputnik's coverage of migration from Central Asia to Russia was pro-EAEU. Azattyk, in contrast, emphasizes the harm that may result from migration. It uses a negative tone in which to report stories about and around migration to Russia. It concentrates primarily on the problems, and interviews migrants who are not happy with their migratory experiences. This creates an image of migration (to Russia) as a dangerous activity. Kyrgyz and Russian versions of the websites mainly coincide on the choice of topics and tone of coverage. The major differences appear in the analysis of Sputnik. Whereas the Russian language version frames migration positively by focusing on the money sent by migrants to their home countries and the opportunities created by the accession to the EAEU, the Kyrgyz version is negative, focusing on the key topics of death, crime, and slavery.

Analysis of Azattyk's and Kloop's coverage of migration revealed a negative bias; their stories concerned blacklists, migrants' children as victims, violations of migrants' rights, violence against women migrants, human trafficking, and slavery. Azattyk also criticized the Kyrgyz government for not protecting migrants' rights and not creating job opportunities in Kyrgyzstan. Although there is negative framing of migration in both Kyrgyz and Russian versions of Azattyk, the Kyrgyz version does show some peculiarities. Negative stories of migrants' arrests, controls by police, deportations, and detentions often pass for the topic of violation of migrants' rights. Two main approaches to the coverage of migration from Central Asia were identified – positive and negative. By choosing specific topics and omitting others, Azattyk (and Kloop) and Sputnik (and VB) highlight certain migratory behaviors and exclude others. The whole picture of what migration from Central Asia looks like emerges when the two discourses complement each other.

As for the theoretical implications of this study, in assessing subtleties in media content this study defined broad and narrow conceptualizations as well as issue-specific frames that may serve as reference points when explicating the nature of the frames. Framing research as a contribution to theory and a tool for media analysis is a work in progress. This chapter is a first attempt to systematically assess issue-specific frames about migration from Central Asia and identify contentious issues for future research to address. This especially refers to the consequences of framing at the individual and societal levels. An individual-level consequence may be altered attitudes about an issue based on exposure to certain frames. At the societal level, frames may contribute to shaping social processes, such as political socialization, decision making, and collective action.

A limitation related to the selection of publications needs to be addressed. During the course of the study, we noticed that some of the articles devoted to migration did not contain any words related to "migration." For example, sometimes migrants were labeled "compatriots" or "Kyrgyzstani," especially if the migration was to Western countries. Although the search criteria were revised every time we found special naming, we cannot predict how many other contextual synonyms for "migration" may exist. This complicated compilation of the finite data set and could have distorted the ratings of the most popular topics and articles. A possible distortion may also appear with regard to the first coding process; the authors compared codes as a means of validating the process, however an independent intercoder reliability check was not conducted. An important limitation needs to be addressed with regard to the results. The time frame of the analysis was short, taking into consideration that the migration from Central Asia started after the collapse of the Soviet Union. It would also have been fruitful to compare more than four media outlets to identify a greater range of perspectives on the issue. Finally, causal relations are hard to ascertain because it is difficult to investigate, using thematic analysis, whether ownership shapes the ideology of media coverage.

References

Bandari, R., Asur, S., & Huberman, B. A. (2012). The pulse of news in social media: Forecasting popularity. *Proceedings of the Seventh International Conference on Weblogs and Social Media.* Retrieved from www.aaai.org/ocs/index.php/ICWSM/ICWSM12/paper/download/4646/4963

Entman, R. B. (1993). Framing: Toward clarification of a fractured paradigm. *Journal of Communication, 43*, 51–58.

Ibraeva, G. (2016). *Media and information space of a Kyrgyz migrant worker in Russia: Experience in issue formulation.* An analytical study of media products for Kyrgyz migrants in Russia commissioned by TSPC, AUCA. Retrieved from https://issuu.com/margaritalazutkina/docs/3e44266b32a3a9

International Migration Report (2017). Department of Economic and Social Affairs, United Nations, New York. Retrieved from www.un.org/en/development/desa/population/migration/publications/migrationreport/docs/MigrationReport2017_Highlights.pdf

Khismatullina, L. G., Garaeva, A. K., & Akhmetzyanov, I. G. (2017). Metaphoric representation of migration in British, American and Russian mass media. *Vestnik Chelyabinskogo gosudarstvennogo pedagogicheskogo universiteta, 2*, 170–176.

King, R. & Wood, N. (2001). Media and migration: An overview. In R. King & N. Wood (Eds.), *Media and migration* (pp. 1–22). London: Routledge.

Kubaeva, Gulaikhan (2015). *Economic Impact of the Eurasian Economic Union on Central Asia.* Central Asia Security Policy Briefs. Bishkek: OSCE Academy in Bishkek. www.osce-academy.net/upload/file/Policy_Brief_20.pdf

Kuckartz, U. (2014). *Qualitative text analysis: A guide to methods, practice and using software.* Thousand Oaks, CA: Sage.

Lerman, K. & Ghosh, R. (2010). Information contagion: An empirical study of the spread of news on digg and Twitter social networks. *Proceedings of the Fourth International Conference on Weblogs and Social Media.* Retrieved from http://arxiv.org/abs/1003.2664

Nam, I. V., Karageorgiy, E. M., Ermolova, A. I., & Nikitina, E. V. (2017). The image of labour migrants constructed by the mass media: The case of Tomsk. *Sibirskie istoricheskie issledovaniya, 1*, 166–192.

National Council for Sustainable Development of the Kyrgyz Republic. (2017). *National sustainable development strategy for the Kyrgyz Republic for the period of 2013–2017.* Retrieved from www.un-page.org/files/public/kyrgyz_national_sustainable_development_strategy.pdf

Pan, Z. H. & Kosicki, G. M. (1993). Framing analysis: An approach to news discourse. *Political Communication, 10*, 55–75.

President of the Kyrgyz Republic. (2015). Retrieved from www.president.kg/ru/news/5882_prezident_almazbek_atambaev_uchastie_kyirgyizstana_v_evraziyskom_ekonomicheskom_soyuze_sootvetstvuet_natsionalnyim_interesam_stranyi

Ryazantsev, S. (2016, August 31). Labour migration from Central Asia to Russia in the context of the economic crisis. *Russia in Global Affairs.* Retrieved from http://eng.globalaffairs.ru/valday/Labour-Migration-from-Central-Asia-to-Russia-in-the-Context-of-the-Economic-Crisis-18334.

Saraeva, O. V. (2011). Construction of the image of migration by Russian mass media. *Vestnik economiki, prava i soziologii, 2*, 245–248.

Scheufele, D. (1999). Framing as a theory of media effects. *Journal of Communication, 49*, 103–122.

Van Dijk, T. A. (1988). *News as discourse.* New York: Lawrence Erlbaum.

Vesti (2014). Top 25 newspapers in circulations in Kyrgyzstan. Retrieved from https://vesti.kg/obshchestvo/item/25830-top-25-tirazhnyih-gazet-kyirgyizstana.html

Vinokurov, E. (2013). The art of survival: Kyrgyz labor migration, human capital, and social networks. *Central Asia Economic Paper*, 7. Retrieved from https://mpra.ub.uni-muenchen.de/49180/

14

KURDISH MEDIA AND KURDISTAN REGIONAL GOVERNMENT EMIGRATION POLICY

The refugee crisis of 2015

Diyako Rahmani

The Syrian civil war that began in 2011 has had deep international, political, and humanitarian consequences, not only for Syria, but also several other Middle Eastern groups/nations such as Kurds in Iraq. As a result of this war, many Syrians had to leave their homes and scattered into neighboring countries such as Jordan, Turkey, Iraq, and Lebanon, and, since 2013, into European and North American countries such as Sweden, the United Kingdom, the United States, Canada, Germany, and others. As of May 1, 2016, about 800,000 refugees had filed for asylum in one of the European countries (Syrian Refugees, n.d.). In 2014, the so-called Islamic State (IS) spread the war to Iraq and this added to the already existing socioeconomic and security problems in Iraqi society. Thus, a large number of Iraqi immigrants joined the Syrians on the trip to Europe. According to the Migration Policy Institute, in 2015 and 2016, 239,415 Iraqi refugees filed applications for asylum in one of the European countries (Migration Policy Institute, n.d.). The Iraqi refugees included different ethnic and religious groups – the Shiite and Sunnis Arabs, and the Iraqi Kurds, along with other religious minorities.

As refugees are registered according to their nationalities, there is no accurate estimation of numbers for each ethnic group within the Iraqi refugees, but the Kurds from the Kurdistan Regional Government (KRG) form a large element of this refugee population (Szlanko, 2016). The refugee's decision to immigrate is based on the information they receive and for different security and economic reasons. The emigration process, from deciding to emigrate, choosing the destination, and means of travel there, is affected by the information they receive from different forms of social and mainstream media. This chapter looks at the emigration process of Kurdish refugees and investigates the role of mass and social media in their emigration process.

Media and emigration policy

The effect of media on emigration policies is multifaceted. Vukov (2003) asserted that, according to governmentality theories, through dramatization of perceived threat among national bodies, governments justify racist policies. The emotional derivations of society can justify such behaviors and there is not an absolute need for a logical reasoning. For example, South African media's non-analytical and anti-immigration coverage of border-crossing has influenced both the public and policymakers (Danso & McDonald, 2001). A study of mass media discourse on immigration in New Zealand showed different phases of content discourse (Spoonley & Butcher, 2009). During the first phase, from 1986–1987, when the country moved towards being more culturally diverse, mass media discourse appeared to be more racialized, compared to the second phase after 2000, when the increasing number of immigrant or immigrant-origin media workers influenced this discourse so as to be more sympathetic and friendly toward immigrants. Spoonley and Butcher reported that New Zealand has recently witnessed been another shift toward "racist othering" by some journalists.

Encouraging depiction

Media can affect the attitude of individuals and their decision to emigrate. One aspect of media influence on encouraging people to emigrate is through advertising a different "lifestyle" and providing individuals with new insights about the values and norms of other countries and societies. Lifestyle emigration has been described as a luxurious North–South trend of human mobility for individuals looking for new life conditions, especially those looking for a desirable retirement lifestyle (Featherstone, 1987), or "residential tourism" (Croucher, 2015). Mostly, previous research approached lifestyle emigration as a trend of human mobility, in which privileged groups of emigrants from the "North" translocate to the "South" as "long-term tourists" (ibid). However, it is more likely that emigration to pursue a different lifestyle, or "lifestyle emigration," is not a unilateral flow of North–South relocation. A study of Filipino nurses in Canada who had experience of working in the Middle East showed that, while their emigration to the Middle East was economically driven, their emigration to Canada was motivated by their desire for a Canadian lifestyle, among other factors (Salami, Nelson, Hawthorne, Muntaner, & McGillis Hall, 2014).

Studies on lifestyle emigration have shown that the decision on destination is usually influenced by the social media profile of the migrants who have already emigrated to that location, and the information provided by the tourism and travel industry (Hayes, 2015). Media could advertise lifestyle either directly (for example, through fashion and lifestyle magazines) or embed it into the content of productions (for example, in movies, TV shows, and news broadcasting).

Media promote lifestyle emigration from developing to developed countries. In the current age of media globalization, media technologies and platforms shape the content and global flow of information, and transform traditional relationships and interactions (Flew & Waisbord, 2015). Individualism is an unavoidable offspring of capitalist globalization, because the free market entails individual consumers' free choice to select from a variety of products (Boettke & Coyne, 2005). In addition, the proliferation of information, wide access to the Internet, and economic booms in societies can change the non-static status of cultures on the individualism–collectivism continuum (Tamis-LeMonda et al., 2008). The discrepancy between globalization as a dominating trend and the cultural characteristics of traditional societies is challenging. This challenge is more prominent among cultures, such as those in the Middle East, which are generally perceived to be more collectivist (Goodall, 2014).

As media influence the public's perception of social realities (Soroka, 2012), depictions of economic prosperity and social security provide strong motivations for individuals from less-advantaged economies, and ethnic, religious and sexual minorities to emigrate (Bashir, Lockwood, Dolderman, Sarkissian, & Quick, 2011; Heller, 2009; Scheepers, Gijsberts, & Hello, 2002; Steel, Silove, Bird, McGorry, & Mohan, 1999). Even those with some level of financial stability are likely to migrate in search of more prosperous conditions (Boneva & Frieze, 2001). Depicting luxury and prosperity in movies, providing news about economic growth, and advertising financial opportunities abroad are typical examples of how the mass media encourages individuals to emigrate to gain economic prosperity. In addition, the social media's tendency towards positive self-presentation provides people in the countries of origin with more positive and encouraging information. Positive self-presentation is defined as highlighting positive rather than negative aspects of self (Shim, Lee-Won, & Park, 2016).

Discouraging depiction

However, media can also discourage people from emigrating. Content describing discrimination toward immigrants and the difficulties and dangers they experience could represent a large barrier to many people's decision to emigrate. In the West, immigration policies are controversial issues mingled with uncertainty and unease about the costs and benefits of accepting immigrants (Artiles & Molina, 2011). Depending on the ideology and political bases, media may depict refugees as the "enemies at the gate" and promote their dehumanization (Esses, Medianu, & Lawson, 2013). Western media's focus on the negative aspects of immigration over the course of recent decades has helped exclude and marginalize refugees and immigrants (Esses et al., 2013). A comparative study of English and Spanish media showed that English media outlets are less positive in their coverage of immigrants (Branton & Dunaway, 2008). Darker skin and Latino immigrants in the US are also frequently negatively portrayed as illegal and criminal foreigners through pan-ethnic labeling and negative stereotyping (Steinberg, 2004). In the same way, the mainstream media have presented a negative representation of Muslims and Middle Eastern individuals, especially following 9/11 (Rettberg & Gajjala, 2016).

By focusing on the difficulties and dangers associated with emigration, the media could discourage individuals from emigrating. Also, developments in ICT have facilitated coverage of these issues and the refugee crisis. For example, during the recent refugee crisis, cellphones recorded unprecedented footage of a catastrophe. The shocking photograph of Alan Kurdi, a three-year-old Syrian Kurdish immigrant who, together with his mother and older brother, drowned and then washed up on a Turkish beach, was a global headline in September 2015. Mass media also played a big role in describing the dangers facing emigrants on their way from the Middle East and Africa to Europe; for example, reports on fake lifejackets provided by smugglers to refugees and overloaded boats from Turkey and Libya were frequently broadcast during the peak of the crisis (Tzafalias, 2016). The media also frequently reports on post-emigration life and the problems associated with adapting to host societies; such data could be extremely disappointing and discouraging for those who want to emigrate.

Ideological and governance variations influence the media's framing of emigration. Mass and mainstream media are owned and governed by a limited number of concentrated conglomerates with interlocking interests, capital intensity, and family-owned structures at three different levels: infrastructural, service, and content (Hamelink, 2015). Online and social media, however, can take a bolder stance in terms of governance. Generally, behavior of social media websites is more publicly determined and collaboratively directed (Leskovec, Huttenlocher, & Kleinberg, 2010). Technological advances in communication have enabled global civil society to be more active and less dependent on the political and institutional powers running the mass media (Castells,

2008). Currently, the most visited social media pages belong to the mass media or the individuals who run or work for influential mass media such as the *New York Times, The Guardian*, the BBC, CNN, Reuters, Associated Press, and so on (Stoddart & Tindall, 2015). In addition, larger social media providers such as Facebook and Twitter have shown a tendency to tailor information and news toward their users (Hamelink, 2015). New technological advancements now give unheard people a voice in the public sphere, and a way to keep in touch with other Internet users. This sphere is characterized by real-time, easy, and comprehensive access to/by other ordinary non-mass media users. Online media have facilitated human interactions and social mobility, as was the case during the Arab Spring (Lim, 2012). In the same way, social media have facilitated communication and information flows based on which individuals and states plan their emigration/immigration policies.

History of emigration from Iraqi Kurdistan

Kurdistan is a land surrounded by Iran, Iraq, Turkey, and Syria. The Kurdish population of these four countries is estimated to be between 25 and 30 million people (Rahmani & Croucher, 2017). Geopolitical interactions after the First World War prevented the formation of an independent Kurdish state and resulted in minority groups residing within the boundaries of the newly-formed countries of Iraq, Turkey, and Syria, while they had already been an ethnic minority in Iran. Kurds have witnessed numerous military and political conflicts and crises and experienced numerous rounds of mass emigration and asylum-seeking.

Since the establishment of Iraq in 1932, the Kurds in Iraq, currently estimated to be 5.2 million in the KRG (Kurdistan Regional Government, n.d.), have been in constant conflict with the central Iraqi government with the aim of securing their ethnic rights (Yildiz, 2007). For example, in 1986, the Iraqi government began the Anfal Campaign against the Kurds, during which more than 182,000, mostly-civilian, Kurds were massacred and more than 5,000 villages destroyed (Fischer-Tahir, 2012). The brutality of this operation and the chemical bombardment of Halabja in 1987 forced many Kurdish people to leave their settlements for the regions controlled by the Peshmerga (Kurdish Militia) and later for Iran. After Saddam Hussein's attack on Kuwait and the first Gulf War in 1991, Kurds revolted against the Ba'athist regime of Baghdad. This uprising was eventually defeated (McDowall, 2004). The Iraqi army killed more than 20,000 Kurdish civilians and more than 1.5 million fled to Iran and Turkey as a result of this brutality (Yildiz, 2007; Yip & Sharp, 1993). Even after the establishment of the KRG in 1992, Kurds continued to emigrate due to the difficult economic situation, lack of financial resources, huge budget deficit, internal conflict, and the 1994 civil war (Olson, 1992).

A combination of long-term economic hardship, political instability, and devastating wars created a situation named by Sirkeci (2005) as the "environment of insecurity." In an environment of conflict, tension, and clashes, the residents do not feel safe in their homeland, so, in search of a better life, they begin their journey toward destinations they perceive as safer and more secure. These destinations are mostly located in Western Europe, the Nordic countries, and/or North America. A study of Iraqi Kurdish immigrants in Greece showed that an immigration peak occurred in 1991–1992 after the First Gulf War, and again in 1996–1998 due to the civil war in the KRG (Papadopoulou, 2004). The same source reported that the UK, Sweden, Germany, and France have been the favored destinations of Kurdish emigrants.

Kurdish media in the KRG

Traditionally, the Kurdish press has faced many technical, political, and financial challenges to its survival (Hassanpour, 1992). Such problems still persist for the independent Kurdish print media in the KRG, where scarceness of readers and censorship have limited the number and circulation of such media (Sheyholislami, 2011). Developments in satellite-mediated broadcasting technology made it possible for Kurds in Europe (in 1995) and then in the KRG (in 1999) to establish TV stations and broadcast programs for the Kurdish population of all four countries and elsewhere. However, such stations (about 50 channels as of 2017) are still mostly run by political parties such as Kurdistan Democratic Party (KDP), Patriotic Union of Kurdistan (PUK), and the recently established Gorran (Change) Movement (Wikipedia, n.d.; Sheyholislami, 2011).

Initially introduced in the mid-1990s, the Internet eventually found its way to the residents of the KRG. The huge Kurdish diaspora living in developed Western countries played an important role in encouraging the spread of Internet (Romano, 2006). Previous research in this area proposed that the Internet has frequently been used to maintain and strengthen Kurdish nationhood among Kurds all over the world (Eliassi, 2015; Romano, 2006; Sheyholislami, 2011). By 2013, out of the 5.6 million residents of the KRG, 2 million people used the Internet, mainly for social networking (Rashid, Faraj, & Shareef, 2016). Among the social networking websites available, Facebook is by far the most popular, and has been used for various commercial, social, political, and cultural reasons (Anwer & Zarro, 2016; Ghafour, 2011).

Media and Kurdish emigration

According to Papadopoulou (2004), during the 1990s potential emigrants gained information about their desired destinations from rumors, smugglers, and other migrants. Immigrants residing in the host countries established ethnic communities and informal social networks, which then played an important role in helping emigrants to choose their migration destination, find travel information, and survive in their new homes (Wahlbeck, 1998). Kurdish people intending to emigrate could also gain information through older means of communication such as meeting with others, talking on the phone, hearing from a relative or friend, and writing letters.

Media content produced by Kurdish refugees in Europe and North America has been an important source of information and encouragement. In preparing this book chapter, some Kurdish immigrants living in Sweden were interviewed about their emigration experiences. Hiwa and Narmin (names are changed upon the request of the interviewees) both emigrated to Sweden in the early 1990s and got married in 1995. They sent a copy of their marriage video back to Kurdistan. According to the couple, their video was so popular that almost every member of their family watched it. Their video was nicely made and represented a group of happy immigrants forming a united community, living in a prosperous and beautiful country, and performing the Kurdish tradition for the marriage ceremony almost entirely. Obviously, the video did not show any of the problems the immigrants were facing at that time.

The spreading of satellite TV stations, the Internet, and online social media in the latter part of the 2000s facilitated communication and information flows. Technological advancement also helped the Kurdish community by offering a diverse range of media channels. Large corporations and political entities run the mainstream media, and ordinary civilians and individuals use social networking to communicate with the world.

The governance of social and mainstream media raises questions regarding their coverage of important issues such as emigration/immigration. As mentioned before, media could encourage or discourage emigration. Thus, it is possible that the governance differences between social and mass media result in a tendency to propagate either encouraging or discouraging emigration messages. Therefore, this chapter answers the following question:

> *RQ*: Was there a difference between Kurdish social media, run by non-professional civilians, and Kurdish mainstream media in terms of encouraging or discouraging emigration during the 2015 refugee crisis?

Method

To answer this question, this chapter applies descriptive thematic and visual analyses to the content of the representative Kurdish mainstream and social media between July and December 2015 during the most intensive period of the recent refugee crisis (Europe Refugees & Migrants Emergency Response, n.d.). Content analysis is a systematic categorization and coding of large amounts of textual information through recognition and categorization of the trends, frequencies, and patterns of words, textual structures, and discursive relationships (Vaismoradi, Turunen, & Bondas, 2013). Specifically, thematic content analysis is a method focusing on describing textual patterns or themes to provide a rich and comprehensive account of data (Braun & Clarke, 2006). As Worring and Snoek (2009) state, "Visual content analysis is the process of deriving meaningful descriptors for image and video data" (p. 3360). The aim of the analyses is to categorize the content of the media as encouraging, discouraging, or neutral regarding the representation of the 2015 refugee crisis. Encouraging content is defined as that which presents a positive and promising image of emigration or the host countries, or a negative and unpromising image of the potential emigrants' homeland. Examples of encouraging content are the "happy and normal lives of immigrants" and "safe border crossings." Discouraging themes mostly portray an ambiguous future for the emigrants and dangerous journeys, and promising homeland perspectives. An example of discouraging content is photographs of "difficult journeys undertaken by emigrants." Neutral content provides messages that are neither encouraging nor discouraging; it simply presents general information about emigration and may be accompanied by images such as political authorities talking about the refugee crisis. To ensure the reliability of coding, two native Kurdish speakers coded 10 percent of content together and developed an agreed upon and mutual understanding of the themes that emerged and the analytical patterns. At the end of the coding process, there was a 76 percent similarity between the coders.

Material

The media chosen for this study are two mainstream Kurdish media outlets based in the KRG and two popular Facebook pages focused on emigration/immigration run by non-professional Kurdish individuals. One main media news outlet affiliated with the KDP is Rudaw (U.S. Department of State, 2016), a media group that covers news of the Kurdish community in Kurdistan and the diaspora in two main Kurdish dialects (Sorani and Kurmanji), as well as in English, Arabic, and Turkish. Rudaw TV broadcasts Kurdish news on both the TV and radio via the Internet and satellite for the Middle East, Europe, and North America. Rudaw also publishes a newspaper for both the KRG and the Kurdish diaspora. Claiming to be the only independent media news outlet in Kurdistan, Nalia Radio and Television (NRT) broadcasts in

Kurdish (both dialects), English, and Arabic for a wide audience in the Middle East, Europe, and North America. Similar to Rudaw, NRT also has applications for both android and IOS platforms. NRT is allegedly connected to the Gorran movement. As a sociopolitical movement in the KRG, Gorran was established in 2009 to protest against the political dominance of the PUK and KDP (Hevian, 2013). It remained an opposition party until 2013, when it took part in the new KRG administration, but has remained very critical of the ruling KDP policies.

Two popular Facebook pages devoted to Kurdish emigration (especially to Europe) were also chosen for this study. Jihiŝtnī Nīŝtiman Erkikī Nīŝtimanīye (Leaving [one's] Homeland is a Patriotic Duty) is a public page with about 21,000 followers (Jihiŝtnī Nīŝtiman Erkikī Nīŝtimanīye, n.d.) This page (hereafter Homeland) covers news about refugees, immigration news, and changes in immigration regulation. The page provides phone numbers and some advertisements directed toward those who are in search of refugee smugglers. Kurdani Aurupa (Kurds in Europe) is also a Facebook page dealing with different issues related to immigration, refugees, and asylum-seekers; it has 65,000 followers.

Results

The results of the analysis revealed some differences between the mass and social media in their approaches to Kurdish emigration. Generally, the investigated mass media showed more cases of discouraging messages compared to the Facebook pages. Table 14.1 shows the frequency and percentage of encouraging, discouraging, and neutral messages in the content produced by each media.

The textual analysis of the news stories and Facebook posts revealed that Rudaw and NRT communicated more messages with discouraging themes related to the 2015 refugee crisis. Rudaw's news stories and TV programs were 74 percent discouraging, 17 percent neutral, and

Table 14.1 Frequency and percentage of encouraging, discouraging, and neutral messages in the content produced by each media

Theme	*Rudaw (n, %)*	*NRT (n, %)*	*Homeland* (n, %)*	*Kurds** (n, %)*
		Text		
Discouraging themes	48(73.85)	20(45.45)	114(25.05)	65(35.91)
Encouraging themes	6(9.23)	17(38.64)	287(63.08)	101(55.8)
Neutral themes	11(16.92)	7(15.91)	54(11.87)	15(8.29)
Total	**65**	**44**	**455**	**181**
		Visual		
Discouraging themes	23(69.7)	18(62.07)	181(39.01)	59(47.97)
Encouraging themes	3(9.09)	6(20.69)	222(47.84)	50(40.65)
Neutral themes	7(21.21)	5(17.24)	61(13.15)	14(11.38)
Total	**33**	**29**	**464**	**123**

* Leaving the Homeland is a Patriotic Duty
** Kurds in Europe

9 percent encouraging on the subject of emigration to Europe. During the same period, 45 percent of NRT broadcasts were discouraging, 39 percent were encouraging, and 16 percent were neutral on the subject of emigration. Despite the similarity between the approach of these two media outlets to emigration, there are obvious differences in their conceptualization of the refugee crisis. This difference can be seen in their choice of themes (see Table 14.2 for details of

Table 14.2 Themes that emerged during media content analysis, June–December 2015

Theme	*Rudaw*	*NRT*	*Homeland**	*Kurds***	*Tone*
	Texts				
Prospect of a more secure Kurdistan, and more dangerous border-crossing to Europe	4	–	1	–	Discouraging
Difficult journeys/insufficient resources/unstable future	25	17	105	41	Discouraging
Immigrants not being welcome in Europe	16	1	1	9	Discouraging
Racist comments against immigrants (by the Kurdish media)	–	–	–	6	Discouraging
Regretful immigrants	3	1	6	9	Discouraging
Terrorists among the immigrants	–	1	1	–	Discouraging
Better life in Europe compared to Kurdistan	–	2	33	20	Encouraging
Challenging idea of staying in the homeland	–	–	25	–	Encouraging
Criticizing KRG authorities	4	8	33	13	Encouraging
Famous people's emigration to Europe	–	–	2	–	Encouraging
Immigrants' happy and normal lives	–	–	82	9	Encouraging
Happy or safe border crossing	–	–	71	1	Encouraging
Nice behavior toward immigrants	–	1	8	23	Encouraging
Opportunities for emigration	2	4	12	12	Encouraging
People's incorrect perception of Europe	–	–	5	4	Encouraging
Smugglers' view	-	2	4	–	Encouraging
Smuggling advertisement	-	–	7	–	Encouraging
Ungrateful immigrants	-	–	5	19	Encouraging
Criticizing other countries over immigration issues	-	2	–	–	Neutral
General news and posts	6	5	54	15	Neutral
Reasons for the immigration crisis	5	–	–	–	Neutral
	Visual				
People experiencing difficulties on their journey	19	17	176	40	Discouraging
Europeans protesting against immigration policies	1	1	–	1	Discouraging
Difficult life in Europe	3	–	4	15	Discouraging
Immigrants causing trouble for the host countries	–	–	1	3	Discouraging
Happy immigrants	0	2	55	21	Encouraging
Beauty and pleasures of Europe	–	1	114	8	Encouraging
Nice behavior toward immigrants	–	1	9	11	Encouraging
Difficulties in Kurdistan life	3	2	44	10	Encouraging
General visual information	7	5	61	14	Neutral

* Leaving the Homeland is a Patriotic Duty
** Kurds in Europe

these themes). Rudaw's discouraging themes often represent the difficulties and problems emigrants face during their trip to Europe, and the unwillingness of Europeans and their governments to receive immigrants from the Middle East and North Africa. However, NRT has mostly been focused on the dangers of emigration routes. It criticizes the KRG for its incompetency in providing Kurds with a stable economy, social welfare, and security, which, according to NRT, are the reasons for Kurdish youth emigration. Figure 14.1 compares the division of theme categories across all media in terms of textual content.

Visually, both media mostly depicted the difficulties and problems emigrants face on their way to Europe. Generally, this includes footage of emigrants (especially children) en route and in crowded refugee camps, and there are frequently graphic images of dead refugees, who lost their lives during their migration, in particular in the Mediterranean Sea. Figure 14.2 compares the division of theme categories across all media in terms of visual content.

The two Facebook pages studied contain more instances of messages encouraging migration (to Europe). About 63 percent of the themes that emerged during analysis of Homeland's content encouraged migration and only 25 percent of messages were discouraging. Analysis of Kurdani Aurupa's page revealed 59 percent of encouraging and 36 percent of discouraging messages (see Table 14.2 for details of the themes). However, there are some differences in the nature of the main themes of these pages. Homeland focuses on an expected happy and normal life after emigration and a safe border crossing and an easy journey. The page's current profile picture is a "selfie" taken by what appears to be a group of emigrants on a boat, supposedly on their way from Turkey to Greece. The page is also filled with photographs of newly-arrived immigrants accompanied by explanations of how they finally made it to Europe and their favorite country, and of how they have begun a new life. These

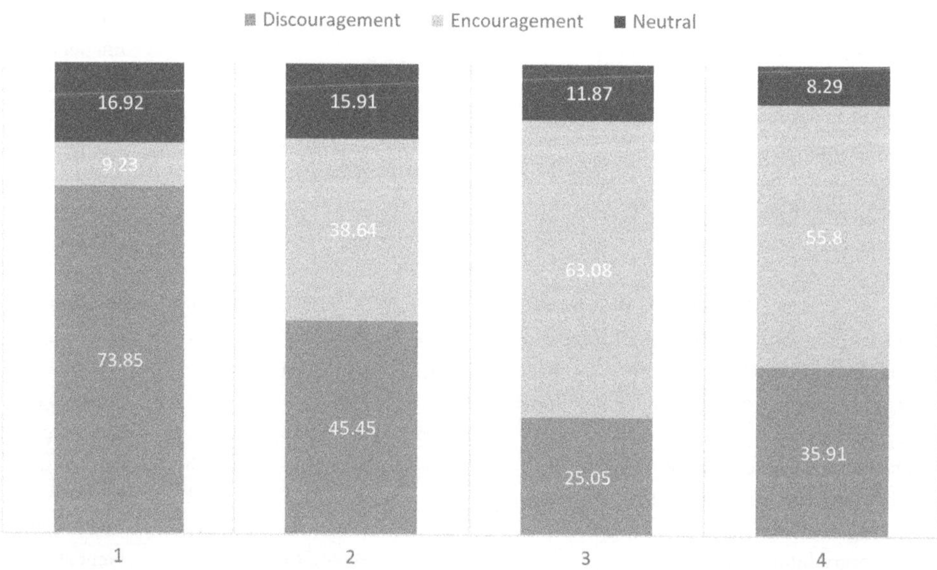

* 1: Rudaw, 2: NRT, 3: Leaving the Homeland is a Patriotic Duty, 4: Kurds in Europe

Figure 14.1 Division of theme categories across all media: textual content

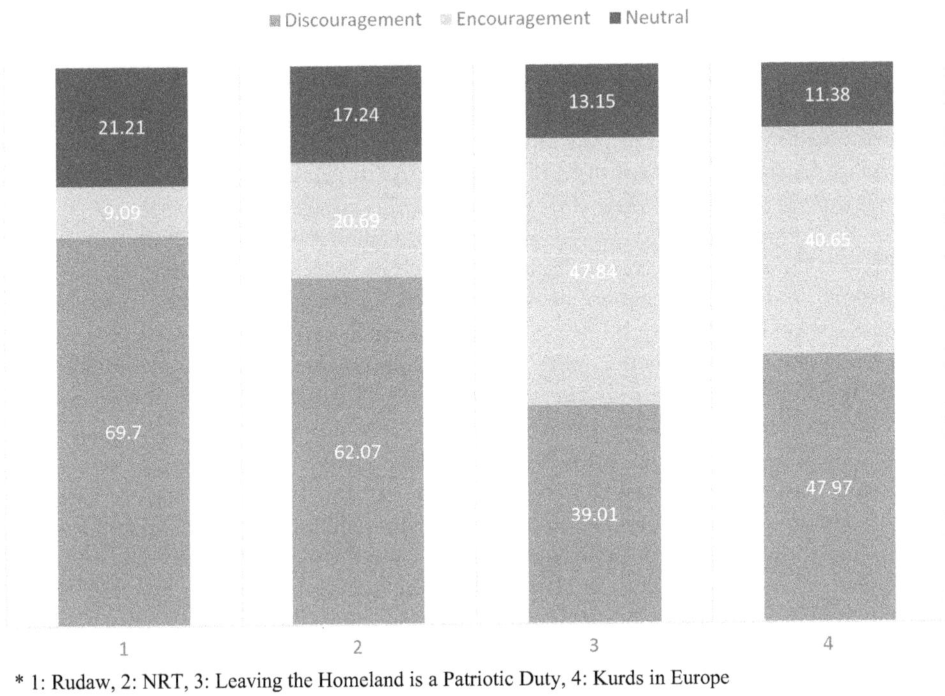

Figure 14.2 Division of theme categories across all media: visual content

photographs are usually taken at tourist sites in big cities. Kurdani Aurupa focuses on comparing the quality of life in Kurdistan and Europe; the philanthropic behavior of Europeans and European governments; and immigrants' ungrateful behavior as evidenced in both their inability to adapt to their new societies and in their expecting too much. Interestingly, this page includes many video messages from immigrants in different European countries, in which they talk about their difficult experiences and wish they had stayed at home. Usually, the administrator(s) of the page scolds such "regretful immigrants" for complaining about their situation, and compare the difficult Kurdistan life with the services they receive in the European refugee camps.

Visual analysis of the content provided by these two Facebook pages revealed different patterns. Kurdani Aurupa reflected more discouraging (49 percent) than encouraging (41 percent) messages because of its reliance on visual content produced by other media (especially mass media such as NRT and Rudaw). This Facebook page frequently used the visual content of the mainstream media and commented on the content to declare its position. Homeland, however, used much of the content and photographs sent to them by immigrant followers or the content they acquired from other Facebook pages. This content is a colorful and positive visualization of migration that encourages individuals from Kurdistan to join others in their "prosperous and joyful European life." Nevertheless, neither of the pages was able to escape from the footage of dangerous journeys on overloaded boats, overcrowded camps and railway stations, and even jails. As mentioned before, Homeland tried to smooth over this image with the "happy immigrant" theme, while Kurdani Aurupa tried to soften discouraging messages through comments and explanations.

Discussion

Analysis of the data revealed a difference in the way Kurdish media present Kurdish emigration/immigration experiences and the tone in which these messages are conveyed. The mass media were generally discouraging of Kurdish migration, as they see it as a disadvantage for the development of Kurdistan and a real danger in the middle of the ongoing war with the terrorist Islamic State (IS). Kurdistan is also engaged in its long-lasting conflict with the government in Baghdad over various issues, such as the right to self-determination, the disputed Kurdish-settled areas, which are outside of the current official KRG borders (e.g., Kirkuk), and budget allocation for the KRG (Katzman et al., 2014; Salih, 2016). Losing a huge human resource during the 2015 refugee crisis had the possibility to affect the strength of the KRG, both in its military conflict with IS and in ongoing multifaceted conflict with the federal authorities in Baghdad. The implementation of Article 140 of the Iraqi constitution is a critical conflict between the KRG and the federal government. This article deals with the status of the strategic oil-rich city of Kirkuk, which underwent the process of Arabization during the Saddam Hussein regime (MacQueen, 2015). During this process, Hussein tried to isolate the Kurds in and around this city and change the demographics of the area by displacing the Kurdish population and replacing them with Arab immigrants from other parts of Iraq. According to Article 140, the process should be reversed and a referendum should determine the status of the city. Therefore, it is critical for the KRG not to lose its main productive resources and workforce to European countries. Emigration could also result in demographic changes within the KRG. In 2015, a video of a woman who was worried about the limited marriage choices of Kurdish women after emigration of young Kurdish men to Europe received widespread attention. Despite its humorous criticism, this video nonetheless addresses a realistic facet of such demographic changes. The discouraging messages of the mass media are in accordance with such realities.

The Kurdish mass media's support of KRG policies is a classic example of the interaction between mass media and institutions of power. Both media studied are linked to political parties and benefit from their political, financial, and technical support. At the same time, they present the ideology of their linked parties to the public and try to influence the public using different (re) framing strategies. Despite the similarities in their stance against Kurdish emigration, they represent basic differences in perception regarding the reasons for emigration. While Rudaw (linked to the ruling KDP) focuses on the consequences of emigration for the future of both emigrants and Kurdistan, the NRT (frequently reported to be linked to the opposition movement, Gorran) staunchly presents the corruption and malfunction of the KRG as the reason for the massive emigration. However, through framing emigration as a dangerous journey with unclear and unpromising outcomes, it seems that the NRT is suggesting one should stay, resist, and change the system. This message is very close to the social and political promises of the Gorran movement.

Along with the problems outside its borders, the KRG has been suffering from a financial crisis and the socio-political consequences thereof since 2014. A large element of the public sector and many governmental institutions such as health and education, are paralyzed as a result of dramatic decreases in oil price, huge budget deficits, the tribal and patronage structures of the KRG, and politically and financially corrupt management (Salih, 2016). Economically, this crisis has led to an increase in the inflation rate and a decrease in quality of life and purchasing power (Akbay, Hussein, Salim, & Latif, 2016). The social consequences of this economic failure and corrupt mismanagement were revealed in a large wealth gap, public dissatisfaction and frustration, and emigration to Europe. These issues were reflected in the numerous references to KRG corruption on the two Facebook pages studied. The Facebook pages encourage and advertise emigration as a form of protest against the existing situation in the KRG. Figure 14.3 is an image frequently used by the two Facebook pages and is captioned: "President! The chair is all yours; just give me enough to pay a smuggler and I will leave."

This represents a difference in the agendas set by social and mass media. Social media provides the traditional audience with the chance to redefine themselves as content contributors and producers, rather than mere media consumers; this heterogeneity defines a more active role for the traditional audience (Arguete, 2017). This diversification challenges the traditional dominant agendas of the mass media by providing various sources of news and empowerment opportunities for those who finally find a chance to be heard (ibid). However, the capability of such media to offer a voice in this way should be viewed with caution; traditional media institutions dominate and use these online platforms to disseminate their content and keep in contact with their readership.

Analysis also showed that social media run by non-professionals depends greatly on mass media content to produce and disseminate its ideas and attract audiences. Various factors, like technical requirements, can restrict the degree to which a non-professional user can produce original content on social media. Production and video editing not only require specialist hardware and software, but also practical know-how. Financial reasons also restrict an individual's ability to support external technical contributions, purchase the copyrighted material, and travel to collect footage. Such limitations force individual Facebook page administrators to use the content of other pages and social network outlets. In the case of this study, the Facebook pages used material from the Kurdish mass media extensively, including, but not limited to, Rudaw and NRT. The pages also used many videos from other Facebook pages.

Despite their dependency on mass media content, the Facebook pages used the borrowed material to build up their own narrative on migration. While the studied mass media discouraged the emigration of Kurds to Europe, the Facebook pages used the content of the same mass media to frame their encouraging messages related to emigration, albeit with differences in the implementation of this strategy. While Kurdani Aurupa used many videos from both Rudaw and NRT, it commented extensively on them to frame its story of emigration. As mentioned before, there are many videos of "regretful immigrants" who find it difficult to adapt to their immigrant lives in Europe. The page has generally commented on such videos to indicate that (1) the immigrants depicted in the videos are emotionally weak,

Figure 14.3 "President! The chair is all yours; just give me enough to pay a smuggler and I will leave"
Source: www.routledge.com/9781138058149

(2) their expectations of their host countries are too high, (3) things will get easier with time, and (4) the little they have in refugee camps is better than what they had in Kurdistan. Homeland, on the other hand, frequently used a special type of video in which the KRG is criticized in relation to the crippled economy, lack of social security, poor quality education and health services, and especially pervasive economic and political corruption.

Conclusion

The media influences the emigration/immigration policies of governments at both local and global levels through framing this subject and building discourses and narratives around it. Based on the differences in governance and agenda, the framing of emigration/immigration can be either encouraging (e.g., lifestyle emigration) or discouraging (e.g., refugees and asylum-seekers).

This study confirmed the differences in the narratives of social and mass media in their representations of Kurdish emigration. The mass media discouraged emigration and framed it as a dangerous journey with unclear outcomes that will hurt Kurdish individuals, and as a demographic transformation with economic, social, and political consequences for Kurdistan. The mass media also used its narration of the immigration crisis to criticize the status quo, and, to invite the public to promote the socioeconomic status of the Kurdistan. The Facebook pages run by Kurdish non-professional individuals represented emigration as a chance to highlight the inefficiency and corruption of the KRG. Their immigration narratives can be summarized as protestation. The administrators of the Facebook pages studied protested social and political inequality and discrimination in Kurdistan through encouraging Kurds to leave the country and emigrate to other countries. This shows that, even in removing the security risks currently threating Kurdistan, people will continue to emigrate in search of higher standards of justice thereby making them feel powerful enough to compete with those benefiting from higher socioeconomic status.

Further studies

As mentioned before, lifestyle emigration is usually perceived as a trend of North–South translocation in search of further amenities. However, with the expansion of media, information, and individualism, not all cases of lifestyle emigration follow the same formula. Lifestyle emigration entails pursuing individual preferences and choices (Featherstone, 1987), thus lifestyle emigration of individuals in more collectivist cultures needs more attention and research. The lifestyle preferences and contradictions between individual choices and cultural norms and values could be important elements to push individuals in general, and the younger generation in particular, toward societies more open to such individual preferences.

Another area of future research is related to the media depiction of destination societies within societies of origin. Seemingly, there are not enough studies that show how the decisions of prospective emigrants are influenced by the local media they consume, both domestic and foreign. This is especially the case with those immigrants who choose to return home after their socioeconomic status as immigrants fails to satisfy their initial expectations. It is likely that their perceptions of the economic and social situation of their destination countries are inaccurate and exaggerated. If this information comes from a media source, which is mostly the case, it is necessary to know more about the discourse of such media depictions to regulate future emigration/immigration policies.

The communication dynamics of online social pages and accounts run by non-professional individuals who are not part of bigger media corporations, and the relationship of such individuals with the mass media, need more in-depth investigation. Such studies will provide us with a better understanding of how such social media administrators attract and interact with their audience, influence their environment, and interact with other media.

References

Akbay, C., Hussein, R. S., Salim, B. T., & Latif, S. (2016). Economic crisis and small business in Erbil-Iraq. *International Journal of Business and Social Research, 6*, 1–7.

Anwer, M. A. & Zarro, R. D. (2016). Effect of different social media interaction factors on promoting SMEs in Kurdistan. *ZANCO Journal of Pure and Applied Sciences, 28*, 72–77.

Arguete, N. (2017). The agenda setting hypothesis in the new media environment. *Comunicación Y Sociedad, 28*, 35–58.

Artiles, A. M. & Molina, O. (2011). Crisis, economic uncertainty and union members' attitudes toward immigrants in Europe. *European Review of Labour and Research, 17*, 453–469.

Bashir, N. Y., Lockwood, P., Dolderman, D., Sarkissian, T., & Quick, L. K. (2011). Emphasizing jobs and trees: Increasing the impact of pro-environmental messages on migrants. *Basic and Applied Social Psychology, 33*, 255–265.

Boettke, P. J. & Coyne, C. J. (2005). Methodological individualism, spontaneous order and the research program of the workshop in political theory and policy analysis. *Journal of Economic Behavior and Organization, 57*, 145–158.

Boneva, B. S. & Frieze, I. H. (2001). Toward a concept of a migrant personality. *Journal of Social Issues, 57*, 477–491.

Branton, R. & Dunaway, J. (2008). English- and Spanish-language media coverage of immigration: A comparative analysis. *Social Science Quarterly, 89*, 1006–1022.

Braun, V. & Clarke, V. (2006). Using thematic analysis in psychology. *Qualitative Research in Psychology, 3*, 77–101.

Castells, M. (2008). The new public sphere: Global civil society, communication networks, and global governance. *Annals of the American Academy of Political and Social Science, 616*, 78–93.

Croucher, S. (2015). The future of lifestyle migration: Challenges and opportunities. *Journal of Latin American Geography, 14*, 161–172.

Danso, R. & McDonald, D. A. (2001). Writing xenophobia: Immigration and the print media in post-apartheid South Africa. *Africa Today, 48*, 115–137.

Eliassi, B. (2015). Making a Kurdistani identity in diaspora: Kurdish migrants in Sweden. In N. Sigona, A. Gamlen, G. Liberatore, & H. Neveu Kringelbach (Eds.), *Diasporas reimagined: Spaces, practices and belonging*. Oxford: Oxford University Press.

Esses, V. M., Medianu, S., & Lawson, A. S. (2013). Uncertainty, threat, and the role of the media in promoting the dehumanization of immigrants and refugees. *Journal of Social Issues, 69*, 518–536.

Europe Refugees & Migrants Emergency Response. (n.d.). Nationality of arrivals to Greece, Italy and Spain, January–December 2015. Retrieved from http://reliefweb.int/sites/reliefweb.int/files/resources/MonthlyTrendsofNationalities-ArrivalstoGreeceItalyandSpain-31December2015.pdf

Featherstone, M. (1987). Lifestyle and consumer culture. *Theory, Culture & Society, 4*, 55–70.

Fischer-Tahir, A. (2012). Gendered memories and masculinities: Kurdish Peshmerga on the Anfal campaign in Iraq. *Journal of Middle East Women's Studies, 8*, 92–114.

Flew, T. & Waisbord, S. (2015). The ongoing significance of national media systems in the context of media globalization. *Media, Culture & Society, 37*, 620–636.

Ghafour, G. S. (2014). Value disclosure of young adults through social media in the Iraqi Kurdistan region as an emerging democracy. *Journalism and Mass Communication, 4*, 303–317.

Goodall, H. (2014). Middle East meets West: Negotiating cultural difference in international educational encounters. *International Review of Education, 60*, 603–617.

Hamelink, C. J. (2015). *Global communication*. Los Angeles, CA: Sage.

Hassanpour, A. (1992). *Nationalism and language in Kurdistan*. San Francisco, CA: Mellon Press.

Hayes, M. (2015). Introduction: The emerging lifestyle migration industry and geographies of transnationalism, mobility and displacement in Latin America. *Journal of Latin American Geography, 14*, 7–18.

Heller, P. (2009). Challenges facing LGBT asylum-seekers: The role of social work in correcting oppressive immigration processes. *Journal of Gay & Lesbian Social Services, 21*, 294–308.

Hevian, R. (2013). The main Kurdish political parties in Iran, Iraq, Syria, and Turkey: A research guide. *Middle East Review of International Affairs, 17*, 94–122.

Jihîŝtnî Nîŝtiman Erkikî Nîŝtimanîye (Leaving [one's] Homeland is a Patriotic Duty). (n.d.). Facebook public page. Retrieved from www.facebook.com/baxer.bo.wlati.baritanya/

Katzman, K., Blanchard, C. M., Humud, C. E., Margesson, R., Tiersky, A., & Weed, M. C. (2014). The "Islamic State" crisis and U.S. policy. Congressional Research Service, Library of Congress. Retrieved from https://fas.org/sgp/crs/mideast/R43612.pdf

Kurdani Auropa (Kurds in Europe). (n.d.). Facebook public page. Retrieved from https://goo.gl/ZdHfs4

Kurdistan Regional Government. (n.d.). People of the Kurdistan region. Retrieved from www.gov.krd/p/p.aspx?l=12&s=020000&r=304&p=214

Leskovec, J., Huttenlocher, D., & Kleinberg, J. (2010). Governance in social media: A case study of the Wikipedia promotion process. *Proceeding of the Fourth International AAAI Conference on Weblogs and Social Media* (pp. 98–105). Washington, DC: George Washington University.

Lim, M. (2012). Clicks, cabs, and coffee houses: Social media and oppositional movements in Egypt, 2004–2011. *Journal of Communication, 62*, 231–248.

MacQueen, B. (2015). Democratization, elections and the "de facto state dilemma": Iraq's Kurdistan Regional Government. *Cooperation and Conflict, 50*, 423–439.

McDowall, D. (2004). *A modern history of the Kurds* (4th ed.). London: I. B. Tauris.

Migration Policy Institute. (n.d.). Moving Europe beyond crisis. Retrieved from https://goo.gl/IaO98i

Olson, R. (1992). The Kurdish question in the aftermath of the Gulf war: Geopolitical and geostrategic changes in the Middle East. *Third World Quarterly, 13*, 475–499.

Papadopoulou, A. (2004). Smuggling into Europe: Transit migrants in Greece. *Journal of Refugee Studies, 17*, 167–184.

Rahmani, D. & Croucher, S. M. (2017). Minority groups and communication apprehension: An investigation of Kurdistan. *Journal of Intercultural Communication, 43*.

Rashid, B. N., Faraj, A. A., & Shareef, T. H. (2016). Investigating and evaluating internet usage in Kurdistan region of Iraq. *International Journal of Multidisciplinary and Current Research, 4*, 474–479.

Rettberg, J. W. & Gajjala, R. (2016). Terrorists or cowards: Negative portrayals of male Syrian refugees in social media. *Feminist Media Studies, 16*, 178–181.

Romano, D. (2006). *The Kurdish nationalist movement: Opportunity, mobilization and identity*. Cambridge: Cambridge University Press.

Salami, B., Nelson, S., Hawthorne, L., Muntaner, C., & McGillis Hall, L. (2014). Motivations of nurses who migrate to Canada as domestic workers. *International Nursing Review, 61*, 479–486.

Salih, M. A. (2016). Low oil prices complicate Iraqi Kurdish independence. Middle East Institute Policy Focus Series. Retrieved from www.mei.edu/sites/default/files/publications/PF7_Salih_KRGeconcrisis.pdf

Scheepers, P., Gijsberts, M., & Hello, E. (2002). Religiosity and prejudice against ethnic minorities in Europe: Cross-national tests on a controversial relationship. *Review of Religious Research, 43*, 242–265.

Sheyholislami, J. (2011). *Kurdish identity, discourse, and new media*. New York: Palgrave Macmillan.

Shim, M., Lee-Won, R. J., & Park, S. H. (2016). The self on the net: The joint effect of self-construal and public self-consciousness on positive self-presentation in online social networking among South Korean college students. *Computers in Human Behavior, 63*, 530–539.

Sirkeci, I. (2005). War in Iraq: Environment of insecurity and international migration. *International Migration, 43*, 197–214.

Soroka, S. N. (2012). The gatekeeping function: Distributions of information in media and the real world. *Journal of Politics, 74*, 514–528.

Spoonley, P. & Butcher, A. (2009). Reporting superdiversity. The mass media and immigration in New Zealand. *Journal of Intercultural Studies, 30*, 355–372.

Steel, Z., Silove, D., Bird, K., McGorry, P., & Mohan, P. (1999). Pathways from war trauma to posttraumatic stress symptoms among Tamil asylum seekers, refugees, and immigrants. *Journal of Traumatic Stress, 12*, 421–435.

Steinberg, S. L. (2004). Undocumented immigrants or illegal aliens? Southwestern media portrayals of Latino immigrants. *Humboldt Journal of Social Relations, 28*, 109–133.

Stoddart, M. C. J. & Tindall, D. B. (2015). Canadian news media and the cultural dynamics of multilevel climate governance. *Environmental Politics*, *24*, 401–422.
Syrian Refugees. (n.d.). A snapshot of the crisis – in the Middle East and Europe. Retrieved from http://syrianrefugees.eu/timeline/
Szlanko, B. (2016, March 7). Kurdish refugees return to Iraqi Kurdistan after Europe disappoints. http://ekurd.net/kurdish-refugees-return-kurdistan-2016-03-07.
Tamis-LeMonda, C. S., Way, N., Hughes, D., Yoshikawa, H., Kalman, R. K., & Niwa, E. Y. (2008). Parents' goals for children: The dynamic coexistence of individualism and collectivism in cultures and individuals. *Social Development*, *17*, 183–209.
Tzafalias, M. (2016). Fake lifejackets play a role in drowning of refugees. *Bulletin of the World Health Organization*, *94*, 411–412.
U.S. Department of State. (2016). Iraq.www.state.gov/j/drl/rls/hrrpt/2015/nea/252925.htm.
Vaismoradi, M., Turunen, H., & Bondas, T. (2013). Content analysis and thematic analysis: Implications for conducting a qualitative descriptive study. *Nursing & Health Sciences*, *15*, 398–405.
Vukov, T. (2003). Imagining communities through immigration policies. *International Journal of Cultural Studies*, *6*, 335–353.
Wahlbeck, O. (1998). Community work and exile politics: Kurdish refugee associations in London. *Journal of Refugee Studies*, *11*, 215–230.
Wikipedia. (n.d.). List of Kurdish-language television channels. Retrieved from https://en.wikipedia.org/wiki/List_of_Kurdish-language_television_channels
Worring, M. & Snoek, C. (2009). Visual content analysis. In L. Liu & M. T. Özsu (Eds.), *Encyclopedia of database systems* (pp. 3360–3365). New York: Springer.
Yildiz, K. (2007). *The Kurds in Iraq: The past, present and future* (revised ed.). London: Pluto Press.
Yip, R. & Sharp, T. W. (1993). Accute malnutrition and high childhood mortality related to diarrhea: Lessons from the 1991 Kurdish refugee crisis. *Journal of the American Medical Association*, *270*, 587–590.

15

LINGUISTIC ANALYSIS OF THE "IMMIGRANT" AS REPRESENTED IN RUSSIAN MEDIA

Cultural semantics

Tatiana M. Permyakova & Olga L. Antineskul

In recent years, the issue of migration has attracted considerable media attention; immigration has become the focus of social, economic, cultural, and linguistic research. While there are numerous studies on public and political discourse about European migration, only a relatively small amount of research appears to concentrate on the specific historical, cultural, and social contexts of the issue in Russia. In view of the above, the research question is: how does the representation of "immigrant" in Russian media reflect the cultural/local/national features of this global phenomenon?

This study has considerable potential for the field of intercultural communication, with its focus on linguistic ethno-relativity when it analyzes the universality and variability of media discourse on migration. Moreover, in this research, the phenomenon under study – the immigrant – is treated as a focal point of intercultural communication. The structure of this chapter is as follows: first, we will explore the concept of the "immigrant" in intercultural communication and media discourse theories; next, we will examine linguistic studies and the methodology used by linguists to analyze the aforementioned concept; finally, we will apply cultural semantic analysis to media discourse, namely, the newspaper subcorpus of the Russian national corpus (RNC).

The "immigrant" in intercultural communication and media discourse studies

There are a number of intercultural communication theories that apply to research on (im) migrants: Kim's (1988) integrative theory of communication and cross-cultural adaptation, Gallois and Callan's (1988) communication accommodation theory, Collier and Thomas's (1988) cultural identity theory, and Ting-Toomey's (1988) face-negotiation theory. These theories focus predominantly on cross-cultural psychology, psychological models of adaptation, and contact with the host culture (Berry, 1997; Kim, 1988, 1989, 2001a, 2001b, 2008).

These theories can, first, be distinguished by their application to individual or group experiences. Kim's integrative theory combines emic (insider) and etic (outsider) approaches with an intercultural personhood that undergoes cross-cultural adaptation as a result of valuable constructs such as host receptivity, host conformity pressure, and ethnic group strength.

Additionally, the theory of cultural adaptation (Kim, 1988, 2001a) has been tested and complemented by other theories, e.g., integrated threat theory in communication science (Croucher, 2013), grounded theory in sociology (Sheridan & Storch, 2009), and uncertainty/anxiety management theory with educational sojourners (Hullett & Witte, 2001). Jandt (2000) raised a terminological issue connected with "immigrant," "tourist," and "sojourner," and goes on to discuss "immigration," "acculturation," and "assimilation" as cultural practices in various countries. His study of group identities showed how language, print, media, marketing, and the Internet collectively contribute to constructing the cultural identities of people who move between countries.

Intercultural theories on immigrants are concerned with developing methods of ethnic identity analysis within interpretative and critical paradigms by incorporating real-life experiences and historical contexts (Davis, Nakayama, & Martin, 2000). Communication adaptation and cultural identity theories are of particular interest to us as they come closer to linguistic analysis and are relevant to studying the role of the media. Another methodological line of study is discourse analysis of immigrants' identity, mediated effects, and language. The cognitive approach to discourse analysis explores language acquisition, and the role of communities in identity construction through language(s), as well as the impact on educational policies (Collier, 1995; Hatch, 1992). The psychological approach to discourse analysis related to immigrants is linked with research on acculturation in anthropology and intergroup relations in sociology (Berry, 2001).

The media plays a key role in how not only media actors and consumers but also migrants and ethnic minority groups themselves perceive migration and its consequences (Wood & King, 2001). Similar to intercultural communication theories, the effects of the media include the "reception" and "social exclusion" of migrants in host societies, as observed in the migratory experiences and the multiple cultural, religious, national, and ethnic identities of diasporic communities. However, in media framing research, Matthes (2009) concluded that a marked rise in quantitative research in framing effects is paralleled by a tendency towards neglecting the qualitative side, which leads to reliability being insufficiently reported. The most significant finding of media framing studies is that immigrants are represented as "others, posing a threat."

Over the last few decades, there has been a growing interest in media representations of immigrants as an object of theoretical study; for example, Grillo (1985) performed a comprehensive anthropological analysis of the representation of immigrants in France. There has also been extensive research on the representation of immigrants on different continents (Khosravinik, 2010; Mahtani, 2008; Martiniello, 2005; Pogliano & Solaroli, 2012). As observed by Riggins (1997), who applies critical discourse analysis to political speeches, language use and political values affecting word choice result in marginalizing immigrant minority groups. Therefore, political discourse analysis highlights the importance of the linguistic perspective in the study of prejudice and social inequality (Chilton, 2004).

A number of studies focusing on the representation of immigrants have adopted linguistic and socio-linguistic perspectives. For instance, according to Santa Ana (1999), metaphor frames applied to immigrants create a public perception that dehumanizes immigrant workers. This echoes the findings of socio-linguistic research on media coverage of immigration policies (Esses, Medianu, & Lawson, 2013): immigrants and refugees are dehumanized by being portrayed as carriers of infectious diseases, potential terrorists, and a threat to Western nations. The results of socio-linguistic studies have been complemented by critical discourse analysis, which has become instrumental in exploring the language of the media with a view to gaining a new perspective on racial and ethnic inequality, as well as social regulation (van Dijk, 1992, 2003). In general, analysis of immigration-related public discourse indicates that the social construction of the news can be biased as it conveys values and stereotypes backed by social and economic factors (Fowler, 2013). These observations are confirmed by recent publications that point out that there is a trend towards globalism, with particular reference to creating discoveries of identity (Manchin & van Leeuwen, 2007).

A study of media discourse about immigration in the national newspaper *Rossiyskaya Gazeta* over a six-year period (2004–2009) found that the subjects of debate on immigration are often linked with law and the economy, that the financial crisis in Russia appears to have reversed the general pro-immigrant trend, and that the debates tend not to make a distinction between immigrants and migrants from other parts of Russia (Berg-Nordlijs, Oslands, & Tkača, 2010).

Although there are many articles about Russian immigrants in the United States, Israel, and the European Union countries (Lesnevskaya, 2013; Mineyeva, 2013), publications about immigration in Russia are rare. The results of sociological research concerning migration in post-Soviet Russia reveal a necessity to shift the focus of study from the structural differences between forced and voluntary migration to the cultural issues inherent in the integration of newcomers who have come to be regarded as a distinct sociocultural "other" group in post-Soviet Russian society (Pilkington, 1998, p. 21). Most of the media framing effects (threat, crime, victim, etc.) are found to apply to the representation of contemporary Russian immigrants (Kosulya, 2011; Sarayeva, 2011; Skrebtsova, 2007).

A study conducted by Sokolsky (2016) includes sociodemographic and geographic overviews of migration history in Russia. The author stressed the fact that many people migrated at the state's behest, while others often did so for their own, often compelling, reasons. Whether people were coerced into moving or did so voluntarily, they developed distinctive ways of dealing with displacement – an aspect of Russian culture that is yet to be explored. Apart from issues arising from conflicts between immigrants and the host population over the course of immigrant adaptation (Kitov & Gasanova, 2014; Koryakin, 2007), another area of immigration-related study is research on the language issues that educational institutions face, which, along with a theoretical background, provide practical recommendations for teaching immigrants' children (Popov, 2008; Streltsova, 2014). As Russia is the EU's neighboring region, it is essential that immigration is explored from the Russian perspective because, on the one hand, it broadens the scope of research and enables it to take a global view of migration cooperation policies and, on the other hand, it contributes to minimizing the limitations of state borders, which often leads to overlooking important aspects of migration issues (Korneev, 2014).

The "immigrant" in language studies

There are various methodological tools for studying immigrant representation in the media, which are aimed at exploring the sociocultural role of language and the specific features of mediated language. These tools are, in effect, intended to address the diverse and complex issue of the immigrant personality, which is typically viewed as being menacing and socially segregated.

Linguistic analysis focuses on the generation of meanings in contexts of power asymmetry, including culture-related assumptions and legal frames of interpretation (Verschueren, 2008).

Another methodological approach to analyzing the linguistic aspect of migration is corpus linguistics (Baker, McEnery & Gabrielatos, 2007). Gabrielatos and Baker (2006) made a significant contribution to migration studies. First, the authors provided a classification of migrants (refugees, asylum seekers, immigrants, and migrants – RASIM) in their study of the construction of minority groups in 175,000 newspaper articles from 1996–2005. Second, the authors determined that a considerable proportion of UK broadsheets and tabloids (sub-corpora) use the same collocations, which implies that there are consistent patterns underlying racist discourses relating to RASIM. Several similar associative meanings of "immigrant" were detected in Russian, Czech, and German corpora (Sibirtseva & Krylova, 2012).

In view of the fact that the representation of immigrants in the media is studied on the basis of a wide range of approaches and methods, we chose the "linguistic personality" approach (Karasik, 2005), which allows analysis to be complemented by interdisciplinary connections. Based on Vygotsky's metatheory of human action (1983), linguistic personality is an interdisciplinary subject covered by psychology, sociology, linguistics, and cultural studies. In cultural studies, linguistic personality is viewed as a *linguistic and cultural type* (LCT) – a generalized representation of a person based on relevant social and ethnic characteristics. LCT is the recognizable character of the representatives of a culture (Dmitrieva, 2007; Horosheva & Biserova, 2013; Ivushkina, 2005; Karasik, 2005; Karaulov & Shmelev, 1987; Larina & Ozyumenko, 2016; Neroznak, 1996).

This chapter focuses on analyzing the linguistic and cultural type "immigrant" by identifying its general and specific features. The importance of studying this linguistic and cultural type lies in the fact that it includes symbolic descriptions of the concept of "immigrant" embedded in language. Thus, the linguistic and cultural type is derived from the cognitive basis of a typified structure in a specific language – Russian. As a result, the individual attributes of a personality are discarded while generalized antipodes remain and constitute representative features that also characterize a typical situation and a broader environment. In this chapter, the generalized dichotomies are analyzed in dictionary definitions, due to the reliability of interpretation, while specific contextual meanings are approached using cultural semantics/pragmatics.

The study of language and intercultural communication incorporates cross-cultural pragmatics, to which cultural semantics belongs, as it relates to cultural values, politeness, and communicative intent (Goddard & Wierzbicka, 2007; Yunxia, 2008). The theory of cross-cultural pragmatics (Wierzbicka, 1991) involves assessing the role of linguistic facts in constructing cultural identities (Danila & Manu-Magda, 2016). Cultural pragmatics and semantics use the notion of "cultural keywords" (Wierzbicka, 1997), i.e., the words that are not culturally neutral, but culture-specific packages of meaning, which are intimately linked with cultural value orientations and cognitive styles. Levinsen (2012) summarized culture-specific semantic items as follows: (1) cultural key-words, (2) ethnopsychological constructs and emotions, (3) social cognition, social interaction, sociality terms, and human social categories, (4) cognitive verbs and cognitive styles, (5) epistemic markers, (6) discourse markers and interjections, (7) sensation and perception, (8) speech act verbs and verbal concepts, (9) memory concepts, (10) religious concepts, (11) visuality and color, (12) grammatical categories and ethnosyntax, (13) the human body, (14) physical activity verbs, (15) ethnobiology and ethnozoology, (16) ethnogeometry, and (17) ethnogeography and landscape terms.

According to Gladkova (2005), semantic analysis of the structure of a language proves that these words in different languages reflect different social attitudes as they are based on different background knowledge. It means semantic descriptions of value words are determined by the "background understanding" of the society or the community in which they function. Value words provide guidelines on how to behave, but they are based on value assumptions of the society in which they exist. These assumptions become part of the semantic explication. In this study, a mixed methodology was applied: the LCT method, which helps to structure the semantics of the Russian language, and cultural pragmatics in identifying keywords and culture-specific semantics, which helps to reconstruct the underlying social and cultural value of the words.

Research data and methods

The study involves a thorough analysis of the contextual use of the term "immigrant" as represented in the newspaper subcorpus of the Russian national corpus (RNC). RNC is an online electronic resource of Russian texts dated between 1767 and 2014. For the purpose of this study, 228 million words from the newspaper subcorpus were used. The search was restricted to the period from 2000 until the present to account for the current use of the terms. The data incorporated 93 subcorpus entries with 85 documents found. The year-by-year distribution of the term is provided in Table 15.1.

The linguistic analysis involved three steps. Following a literature review on the interdisciplinary approach to "immigrant," the first step was to analyze 61 definitions of the word "immigrant" selected from various Russian dictionaries. According to Karasik (2005), dictionary articles help to narrow the meanings of complex LCTs, which are usually broadly defined and flexibly interchanged in academic literature and the media. Subsequently, we conducted an in-depth analysis of only a limited, confirmed set of meanings of "immigrant" found in authoritative national language dictionaries. The second step consisted of analyzing the contextual and culture-specific meanings of "immigrant" in Russian newspapers, presented as areas of tension, either negative or positive. The third step was to summarize the meanings of dichotomies and categorized cultural keywords in the representation of "immigrant" in Russian.

Findings

Component analysis of the selected lexical sources revealed that the LCT structure has nuclear features and a cluster of peripheral elements. For example, the core "иммигрант" can mean "moving" (Nail, 2015) and "foreign country": *Immigrant –* ***a foreigner who has arrived in a country*** *for permanent residence.* However, the conceptual core has markedly different semantics – "citizen" in Russian: *Immigrant – a collective term for* ***citizens of other countries*** *or* ***persons without citizenship.***

The frequency of "citizen" in Russian indicates the importance of immigration formalities to the Russian mentality. This meaning is consistent in all of the lexicographic sources explored (Bosniak, 1991; Lipman, 2006). The closer periphery of the concept contains the themes "foreigner," "duration of stay," and "reason": *Immigrants –* ***citizens*** *of a state who settle* ***permanently or on a long-term basis*** *in the territory of* ***another state.***

Table 15.1 Distribution of the term "immigrant" in the RNC newspaper subcorpus, 2000–2013

2013	2012	2011	2010	2009	2008	2007
13	8	4	6	4	6	12
2006	2005	2004	2003	2002	2001	2000
9	11	4	2	4	8	2

Further periphery sets are characterized by low frequency, with each distributed lexical unit included in dictionaries only once. The marginal periphery contains words that have a stylistic, emotional, and expressive effect, which includes the following: (1) the assessment of immigrant labor as low quality ("unskilled"); (2) the assessment of immigrants' standard of living as low level; and (3) identification of ethnic origin. It is clear that the boundaries between the peripheries are blurred because they include factors such as an individual's ethnic identity, residence, and nationality. Overall, thesaurus definitions highlight the nuclear features of the concept of the "immigrant" in Russian.

We will now focus on the contextual use and semantic features of the term "immigrant" in the newspaper subcorpus of the RNC. Russian print media reveal polar characteristics of the "immigrant," which characterize the components of the phenomenon under study as being simultaneously contradictory and interdependent (Horosheva & Biserova, 2013). These two patterns exist against a backdrop of tension that manifests itself in the following dichotomies: (1) victim–offender, (2) Europe–Russia, (3) inclusion–exclusion, and (4) threat–prosperity.

On the negative pole of the dichotomies, Russian print media reveal the cultural and historical background as well as the political and economic links that have contributed, historically, to forming the cultural context as well as attitudes towards people of different nationalities: Russian cultural immigrants are mostly natives of Asia and the Caucasus (Tajiks, Azeris, etc.). The article below contains culture-specific words:

Marina Shimadina's "Put in a word for the **poor** Tajik" (1):

> In fact, "Angst essen Seele auf" is, in its turn, a remake of the Hollywood classic "All that Heaven Allows" directed by Douglas Sirk. However, Fassbinder replaced the traditional **social status** conflict (2) (a rich widow and a gardener) with a national conflict (a German cleaner and an Arab immigrant), thus injecting a significant dose of anaesthetic into the melodramatic plot and turning it into a social pamphlet about a closed society, steeped in **prejudice** (3) and unwilling to accept **aliens**. (4)
>
> (*Izvestia, June 26, 2013*)

In (1), besides the qualifying direct meaning of "poor" + ethnonym:
Bedny (poor):

1) Lacking sufficient money to live at a standard considered comfortable or normal in a society
2) (Of a person) deserving of pity or sympathy,

the culture-specific feature is embedded in a fixed phrase that alludes to the lyrics of a famous Russian love song, and can also be found in the title of a Russian historical movie, thus being an essential component of the collective construal of value. This cultural and historical significance is enhanced by the use of the word "soslovie/social status" (2):
Sosloviye (social status/class/estate):

1) A particular class or category of people in society with legally determined hereditary rights and duties
2) An occupational group

Though the article is about a European theatrical production, the contextual effect of expressing a certain attitude to immigrants is clearly negative – prejudice (3) and alienation (4), which are also specifically Russian forms of linguistic representation:

Predrassoudok (prejudice):

1) Preconceived opinion that is not based on reason or actual experience
2) Dislike, hostility, or unjust behavior formed on such a basis

Chouzhak (alien):

1) A person who does not know, or is not known in, a particular place or community
2) A person belonging to a different country, race, or group, usually one you do not like or are frightened of
3) An outsider

One of the key features making the representation of "immigrant" provided by Galina Sapozhnikova's "Will Russians **venerate the Quran** and **eat rice with chopsticks**?" (5), below, culture-specific is the obvious references to religious aspects (5, 7): //

> All European conventions are full of clauses on immigrants' rights. Their responsibilities are not mentioned for some reason, though. But if in a bar in the centre of Moscow **a woman, apparently of Transcaucasian descent** (6), **sings something tender about jihad** (7) **into a microphone**, and the male members of the audience give her a round of applause indicative of passion and understanding, aren't we entitled to remind them who is who? Shouldn't an immigrant arriving here leave **their religious principles and other preferences behind, in the country they have said goodbye to**? From a European legal perspective, what I am writing is sheer sedition, but that's what I really think. The forecast is far from optimistic.
>
> (Komsomolskaya Pravda, *July 9, 2003)*

The description of the woman's appearance also contains elements that are of cultural significance to Russian discourse (6): a Transcaucasian national (a person of Transcaucasian origin/descent, a person from the Caucasus) is an expression formed by analogy with "a person of Jewish origin/descent" – an administrative and political cliché coined in the 1920s. It is used in modern Russian mainly as a derogatory reference to immigrants from a number of CIS (Commonwealth of Independent States) countries located in the Caucasus and Transcaucasia.

Alexander Kots' "Chinese border approaching Moscow" below contains lexical units that fall into the "ethnogeography and landscape terms" category as per Levinsen's (2012) classification:

> We have thousands of hectares of **vacant agricultural land** (8), **–** Sergey Chemezov, Minister of Agriculture for the Sverdlovsk Region, reports. – We could rent it out to Chinese immigrants for a period of 49 years. Why not 50 or 60? Because by that time the immigrant **will have settled down in the Urals** (9) **with a family and children, and it will be difficult to tear him away from this land. As a result we are going to have a miniature Harbin** (10) **in the centre of the country**.
>
> (Komsomolskaya Pravda, *August 3, 2006)*

The basis for associating immigration in Russia with these terms is Russia's vast territory (8, 9), and the ongoing influx of Chinese immigrants (10).

Another distinctive feature of Russian media discourse with regard to the representation of "immigrant" is frequent comparisons of the social consequences of immigration in the EU and Russia, indicative of negative attitudes toward immigrants, who are viewed as a threat to host countries. "French lesson for Russia", for example, states:

> **Black banners** (11) **were billowing over the demonstrators, revealing the slogans "Russia is for Russians," "Immigrant, get lost!**" This offer is addressed to at least 10 million illegal immigrants – the estimated number of immigrants currently staying in Russia. The escalating aggression of Le Pen's Russian supporters towards this seemingly silent, featureless mass of people may backfire. Rather than getting lost, the immigrant, armed with a bottle of petrol, will go to the nearest petrol station, which is all the more likely in view of the fact that Russia still doesn't have a clear-cut immigration policy backed up by appropriate legislation, as some of the leading politicians, e.g., senator Mihail Margelov, admit. While the government and legislature see eye to eye about how Russia can benefit from labour migration, what is often ignored is the fact that **uncontrollable import of cheap labour force is a two-edged sword** (12). A barely manageable **army of "aliens"** (13) is growing within the country, and is **scapegoated by unemployed Russians for all their woes**. (14)
>
> (RIA Novosti, *November 9, 2005)*

The above extract comprises a reference to the category of "visuality and color" (11), as defined by Levisen (2012), which can be interpreted as both culture-specific and cross-cultural. Interestingly, the article touches upon the socio-economic reasons for migration, and sounds a warning note over the implications of economic migration for the domestic labor market, the connotation being clearly negative (12). The metaphor describing the immigrant population in Russia (13) springs from the military domain and implies being at war with immigrants ("army of aliens" = enemies). The author of this article also uses idiomatic expressions that reinforce associations with hostility and war (12), (14).

Igor Karaoulov's "**Olivier salad, Depardieu** (15) and Polonsky on board a **shallop**" provides examples of irony:

> It was **snowy but not too frosty** (16). The President was talking about mercy, and the first sensation of 2013 was, thank God, not a terrorist attack, not a natural disaster, not even a new ban on something previously allowed. The first piece of news which tore my fellow citizens away from their bowls of healthy and unhealthy salads is perfectly in line with the New Year celebrations, the sparkles of champagne, and the downpour of confetti: Depardieu chooses Russia. Thus "Olivier" has been rhymed with Depardieu, and Russia has got its first **"sausage immigrant"** (17) from a **European country** (18). This is what seems to have driven some progressive thinkers in a matter of hours from shrugging their shoulders in perplexity to utter indignation: granting citizenship to Gérard **Xavierovich** (19) is equated with **insulting** both the **more deserving candidates** (20) for receiving the Russian passport and its current owners, as well as the sacred notion of Russian citizenship. It makes you wonder why no one has mentioned **Nasser and the Order of Lenin awarded to him** (21) yet.
>
> (Izvestia, *January 1, 2013)*

The example provided above is imbued with a sense of irony specific to Russian media discourse: the New Year – the biggest national holiday in Russia – is mentioned alongside a terrorist attack and a natural disaster; "Olivier salad" – a dish traditionally associated with New Year celebrations – is rhymed with "Depardieu" (15); Gérard Depardieu is jokingly given a middle name – Xavierovich (19) – formed by analogy with a Russian patronymic. The extract also alludes to a period in Russian history when an economic crisis and social instability were paralleled by a wave of economic migration, the so-called "sausage emigration" (17). The term per se is bitterly ironic as it can be taken to symbolize highly desirable yet unattainable welfare. Another issue that Karaoulov raises is the social impact of granting Russian citizenship to immigrants, which appears to insult Russian citizens (20), (21). Notably, the Europe–Russia dichotomy also comes through (18), and an ethnogeographic reference is made (16). Nikolaeva's article uses collocations to underline dichotomy.

Irina Nikolaeva's "Russians protesting against Santa Claus":

> **Russia is meant for Father Frost**, and **Santa Claus is an illegal immigrant** (22). Patriotic citizens are calling for protests against the Western symbol of Christmas. There is even a website (ZaDedaMoroza.ru) that offers legal advice on how **to wage war on toy Santas in shops, urging people to buy Father Frosts only and providing guidelines on how to tell the correct "Grandfather" from his foreign counterpart** (23). Santa Claus is viewed as a glam star. Interestingly, Russia is not the only country protesting against Santa Claus – for instance, Austria has, for years, been in favour of replacing Santa Claus with St. Nicholas, a saint worshipped by the Catholic church.
>
> (RBK Daily, *December 24, 2010)*

As is evident from this extract, "illegal immigrant" has come to be used as a common collocation (22). Another interesting phenomenon that can be observed here is a religious concept (the reference to Santa Clause as the Western symbol of Christmas) viewed through the prism of the Europe–Russia dichotomy (23). Similar to the previous example, there is an implicit ethnogeographic reference to the Russian winter as a backdrop to the story.

Let us now turn to the positive pole of the dichotomies. Interestingly, a specific term – Gastarbeiter, a borrowing from German (24) – is used to denote integration of immigrants into the host culture in Vladimir Dergachev's "Public funds to be allocated for immigrant adaptation":

> Politologist Gleb Pavlovsky ... is sure it is a dead-end experiment. However, NCA [national and cultural autonomy] representatives are ready to help **Gastarbeiters**. (24) Ruslan Sunovarov, Head of "Vatan," the Rostov Regional Tajik National and Cultural Autonomy, approves of the legislators' initiative. "An immigrant who feels **cosy** is a **boon** to Russia" (25), – he reckons. – And he will only feel cosy when he knows the legislation and the Russian language. And when he knows both he will be able to contribute more to the country.
>
> (Izvestia, *February 11, 2013)*

Gastarbeiter: Guest worker (commonly associated with an immigrant from one of the CIS countries)
Ouyutny (cosy): Giving a feeling of comfort, warmth, and relaxation; homely
Blago (boon): 1) Good, happiness; 2) Welfare, benefit, boon

An important point that Dergachev makes is that the idea of positive adaptation (25) is linked with the need for good knowledge of the host country's legislation and language. The Russian cultural context indicates a low level of linguistic competence initially and, hence, a low degree of integration into the host culture. It is worth noting at this point that some researchers view the role of language as a catalyst for international migration (Adsera & Pytlikova, 2012; Kerswill, 2006), on the grounds that proximity of a prospective migrant's native language to the language of the prospective host country should facilitate integration into the host culture. However, the findings of this study show that the primary driving force behind migration, from a media perspective, is the labour market and the prospect of financial gain (Table 15.2). Linguistic competence, in the context of immigration-related media discourse, is regarded as a major intercultural factor (Esser, 2006; Tomas, 2005) and an indicator of immigrant integration.

"Presidential address to the Federal Assembly of the Russian Federation" states:

> A **garden house** (26) is not an option either: it is so expensive that most people can't afford it. I also believe that an increase in population numbers should be paralleled by a meaningful strategy with regard to the immigration policy. We are interested in the arrival of qualified legal labor force. However, a lot of Russian entrepreneurs still **tend to take advantage of illegal migration as no one could be easier to exploit uncontrollably than an immigrant deprived of civil rights** (27), who is, by the way, also a potential **criminal threat to society** (28). Having said that, what we should focus on is not just reducing the size of the "shadow sector," but also the real benefits to the state and to Russian people. After all, every legal immigrant should have an opportunity to become a Russian citizen.
>
> (RIA Novosti, *April 25, 2005)*

Table 15.2 Distribution of culture-specific words in LCT components

LCT components	*Culture-specific semantic items*	*Examples*	*Frequency (%) (N = 123)*
Citizen	Social categories Ethnopsychological constructs Memory concepts	Soslovie (social status)	15.4
Another country	Ethnogeography Ethnopsychological constructs	Arab China	40.6
Person	Religious concepts	Olivier salad Transcaucasian	9.
Job search	Ethnogeography	Vacant land in the Urals Belarus bank	18.6
Formal status	Ethnopsychological constructs and emotions	Dacha (garden house)	9
Language level	Religious concepts	Blago (boon)	2.6
Social consequences	Visual perception and color Religious concepts Ethnopsychological constructs and emotions	Holidays War/woe/alien Insult Civil rights	4.8

Here, a cultural construct rendered in history, arts, and everyday life (26) is seen as an element of the current immigration policy; however, the other side of the coin is a violation of civil rights (27), which is viewed as a potential source of criminal threat to the host culture (28).

Ksenia Novozhilova's "Immigrants to be granted tax benefits" states:

> The stock purchased before that date will bring him dividends. Until 2014 he will be exempt from paying tax on this income provided he deposits the money in a bank account. However, if he becomes a shareholder in 2010, his dividends will be taxed. An immigrant **will only be exempt from paying income tax on the money he/she receives from overseas** (29). They will have to provide documents proving that the contract yielding cash returns was made before their arrival. Another mandatory condition is that the money should be deposited in a **Belorussian bank** account (30), whatever the amount of income.
>
> (Komsomolskaya Pravda, *March 12, 2010)*

This example focuses on a positive aspect of Russian immigration policy – tax benefits (29). It also contains an ethnogeographic reference to Belarus, a Slavic country that has close historical links with Russia (30).

The quantitative findings of the cultural semantic analysis are summarized in Table 15.2.

As is evident from Table 15.2, the culture-specific concepts prevalent in Russian media discourse are those relating to history, religion, national holidays, cultural constructs, and ethno-geography. In line with the observations made previously in a number of studies, the research findings show that, by and large, immigrants in Russia are perceived as a source of danger, crime, and social tension. On the other hand, the political and social adaptation measures taken by the Russian government are viewed as a positive factor. Table 15.3 illustrates dichotomies observed in the sample and the ratio of the parts.

The first conclusion that can be drawn from Table 15.3 is that, in Russian print media, immigrants are represented as offenders just over twice as often as victims. The majority of offense-related representations are criminal cases – bank robberies, car thefts, and attacks on the native population of the host country. Many of the narratives of victims come from criminal records too: Neo-Nazis attacking immigrants, the police putting pressure on illegal immigrants, and intragroup violence. The second point that can be inferred from the table is that migration in Europe appears to be a focus of attention for Russian media significantly more often than migration in Russia. The country mentioned most frequently in media coverage is France, followed by the UK, Greece, Spain, Italy, Germany, and Sweden. There are occasional references to Russian immigrants in Europe, mostly with a negative connotation. Interestingly, European multiculturalism is regarded as a political failure, whereas Russia's immigration policy tends to be portrayed favorably. However, the proportion of

Table 15.3 Dichotomies observed in the sample and ratio of the parts

Dichotomy tensions	*Ratio of parts*
Victim–Offender	5:12
Europe–Russia	25:16
Inclusion–Exclusion	13:16
Threat–Prosperity	19:22

cases relating to the exclusion/inclusion of immigrants from/in the host society is more balanced than in the previous two dichotomies. In the final dichotomy, immigrants are regarded not so much as a threat but as a benefit to society, especially from an economic perspective. Thus, the analysis of Russian media discourse reveals, on the one hand, signs of tolerance towards immigrants and, on the other hand, a tendency towards rejecting immigrants. This ambiguity, as is evident from the analysis of the selected samples, is a factor that, directly or indirectly, provokes a sociocultural conflict.

Discussion and conclusions

To summarise, not only does Russian media reflect the actual situation, but it also "interpret[s] it through the prism of a particular system of cultural values" (Dobrosklonskaya, 2005, p. 22). The findings confirm and develop the main premises of the integrative theory of the intercultural personhood of an immigrant who conforms to ethnic groups and is viewed as an outsider by the host culture. The cultural identity of an immigrant constructed by the media language in Russia is largely universal (Permyakova & Antineskul, 2016).

Based on the results of the linguistic analysis of the representation of the "immigrant" in Russian print media, the following key conclusions can be drawn. The semantic structure of the representation of "immigrant" in Russian through dictionary definitions shows distinct nuclear features of the concept. However, the boundaries between the peripheries are blurred because they include items relating to ethnic identity, nationality, and residence.

The cultural semantic analysis reinforces the results of analyzing the LCT structure: the economic purpose behind migration (seeking employment) is not always accepted socially; The respective approaches to immigration policy of Europe and Russia are indirectly opposed, which may complicate communication on the international arena; although the media offers a predominantly negative portrayal of immigrants, it also consistently avoids "blaming the others" strategies. Overall, in terms of attitude patterns existing between the host culture and immigrants, the media representation of immigrants is bifurcated. The culture-specific concepts that account for this bifurcation are those relating to history, religion, cultural constructs, and ethnogeography.

From a theoretical perspective, this study contributes to enhancing research methodology by combining the LCT method with cultural semantic analysis to determine the culture-specific vocabulary classes that play a significant role in Russian media discourse on immigrants. Furthermore, the application of these combined methods to the newspaper subcorpus of the Russian national corpus yields results demonstrating the discourse of power, as certain dichotomies in immigrant representation prevail both quantitatively and qualitatively. Thus, the Russian media, while portraying immigrants in Russian localities only, predominantly approaches immigration as a global issue. On the other hand, since the Russian language does not dominate the world's largest media outlets, the study indicates that culture-specific ways of representing immigrants are valid for agenda-setting and conflict-resolution on a global scale.

Despite certain unavoidable limitations, e.g., a limited sample in the Russian national corpus, this research provides a new perspective on immigration: its results indicate the cultural traits associated with immigrants, and also show that the media can reduce a subject with broad social implications to a limited stereotyped story (Glick Schiller, 2015). This chapter can therefore be regarded as contributing to the field of migration studies. In the context of transnational migration, another interesting aspect emerges, that of the "immigrant." In addition to being a specific linguistic and cultural type, the "immigrant" seems highly likely to further develop into a global metaphor for a person crossing borders in search of new horizons. Given the fact that looking for employment remains a major driving force behind migration, it is only logical that work should be regarded as a cultural code that can be instrumental in reducing the ambiguity inherent in the cultural transfer of an "immigrant" into a different space.

The potential of this research lies, first, in enriching the methodology, which can be achieved by applying a humanistic theory and by incorporating "personalized" research methods, e.g., case studies or immigrant narratives, with the purpose of exploring the issue in a micro context as well as providing new insights into immigration-related conflict dynamics. Second, in addition to increasing the corpus sample, the research could be extended to include other languages in order to broaden the scope of analysis by drawing cross-cultural comparisons, and also to cover a wider range of media discourses, e.g., TV, blogs, and social media networks.

Given the current focus of media discourse on immigration viewed from a host country's perspective, it might also be worthwhile to explore "the other side of the story" by examining the media representation of "immigrant" in some of the countries that people tend to emigrate from. Examining a broader cross-section of the immigrant population would also provide a more comprehensive and balanced view and add a new dimension to the intercultural perspective on the issue.

In practical terms, the study findings could be taken into consideration by journalists and reporters when covering controversial and sensitive issues in order to reduce tension and/or prevent conflict. The results of the analysis might also be of relevance to social and civil workers dealing with immigrants in helping them identify potential areas of socio-ethnic polarization. In addition to the above, the research data could be used for intercultural education purposes.

References

Adsera, A., & Pytlikova, M. (2012). The role of language in shaping international migration. *Economic Journal, 125*, 49–81.

Baker, P., McEnery, T., & Gabrielatos, C. (2007). Using collocation analysis to reveal the construction of minority groups: The case of refugees, asylum seekers and immigrants in the UK press. Paper presented at Corpus Linguistics 2007, University of Birmingham, UK.

Berg-Nordlijs, M., Oslands, I., & Tkača, O. (2010). Compatriots or competitors? A glance at Rossiyskaya Gazeta's immigration debate 2004–2009. *Social Sciences Bulletin/Socialo Zinatnu Vestnesis, 11*, 7–26.

Berry, J. W. (1997). Immigration, acculturation and adaptation. *Applied Psychology: An International Review, 46*(1), 5–34.

Berry, J. W. (2001). A psychology of immigration. *Journal of Social Issues, 57*, 615–631.

Bosniak, L. S. (1991). Human rights, state sovereignty and the protection of undocumented migrants under the international migrant workers convention. *International Migration Review, 25*, 737–770.

Chilton, P. (2004). *Analysing political discourse: Theory and practice.* London: Routledge.

Collier, M. J., & Thomas, M. (1988). Cultural identity: An interpretive perspective. In Y. Y. Kim & W. B. Gudykunst (Eds.), *Theories in intercultural communication* (pp. 99–122). Newbury Park, CA: Sage.

Collier, V. P. (1995). Acquiring a second language for school. *Directions in Language and Education, 1*(4), 1–14.

Croucher, S. M. (2013). Integrated threat theory and acceptance of immigrant assimilation: An analysis of Muslim immigration in Western Europe. *Communication Monographs, 80*, 46–62.

Danila, A., & Manu-Magda, M. (2016). The use of language in constructing hybrid identities. Local and global in German and Romanian written press in Romania. *Bulletin of the Transilvania University of Brasov, Series IV: Philology & Cultural Studies, 9*(58), 103–132.

Davis, O. I., Nakayama, T. K., & Martin, J. N. (2000). Current and future directions in ethnicity and methodology. *International Journal of Intercultural Relations, 24*, 525–539.

Dijk, T. A. van (1992). Discourse and the denial of racism. *Discourse and Society, 3*, 87–118.

Dijk, T. A. van(2003). Critical discourse analysis. In D. Schiffrin, D. Tannen, & H. E. Hamilton (Eds.), *The handbook of discourse analysis* (pp. 352–372). Oxford: Blackwell.

Dmitrieva, O. A. (2007). *Lingvokul'turnye tipazhi Rosiji i Frantsii XIX veka* [Linguistic and cultural types of Russia and France of XIX century: A monograph]. Volgograd: Peremena.

Dobrosklonskaya, T. G. (2005). *Voprosy izucheniya mediatekstov: Opyt issledovaniya sovremennoi angliiskoi mediarechi* [Issues of media text studies: The practice of modern English media speech]. Moscow: Editorial URSS.

Esser, H. (2006). *Migration, language and intergration*. AKI Research Review 4. Berlin: Social Science Research Center.

Esses, V. M., Medianu, S., & Lawson, A. S. (2013). Uncertainty, threat, and the role of the media in promoting the dehumanization of immigrants and refugees. *Journal of Social Issues, 69*, 518–536.

Fowler, R. (2013). *Language in the news: Discourse and ideology in the press*. London: Routledge.

Gabrielatos, C., & Baker, P. (2006). Representation of refugees and asylum seekers in UK newspapers: Towards a corpus-based comparison of the stance of tabloids and broadsheets. *First International Conference: Critical Approaches to Discourse Analysis across Disciplines (CADAAD 2006)*. University of East Anglia, Norwich, UK.

Gallois, C., & Callan, V. J. (1988). Communication accommodation and the prototypical speaker: Predicting evaluations of status and solidarity. *Language and Communication, 8*, 271–283.

Gladkova, A. (2005). New and traditional values in contemporary Russian: Natural semantic metalanguage in cross-cultural semantics. In I. Mushin (Ed.), *Proceedings of the 2004 Conference of the Australian Linguistics Society*. Retrieved from http://ses.library.usyd.edu.au/handle/2123/93

Glick Schiller, N. (2015). Explanatory frameworks in transnational migration studies: The missing multi-scalar global perspective. *Ethnic and Racial Studies, 38*, 2275–2282.

Goddard, C., & Wierzbicka, A. (2007). Semantic primes and cultural scripts in language learning and intercultural communication. In G. Palmer & F. Sharifian (Eds.), *Applied cultural linguistics: Implications for second language learning and intercultural communication* (pp. 105–124). Amsterdam: John Benjamins.

Grillo, R. D. (1985). *Ideologies and institutions in urban France: The representation of immigrants*. Cambridge: Cambridge University Press.

Hatch, E. (1992). *Discourse and language education*. Cambridge: Cambridge University Press.

Horosheva, N. V., & Biserova, N. M. (2013). Reprezentatsia lingvokul'turnogo tipazha "immigrant" v mediadiskursah Frantsii i Rossii [The representation of the linguo-cultural type "immigrant" in French and Russian media discourses]. *Perm University Herald, Russian and Foreign Philology, 4*(24), 116–120.

Hullett, C. R., & Witte, K. (2001). Predicting intercultural adaptation and isolation: Using the extended parallel process model to test anxiety/uncertainty management theory. *International Journal of Intercultural Relations, 25*, 125–139.

Ivushkina, T. A. (2005). Lingvokul'turnyi tipazh "angliiskiy aristocrat" [Linguistic and cultural type "English aristocrat"]. In V. I. Karasik (Ed.), *Axiologic linguistics: Linguistic and cultural types* (pp. 62–74). Volgograd: Paradigma.

Jandt, E. (2000). *Intercultural communication: An introduction* (3rd ed.). London: Sage.

Karasik, V. I. (2005). Lingvokul'turnyi tipazh: K opredeleniyu ponyatiya [Linguistic cultural type: Towards definition]. In V. I. Karasik (Ed.), *Axiologic linguistics: Linguistic and cultural types* (pp. 5–25). Volgograd: Paradigma.

Karaulov, Y. N., & Shmelev, D. N. (1987). *Russkiy yazyk i yazykovaya lichnost* [The Russian language and linguistic personality]. Moscow: Nauka.

Kerswill, P. (2006). Migration and language. In K. Mattheier, U. Ammon, & P. Trudgill (Eds.), *Sociolinguistics/Soziolinguistik: An international handbook of the science of language and society* (2nd ed., Vol. 3, pp. 2271–2285). Berlin: De Gruyter.

Khosravinik, M. (2010). The representation of refugees, asylum seekers and immigrants in British newspapers: A critical discourse analysis. *Journal of Language and Politics, 9*, 1–28.

Kim, Y. Y. (1988). *Communication and cross-cultural adaptation: An integrative theory*. Clevedon: Multilingual Matters.

Kim, Y. Y. (1989). Personal, social and economic adaptation: 1975–1979 arrivals in Illinois. In D. Haines (Ed.), *Refugees as immigrants: Cambodians, Laotians and Vietnamese in America* (pp. 86–104). Totowa, NJ: Rowman & Littlefield.

Kim, Y. Y. (2001a). *Becoming intercultural*. Thousand Oaks, CA: Sage.

Kim, Y. Y. (2001b). *Adapting to an unfamiliar culture: An interdisciplinary overview*. London: Sage.

Kim, Y. Y. (2008). Intercultural personhood: Globalization and a way of being. *International Journal of Intercultural Relations, 32*, 359–368.

Kitov, Y. V., & Gasanova, N. K. (2014). Praktiki kulturnoy politiki: Rossiyskiy opyt [The practices of cultural policy: Russia's experience]. *Cultural Life of Southern Russia, 1*, 45–49.

Korneev, O. (2014). Exchanging knowledge, enhancing capacities, developing mechanisms: IOM's role in the implementation of the EU–Russia readmission agreement. *Journal of Ethnic and Migration Studies, 40*, 888–904.

Koryakin, K. V. (2007). *Sotsialnye i kulturnye aspekty adaptatsii migrantov-armyan v Krasnodarskom kraye (1988–2006)* [The social and cultural aspects of Armenian migrants' adaptation in the Krasnodarsk Region (1988–2006)]. Moscow: Institute of Sociology, Russian Academy of Sciences.

Kosulya, I. Y. (2011). Konfliktogennost migratsii: Problema mezhetnicheskoy tolerantnosti v sovremennoy Yevrope [Conflictogenity of migration: The problem of interethnic tolerance in present-day Europe]. *Harkov State University Herald, 941*, 34–40.

Larina, T. V., & Ozyumenko, V. I. (2016). Enticheskaya identichnost i eye proyavlenye v yazyke I kommunikatsii [Ethnic identity and its manifestation in language and communication]. *Cuadernos de Rusística Española, 12*, 57–68.

Lesnevskaya, D. (2013). Russkoye zarubezhye v epohu globalizatsii [Russian émigrés in the globalization era]. In P. Bunyak (Ed.), *Russian émigrés (diaspora) and the slavic world* (pp. 22–33). Belgrade: Slavistichko drushtvo Sebije.

Levisen, C. (2012). *Cultural semantics and social cognition: A case study on the Danish universe of meaning*. Berlin: Mouton de Gruyter.

Lipman, F. J. (2006). The taxation of undocumented immigrants: Separate, unequal, and without representation. *Harvard Latino Law Review, 9*, 1–58.

Mahtani, M. (2008). How are immigrants seen – and what do they want to see? Contemporary research on the representation of immigrants in the Canadian English-language media. In J. Biles, M. Burstein, & J. Frideres (Eds.), *Immigration and integration in Canada in the twenty-first century* (pp. 231–251). Montréal: McGill Queens University Press.

Machin, D., & Van Leeuwen, T. (2007). *Global media discourse: A critical introduction*. London: Taylor & Francis.

Martiniello, M. (2005). *Political participation, mobilisation and representation of immigrants and their offspring in Europe*. No. 1/05. Malmö: Malmö University.

Matthes, J. (2009). What's in a frame? A content analysis of media framing studies in the world's leading communication journals, 1990–2005. *Journalism & Mass Communication Quarterly, 86*, 349–367.

Mineyeva, I. N. (2013). Fenomen emigratsii v russkoy culture XX–XXI vv: Genezis, semantika, interpretatsii [The phenomenon of emigration in the Russian culture of the 20th and 21st centuries: Genesis, semantics, interpretations]. In P. Bunyak (Ed.), *Russian émigrés (diaspora) and the slavic world* (pp. 40–50). Belgrade: Slavistichko drushtvo Sebije.

Nail, T. (2015). *The figure of the migrant*. Redwood City, CA: Stanford University Press.

Neroznak, V. P. (1996). Lingvisticheskaya personologiya: K opredeleniyu statusa distsipliny [Linguistic personality studies: Towards discipline status]. In V. P. Neroznak (Ed.), *Language. Poetics. Translation* (Vol. 426, pp. 112–116). Moscow: Moscow Linguistic University Press.

Permyakova, T. M., & Antineskul, O. L. (2016). "Immigrant" in Russian and French print media (Linguistic and visual composition analyses). *Journal of Intercultural Communication Research, 45*, 319–337.

Pilkington, H. (1998). *Migration, displacement, and identity in post-Soviet Russia*. London: Routledge.

Pogliano, A., & Solaroli, M. (2012). The visual construction of immigration in the Italian press: News photography and meta-communicative cultural frames. *Studi culturali, 9*, 371–400.

Popov, L. N. (2008). Russkaya intonatsiya kak neobhodimoye sredstvo formirovaniya kommunikativnogo soznaniya i povedeniya migrantov [Russian intonation as an indispensable element of forming the communicative consciousness and behavior of migrants]. *Linguoculturology, 2*, 172–177.

Riggins, S. H. E. (1997). *The language and politics of exclusion: Others in discourse*. Thousand Oaks, CA: Sage.

Santa Ana, O. (1999). "Like an animal I was treated": Anti-immigrant metaphor in US public discourse. *Discourse & Society, 10*, 191–224.

Sarayeva, O. V. (2011). Konstruirovaniye obraza migratsii rossiyskimi SMI [Construction of the image of migration by Russian mass media]. In *Economics, law and sociology herald* (Vol. 2, pp. 245–249). Kazan: Expert 16.

Sheridan, V., & Storch, K. (2009). Linking intercultural and grounded theory: Methodological issues in migration research. *Qualitative Social Research, 10*(1), 1–22.

Sibirtseva, V. G., & Krylova, L. K. (2012). Migrant" i "migratsiya" po dannym slovarey I lingvisticheskih korpusov russkogo, cheshskogo i nemetskogo yazykov [Migrant and "migration" according to dictionaries and the linguistic corpora of Russian, Czech and German]. *Financial University Herald, 2*, 73–78.

Skrebtsova, T. G. (2007). Obraz migranta v sovremennyh rossiyskih SMI [The image of the migrant in the modern Russian mass media]. *Political Linguistics*, *3*(23), 115–118.

Sokolsky, M. (2016). Broad is my native land: Repertoires and regimes of migration in Russia's twentieth century. *Journal of Social History*. doi: http://dx.doi.org/10.1093/jsh/shv089

Streltsova, Y. (2014). The adaptation of immigrants in Russia: The language aspect. *Russian Politics & Law*, *52*(6), 24–41.

Ting-Toomey, S. (1988). A face negotiation theory. In Y. Y. Kim & W. B. Gudykunst (Eds.), *Theories in intercultural communication* (pp. 47–92). Thousand Oaks, CA: Sage.

Tomas, K. (2005). *Displaced self: The impact of language-migration on self-identity* Master's thesis, School of Communication and Creative Arts, Deakin University, Australia.

Verschueren, J. (2008). Intercultural communication and the challenges of migration. *Language and Intercultural Communication*, *8*(1), 21–35.

Vygotsky, L. S. (1983). *Istoriya razvitiya vysshiykh psykhicheskikh funktsiy* [History of superior psychological functions development] (Vol. 3). Moscow: Pedagogy.

Wierzbicka, A. (1991). Japanese key words and core cultural values. *Language in Society*, *20*(3), 333–385.

Wierzbicka, A. (1997). *Understanding cultures through their key words*. Oxford: Oxford University Press.

Wood, N., & King, R. (2001). *Media and migration: Constructions of mobility and difference*. London: Routledge.

Yunxia, Z. (2008). Revisiting relevant approaches for the study of language and intercultural communication. *International Journal of English Studies*, *8*(2), 25–42.

16
APPLICATIONS OF MUSIC FOR MIGRANTS

Elsa A. Campbell

With current possibilities for worldwide travel, *intra*- and *inter*cultural exchange has become an increasingly important topic in today's society. Several issues arise relating to the political ramifications of mass forced migration or asylum seeking; however, when focusing on other reasons for migration – such as the search for employment – issues such as identity formation, cultural fusion, and personal and group expression nevertheless remain integral. Indeed, around 3 percent of the world's population comprises migrants (Castles & Miller, 2009) and we are urged to consider how migration influences our conceptualization of community and indeed music (Phelan, 2012).

The way in which indigenous music is introduced to a new culture may be seen as a metaphorical and artistic representation of the introduction of the "other." Immigrants in Europe were seen solely as workers and were not expected to be stakeholders in arts or culture. This has developed over generations to unveil their influence on multiculturalism. The fusion of their histories with the receiving community, such as in stories of migration and/or discrimination, cultural fusion and their unique way of influencing musical output and artistic exchange, may be shown in examples such as the incorporation of jazz music into mainstream American popular culture (Martiniello & Lafleur, 2008). The fluidity of music and its change under various influences becomes increasingly complex the more influences are imposed upon it (Phelan, 2012). Yet, the question arises: how can music be utilized as a means of helping migrants become a member of their adoptive culture? This chapter addresses how cultural fusion can be compared to musical output, how it can be both creative as well as a tool for creating connections between individuals, a means of understanding ourselves and others in contexts of migration, and how music – the universal language – can be a way to traverse barriers in communication. Community music initiatives are presented as a way to contextualize these concepts, highlighting how music-making encourages and fosters self-discovery, socializing, and bonding.

Music in communication

Juliette Alvin – a pioneer in music therapy – considered music a means of discovering oneself. Playing or engaging in music without the imposition of rules and regulations displays our characters, pathologies, and inner conflicts/issues as a sonic product (Kim, 2016). This product is a representation of one's inner being and is translated into a language that others can more easily comprehend. Music may thus be considered a *lingua franca*, which displays the delicate nuances of expressing emotions and experiences.

Understanding how individuals are affected by geographical, social and emotional change helps decrease the divide between "us and the other." Creating a therapeutic space and relationship conducive to change through creative output and communication helps reduce this divide and affords self-discovery and support during a time of change. Music therapy is one such therapeutic and creative process used with migrants.

Music has long been used as a medium for therapy – both within clinical settings or used for individual emotion regulation (Wigram, Nygaard Pedersen, & Bonde, 2002). However, even though there has been relatively little research on the use of music therapy with migrants, several aspects are to be considered. Although these aspects are nonetheless important in clinical work as such, cultural background and its effects on therapeutic relationship building may be especially important as a focus within this particular context (Hunt, 2005). Additionally, identity formation – or rather identity reconstruction – and the new environment, peer acceptance and migrants' experiences of being such are also to be considered.

Migrants are often viewed as problems for the receiving country and portrayed as victims (Kiwan & Meinhof, 2011). The narrative presented as regards how migrants are or wish to be perceived may be somewhat taut, as communication between the "host" country and the "visitors" may be hindered by cultural, social or linguistic differences. Music – often considered a universal language – helps to break down these barriers, working towards creating social harmony.

Adaptation

The process of acculturation (Kim, 2001) – our process of learning social norms and adapting to elements of a host society – begins when we enter a new culture. This includes the *un*learning of familiar customs and identities to be replaced with the new. According to Kim, forming a new identity requires, to a certain extent, losing our old one; a process of acculturation through deculturation. However, this definition and conceptualization of this process eludes the ability of humans to react to new situations based on previous knowledge and experiences, how we as humans learn by experience. By dismissing that which was learned as children and starting the process from the beginning would mean that we are to define our world view and ourselves as only relative to the adoptive culture, rather than using the past experiences as a means of broadening our knowledge when combined and fused with experiences we encounter in our future. This reductionist approach ignores our ability to adapt – Darwin's theory of evolution propagated nature's ability to adapt to new situations based on a change in its environment, meaning that change and learning from and developing from previous scenarios are necessary for adapting to one's new environment. We do not forget or dismiss what we have previously learned; rather, we use that knowledge as a calibration tool. Previous experiences and learned behaviors are the basis from which we can move towards future understanding and communication. As Croucher and Kramer (2017) highlighted, cultural adaptation does not account for how the "other" impacts the adoptive culture. The abandonment of one's previous cultural knowledge in an attempt to assimilate disregards the process through which both "host" and "newcomer" go (ibid). For migrants, music's place in cultural and personal identity acts as a means to opening dialog and expression of both "new" and "old" cultures.

Music as a tool in cultural adaptation

Music does not only serve the purpose of entertainment; rather, the effects reach much farther. Music's role in rites or rituals, religious practices, and military arousal, to name a few, show the pertinence of music application for regulating and establishing coherency between and among groups of people (Spintge & Droh, 1987, p. 12). Indeed, Stige (2015) insisted that culture is not only a construct that influences our behavior, but is also an integral part of human interaction and creativity. Taking this thought further, music is not only a tool that can be used to mold us and our behaviors but can also be used as a means of understanding ourselves via human and musical interaction, with cultural cohesion, communication and comprehension at the core.

Music can be used both by individuals outside of the therapeutic setting as part of everyday life, e.g., adolescents using listening to music as a method of emotion regulation (Saarikallio & Erkkilä, 2007), or within clinical music therapy practice itself (Moore, 2013). Knowledge on how to regulate or elicit specific emotional reactions, however, is needed for regulatory music to be effective. In this vein, preferred music produces desirable activation, whilst complex, dissonant music with surprising musical events can be considered as inducing undesired activation (ibid). These are not as universal as once thought; the cultural ties one has to music are instrumental.

The therapeutic use of music has often been used in nursing practice in the United States; however, the idea that certain musics are universally liked and equally therapeutic has pervaded. This has also presumed that others hold similar beliefs and values, if this fundamental universality is present (Good, Picot, Salem, Chin, Picot, & Laneet, 2000). In fact, these authors explained that there are significant cultural differences in musical preference regarding therapeutic purposes and the use of music for pain relief. For example, orchestral and popular piano music were important to Caucasian Americans in this respect, whilst jazz was most frequently chosen by African Americans, followed by gospel music used for the same purpose (ibid).

Much of previous research on creativity and migration relating to music has focused on song lyrics (Bailey & Collyer, 2006). There is a strong connection between song-writing/composition and social experiences, as both may be driven by either positive or negative emotional experiences as well as identity. Lomax (1959, p. 929) expressed this connection succinctly in the ability of music to serve as a function of society:

> from the point of view of its social function, the primary effect of music is to give the listener a feeling of security, for it symbolizes the place where he was born, his earliest childhood satisfactions, his religious experience, his pleasure in community doings, his courtship and his work – any or all of these personality-shaping experiences.

His explanation underlines the importance of one's roots as a facet of personal experiences – one's way of understanding one's own place within one's own culture and community. In entering a new culture, a new society, one's past may inevitably become a source of comfort and is the foundation upon which new experiences are built. This underscores the importance of previous experiences and learned behaviors from one's home culture in providing solace and a sense of familiarity in the adoptive one. The process of migration is not an individual endeavor; rather, it is a group process resultant of social change, affecting not only the person migrating but also those receiving this new culture (Castles & Miller, 2009; Croucher & Kramer, 2017). Music is a source of social stability and means of communication within this chaotic social change.

Music therapy can focus on relationships and all these encapsulate. As Bruscia (1998) explains, music experiences can be created, molded, and designed to highlight relationships within a person, between a group of people, and between a person and their (new) environment, as well as to explore one's feelings and emotional responses. Although these types of exploration need not be led by a therapist, rather can be a solo act and means of self- and individual discovery (Wersal, 2006), music-making can be a powerful way to discuss and dissect relationships, as music is inherently a social activity, either as a group playing/experiencing or as a relationship between the listener and the artist.

Music-making as an individual and collective action

As moving itself is constituted as a collective action, so too can music-making and music reception occur as a collective. Several methods are used within music therapy for migrants, such as improvisation, song singing and writing, music and movement, as well as in various genres such as hip hop and rap. In cases where traumatic experiences are part of the narrative, methods such as holding (where the musical improvisation serves as a means of providing comfort; see Bruscia, 1998) or guided imagery are used (Orth, 2005).

The ever-changing, adaptive nature of humans leads to a complex phenomenon when this is intermingled with the upheaval associated with migration. The collective nature of this act – a geographical move and a social change – is allegorically represented in group music-making and the possible therapeutic change and exchanges occurring within group music therapy. In individual therapy – one-on-one sessions – the music acts as a means of explaining that which cannot be verbally described. As Hans Christian Andersen famously wrote, where words fail, music speaks (Hans Christian Andersen Center, n.d.). In music therapy practice, music-making and music reception are regarded as ways to initiate meaningful discussions and interactions; music opens us up and acts as a way to express our innermost thoughts and feelings in a safe and nurturing environment. Music-making acts as a bridge between therapist and client and is capable of addressing psychological, physical, social, and spiritual issues (Bruscia & Burnett, 2014). This therapeutic appositeness affords flexibility in approaches and target groups. Music therapy can be seen as a psychotherapeutic method in which the musical interaction, for example improvisation – as well as verbal discussion – is used as a means of communication (Erkkilä et al., 2008).

Improvisation may have several connotations; however, it serves a different function than entertainment. Regarding musical improvisation, the various interrelated and interacting mechanisms at play offer a plethora of possibilities; even though the act of producing music may not be considered taxing, the responsiveness necessary to improvise with another is indicative of the willingness to disclose and discover oneself mirrored in one's own creative output. MacDonald and Wilson (2014) presented various ways of defining or understanding improvisation, highlighting the importance of the social aspects of this practice:

Most musical improvisation is social, involving the idiosyncratic contributions of two or more individuals, each interpreting and musically responding to the other(s) and their playing. It is spontaneous in that music is formed as it is played through moment-by-moment responses to immediate musical contexts. It is creative in that improvising musicians produce novel music each time they play that may be similar to, but is different from, any previous performance. Finally, while masterful improvisation garners most attention and may be what comes to mind first when considering this musical practice, musical improvisation is something in which anyone can engage.

The social, creative, and accessible nature of improvisation within a music therapy context means that this can be a suitable way of building contact and relationships with migrants. As migration may often take place because of political or social persecution, the traumatic, cultural, social, and physical upheaval resultant of these experiences can be addressed through and with musical activities.

Making time, making music

The happenings within time on a social level may be understood and tolerated through musical expression and reception. If the possibility to return to one's origins and familiarity does not exist, the absence of home can lead to an experience of limbo – neither being a part of the home community nor truly accepted in the new one (Baily & Collyer, 2006). Perhaps the lack of predictability connected to migration and the feelings associated with displacement may be regulated by the temporal and spatial regularity of music. Music and sounds are sometimes conceived as ways in which humans understand time, as musical compositions present themselves as, among other things, a manipulation of time conveyed through frequency, rhythms, beats, and so forth (Eagle & Harsh, 1988). Therefore, if music were used as a tool through which one could understand one's current situation and place within time, it may be argued that this exploration of the current situation is a gateway to exploring past times, past experiences, and past manifestations of self – the music is used as a temporal reference point.

Musical and cultural fusion

Fusing experiences and knowledge gained in migrants' home contexts with those they gain in their "host" countries is represented also in musical contexts. "Host" countries give migrants a voice – in all senses of the phrase – through music; it helps bridge the gap between the past and present, former and current, the familiar and unfamiliar. In this way, cultural fusion and adaptation are representative of music fusion. In mixing traditional Irish jigs and reels with arrangements of jazz, popular music, Irish-American ballads, and classical music, Irish musicians Frankie Gavin and De Dannan underscored the passion for what is beloved and known with a simultaneous igniting of a passion for new and undiscovered territory (Haynes, 2017). In this way, the musical output acts as both a reference to what came before and a presentation and discussion of development. The same can be said of migrants' music becoming a fusion of previous experiences with new ones.

In one survey on goals for song-writing within clinical music therapy settings with various target groups (Baker, Wigram, Stott, & McFerran, 2008), reasons such as *developing self-confidence, enhancing self-esteem, choice and decision making, telling the client's story*, and *gaining insight* were cited. The intention to gain insight is inherently one of the main goals in therapeutic activities; however, with respect to migrants, the goal of telling the client's story or stories is perhaps most intriguing.

Song-writing and singing are powerful tools of self-expression within clinical music therapy. Singing, as Austin (2002) explains, facilitates deep breathing, which slows the heart rate and calms the autonomic nervous system, and stills the mind and body. In a sense, singing bridges the division between mental and physical manifestations of experiences. It is a very personal way of making music and communicating, as it uses our own voice as a means of conveying a message. Musical instruments, such as the piano, which we use as self-expressive vehicles, are extensions of our physical selves. They are tools we use to communicate. Our own voices are however inherently ours, and this ownership may be taken as an important mode of communication, particularly for those who have figuratively lost their voice or feel unable to express themselves in their newly-adopted foreign culture and country. Relating to Lomax (1959), this personal expression may be connected to home, to one's origins and roots, to all ways one can be defined as being oneself. The new context in which these are then sung bridges the gap between old and new, past and present, and paves the way towards integrating these previous aspects of self with those yet to develop.

Song-singing may not be the final product or intention – improvisation on the themes brought up through song-singing and song-writing creates a possibility for deeper exploration (Orth, 2005). Aiming at a clearer picture between the blurry lines of belonging and newcomer, the lyrics of the song could be seen as the narrative which the client or group of clients present to the therapist. Orth further discussed that traumatized refugees are not always capable of discussing their experiences. Music as the tool through which therapeutic rapport is built lends itself to the creation of a safe mode of expression. Traumatized refugees find it difficult to talk about their issues and trauma, but singing – although certainly personal – is not as invasive.

Music as language

On a practical level, the divide is not simply a cultural one; rather, it is also a linguistic one. The beauty of music therapy lies in the ability of this expressive art form to be an international mode of communication – thus, if there is no common spoken language, this is not always a hindrance. Orth (2005) also explained that, although the therapist may not understand a client as they express their thoughts, memories, feelings, and experiences in their mother tongue, the expression is more fluid and natural as a result of using their native language. The lack of a common language is not a barrier, it is a safety net. The music and language barrier initially create a space in which the migrant can feel heard, not berated. As the therapeutic relationship develops within this safe space and the client is attempting to integrate with the new culture, the client's ability to slowly leave the safety net and enter a common space of understanding and communication is supported.

Traversing communication barriers

The question of how much of oneself is lost in translation is another issue to be addressed. Migration influences the place of both origin and destination, which results in a deficit in development of one and a gain in the other. On an individual and personal level, cultural fusion theory (Croucher & Kramer, 2017) accounts for the merging of the origin culture with that of the host culture so that elements of both are present. The movement, flow, and rhythm of social, cultural, economic, and political exchange acts as both an inhibitor and an enabler of communication between the host country and migrant newcomers (Castles & Miller, 2009). However, identity boundaries become blurred when these collide and intersect; how much of one's own culture need be adapted to conform to the new? Can a migrant truly become assimilated into the new culture, and even if this were possible, is it necessary or even desired? In discussing this issue in relation to music and clinical music therapy, fusion – as also in the musical sense – is the means of combining two separate entities, a mutual effort resulting in a combination of both sources (ibid). In musically combining these, we may view the migrant's narrative as either diluted or enriched. The musical expression may sound different to the original; however, the perspective of adding something to this expression (the musical style or context of the host, for example), rather than losing something, builds upon and enriches expression and experiences – a fusion of musical styles rooted in the fusion of cultural exchange. When musical expression and output adapts, conforms, or includes elements of the adopted culture, it becomes a metaphorical symbol and a memento and representation of an experience or series of experiences.

Music therapists afford a space within which clients can explore themselves and their context. They enable the discussion of mutual musical creations. The therapist is an active participant in the migrant's identity (re)formation within the new context. Castles and Miller discussed how a failure to learn the new language, or a staunch retention of the mother tongue, can be perceived as the migrant's unwillingness to integrate into the adoptive culture. The retention of culture and associations to one's own culture and language are needed in order to deal with resettlement, and Castles and Miller in fact suggest that this problematic integration of immigrants is also a reflection of the host community's inability or unwillingness to deal with the situation. Social exclusion and discrimination may impact heavily upon one's ability to integrate into society. However, the opposite – loosening ties on culture and one's associations thereto – may also be effective in creating cohesion and dealing with re-settlement.

Creating social and musical harmony

Themes of discrimination and integration emerged quickly in one group in the Republic of Ireland called *Comhceol*, meaning "harmony" in Gaelic. This community music initiative brought together members of Irish ethnic travelers and African asylees. They had weekly meetings at the Irish World Academy of Music and Dance at the University of Limerick. The repertoire was constructed of exchanges from different cultures and, after one year, their efforts culminated in a performance at the Festival of Community Music in Limerick. Members of the group explicated that they had previously felt discriminated against, however the success of this group in reducing these tensions led to some members continuing this tradition and developing other community groups (Phelan, 2012). In this instance, music acted as a way of bringing people and communities together, building an understanding of each other, especially in the context of migration. Amit and Rapport (2002, p. 64) suggest that, even if our networks are developing and changing over time, with some entering and others leaving, it may be this process of formulating collective experiences as personal intimacies that affords a sense of personal continuity in the context of this migratory process. Therefore, the constant movement of peoples, ideas and identities may be a means for us to create a unique bond and definition of self and experience – both inter- and intra-personally. By not constricting the definition of community, we are allowing a much broader scope for human interaction. This is evidenced in the *Comhceol* project in which Igbo, Yoruba, Romanian, and Irish songs were mixed or fused with the travelers' traditional language, Cant. Ultimately, music became the language through which they communicated, with representatives from each affording unique insight that would otherwise have been left undiscovered. It beautifully represents how music can be a common language even when many languages are fused together; the final product is a form of creative catharsis.

Music and social exclusion

Interest in social exclusion has been developing in recent times as such topics as unemployment, cutbacks in social welfare and support, and greater numbers of migrant movement have been increasingly present in the media (Belfiore, 2002). Migratory movement results in the formation of ethnic communities and minority settlements in a new country. Identity is not stationary; rather, it flows, modulates, and is influenced by a variety of factors, resulting in migrants' fusion with their adoptive culture. Cultural traditions have been receiving a facelift of sorts after the introduction of ethnic minorities' artistic productions, which emerged based on themes of discrimination or migration. One example is the incorporation of jazz into American popular culture; as Martiniello and Lafleur (2008) put it: "studying the artistic production of racialised and dominated ethnic and racial minorities, and studying African-American music, Anglo-Pakistani cinema or post-colonial literature in France, have certainly been part of a process of identity claim making" (p. 1192). Music and the arts have become an important aspect of identity formation, cultural fusion, and even political action (Baily & Collyer, 2006). The changes in artistic production in the face of adversaries and discrimination have led to an alternative perception of cultural influx; rather than being a problem, it may be seen as an opportunity for growth and positive change. Griffiths (cited in Cathro & Devine, 2012) noted that creativity and creative activities can be used as both mediums of treatment and connectors to others within a community. In another project on music and social inclusion, an occupational therapy and nursing initiative in the form of a community percussion-based group for adults aged 18–65 with mental health issues, gathered together 20 participants who reported positive experiences such as "socialising in the group made me feel less lonely" and "[the group] made me feel more positive" (Cathro & Devine, 2012, p. 36). Although this target group had not undergone a change in geographical location, feelings of social isolation and loneliness are issues common with migrants and marginalized groups, as evidenced in the *Comhceol* project. Interventions that take the form of group activities, especially those centering on creative output, help to promote positive experiences and encourage socialization and social bonding.

Conclusion

The ability of music to act as a medium for cultural exchange through musical fusion, as a means of mirroring and expressing one's inner self, and of offering feelings of security and comfort, whilst being able to encourage social integration and bonding, has been presented here. Fusion of aspects from the "old" and "new" enables us to re-examine how we view ourselves within the context of others. The *Comhceol* project is just one example of how group music-making can give a voice to the voiceless, and can help to work towards positive community change and development. Fusion of cultures – as with music – affords a creative passage towards understanding both the migrant and home cultures, as well as the human interaction and creativity that are integral to those cultures.

References

Amit, V. & Rapport, N. (2002). *The trouble with community: Anthropological reflections on movement, identity and collectivity*. London: Pluto Press.

Austin, D. (2002). The voice of trauma: A wounded healer's perspective. In J. P. Sutton (Ed.), *Music, music therapy and trauma: International perspectives* (pp. 231–259). London: Jessica Kingsley.

Baily, J. & Collyer, M. (2006). Introduction: Music and migration. *Journal of Ethnic and Migration Studies*, *32*, 167–182.

Baker, F., Wigram, T., Stott, D., & McFerran, K. (2008). Therapeutic songwriting in music therapy. *Nordic Journal of Music Therapy*, *17*, 105–123.

Belfiore, E. (2002). Art as a means of alleviating social exclusion: Does it really work? A critique of instrumental cultural policies and social impact studies in the UK. *International Journal of Cultural Policy*, *8*, 91–106.

Bruscia, K. E. (1998). *Defining music therapy* (2nd ed). Gilsum, NH: Barcelona Publishing.

Bruscia, K. E. & Burnett, J. (2014). *Defining music therapy* (3rd ed). University Park, IL: Barcelona Publishers.

Castles, S. & Miller, M. J. (2009). *The age of migration: International population movements in the modern world* (4th ed). Basingstoke: Palgrave Macmillan.

Cathro, M. & Devine, A. (2012). Music therapy and social inclusion. *Mental Health Practice, 16*, 33–36.

Croucher, S. M. & Kramer, E. (2017). Cultural fusion theory: An alternative to acculturation. *Journal of International and Intercultural Communication, 10*, 97–114.

Eagle, C. T. & Harsh, J. M. (1988). Elements of pain and music: The Aio connection. *Music Therapy, 7*, 15–27.

Erkkilä, J., Gold, C., Fachner, J., Ala-Ruona, E., Punkanen, M., & Vanhala, M. (2008). The effect of improvisational music therapy on treatment of depression: Protocol for a randomized controlled trial. *BMC Psychiatry, 8*.

Good, M., Picot, B. L., Salem, S. G., Chin, C. C., Picot, S. F., & Lane, D. (2000). Cultural differences in music chosen for pain relief. *Journal of Holistic Nursing, 18*, 245–260.

Hans Christian Andersen Center. (n.d.). *Thirty-second evening: A translation of Hans Christian Andersen's "to og tredivte aften" by Jean Hersholt*. Retrieved from www.andersen.sdu.dk/vaerk/hersholt/ThirtySecondEvening_e.html

Haynes, S. (2017). *Irish music today is a global brand*. Retrieved from www.frankiegavinanddedannan.ie

Hunt, M. (2005). Action research and music therapy: Group music therapy with young refugees in a school community. *Voices: A world forum for music therapy, 5*.

Kim, J. (2016). Psychodynamic music therapy. *Voices: A World Forum for Music Therapy, 16*.

Kim, Y. Y. (2001). *Becoming intercultural: An integrative theory of communication and cross-cultural adaptation*. Thousand Oaks, CA: Sage.

Kiwan, N. & Meinhof, U. H. (2011). Music and migration: A transnational approach. *Music and Arts in Action, 3*, 3–20.

Lomax, A. (1959). Folk song style. *American Anthropologist, 61*, 927–954.

MacDonald, R. A. R. & Wilson, G. B. (2014). Musical improvisation and health: A review *Psychology of Well-being, 4*.

Martiniello, M. & Lafleur, J. (2008). Ethnic minorities' cultural and artistic practices as forms of political expression: A review of the literature and a theoretical discussion on music. *Journal of Ethnic and Migration Studies, 34*(8), 1191-1215.

Moore, K. S. M. M. (2013). A systematic review on the neural effects of music on emotion regulation: Implications for music therapy practice. *Journal of Music Therapy, 50*, 198–242.

Orth, J. (2005). Music therapy with traumatized refugees in a clinical setting. *Voices: A World Forum for Music Therapy, 5*.

Phelan, H. (2012). Sonic hospitality: Migration, community, and music. Oxford Handbooks Online. Retrieved from fromwww.oxfordhandbooks.com/view/10.1093/oxfordhb/9780199928019.001.0001/oxfordhb-9780199928019-e-12

Saarikallio, S. & Erkkilä, J. (2007). The role of music in adolescent's mood regulation. *Psychology of Music, 35*, 88–109.

Spintge, R. & Droh, R. (Eds). (1987). *Musik in der medizin: Neurophysiologische Grundlagen, klinische Applikationen, geisteswissenschaftliche Einordnung [Music in medicine: Neurophysiological basis, clinical applications, aspects in the humanities]*. Berlin: Springer-Verlag.

Stige, B. (2015). Culture-centered music therapy. Oxford Handbooks Online. Retrieved from fromwww.oxfordhandbooks.com/view/10.1093/oxfordhb/9780199639755.001.0001/oxfordhb-9780199639755-e-1

Wersal, L. (2006). Song and self-discovery: Touching the pattern that connects. *Voices: A World Forum for Music Therapy, 6*.

Wigram, T., Nygaard Pedersen, I., & Bonde, L. O. (2002). *A comprehensive guide to music therapy: Theory, clinical practice, research and training*. London: Jessica Kingsley.

PART IV

Case studies on migration

17

PATTERNS OF POLITICAL TRANSNATIONALISM IN A NON-TRADITIONAL DIASPORA

The case of Swiss citizens in Latin America[1]

Pablo Biderbost, Claudio Bolzman, & Guillermo Boscán

Switzerland is nowadays recognized worldwide as a common migrant destination. Of its 8.41 million inhabitants in 2016, 24.9 percent were foreigner. European countries are the main countries of origin for its migrants; 55.2 percent of the total number of immigrants[2] in the Swiss Confederation come from Italy, Germany, Portugal, France, and Kosovo (State Secretariat for Migration, 2017). In recent decades, the increasing percentage of aliens has provoked an endless number of federal referendums and popular initiatives aimed at changing the way in which different dimensions of migration processes are politically managed[3] (Arrighi, 2016; Gadient & Milani, 2015).

Nevertheless, Switzerland is not only a host society. Across its history, it has also had a clear pattern as an emigration country. From Swiss mercenaries who looked for economic opportunities on far battlefields (Casparis, 1982; Echevarría, 2016) to current expatriates after retirement (Huber & O'Reilly, 2004; Vogler, 2015), there are manifold examples of former and present members of the Swiss diaspora. For the purposes of this chapter, one specific target of Switzerland's emigration is going to be explored: the Swiss living in Latin America. The purpose of this study is specifically to contribute to a preliminary understanding of how this diasporic group is related to the *sui generis* political system of its motherland.[4] These links are analysed through the use of the concept of civic competencies (Biderbost, 2014; Fratczak-Rudnicka & Torney-Purta, 2002; Janmaat, 2011; Naval & Ugarte, 2012).

The remainder of this chapter is structured as follows. First, a short story about the studies of political transnationalism is described. Second, civic competencies are theoretically and empirically contextualized. Third, the profile of Swiss citizens living in Latin American countries is described. At the same time, characteristics and reasons for the choice of quantitative methods applied are mentioned. Fourth, the main findings about the political profile of "Swiss Latinos" are discussed. Finally, some concluding remarks are made with suggestions on future research avenues.

Political transnationalism and "non-traditional diasporas"

A general view

The recognition of voting rights for citizens living outside of the national borders was the legislative change which created the opportunity and necessity of understanding the ways in which emigrants are related to the political systems of their birth countries (Bauböck, 2007, 2010a; Biderbost & Boscán, 2011; Escobar, 2007; Lafleur, 2013; Parra, 2006). In a formal sense, it represents a kind of departing point for the studies about political transnationalism. Studies about it are, in a general sense, divided among those that try to understand conditions that create political transnational devices (such as the extension of voting rights to expatriates) and those that look towards describing and explaining political transnational practices at both the individual and organization level.

Since the inception of the research on this matter, there has been a strong focus on trying to identify political patterns of migrants (and also the organizations to which they belong) from the "Global South" who are settled in developed countries (Dumont, 2008; Guarnizo, Portes, & Haller, 2003; Hartmann, 2015; Itzigsohn, 2000, Jaulin, 2016; Østergaard-Nielsen, 2001; Toivanen, 2016). Among them, the Latin American community has been more widely studied (Boccagni, 2011; Bolzman, 2011; Calderón Chelius, 2003; Escobar, Arana, & McCann, 2015; Itzigsohn & Villacrés, 2008; Lafleur, 2011; Lieber, 2010; Morales & Pilati, 2014).

In contrast, few studies concentrated efforts on migrant flows in the opposite direction; those composed of citizens from countries in the "Global North" who live in developing nations. In relation to emigrants coming from traditional settlement societies, the case of the United States citizens is, although with many aspects still to be covered, the most studied. Interesting contributions are those made by Croucher (2009) and von Koppenfels (2014), which tried to distinguish political patterns among American expatriates living in Mexico and Europe, respectively.[5]

In recent years, although in a more limited extension, the political transnationalism panorama among the citizens of highly developed Asian countries has also been studied. Ju Rhee (2014) offered an interesting explanation for understanding the recent low turnout among Korean expatriates in the first assembly and presidential election in which they had voting rights. The Japanese case has attracted the attention of Hotaka Roth (2003) and Kalicki (2008, 2009). The former described the manner in which Japanese citizens who are residents in Brazil participated in elections in their country of origin. The latter explained the dynamics that promoted, at the end of the twentieth century, the participation of non-resident citizens in Nipponese politics.

The profile of external voters from European countries, in which the reception of migrants in comparison to the US and other traditional settlement societies[6] is a more recent phenomenon, has also attracted the interest of some scholars. Tintori (2011) described the political practices of Italian citizens with Latin American backgrounds and the way in which they have created overlapping polities. Lafleur (2013), in his research about the political process promoting the recognition of external voting rights in Italy, identified the causal configurations that produced restrictive or expansive answers over time from the political system in relation to the recognition of these rights.

The Irish case is covered by Honohan (2011). In her study, she theoretically discusses the convenience of a hypothetical extension of voting rights to expatriates in one of the few

European countries in which these are recognized only for military and diplomatic personnel appointed abroad. Lafleur (2011), in an interesting comparative contribution, offered an explanation for understanding the late inclusion of this recognition in Belgian law. In his opinion, the presence of external pressures from a supranational organization such as the European Union for the extension of voting rights to non-citizen residents was the window of opportunity used by non-resident citizens for the obtaining of political rights while living abroad. Lisi et al. (2015) analysed the interaction between, on one side, the procedural and organisztional aspects of the electoral laws and, on the other side, the socio-economic, geographic features and political behaviour of Portuguese expatriates.

The Swiss case

Switzerland's Federal Department of Foreign Affairs (2017) estimated that each year 28,000 Swiss citizens move abroad to work, study, enjoy retirement, or create a new family. In total, there were 761,930 Swiss nationals living outside of the country on December 31, 2015.[7] This figure represents around 9 per cent of the population in Swiss territory and increases to 12 per cent when only Swiss passport holders living in Switzerland are considered.

Of the Swiss expatriates, 61.97 per cent are settled in European states. The second receptor continent of Swiss expatriates is America, with 24.11 per cent (183,072 individuals). Specifically, in the case of Swiss Latin Americans, the Federal Government reports that 63,615[8] citizens officially lived in this region of the world on December 31, 2015 (8.34 per cent of the Swiss diaspora around the world). Argentina, Brazil, and Mexico, the three biggest countries in the region, are also those with the large Swiss populations in this area of the world (15,865, 15,730 and 5,366, respectively).

Many indicators describe the social and political importance of the Swiss community settled around the globe. First, the Swiss Federal Government considers its population living outside of its borders to be the fifth region of the country[9] (Schönenberger & Efionayi-Mäder, 2010). Second, Swiss residents abroad are organized in local associations, which are, at the same time, composing a kind of umbrella institution (Organisation of the Swiss Abroad[10]) with a direct interlocution to the Swiss authorities.

Third, the Swiss Foreign Affairs Ministry has a special section (Swissemigration EDA) concentrating on serving its citizens residing outside its borders. The Delegate for Relations with the Swiss Abroad is responsible for this population.[11] Fourth, there is a battery of state-funded mass media with the purpose of keeping active the links between all members of the Swiss community.[12] Finally, each year, when the national holiday is celebrated (August 1), the president of the country directs two speeches: one to the whole Swiss population and another one exclusively prepared for the population residing overseas.

Swiss citizens abroad have, in Honohan's (2011) opinion, substantial external voting rights for federal elections.[13] The process for gaining this recognition was gradual (Braun, 2013). In the period between 1977 and 1992, Swiss expatriates were obliged to return to Swiss territory to cast their vote. Since July 1, 1992, they have been able to vote from their countries of residence via the post.[14] The right to vote is not immediate; Swiss citizens have to request it. The possibility of being active or passive electors is allowed for all Swiss nationals living in a foreign country who are older than 18 years of age and, at the same time, are registered as expatriates in embassies or consulate-generals. In the first semester of 2016, 156,534[15] Swiss voters were registered (20.54 per cent of the total Swiss expatriates officially recorded).

Specifically, at the federal level, Swiss expatriates can vote for members of the National Council, in constitutional (mandatory) and facultative referendums, and in ballots related to popular initiatives (Federal Department of Foreign Affairs, 2016). As is the case for their Switzerland-residing Swiss counterparts, in order to promote enlightened participation, they receive the official voting papers and explanatory brochure provided by the Federal Council via post, some weeks before each election. Furthermore, they can sign sheets for promoting popular initiatives and facultative referendums. In other words, they also have policy-shaping capabilities even when residing overseas. Swiss expatriates can also send individual and collective petitions[16] to the political authorities.

Despite, on one side, the strong relationship between Switzerland and its diaspora around the world and, on the other side, the wide range of political rights recognized for Swiss expatriates, there are few academic efforts focused on generating empirical evidence on their patterns of political transnationalism. Most of them rely exclusively on the study of the process of incorporation of e-voting techniques for facilitating Swiss vote casting in general, with special mention of expatriates (Braun & Brändli, 2006; Gerlach & Gasser, 2009; Serdült, Germann, Mendez, Portenier, & Wellig, 2015) and the Swiss abroad[17] in particular (Driza-Maurer, Spycher, Taglioni, & Weber, 2012; Serdült, 2010).

Some of the studies included in the latter group offered interesting insights into the profile of politically active expatriates. The use of Internet voting by Swiss expatriates tends to increase relative to geographical distance to the home country. As expected, knowledge of IT increases the chances of utilizing this channel (Germann, Conradin, Wellig, & Serdült, 2014a). Those casting their vote via the Internet also tend to be young, male, and members of the upper classes. At the same time, e-voting does not seem to affect electoral mobilization of overseas Swiss (Germann et al., 2014b). Only Germann et al. (2014a) applied some conceptual categories of interest for the field of political transnationalism. These scholars found that, among expatriates, those who vote online, in comparison to those who vote via post, have a higher level of political knowledge and political interest (attention), two of the civic competencies analysed in our research.

It is difficult to find studies about Swiss expatriates in which online voting is not the main focus.[18] One of them is the short note of Nadja Braun (2013). She presented the history of the Swiss population living abroad in a very structured way and, at the same time, described some political patterns of the members of this European diaspora; namely, its levels of (1) enrolment for casting, (2) voting, and (3) presence in the Swiss parliament. Hermann (2012) and Milic (2015b) described the ideological voting pattern of Swiss expatriates in the federal elections of 2011 and 2015, respectively.[19] At the same time, Milic explored levels of political interest in the Swiss political system of the diaspora. In this sense, he found a high degree of similarity in the way in which compatriots see problems within and outside of the Swiss border.[20]

As it is easy to detect, most of the empirical evidence about the political profile of the Swiss abroad is concentrated on those expatriates who have participated in recent electoral processes. Until this point of time, there has only been one research effort with a focus on detecting political patterns among Swiss expatriates beyond their condition as electors/voters (Schlenker, Blatter, & Birka, 2017). At the same time, its authors focused their attention, not on the entire diaspora, as in the previously mentioned studies, but on specific countries with Swiss emigrant settlers. Nevertheless, their analysis only explored patterns of political transnationalism among Swiss emigrants residing in other developed countries (the US, France, Italy, and Germany). In contrast, this chapter is part of a major academic research project in which, through screening of the civic competencies of Latin American Swiss, the main purpose is to generate data about the political transnationalism trends of Switzerland's diaspora settled in developing countries.

Civic competencies as indicators of political transnationalism patterns

Civic competencies are the personal skills relevant for the facilitation of citizens' lives in democratic contexts. These are the assets through which individuals can have a voice in political systems. An adequate level of their distribution among the population is deemed the best instrument for the promotion of a healthy democratic regime (Lipset, 1987; Tocqueville, 1956; Torney-Purta, Barber, & Wilkenfeld, 2007; Waldstein & Reiher, 2001).

Good marks awarded to democratic quality are only guaranteed by the existence of an active citizenry selecting and controlling political authorities and the manner in which they design and execute public policies (Levine & Molina, 2011). Citizens are able to act in such a way because they possess civic competencies. As a consequence, when the political integration of migrants in settlement societies is studied, it is common practice to measure their level of civic competency as an indicator of their incorporation into the host democratic political system[21] (Biderbost, 2010b; Fennema & Tillie, 1999; Torney-Purta, Barber, & Wilkenfeld, 2006; Torney-Purta et al., 2007). Civic competencies are presented among migrants in general with some kind of circularity (a civic competency tends to produce other civic competencies) and it is expected to find in one specific individual a similar (positive or negative) sign (but not intensity) for each one of his or her civic assets (Biderbost, 2014; Finkel & Ernst, 2005; Gastil & Xenos, 2010).

If civic competencies are useful for identifying the type of relationship between non-citizen residents (immigrants) and the political system of the host societies, there is theoretically no obstacle to making use of them for measuring the same link between non-resident citizens (expatriates) and the political system of their home countries. The quality of the democracy of sending societies is expanded when expatriates overseas also express interest in political mechanisms in their societies of origin. Political transnationalism patterns of members of any diaspora may be explored perfectly through these capabilities.

Under the conceptual umbrella of civic competencies, different authors have listed a limited number of skills considered necessary for allowing citizens to have a real voice in politics. In general, among these competencies of a political nature are two subgroups: one composed of attitudinal elements and the other of behavioural components (Morales & Morariu, 2011). At the same time, these civic assets cover one type (the broad one) of transnational political practices described in the literature (Itzigsohn, 2000).

First, authors have talked about the importance of *political knowledge.* This refers to the quantity of information that it is possible to detect in one specific citizen or community regarding political reality and the capacity to make connections within it. Those societies better equipped with political knowledge have more tools with which to ensure their political representatives are accountable (Fraile, Ferrer, & Martín, 2007; Langton & Jennings, 1968).

A second important competency is *political attentiveness.*[22] This refers to the level of interest that individuals demonstrate in relation to political processes and the mechanisms used for obtaining political information (Giugni & Morales, 2011; Torney-Purta et al., 2007). Those who demonstrate high levels of political attentiveness can easily take decisions linked to political matters; in comparison to other civic capabilities, it is the one requiring the least level of effort (Biderbost, 2014; White, Nevitte, Blais, Gidengil, & Fournier, 2008).

Political efficacy is the third relevant competency. It has two dimensions (Balch, 1974; Wu, 2003). The internal one is related to individuals' self-described capacity for understanding politics. The external one is linked to self-described capacity for influencing the political scene (Craig & Maggiotto, 1982; Easton & Dennis, 1967; Pasek, Feldman, Romer, & Hall, 2008). Without a good combination of both sorts of efficacy, people would respond in an apathetic way to the stimulus offered by the democratic political process (Craig, Niemi, & Silver, 1990).

A fourth civic skill is the classic *political participation*.[23] This concept covers all the practical activities of a political nature with which a person is involved with the purpose of having an impact on the political agenda or, at the very least, expressing adherence to some political ideology. These activities can be classified by taking their grades (intensity or compromise demanded of the people executing them) into account (Burns, Schlozman, & Verba, 2001; Conge, 1988). Different grades denote, at the same time, different levels of personal involvement by the citizens (from casting a ballot to being an elected public official) (Gastil & Xenos, 2010; Milbrath & Goel, 1977; Verba, Schlozman, & Brady, 1995).

These four civic competencies were those explored among the Swiss diaspora living in Latin American countries in order to identify the pattern of their relationships with the political institutions of their home country. The Swiss political system, as an effect of the institutions of direct democracy that it includes, favours (at least, from a theoretical point of view) an active role on the part of its citizens. This text is part of a research effort to test this idea with one specific segment of Switzerland's emigrants. Figure 17.1 mentions one theoretical descriptor for each competency and exhibits the expected causal relationships among them, taking a recent revision of the literature on this matter (Biderbost, 2014) into account.

The possession of civic competencies can be seen as the consequence of different experiences of political socialization (Biderbost, 2014; White et al., 2008). In the specific case of expatriates, the level of political assets could be explained by exposure theory. This suggests that the length of time overseas migrants have been exposed to the political system of the society of origin is a good predictor of their political ties to the home country. The transference theory offers another explanation for expatriates' political transnational patterns. For this, the socio-demographic background of the host society could contribute to understanding of the political attachment to their motherland.

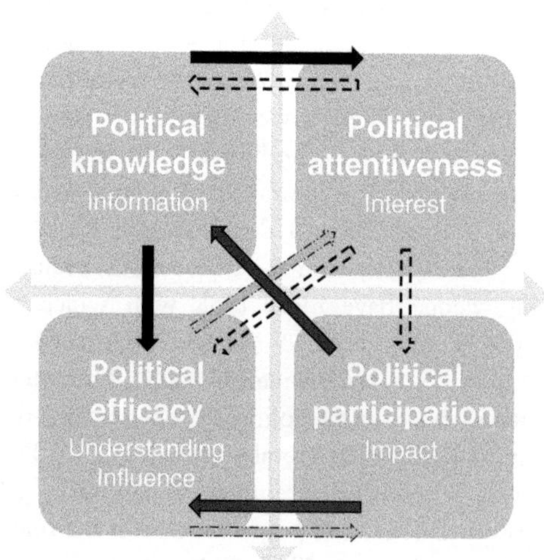

Figure 17.1 Theoretical descriptors and causal relationships among civic competencies

Data and methods

Among the Swiss settled in Latin America, 48,344 were potentially voters in December 31, 2016, because they were 18 years or older at that moment. This appears a small number but, in fact, it represents more than the population of five cantons (Uri, Obwalden, Nidwalden, Glarus, and Appenzell Innerrhoden), and exceeds the number of inhabitants in cities such as Fribourg, La Chaux-de-Fonds, Locarno, Neuchâtel, and Aarau (Swiss Federal Statistical Office, 2017).[24]

A virtual survey was administered via SurveyMonkey in summer 2016 to detect the political transnational patterns of Swiss citizens in Latin America. The questionnaire was delivered in Spanish and Portuguese. The channels used for accessing potential respondents were the official and non-official Swiss societies/associations in this region.[25] Swiss expatriates were also contacted personally via Facebook and SwissCommunity.org, the social network of the Swiss diaspora. At the same time, the Spanish version of Swissinfo promoted the research by reporting on it.[26] Making use of a snowball strategy, each respondent was invited to re-send the survey to a compatriot fulfilling the same requirements (residence in Latin America).

In total, 622 responses were collected. Some of them were eliminated because the respondents did not hold, at that moment, a Swiss passport. A total of 539 cases were included in the final sample. They covered, with the exception of Cuba, all the Latin American countries. Data were collected about different groups of variables of interest: sociodemographic background, migratory trajectory, civic competencies, and ideological identity.[27] Migrants were also invited to include any impressions about the survey in a section for comments.

Data are first analysed through indicators of descriptive statistics. Their application allowed us to obtain a general landscape of the main characteristics of the survey respondents. Second, multiple correspondence analysis (MCA) was used. This tool is frequently used in analysing a set of observations described by a set of nominal variables. MCS is helpful for both exploring the sample and distinguishing conceptual components within it (Abdi & Valentin, 2007; Husson & Josse, 2014). MCA was applied in order to identify the relationship between, on one side, the demographic and migratory group of variables and, on the other, the whole toolkit of civic competencies. Data were processed using IBM SPSS 24.0.

Findings and analysis

First, findings on sociodemographic background are analysed and described. Second, the migratory background of the respondents is reported and systematized. Third, the distribution of civic competencies among Swiss expatriates in Latin America is introduced. Finally, the results of the MCA analysis are interpreted, commented on, and discussed.

Sociodemographic background

Swiss citizens born in Latin American countries represents 60.9 per cent of the final sample. The remaining respondents (39.1 per cent) are Swiss nationals born in the mother country.[28] In the Swiss social and political tradition, a citizen's canton of origin resembles a distinct stamp. Regardless of his or her real birthplace, the former is the person's place of origin written on the identification (ID) card. Cantons of origin could also be identified as a useful (but not flawless) heuristic for tracking Swiss nationals' urban–rural and cultural–linguistic backgrounds. The distribution of cantons of origin among respondents is representative of the current proportion of population by district in the native land. This similarity makes of "canton of origin" a variable theoretically not relevant for explaining dissimilarities among Swiss abroad and in the home country using aggregate values. Table 17.1 summarizes the information related to the last point in relation to the six cantons with more subjects in the sample.

The gender distribution of the answers to the survey is male biased (56.8 per cent of respondents). If responding to a questionnaire of this kind is considered an indicator of political interest, these results are not incongruent with patterns historically reported by Political Science studies (Bennett & Bennett, 1989; Verba, Burns, & Schlozman, 1997). Similar results have also been found in previous studies on the online voting performance of the same cohort as is addressed in this study (Driza-Maurer et al., 2012; Germann et al., 2014a).

Age distribution among respondents does not reveal any peaks or troughs. Answers of young, middle-aged, and older adults are equally represented in the sample. This pattern echoes previous findings in research on the online political behaviour of Swiss expatriates. As Germann et al. (2014a) suggested, the use of a virtual channel for collecting information could be acting as compensation for age effects.

In contrast, when the educational level of respondents is taken into account, 67.4 per cent of those surveyed have a Bachelor's degree at the very least. Furthermore, 24.4 per cent of the sample hold a postgraduate diploma. Respondents' occupations are more diverse. The three most frequent job profiles are those of private sector employee (23.3 per cent), independent professional (20.7 per cent), and entrepreneur/businessperson (17.0 per cent).

Mastery of the Swiss languages is another interesting indicator of the socio-demographic profile of the Helvetic population abroad. The distribution of verbal skills in Switzerland's official languages shows a similar, but not identical, pattern to that seen in the home country (Federal Statistical Office, 2016). A high level of German competency is reported by 36.3 per cent of respondents. A high level of French competency is reported by 27.3 per cent of the sample. Only 8.6 per cent of respondents say that they are fluent Italian speakers. Fluent Romansh is reported by just 0.6 per cent of the sample.

Migratory background

The sample shows that, contrary to belief, Swiss Latin Americans are mostly composed of first (43.1 per cent) and second (25.2 per cent) generation migrants coming from the motherland.[29] Moreover, 31.4 per cent of those surveyed have lived in the country of origin for at least 20

Table 17.1 Proportion of respondents by canton of origin versus distribution of Swiss population in the home country

Canton of origin	*% of respondents*	*% of population of the canton in relation to whole Swiss population*	*Difference*
Bern	15.5	12.2	+3.3
Zürich	15.0	17.6	–2.6
St. Gallen	10.3	5.9	+4.4
Argau	8.2	7.8	+0.4
Ticino	8.2	4.2	+4.0
Valais	5.1	4.3	+0.8

years. This closeness of "personal history" to Switzerland's political reality could act, as exposure theory suggests, as an activator of transnational political practices.

Of the respondents, 32.45 per cent had left Switzerland at least 11 years previously. Similar figures (26.7 per cent) describe the number of years (at least 11) that migrants have been settled in the host society. This finding could indicate the activation of an opposite mechanism to the one described in the previous paragraph: the longer the time since leaving the home country, the less attached one is to the current Swiss political reality. This may even be the case for first-generation Swiss.

The main drivers of migration have been, taking the voice of the respondents into account, first, seeking economic and job opportunities (46.7 per cent) and, second, family reasons (21.9 per cent). The thirst for new experiences is the third most cited reason for leaving Switzerland (16.4 per cent). From a theoretical point of view, none of these reasons could be exclusively understood as motivation or demotivation for transnational political practices.

Civic competencies

Levels of political knowledge among Swiss Latin Americans are high. However, percentages of correct answers tended to diminish when the questions posed were worded in a more sophisticated manner. Civic competency was measured using three different indicators. First, respondents were asked if they could name a referendum or population initiative election that had taken place in the previous five years. Of respondents, 76.4 per cent said they were able to remember one of these events and, at the same time, could describe some features of a specific ballot.

Second, a similar percentage can be found in relation to how well Swiss Latin Americans know the length of the term of office of the Swiss president; 73.9 per cent answered correctly – that it lasts one year. Nevertheless, in the case of the third indicator, the percentage of adequate answers diminished to 64.7 per cent when respondents were asked about the process through which members of the Federal Council (equivalent to ministers) are chosen.

It is important to note that, at least in this sample of Swiss Latin Americans, levels of political knowledge seem to be higher than among Swiss citizens living in developed countries such as the US, France, Italy, and Germany (Schlenker et al., 2017).[30] At the same time, similar results have been found in studies on levels of political knowledge among the Swiss young adult population residing in the home country (Koller, 2014).

Swiss migrants settled in Latin America said they are politically attentive. This civic competency was measured through two indicators: the frequency with which respondents follow Swiss political news in different mass media and the frequency of talking about Swiss politics to members of their social circle. In the case of the former, expatriates stated that they look for information with a focus on Swiss political reality on a regular basis (56.8 per cent of total respondents). This percentage increases to 90.4 per cent when those occasionally consuming Swiss political news are also included. Only 9.6 per cent declared not having or having only intermittent contact with Swiss news.

In the case of the latter, the percentages were much lower. Only 21.5 per cent discuss Swiss politics with relatives, friends, or work colleagues on a regular basis. When occasional discussants are included, the percentage grew to 71.5 per cent. Those who did not wish to talk about Swiss political reality formed 28.4 per cent of the sample. This divergent pattern among the two indicators of political attentiveness seems to have an obvious explanation. While following political news is a non-demanding individual activity, discussing or talking about politics requires more effort (at least two interested people who make this topic the focus of their conversation).

Regardless of the divergence between the two indicators of political attentiveness, the results are congruent with former empirical evidence in which this civic competency showed a higher value in comparison to the remaining civic assets, because it requires less personal effort (Biderbost, 2014; Morales & Morariu, 2011; White et al., 2008). Similar levels of political attentiveness to those found for Swiss Latin Americans in this research have been detected among the Swiss population residing in Switzerland (Blais, 2014) and for Swiss emigrants living in developed host states (Schlenker et al., 2017).

Both dimensions of political efficacy were measured among Swiss Latin Americans. Although internal dimensions showed a slightly higher value than external dimensions (73.9 per cent versus 71.0 per cent), Swiss expatriates in this region of the world declared having a deep understanding of the features of the Swiss political system and, at the same time, expressed having a voice in Swiss politics. These results are not surprising in the current context. Swiss emigrants are increasingly aware of their electoral power and have become a strong political lobbying group for the promotion of a universal extension of e-voting mechanisms (Swissinfo, 2017b).

When these figures are compared to equivalent results among the Swiss population in the motherland, the analysis showed that Latin American expatriates performed 30 per cent better (Blais, 2014). A reason for this difference may be found in the fact that Swiss expatriates are mostly only exposed to the political complexities of the federal level of government. In contrast, Swiss citizens residing in the home country are exposed to the complexities of a multilevel direct democracy political system. Nevertheless, this explanation must be considered with caution because it may result from a divergence in operational definitions, even though the conceptual definition of political efficacy is similar among different researchers (Biderbost, 2014). Only a future survey in which Swiss settled in both the home country and abroad are equally included will generate credible comparable empirical evidence. Regrettably, there are no records of this kind for Swiss emigrants living in developed countries.

The last civic competency included in the survey is political participation. This is the asset with the worst performance among Swiss expatriates. It was measured using three different indicators. Only 51.7 per cent of respondents have formally activated, via a request to the Swiss embassies in the countries where they are settled, their right to vote. In the last five years, 40.9 per cent of respondents have voted at least once in a referendum or election related to a population initiative process (typical instruments in the Swiss direct democracy political system). This percentage diminished to a poor 18.4 per cent of positive answers when emigrants were asked if they voted in the last federal election (October 2015).

The gap between the Swiss Latin Americans who requested the vote and those who actually voted is explained by the difficulties associated with utilising the ballot system via mail. Generally, the ballots arrive in Latin American countries after the elections in the home country have taken place or they arrive with too little time for expatriates returning them to the canton of origin to be included in the final records.

These figures do not coincide with Swiss turnout standards in general. Swiss average participation in ballots is historically low in comparison to other Western countries. Voter fatigue (because of the frequent organization of elections due to the direct democracy system), complexity of the political system, and use of the magic formula[31] for appointing political representatives to the cabinet have been described as the factors explaining this limited turnout (Blais, 2014).

In comparison to previous civic competencies, Swiss Latin Americans fall behind their fellows residing in developed countries. While only 18.4 per cent voted in the federal election among those composing the former group, 61 per cent did so in the case of the latter (Schlenker et al., 2017). Two explanations can be offered here. On one hand, geographical closeness to the home country may stimulate political participation. For example, many Swiss settled in European countries are *frontaliers* or, in other words, they live in a foreign country (France, Italy, or Germany) but work in Swiss cantons (Geneva, Ticino, or Zürich). They are not really disconnected from Swiss reality. On the other hand, the Swiss residing in European countries do not experience the problems associated with delivery by mail of official ballots, as described above. That clearly acts as a catalyst for their voting behaviour.

Nevertheless, at this point, it is important to remember that the samples were not gathered using similar criteria. The sample including Swiss expatriates in the US, Italy, Germany, and France exclusively includes citizens recorded in Swiss consulates. In other words, there is a bias in favour of those emotionally connected to the motherland. In contrast, the sample incorporating Swiss Latin Americans was created with the support of organizations within the Swiss diaspora.

>When different components of each civic competency are added, two interesting patterns can be detected. First, values of attitudinal civic competencies (knowledge, attentiveness, and efficacy) are similar (between 0.7 and 0.8 points). This could be understood as the existence of a clear disposition for engaging in political activities. However, these expectations are not realized. On the contrary, behavioural civic competencies *stricto sensu* (participation) represent only half of the values (0.37) of the former group. Second, higher values of civic attitudes are demonstrated by citizens who are not directly related to (or interacting with) political institutions in the home country. Lower values are shown for the opposite group, as revealed in conduct demonstrating that Swiss expatriates are more closely connected to national polities. Figure 17.2 describes the performance of Swiss expatriates in Latin America in the different civic competencies.

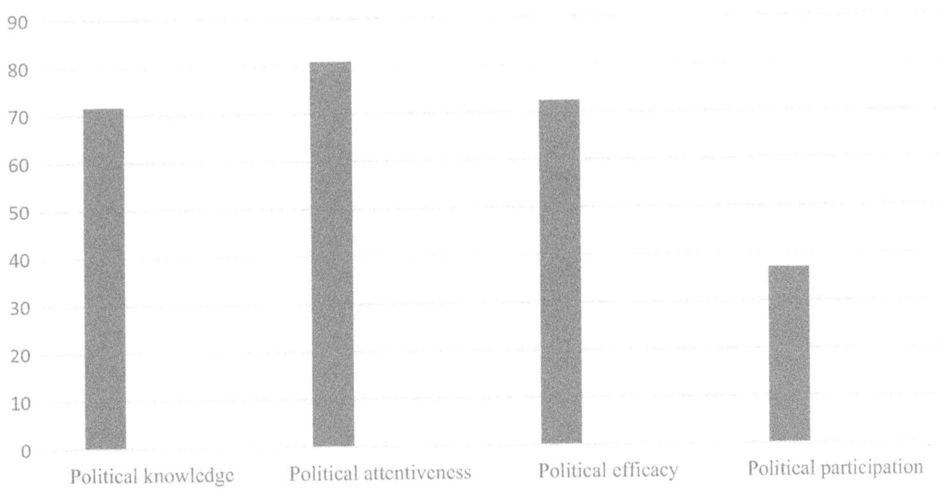

Figure 17.2 Performance of Swiss expatriates in Latin American countries

Multivariate findings

The application of multiple correspondence analysis reveals the presence of two analytical dimensions. One of them is composed of variables related to the previously mentioned theory of exposure. Attitudinal civic competencies (internal dimension of political efficacy and political knowledge) seem to be better explained by the quantity of time that the expatriate has been under the influence of Swiss society. Added to this, mastery in the use of German and French is a resource through which Swiss emigrants have a better understanding of the Helvetic political system.

A second dimension is composed, using a *lato sensu* definition, of civic competencies of a behavioural nature, such as political participation, the external dimension of political efficacy, and political attentiveness. Education is a clear explanatory variable in this second group. This could be understood, although in a limited way, as an indicator of some explanatory power recognized in the theory of transference (that based on sociodemographic factors). Nevertheless, the empirical evidence is limited and data has to be studied more intensively.

Latin American country of residence is an explanatory factor for this second dimension. Two hypotheses, although not exclusively, can be expressed in relation to this fact. The strength of Swiss associations in the host country could act as a promoting variable in relation to proactive political behaviour. The performance of the local postal service could be another factor affecting the nature of the voting process for Swiss citizens abroad.

Data on ideology and gender had no capacity to explain the transnational political practices of Swiss expatriates in Latin American countries. The male condition is not, in comparison to previous research on the Swiss abroad, an activator of civic competencies in relation to the political system of the home country (Driza-Maurer et al., 2012; Germann et al., 2014a). Nor is canton of origin relevant to any dimension. Figure 17.3 provides a visual representation of both dimensions identified using multiple correspondence analysis.

Concluding remarks

This chapter is part of a bigger, innovative research effort tracing the transnational political practices of a Northern diaspora settled in developing countries. In this sense, this research intends to break the institutionalized approach to studying transnationalism that focuses mainly on the detection of patterns of political behaviour of "South going North" migrants.

The civic competencies of an attitudinal nature among Swiss citizens in Latin America describe the clear intention of this diaspora to be connected to the political system of the motherland. However, levels of participation are surprisingly low. A first plausible hypothesis to explain this finding is related to two aspects of the system for voting abroad: first, the right to vote is not automatic following registration in a Swiss embassy (a second step is required) and, second, ballots must be returned via the postal service.

The application of multiple correspondence analysis provides preliminary support for the two theories of political socialization traditionally used for studying the integration of migrants in receiving societies. On one hand, variables related to the theory of exposure explain better civic competencies of an attitudinal nature; the length of time a Swiss citizen lives in Switzerland is reflected in the high values they score on political knowledge and the internal dimension of political efficacy. On the other hand, level of education, a typical variable of the theory of transference, seems to be the main driver of civic competencies of a behavioural nature (*lato sensu*). The Latin American country of residence of the Swiss citizens

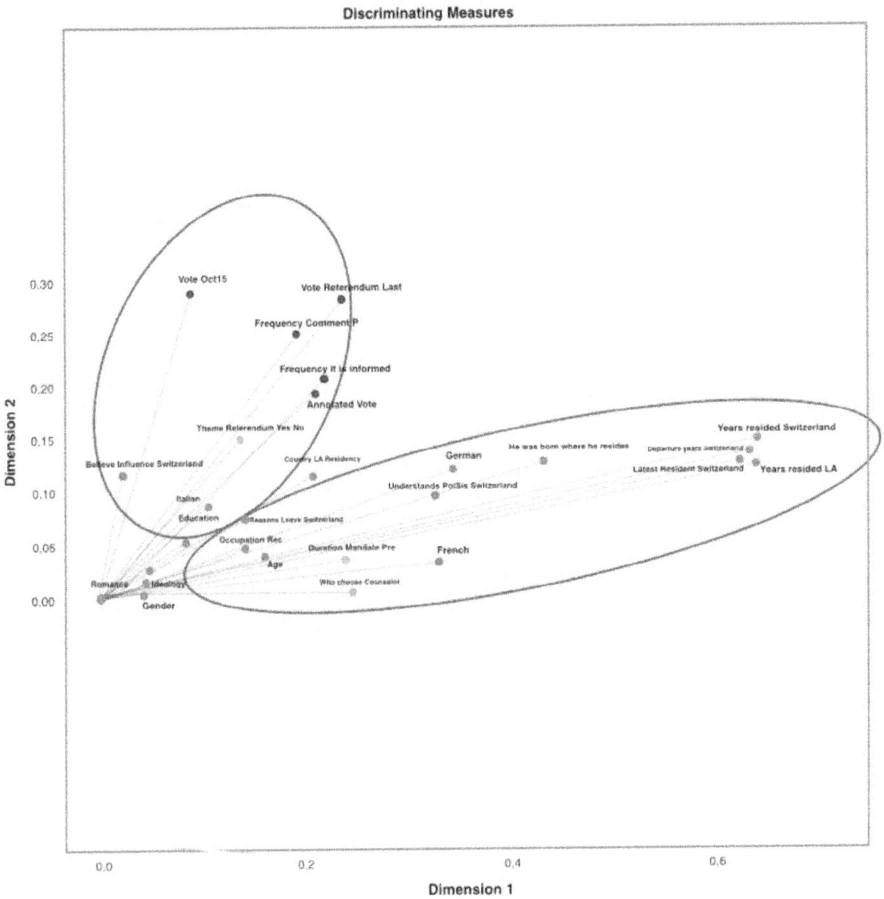

Figure 17.3 Dimensions identified using multiple correspondence analysis

also promotes this second type of competency. Nevertheless, there is not yet enough information to describe the ways in which the settlement environment is producing this result.

To better contextualize the political performance of Swiss Latin Americans, more comparative studies are needed. They have to be designed at two levels. First, transnational political practices must be identified and compared among Swiss expatriates across different continents and, consequently, including countries with different political (democracy versus authoritarian regimes) and economic (developed versus developing societies) backgrounds. Second, political attitudes and behaviours of Swiss citizens, regardless of their place of residence, must also be screened. Only in this manner can indicators of the different civic competencies be compared among Swiss citizens residing in Switzerland and overseas.

No one doubts the high quality of democracy in the Swiss political system. Citizens of this country can access different mechanisms for participating in the political scenery and also for ensuring the accountability of their representatives. The formal extension of voting rights for Swiss expatriates is itself an example of the expansionary democratic logic of the Swiss regime. Nevertheless, the limited empirical evidence suggests that, actually, for some

Swiss expatriates, some practical features of the system for voting abroad are frustrating their intention to have a say in the political system of the home country. The gradual continuity of the research agenda previously described could act as a generator of new data explaining the mechanisms through which these gaps between the formal recognition and practical use of political rights are shaped.

Notes

1 This article is a product of the "Establishing a joint research partnership about political transnationalism" project. It was funded by the Swiss National Science Foundation (IZK0Z1_164827).

2 The total number of migrants in Switzerland, taking into account official figures of the State Secretariat for Migration, was 2.09 million people on July 31, 2017.

3 The most famous popular initiative of this kind, as a consequence of its unexpected result, was the one that took place on February 14, 2017 (against mass immigration). In that opportunity, a majority of people (50.3 per cent) and a majority of cantons (16) decided to include in the Constitution an article in which residence permits for foreigners must be limited to annual quotas. The particularities of this election process have generated a huge interest among social scientists in terms of clarifying its causes and consequences (Abberger, Dibiasi, Siegenthaler, & Sturm, 2014; Ackermann & Freitag, 2015; Mazzoleni & Pilotti, 2015; Milic, 2015a).

4 The main feature of the Swiss political system is its direct democracy. This is composed of four juridical elements: constitutional referendum, optional referendum, popular initiative, and right of petition. They allow Swiss citizens, on one hand, to have the final word on many political issues and, on the other hand, to maintain regular contact with their political representatives.

5 Interest in the political behaviour of US expatriates gained renewed attention after overseas votes decided the result of the presidential race between George W. Bush and Al Gore in 2000 (Imai & King, 2004).

6 Two groups of countries can be distinguished under the umbrella of traditional settlement societies. It is possible to detect a common pattern in the origin of these nations: the massive arrival of people from overseas. On one side, there is a group composed of highly-developed Anglo-Saxon countries such as the US, Canada, Australia, and New Zealand. On the other side, there is a group composed of middle–high income Latin American countries such as Argentina, Brazil, and Uruguay. Despite its Anglo-Saxon cultural roots and taking into account its level of development, South Africa may be included in this second group.

7 Among them, 73.5 per cent are dual nationals and 26.5 per cent hold only Swiss nationality (Swissinfo, 2017a).

8 This number of people is larger than the population in six Swiss cantons (Federal Statistical Office, 2017).

9 The other four Swiss regions are those related to each one of the officially recognized national languages (German, French, Italian, and Romansh).

10 This organization is also known by its acronym, OSA.

11 More information about the role expected of this official by the government is described here: www.eda.admin.ch/eda/en/home/fdfa/organisation-fdfa/directorates-divisions/cd/delegate-relations-swiss-abroad.html

12 Swissinfo (www.swissinfo.ch) is a virtual journal published in ten different languages. Its main aim is promoting different concepts related to Swissness such as direct democracy, innovation, quality of life, and productivity. The *Swiss Review* (www.revue.ch) magazine is published six times a year, freely delivered to the Swiss population worldwide. It has two versions: print and virtual. SwissCommunity (www.swisscommunity.org) is a social network in which Swiss expatriates have a personal profile and can exchange information with other nationals living abroad.

13 Some cantons let their expatriates participate in cantonal elections. Until August 18, 2017, this was a right recognized in Zurich, Berne, Schwyz, Fribourg, Soleure, Bâle-Campagne, Grisons, Tessin, Neuchâtel, Genève, and Jura (Federal Department of Foreign Affairs, 2017).

14 Swiss expatriates, if they are temporarily in Switzerland at the time of elections, can also vote in person at the polling station. At the same time, some cantons began to increasingly include the possibility of e-voting in federal referendums and elections.

15 When voting rights for Swiss expatriates were originally recognized through the "Loi fédérale sur les droits politiques des Suisses de l'étranger," only 2,272 people were recorded for voting in the first

turnout (March 13, 1977). In the last federal turn of referendums (May 21, 2017), the total number of voters registered was 163,601 (Chancellerie fédérale, 2017).

16 This is a right recognized in the Swiss constitution for all persons regardless of their nationality. The petitions may take the form of a demand, suggestion, or complaint. Authorities are formally obliged to notify the reception of the petition but they are not obliged to answer it. Nevertheless, in general, authorities respond in some way to the petitioners. It must not be conflated to the popular initiative dispositive, whose aim is to organize a universal election on one particular topic. Swiss abroad used it in order to promote the expansion of e-voting ballots in 2012. More information about the punctual use of this political dispositive can be found at: http://aso.ch/en/politics/petition-evoting

17 The expressions "Swiss abroad" and "Swiss expatriates" are used interchangeably in this chapter.

18 Under the format of divulgation articles in non-scientific magazines related to the Swiss diaspora community, information is published on the political behavioural patterns of Swiss expatriates (Jaberg, 2017; Mariani, 2015; Milic, 2016; Raaflaub, 2017). These publications always place a strong emphasis on reportage of voting behaviour of diaspora members.

19 Milic (2016) suggested that, despite recent gains in popularity by the Swiss People's Party among expatriates, members of the diaspora tend to vote with a more leftist bias, with a clear preference for the Social Democrats. The Green Party also performed better among voters overseas than with voters in the home country.

20 In spite of this overlapping in outlook, there are some topics in which the distance between the Swiss abroad and those in the home country is significant. Those thematic areas are the European Union and migration/refugee dynamics (Milic, 2016).

21 Sometimes, these civic competencies are named in these studies under the conceptual umbrella of political attitudes (González-Ferrer, 2011; Maxwell, 2010; Morales, 2011).

22 In this text, political attentiveness, political attention, and political interest are interchangeably used.

23 Some scholars add political tolerance as the fifth civic competence (Biderbost, 2014; Torney-Purta et al., 2007). It is described as individuals' expressions of their capability to accept the presence/existence of political ideas opposed to their own ideas or preferences.

24 If, as an estimator for the real number of registered voters in Latin America, a similar percentage (20.54 per cent) of electors to that found for the entire population of the Swiss abroad is used, around 13,066 expatriates could have acquired the right in this region. Information about real quantity of voters (those who have acquired that right) in each country (or region) of the world is not easily constructed. This is due to the fact that the data about Swiss expatriate voters is compiled at the communal and cantonal levels.

25 The distinction between them is based on the fact that the former are affiliated to the Organisation of the Swiss Abroad; 38 official Swiss societies were active in 2018 in the region.

26 www.swissinfo.ch/spa/la-v-suiza-y-la-pol%C3%ADtica_encuesta-para-los-suizos-en-am%C3%A9rica-latina/42293444

27 This last dimension was collected in order to detect continuities and discontinuities among societies of origin and societies of reception in the ideological self-placement of the respondents. Results about this dimension are not included in this document.

28 The percentage distribution of the respondents, taking into account their countries of settlement, is similar to that identified for the general Swiss population in the region.

29 As is very common when studying migration processes, these percentages do not exactly describe the first people who began the movement among countries. In many cases, Swiss descendants of first migrants have returned to the home country during specific periods of time during their lives. Of course, this situation increases the number of those who are incorporated into the category of first-generation migrants. What is important, in research of this kind, is capturing closeness to the Swiss political reality in personal biographies.

30 When the average of the answers to the three indicators is generated, the value of political knowledge for the Swiss Latin Americans is around 71.66 per cent. This percentage declines to 54.0 per cent in the case of Swiss citizens living in neighbouring European countries plus the US. More insights are needed in order to explain this wide gap. Further samples must include Swiss expatriates living in countries with different political and economic features.

31 The magic formula is the expression used to describe the way in which the Federal Council (Executive Branch) of the Swiss Confederation is composed. Although not a formal rule, this is an informal institution through which the presence of politicians representing the four most voted for political parties *and* the linguistic areas are guaranteed in the Executive branch.

References

Abberger, K., Dibiasi, A., Siegenthaler, M., & Sturm, J. E. (2014). *The Swiss mass immigration initiative: The impact of increased policy uncertainty on expected firm behaviour (research collection)*. Zürich: ETH.

Abdi, H. & Valentin, D. (2007). Multiple correspondence analysis. In N. J. Salkind (Ed.), *Encyclopedia of measurement and statistics* (pp. 651–657). Thousand Oaks, CA: Sage.

Ackermann, M. & Freitag, M. (2015). What actually matters? Understanding attitudes toward immigration in Switzerland. *Swiss Political Science Review, 21*(1), 36–47.

Arrighi, J.-T. (2016). *Dataset on migration referendums and initiatives in Switzerland*. Neuchatel: Nccr – On the move. Retrieved from http://nccr-onthemove.ch/research/projects/dataset-on-migration-referendums-and-initiatives/

Balch, G. I. (1974). Multiple indicators in survey research: The concept “sense of political efficacy”. *Political Methodology, 1*, 1–43.

Bauböck, R. (2007). Stakeholder citizenship and transnational political participation: A normative evaluation of external voting. *Fordham Law Review, 75*, 2393–2447.

Bennett, L. L. & Bennett, S. E. (1989). Enduring gender differences in political interest: The impact of socialization and political dispositions. *American Politics Quarterly, 17*, 105–122.

Biderbost, P. (2010a). El estudio de las migraciones en la ciencia política, un intento de sistematización. *Ciencia Política, 9*, 9–34.

Biderbost, P. (2010b). La cultura política de los jóvenes inmigrantes latinoamericanos en España. El desarrollo cívico como indicador de su integración política. In A. En Ayuso & G. Pinyol (Eds.), *Inmigración latinoamericana en España. El estado de la investigación* (pp. 167–215). Barcelona: Fundació CIDOB, Edicions Bellatera y Fundación Carolina.

Biderbost, P. (2014). *La integración política del adolescente. Las competencias cívicas de los inmigrantes en la escuela secundaria española*. Doctoral dissertation, Universidad de Salamanca.

Biderbost, P. & Boscán, G. (2011). Comunicación política, emigración y voto en América Latina. *Revista El Molinillo*, (33).

Blais, A. (2014). Why is turnout so low in Switzerland? Comparing the attitudes of Swiss and German citizens towards electoral democracy. *Swiss Political Science Review, 20*, 520–528.

Boccagni, P. (2011). Reminiscences, patriotism, participation: Approaching external voting in Ecuadorian immigration to Italy. *International Migration, 49*(3), 76–98.

Bolzman, C. (2011). The transnational political practices of Chilean migrants in Switzerland. *International Migration, 49*(3), 144–167.

Braun, N. (2013). Switzerland: External voting in a federal state with direct democracy. *IDEA*, 230–231.

Braun, N. & Brandli, D. (2006). Swiss e-voting pilot projects: Evaluation, situation analysis and how to proceed. In R. Krimmer (Ed.), *Proceedings of Electronic Voting 2006: 2nd International Workshop* (pp. 27–36). Bonn: Gesellschaft fur Informatik..

Burns, N., Schlozman, K. L., & Verba, S. (2001). *The private roots of public action: Gender, equality, and political participation*. Cambridge, MA: Harvard University Press.

Calderón Chelius, L. (2003). *Votar en la distancia: La extensión de los derechos políticos a migrantes, experiencias comparadas*. México City: Instituto Mora/Consejo Superior de Investigaciones Científicas.

Casparis, J. (1982). The Swiss mercenary system: Labor emigration from the semiperiphery. *Review (Fernand Braudel Center), 5*, 593–642.

Chancellerie fédérale. (2017). *Répertoire chronologique du votations*. Retrieved from www.admin.ch/ch/f/pore/va/vab_2_2_4_1_gesamt.html

Conge, P. J. (1988). The concept of political participation: Toward a definition. *Comparative Politics, 20*, 241–249.

Craig, S. C. & Maggiotto, M. A. (1982). Measuring political efficacy. *Political Methodology, 8*(3), 85–109.

Craig, S. C., Niemi, R. G., & Silver, G. E. (1990). Political efficacy and trust: A report on the NES pilot study items. *Political Behavior, 12*, 289–314.

Croucher, S. (2009). Migrants of privilege: The political transnationalism of Americans in Mexico. *Identities: Global Studies in Culture and Power, 16*, 463–491.

Driza-Maurer, A., Spycher, O., Taglioni, G., & Weber, A. (2012). E-voting for Swiss abroad: A joint project between the Confederation and the cantons. In *5th International Conference on Electronic Voting 2012 (EVOTE2012)* (pp. 173–187), Bregenz, Austria.

Dumont, A. (2008). Representing voiceless migrants: Moroccan political transnationalism and Moroccan migrants’ organizations in France. *Ethnic and Racial Studies, 31*, 792–811.

Easton, D. & Dennis, J. (1967). The child's acquisition of regime norms: Political efficacy. *American Political Science Review*, *61*(1), 25–38.

Echevarría, J. B. (2016). Los regimientos suizos al servicio de España en las guerras de Italia (1717–1748) [The Swiss regiments in service to Spain during the Italian Wars (1717–1748)]. *Cuadernos de Historia Moderna*, *41*, 295–312.

EDA Auslandschweizerbeziehungen. (2016). *Auslandschweizerstatistik 2015 nach Wohnländern und Konsularbezirken*. Retrieved from www.eda.admin.ch/content/dam/eda/de/documents/publications/AuslandschweizerinnenundAuslandschweizer/Auslandschweizerstatistik/2015-Auslandschweizerstatistik_de.pdf

Escobar, C. (2007). Extraterritorial political rights and dual citizenship in Latin America. *Latin American Research Review*, 43–75.

Escobar, C., Arana, R., & McCann, J. A. (2015). Expatriate voting and migrants' place of residence: Explaining transnational participation in Colombian elections. *Migration Studies*, *3*(1), 1–31.

Federal Department of Foreign Affairs. (2016). *Droits politiques pour les Suissesses et les Suisses de l'étranger*. Retrieved from www.eda.admin.ch/content/dam/countries/eda-all/fr/20151110-politische-rechte-der-AS_FR.pdf

Federal Department of Foreign Affairs. (2017). *Swiss emigration data*. Retrieved from www.eda.admin.ch/eda/en/home/living-abroad/information-and-advice.html

Federal Statistical Office. (2016). *Pratiques linguistiques en Suisse*. Retrieved from www.bfs.admin.ch/bfsstatic/dam/assets/1000171/master

Federal Statistical Office. (2017a). *Regional comparison of selected indicators, 2017 (cantons)*. Retrieved from www.bfs.admin.ch/bfs/en/home/statistics/regional-statistics/regional-portraits-key-figures/cantons.assetdetail.1922815.html

Federal Statistical Office. (2017b). *STAT-TAB – Interactive tables (FSO)*. Retrieved from www.bfs.admin.ch/bfs/en/home/services/recherche/stat-tab-online-data-search.html

Fennema, M. & Tillie, J. (1999). Political participation and political trust in Amsterdam: Civic communities and ethnic networks. *Journal of Ethnic and Migration Studies*, *25*, 703–726.

Finkel, S. E. & Ernst, H. R. (2005). Civic education in post-apartheid South Africa: Alternative paths to the development of political knowledge and democratic values. *Political Psychology*, *26*, 333–364.

Fraile, M., Ferrer, M., & Martín, I. (2007). *Jóvenes, conocimiento político y participación*. Madrid: Centro de Investigaciones Sociológicas.

Fratczak-Rudnicka, B. & Torney-Purta, J. (2002). *Competencies for civic and political life in democracy*. Zurich: Swiss Federal Statistical Office/OECD Program DeSeCo.

Gadient, I. & Milani, P. (2015). Letter from Switzerland. *Political Quarterly*, *86*, 468–471.

Gastil, J. & Xenos, M. (2010). Of attitudes and engagement: Clarifying the reciprocal relationship between civic attitudes and political participation. *Journal of Communication*, *60*, 318–343.

Gerlach, J. & Gasser, U. (2009). *Three case studies from Switzerland: E-voting*. Berkman Center Research Publication No. 3. Retrieved from https://cyber.harvard.edu/sites/cyber.harvard.edu/files/Gerlach-Gasser_SwissCases_Evoting.pdf

Germann, M. & Serdült, U. (2014b). Internet voting for expatriates: The Swiss case. *JeDEM-eJournal of eDemocracy and Open Government*, *6*, 197–215.

Germann, M., Conradin, F., Wellig, C., & Serdült, U. (2014a). Five years of Internet voting for Swiss expatriates. In *CeDEM14: Conference for E-Democracy and Open Government* (pp. 127–140). Retrieved from www.researchgate.net/publication/280677037_Five_years_of_internet_voting_for_Swiss_expatriates

Giugni, M. & Morales, L. (2011). Conclusion. Towards an integrated approach to the political inclusion of migrants. In M. Giugni & L. Morales (Eds.), *Social capital, political participation and migration in Europe: Making multicultural democracy work?* (pp. 262–274). Basingstoke: Palgrave Macmillan.

González-Ferrer, A. (2011). The electoral participation of naturalized immigrants in ten European cities. In L. Morales & M. G. Giugni (Eds.), *Social capital, political participation and migration in Europe: Making multicultural democracy work?* (pp. 63–84). Basingstoke: Palgrave Macmillan.

Guarnizo, L. E., Portes, A., & Haller, W. (2003). Assimilation and transnationalism: Determinants of transnational political action among contemporary migrants. *American Journal of Sociology*, *108*, 1211–1248.

Hartmann, C. (2015). Expatriates as voters? The new dynamics of external voting in sub-Saharan Africa. *Democratization*, *22*, 906–926.

Hermann, M. (2012). *Das politische Profil der Auslandschweizer*. Zürich: Sotomo. Retrieved from www.infosperber.ch/data/attachements/Das_politische_Profil_der_Auslandschweizer.pdf

Honohan, I. (2011). Should Irish emigrants have votes? External voting in Ireland. *Irish Political Studies*, *26*, 545–561.

Hotaka Roth, J. (2003). Urashima Taro's ambiguating practices: The significance of overseas voting rights for elderly Japanese migrants to Brazil. In J. Lesser (Ed.), *Searching for home abroad: Japanese Brazilians and transnationalism* (pp. 103–120). Durham, NC: Duke University Press.

Huber, A. & O'Reilly, K. (2004). The construction of Heimat under conditions of individualised modernity: Swiss and British elderly migrants in Spain. *Ageing & Society*, *24*, 327–351.

Husson, F. & Josse, J. (2014). Multiple correspondence analysis. In M. Greenacre & J. Blasius (Eds.), *Visualization and verbalization of data* (pp. 163–181). London: Chapman & Hall/CRC.

Imai, K. & King, G. (2004). Did illegally counted overseas absentee ballots decide the 2000 U.S. presidential election? *Perspectives on Politics*, *2*, 537–549.

Itzigsohn, J. (2000). Immigration and the boundaries of citizenship: The institutions of immigrants' political transnationalism. *International Migration Review*, 1126–1154.

Itzigsohn, J. & Villacrés, D. (2008). Migrant political transnationalism and the practice of democracy: Dominican external voting rights and Salvadoran home town associations. *Ethnic and Racial Studies*, *31*, 664–686.

Jaberg. (2017). *Swiss abroad vote for facilitated naturalisation.* Swissinfo. Retrieved from www.swissinfo.ch/eng/voting-analysis_swiss-abroad-vote-for-facilitated-naturalisation/42957342

Janmaat, J. G. (2011). Ability grouping, segregation and civic competences among adolescents. *International Sociology*, *26*, 455–482.

Jaulin, T. (2016). Geographies of external voting: The Tunisian elections abroad since the 2011 uprising. *Comparative Migration Studies*, *4*(1), 14.

Kalicki, K. (2008). Voting rights of the "marginal": The contested logic of political membership in Japan. *Ethnopolitics*, 7, 265–286.

Kalicki, K. (2009). Ethnic nationalism and political community; The overseas suffrage debates in Japan and South Korea, *Asian Studies Review*, *33*, 175–195.

Koller, D. (2014). *Analysing the effects of gender differences in political knowledge in Switzerland.* ECPR Graduate Student Conference, Innsbruck. Retrieved from https://ecpr.eu/filestore/paperproposal/995bf50e-f046-40cf-b603-cc199aa6b994.pdf

Koppenfels, A. K. V. (2014). Political transnationalism and political engagement. In *Migrants or expatriates? Migration, diasporas and citizenship series.* London: Palgrave Macmillan.

Lafleur, J. M. (2011). The transnational political participation of Latin American and Caribbean migrants residing in Europe. *International Migration*, *49*(3), 1–9.

Lafleur, J. M. (2013). *Transnational politics and the state. The external voting rights of diasporas.* New York: Routledge.

Langton, K. P. & Jennings, M. K. (1968). Political socialization and the high school civics curriculum in the United States. *American Political Science Review*, *62*, 852–867.

Levine, D. H. & Molina, J. E. (2011). *The quality of democracy in Latin America.* London: Lynne Rienner Publishers.

Lieber, M. A. (2010). *Elections beyond borders: Overseas voting in Mexico and the Dominican Republic, 1994–2008*, Doctoral dissertation, Brown University.

Lipset, S. M. (1987). *El hombre político: Las bases sociales de la política.* Madrid: Tecnos.

Lisi, M., Belchior, A. M., Abrantes, M., & Azevedo, J. (2015). Out of sight, out of mind? External voting and the political representation of Portuguese emigrants. *South European Society and Politics*, *20*, 265–285.

Mariani, D. (2015). *Have the Swiss abroad votes made all the difference?* Swissinfo. Retrieved from www.swissinfo.ch/eng/politics/radio-tv-licences_have-the-swiss-abroad-votes-made-all-the-difference-/41505542

Maxwell, R. (2010). Evaluating migrant integration: Political attitudes across generations in Europe. *International Migration Review*, *44*(1), 25–52.

Mazzoleni, O. & Pilotti, A. (2015). The outcry of the periphery? An analysis of Ticino's no to immigration. *Swiss Political Science Review*, *21*(1), 63–75.

Milbrath, L. & Goel, M. (1977). *Political participation: How and why do people get involved in politics?* Lanham, MD: University Press of America.

Milic, T. (2015a). "For they knew what they did." What Swiss voters did (not) know about the mass immigration initiative. *Swiss Political Science Review*, *21*(1), 48–62.

Milic, T. (2015b). *Analyse des meinungsbildungsprozesses der auslandschweizerinnen vor den wahlen 2015.* Aarau: Centre for Democracy Studies Aarau.

Milic, T. (2016). How the Swiss abroad voted. *Revue Suisse*, Vol. I. Retrieved from www.revue.ch/en/editions/2016/01/detail/news/detail/News/how-the-swiss-abroad-voted/

Morales, L. (2011). Conceptualizing and measuring migrants' political inclusion. In L. Morales & M. G. Giugni (Eds.), *Social capital, political participation and migration in Europe: Making multicultural democracy work?* (pp. 19–42). Basingstoke: Palgrave Macmillan.

Morales, L. & Morariu, M. (2011). Is home a distraction? The role of migrants' transnational practices in their political integration into receiving-country politics. In L. Morales & M. G. Giugni (Eds.), *Social capital, political participation and migration in Europe: Making multicultural democracy work?* (pp. 140–171). Basingstoke: Palgrave Macmillan.

Morales, L. & Pilati, K. (2014). The political transnationalism of Ecuadorians in Barcelona, Madrid and Milan: The role of individual resources, organizational engagement and the political context. *Global Networks, 14*(1), 80–102.

Naval, C. & Ugarte, C. (2012). The development of civic competencies at secondary level through service-learning pedagogies. In M. Print & D. Lange (Eds.), *Schools, curriculum, and civic education for building democratic citizens* (pp. 99–112). Rotterdam: Sense Publishers.

Østergaard-Nielsen, E. K. (2001). Transnational political practices and the receiving state: Turks and Kurds in Germany and the Netherlands. *Global Networks, 1*, 261–282.

Parra, J. (2006). Discursos y modelos sobre la ampliación de los electorados: El voto en el extranjero a ciudadanos emigrantes en perspectiva comparada. *Studia Politicae, 6*, 105–132.

Pasek, J., Feldman, L., Romer, D., & Hall, K. (2008). Schools as incubators of democratic participation: Building long-term political efficacy with civic education. *Applied Development Science, 12*(1), 26–37.

Raaflaub, C. (2017). *E-voting pilot project seen as a big success.* Retrieved from www.swissinfo.ch/eng/council-of-the-swiss-abroad_e-voting-pilot-project-seen-as-a-big-success/43408512

Rhee, J. (2014). *Voting from abroad: 2012 elections and the overseas Koreans' vote.* Retrieved from https://ssrn.com/abstract=2476145

Sanchez, G. C. & Brown, T. N. (1994). Nostalgia: A Swiss disease. *American Journal of Psychiatry, 151*(11), 1715.

Schlenker, A., Blatter, J., & Birka, I. (2017). Practising transnational citizenship: Dual nationality and simultaneous political involvement among emigrants. *Journal of Ethnic and Migration Studies, 43*, 418–440.

Schönenberger, S. & Efionayi-Mäder, D. (2010). *Die Fünfte Schweiz.* Université de Neuchâtel, Swiss Forum for Migration and Population Studies.

Serdült, U. (2010). Internet voting for the Swiss abroad of Geneva: First online survey results. In J.-L. Chappelet et al. (Eds.) *Electronic government and electronic participation: Joint Proceedings of Ongoing Research and Projects of IFIP EGOV and ePart 2010.* Schriftenreihe Informatik, 33. Linz: Trauner Verlag, 319–325.

Serdült, U., Germann, M., Mendez, F., Portenier, A., & Wellig, C. (2015). Fifteen years of internet voting in Switzerland (history, governance and use). In *2015 Second International Conference on Edemocracy & Egovernment (ICEDEG)* (pp. 126–132). IEEE. Retrieved from www.researchgate.net/publication/283878260_Fifteen_Years_of_Internet_Voting_in_Switzerland_History_Governance_and_Use

State Secretariat for Migration. (2017). *Statistique sur les étrangers, juillet.* Retrieved from www.sem.admin.ch/sem/fr/home/publiservice/statistik/auslaenderstatistik/archiv/2017/07.html

Swissinfo. (2017a). *Expat delegates give pension reform thumbs up.* Retrieved from www.swissinfo.ch/eng/swiss-abroad-council_expat-delegates-give-pension-reform-thumbs-up/43408726

Swissinfo. (2017b). *How long before all Swiss expats can use e-voting?* Retrieved from www.swissinfo.ch/eng/citizen-participation_how-long-before-all-swiss-expats-can-use-e-voting-/43503442

Tocqueville, A. (1956). *Democracy in America.* London: Penguin Classics.

Toivanen, M. (2016). Political transnationalism as a matter of belonging: Young Kurds in Finland. In P. Ahponen, P. Harinen,& V.-S. Haverinen (Eds.), *Dislocations of civic cultural borderlines* (pp. 87–106). Berlin: Springer.

Torney-Purta, J., Barber, C., & Wilkenfeld, B. (2006). Differences in the civic knowledge and attitudes of adolescents in the United States by immigrant status and Hispanic background. *Prospects, 36*, 343–354.

Torney-Purta, J., Barber, C., & Wilkenfeld, B. (2007). Latino adolescents′ civic development in the United States: Research results from the IEA Civic Education Study. *Journal of Youth and Adolescence, 36*(2), 111–125.

Verba, S., Burns, N., & Schlozman, K. L. (1997). Knowing and caring about politics: Gender and political engagement. *Journal of Politics, 59*, 1051–1072.

Verba, S., Schlozman, K. L., & Brady, H. E. (1995). *Voice and equality: Civic voluntarism in American politics.* Cambridge, MA: Harvard University Press.

Vogler, C. (2015). Change and challenges for foreign retirees in Thailand. An interview with Nancy Lindley. *Austrian Journal of South-East Asian Studies, 8*, 209–214.

Waldstein, F. A. & Reiher, T. C. (2001). Service-learning and students' personal and civic development. *Journal of Experiential Education*, *24*(1), 7–13.

White, S., Nevitte, N., Blais, A., Gidengil, E., & Fournier, P. (2008). The political resocialization of immigrants: Resistance or lifelong learning? *Political Research Quarterly*, *61*, 268–281.

Wu, C. (2003). Psycho-political correlates of political efficacy. The case of the 199 New Orleans mayoral election. *Journal of Black Studies*, *33*, 729–760.

Appendix: summary of variables

Items and wording of questions

Possession of Swiss citizenship

Yes – No

Variables related to sociodemographic factors

Age: age in years

Gender: Male – Female

Canton of origin in Switzerland: Which is your canton of origin in Switzerland?

Education: No training, Primary incomplete, Primary complete, Secondary incomplete, Secondary complete, University incomplete, University complete, Postgraduate studies.

Occupation (not exclusive categories): Independent professional, Public sector employee, Private sector employee, Entrepreneur/Businesspersonn, Retired, Domestic work, Student, Unemployed, Other.

Levels of knowledge of German/French/Italian/Romansh: No knowledge, Low, Medium, High.

Variables related to migratory background

Migrant generation: First, Parents, Grandparents, Great grandparents, Parents of great grandparents.

Reasons for migrating of the first Swiss emigrant: Economic/job reasons, Family reasons, Political reasons, Studies, New experiences, Others.

Length of time lived in Switzerland: How many years did you live in Switzerland?

Length of time out of Switzerland: How many years ago did you depart from Switzerland?

Latin American country of settlement: In which Latin American country do you reside?

Birth in the country of residence: Were you born in the country in which you reside? Yes – No

Length of time in the country of residence: How many years have you lived in the country of residence?

Variables related to civic competencies

Frequency of reading newspapers, listening to radio, watching TV and surfing Internet for Swiss political news: never, almost never, sometimes, almost always, always.

Frequency of talking about Swiss politics to relatives, friends, and colleagues: never, almost never, sometimes, almost always, always.

Knowledge about direct democracies ballots: Could you cite a topic submitted to a national ballot as a referendum or popular initiative? Yes – No. Which?

Knowledge of the term in office of the Swiss president: How long is the term in office of the Swiss president? 1 year, 3 years, 5 years?

Knowledge about selection of federal councillors: How are federal councillors selected? By communes and cantons – By citizens in a direct ballot – By the federal parliament

Political participation I: Are you registered to vote in Swiss elections? Yes – No

Political participation II: Did you vote in the last federal election (October 2015)? Yes – No

Political participation III: Have you voted at least once during the last five years in one referendum or ballot related to a popular initiative? Yes – No

Internal dimension of political efficacy: Do you believe that you understand the functioning of the Swiss political system? Yes – No

External dimension of political efficacy: Do you believe that your vote is influential in the Swiss political system? Yes – No

18

NICARAGUAN IMMIGRATION TO COSTA RICA

Understanding power and race through language

Anthony T. Spencer

When people around the world hear Costa Rica, they tend to think of natural beauty and peace. Costa Ricans refer to this concept as *pura vida* or *the good life*. This life-loving attitude attracts and lures immigrants, expatriates, and long-term tourists from around the globe. This idea is a particularly strong draw for North Americans who have altered the ethno-linguistic and media landscape of the nation. Many people from North America do migrate to Costa Rica. Three of the largest contemporary immigrant groups are from the US, Colombia, and Nicaragua. However, according to the major English-language newspaper in the country, the *Tico Times* (Arias, 2014), the largest immigrant group is from Nicaragua. Costa Rica has – for a Latin American country – the highest percentage of immigrants at its borders (9 percent). It is this lesser discussed Nicaraguan immigrant population (Kron, 2011) that is the focus of this chapter.

Costa Rica and Nicaragua are neighboring countries in Central America. Nicaragua is just south of Honduras and north of Costa Rica. Costa Rica is located between Nicaragua and Panama. They share a long and complicated history. According to the *CIA World Factbook* (2017), Nicaragua has a population of just over 6 million while Costa Rica's population is just under 5 million. Nicaragua is the poorest country in the mainland Americas but also one of the safest in Central America (*The Economist*, 2012). It is the poverty that has propelled so many Nicaraguans to travel to Costa Rica looking for work. Costa Rica is a tropical paradise just south of Nicaragua, which has lured investors and tourists for decades (Miranda & Penland, 2016). It is this prosperity that makes the prospect of employment (both formal and informal) for Nicaraguans so attractive.

The process of classifying and delineating racial and ethnic categories is an arbitrary and contentious process. Racial and ethnic categories are social constructs, not inherent biological qualities. According to Omi and Winant (2005), race stems from social and historical forces that are essentially manipulated. In many ways, we can better understand the Nicaraguan immigration population in juxtaposition with the other non-Costa Ricans in the country, particularly US citizens. The position of Nicaraguans in Costa Rica is a historically delicate and precarious situation made more culturally charged by an economic downturn in Costa Rica in 2011 (Voorend, 2013). Sandoval Garcia (2013) writes that Nicaraguans in Costa Rica represent a salient and timely example of immigration. There is an increase in Nicaraguan immigration, and negative attitudes persist toward Nicaraguans. I argue that many of these attitudes are based on language.

Costa Rica prides itself on not having a military, on possessing incredible ecological diversity, and on the concept of being a *Tico*. Simply put, a *Tico* is a person from Costa Rica. The correct term for a Cost Rican in Spanish is a *Costarricense*. However, Costa Ricans most often refer to themselves as *Ticos*, which evolved from the way they form the diminutive of nouns in their dialect of Spanish; non-Costa Ricans will hear non-immigrants proudly refer to themselves by this name. Costa Rican writer Alf Alexander (cited in Giebler Simonet, 2005) published a popular guide to the Costa Rican dialect of Spanish, titled *A lo Tico: Costarriqeñismos y otras vainas*, to preserve the country's linguistic heritage and to teach outsiders how to speak like a *Tico*. The guide and others like it write for the large and visibly high-end US citizen immigration group, not for the Spanish-speaking, Nicaraguan immigrants (Spencer, 2011).

Language is not the only way Costa Ricans mark themselves as unique from their Spanish-speaking Central American neighbors. While simultaneously acknowledging that they are Latinos, Costa Ricans overwhelmingly refer to themselves as White. Biesanz, Biesanz, and Biesanz (1999) delve further into this racial construction of Costa Rican identity in their exhaustive text, *The Ticos: Culture and social change in Costa Rica*: "They feel set apart from (and superior to) their Central American neighbors not only because of the lighter skin of the average Costa Rican but also because of cultural differences" (p. 6). A recent *BBC Mundo* article (Wallace, 2017) explored historical and contemporary logic for a White construction of identity in Costa Rica. Race has long been an issue in Costa Rica as in much of the Colonial Americas. According to Cottrol (2013), Costa Rica enacted an immigration ban as early as 1862, restricting Africans and Asians from settling in the country. These cultural and linguistic attributes combined with a perception of Whiteness are important to understanding the Costa Rican national identity as well as current issues of immigration and intercultural communication.

Nicaraguan immigration

Around the globe most people understand immigration discourse in terms of Global North to Global South, which implies that most often immigrants make a metaphorical and/or literal journey from the South to the North (Moreman, 2008; Moreman & Calafell, 2008; Santa Ana, 1999). However, much of the world's immigration patterns are South to South (Gindling, 2009), meaning that many immigrants from developing nations emigrate to other, more prosperous developing nations; such is the case with Nicaraguans who move to Costa Rica looking for employment and a higher standard of living (Garcia Sandoval, 2013; Molina & Palmer, 2006). Since Nicaraguans speak a markedly different dialect of Spanish from Costa Ricans and are perceived to be non-White, they are racialized in Costa Rica (Sandoval Garcia, 2004). Costa Ricans and Nicaraguans both admit they perceive discrimination in Costa Rica.

While most people outside of Central America may be unaware of the South to South migration taking place in that region, journalists in mainstream English-language media began to report on this phenomenon as long ago as 2010 in the newspaper *USA Today*. Hawley (2010, para. 5), for example, notes the income difference between Nicaragua and Costa Rica and the impact on immigration: "The disparity has drawn about 74,000 migrants to Costa Rica since 2002, swelling its population of foreign-born people by 26%." Since this article was published, immigration has continued to be a major issue facing the two nations.

For a relatively small country, this influx of both documented and undocumented immigrants not only impacts the Costa Rican labor market, but also influences the national psyche and the previously mentioned *Tico* cultural identity. Many Costa Ricans and US high-end immigrants (Spencer, 2013) in the country frame the immigration scenario by drawing comparisons to Mexican immigration to the US. Paniagua (2007) nuanced this situation by exploring the economic need for Nicaraguan labor in Costa Rica in the sectors of agriculture, construction, and domestic employment, while simultaneously highlighting the discrimination Nicaraguans encounter in Costa Rica resulting from taking those "typical" immigrant jobs. They are viewed as non-White, poor, and illiterate.

Thirty-nine-year-old business manager Yolanda was born in Nicaragua. She has lived in Costa Rica almost her entire life. She self identifies as a *Nica*. Much as a *Tico* is the name for a person from Costa Rica, *Nica* is the informal term for a *Nicaragüense*, someone from Nicaragua. Nicaraguans use this term without prejudice or malice. This is simply a way people refer to themselves. However, because of the linguistic and racial overtones of the image of a Nicaraguan in Costa Rica, the term *Nica* has come to imply someone who is poor, generally illiterate, and non-White. Yolanda explains how she feels when someone in Costa Rica refers to her as a *Nica*:

> Yolanda: Here *Nica* is questioned, is criticized, it is when they tell you *Nica*, it is…, just by telling you *Nica* it is strong so that you feel it like an offense

In present day Costa Rica, Yolanda's heart-felt admission is critical to understanding and exploring the current intercultural interactions between Nicaraguans and Costa Ricans.

I believe it is imperative to explain my own position as I conduct research into this intercultural phenomenon. I am undoubtedly an outsider. I am a white, male PhD-trained scholar. Even though I have lived in both Costa Rica and Nicaragua extensively and speak Spanish, I am still an outsider. I collect and analyze data from the perspective of a white, English-speaking foreigner. I struggle with my own linguistic and cultural acceptance in Central America as a privileged foreigner who has lived on the margins, admittedly high-end margins, of society. I wanted to draw upon the real fabric of the nation's cultural and linguistic identity to understand the way in which *Ticos* weave their complex image of racial and linguistic identities. I turn to the work of a scholar whose context was very different from my own, but whose research provides an ideal framework for this study. In his research of the Western Apache, Basso (1984) focused on how language impacts social interaction through the eyes of those being observed; however, this is filtered through an outsider's perspective. I am also an outsider looking in, but hopefully bring a unique perspective to exploring this phenomenon. While I am not a linguist, my work is in line with fellow qualitative intercultural communication scholars who use qualitative interviewing research methods to "allow participants to organically discuss their lived experiences" (Moreman, 2011, p. 1999).

As modeled by Halualani (2008), qualitative interviewing allows for the understanding of how cultural groups constitute and reconstitute themselves via their communicative practices.

Within Costa Rican everyday intercultural interactions, the classification and delineation of racial and ethnic categories are often constructed through language usage. In general terms, Costa Ricans react differently to each of three predominant immigrant groups in the country. Americans are inherently marked with an outsider status as they are overwhelmingly native English speakers. Although Nicaraguans and Colombians are native Spanish speakers, their accent/dialect clearly marks them as outgroup members. While Colombian immigration to Costa Rica is worthy of exploration, it is outside the scope of this study.

Language ideology

I examine the intercultural interactions of Costa Ricans and Nicaraguans through the framework of language ideology (Blommaert & Verschueren, 1998; Hansen-Thomas, 2007; Hill, 1998; Irvine & Gal, 2000; Schieffelin et al., 1998; Silverstein, 1998b; Trenchs-Parera & Newman, 2009). This theoretical lens allows researchers to examine concepts and constructs that manifest themselves through discourse. Scholars can better understand those such as race, class, and in/outgroup behavior by applying these to lived experiences through field research. Woolard (1998) writes that language ideology is a bridge between linguistic theory and social theory. Through the concept of language ideology, scholars connect communication with social power and inequality. Although the immigrant Nicaraguans and the Costa Ricans in the host country are all native Spanish speakers, their dialects are apparent and important to the constructions of ethnic identity and the basis for the claims of White for Costa Rican and non-White for Nicaraguan identities. I also aim to expand upon and nuance the theory by applying it to two dialects of the same language; traditionally research has focused on different languages rather than dialects.

Bourdieu (1991) establishes the symbolic power of language and the process of its exchange. He does this by illustrating how the relationships established through linguistic exchange are like those involved in economic transactions. Thus, according to Bourdieu, language operates as an arena where power struggles are waged among speakers; also, language becomes a site of competition and contestation. Sandel (2011) expanded on this concept and tied it to the field of Communication when exploring local languages and dialects in Taiwan as they relate to linguistic capital. I argue that the differences in dialects between Costa Ricans and Nicaraguans can be viewed as a contestation of cultural space and privilege in society. Benedict Anderson ([1983] 1991) explains the relationship of language development and standardization and the subsequent valuation of dialects and languages in his foundational study of nationalism, *Imagined Communities*.

Silverstein (1998b) wrote, "ideology is an intentional characteristic, predictable of a society or of a group in a social formation abstracted from society" (p. 125). His goal is to illustrate that ideologies often emerge from social groups and their language rather than being a force of external oppression. These points of linguistic contestation allow scholars to examine identity and power as they manifest themselves through language. Culture and language constitute both ontological and epistemological understandings of the relative power in language ideologies.

Irvine and Gal (2000) build on the theoretical notions of language and identification. Focusing much of their research on present-day Macedonia, these scholars examine how cultural identification and language are inherently connected but are also fluid concepts. All speakers navigate interactions and establish identity through the linguistic tools they find at their disposal. Language ideologies are adaptable and historical; thus, they can change from one time to another, or take on different meanings. Hill (1998) furthers explores the ways in which language mediates interactions by illustrating how the type of language or even the language itself that is chosen can show either respect or disrespect. The construction of race through language subsequently manifests in the concepts of money and power. This creation of privileged space in language parallels Hill's (1999) finding of the emergence of whiteness through intercultural discourse among Spanish speakers in the United States.

Through similar linguistic interactions, Costa Ricans construct themselves as dominant and White, while silencing the voice of the Nicaraguans and constructing them as a non-White

Other in the country. In order to make the analysis clearer for the reader, I want to explain some important yet subtle variations between the dialects. These distinctions include the pronunciation of the letter "s" (Nicaraguan characteristic), use of the verb form *vos* (somewhat shared characteristic), and the pronunciation of the "r"/"rr" (Costa Rican characteristic). These three qualities are imperative to understanding, interpreting, and explicating the ideologies that surround each dialect and impact the linguistic and power intersections.

Costa Rican versus Nicaraguan Spanish

The "s"

According to Lipski (1985) and Qesada Pacheco (2008), Central American dialects of Spanish have traditionally been among the least studied. Lipski also addresses one of the primary characteristics of Nicaraguan Spanish that makes it different from most Costa Rican speakers: the dropped "s" at the end of words. For most Nicaraguans, the final "s" is barely pronounced, causing many non-Nicaraguans to claim that they do not pronounce it or "drop it." In daily discourse, Costa Ricans refer to this as the "Nicaraguan pronunciation." This "dropping" or light pronunciation of the final "s" at the end of words is one of the simplest yet most value-laden of the ways in which Nicaraguans are seen as different.

The *vos* form

The singular informal form varies within Latin America. The standardized way of speaking in Spanish is by using *tú* as the informal singular. Almost all Nicaraguans (Benavides, 2003), as well as many Costa Ricans (Giebler Simonet, 2005), use *vos* as the informal form. To conjugate this verb form, the final "r" is dropped from the infinitive verb and the final syllable is accented and an "s" is added. Unlike other forms of Spanish, the stem of the verb does not change. For example, to conjugate the verb *tener* (to have) you would say, tu *tienes* but *vos tenés*. This is not a form of Spanish taught in textbooks; however, many countries use the *vos* as a standard for the informal in everyday conversation.

Even for these Spanish speakers, there is a varying degree of intimacy or distance associated with this usage (Rojas Blanco, 2003). Some speakers, especially those in poorer rural areas of Costa Rica, tend to use the formal form with everyone, much as English stopped using the informal thou (Silverstein, 1998b). Thus, much of the Costa Rican population would use the *usted* (formal) form in all cases, while the rest of Costa Ricans would use the *vos* (informal) form to conjugate verbs when speaking to friends or family members. This usage of *vos* illustrates a similarity between the dialects as well as a difference: Nicaraguans are much more likely to use *vos* in all friendship and family interactions of equal level.

The "r" and "rr"

One of the primary linguistic distinctions of Costa Rican Spanish is the pronunciation of the letters "r" and "rr" (Van Rheenen, 2004). It is a sure sign of someone who speaks the Costa Rican dialect of Spanish when they neither roll the "rr," nor pronounce the "r" with a trill sound that most native Spanish speakers use. Costa Ricans tend to pronounce these letters in a semi-rolled and more aspirated fashion. Nicaraguans do not pronounce either letter in this way. They use a more standard traditional Spanish pronunciation of both the "r" and "rr."

This linguistic feature further marks Nicaraguans as outgroup (Tajfel & Turner, 1986) members in Costa Rica.

Much as Schieffelin and Doucet (1998) explore the prestige of language dialects such as Haitian Creole and Parisian versus Creole French, I will illustrate the ways in which Nicaraguans are racialized based upon their dialect of Spanish. This impacts their subsequent social interactions with the host Costa Ricans. I argue that Nicaraguans form a local language community (Silverstein, 1998a) within the larger host culture. Tajfel and Turner (1986) put forth three basic assumptions of group identity. These are: "individuals strive to maintain or enhance self-esteem," "social groups or categories and the membership of them are associated with positive or negative value connotations," and "the evaluation of one's own group is determined in reference to other groups" (p. 16). Based upon linguistic, as well as perceived, ethnic differences, Nicaraguans and Costa Ricans acknowledge that Nicaraguans are outgroup members. To better analyze the interactions between the groups and the subsequent claim of marginalization based on language and the connected perception of race, I present the following research question: How do Costa Ricans marginalize Nicaraguan immigrants based upon linguistic and ethnic perceptions?

I will examine how Costa Ricans marginalize Nicaraguan immigrants based upon linguistic and ethnic perceptions.

Method

I utilize ethnographic and interview methods of research in this study. These forms of data collection are appropriate to answer the above-mentioned research question as they allow for an understanding of the "thick description" (Geertz, 1973) of this important and interesting social phenomenon. Scholars can uncover key points of cultural interaction by collecting and analyzing observational and interview data (O'Reilly, 2004). Essentially, we as researchers become the "eyes and ears" in the field for our audiences as we observe, note, and record human interactions.

Geertz believed that the most effective way to understand a culture was by immersion. According to Hymes (1974), one of the most effective methods for tapping into this cultural richness is to examine speech acts as they occur in communicative events. Woolard (1998) writes that language ideology is a bridge between linguistic theory and social theory. It is through the concept of language ideology that scholars can connect the related concepts of communication, social power, and inequality. Thus, communicative practices under the theoretical lens of language ideology guide this study. I conducted the observations and interviews for this study from June through August 2009. These methods for gathering qualitative data are particularly well suited to exploring culture (Briggs, 1986; Halualani; 2008; Lofland & Lofland, 1995; Spradley & McCurdy, 1988).

During this time period, I lived in a suburb of Costa Rica's capital, San José. While three months may seem a short period of time, I have, however, lived in Costa Rica and Nicaragua for several years over the past two decades. I speak fluent Spanish and have a long-standing relationship with the Costa Rican host culture as well as the immigrant Nicaraguan culture.

Site

The site for this project includes, in general terms, the entire country of Costa Rica, where Nicaraguans serve as guest workers and long-term members of the immigrant community. I conducted observations in the heavily populated Central Valley, on the Pacific and Caribbean coasts, and in the northern area of Costa Rica. I also made the arduous border crossing between Costa Rica and Nicaragua as part of the data collection process. All interviews took place in the capital city of San José and its surrounding suburbs. This metropolitan area is in the country's Central Valley and is the most populated region of the nation.

Participants

Twenty participants took part in this project. I attempted to provide a numerical balance of perspectives in the sample by interviewing ten Nicaraguan immigrants and ten Costa Ricans. I further stratified the sample by purposefully attempting to include a variety of socio-demographic variables including gender, education, and socio-economic status. While this effort is well intended, I acknowledge that, regarding education and socio-economic status, the participant pool is inherently skewed toward higher levels in Costa Rican participants than in their Nicaraguan counterparts. More than 60 percent of Nicaraguan immigrants in Costa Rica have completed primary school or less (Gindling, 2009). Thus, I purposefully sought out some Nicaraguans who had completed some level of secondary education. The average age of the Costa Rican respondents (38.9) was higher than the average age of the Nicaraguan participants (27.7).

It is imperative to acknowledge that this type of research is very sensitive in Costa Rica. Therefore, I searched for participants who showed a genuine interest in the project and who felt comfortable expressing their views regarding the interactions between Costa Ricans and Nicaraguans. Many people from both groups often commented on and shared concerns but did not want to take part in recorded interviews. The sample includes more men than women. This is not intentional. However, it is vital to note that, of the seven women who participated in recorded interviews, five are Nicaraguan. The Nicaraguan women in this study displayed more interest in the project; I can only assume this is because they perceived the research focus to be more salient to their everyday lives. Participant demographic information is displayed in Table 18.1. Each participant agreed to formal recorded interviews and gave permission for their first name to be used in this study.

Protocol

Interviews followed a semi-structured format. I asked all participants about their pertinent personal demographic information and followed a script posing questions that focused on their perceptions of immigration, interaction between the groups, and what they thought were inequities in those interactions. As Briggs (1986) recommends, I attempted to make the interviews as organic as possible by conducting the taped interviews in settings where participants would feel most comfortable and at ease. We talked in a variety of locations, including workplaces, restaurants, hair salons, and other public sites. I conducted all interviews in Spanish except three; in these cases, the participants were bilingual and spoke to me in English as a courtesy so I would not have to translate the interviews. Even in those two cases, the participants would often revert to Spanish to express themselves more clearly. All translations used in this chapter are my own.

Findings

Following a careful and exhaustive analysis of the ethnographic data and the interviews and their transcriptions, I have arranged the findings from this data set by theme. The two primary themes that emerged from the data set are language and race. As I will illustrate in

Table 18.1 Participant data

Name	*Age*	*Gender*	*Profession*	*Nationality*
Monica	18	F	Kitchen assistant	Costa Rica
Juan Diego	36	M	Visual arts coordinator	Costa Rica
Jose	37	M	Volunteer coordinator	Costa Rica
Robert	42	M	Art professor	Costa Rica
Juan Pablo	34	M	Business administrator	Costa Rica
Carlos	44	M	Supervisor	Costa Rica
Henry	42	M	Professor	Costa Rica
Gloria	56	F	Business owner	Costa Rica
Hugo	34	M	Graphic designer	Costa Rica
Carlos	46	M	Art professor	Costa Rica
Martha	32	F	Cook	Nicaragua
Aldo	41	M	Hair stylist	Nicaragua
Walkenia	19	F	Student	Nicaragua
Michelle	21	F	Student	Nicaragua
Fabricio	23	M	Service worker	Nicaragua
Carlos	21	M	Hair stylist	Nicaragua
Marcela	36	F	Housewife	Nicaragua
Christian	21	M	Service worker	Nicaragua
Yolanda	39	F	Business administrator	Nicaragua
Francisco	24	M	Student	Nicaragua

this analysis, those two constructs often intertwine and overlap with one another. While it would be impractical to include all the findings that relate to a particular theme, I have chosen the excerpts that best highlight the respective topic.

Language

I analyze the participant interview data in this section to illustrate that, although Costa Ricans and Nicaraguans speak Spanish as native speakers, their linguistic markers nevertheless identify them as belonging to one group or the other. In this first transcript, I asked a Nicaraguan if he could more easily integrate than could English-speaking Americans.

RESEARCHER: Can a Nicaraguan integrate more easily into Costa Rican society [than an American]?

CHRISTIAN: No, less because what happens is that she or he has a pronounced accent.

RESEARCHER: But, those who live here and come at a young age? They can integrate, right?

CHRISTIAN: Well I know people who are, let's say, very white, light eyes, that do not look like Nicaraguans but they have been here for years or grew up in Costa Rica and by only opening their mouth we realize that they are Nicaraguans.

Christian ends his statement by saying "that they are Nicaraguans." As soon as the Nicaraguans speak they are instantly seen as non-Costa Rican and viewed as outsiders. Even if they have White skin they are deemed to be non-White because of the dialect in which they speak Spanish. Costa Rican, Juan Pablo, agrees. His transcript illustrates the acceptance of non-native Spanish speakers in Costa Rica and the subsequent rejection of the native-speaking Nicaraguans:

> Juan Pablo: People here love a foreigner's accent in Spanish. But, if it is a Nicaraguan, they speak with an "accent" and here comes the prejudice, the xenophobia, but if a *Gringo* [American] or European comes and speaks Spanish with an accent, then we say, ah [pronounced with a smile] it's a foreigner. That's the way it is.

Juan Pablo provides us with an interesting dichotomy of analysis. A different accent is perceived as good or interesting in Costa Rica if it is a non-native accent. The Nicaraguan accent is seen as "the foreigner" even though the Gringos and Europeans are foreigners as well. Lee (1992) notes how the use of a language can mark distance or intimacy between communicators. Essentially, a non-native Spanish speaker can integrate and be seen as having a good albeit foreign accent in Spanish, while the native Nicaraguan speaker is perceived as having an undesirable accent and is marked as a "foreigner." This equates to a negative connation for the native speaker and a positive one for the presumably White foreigner.

Twenty-four-year-old Nicaraguan, Juan, was studying at a local university. He spoke to me one afternoon at a local coffee shop. In this informal environment, he opened up. Juan admitted he felt discrimination for both his phenotype and accent in Spanish. He was very willing to participate in the study but also became very emotional. Juan confessed that what really bothered him were the jokes Costa Ricans told about the way Nicaraguans spoke Spanish, lived in poor conditions, and had limited education:

JUAN: Here in Costa Rica there is not that difference like the color of the skin.
RESEARCHER: You cannot tell someone is from Nicaragua just by looking at them.
JUAN: No.
RESEARCHER: Really?
JUAN: Well, maybe. But not much for that. Instead the way of the talking.
RESEARCHER: So, you think language is the most important thing, not the skin color? But you think that is important?
JUAN: Well, it is important.
RESEARCHER: But you don't like to talk about that. You seem hesitant.
JUAN: Yeah, maybe that. Because I think it is a very sad thing.

Juan provides a fascinating glimpse into the emotional distress many Nicaraguans confessed they had felt but had not had the opportunity to articulate. Juan told me he participated in this interview to attempt to stop the discrimination Nicaraguans faced in Costa Rica.

To supplement the interview data with an ethnographic observation, my interviewee, Henry, arrived at a local mall's food court to speak with me while a Nicaraguan interactant was present. They exchanged greetings and the Nicaraguan left the food court. Henry turned to me and said, "He's Nicaraguan, isn't he?" The comment was not intended to convey malice; however, it clearly illustrates and supports the above-mentioned data that, based on linguistic cues alone, Nicaraguans stand out as different and marked by their accent and vocabulary usage. They are essentially racialized by the way they speak Spanish as a non-White speaker.

Racial features

In addition to the linguistic differences perceived by both groups, there are racial characterizations ascribed to each group. Costa Ricans view themselves as White and they view Nicaraguans as non-White. Costa Ricans are the dominant and empowered group; thus, they can control more of the perceptions of each group. We, as outsiders, must first understand how the Nicaraguans are assigned to their group status (Tajfel & Turner, 1986). Even if they have a lighter skin color and can "pass" as Costa Rican, as the data above indicate, they are marginalized and racialized based on the way they speak. Only after establishing the linguistic othering is it possible to examine how Nicaraguans are racialized based on their physical characteristics. Next, I examine the interview transcript of a 21-year-old hair stylist who had been in Costa Rica for a year. As a relative newcomer to the country, I asked him to compare the perceptions Costa Ricans hold of the two largest immigrant groups to the country:

RESEARCHER: Describe a typical Gringo.
CARLOS: *Blanco* [White], tall, blue eyes, and blond hair.
RESEARCHER: And what does the typical Nicaraguan look like?
CARLOS: *Moreno* [Dark]. Like the stereotypical Nicaraguan.

In a separate but thematically consistent interview, 41-year-old Nicaraguan, Aldo, added to the story Carlos started. Aldo had lived in Costa Rica for eight years at the time of our interview.

RESEARCHER: What is the image of a typical Nicaraguan?
ALDO: Image in what way?
RESEARCHER: In whatever way. The stereotype, let's say.
ALDO: Physically?
RESEARCHER: Yes.
ALDO: Indians. Really ugly.
RESEARCHER: And Gringos, how are they physically?
ALDO: Beautiful. Foul-smelling, but beautiful.
RESEARCHER: What color of skin do they have?
ALDO: Light skin, blue eyes.

As Carlos and Aldo illustrate, the Nicaraguans view themselves as non-White and, in the current climate of Costa Rican society, compare themselves to the Americans or Gringos who are flooding the country to visit and/or live. I next turn to the interview of another Nicaraguan who compares marginalization of the Nicaraguan not only in terms of phenotype but also introduces the implied understanding of financial power perceived to be inherent to physical characteristics and national identity. Gringos are perceived as White and relatively affluent, while Nicaraguans are thought to be non-White and poor.

RESEARCHER: What are the differences between Gringos and Nicaraguans [in Costa Rica]?
CHRISTIAN: Economics.
RESEARCHER: And skin color, no?
CHRISTIAN: As well.
RESEARCHER: What is a typical Gringo like?
CHRISTIAN: White, blue eyes, tall.

RESEARCHER: And the typical Nicaraguan?
CHRISTIAN: *Morenito* [Dark], ugly.
RESEARCHER: Why ugly?
CHRISTIAN: Well, because people from the North are more elegant, whiter, have light eyes.

Thirty-six-year-old Marcela further expands on the differences between the physical and economic perceptions of these groups:

RESEARCHER: How is the typical Gringo physically?
MARCELA: He is handsome and polite.
RESEARCHER: Is he black or white?
MARCELA: White
RESEARCHER: And Nicaraguans, what do they look like?
MARCELA: *Morenos* [Dark]. We are almost all *morenos* [dark].
RESEARCHER: And what is the biggest difference between Nicaraguans and Gringos in Costa Rica?
MARCELA: For me, the biggest difference is that we have little education, communication [skills], and few resources. And really the people who emigrate from Nicaragua – we are the poorest people there. The Gringo can develop himself here because he knows English, which is becoming like the official language [here].

After extracting the concepts of Whiteness and money and dark and poor that emerged during the interviews with the Nicaraguan participants, I decided to ask Costa Ricans if they also noticed these social constructs. All the Costa Rican participants agreed that these connotations were part of their everyday discourse about immigration.

I interviewed 42-year-old professor, Robert, and 34-year-old graphic designer, Hugo, at the same time. This method of interviewing participants in pairs or triads can often be extremely enriching, as they will respond to what another says in the same interview.

RESEARCHER: In Costa Rica there is a concept called whitening. What does this mean to you?
ROBERT: It is negation.
RESEARCHER: Of what?
HUGO: Of diversity.
ROBERT: And it is segregation. It is...
HUGO: It is to want to have a sense of superiority over others.
ROBERT: To take away liberties and opportunities.
HUGO: In any case, it is to follow a pyramid system in relation to others. Right? In general, we want to be on top of others.

The data Robert and Hugo provide are consonant with the claim Biesanz, Biesanz, and Biesanz (1999) posit about how Costa Ricans consider themselves both White and superior to other Central Americans. Perhaps this discourse is beginning to change within Costa Rican society. Thirty-seven-year-old Costa Rican, José, responded to this construction of real and/or perceived Whiteness in Costa Rican culture, particularly as juxtaposed to the non-Whiteness of neighboring countries:

> José: I think that happened before, this idea of *blanqueamiento* ["whitening" is stated in Spanish, though the interview took place in English], or this idea that we were

> more European because we were lighter than other Central Americans. I don't see that, I don't hear that as often as I heard it maybe ten years ago. I think Costa Ricans are little by little understanding our identity is not only as Costa Ricans but as Central Americans and I think that we're embracing more people from Central America, even in many cases with certain idea of superiority, because of access to education or health care or living in a country without an army, but I think this idea of *blanqueamiento* is not as strong as it was before and I think it has to do with we accepting who we are now better to not comparing to Europe or the States.

José eloquently and directly confronts and interrogates this concept of Costa Ricans as White and the understanding of whitening within his culture. This mentality of whitening is not unique to Costa Rica. *Blanqueamiento* can be found in various parts of Latin America. According to Johnson (2007), "Mestizaje [racial and cultural mixture] and Blanqueamiento [an orientation towards whiteness] evolved as the basis of national identity, resulting in an ambiguous ideological construction of race where who is Black, White or Indigenous is not self-evident" (p. 48). When these constructions of race are not self-evident, one might use language as a way to understand race and group membership.

Implications

As the ethnographic and interview data illustrate, language and race are interrelated concepts of identity construction between Nicaraguans and Costa Ricans. Nicaraguan immigrants feel they are marginalized based on the dialect in which they speak Spanish. These immigrants believe that, after identifying them by language, Costa Ricans next racialize and *Other* them based upon those linguistic traits. Nicaraguan sisters, nineteen-year-old Walkenia and 21-year-old Michelle, have lived their entire lives in both countries because of family circumstances and by virtue of having relatives on both sides of the border. I asked them to speak about how foreigners are treated in Costa Rica.

MICHELLE: It depends on their nationality. If it is a foreigner that is not Nicaraguan, they are treated well.
WALKENIA: Let's speak directly about this.
MICHELLE: Yes [with slight hesitation].
WALKENIA: Every time that I have come here they have treated me . . . fine but it shows up on their face . . . ah, a *Nica*.
RESEARCHER: How do they know? From your accent?
MICHELLE: [laughs] Yes.
WALKENIA: Of course, they know by the accent.

Costa Ricans and Nicaraguans contributed to this study. Both groups agree, with Nicaraguans being more vocal, whether purposefully or inadvertently, that Costa Ricans discriminate against Nicaraguans and view them as less White based on language and skin color. I personally applaud the participants for their willingness to speak about what is a tension and problem between the two groups.

Immigrant discrimination has been apparent in everyday discourse in the US for decades. However, in the twenty-first century other countries have come to grapple with the integration of various linguistic and cultural groups, such as in Canada (Croucher, 2008), Germany (Hansen-Thomas, 2007), Spain (Trenchs-Parera & Newman, 2009), and Italy (Sinea, 2011) – just to name a few. Intercultural scholars tend to focus on the US or Western Europe when they investigate immigration issues. However, as Gindling (2009) reminds us, immigration is much more complex and nuanced than a mere North to South phenomenon. Researchers must acknowledge and explore the situations of South to South immigration as well.

Costa Rican authorities do not have reliable immigration numbers because many Nicaraguans cross the border illegally, others obtain a tourist visa and simply do not return home, and many immigrants have legal residency in both countries. The Nicaraguan government even produces promotional materials, including a poster entitled, "*Lo que debes saber antes de migrar a Costa Rica*" (What you should know before migrating to Costa Rica), with basic tips. This poster indicates that the Nicaraguan government apparently does not anticipate a decrease in immigrants to Costa Rica in the near future if it continues to prepare its citizens to undertake the trip.

This study adds to the development of both theory and context concerning language and racialization of immigrants. As Geertz (1973) reminds us, "Ethnographic findings are not privileged, just particular; another country heard from" (p. 23). In this study, I aim to use these findings to understand language ideology in this context. First, the data presented inform and nuance our understanding of language ideology. Not only do languages compete, they are also vehicles of ideological assumptions; dialects within the same language can compete and impart ideologies as well. Also, this study conveys contextual knowledge for intercultural communication scholars. Immigration takes places in the US and Europe; however, the flow of peoples is not limited to those Western nations. As scholars begin/continue to examine intercultural communication in international contexts, it becomes apparent that identity of *Latinos(as)* is not as homogenous as many might believe. *Latinidad* (concept of being Latino) covers many types of Spanish speakers and/or those who have lived a Latin experience. Not all *Latinos(as)* identify with one another, nor do they see themselves as one unified group.

Discussion

While Costa Ricans and Nicaraguans all ascribe as Latinos, they do so in respect to both White and non-White labels. If we understand the fluidity and complexity of *Latinidad* we can best investigate this Central American phenomenon. For both the White and non-White immigrant, Nicaraguans' and Costa Ricans' intercultural interactions viewed through a lens of language ideology are important daily concerns. When referring to problems related to immigration and intercultural acceptance, 36-year-old Costa Rican, Juan Diego, says: "I don't know what to say but it is something we confront every day." The aforementioned BBC Mundo article (Wallace, 2017) illustrates that this topic continues to be of interest in the region. The article even argues that the Nicaraguan population might actually have more White heritage than Costa Rica. This is one way in which people in the region are starting to confront cultural stereotypes and myths.

The Costa Ricans who take part in this dialogue consider themselves White and relatively privileged. It takes a great deal of courage on their part to participate in a conversation that requires them to "deprivilege" their own identities and voice. Most importantly, they have started the dialogue. By acknowledging how various discourses can compete in one single linguistic construction, Bakhtin (1980) allows us to better understand that processes of ideological production as "social languages" (p. 275) can be found within and alongside "official" national languages. To maintain the dialogic spirit of this research, I invited both Costa Ricans and Nicaraguans to read the data and to make comments during the writing and editing process for this chapter. As Woolard (1998) states,

> In much recent theory, ideology is not necessarily conscious, deliberate, or systematically organized thought, or even thought at all; it is behavioral, practical, prereflective, or structural. Signification – or, more simply, meaning – rather than ideation in a mental sense is the core phenomenon in these contemporary uses.
>
> (p. 6)

It is this shared approach with participants in the study that allows us to understand behaviors and practices associated with language and immigration regarding Nicaraguans in Costa Rica. This project has been a collaboration with the various participants (both Nicaraguan and Costa Rican). They have opened up about their linguistic and intercultural interactions because they want to work together to improve the situation.

In Costa Rica, as well as in other countries, including the United States, the interrogation of the concept of race is complex and ongoing. Leeman (2004) writes, "Whereas the primary racial distinction in the US has been between groups constructed as White and those constructed as non-White, differences among groups now classified as White have also been constructed as racial" (p. 509). Just as many of us in the US struggle to interrogate race and identity beyond the concept of whiteness, so too do Costa Ricans.

I encourage researchers to explore immigration and the phenomenon of ideologies as they manifest themselves through language in other regions of the world, particularly regarding South to South immigration. I acknowledge limitations of time, sample size, and my own "White" body. I hope to further conversations already taking place in Central America: in the classrooms, academic investigations, and on the streets in daily discourse. The more we understand regarding the dual, yet interconnected, concepts of immigration and language ideology, the closer we will be to obtaining a *pura vida* lifestyle for immigrants in Costa Rica and beyond.

Note

This chapter was written before the protests that led to government violence and protester deaths starting on April 18, 2018.

References

Anderson, B. ([1983] 1991). *Imagined communities*. New York: Verson.

Arias, L. (2014, November 23). Costa Rica has the highest percentage of migrant population in Latin America, study finds. *Tico Times*. Retrieved from www.ticotimes.net/2014/11/23/costa-rica-has-the-highest-percentage-of-migrant-population-in-latin-america-study-finds

Bakhtin, M. M. (1980). *The dialogic imagination*. Austin, TX: University of Texas Press.

Basso, K. H. (1984). Stalking with stories: Names, places, and moral narratives among the Western Apache. In E. M. Bruner & S. Plattner (Eds.), *Text, play, and story: The construction and reconstruction of self and society* (pp. 19–55). Washington, DC: American Ethnological Society.

Benavides, C. (2003). La distribución del voseo en Hispanoamérica. *Hispania, 86*, 612–623.

Biesanz, M. H., Biesanz, R., & Biesanz, K. Z. (1999). *The Ticos: Culture and social change in Costa Rica*. Boulder, CO: Lynne Rienner Publishers.

Blommaert, J., & Verschueren, J. (1998). The role of language in European nationalist identities. In B. B. Schieffelin, K. A. Woolard, & P. V. Kroskrity (Eds.), *Language ideologies: Practice and theory* (pp. 189–210). New York: Oxford University Press.

Bourdieu, P. (1991). *Language and symbolic power*. Cambridge, MA: Harvard University Press.

Briggs, C. (1986). *Learning how to ask: A sociolinguistic appraisal of the role of the interview in social science research*. Cambridge: Cambridge University Press.

CIA Factbook. (2017). *The world factbook 2017*. Washington, DC: Central Intelligence Agency. Retrieved from www.cia.gov/index.html/

Cottrol, R. J. (2013). *Long, lingering shadow: Slavery, race, and law in the American hemisphere.* Retrieved from http://ebookcentral.proquest.com.ezproxy.lib.ou.edu

Croucher, S. M. (2008). An analysis of Montréal's Quartier Chinois and sense of self: Une Loi peut faire mal au dragon, mais La Loi ne peut pas tuer le dragon. *Chinese Journal of Communication, 1*, 213–223.

Geertz, C. (1973). *The interpretation of cultures.* New York: Basic Books.

Giebler Simonet, A. A. (2005). *A lo Tico: Constarriqueñismos y otras vainas.* San José, Costa Rica: Grupo Diseños Impresos.

Gindling, T. H. (2009). South–South migration: The impact of Nicaraguan immigrants on earnings, inequality and poverty in Costa Rica. *World Development, 37*(1), 116–126.

Hallualani, R. T. (2008). "Where exactly is the Pacific?" Global migrations, diasportic movements, and intercultural communication. *Journal of International & Intercultural Communication, 1*, 3–22.

Hansen-Thomas, H. (2007). Language ideology, citizenship, and identity: The case of modern Germany. *Journal of Language and Politics, 6*, 249–264.

Hawley, C. (2010, December 30). Costa Rica copes with its own immigration ills. *USA Today*. "The disparity has drawn about 74,000 migrants to Costa Rica since 2002, swelling its population of foreign-born people by 26%." www.usatoday.com/news/world/2010-12-30foreignimmigration30_ST_N.htm

Hill, J. (1998). Today there is no "respect": Nostalgia, "respect" and oppositional discourse in Mexicano (Nahautl) language ideology. In B. B. Schieffelin, K. A. Woolard, & P. V. Kroskrity (Eds.), *Language ideologies: Practice and theory* (pp. 68–86). New York: Oxford University Press.

Hill, J. (1999). Language, race and white public space. *American Anthropologist, 100*, 680–689.

Hymes, D. (1974). *Foundations in sociolinguistics: An ethnographic approach.* Cinnaminson, NJ: University of Pennsylvania Press.

Irvine, J. T., & Gal, S. (2000). Language ideology and linguistic differentiation. In P. V. Kroskrity (Ed.), *Regimes of language: Ideologies, politics, and identities* (pp. 35–83). Santa Fe, CA: School of American Research Press.

Johnson, E. (2007). Schooling, blackness and national identity in Esmeraldas, Ecuador. *Race, Ethnicity and Education, 10*, 47–70.

Kron, S. (2011). Gestión Migratoria en Norte Centroamerica: Manifestaciones y contestaciones. *Anuario De Estudios Centroamericanos, 37*, 53–85.

Lee, D. (1992). *Competing discourses: Perspective and ideology in language.* New York: Longman.

Leeman, J. (2004). Racializing language: A history of linguistic ideologies in the US Census. *Journal of Language & Politics, 3*, 507–534.

Lipski, J. M. (1985). Central American Spanish. *Hispania, 68*, 143–149.

Lofland, J., & Lofland, L. H. (1995). *Analyzing social settings: A guide to qualitative observation and analysis.* Belmont, CA: Wadsworth Publishing.

Miranda, C. R., & Penland, P. R. (2016). *Costa Rica.* New York: Lonely Planet.

Molina, I., & Palmer, S. (2006). *The history of Costa Rica.* San José, Costa Rica: Editoral De Universidad De Costa Rica.

Moreman, S. T. (2008). Hybrid performativity, South and North of the border: Entre la teoría y la materialidad de hibridación. In A. N. Valdivia (Ed.), *Latina/o communication studies today* (pp. 91–111). New York: Peter Lang.

Moreman, S. T. (2011). Qualitative interviews of racial fluctuations: The "how" of Latina/o-White hybrid identity. *Communication Theory, 21*(2), 197–216.

Moreman, S. T., & Calafell, B. M. (2008). Buscando para nuestra latinidad: Utilizing La Llorona for cultural critique. *Journal of International & Intercultural Communication, 1*, 309–326.

Omi, M., & Winant, H. (2005). The theoretical status of the concept of race. In C. McCarthy, W. Crichlow, G. Dimitriadis, & N. Dolby (Eds.), *Race, identity and representation in education* (2nd ed., pp. 3–12. New York: Routledge.

O'Reilly, K. (2004). *Ethnographic methods.* London: Routledge.

Paniagua Arguedas, L. (2007). Situación sociolaboral de la población Nicaragüense en Costa Rica. *Revista de Ciencias Sociales Universidad de Costa Rica, 117/118*, 57–71.

Quesada Pacheco, M. A. (2008). El español de América Central ayer, hoy y mañana. *Boletín de Filología, 43*, 145–174.

Rojas Blanco, L. (2003). A propósito del voseo: Su historia, su morfología y su situación en Costa Rica. *Revista Educación, 27*(2), 143–163.

Sandel, T. L. (2003). Linguistic capital in Taiwan: The KMT's Mandarin language policy and its perceived impact upon the language practices of bilingual Mandarin and Tai-gi speakers. *Language in Society*, *32*, 523–551.

Sandoval Garcia, C. (2004). Contested discourses on national identity: Representing Nicaraguan immigration to Costa Rica. *Bulletin of Latin American Research*, *23*, 434–445.

Sandoval Garcia, C. (2013). To whom and to what is research on migration a contribution? *Journal of Ethnic and Racial Studies*, *36*, 1429–1445.

Santa Ana, O. (1999). Like an animal I was treated: Anti-immigrant metaphor in US public discourse. *Discourse & Society*, *10*, 191–224.

Schieffelin, B. B., Woolard, K. A., & Kroskrity, P. V. (Eds.) (1998). *Language ideologies: Practice and theory*. New York, Oxford: Oxford University Press.

Silverstein, M. (1998a). Contemporary transformations of local linguistic communities. *Annual Review of Anthropology*, *27*, 401–426.

Silverstein, M. (1998b). The uses and utility of ideology: A commentary. In B. B. Schieffelin, K. Woolard, & P. V. Kroskrity (Eds.), *Language ideologies: Practice and theory* (pp. 123–145). New York: Oxford University Press.

Sinea, A. (2011). What about the Roma people? The enigma of an Italian crisis. Context. Response. Effects? *Journal of Media Research*, *4*, 73–92.

Spencer, A. T. (2011). Americans create hybrid spaces in Costa Rica: A framework for exploring cultural and linguistic integration. *Language & Intercultural Communication*, *11*, 59–74.

Spencer, A. T. (2013). High-end immigrants create an imagined community in Costa Rica: Examining the evolving discourse in ethnic-minority media. *Human Communication*, *16*, 13–30.

Spradley, J. P., & McCurdy, D. W. (1988). *The cultural experience: Ethnography in complex society*. Prospect Heights, IL: Waveland Press.

Tajfel, H., & Turner, J. (1986). The social identity theory of intergroup behavior. In S. Worchel & W. Austin (Eds.), *Psychology of intergroup relations* (2nd ed.), pp. 7–24. Chicago, IL: Nelson-Hall.

The Economist. (2012, January 28). A surprising safe haven: How Central America's poorest country became one of its safest. Retrieved from www.economist.com/node/21543492/

Trenchs-Parera, M., & Newman, M. (2009). Diversity of language ideologies in Spanish- speaking youth of different origins in Catalonia. *Journal of Multilingual and Multicultural Development*, *30*, 509–524.

Van Rheenen, E. (2004). *Living abroad in Costa Rica*. New York: Avalon Publishing Group.

Voorend, K. (2013). "Shifting in" migration control: Universalism and immigration in Costa Rica. *ISS Working Paper Series/General Series*, *564*(564), 1–31.

Wallace, A. (2017). Qué tan diferentes son en realidad los habitantes de Costa Rica a los del resto de los países centroamericanos? *BBC Mundo*. Retrieved from www.bbc.com/mundo/noticias-america-latina-40017780

Woolard, K. A. (1998). Language ideology as a field of inquiry. In B. B. Schieffelin, K. A. Woolard, & P. V. Kroskrity (Eds.), *Language ideologies: Practice and theory* (pp. 3–47). New York: Oxford University Press.

19

INDIVIDUAL AND CONTEXTUAL EXPLANATIONS OF ATTITUDES TOWARD IMMIGRATION

Eva G. T. Green & Oriane Sarrasin

Largely due to immigration, virtually all contemporary societies are becoming more and more culturally diverse. Immigration is frequently triggered by societal circumstances such as armed conflicts, global economic downturns, or environmental crises and can result in large flows of immigrants crossing international borders. The refugee crisis that started in 2015 notably exemplifies a dramatic consequence of such events. Accordingly, immigration has become one of the most polarizing topics in political and societal debates in receiving societies across the globe. Public opinion varies from exclusive to inclusive when it comes to receiving immigrants, providing them support, or granting them rights. Currently, however, anti-immigrant attitudes are on the rise and, in Europe in particular, right-wing populist parties are gaining support. Such a trend is clearly a risk for social cohesion and increases the stigmatization immigrants endure in the receiving societies. Uncovering the multiple reasons that explain the rise of intolerance toward immigrants is a major challenge.

The key question is thus which factors explain how members of receiving societies react to the increased and diversified immigrant presence. This chapter presents a multilevel research approach – in a non-statistical conceptual manner – for studying how the interplay of individual and contextual factors accounts for anti-immigration prejudice among members of the national majority (i.e. citizens with no foreign roots). Radical right voting can be seen as a behavioural manifestation of anti-immigration stances. Therefore, we also refer to multilevel research examining radical right voting intentions.[1] Though immigration is a global phenomenon, as large scale international surveys on immigration attitudes have been mainly conducted in the global North, the existing multilevel research focuses on receiving countries in Europe. We first define a multilevel approach for studying immigration attitudes. Second, based on multilevel survey research drawing on social and political psychology, we present individual-level determinants of these viewpoints (i.e. threat perceptions, intergroup contact with immigrants, ideological orientations such as national attachment) that have been evidenced to play an important role in shaping immigration attitudes. Third, extending the theorization used to conceptualize individual-level explanations to a contextual level, we examine how individuals' attitudes are shaped by the contexts in which they are embedded.

In parallel, to illustrate this research approach, we present four examples of our recent research conducted on attitudes regarding immigration and radical right support in Switzerland. Switzerland is a highly relevant national context for studying immigration attitudes and radical right support with a multilevel perspective. Indeed, the proportion of immigrants within the Swiss population has historically been high (Piguet, 2009). In 2015 a quarter of the resident population (24.6 per cent) did not possess Swiss citizenship (Swiss Federal Statistical Office, 2017a). Both strict naturalization policies and continued emigration to Switzerland (in 2015 most immigrants – 80.6 per cent – were born abroad) explain this high immigrant proportion. Moreover, Switzerland is a decentralised federal state, in which political deliberation frequently occurs at the local regional level. Due to the political system practising direct democracy, Swiss citizens have opportunities to express their views concerning immigration in local or national referenda. These referenda have frequently been initiated by the radical right Swiss People's Party (in German, *Schweizerische Volkspartei*, SVP), the largest party in the Federal assembly (32.5 per cent of the seats). In this context, radical right voting can be seen as a behavioural expression of anti-immigration prejudice. Note also that the Swiss national majority is composed of four language groups (approximately 63 per cent Swiss German speakers, 23 per cent French speakers, 8 per cent Italian speakers, and less than 1 per cent Romansh speakers; Swiss Federal Statistical Office, 2017b), more or less located in linguistic regions. This both enriches and renders complex the study of immigration attitudes.[2]

A multilevel approach to studying immigration attitudes

A multilevel approach takes into account the impact of both individual and contextual factors on immigration attitudes (see Christ et al., 2016; Pettigrew, 2006). The basic premise is that individuals are part of broader social contexts, which have the power to shape their attitudes (Hox, 2010). Thus it is likely that attitudes of individuals living within a given geographically delimited contextual unit are dependent. The characteristics of these units are assumed to explain a part of individuals' attitudes, over and above individual determinants. Contextual units can be distal, such as nations or regions, or more proximal, such as districts, municipalities, or neighbourhoods. The choice of the level(s) of units to be examined in a specific study is driven by both conceptual (e.g. research questions) and methodological (e.g. data sampling) considerations. Figure 19.1 summarizes the basic multilevel model to which we refer throughout the chapter. Note that, because we present results of multilevel regressions based on cross-sectional data, causality cannot be established. However, when discussing literature on antecedents of immigration attitudes in the next sections, we discuss theory-driven claims that imply direction.

While the importance of examining and articulating different levels of analysis in social psychology has been acknowledged and theorised previously (e.g. Doise, 1986; see Pettigrew, 2006), analytical techniques allowing for the empirical investigation of multilevel models have become available only in the last 20 years. In statistical terminology, data requiring a multilevel approach is *hierarchical*, and individuals are *nested* within contextual (macro) units. Explanations can be conceptualised and variables can be defined at any level of this hierarchy. Preliminary tests ensure that a significant part of an individual's attitudes is due to them living within a given unit. If not, basic statistical tests (e.g. OLS regressions) can be performed and only the impact of individual characteristics is investigated. =However, if such tests – based on the assumption of independence – are performed on data that are not independent, the findings reached are

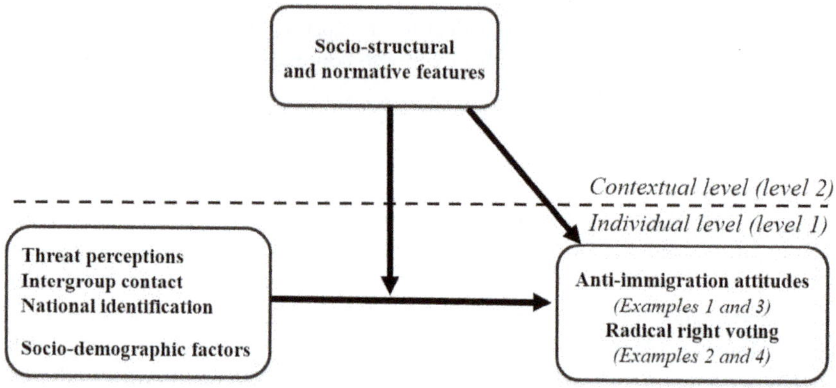

Figure 19.1 Multilevel model

unreliable (i.e. the standard errors of conventional statistical tests are too small; see Hox, 2010). Instead, in these cases, multilevel research designs that combine individual-level (so-called level 1) predictors with macro-level (level 2) factors in a single explanatory model should be applied (see Figure 19.1). Such models can be implemented straightforwardly with a number of statistical software packages, such as STATA, SPSS, LISREL, MLwin, MPlus and R, to mention just a few of those most used in the social sciences.

The advancement of software coincided with the development of high-quality large-scale, international social surveys on immigration, which prompted a surge of cross-national and cross-regional research that simultaneously takes into account the impact of individual and contextual factors on attitudes. The European Social Survey (ESS – www.europeansocialsurvey.org/) has monitored bi-annually the attitudes and practices of Europeans on a range of topics since 2002. An immigration module has been fielded twice, in 2002/2003 (Round 1, 22 countries) and 2014/2015 (Round 7, 22 countries), partially repeating and developing the original module (see Heath et al., 2012). The ESS has become the reference for cross-national research on immigration attitudes and explicitly encourages cross-national multilevel research by providing nation-level contextual variables. The International Social Survey Programme (ISSP – www.issp.org), in turn, is the biggest and most extensive cross-national social survey endeavour, conducting surveys on an annual basis. The ISPP network was initiated in 1984 and currently includes around 50 countries worldwide. A National Identity module, that includes questions regarding attachment to the nation as well as attitudes toward immigrants, has been fielded three times (1996, 2003, 2013). Other collective survey endeavours such as the World Values Survey (WVS – www.worldvaluessurvey.org) and the European Values Study (EVS – www.europeanvalues study.eu/) also contain questions tapping into immigration attitudes, and have been widely used.

Individual-level explanations of immigration attitudes

Many individual-level, socio-demographic and attitudinal factors as well as contextual characteristics have been put forward to explain immigration attitudes and radical right voting. With a focus on three key social psychological explanations – threat perceptions, intergroup contact and national attachment (see also Green, Sarrasin, & Fasel, 2015) – we now discuss individual-level antecedents of anti-immigration stances (Figure 19.1, bottom).

Building on this discussion, in the following section, contextual explanations using a multi-level approach are overviewed.

Threat perceptions

Perceptions that immigrants *threaten* the national majority are frequently argued to explain individuals' anti-immigrant attitudes.[3] A number of theoretical approaches, such as integrated threat theory (Stephan, Renfro, & Davis, 2008) and ethnic competition theory (Scheepers, Gjisberts, & Coenders, 2002) have elaborated on the role of threat in determining immigration attitudes, albeit with somewhat different reasoning and focus. Threats are usually grouped into two major categories: realistic, material threats and symbolic, cultural threats (Riek, Mania, & Gaertner, 2006).[4] Material threat is associated with perceived competition for tangible, limited resources, such competition being between immigrants and the national majority population in the labour and housing markets, as well as the perceived fiscal burden of welfare benefits such as health care or integration measures for immigrants. Resources are thus conceived as zerosum; that is, an advantage for immigrants by default implies a disadvantage for the national majority (Esses, Jackson, & Armstrong, 1998). The fear of immigrants accessing power and status, for example by claiming civic rights, is also in the realm of material threat. Cultural threat, in turn, derives from supposed differences between immigrants and natives in traditions, language and religion, and thus the perception that immigrants undermine the values of the national majority. Fear of crime and terrorism – conveying material, physical threats as well as a symbolic threat of collapsing values – also underlie negative immigration attitudes. The populist right campaigns frequently present immigrants as both material and cultural threats thereby fostering harsh views concerning immigration.

Beneficial effects of intergroup contact

Whereas there is ample evidence that threat perceptions predict increased anti-immigration prejudice (Riek et al., 2006; Stephan et al., 2008) and radical right voting intentions (e.g. Lucassen & Lubbers, 2012), other factors have the potential to curb anti-immigration stances. Indeed, there is evidence from over 60 years of research on intergroup contact that positive intergroup encounters with outgroup members reduce prejudice (Allport, 1954; Hewstone & Swart, 2011; Pettigrew & Tropp, 2006). Positive intergroup contact with immigrants has been shown to improve attitudes of the national majority (e.g. McLaren, 2003; Voci & Hewstone, 2003) by reducing perceptions of threat and anxiety associated with immigrants and increasing empathy toward them (see Pettigrew & Tropp, 2008, for a meta-analysis). Cross-group friendships – conveying deep and intimate encounters a national majority member can have with an immigrant outgroup member – are particularly powerful for reducing anti-immigrant attitudes (see Davies, Tropp, Aron, Pettigrew, & Wright, 2011 for a meta-analysis). Indeed, analyses performed on the ESS immigration modules have demonstrated that having friends with foreign origins relates negatively to a range of anti-immigration viewpoints (Schneider, 2008; Semyonov & Glickman, 2009), but the link to radical right support is equivocal (e.g. Rydgren, 2008). The ESS repeat module on immigration (Heath et al., 2012) contains a wider range of measures on different forms of intergroup contact that allow, for example, distinguishing close (i.e. intergroup friendships) as well as mundane contact experiences (i.e. on public transport, in the street, in shops or in the neighbourhood).

National attachment as an ideology

Both threat perceptions and intergroup contact are related to how one perceives and interacts with immigrant *outgroups*. Yet, the way in which one relates with the national *ingroup* also plays a role for immigration attitudes. National attachment has been shown to relate to attitudes toward immigrants; however, whether the relationship is positive or negative depends on the nature of national attachment. Two forms of national attachment – nationalism and patriotism – are generally distinguished (e.g. Blank & Schmidt, 2003; Davidov, 2009; Wagner, Becker, Christ, Pettigrew, & Schmidt, 2010). Nationalism refers to an uncritical attachment to and idealisation of the nation, as well as a sense of national superiority with respect to other countries. This form of national attachment has consistently been associated with anti-immigration attitudes (Blank & Schmidt, 2003). Patriotism, in turn, reflects pride in one's country, particularly in its democratic political institutions and does not involve comparisons with other countries (e.g. Mummendey, Klink, & Brown, 2001). This form of attachment reflects a constructive and critical view of the nation. It is congruent with tolerance toward immigrants and frequently unrelated to immigration attitudes (e.g. de Figueiredo & Elkins, 2003) or even linked to positive immigration attitudes (e.g. Blank & Schmidt, 2003; see also Green, Sarrasin, Fasel, & Staerklé, 2011). The ISSP national identity modules include questions tapping into these forms of national attachment, as well as others, and have thus prompted cross national multilevel studies examining the predictive power of both nationalism and patriotism, as well as their antecedents.

Whereas nationalism and patriotism convey ideological beliefs related to nationhood, it is important to acknowledge that other ideological beliefs underlie immigration attitudes too. For example, right-wing authoritarianism, concerned with conformity and cohesion (Altermeyer, 1998), and social dominance orientation, a preference for group dominance and hierarchy (Sidanius & Pratto, 1999), are also crucial antecedents of anti-immigration prejudice (Cohrs & Stetzl, 2010; Sibley et al., 2013). Similarly, conservative values have been linked to anti-immigration attitudes (e.g. Fasel, Green, & Sarrasin, 2013).

Socio-demographic antecedents of anti-immigration attitudes

Socio-demographic variables are routinely added to multilevel models as predictors. Unlike in comparative sociology, their impact is more rarely theorised in social psychological research. Nevertheless, some elaboration is in order. The role of individuals' socioeconomic status on immigration attitudes is well studied (Ceobanu & Escandell, 2010). The basic argument has been that citizens with a low status are more likely than their high-status compatriots to experience competition with immigrants in the job and housing markets, and therefore they should experience immigrants as more threatening and be more inclined to express an exclusionary anti-immigrant stance (Scheepers et al., 2002; see Lubbers, Gjisberts, & Scheepers, 2002 regarding radical right support). While education, labour force status, occupation and income are all intertwined manifestations of social status, their effects on immigration attitudes are not uniform (see Ceobanu & Escandell, 2010). Higher level of education is quite systematically related to reduced expressions of anti-immigration stances (although attitudinal differences exist prior to entering education; Lancee & Sarrasin, 2015), but the effects of other social status markers are inconsistent. Age and gender effects are also typically accounted for in multilevel studies on immigration attitudes. Older people often hold more conservative worldviews than younger people, which can explain harsher attitudes toward immigrants, and men express more negative attitudes than women (Ceobanu & Escandell, 2010).

Contextual explanations of anti-immigration attitudes

The rationale of threat, intergroup contact and ideological beliefs (such as national attachment) driving immigration attitudes outlined above can be extended to a contextual level (see Figure 19.1, top). We now discuss how contextual characteristics shape individuals' attitudes to immigration and radical right support. Multilevel survey research has focused heavily on the role of immigrant presence, typically assessed with the proportion of immigrants or increase in proportion, as characteristics of a given macro context, to understand negative attitudes toward immigrants (see Fasel et al., 2013 for an overview). The role of normative contexts in relation to immigration attitudes, in turn, has only received attention more recently. We provide four examples from our research conducted in Switzerland that have contributed to this body of research.

Presence of immigrants: threat or opportunity?

Threat reasoning has been applied in multilevel research to explain the impact of immigrant presence, with the rationale being that a higher or an increasing ratio of immigrants triggers concerns over competition for scarce resources and fears of eradication of native traditions. Indeed, multilevel research across European countries has found evidence that immigrant ratios are related to increased threat perceptions and stronger anti-immigrant stances (e.g. Green, 2009; Quillian, 1995; Scheepers et al., 2002) and radical right support (Lubbers et al., 2002). Perceptions of the number of immigrants explains part of this effect (*mediates*, in statistical terms). The greater the actual presence of immigrants in a given place, the greater their perceived presence, which then drives more expressions of anti-immigrant stances (e.g. Semyonov, Raijman, & Gorodzeisky, 2006).

Besides direct and indirect effects on immigration attitudes, contextual characteristics can also have interactive effects (*level-2 interactions* in multilevel terminology). That is, one contextual characteristic can curb or intensify the effect of another characteristic. Indeed, in support of threat reasoning, a seminal study across 12 European countries conducted by Quillian (1995) demonstrated that, while the proportion of immigrants from non-European countries increased racial prejudice, this relationship was enhanced in countries with poor economic conditions. The same pattern was found for anti-immigrant prejudice, but the effect was less prominent.

Intergroup contact theory has argued, however, that immigration can have the opposite effect to that just described: a strong immigrant presence provides contact opportunities and thereby facilitates positive intergroup encounters, which, in turn, reduce anti-immigrant attitudes. In a study across German districts, Wagner, Christ, Pettigrew, Stellmacher, and Wolf (2006) demonstrated that the proportion of immigrants was negatively related to immigrant prejudice. This relationship was explained by enhanced encounters with immigrants at the workplace and in neighbourhoods. Moreover, intergroup contact was related to improved attitudes toward immigrants by reducing perceived threat (see also Christ et al., 2014; Schmid, Al Ramiah, & Hewstone, 2014). These seemingly contradictory threat and intergroup contact approaches can be reconciled as immigrant presence yields simultaneously different outcomes. Schlueter and Wagner (2008), for example, found that the proportion of immigrant populations at the regional level within European countries was related to both intergroup contact and perceived threat.

Example 1: disentangling threat and contact effects

In our research conducted in Switzerland (see Green, Fasel, & Sarrasin, 2010 for details), we attempted to untangle the potential threat and contact effects of immigrant presence by differentiating between types of immigrant group. To do so, we compared the impacts of the presence of devalued, stigmatised groups and of valued, culturally-close immigrants (e.g. Montreuil & Bourhis, 2001) on threat perceptions and contact underlying anti-immigrant attitudes. Muslims – in Switzerland, mainly originating from Turkey, the former Yugoslavia and Albania – are more stigmatised than other immigrant groups in Switzerland (Helbling, 2010; Stolz, 2005)[5] as well as elsewhere in Europe (e.g. Spruyt & Elchardus, 2012). Indeed, a uniform group of Muslims does not exist, as Muslim immigrants vary in economic, political and social status and as a function of the national context. Yet, while attitudes vary when it comes to specific Muslim groups or individuals, for example due to visible signs of religion (such as wearing a head scarf) or associations with terrorism, the national majority *representations* of Muslims and Islam as a religion are quite homogeneous. Perceived as culturally similar, highly-skilled immigrants from neighbouring Northern and Western European countries are appreciated to a greater degree (e.g. Deschamps, Vala, Marinho, Costa Lopes, & Cabecinhas, 2005; see, however, Binggeli, Krings, & Sczesny, 2014; Matser, van Oudenhoven, Askevis-Leherpeux, Florack, & Rossier, 2010). We used the first round of ESS data from Switzerland and examined the views of 1,472 Swiss citizens across 185 municipalities to uncover how the presence of immigrants of different origins shapes citizens' attitudes. Municipalities are a relevant contextual unit for comparing intergroup contact and the threat rationale because, when looking at immigrant presence at the municipality level, it is plausible that encounters with immigrants occur in everyday life (see Wagner et al., 2006). This may not necessarily be the case when considering immigrant presence at the national level (see, however, Pottie-Sherman & Wilkes, 2017). The presence of immigrants in one part of the country does not necessarily translate into contact opportunities elsewhere. We found that the presence of valued, culturally-close immigrants was related to heightened intergroup contact in municipalities. Indeed, it is likely that similarity and absence of a priori prejudice facilitate encounters. Contact was further associated with more inclusive immigration attitudes as a result of reduced threat perceptions. The presence of devalued immigrants in municipalities, however, yielded a more intricate pattern. On the one hand, it was related to perceived threat, which, in turn, was associated with increased anti-immigration prejudice (see also Savelkoul, Scheepers, Tolsma, & Hagendoorn, 2011). On the other hand, presence of stigmatized immigrants was related to increased intergroup contact. These findings show that exposure to dissimilar types of immigrant group differently shape immigration attitudes. More crucially, however, these findings imply that encouraging and enabling encounters with stigmatised immigrants is a route for more harmonious intergroup relations. Yet, as the focus of the study was on attitudinal outcomes, we cannot conclude whether these processes play out when considering actual behaviour. We thus extended our research to political behaviour by examining voting intentions.

Example 2: from attitudes to political behaviour

Radical right campaigning in Switzerland, like elsewhere, uses images and rhetoric of threat extensively when addressing immigration-related issues, and, in particular, when referring to immigrants of Balkan and Muslim origin (see Ruedin, 2013 for an analysis of party manifestos; Sarrasin, Fasel, Green & Helbing, 2015 for a study on the impact of the radical right SVP campaign posters). Thus, to further extend our examination of the impact of the presence of stigmatised immigrants, we examined whether the proportion of stigmatised immigrants, from the former Yugoslavia and Albania, is associated with intentions to vote for the radical right, that is, the SVP (for details, see Green, Sarrasin, Baur, & Fasel, 2016). We investigated this issue using Swiss Election Studies data for 2011 on 1,736 Swiss citizens from 136 districts. We found that presence of former Yugoslavian and Albanian immigrants was related to increased intention to vote for the radical right as a result of increased threat perception (see also Ford & Goodwin, 2010). However, having positive intergroup encounters with former Yugoslavian and Albanian immigrants was related to reduced intention to vote for the radical right. While actual presence of former Yugoslavian and Albanian immigrants was unrelated to contact, in districts with overall more positive encounters with former Yugoslavian and Albanian immigrants, threat perceptions and support for the radical right were lower. Our findings again speak to the importance of intergroup encounters in reducing anti-immigrant prejudice and in attenuating support for the radical right, and thus potentially curbing the rise of the populist right. While these findings on immigrant presence in Switzerland are promising, one cannot directly generalise from them to other countries. Indeed, in a recent meta-analysis, Pottie-Sherman and Wilkes (2017) revealed that type of immigrant presence is not a definite explanation for varying findings of immigrant presence found in the literature. While generalisation is not possible, the findings of the two examples show that 'valued' and 'devalued' immigrants in the Swiss context relate to different reactions among the national ingroup. As whether a group is valued or devalued will vary across contexts, further research in different countries is needed to pursue this interpretation. Importantly, normative climates need to be considered too.

Normative climates and immigration

So far, most multilevel research has focused on the impact of socio-structural features of national and regional contexts, such as immigrant ratio. Besides these features, contexts also have normative or ideological characteristics, referred to as normative climates. Individuals are embedded in these environments, which provide guidance and information regarding the appropriate way to think about and deal with immigration (e.g. Green & Staerklé, 2013; Guimond, de la Sablonnière, & Nugier, 2014; Pettigrew, 2006). Indeed, normative characteristics manifest themselves in different ways, and potentially have a huge impact on shaping immigration attitudes. Normative contexts are formed, for example, by institutions, political parties and the attitudinal climate derived from the beliefs and values shared by fellow ingroup members. We now consider these different features and how they jointly influence individuals' attitudes regarding immigration.

Institutional features of normative climates are conveyed through legislation and policies. They express governmental viewpoints on and action toward cultural diversity and immigration, and thereby orient citizens' stances on immigration. In a study across four countries, Guimond, Dambrun, Michinov, and Duarte (2013) showed that actual integration policies of countries affected perceived integration norms, which then predicted attitudes toward immigrants. These findings suggest that citizens have some awareness of and are guided by the surrounding policy context when forming views regarding immigration.

Indeed, in a study across 27 European countries, Schlueter, Meuleman, and Davidov (2013) considered that more inclusive integration policies reflect tolerant institutionalised norms (measured by the Migrant Integration Policy Index (MIPEX), www.mipex.eu; Niessen, Huddleston, & Citron, 2007), and found that they were related to reduced threat perceptions. The official views of political parties also convey visions of how cultural diversity and immigration should be dealt with. A high presence of radical right parties in countries (Semyonov et al., 2006) has been used to measure exclusionary, normative climates. Indeed, such climates foster anti-immigrant attitudes beyond the individual characteristics driving such attitudes.

Whereas policies and political parties express a normative climate that is defined top-down, shared ideological beliefs and values, in turn, circulating through citizens' everyday conversations and expressions regarding immigration within a given context, convey bottom-up normative climates. Shared ideological beliefs can be conceived broadly on a continuum from conservative and exclusive to progressive and inclusive. For example, shared exclusionary conceptions of who belongs to the national ingroup, measured with aggregated support for strict nationhood criteria (Pehrson, Vignoles, & Brown, 2009) and an aggregated right-wing stance in countries and regions (Van Assche, Roets, De Keersmaecker, & Van Hiel, 2016) have been used to depict bottom-up exclusionary normative climates. In the following two examples we consider the impact of both bottom-up and top-down forms of normative climates in Switzerland.

Example 3: referenda results as normative climate

In our research comparing Swiss municipalities, we studied both the impact of immigrant presence and conservative versus progressive normative climate on anti-immigrant views; more precisely, opposition to anti-racism laws (for details, see Sarrasin et al., 2012). With data from the first round of the ESS we studied the views of 1,711 Swiss citizens from 176 municipalities.[6] We measured municipality-level conservative versus progressive normative climates via national referendum results on a range of political topics (excluding referenda on immigration to avoid tautology in our analysis) over a period of ten years. Over and above individual-level antecedents, opposition to anti-racism laws was greater in conservative municipalities and intergroup friendships more frequent when proportion of immigrants was high. In addition, an interplay of municipality-level normative climate and proportion of immigrants (that is, a level-2 interaction in multilevel terminology) was revealed. In municipalities with a high immigrant proportion, conservative normative climates were unrelated to having friendships with immigrants, whereas in municipalities with a low proportion of immigrants, the more conservative the municipality, the less frequent were intergroup friendships. Put differently, in conservative municipalities with a low portion of immigrants, intergroup friendships were the rarest. Presence of immigrants thus seemed to buffer the impact of conservative contextual norms. Here, we examined referenda results as a bottom-up manifestation of the normative climate in municipalities, while in the next example we investigate the role of both top-down and bottom-up normative climates.

Example 4: comparing features of normative climates

Extending our work on contextual norms as antecedents of attitudes to examine political behaviour, we decided to study the relationship between normative climates and radical right voting intentions across Swiss cantons (for details, see Baur, Green, & Helbling, 2016). Moreover, whether top-down and bottom-up normative climates have similar effects on immigration-related attitudes begged further inquiry. We thus set out to test whether canton-level institutionalised norms (top-down climates) and shared conservative values (bottom-up climates) similarly shape immigration attitudes and radical right voting intentions. We investigated these issues using 2011 Swiss Election Studies data on 3,653 Swiss citizens in the 26 Swiss cantons.[7] The institutional normative climate was measured with an integration policy index developed by Manatschal (2011) and shared conservative values were based on aggregated attitudes from prior waves of the Swiss Election Studies survey (i.e. items measuring preferences for a strong military, for law and order, preference for Swiss traditions, and for Swiss citizens having better chances than foreigners). As anticipated, in more exclusionary cantonal contexts (both institutionally more exclusive and with entrenched conservative beliefs) support for the radical right was greater than in more inclusive cantons, over and above the impact of individual political orientation or socio-demographic characteristics. Exclusionary cantonal norms were related to an anti-immigrant stance, which further fostered radical right voting intentions. Furthermore, we found that the relationship between immigration attitudes and radical right voting was reinforced in cantons with exclusionary normative climates (in multilevel modelling terminology, a *cross-level interaction* was revealed). This implies that individuals' attitudes toward immigration are a stronger driver of their voting intentions in exclusionary rather than in inclusionary contexts. This finding suggests that when individuals' attitudes match the surrounding normative climate they translate more readily into action – here, voting for the radical right.

Conclusion

The aim of the current chapter was to showcase a multilevel approach that allows for studying the impact of individual- and context-level factors on shaping attitudes toward immigration and radical right support. While the focus here was on predictors of negative immigration attitudes, one must recall that there are also individuals and popular movements reducing social inequalities, providing equal opportunities and fighting discrimination. After describing the basic rationale of multilevel analyses, we overviewed both cross-national and cross-regional research on immigration attitudes and the principal explanations put forward by this approach. We focused on immigrant ratio and normative climates as context-level characteristics driving immigration attitudes. Our recent study in Switzerland was showcased with four examples of this research approach. The decentralised political system that allows decision making regarding immigration at the local level makes Switzerland a fascinating context for studying regional-level variation in immigration attitudes. As mentioned at the outset of the chapter, the cited multilevel research focuses on the standpoint of national majorities in receiving societies in the global North. We acknowledge that immigration between countries of the global South is at least, if not more, frequent than South–North immigration. However, currently most international large data collection projects (ESS and ISSP) that allow for multilevel modelling have been carried out in the global North. The issues of national majorities in relation to immigration, as well as the contextual features driving stances on immigration, may differ drastically from those in the global South. To gain a comprehensive view of individual and contextual antecedents of immigration attitudes, it is imperative to broaden the sampling of countries.

There are a number of extensions of multilevel modelling that have been used to study immigration attitudes and related topics that are beyond the scope of this chapter. Indeed, multilevel structural equation modelling (Christ et al., 2016) allows testing for more complex modelling. For example, multiple indirect effects (i.e. mediations) as well as multiple dependent variables (i.e. outcomes, such as different attitude constructs related to immigration) can be examined simultaneously. To this end, Schmid et al. (2014) examined effects of neighbourhood ethnic diversity on different forms of trust as well as on outgroup attitudes, and showed that intergroup contact and perceived threat mediated these relationships. Moreover, it is important to take stock of the body of multilevel immigration research. Meta-analyses are tools well-suited to this task because they allow for exploring plausible explanations for contrasting findings and provide guidance on the generalisability of findings from individual studies. A multilevel meta-analysis, briefly evoked in the current chapter, has been conducted recently to statistically summarise research on the impact of immigrant presence on immigration attitudes (Pottie-Sherman & Wilkes, 2017).

Whereas the chief asset of multilevel modelling is the possibility it provides to jointly model macro- and individual-level explanations of individual attitudes, we acknowledge that no method alone permits unequivocal interpretations of the construction of attitudes toward immigration. Cross-sectional surveys need to be complemented with longitudinal surveys (allowing multilevel modelling) and experimental methods to determine causality. Moreover, self-report measures – such as survey questionnaires (whether administered via the telephone or face-to-face; self-administered with a paper-and-pencil; or taken online) – need to be complemented: interviews, for example, would allow the researcher to gain a deeper understanding of the reasoning and reflections underlying individuals' stances regarding immigration. We examined radical right voting intentions to tap into actual political behaviour related to immigration. These intentions can have tangible consequences for the organisation of society. Observational studies, however, would allow further insights regarding actual behaviour. Yet it is obvious that no research programme can combine all these methods. Using a multilevel approach in conjunction with another approach – be it a social psychological experiment to test causal claims or a discursive analysis of everyday reactions to immigration – and triangulating the findings would be an ideal approach to aim for.

Notes

1 We focus on antecedents of anti-immigration prejudice, as the consideration of other factors underlying radical right voting, such as political dissatisfaction, Euroscepticism and distrust of elites, as well as party characteristics or electoral competition, is beyond the scope of this chapter. In the current chapter, the term radical right is used to refer to political parties with an explicit anti-immigration agenda, and that have become mainstream political actors in Western countries. Right-wing extremist parties, that openly endorse, for example, neo-Nazi or racist viewpoints, are not considered here.

2 The differences between linguistic regions in Switzerland are beyond the scope of this chapter. However, differences between linguistic regions are accounted for in the original papers of our research showcased here. In short, linguistic regions frequently differ in outcomes of referenda results concerning immigration as well as in attitudes examined in social surveys. The German-speaking regions, for example, come across as having more negative views on immigration than the French-speaking regions. Yet, it is not possible to attribute these differences to language as the regions differ on other aspects too, with the Swiss-German region, for example, being markedly more rural than the Swiss-French region.

3 Note that threat can be conceptualised as an antecedent as well as a depiction of anti-immigration stances.

4 Despite conceptually differentiating between dimensions of threat, empirically these dimensions frequently overlap, for example in factor analyses loading on the same factor. Thus general immigration threat is frequently studied (as a predictor or an outcome).

5 Immigrants from the former Yugoslavia and Albania report discrimination twice as often as West European or less recent immigrant groups (Swiss Federal Statistical Office, 2014). While the nationalities from this region differ in terms of language and religion, the representations of these immigrant groups among the Swiss majority do not differ. Indeed, even the statistics on discrimination experiences of immigrants from different countries of the former Yugoslavia and Albania are grouped together, suggesting similar reactions on the part of the national majority.

6 Note that, despite using the same data set, the *N*s in Examples 1 and 3 differ because the variables used in the respective studies were not the same.

7 Albeit using the same data set, the *N*s in Examples 2 and 4 differ because the variables used in the respective studies were not the same.

References

Allport, G. W. (1954). *The nature of prejudice*. New York: Doubleday.

Altemeyer, B. (1998). The other "authoritarian personality". *Advances in Experimental Social Psychology, 30*, 47–92.

Baur, R., Green, E. G. T., & Helbling, M. (2016). Immigration-related political culture and support for radical right parties. *Journal of Ethnic and Migration Studies, 42*, 1748–1773.

Binggeli, S., Krings, F., & Sczesny, S. (2014). Perceived competition explains regional differences in the stereotype content of immigrant groups. *Social Psychology, 45*, 62–70.

Blank, T. & Schmidt, P. (2003). National identity in a united Germany: Nationalism or patriotism? An empirical test with representative data. *Political Psychology, 24*, 289–312.

Ceobanu, A. M. & Escandell, X. (2010). Comparative analyses of public attitudes toward immigrants and immigration using multinational survey data: A review of theories and research. *Annual Review of Sociology, 36*, 15.11–15.20.

Christ, O., Hewstone, M., Schmid, K., Green, E. G. T., Sarrasin, O., Gollwitzer, M., & Wagner, U. (2016). Advanced multilevel modeling for a science of groups: A short primer on multilevel structural equation modeling. *Group Dynamics: Theory, Research, and Practice, 21*, 121–134.

Christ, O., Schmid, K., Lolliot, S., Swart, H., Stolle, D., Tausch, N., ... Hewstone, M. (2014). Contextual effect of positive intergroup contact on outgroup prejudice. *Proceedings of the National Academy of Sciences, 111*, 3996–4000.

Cohrs, J. C. & Stelzl, M. (2010). How ideological attitudes predict host society members' attitudes toward immigrants: Exploring cross-national differences. *Journal of Social Issues, 66*, 673–694.

Davidov, E. (2009). Measurement equivalence of nationalism and constructive patriotism in the ISSP: 34 countries in a comparative perspective. *Political Analysis, 17*(1), 64–82.

Davies, K., Tropp, L. R., Aron, A., Pettigrew, T. F., & Wright, S. C. (2011). Cross-group friendships and intergroup attitudes: A meta-analytic review. *Personality and Social Psychology Review, 15*, 332–351.

Deschamps, J.-C., Vala, J., Marinho, C., Costa Lopes, R., & Cabecinhas, R. (2005). Intergroup relations, racism and attribution of natural and cultural traits. *Psicologia Politica, 30*, 27–39.

Doise, W. (1986). *Levels of explanation in social psychology*. Cambridge: Cambridge University Press.

Esses, V. M., Jackson, L. M., & Armstrong, T. L. (1998). Intergroup competition and attitudes toward immigrants and immigration: An instrumental model of group conflict. *Journal of Social Issues, 54*, 699–724.

Fasel, N., Green, E. G. T., & Sarrasin, O. (2013). Facing cultural diversity. Anti-immigrant attitudes in Europe. *European Psychologist, 18*, 253–262.

Figueiredo, R. J. P. D. & Elkins, Z. (2003). Are patriots bigots? An inquiry into the vices of in-group pride. *American Journal of Political Science, 47*, 171–188.

Ford, R. & Goodwin, M. J. (2010). Angry white men: Individual and contextual predictors of support for the British National Party. *Political Studies, 58*(1), 1–25.

Green, E. G. T. (2009). Who can enter? A multilevel analysis of public support for immigration criteria across 20 European countries. *Group Processes & Intergroup Relations, 12*, 41–60.

Green, E. G. T. & Staerklé, C. (2013). Migration and multiculturalism. In L. Huddy, D. O. Sears, & J. Levy (Eds.), *Oxford handbook of political psychology* (pp. 852–889). Oxford: Oxford University Press.

Green, E. G. T., Fasel, N., & Sarrasin, O. (2010). The more the merrier? The effects of type of cultural diversity on exclusionary immigration attitudes in Switzerland. *International Journal of Conflict and Violence, 4*, 177–190.

Green, E. G. T., Sarrasin, O., Baur, R., & Fasel, N. (2016). From stigmatized immigrants to right-wing voting: A multilevel study on the role of threat and contact. *Political Psychology, 37*, 465–480.

Green, E. G. T., Sarrasin, O., & Fasel, N. (2015). Immigration: Social psychological aspects. In J. D. Wright (Ed.), *International encyclopedia of the social and behavioral sciences* (2nd ed). New York: Elsevier.

Green, E. G. T., Sarrasin, O., Fasel, N., & Staerklé, C. (2011). Nationalism and patriotism as predictors of immigration attitudes in Switzerland: A municipality-level analysis. *Swiss Political Science Review, 17*, 369–393.

Guimond, S., Dambrun, M., Michinov, N., & Duarte, S. (2013). Does social dominance generate prejudice? Integrating individual and contextual determinants of intergroup cognitions. *Journal of Personality and Social Psychology, 84*, 697–721.

Guimond, S., de La Sablonnière, R., & Nugier, A. (2014). Living in a multicultural world: Intergroup ideologies and the societal context of intergroup relations. *European Review of Social Psychology, 25*, 142–188.

Heath, A., Schmidt, P., Green, E. G. T., Ramos, A., Davidov, E., & Ford, R. (2012). *Attitudes towards immigration and their antecedents.* European Social Survey Round 7 Question Module. Retrieved from www.europeansocialsurvey.org/docs/round7/questionnaire/ESS7_immigration_final_module_template.pdf

Helbling, M. (2010). Islamophobia in Switzerland: A new phenomenon or a new name for xenophobia. In S. Hug & H. Kriesi (Eds.), *Value change in Switzerland* (Vol. 65–80). Lanham, MD: Lexington Press.

Hewstone, M. & Swart, H. (2011). Fifty-odd years of inter-group contact: From hypothesis to integrated theory. *British Journal of Social Psychology, 50*, 374–386.

Hox, J. (2010). *Multilevel analysis: Techniques and applications.* New York: Routledge Academic.

Lancee, B. & Sarrasin, O. (2015). Educated preferences or selection effects? A longitudinal analysis of the impact of educational attainment on attitudes towards immigrants. *European Sociological Review, 31*, 490–501.

Lubbers, M., Gijsberts, M., & Scheepers, P. (2002). Extreme right-wing voting in Western Europe. *European Journal of Political Research, 41*, 345–378.

Lucassen, G. & Lubbers, M. (2012). Who fears what? Explaining far-right-wing preference in Europe by distinguishing perceived cultural and economic ethnic threats. *Comparative Political Studies, 45*, 547–574.

Manatschal, A. (2011). Taking cantonal variations of integration policy seriously – or how to validate international concepts at the subnational comparative level. *Swiss Political Science Review, 17*, 336–357.

Matser, C., Van Oudenhoven, J. P., Askevis-Leherpeux, F., Florack, A., Hannover, B., & Rossier, R. J. (2010). Impact of relative size and language on the attitudes between nations and linguistic groups: The case of Switzerland. *Applied Psychology, 59*, 143–158.

McLaren, L. M. (2003). Anti-immigrant prejudice in Europe: Contact, threat perception, and preferences for the exclusion of migrants. *Social Forces, 81*, 909–936.

Montreuil, A. & Bourhis, R. Y. (2001). Majority acculturation orientations toward "valued" and "devalued" immigrants. *Journal of Cross-Cultural Psychology, 32*, 698–719.

Mummendey, A., Klink, A., & Brown, R. (2001). Nationalism and patriotism: National identification and out-group rejection. *British Journal of Social Psychology, 40*, 159–171.

Niessen, J., Huddleston, T., & Citron, L. (2007). *Migration integration policy index.* Brussels: British Council and Migration Policy Group.

Pettigrew, T. F. (2006). The advantages of multilevel approaches. *Journal of Social Issues, 62*, 615–620.

Pettigrew, T. F. & Tropp, L. R. (2006). A meta-analytic test of intergroup contact theory. *Journal of Personality and Social Psychology, 90*, 751–783.

Pettigrew, T. F. & Tropp, L. R. (2008). How does intergroup contact reduce prejudice? Meta-analytic tests of three mediators. *European Journal of Social Psychology, 38*(6), 922–934.

Piguet, E. (2009). *L'immigration en Suisse: Soixante ans d'entrouverture* (Vol. 24). Lausanne, Switzerland: Collection le savoir suisse.

Pottie-Sherman, Y. & Wilkes, R. (2017). Does size really matter? On the relationship between immigrant group size and anti-immigrant prejudice. *International Migration Review, 51*, 218–250.

Quillian, L. (1995). Prejudice as a response to perceived group threat: Population composition and anti-immigrant and racial prejudice in Europe. *American Sociological Review, 60*, 586–611.

Riek, B. M., Mania, E. W., & Gaertner, S. L. (2006). Intergroup threat and outgroup attitudes: A meta-analytic review. *Personality and Social Psychology Review, 10*, 336–353.

Ruedin, D. (2013). Obtaining party positions on immigration in Switzerland: Comparing different methods. *Swiss Political Science Review, 19*(1), 84–105.

Rydgren, J. (2008). Immigration sceptics, xenophobes or racists? Radical right-wing voting in six West European countries. *European Journal of Political Research, 47*, 737–765.

Sarrasin, O., Fasel, N., R Green, E. G. T., & Helbling, M. (2015). When sexual threat cues shape attitudes toward immigrants: The role of insecurity and benevolent sexism. *Frontiers in Psychology. Personality and Social Psychology*, doi: 10.3389/fpsyg.2015.01033

Sarrasin, O., Green, E. G. T., Fasel, N., Christ, O., Staerklé, C., & Clémence, A. (2012). Opposition to anti-racism laws across Swiss municipalities: A multilevel analysis. *Political Psychology, 33*, 659–681.

Savelkoul, M., Scheepers, P., Tolsma, J., & Hagendoorn, L. (2011). Anti-Muslim attitudes in the Netherlands: Tests of contradictory hypotheses derived from ethnic competition theory and intergroup contact theory. *European Sociological Review, 27*, 741–758.

Scheepers, P., Gijsberts, M., & Coenders, M. (2002). Ethnic exclusion in European countries. Public opposition to civil rights for legal migrants as a response to perceived ethnic threat. *European Sociological Review, 18*, 17–34.

Schlueter, E. & Wagner, U. (2008). Regional differences matter: Examining the dual influence of the regional size of the immigrant population on derogation of immigrants in Europe. *International Journal of Comparative Sociology, 49*(2–3), 153–173.

Schlueter, E., Meuleman, B., & Davidov, E. (2013). Immigrant integration policies and perceived group threat: A multilevel study of 27 Western and Eastern European countries. *Social Science Research, 42*, 670–682.

Schmid, K., Al Ramiah, A., & Hewstone, M. (2014). Neighborhood ethnic diversity and trust: The role of intergroup contact and perceived threat. *Psychological Science, 25*, 665–674.

Schneider, S. L. (2008). Anti-immigrant attitudes in Europe: Outgroup size and perceived ethnic threat. *European Sociological Review, 24*(1), 53–67.

Semyonov, M. & Glikman, A. (2009). Ethnic residential segregation, social contacts, and anti-minority attitudes in European societies. *European Sociological Review, 25*, 693–708.

Semyonov, M., Raijman, R., & Gorodzeisky, A. (2006). The rise of anti-foreigner sentiment in European societies, 1988-2000. *American Sociological Review, 71*, 426–449.

Sibley, C. G., Duckitt, J., Bergh, R., Osborne, D., Perry, R., Asbrock, F., . . . Barlow, F. K. (2013). A dual process model of attitudes towards immigration: Person × residential area effects in a national sample. *Political Psychology, 34*, 553–572.

Sidanius, J. & Pratto, F. (1999). *Social dominance: An intergroup theory of social hierarchy and oppression.* New York: Cambridge University Press.

Spruyt, B. & Elchardus, M. (2012). Are anti-Muslim feelings more widespread than anti-foreigner feelings? Evidence from two split-sample experiments. *Ethnicities, 12*, 800–820.

Stephan, W. G., Renfro, C. L., & Davis, M. D. (2008). The role of threat in intergroup relations. In U. Wagner, L. R. Tropp, G. Finchilescu, & C. Tredoux (Eds.), *Improving intergroup relations: Building on the legacy of Thomas F. Pettigrew.* Oxford: Blackwell.

Stolz, J. (2005). Explaining Islamophobia: A test of four theories based on the case of a Swiss city. *Schweizerische Zeitschrift für Soziologie, 31*, 547–566.

Swiss Federal Statistical Office. (2014). *Integration Indikatoren.* Retrieved from www.bfs.admin.ch/bfs/portal/de/index/themen/01/07/blank/ind43.indicator.430114.430230.html

Swiss Federal Statistical Office. (2017a). *Population by place of birth.* Retrieved from www.bfs.admin.ch/bfs/fr/home/statistiques/population/migration-integration/selon-lieu-naissance.html

Swiss Federal Statistical Office. (2017b). *Population: Panorama.* Retrieved from www.bfs.admin.ch/bfs/fr/home/statistiques/population.assetdetail.2241465.html

Van Assche, J., Roets, A., De Keersmaecker, J., & Van Hiel, A. (2016). The mobilizing effect of right-wing ideological climates: Cross-level interaction effects on different types of outgroup attitudes. *Political Psychology, 38*, 757–776.

Voci, A. & Hewstone, M. (2003). Intergroup contact and prejudice toward immigrants in Italy: The mediational role of anxiety and the moderational role of group salience. *Group Processes & Intergroup Relations, 6*, 37–54.

Wagner, U., Becker, J. C., Christ, O., Pettigrew, T. F., & Schmidt, P. (2010). A longitudinal test of the relation between German nationalism, patriotism, and outgroup derogation. *European Sociological Review, 28*, 319–332.

Wagner, U., Christ, O., Pettigrew, T. F., Stellmacher, J., & Wolf, C. (2006). Prejudice and minority proportion: Contact instead of threat effects. *Social Psychology Quarterly, 69*, 380–390.

20

THE POLITICS AROUND ROMANI MIGRATION

European and national perspectives

Julija Sardelić

The politics of fear around a "poor migrant"

Approximately a decade ago, Frank Furedi (2005) stated that contemporary politics is often reduced to risk management by treating people as vulnerable subjects in need of protection; thus, one of the main approaches of different political authorities across the left–right spectrum is the politics of fear. Since the turn of the millennium, the approach of the politics of fear has been particularly visible in the way different states govern migration. This approach became securitized (Huysmans, 2006) in the cases of migrants belonging to unwanted populations such as Muslims, certain asylum seekers, or even economic migrants. All of these populations fall under the societal trope of what Bauman calls "strangers at our door" (Bauman, 2016). While migration is certainly one of the realities of this age, the politics around migration surpass the frame of this reality. It is also present in the cases where migration numbers are low, but the perceived risk connected to such migration is high (Carens, 2009). This chapter highlights one such instance of the politics around migration: politics connected to the management and governance of mobility of the most marginalized minority in Europe: Romani migrants from different European countries.

This chapter maps discourses on the legal and political governance of the phenomenon of Romani migration at the intersection of European Union and national policies and politics, which I mark as the politics around Romani migration. I claim that such governance is not dealing with Romani migration per se, but usually has a normative connotation, which dubs such migration an anomaly. It focuses on the question of why, after the 2004 and 2007 EU enlargements, the mobility of Romani individuals (especially those perceived as the most socio-economically deprived, socially marginalized, and culturally stigmatized) was increasingly highlighted despite the fact that a very small number of Romani individuals leave their own country and migrate to another place (Cahn & Guild, 2008; Pantea, 2013). In the first section, the chapter argues that the politics around Romani migration were not created only in anticipation of EU enlargement; on the contrary, throughout different historical periods, Romani migration has been scrutinized by policies and politics on unwanted migration (Crowe, 2007; Sardelić, 2017a). Second, it investigates in what ways Roma have been positioned as intra-EU migrants in different EU Member States, such as Italy, France,

Germany, and the UK. It analyzes how different states hinder the freedom of movement of Roma, although it is their right as EU citizens. It then focuses on the legal approaches that have been taken to restrict the access to social welfare benefits of marginalized intra-EU migrants (for example, the case of *Elisabeta Dano v. Jobcenter Leipzig* heard at the EU Court of Justice – CJEU). In the final analysis, the chapter also maps the position of Roma as forced migrants and the accompanying politics of Romani migration. It scrutinizes the case of Romani asylum seekers in Canada who came from Hungary. Furthermore, it offers an overview of how Romani individuals from the post-Yugoslav states found themselves in a tense political relationship between the EU and the countries on its outskirts. Finally, it presents how the so-called refugee crisis in Europe impacted the position of Romani migrants and asylum seekers.

On the basis of the mapping, I claim that the Romani migration(s) was used and abused as a symptom within broader political debates on migration governance. Taken from the perspective of risk management and securitization, the politics around Romani migration in many cases presented the limits of when certain rights should apply to migrants in general, not only to Roma.

Historical accounts of politics around Romani migration

In different folk stories, as well as classical literature, Roma were perceived as frivolous vagrants; this was considered as behavior based on their culture. While it is highly questionable whether Romani culture is inherently nomadic, socio-historical research shows that from the Middle Ages onwards a certain type of securitized approach has existed that could be labelled as politics around Romani (gypsy) migration (Lucassen, Willems, & Cotaar, 1998). In different historical periods, European state formations and their authorities developed a variety of policing approaches for dealing with poor "itinerant" populations. In many cases, gypsies (as they were named by these authorities) were given a certain amount of money so they would not enter a city. For example, historical sources show that, in 1463, the authorities in the city of Bamberg paid "gypsy nomads" a certain amount of money so they would leave the city as soon as possible (Fact Sheets on Romani History, n.d.). In other cases, such as in Lindau in 1482, Roma were forbidden to stay in the territory by a legal decree (ibid). In the most extreme example, while many Roma were forced to flee their homes because of the Thirty Year War (1618–1648), their migration caused even more resentment towards them. In the territory of today's Slovakia, an extreme law was introduced in 1697 according to which all Roma migrants should either be expelled or executed by hanging (ibid). Throughout history, the politics around "gypsy migration" were centred on the abolishment of unwanted societal elements, which in many cases society itself constructed (Lucassen et al., 1998).

Many different scholarly accounts showed that socialist state policies to a large extent limited migration of Romani minorities (Sardelić, 2015; Stewart, 1997). Yet such restrictions should be understood as part of the politics around Romani migration as well as part of the politics of migration in general. Different socialist state systems controlled migration of their citizens, not just Roma (King, 1993). After the fall of the Berlin Wall, the control of Romani migration was framed as a question of human rights attached to an ethnic minority rather than to a socio-economically deprived group (Simhandl, 2008). In anticipation of EU enlargement following acceptance of the former socialist countries, the European Community developed the Copenhagen Criteria for EU membership, which also included a criterion relating to respect of minority rights (Ram, 2013; Spirova & Budd, 2008). Some authors argued that the focus on the position of Roma was not simply because of humanitarian concerns, but was also based on the fear of possible mass migration towards the West (Guiglielmo & Waters, 2005). While mass migration never happened, there are studies that show that Roma have become victims of the new extremist nationalist politics in different post-socialist countries (Stewart, 1997, 2012) as a result of also being perceived by the EU as a privileged minority (Vermeersch, 2012).

EU politics of free movement and the position of Roma as EU citizens

The prospects of the new enlarged EU were also supposed to bring new possibilities for the most marginalized EU citizens (Sobotka & Vermeersch, 2012; Vermeersch, 2006). Many EU institutions, ranging from the European Commission to the EU Agency for Fundamental Rights (FRA), emphasized that the EU has a commitment not only to end discrimination and human rights violations towards Romani EU citizens but also to improve the living conditions and integration of the EU's largest ethnic minority. Following the experience of the Decade of Roma Inclusion (2005–2015), which was led primarily by the Open Society Foundation, the European Union introduced the EU Framework for National Roma Integration Strategies by 2020 (COM 2011/173), each EU Member State should now address the disadvantaged position of citizens who are of Romani background. The communication on integration strategies acknowledged that many Roma who live in the EU are not EU citizens, but third-country nationals, i.e. migrants. It highlighted that countries should focus on tackling discrimination and violation of the human rights of Roma, as well as on improving their living conditions. The responsibility towards Roma was delegated from the EU to the countries themselves. However, there was no particular conclusion on how countries should treat Roma individuals who are EU citizens but reside in an EU Member State other than their own.

The politics of intra-EU Romani migration are always connected to the question of rights associated with EU citizenship (Aradau, Huysmans, Macioti, & Squire, 2013; Parker & Toke, 2013; Ram, 2012). In particular, they are connected to the right of freedom of movement granted to all EU citizens, including Roma. The 2004/38/EC Directive enshrined, with certain limitations, the right of EU citizens to move and reside freely in other EU Member States of which they do not hold citizenship. The EU Citizenship Directive, or the EU Freedom of Movement Directive, carried with it a new promise, even for the Roma. As shown in the previous section, different policies throught history manifestly limited and punished their free movement and migration. Yet, this EU directive also gave them the right to move and reside freely in other countries, seemingly irrespective of their ethnicity or socio-economic status. While previous EU policies were primarily addressing the free movement of workers, the EU Citizenship Directive constructs free movement as a right of an EU citizen. However, the political reality of Romani migration was that different EU Member States tried to limit migration of unwanted EU citizens such as Roma (Sardelić, 2016).

The politics of intra-EU Romani migration, in which Roma were very clearly constructed as unwanted migrants, became evident in Italy after Romania and Bulgaria joined the EU in 2007. According to the European Roma Rights Centre (ERRC, 2013), between 55,000 and 90,000 Romani individuals live in Italy and are not Italian citizens. This represents a small proportion of the approximately 5 million international migrants who currently reside in Italy (Pew Research Center, 2016). The majority of Romani individuals without an Italian passport either came to Italy during the Yugoslav wars (Sigona, 2003; Solimene, 2011) or under the policy of EU freedom of movement. Romani individuals, who fled to Italy because of the Yugoslav wars, still live in camps and face many difficulties in obtaining the most basic personal documents and are on the verge of statelessness (Sigona, 2015). However, in the case of the Roma who came to Italy from Romania and Bulgaria as EU citizens, the Italian state reacted by adopting emergency measures. In 2007, an Italian woman was allegedly killed by a Romanian Roma from one of the so-called "nomad camps." With fomenting anti-Roma public sentiment, different regions in Italy passed the "Nomad Emergency Decree," according to which these camps were to be dismantled and Roma from other EU countries deported and repatriated (Hepworth, 2012). As Hepworth argued, while all EU citizens should be entitled to free movement within the EU, the Italian emergency laws, which collectively addressed all the "nomads" despite murder being an act of a single person, hindered their movement and made them abject citizens. The politics around Romani migration in Italy also made a clear statement about the understanding of EU citizenship in practice: "In regulating and attempting to hinder the mobility of Romanian Roma, these laws (and the practices they subsequently enabled) constituted them as abject *European* citizens, in turn defining the limits of European citizenship" (p. 442).

In another national context, Romani EU migrants were again subject to politics of migration and were treated as abject European citizens, to use Hepworth's term. In France in 2010, the politics of Romani migration became known as *L'Affaire des Roms* (Faure Atger, 2013; Sardelić, 2016). While in theory all EU citizens were entitled to freedom of movement, according to the 2004/38/EC Directive, these rights had certain limitations: EU citizens of other Member States should not pose a threat to public health and order or constitute an unreasonable burden for the host states. As argued elsewhere (Sardelić, 2016), the French authorities used these provisions from the Directive to *irregularize* the position of EU Romani migrants and to make them deportable. In 2010, French president at the time Nicholas Sarkozy called for the dismantling of the camps where Romani migrants resided. In turn, Romani migrants were declared a threat to public health and order, which gave the French authorities the right to expel them. However, such expulsion, which clearly targeted Romani migrants, was criticized by both international organizations and human rights non-governmental organizations (NGOs) (Parker & Toke, 2013; Ram, 2012; Sardelić, 2016). While overt expulsions ceased, the French Office for Immigration and Integration found a more innovative way to send Romani migrants back to their countries of citizenship; this approach was funded by the European Commission (Sardelić, 2016, p. 8). With the notion of voluntary repatriation, the French authorities paid Romani migrants a one-way ticket back to Romania or Bulgaria and also compensated them with a small monetary payment that was supposed to help them start a business in their country of origin (Sardelić, 2016). While occurring in a different era, these politics of Romani migration have an uncanny resemblance to an event that happened many centuries before: in 1463, the authorities of the city of Bamberg paid Romani migrants to leave the city. The practice whereby certain populations are expected to leave seems to occur through the different centuries.

Romani migrants were also caught up in the debate on what social welfare an intra-EU migrant is entitled to. According to Article 24 of Directive 2004/38/EC, EU citizens should be treated on the same terms as apply to the citizens of the country in which they reside. However, this equal treatment is not absolute, but has certain limitations as enshrined in the second paragraph of Article 24:

> By way of derogation from paragraph 1, the host Member State shall not be obliged to confer entitlement to social assistance during the first three months of residence or, where appropriate, the longer period provided for in Article 14(4)(b), nor shall it be obliged, prior to acquisition of the right of permanent residence, to grant

> maintenance aid for studies, including vocational training, consisting in student grants or student loans to persons other than workers, self-employed persons, persons who retain such status and members of their families.

Article 7 also states that intra-EU migrants need to have "sufficient resources" so as to avoid becoming a burden on the social assistance provided in the host country even after the period of three months. In 2013, the question regarding access to social welfare for intra-EU migrants in Germany was referred to the CJEU in Case C-333/13, *Elisabeta Dano v. Jobcenter Leipzig*. Elisabeta Dano was a Romanian citizen. She had resided in Germany since 2010, with her son Florin, in the apartment of her sister, who provided for them materially. In 2011, she applied for social assistance at the Jobcenter Leipzig, but was refused since she was economically inactive. She had not finished primary school, and had oral but not written proficiency in the German language. In November 2014, the CJEU decided that Germany was not obliged to pay social assistance to Dano and her son. Most media outlets in Europe labeled this case a judgment on "benefit tourism." Yet two things were far less discussed in relation to this case. First, it showed that equal treatment of EU citizens is still, in certain areas, conditional on economic grounds. Second, the CJEU court decision – as well as public opinion – identified Dano as a Romanian citizen, but none of the CJEU documents mentioned that she might a be Roma. Yet an assumption that she was Roma was evident in the media based on the following stereotypes: Roma are nomadic (and hence become migrants), do not wish to be gainfully employed, and, as nomads, would rather beg or live on social assistance. Most mainstream European media outlets did not discuss her ethnicity. That was also the case with the European media portal, EURACTIV (2014). However, although the article did not discuss Dano's ethnicity, it was nevertheless accompanied by a photograph featuring a Roma beggar, captioned "Roma panhandler in Sweden, 2013." Some British tabloids, such as the *Daily Mail*, did not shy away from identifying Dano as a Roma: "The Roma gipsy who sparked a crackdown on benefit tourism: Elisabeta Dano, 25, tracked down to German city after finding herself at centre of landmark welfare case" (Bentley, 2014). Dano was considered a Romani migrant only if she fitted the stereotypical characteristics of Roma. As Stefan Luca commented in his ERRC blog: "Around the Western European capitals the ruling was hailed as timely vindication for efforts to stem the tide of 'benefit tourism,' a label often applied to Roma migrants" (Luca, 2014). While EU institutions commit to improving the position of Roma, in this case they failed to discuss the discrimination Roma face in the labor market. The politics of Romani migration were here reduced to a debate on welfare tourism without taking into account any other factors about the position of Romani minorities. As Luca pointed out, while there is no firm definition of "unreasonable burden," and it is more in the domain of politics than law, the position of Romani migrants was abused to curb the rights to social welfare of all intra-EU migrants.

While the case of *Elisabeta Dano vs Jobcenter Leipzig* had a direct impact in Germany, it also echoed in the UK with regard to debates on welfare or benefit tourism. In the beginning of 2014, the UK put an end to the job market restrictions applied to Bulgarian and Romanian citizens, which generated fear that huge numbers of such would migrate to the UK and subsequently overburden both the labor market and the social welfare system. Romani migrants also found themselves in the middle of this debate. A *Guardian* article published on January 1, 2014, titled "Alarm sounded on anti-Roma rhetoric as door opens to more EU workers," identified the anti-Roma rhetoric used by those Members of Parliament (MPs) who formed the Ministerial Working Group on Gypsies and Travellers

> [A] prominent Tory council leader suggested that some Roma are planning to come to the UK to "pickpocket and aggressively beg following the end of labour market controls on the two Eastern European countries." On Tuesday, ahead of the restriction expiring at midnight, Philippa Roe, leader of Westminster City Council, blamed Roma in central London of already causing "a massive amount of disruption and low-level crime", including defecating on doorsteps. Speaking on the BBC, she called for more limits on benefits for new arrivals from EU countries.
>
> *(Mason & Malik, 2014)*

Alongside the rising voice of the UK Independence Party (UKIP) in 2014, David Cameron, then Conservative Prime Minister, initiated a policy to curb the benefit entitlements of EU migrants. In the beginning of 2016, just before the UK's EU membership referendum, he negotiated the so-called "emergency brake," according to which EU migrants in the UK have to work and contribute to the UK tax system for four years before they are entitled to social housing and welfare benefits. Even before these negotiations, party colleague Theresa May had emphasized that the problem of "benefit tourism" could have a devastating impact on the UK social welfare system. While discussing benefit tourism, proponents of limiting intra-EU free movement often quoted the case of Lavinia Olmazu. Olmazu was a Romanian human rights activist who was imprisoned for benefit fraud amounting to £2.9 million. According to available sources, she was sentenced because she was involved in the forging of employment documents for 172 Romanian Roma individuals, who could – on the basis of these documents – claim benefits in the UK. According to newspaper sources, this case was also quoted by then Home Secretary, Theresa May. Many academic studies, however, including one conducted by the Centre for Research and Analysis of Migration (CReAM), University College London (UCL), showed that benefit tourism is in fact negligible when compared to the £20 billion that EU migrants had contributed to the UK economy in only one decade. UCL's study also revealed that EU migrants are – on average – better educated than UK citizens (Dustman & Frattini, 2014). May was later accused by other MPs of manipulating crucial data on EU migration in order to make benefit tourism seem like a bigger problem than it is in reality (Agerholm, 2016) and undermining the benefits EU migrants bring to UK society in order to build a stronger argument for Brexit. Although Olmezu was an isolated case and Roma themselves were the victims, they were used as scapegoats to make a case against intra-EU migration and consequentially also to demonstrate why the UK should stop being an EU Member State.

Roma as asylum seekers and the politics around forced migration

The politics around Romani migration were not limited to the case of intra-EU migration, but were also evident when dealing with forced migration; that is, Romani individuals with the status of asylum seekers and forced migrants entitled to international protection (which is usually different to refugee status). One such case that received significant media attention involved Romani individuals from the Czech Republic and Hungary, who sought asylum in Canada. Before the 1990s, citizens of different socialist states sought asylum in Canada citing anti-communism as the grounds of their persecution; they were duly granted asylum as they were perceived to be fleeing non-democratic states. According to Lee (2000), these individuals also included those who belonged to Romani minorities but their ethnicity was not highlighted. This changed after the collapse of socialism in the 1990s (ibid). Since then, Romani migrants have sought asylum on the basis of racial and ethnic persecution. In Canada, the cases of Romani asylum seekers were individually processed until 1997. In 1997, approximately 1,500 asylum seekers from the Czech Republic came to Canada, at which point the national Canadian media started reporting on "gypsy invasion." Media reports questioned whether Roma are in Canada on economic grounds rather than as the result of persecution and also claimed they represented a drain on the economy. While previously citizens of the Czech Republic and Hungary did not require a visa to enter Canada, this "incident" led to reintroduction of visas for the two countries in question (Lee, 2000; Toth, 2010).

The case of Romani asylum seekers in Canada became more complicated after the Czech Republic and Hungary joined the EU in 2004. To ensure the Canada–EU free trade agreement, Canada agreed to abolish visa restriction for the two countries in question (Beaudoin, Danch, & Rehaag, 2015; Levin-Rasky, Beaudoin, & St Clair, 2014). Both countries had to comply with the Copenhagen Criteria, according to which they had to demonstrate their respect for minority rights. In the international arena, that meant that these countries were designated as safe and free from minority persecution. Yet this became questionable in 2008 in Hungary, when an organized extremist group committed a series of murders in which Roma were targeted on the basis of their ethnic group. With the visa restriction lifted, the number of asylum seekers from Hungary self-identifying as belonging to Romani minorities increased. As a result of the 2008 murders, they could legitimately claim persecution on the basis of race in Hungary. Yet once again they were initially proclaimed as "bogus" asylum seekers as no clear definition existed regarding discrimination and persecution in their case (Beaudoin et al., 2015). To decrease the number of asylum seekers from Hungary, the Canadian government decided to erect billboards in the Hungarian town of Miskolc discouraging Roma from seeking asylum in Canada. While the Canadian press demonstrated a generally negative attitude toward Roma (Levin-Rasky et al., 2014), there was another issue at stake in the case of the politics around Romani migration. Granting asylum to Romani citizens of Hungary would effectively mean that a country like Canada granted asylum to EU citizens. It would also mean that a particular part of the EU would be internationally recognized as unsafe for minorities and, hence, would question EU policies relating to respect for diversity and protection of vulnerable minorities such as Roma. However, in 2015 Canadian politics in relation to Romani migration changed slightly, in favor of Romani asylum seekers: although there was still no en masse acceptance that Romani individuals can be legitimate asylum seekers, a paper reported that the Canadian Immigration and Refugee Board accepted 68 percent more asylum seekers from Hungary in 2014 as evidence accumulated that Hungary was not a safe country for Roma (Romea, 2015). Still, accepting Romani asylum seekers in Canada remained a controversial issue (Beudoin, Danch, & Rehaag, 2015, p. 771):

> [O]ver 11,000 Hungarians made refugee claims in Canada, primarily on the basis that they feared persecution on account of their Romani ethnicity. While hundreds succeeded with their refugee claims, most did not. Instead, they encountered racist rhetoric that drew on stereotypes about Roma being fraudsters, beggars, and criminals, and which presented Hungarian Romani refugee claimants as "bogus." These stereotypes have now been enshrined in Canada's new refugee-determination process, which limits the procedural and substantive rights of refugee claimants from designated countries of origin, including Hungary, on the theory that asylum seekers from these countries are taking advantage of Canadian generosity.

Another example of the complex politics surrounding Romani migration is connected to the relations between the EU and the non-EU former Yugoslav states on its margins. The post-Yugoslav conflicts and subsequent state disintegration also profoundly affected the position of Roma, but it was only with the EU membership negotiations and visa liberalization (Kacarska, 2012; Sardelić, 2015) that their position came under the spotlight. As previously argued (Sardelić, 2017a), the migration of Roma has a longer history and is not simply connected to Yugoslav disintegration. During the Yugoslav period, a number of Roma were already migrating to some Western European states, notably Germany, as Yugoslav migrant workers. Yugoslavia was the only socialist country that concluded bilateral agreements on temporary workers with a few European Community countries and this was one of the instruments for addressing the unemployment of rural populations as well as marginalized minorities such as Roma. While Roma were not nominally involved in the post-Yugoslav conflicts, they were invisible victims of it and became forcedly displaced for longer periods. Because births were not registered during the conflict, many Romani forced migrants were left without essential identification documents and fell into the group of legally invisible persons (Sardelić, 2015). During the Schengen visa liberalization process for some of the western Balkan countries such as Macedonia and Serbia, one of the requirements was to provide all citizens with identification documents (Kacarska, 2012), which would effectively mean solving the position of legally invisible Roma. When the visa restrictions were lifted in 2010, the number of asylum seekers in the EU from the two countries in question increased. The majority of these asylum seekers self-identified as Roma (Sardelić, 2017b). This generated a debate in the European Parliament on the possibility of reintroducing visa requirements for Serbia and Macedonia. The result of this debate was a decision to reintroduce the visa-free suspension mechanism in case a large number of Romani asylum seekers continued to approach EU countries. The European Parliament requested Serbia and Macedonia to improve the position of their minorities so they would no longer seek asylum in the EU. In turn, the Serbian government placed tri-lingual posters (in Serbian, Albanian, and Romani) at border crossings and airports entitled, "I do not want to seek asylum in the EU." The posters explained how Serbia respects minority rights and does not discriminate against minorities. However, both Serbia and Macedonia were aware that the integration of marginalized Romani minorities was a long-term process and could not be a quick solution to prevent Roma from seeking asylum in the EU. Macedonian border patrols therefore started to apply racial profiling at the borders, thereby preventing certain Romani individuals from leaving their country on the basis of their skin colour, last name, and address. Romani individuals who were citizens of Serbia and Macedonia thus found themselves in more politicized juggling between the EU and the post-Yugoslav states. The European Parliament stated that if the Serbian and Macedonian authorities wanted to maintain freedom of movement for all of their citizens, they needed to improve the position of their minority citizens. However, to maintain the visa-free regime for all citizens, these countries started hindering the free movement of some of them, that is, Romani citizens.

The politics of Romani migration were also indirectly impacted by the so-called European refugee crisis (Sardelić, 2017) in several different ways. While Germany was accepting the largest number of Syrian refugees in the autumn of 2015, it simultaneously changed its asylum law by adding all western Balkan states to the list of safe third countries. Many of the previous forced migrants and asylum seekers from these countries were identified as Roma and were therefore deemed to have returned to their country of origin. Such returns transpired to be problematic because it was questionable whether, first, these countries were indeed safe for Roma to be returned to, and, second, they could still be considered as countries of origin: many of them had started families in destination countries and their children had never been to what were considered their countries of origin. Romani migrants were, however, caught up in the politics of EU accession and visa liberalization even before, which are usually connected to agreements on repatriation of one's own citizens.

Conclusion

In this chapter I analyzed different examples highlighting the intersection between European and national perspectives on the politics around Romani minorities. In the first section of the chapter I tried to show that a historical common thread views Romani migration as migration of unwanted poor migrants. This view persists to the present day despite the fact that the legal framework has changed. In the EU, freedom of movement was developed as a right of all citizens. Yet the examples from the politics of Romani migration show that states developed different approaches to limit this right by excluding those who are perceived as a burden on the economy and the social welfare system rather than as contributors to them (although, in most instances wrongfully so). The perceived position of Romani migrants (as social benefit abusers) is manipulated to craft broader politics on migration and to limit the rights of all migrants, not just the Roma themselves. Similarly, as in the case of intra-EU migration, the politics around Romani migration are symptomatic of broader questions on the politics of forced migration. This is shown by the examples of Romani asylum seekers fleeing Hungary to Canada and fleeing the post-Yugoslav space towards EU countries. Both raise a question of the notion of a safe country (within and outside the EU) and the individualized approach to asylum claims. Yet the politics around Romani migration are not only a symptom of broader politics around migration – they are also a symptom of the deeply rooted stereotypes applied to Roma and the prejudice leveled against them, which are the basis of discrimination and persecution. It reveals that previous inclusion policies have not ensured equal treatment of Roma or have simply failed completely.

References

Agerholm, H. (2016, September 28). Theresa May accused of manipulating crucial immigration report before Brexit vote. *Independent*. Retrieved from www.independent.co.uk/news/brexit-immigration-theresa-may-report-liberal-democrats-accuse-pm-manipulation-a7334466.html

Aradau, C., Huysmans, J., Macioti, P., & Squire, V. (2013). Mobility interrogating free movement: Roma acts of European citizenship. In E. Isin & M. Saward (Eds.), *Enacting European citizenship* (pp. 132–154). Cambridge: Cambridge University Press.

Bauman, Z. (2016). *Strangers at our door*. Cambridge: Polity Press.

Beaudoin, J., Danch, J., & Rehaag, S. (2015). No refugee: Hungarian Romani refugee claimants in Canada. *Osgoode Hall Law Journal, 52*, 705–774.

Bentley, P. (2014, November 15). The Roma gipsy who sparked a crackdown on benefit tourism: Elisabeta Dano, 25, tracked down to German city after finding herself at centre of landmark welfare case. *Daily Mail*. Retrieved from www.dailymail.co.uk/news/article-2835442/The-Roma-gipsy-sparked-crackdown-benefit-tourism-Elisabeta-Dano-25-tracked-German-city-finding-centre-landmark-welfare-case.html

Cahn, C., & Guild, E. (2008, December 10). *Recent migration of Roma in Europe*. Retrieved from www.gfmd.org/recent-migration-roma-europe-claude-cahn-and-elspeth-guild

Carens, J. (2009). Fear versus fairness: Migration, citizenship and the transformation of political community. In N. Holtug, K. Lippert-Rasmussen, & S. Lægaard (Eds.), *Nationalism and multiculturalism in a world of immigration* (pp. 151–173). London: Palgrave Macmillan.

Crowe, D. M. (2007). *A history of the gypsies of Eastern Europe and Russia*. New York: Palgrave Macmillan.

Dustmann, C., & Frattini, T. (2014). The fiscal effects of immigration to the UK. *Economic Journal, 124*, 593–643.

EURACTIV. (2014, November 12). *EU judges rule against "welfare tourists" in nod to Cameron*. Retrieved from www.euractiv.com/section/justice-home-affairs/news/eu-judges-rule-against-welfare-tourists-in-nod-to-cameron/

Fact Sheets on Romani History. (n.d.). Retrieved from http://romafacts.uni-graz.at/index.php/history/general-introduction/general-introduction

Faure Atger, A. (2013). European citizenship revealed: Sites, actors and Roma access to justice in the EU. In E. Isin & M. Saward. (Eds.), *Enacting European citizenship* (pp. 178–194). Cambridge: Cambridge University Press.

Furedi, F. (2005). *The politics of fear: Beyond left and right*. London: Continuum.

Guglielmo, R., & Waters, T. W. (2005). Migrating towards minority status: Shifting European policy towards Roma. *Journal of Common Market Studies, 43*, 763–785.

Hepworth, K. (2012). Abject citizens: Italian "Nomad emergencies" and the deportability of Romanian Roma. *Citizenship Studies, 16*, 431–449.

Huysmans, J. (2006). *The politics of insecurity: Fear, migration and asylum in the EU*. London: Routledge.

Kacarska, S. (2012). *Europeanisation through mobility: Visa liberalisation and citizenship regimes in Western Balkans*. CITSEE Working Paper No. 2012/21. Edinburgh: Edinburgh University Press.

King, R. (1993). From another place: Migration and the politics of culture. *Urban Studies, 30*, 1612–1613.

Lee, R. (2000). Post-communism Romani migration to Canada. *Cambridge International Relations Review, 13*(2), 51–70.

Levin-Rasky, C., Beaudoin, J., & St Clair, P. (2014). The exclusion of Roma claimants in Canadian refugee policy. *Patterns of Prejudice, 48*, 67–93.

Luca, S. (2014, December 19). *EU court ruling on "benefit tourism" – Is Dano about law or politics?* Retrieved from www.errc.org/blog/eu-court-ruling-on-benefit-tourism-%E2%80%93-is-dano-about-law-or-politics/48

Lucassen, L., Willems, W., & Cottaar, A. (1998). *Gypsies and other itinerant groups*. Basingstoke: Macmillan.

Mason, R., & Shiv, M. (2014). Alarm sounded on anti-Roma rhetoric as door opens to more EU workers. *The Guardian*. Retrieved from www.theguardian.com/uk-news/2013/dec/31/mps-anti-roma-rhetoric-romania-bulgaria

Parker, O., & Toke, D. (2013). The politics of a multi-level citizenship: French republicanism, Roma mobility and the EU. *Global Society, 27*, 360–378.

Pew Research Center. (2016). *International migrants by country*. Retrieved from www.pewglobal.org/interactives/migration-tables/

Ram, M. H. (2012). Lost in transition? Europeanization and the Roma. *L'europe En Formation, 364*, 417.

Ram, M. H. (2013). European integration, migration and representation: The case of Roma in France. *Ethnopolitics, 13*, 203–224.

Romea, C. Z. (2015, August 26). Canada now accepting more Roma asylum-seekers from Hungary as evidence of persecution accumulates. *Romeacz*. Retrieved from www.romea.cz/en/news/world/canada-now-accepting-more-roma-asylum-seekers-from-hungary-as-evidence-of-persecution-accumulates

Sardelić, J. (2015). Romani minorities and uneven citizenship access in the post-Yugoslav space. *Ethnopolitics, 14*, 159–179.

Sardelić, J. (2016). The position and agency of the "irregularized": Romani migrants as European semi-citizens. *Politics, 37*, 332–346.

Sardelić, J. (2017a). Romani minorities in war conflicts and refugee crises of the (post)-Yugoslav space: A comparative socio-historical perspective. *Roma Rights, 1*, 35–41.

Sardelić, J. (2017b). In and out from the European margins: Reshuffling mobilities and legal statuses of Romani minorities between the post-Yugoslav space and the European Union. *Social Identities*, 1–16.

Sigona, N. (2003). How can a "nomad" be a "refugee"? Kosovo Roma and labelling policy in Italy. *Sociology, 37*, 69–79.

Sigona, N. (2015). Everyday statelessness in Italy: Status, rights, and camps. *Ethnic and Racial Studies, 39*, 263–279.

Simhandl, K. (2008). Beyond boundaries? Comparing the construction of the political categories "Gypsies" and "Roma" before and after EU enlargement. In N. Sigona & N. Trehan (Eds.), *Romani politics in contemporary Europe: Poverty, ethnic mobilization and the neoliberal order* (pp. 72–93). Basingstoke: Palgrave Macmillan.

Sobotka, E., & Vermeersch, P. (2012). Governing human rights and Roma inclusion: Can the EU be a catalyst for local social change? *Human Rights Quarterly, 34*, 800–822.

Solimene, M. (2011). "These Romanians have ruined Italy": Xoraxané Romá, Romanian Roma and Rome. *Journal of Modern Italian Studies, 16*, 637–651.

Spirova, M., & Budd, D. (2008). The EU accession process and the Roma minorities in new and soon-to-be member states. *Comparative European Politics, 6*, 81–101.

Stewart, M. (1997). *The time of the gypsies*. Boulder, CO: Westview Press.

Stewart, M. (2012). *The gypsy "menace."* New York: Columbia University Press.

Toth, J. (2010, November 5). *The incomprehensible flow of Roma asylum-seekers from the Czech Republic and Hungary to Canada*. Retrieved from www.ceps.eu/publications/incomprehensible-flow-roma-asylum-seekers-czech-republic-and-hungary-canada

Vermeersch, P. (2006). *The Romani movement*. New York: Berghahn Books.

Vermeersch, P. (2012). Reframing the Roma: EU initiatives and the politics of reinterpretation. *Journal of Ethnic and Migration Studies, 38*, 1195–1212.

21

EXPLORING THE RELATIONSHIP BETWEEN ACCULTURATION PREFERENCES, THREAT, INTERGROUP CONTACT, AND PREJUDICE TOWARD IMMIGRANTS IN FINLAND

Elvis Nshom Ngwayuh & Stephen M. Croucher

Immigration is a critical issue in most contemporary societies. In 2015 alone, more than 1 million refugees made their way to Europe (BBC, 2015). According to a 2017 Eurostat report, "In 2016, 1,204,300 first time asylum seekers applied for international protection in the Member States of the European Union (EU)." Rising irregular immigration is a critical political, economic, and social issue in the European Union. In Finland, immigration has been received with mixed feelings. Attitudes in Finland, as well as in many other European countries, toward immigrants have hardened during this crisis (BBC, 2015). The current political, economic, and social situation surrounding migration to Europe points to the necessity for empirically and theoretically grounded research that helps us understand important aspects of the relationship between immigrants and members of the host societies. Under investigation in this study is the relationship between the immigrant acculturation preferences (assimilation/integration) of majority Finnish adolescentstoward, the perceived threat (realistic threat and symbolic threat) posed by immigrants, prejudice toward immigrants, and intergroup contact. By studying these relationships among Finnish adolescents in particular, we gain insights into important aspects of the relationships between Finns and immigrants living in Finland from the majority's perspective. This is especially useful for understanding majority attitudes toward the integration of immigrants into Finnish society.

The Finnish context is particularly important and unique because Finland has traditionally been a homogeneous country and a country of emigration excluded from the challenges of mass immigration (Jasinskaja-Lahti, 2000). However, things have changed. For example, the immigrant population in Finland increased threefold from 1990 to 2002 (Ervasti, 2004) and continues to rise. "The share of people with foreign background in Finland's population has grown from 0.8 to 6.2% in the course of 1990 to 2015" (Statistics Finland, 2015). Currently, there are more than 200,000 immigrants living in Finland (ibid), representing about 6 percent of the population (Statistics Finland, 2017).

According to the BBC (2015), the current surge in immigration has provoked vibrant internal discussion and debate on how to respond to immigration challenges in Finland. These discussions intensified when the Finnish government said it would take double the number of asylum seekers, rising from 15,000 to 30,000. This decision was highly criticized by the coalition anti-immigration True-Finns party. For example, one True-Finns Member of Parliament (MP) said immigrants, particularly Muslim immigrants, did not acculturate into Finnish society. Another MP from the same political party described multiculturalism as a nightmare on his social media page. His statement sparked public debate and concerns about immigration and how immigrants should acculturate. A clear divide has grown in Finland, with some people being for and others against cultural maintenance or pluralism. Some Finnish cities have hosted marches in favor of multiculturalism and others against it.

Apart from issues of cultural plurality, other concerns voiced by Finns are often related to the threat immigrants pose to Finnish society. For example, some Finns believe immigration will lead to more crime, fewer benefits for the unemployed, increased taxes, and increased government spending (ibid). Clearly, these fears are symbolic or realistic in nature. Nshom and Croucher (2017) carried out an empirical investigation into this issue and found that Finnish adolescents are more likely to perceive immigrants as a realistic threat and a symbolic threat than to negatively stereotype them. In the current study, we argue that the immigrant acculturation preferences (assimilation/integration) of majority Finnish adolescents can be associated with the threat they perceive immigrants to pose to Finnish society. Understanding the relationships between the perceived threat (realistic threat and symbolic threat) posed by immigrants, immigrant acculturation preferences (assimilation and integration) of majority Finnstoward, and prejudice toward immigrants in Finland is not only crucial but also timely amidst the current immigration crisis and the rhetoric in Europe – and Finland in particular.

Acculturation preferences

Brown and Zagefka (2011, p. 131) defined acculturation as "the processes by which different cultural groups adapt to one another." The question of how people prefer to acculturate has been examined with respect to two main factors: cultural maintenance and participation or contact with other groups. Cultural maintenance refers to the extent to which a person desires to maintain important elements of their culture and identity. Contact or participation is the extent to which a person desires to have contact and become involved with other groups (Berry, 1997, 2001). According to Brown and Zagefka (2011), a combination of these two factors indicates the extent to which a minority culture is accepted and recognized. According to Berry (1997, 2001, 2005), the interplay between these two factors produces four acculturation preferences or strategies: assimilation, integration, separation, and marginalization.

Within the context of this study, and from the majority's perspective, *assimilation* is a preferred strategy of acculturation in relation toward immigrants whereby Finns do not want immigrants to maintain their cultural identity but, instead, want them to maintain contact and participation with Finns. On the other hand, if Finns want immigrants to maintain their cultural identity to some degree while at the same time striving to participate as an integral part of the larger Finnish society, it implies Finns prefer *integration* on the part oftoward immigrants. *Separation* is preferred if Finns think it is important for immigrants to maintain their cultural identity and at the same time avoid contact and involvement with and participation with larger Finnish society. Lastly, *marginalization* is preferred if Finns place no value on cultural maintenance or participation with larger Finnish society. In this study, we focus particularly on assimilation and integration. The acculturation debate in Finland has centered on a preference for assimilationist or integrationist views (BBC, 2015). Moreover, assimilation and integration are considered the most popular strategies among dominant and non-dominant groups (Callens, Meulleman, & Valentova, 2014; Van Oudenhoven & Eisses, 1998). While the literature on acculturation preferences of immigrant groups is exhaustive, studies on dominant or majority group preferences toward minority groups is lacking (Zagefka, Tip, González, Brown, & Cinnirella, 2012).

Integrated threat theory (ITT)

Since 2011, many European Union countries such as Finland have witnessed an outbreak of anti-immigrant demonstrations (EURACTIVE, 2015; Yle, 2015). In such circumstances, negative attitudes such as prejudice from majority members are often motivated by the threat immigrants are perceived to pose to the wider society (Stephan, Diaz-Looving, & Duran, 2000). Within the context of this study, prejudice is:

> [a]n aversive or hostile attitude toward a person who belongs to a group, simply because he belongs to that group, and is therefore presumed to have the objectionable qualities ascribed to the group ... Ethnic prejudice is an antipathy based upon a faulty and inflexible generalization. It may be felt or expressed; it may be directed toward a group as a whole, or toward an individual because he is a member of that group.
>
> *(Allport, 1954, p. 7)*

According to integrated threat theory (ITT; Stephan & Stephan, 1996, 2000; Stephan, Ybarra, Martinez, Schwarzwald, & Turk-Kaspa, 1998), these threats can be classified as realistic, symbolic, negative stereotype, or intergroup anxiety. *Realistic threats* are threats to the economic and physical wellbeing and political power of the ingroup. For instance, if Finns believe immigrants are taking their houses and jobs and causing a rise in unemployment, it is a perceived realistic threat. *Symbolic threats* are threats to the way of life, culture, language, and beliefs of the ingroup. For example, immigrants from Muslim countries, in particular, are often perceived as a symbolic threat to Christian Europe on the basis of religious differences (Croucher, 2013; Jaakkola, 2009). *Negative stereotype* are fears that arise from the negative stereotypical perceptions the ingroup has of an outgroup. During interaction, they may expect negative consequences (Stephan & Stephan, 2000). For example, if Finns think immigrants are violent and exploitative, they (Finns) may expect a violent and exploitative interaction with the immigrant outgroup. Lastly, *intergroup anxiety* refers to anxiety that may arise during interaction between ingroup members and outgroup members, especially if the groups have a history of antagonism.

The conceptualization of negative stereotypes and intergroup anxiety have been discussed as threat antecedents of prejudice (see Redmond, 2011; Riek, Mania, & Gaertner, 2006). The ITT model has since been modified and realistic threat and symbolic threat have been retained as the two main threats explaining negative attitudes toward immigrants and minorities (Stephan & Renfro, 2002; Stephan, Ybarra, & Rios Morrison, 2009). In this study, we utilize the most recent conceptualization of ITT, with realistic and symbolic threats as the those explaining social attitudes (Stephan et al., 2009). In addition, research has shown that Finnish adolescents are more likely to perceive immigrants as symbolic and realistic threats than to negatively stereotype them (Nshom & Croucher, 2017). In their study, Nshom and Croucher (2017) found that perceived threat (realistic and symbolic threats) and prejudice toward immigrants were prevalent in Finland. However, research has not considered the extent to which these threats are associated with the acculturation preferences of majority Finns toward immigrants.

Research hypotheses

Research in the field of acculturation suggests there exists a relationship between acculturation preferences, perceived threat, and attitudes toward minorities (e.g., Brown & Zagefka, 2011; Ljujic, Vedder, Dekker, & Van Gael, 2012; Piontkowski, Rohmann, & Florack, 2002; van Osch & Breugelmans, 2012; Zagefka, Gonzalez, Brown, & Cinirella, 2012). According to Aronson and Brown (2013), a preference for cultural maintenance and contact (integration) among majority members predicts the most favorable social attitudes toward immigrants. This is, of course, not surprising because "if majority members endorse culture maintenance as their preferred strategy for the minority group, then it implies an acceptance of that minority group culture. This is likely to lead to more tolerant intergroup attitudes" (Brown & Zagefka, 2011, p. 142).

In another study, Zick, Wagner, Dick, and Petzel (2001), found assimilation to be positively related to prejudice and discriminatory behavior, and integration to be negatively correlated with prejudice in a number of samples. Piontkowskia, Floracka, Hoelkera, and Obdrzälek (2000) also studied acculturation preferences among majority members in Germany, Slovakia, and Switzerland and observed that integration was less likely to be associated with ingroup bias and more likely to be associated with perceived intergroup similarity. In another study carried out in Germany, integration was found to be associated with more favorable intergroup relations between majority and minority members (Zagefka & Brown, 2002). Moreover, Kim (1988) and Piontkowskia et al. (2000) also argued that, if the majority perceives the minority to be different or threatening, they are likely to pressurize the minority group to assimilate. In the same light, Piontkowskia et al. (2000, p. 7) stated:

> If the dominant group thinks the non-dominant group to be a greater enrichment than a threat, an integration attitude is probable. On the other hand, if the perceived threat exceeds the perceived enrichment, separation or marginalization will be preferred. Assimilation could also be an option, if the dominant group wants to control the resources.

For instance, Callens, Meuleman, and Valentova (2015) studied acculturation preference (assimilation and integration) in relation toward immigrants in Luxembourg and found that assimilation was positively related to threat while integration was negatively related to threat. Based on the findings of their study, it was concluded that, "when the majority feels that the minority group is threatening their economic, cultural and future societal position, they become less open to diversity and prefer assimilative integration strategies" (p. 19). In fact, Piontkowskia et al. (2000) found in their study that those who scored lower on cultural maintenance of minority culture and social contact and participation with host culture (integration) felt more threatened bytoward minorities. Gonzalez, Verkuyten, Weesie, and Poppe (2008), on the other hand, found that Dutch adolescents who scored higher on integrationist attitudes felt less threatened by and displayed less prejudice toward culturally distinct minorities.

Studies in Finland suggest that majority Finnish adolescents have prejudicial attitudes toward immigrants and that the perception of threat (realistic threat and symbolic threat) from immigrants is high (Nshom & Croucher, 2017). In the current study, we attempt to understand the extent to which threat and prejudice are related to their acculturation preferences in relation toward immigrants amidst the ongoing rhetoric on multiculturalism in Finland. It is expected, based on previous findings, that those who prefer assimilation will experience greater feelings of threat (realistic and symbolic threats) while those who prefer integration will experience less. Similarly, it is expected that those who prefer assimilation will feel more prejudice toward immigrants while those who prefer integration will feel less. Based on these expectations, the following hypotheses are posed:

H1a: Preference for assimilation is positively related to levels of threat toward immigrants.
H1b: Preference for integration is negatively related to levels of threat toward immigrants.
H2a: Preference for assimilation is positively related to feelings of prejudice toward immigrants.
H2b: Preference for integration is negatively related to feelings of prejudice toward immigrants.

In addition to these hypotheses, Ford (2012) argued that adolescents in Europe might be more tolerant of cultural diversity and multiculturalism in response to increased possibilities for intergroup contact with immigrants. Immigration is on the rise and, as a result, Europe is becoming more culturally diverse.

In Finland, the number of people with foreign backgrounds has grown significantly since 1990 (Statistics Finland, 2015). European adolescents have more opportunities for intergroup contact. Adolescents experience diversity more than do other age groups (Ford, 2012). Intergroup contact can be direct or indirect. According to Harwood (2008), there are three main sources of indirect contact: media contact effects, knowledge of ingroup friend's intergroup relationship, and broader cultural contact. There is sufficient research pointing to the notion that intergroup contact between majority and minority members leads to more favorable social attitudes and acceptance of immigrant groups (Pettigrew & Tropp, 2006, 2008). Researchers have argued that not all contact has the ability to influence social attitudes. Brown and Hewstone (2005) observed that intergroup contact would affect attitudes and stereotypes only when the following conditions are in place: (1) group membership is salient during the interaction, (2) the communicator views the outgroup member as typical of the stereotyped group, (3) interaction with the outgroup member is sufficiently frequent, and (4) interaction with the outgroup member is assessed positively by the communicator.

However, the ability of intergroup contact to positively affect the perception of threat and prejudice in relation toward outgroups such as immigrants has been supported by an abundance of research (see González et al., 2008; Riek et al., 2006; Stephan, Diaz-Loving, & Duran, 2000). Research on acculturation also suggests that the more contact an individual has with an outgroup, the more likely they are to support integrationist tendencies such as diversity, cultural pluralism, or multiculturalism (Aronson & Brown, 2013; Callens et al., 2015; González et al., 2008; Piontkowski et al., 2002; Verkuyten & Martinovic, 2006; Ward & Masgoret, 2006). For instance, Callens et al. (2015) found that, "having more intense friendship contact leads to a reduction in threat perceptions and then again to less support for assimilation and more support for multiculturalism" (pp. 18–19). This suggests that intergroup contact has a significant effect on the relationship between threat and acculturation preferences. In the current study, we expect contact with immigrants to be negatively associated with a preference for assimilation and to be positively associated with a preference for integration. In addition, it is expected that intergroup contact will moderate the relationship between perceived threat and acculturation preferences, and the relationship between acculturation preferences and prejudice. For this reason, the following hypotheses are proposed:*H3a*: Intergroup contact will moderate the relationship between perceived threat and acculturation preferences.*H3b*: Intergroup contact will moderate the relationship between acculturation preferences and prejudice.

Method

Participants and procedures

Data were collected from Finnish adolescents between grades six to upper secondary school from three Finnish cities: Jyväskylä, Helsinki, and Joensuu. Participants' ages ranged from 11 to 19 years and all were native Finns. The data were collected only after the principal researcher obtained the required official authorization from the city councils and educational institutions. After the necessary authorization was obtained, the principal researcher then organized data collection trips to the various schools. Data were collected through self-administered questionnaires and the principal researcher ensured it conformed to the established institutional ethical guidelines. Completing the questionnaire took 10 to 15 minutes. Before participation, participants were introduced to the purpose of the study and were told participation was voluntary, anonymous, and without charge. A pre-test was conducted to make sure participants fully understood the questions. The results of the pre-test indicated that the questions were understood correctly. In total, there were 795 participants in this study. Of these, 459 (57.7 percent) were female and 336 (42.3 percent) were male.

Measures

The questionnaire used in this study included: demographics, a measure of symbolic threat (González et al., 2008), a measure of realistic threat (González et al., 2008), a measure of prejudice (Stephan & Stephan, 2000), a measure of intergroup contact (González et al., 2008), a measure of assimilation (Berry, Phinney, Sam, & Vedder, 2006), and a measure of integration (Berry et al., 2006). The original survey was in English but was translated/back-translated into Finnish by native speakers of Finnish-English. See Table 21.1 for the means, standard deviations, correlations, alphas, and kappas for the study variables.

Table 21.1 Means, standard deviations, correlations, and alpha reliabilities for study variables

Variable	*M*	*SD*	*α*	*(1)*	*(2)*	*(3)*	*(4)*	*(5)*	*(6)*
(1) Realistic threat	3.60	1.23	0.89	–					
(2) Symbolic threat	3.74	1.32	0.95	0.82**	–				
(3) Assimilation	2.57	1.03	0.73	−0.19**	−0.18**				
(4) Integration	4.21	0.87	0.85	0.23**	0.24**	−0.06	-		
(5) Prejudice	3.85	0.69	0.71	0.21**	0.25**	−0.38**	0.42**	–	
(6) Contact	1.80	0.67	0.73	0.11**	0.08*	−0.16**	0.17**	0.24**	–

*$p < 0.05$; **$p < 0.01$.

Realistic threat

To measure realistic threat, participants were asked to respond to three statements: "Because of the presence of immigrants, Finns have more difficulty finding a job," "Because of the presence of immigrants; Finns have more difficulty finding a house," and "Because of the presence of immigrants, unemployment in Finland is increasing." This scale was adapted from González et al. (2008) and showed an alpha reliability of 0.80 in that study and an alpha reliability of 0.89 in the current study. Responses ranged from (1) strongly disagree to (5) strongly agree, and higher scores meant more perceived threat and lower scores meant less perceived threat.

Symbolic threat

For symbolic threats, participants were given three statements adapted from González et al. (2008): "Finnish identity/culture is threatened because there are too many immigrants today," "Finnish norms and values are threatened because of the presence of immigrants today," and "Immigrants are a threat to Finnish culture." This scale in the original González et al. study showed an alpha reliability of 0.89 and an alpha reliability of 0.85 in the current study. Responses ranged from (1) strongly disagree to (5) strongly agree, and higher scores meant more perceived threat and lower scores meant less perceived threat.

Prejudice

To measure prejudicial feelings, participants were given six evaluative and emotional reactions adapted from Stephan and Stephan (2000) and were asked to indicate the extent to which these items reflected how they felt toward immigrants: "Acceptance, approval, admiration, antipathy, disdain, and disrespectful." Acceptance, approval, and admiration were reverse-scored. This scale showed an alpha reliability coefficient of 0.71 in the current study. Responses ranged from (1) totally disagree to (5) absolutely agree. Higher scores meant more feelings of prejudice toward immigrants while lower scores meant less.

Assimilation

Four items measured assimilation. These items were adapted from Berry et al. (2006). The response category ranged from (1) absolutely disagree to (5) totally agree. The items for this scale were: "I want immigrants to adopt the Finnish culture and not keep their own," "I want immigrants to be more fluent in our [Finnish] language than in their own," "I want immigrants to take part in social activities which do not involve immigrants," and "I want immigrants to be friends with Finns." The alpha reliability for this scale in the current study was 0.61. One item was deleted and the reliability rose to 0.73.

Integration

Four items measured integration, which were adapted from Berry et al. (2006). Responses ranged from (1) absolutely disagree to (5) totally agree. The items for this scale were: "I want immigrants to keep their own culture, but also to adapt to ours," "I want immigrants to be fluent in their own and our [Finnish] language," "I want immigrants to take part in social activities which involve both immigrants and Finns," and "I want immigrants to be friends with Finns and other immigrants." The alpha reliability obtained for this scale in the current study was 0.85.

Intergroup contact

The four items used to measure intergroup contact were adapted from González et al. (2008). The first two items were: "How many immigrant friends do you have?" and "Do you have contact with immigrants?" These were rated from (1) none to (4) only immigrant friends. The other three items were: "Do you have contact with immigrants at school?", "Do you have contact with immigrants in your neighborhood?" and "Do you have contact with immigrants somewhere else such as during activities?" Responses ranged from (1) never to (4) often. The original González et al. (2008) study had an alpha reliability of 0.70 and the current study had an alpha reliability of 0.73. Table 21.1 contains the means, standard deviations, alphas, and correlations for all variables in this study.

Results

To confirm the hypotheses, two hierarchical regressions were constructed, each with three steps. In the first regression (Table 21.2), preference for assimilation served as the criterion variable and, in the second regression (Table 21.3), preference for integration served as the criterion variable. The following predictor variable was entered in model 1: age. In model 2, symbolic threat, realistic threat, contact, and prejudice were entered. In model 3, the interactions between contact and symbolic threat, contact and realistic threat, and contact and prejudice were entered. Symbolic threat, realistic threat, contact, and prejudice were mean-centered before testing for interaction effects (Cohen, Cohen, West, & Aiken, 2003).

For preference for assimilation, in model 1 age was entered as a predictor variable ($b = -0.12$, $p = 0.004$, $R^2_{adj} = 0.01$; $F = 8.40$). In model 2, symbolic threat ($b = -0.03$, $p = 0.68$), realistic threat

Table 21.2 Regression predicting preference for assimilation

Model 1				*Model 2*			*Model 3*		
Variable	*b*	*SE*	*t*	*b*	*SE*	*t*	*b*	*SE*	*t*
Age	−0.12**	0.06	−2.90	−0.07	0.06	−1.78	−0.07	0.06	−1.89
Symbolic threat				−0.03	0.05	−0.42	−0.01	0.14	−0.02
Realistic threat				−0.07	0.05	−1.09	−0.07	0.15	−0.36
Contact				−0.09*	0.06	−2.30	0.28	0.36	1.21
Prejudice				−0.35***	0.06	−8.89	−0.21	0.16	−1.95
Contact*Symbolic Threat							−0.04	0.08	−0.15
Contact*Realistic Threat							−0.01	0.08	−0.01
Contact*Prejudice							−0.40	0.09	−1.48
F		8.40**			26.50***				16.88**
R^2	0.01			0.18			0.18		
R^2_{adj}	0.01			0.17			0.17		

*$p < 0.05$; **$p < 0.01$; ***$p < 0.001$.

Table 21.3 Regression predicting preference for integration

Model 1				*Model 2*			*Model 3*		
Variable	*b*	*SE*	*t*	*b*	*SE*	*t*	*b*	*SE*	*t*
Age	0.19***	0.05	4.79	0.14***	0.05	3.79	0.13***	0.05	3.69
Symbolic threat				0.05	0.04	0.78	0.14	0.12	0.74
Realistic threat				0.07	0.04	1.19	–0.03	0.13	–0.16
Contact				0.08*	0.05	2.12	0.52*	0.23	2.29
Prejudice				0.35***	0.05	9.09	0.54***	0.13	5.31
Contact*Symbolic Threat							–0.15	0.07	–0.53
Contact*Realistic Threat							0.19	0.07	0.64
Contact*Prejudice							–0.55*	0.07	–2.08
F		22.99**			32.46***				20.95**
R^2	0.04			0.21			0.22		
R^2_{adj}	0.03			0.20			0.21		

*$p < 0.05$; **$p < 0.01$; ***$p < 0.001$.

($b = -0.07, p = 0.28$), contact ($b = -0.09, p = 0.02$), and prejudice ($b = -0.35, p = 0.0001$) were added to the regression ($R^2_{adj} = 0.17$; $F = 26.50$). Model 2 was a significant improvement over model 1 ($\Delta F = 30.61, p = 0.001$). In model 3, interaction between contact and symbolic threat ($b = -0.04$, $p = 0.88$), contact and realistic threat ($b = -0.01$, $p = 0.99$), and contact and prejudice ($b = -0.40, p = 0.14$) were added to the regression ($R^2_{adj} = 0.17$; $F = 16.88$). Model 3 was not a significant improvement over model 2 ($\Delta F = 0.88$, $p = 0.45$). Thus, model 2 was retained for final analysis. Based on model 2, *H1a* is not confirmed, as threat (realistic and symbolic) does not significantly relate to preference for assimilation in relation toward immigrants. Moreover, regarding *H2a*, the opposite result was found. In the current study, it was proposed that preference for assimilation would be positively related to feelings of prejudice toward immigrants. Instead, prejudice had a significant negative effect on preference for assimilation ($b = -0.35$, $p = 0.0001$). For full regression results, see Table 21.2.

For preference for integration, in model 1 age was entered as a predictor variable ($b = 0.19$, $p = 0.0001$, $R^2_{adj} = 0.03$; $F = 22.99$). In model 2, symbolic threat ($b = 0.05$, $p = 0.78$), realistic threat ($b = 0.07$, $p = 0.23$), contact ($b = 0.08$, $p = 0.04$), and prejudice ($b = 0.35$, $p = 0.0001$) were added to the regression ($R^2_{adj} = 0.20$; $F = 32.46$). Model 2 was a significant improvement over model 1 ($\Delta F = 33.61$, $p = 0.001$). In model 3, interaction between contact and symbolic threat ($b = -0.15$, $p = 0.60$), contact and realistic threat ($b = 0.19$, $p = 0.53$), and contact and prejudice ($b = -0.55$, $p = 0.04$) were added to the regression ($R^2_{adj} = 0.17$; $F = 16.88$). Model 3 was not a significant improvement over model 2 ($\Delta F = 1.62$, $p = 0.18$). Thus, model 2 was retained for final analysis. Based on model 2, *H1b* is not confirmed, as threat (realistic and symbolic) does not significantly relate to preference for integration in relation toward immigrants. Moreover, regarding *H2b*, the opposite result was found. In the current study, it was proposed that preference for integration would be negatively related to feelings of prejudice toward immigrants. Instead, prejudice had a significant positive effect on preference for assimilation ($b = 0.35$, $p = 0.0001$). For full regression results, see

Table 21.3.*H3a* proposed that intergroup contact would moderate the relationship between perceived threat and acculturation preferences. Regression analysis revealed non-significant moderation. *H3b* proposed that intergroup contact would moderate the relationship between acculturation preferences and prejudice. Regression analysis revealed non-significant moderation.

Discussion

This study set out to examine the relationship between acculturation preferences (assimilation and integration), perceived threat (realistic and symbolic threats), and prejudice toward immigrants living in Finland. Another aim of this study was to examine the moderating effect of intergroup contact on the aforementioned relationships. Based on previous literature, *H1a* argued that a preference for assimilation would be positively related with perceived threat, while *H1b* argued that a preference for integration would be negatively related to perceived threat. On the other hand, *H2a* argued that a preference for assimilation would be positively related to feelings of prejudice, while *H2b* argued that a preference for integration would be negatively related to feelings of prejudice toward immigrants. Based on the findings of this study, none of the above hypotheses (*H1a, H1b, H2a* or *H2b*) were supported.

According to the findings of this study, there was a non-significant relationship between a preference for assimilation and perceived threat and between a preference for integration and perceived threat. Moreover, contrary to what was expected, this study revealed a significant negative relationship between assimilation and prejudice and a significant positive relationship between integration and prejudice toward immigrants. These results are in direct contrast to those hypothesized and also contrary to previous literature on acculturation preferences, threat, and prejudice. Previous research found a significant positive relationship between a preference for assimilation and perceived threat and a significant negative relationship between a preference for integration and perceived threat (Brown & Zagefka, 2011; Ljujic et al., 2012; Piontkowski et al., 2002; van Osch & Breugelmans, 2012; Zagefka et al., 2012). For example, Callens et al. (2015) studied acculturation preference (assimilation and integration) in relation toward immigrants in Luxembourg and found assimilation was positively related to threat while integration was negatively related to threat. However, the findings of this study suggest perceived threat must be related to acculturation preferences, particularly within the context of this study. This points to the need to investigate the extent to which other possible antecedents to acculturation influence attitudes toward immigrants in Finland. This is an important endeavor in an attempt to improve intergroup relations between Finns and immigrants living in Finland. Research has identified several such factors that could possibly be related to acculturation preferences. For instance, Navas, Rojas, Garcia, and Pumares (2007, p. 70) identified the following factors as possible antecedents of acculturation preferences:

> Individual (e.g., age, sex, time in the host country, education, ethnocultural origin), psychosocial (e.g., intergroup bias, intergroup contact, mutual prejudice, perceived similarity, cultural enrichment perceived, intergroup identification, visibility, group status, etc.) or group/context (e.g., specific peculiarities of each immigrant and/or host group country, political context, cultural distance, regulations, predominant ideologies, etc.

Unfortunately, most of these factors have not been investigated within the Finnish context among majority Finns, and they should be to better understand acculturation preferences. This study also indicated that those Finns who preferred integration for immigrants had more feelings of prejudice toward them while those who preferred assimilation had less feelings of prejudice toward them. This result is in contrast to previous research identifying a significant negative relationship between prejudice and a preference for integration and a significant positive relationship between prejudice and a preference for assimilation (Callens et al., 2015). For example, Zick et al. (2001) found assimilation to be positively related to prejudice and discriminatory behavior, and integration to be negatively correlated with prejudice in a number of samples in Germany. The opposite finding in this study can be explained by the fact that majority Finns may have prejudicial attitudes toward a particular immigrant group (for example, Muslim immigrants) but at the same time may think the immigrant group is unable to assimilate into Finnish society. Hence, they may predominantly be in support of integration since assimilation is not an option. One limitation of this study is that we focused on immigrants in general and not on a particular immigrant group. It can be expected that attitudes toward different immigrant groups will differ. Moreover, people may be in support of assimilation because it is perceived to be more practical and not necessarily because they dislike the outgroup. In this way, more support for assimilation can be negatively related to prejudice. In addition, support for assimilation may be negatively related to prejudice because of the possible effect of intervening factors such as religiosity and social desirability on prejudice, especially when we consider the nature of the Finnish context.

Another aspect of this study was investigating the moderating role of intergroup contact on the relationship between acculturation preferences and threat and the relationship between acculturation preferences and prejudice. Based on previous literature (Pettigrew & Tropp, 2006, 2008), we hypothesized that intergroup contact would moderate the relationship between perceived threat and acculturation preferences (*H3a*) and the relationship between acculturation preferences and prejudice (*H3b*). The findings of this study revealed that contact with immigrants had no significant moderating effect. This finding is different from other studies that have found intergroup contact to have a significant effect on acculturation preferences, prejudice, and threat (Aronson & Brown, 2013; Callens et al., 2015; González et al., 2008; Piontkowski et al., 2002; Verkuyten & Martinovic, 2006; Ward & Masgoret, 2006). Callens and colleagues (2015) found that "having more intense friendship contact leads to a reduction in threat perceptions and then again to less support for assimilation and more support for multiculturalism" (pp. 18–19). However, the findings in this study emphasize the need to consider contextual factors when studying attitudes such as prejudice, acculturation preferences, and threat. The findings in this study indicate that results also may not be in line with theoretical expectations and previous applications in other contexts. Most of the scales used in this study have been developed for and widely applied within the US context. These scales may not always work when applied in other contexts. Even though we obtained high alpha reliability coefficients for the scales in this current study, we cannot ignore this possibility of a contextual misfit. Future research should consider contextual issues when adapting a scale to a particular context.

The importance of this study cannot be underestimated. It is the first time that the relationship between four different intergroup phenomena has been examined within the Finnish context: ITT (Stephan & Stephan, 1996), acculturation (Berry, 1997), intergroup contact (Allport, 1954), and prejudice (Allport, 1954).

Bibliography

Allport, G. (1954). *The nature of prejudice*. Cambridge, MA: Addison-Wesley.

Aronson, M. & Brown, R. (2013). Acculturation and social attitudes among majority children. *International Journal of Intercultural Relations, 37*, 313–322.

BBC (2015). *Migrant crisis: Finland's case against immigration*. Retrieved from www.bbc.com/news/world-europe-34185297.

Berry, J. W. (1997). Immigration, acculturation, and adaptation. *Applied Psychology: An International Review, 46*, 5–68.

Berry, J. W. (2001). A psychology of immigration. *Journal of Social Issues, 57*, 615–631.

Berry, J. W. (2005). Acculturation: Living successfully in two cultures. *International Journal of Intercultural Relations, 29*, 697–712.

Berry, J. W. (2006). Contexts of acculturation. In D. L. Sam & J. W. Berry (Eds.), *Cambridge handbook of acculturation psychology* (pp. 27–42). Cambridge: Cambridge University Press.

Berry, J. W., Phinney, J. S., Sam, D. L., & Vedder, P. (2006). Immigrant youth: Acculturation, identity, and adaptation. *Applied Psychology, 55*, 303–332.

Brown, R. J., & Hewstone, M. (2005). An integrative theory of intergroup contact. In M. Zanna (Ed.), *Advances in experimental social psychology* (pp. 255–331). San Diego, CA: Academic Press.

Brown, R. J. & Zagefka, H. (2011). The dynamics of acculturation: An intergroup perspective. In M. P. Zanna & J. M. Olson (Eds.), *Advances in experimental social psychology* (pp. 129–184). San Diego, CA: Elsevier Academic Press.

Bunikowski, D. (2016). *Finland's immigration crisis*. Retrieved from www.gatestoneinstitute.org/7559/finland-migrant-crisis

Callens, M., Meuleman, B., & Valentova, M. (2015). *Perceived threat, contact and attitudes toward the integration of immigrants: Evidence from Luxembourg*. Luxembourg Institute of Socio-Economic Research (LISER), Working Paper Series 2015–01. Retrieved from file:///C:/Users/KNOWHOW/Downloads/perceived-threat-contact-and-attitudes-towards-the.pdf

Callens, M., Valentova, M., & Meuleman, B. (2014). Do attitudes toward the integration of immigrants change over time? A comparative study of natives, second-generation immigrants and foreign-born residents in Luxembourg. *Journal of International Migration and Integration, 15*, 135–157.

Cohen, J., Cohen, P., West, S. G., & Aiken, L. S. (2003). *Applied multiple regression/correlation analysis in the behavioral sciences* (3rd ed.). Mahwah, NJ: Lawrence Erlbaum.

Croucher, S. M. (2013). Integrated threat theory and acceptance of immigrant assimilation: An analysis of Muslim immigration in Western Europe. *Communication Monographs, 80*, 46–62.

Croucher, S. M., Aalto, J., Hirvonen, S., & Sommier, M. (2013). Integrated threat and intergroup contact: An analysis of Muslim immigration to Finland. *Human Communication, 16*, 109–120.

Dovidio, J. F., Eller, A., & Hewstone, M. (2011). Improving intergroup relations through direct, extended and other forms of indirect contact. *Group Processes & Intergroup Relations, 14*, 147–160.

Ervasti, H. (2004). Attitudes toward foreign-born settlers: Finland in a comparative perspective. In I. S. Teoksessa (Ed.), *Yearbook of population research in Finland* (pp. 25–44). Helsinki: Väestöliitto, Väestöntutkimuslaitos.

Eurostat (2017). *Asylum in the EU Member States*. Retrieved from http://ec.europa.eu/eurostat/documents/2995521/7921609/3-16032017-BP-EN.pdf/e5fa98bb-5d9d-4297-9168-d07c67d1c9e1

Ford, R. (2012). *Europe's young cosmopolitans: Explaining generational differences in immigration attitudes*. Institute of Social Change Working Paper. Manchester: Manchester University Press.

González, K. V., Verkuyten, M., Weesie, J., & Poppe, E. (2008). Prejudice toward Muslims in the Netherlands: Testing integrated threat theory. *British Journal of Social Psychology, 47*, 667–685.

Harwood, J. (2008). Intergroup contact and communication. In D. Wolfgang (Ed.), *The International Encyclopedia of Communication*. Blackwell. Retrieved from www.blackwellreference.com/subscriber/tocnode.html?id=g9781405131995_chunk_g978140513199514_ss58-1

Jaakkola, M. (2009). *Maahanmuuttajat suomalaisten näkökulmasta. Asennemuutokset, 1987–2007* [Finnish attitudes toward immigrants, 1987–2007]. Helsinki: City of Helsinki Urban Facts Research Series.

Jasinskaja-Lahti, I. (2000). *Psychological acculturation and adaptation among Russian speaking immigrant adolescents in Finland*. Helsinki: Helsingin yliopiston verkkojulkaisut.

Kim, Y. Y. (1988). *Communication and cross-cultural adaptation: An integrative theory*. Philadelphia, PA: Multilingual Matters Limited.

Ljujic, V., Vedder, P., Dekker, H., & Van Geel, M. (2012). Serbian adolescents' Romaphobia and their acculturation orientations toward the Roma minority. *International Journal of Intercultural Relations, 36*, 53–61.

Navas, M., Rojas, A. J., Garcıa, M., & Pumares, P. (2007). Acculturation strategies and attitudes according to the Relative Acculturation Extended Model (RAEM): The perspectives of natives versus immigrants. *International Journal of Intercultural Relations, 31*, 67–86.

Nshom, E. (2016). Predictors of Finnish adolescents' prejudice toward Russian immigrants and the role of intergroup contact. *Journal of Intercultural Communication Research, 45*, 31–44.

Nshom, E. & Croucher, S. M. (2014). Threats and attitudes toward Russian-speaking immigrants: A comparative study between younger and older Finns. *Russian Journal of Communication, 6*, 308–317.

Nshom, E. & Croucher, S. M. (2017). Perceived threat and prejudice toward immigrants in Finland: A study among early, middle and late Finnish adolescents. *Journal of International and Intercultural Communication, 10*, 309–323.

Osch, Y. M. J. van & Breugelmans, S. M. (2012). Perceived intergroup difference as an organizing principle of intercultural attitudes and acculturation attitudes. *Journal of Cross-Cultural Psychology, 43*, 801–821.

Pettigrew, T. F. & Tropp, L. R. (2006). A meta-analytic test of intergroup contact theory. *Journal of Personality and Social Psychology, 90*, 751–783.

Pettigrew, T. F. & Tropp, L. R. (2008). How does intergroup contact reduce prejudice? Meta analytic tests of three mediators. *European Journal of Social Psychology, 38*, 922–934.

Piontkowski, U., Rohmann, A., & Florack, A. (2002). Concordance of acculturation attitudes and perceived threat. *Group Processes and Intergroup Relations, 5*, 221–232.

Piontkowskia, U., Florack, A., Hoelkera, P., & Obdrzälek, P. (2000). Predicting acculturation attitudes of dominant and non-dominant groups. *International Journal of Intercultural Relations, 24*, 1–26.

Redfield, R., Linton, R., & Herskovits, M. J. (1936). Memorandum for the study of acculturation. *American Anthropologist, 38*, 149–152.

Redmond, B. F. (2011). *Intergroup theories (integrated threat, social identity, and social dominance)*. Retrieved from https://wikispaces.psu.edu/display/PSYCH484/8.+Intergroup+Theories+(Integrated+Threat,+Social+Identity,+and+Social+Dominance)

Riek, B. M., Mania, E. W., & Gaertner, S. L. (2006). Intergroup threat and the integrated threat theory: A meta-analytic review. *Personality and Social Psychology Review, 10*, 336–353.

Schcibncr, G. & Morrison, T. (2009). Attitudes toward Polish immigrants to the Republic of Ireland: An integrated threat analysis. *Ethnic and Racial Studies, 32*, 1431–1448.

Statistics Finland. (2015). *Immigrants and integration*. Retrieved from www.stat.fi/tup/maahanmuutto/immigration/index_en.html

Statistics Finland. (2017). *Foreigners in Finland*. Retrieved from www.stat.fi/tup/suoluk/suoluk_vaesto_en.html#foreignersinfinland

Stephan, W. G. & Renfro, C. L. (2002). The role of threat in intergroup relations. In D. Mackie & E. R. Smith (Eds.), *From prejudice to intergroup emotions: Differentiated reactions to social groups* (pp. 191–207). New York: Psychology Press.

Stephan, W. G. & Stephan, C. W. (1996). Predicting prejudice. *International Journal of Intercultural Relations, 20*, 409–426.

Stephan, W. G. & Stephan, C. W. (2000). An integrated threat theory of prejudice. In S. Oskamp (Ed.), *Reducing prejudice and discrimination* (pp. 225–246). Hillsdale, NJ: Lawrence Erlbaum.

Stephan, W. G., Diaz-Looving, R., & Duran, A. (2000). Integrated threat theory and intercultural attitudes: Mexico and the United States. *Journal of Cross-Cultural Psychology, 31*, 240–249.

Stephan, W. G., Ybarra, O., Martinez, C., Schwarzwald, J., & Turk-Kaspa, M. (1998). Prejudice toward immigrants to Spain and Israel: An integrated threat theory analysis. *Journal of Cross-Cultural Psychology, 29*, 559–576.

Stephan, W. G., Ybarra, O., & Morrison, R. (2009). Intergroup threat theory. In T. Nelson (Ed.), *Handbook of prejudice* (pp. 43–59). Mahwah, NJ: Lawrence Erlbaum.

Van Oudenhoven, J. P. & Eisses, A. (1998). Integration and assimilation of Moroccan immigrants in Israel and the Netherlands. *International Journal of Intercultural Relations, 22*, 293–307.

Verkuyten, M. & Martinovic, B. (2006). Understanding multicultural attitudes: The role of group status, identification, friendships, and justifying ideologies. *International Journal of Intercultural Relations, 30*, 1–18.

Ward, C. & Masgoret, A. (2006). An integrated model of attitudes toward immigrants. *International Journal of Intercultural Relations, 30*, 671–682.

Yle (2015). *Anti-immigration protest draws 200 in Helsinki*. Retrieved from http://yle.fi/uutiset/anti-immigration_protest_draws_200_in_helsinki/8317805

Zagefka, H., & Brown, R. (2002). The relationship between acculturation strategies, relative fit and intergroup relations: Immigrant-majority relations in Germany. *European Journal of Social Psychology, 32*, 171–188.

Zagefka, H., Tip, L., González, R., Brown, R., & Cinnirella, M. (2012). Predictors of majority members' acculturation preferences: Experimental evidence. *Journal of Experimental Social Psychology, 48*, 654–659.

Zick, A., Wagner, U., Dick, R., & Petzel, T. (2001). Acculturation and prejudice in Germany: Majority and minority perspectives. *Journal of Social Issues, 57*, 541–557.

22

(RE)FRAMING CULTURAL INTELLIGENCE IN ORGANIZATIONS

Migration, negotiation, and meaning-making of female migrants from North East India

Debalina Dutta

Cultural scholars have paid particular attention to the sites and structures of migration in the global south, particularly in the context of India (Harvey, 2003). In particular, scholars have noted that migrants from the North Eastern[1] region[2] (NE) of India have entered, altered, and contributed to the labor market of Indian metropolitan cities (Zou & Kumar, 2011). According to a 2011 North East Support Centre and Helpline (NESCH) survey, over 414,850 migrants from the North East have "resited" themselves in the other main Indian cities. Limited educational and employability opportunities, insurgency, conflict, corruption, and lack of infrastructure are reasons that frame the logic of migration from home states propelled by economic opportunities in the host states (McDuie-Ra, 2013). However, Baruah (2005) identified that the false unification of the different regions and states from North East India delegitimizes the diversity and cultural differences of the region. The unique "mongoloid" physical characteristics and language act as distinct markers, drawing invisible social and cultural boundaries between "mainland" Indians and "North East" Indians, who are otherwise bound together by citizenship. In addition, the artificial clustering based on these racial features, which distances the "North East" from the rest of India (Eriksen, 2002), ascribes a kind of foreignness particular to the migrants of this region (as compared to migrants from the rest of India), which means they are often subjected to discrimination, racism, and violence by their own countrymen (see McDuie-Ra, 2015a, 2016; Ngaihte & Hanghal, 2017; Wouters & Subba, 2013). Through these everyday, often violent, "acts" of racial purging, exclusion, prejudice, and subjugation against the migrants from the NE, the ideals of "false" mainstream nationality is managed and secured.

Research also shows that most of these acts of violence are gendered in nature, directed at women from the NE whose exotic looks and "Westernized" manner of dressing and comfort with the English language stand out among mainstream societies where women are subjected to patriarchal ideologies (McDuie-Ra, 2013; Merelli, 2011). These patriarchal mainstream ideologies produce and reproduce certain norms whose violation sanctions sexual violence and gendered subjugation through moral policing (NESCH, 2011). Women from the NE, especially those belonging to Mon-Khmer, Tai, and Tibeto Burmese roots, are stereotyped as immoral, exotic, of low calibre, and open to having multiple relationships. Such imagery leads to everyday social and sexual harassment of female NE migrants in urban spaces, which are often not reported to the police from fear of inaction and backlash (McDuie-Ra, 2013, 2015a). However, most studies have highlighted racism in attempts to understand the experiences of migrants from the NE in other Indian cities and researchers have paid attention to cultural differences, sites of differentiation, and discrimination in the context of migration rather than gender. Also, most research examines the work and migration trajectories of people from the NE belonging to lower-middle-class and poor families (see McDuie-Ra, 2013) and there exists a gap in our understanding of professional NE migrants. Therefore, the current study bridges our understanding of how gender operates in the context of professional organizations especially for NE women. For the purpose of my research, I examine women from the NE who are working in professional organizations as scientists, engineers, doctors, and professors after receiving their professional degrees from reputable institutions in India. In doing so, I invoke the theoretical lens of cultural intelligence (Earley & Ang, 2003) as successful adaption to transnational organizations by individuals. I critique the stabilization of cultural intelligence (CQ) as a trait-based linear articulation of individual cultural management in organizations. As researchers argue (Dutta & Dutta, 2013), CQ is framed as a competitive and advantageous tool for professional organizations that underplays vulnerability and exploitation of employees. The logic of CQ is then essentially flawed because it rewards strategic and goal-driven Eurocentric biases of "fitting in" and assuming CQ is value neutral. In this context, I pay attention to the materialities and discourses performed by the organization members that act as barriers in the organization site where the minority entrant organization members are supposed to practice cultural intelligence. As a result, this interrogates the value neutrality of CQ. Furthermore, I attend to the discourse of organizational space as a site of systems and structures where the everyday cultural practices and power relations play an important role in how individuals might practice CQ tied to the organizational structures of power and control.

The study offers important theoretical and practical contributions to our understanding of how dominant organizational culture plays an important role in how women from a different cultural context practice CQ in these organizations. The study also aims to contribute to our present limited understanding of how professional women from the NE describe and interpret interactions and situations in the organizations in which they are employed. In addition, the goal of this chapter is to examine and interrogate how cross-cultural experiences and adaptations are localized in professional organizations by exploring the role of gender in CQ. The findings inform retention and mentoring of women from the NE who are employed in these organizations, thus offering practical implications for the study. Thus, policy makers and government and non-government agencies can offer strategic resources that can benefit potentially vulnerable employees and organizations in the context of talent and diversity management. Therefore, I begin by offering a critique of CQ, suggesting that organizations become the visible sites of everyday cultural struggles of (un)belonging. I then offer a detailed report of the findings of in-depth interviews with 20 women from the NE employed in professional organizations in the rest of India.

Literature review

Women from the North East

Historically, women from the North East occupy a special position in the geopolitical landscape of India. Most tribes in the region are matrilineal in nature whereby women inherit property (Fox, 1967) and societal practices empower and emancipate women. Research has shown women who are in the NE region of India are more exposed to public life than women belonging to central and northern India (Ray & Jyrwa, 2008). Such exposure implies active participation in the social and educational spaces and, coupled with matrilineal traditions in some societies, women in the NE have access to better societal conditions. Mahanta and Nayak (2013) noted the comparatively lesser degree of discrimination against women and young girls with respect to access to education in the region. Discourses of choice and freedom also inform the vocabulary of these women. In addition they practice their own curation of fashion, language, and social habits that often do not align with mainstream Indian traditions and customs (especially those of the northern region). Insurgency, political unrest, limited educational, and employability opportunities have led to more and more women from NE India migrating to mainland India in search of better opportunities (McDuie-Ra, 2012). Government-sanctioned reservation practices, popularly known as "quotas", help indigenous groups secure admission to educational institutions.

Remesh (2012) noted that, when women from the NE migrate to the major Indian cities, they often attempt to culturally adjust to better acquaint themselves with their immediate social environment (which is patriarchal in nature). However, such moments of interaction between NE women and the broader "mainstream" Indian societies are often considered transgressions and are resisted by acts of violence by the "local" keepers of morality against what is stereotypically perceived as the epitome of Western modernities. Such modernities (wearing Western clothes, speaking fluent English, and being comfortable around men) are marked as not congruent with the traditions and customs that define India. Such unnecessary and problematic correlations between modernity and morality lead to a false sense of nationalist logic, which, according to McDuie-Ra (2012), is at the core of the acts of violence against women from the NE in the metropolitan Indian cities. These acts are manifested in everyday social interactions in the cities, where the women are subjected to inappropriate, racist, and lewd comments, are harassed in public places and become the victims of sexual crimes on accouunt of their looks, clothes, and mannerisms. Generally, the government's response to their situation is apathetic; public silence suppresses their voices; and most crimes against them go unreported (Dholabhai, 2007; Smith & Gergen, 2015).

(Re)framing cultural intelligence

Earley and Ang (2003) defined cultural intelligence as "a person's capability for successful adaptation to new cultural settings" (p. 9). According to them, a high CQ implies that an individual is likely to succeed and work effectively with other cultures and can adapt to a normatively different organizational environment. Research in cultural intelligence has highlighted the need to span cultural boundaries in organizations in order for people to work effectively with others who usually subscribe to different norms (Middleton, 2014). The framework of CQ exclusively focuses on the individual as the expert in navigating cultural differences and adapting to organizations (Ang & Van Dyne, 2008), thus stabilizing the notion of culture as an entity to be managed in those spaces. CQ evokes the imagery of individual survival, thus valorizing and rewarding the populist notion of agency and willingness to adapt and succeed (Ang & Van Dyne, 2015). The view of the "individual as expert" in terms of adapting to organizational cultural norms has been prioritized in hiring decisions, evidenced by a willingness to favor recruits who demonstrate high CQ. However, in placing importance on individual capabilities and intelligence, the organization becomes framed as a site of cultural management.

Such uncritical framing of problem solving by individual entrants assumes that the issues to be addressed for successful cultural adaptation are discrete and out there in organizational spaces. Moreover, cultural intelligence as a framework standardizes and stabilizes culture-based differences (Dutta & Dutta, 2013). In doing so, the framework of cultural intelligence focuses primarily on individualization of cultural features hereby erasing the structural context. For instance, studies show that organizations are complex political and cultural sites shaped by a nexus of everyday interactions and power relations (see Mumby, 2010). Other studies, however, uphold the existence of multiple forms of discrimination in response to the perception of cultural otherness in the same organizations. I interrogate the existing framework of CQ by foregrounding the cultural biases and stereotypes that impede the integration of minority members, whereby disenfranchised and under-represented members have to navigate the organization and adapt. By examining the lived experiences of women from the NE who are employed in professional organizations in mainstream India, I aim to understand the existing organizational cultural complexities and potentially elucidate the organizational structural and cultural challenges that exist for individuals with CQ.

Method

Recruitment

After receiving institutional review board[3] approval, I contacted friends and acquaintances and asked them to participate in the interview. I contacted participants by phone, email and Facebook, and, upon receiving their verbal consent, set up an interview date and time by Skype or phone. In order to participate, the participants had to be over 18 years of age, belong to ethnic communities of the Indian states of Assam, Meghalaya, Manipur, Nagaland, Arunachal Pradesh, Mizoram, or Tripura, and be working in organizations in India outside of the NE region. I interviewed 22 female participants whose age ranged between 27 and 40 years, with an average age of 32 years. The interviews ranged in duration from 30 to 60 minutes. All interviews were audio-recorded and pseudonyms were used to protect the identity of the participants. The participants were not reimbursed for taking part in the interviews. Information on the participants is provided in Table 22.1.The interviews addressed the following questions: What were the experiences of the participants in the organizations? How did their colleagues interact with them in these professional spaces? In what ways were these experiences potentially different from those experienced by other women who were employed in these organizations? Some participants contacted me later if they had anything else to share. The interviews were conducted in English. The audio-recordings were then transcribed verbatim and compared to the audio-recordings to ensure accuracy.

Table 22.1 Participant data

Name	*State*	*Employed as*
Lal	Mizoram	Engineer/Engineering consultancy firm
Loya	Nagaland	Engineer/Construction firm
Monika	Manipur	Scientist/Research & Development firm
Sayonbi	Manipur	Scientist/Educational institution
Lalringa	Mizoram	Scientist/Private R & D firm
Prema	Manipur	Engineer/Construction firm
Putoli	Arunachal Pradesh	Scientist/R & D firm
Reema	Assam	Engineer/R & D firm
Aainu	Arunachal Pradesh	Scientist/Manufacturing firm
Anika	Manipur	Scientist/Educational institution
Aiko	Nagaland	Engineer/R & D firm
Yagum	Arunachal Pradesh	Engineer/Power plant
Lily	Manipur	Engineer/Consultancy firm
Yutika	Assam	Scientist/Chemical manufacturing firm
Akokla Lucy	Nagaland	Scientist/Manufacturing firm
Thoibi	Manipur	Engineer/Logistics firm
Taba	Arunachal Pradesh	Engineer/Construction firm
Jonaki	Assam	Engineer/Consultancy firm
Purno	Mizoram	Scientist/Educational institution
Mary	Mizoram	Engineer/Manufacturing firm
Rani	Nagaland	Scientist/Start-up organization
Patricia	Meghalaya	Engineer/Construction firm

Data analysis

After a thorough reading of the transcripts to gain a holistic sense of their content, I conducted line-by-line open coding (Tracy, 2013). During the interviews, I noted down the themes and patterns and these became the basis of my transcript analysis. Based on my reading and initial notes, I paid attention to the instances where the women commented on their everyday experiences of racism and discrimination. Using this constant comparative method, I looked for patterns and similarities in the codes generated. Finally, I checked the validity of my study through an audit trail (Bowen, 2009). During data analysis, I got in touch with some of my participants to check some of the codes I had generated. The additional conversations became the basis for checking some of the codes for further clarity. The findings were discussed with a senior colleague for in-depth understanding of the major themes and the connections between significant findings. I offer my in-depth perspective as researcher in the next section, documenting my role and reflexivity in conducting the interviews and the analysis.

My role as researcher

Most of the women I contacted for the interview are known to me, as I grew up in a state in the NE. Some of these interviewees were my childhood friends, their friends and their siblings, and they readily agreed to the interview. Using snowball sampling, I also contacted other women who were employed in professional organizations. Because I have also worked for some time in an organization in one of the metropolitan cities in India, I am deeply aware of the discrimination and everyday harassment experienced by women from the NE in particular. However, I am also cognizant of the fact that, although I share roots in the NE, I am an upper caste Bengali woman and my features are distinctly different from the indigenous communities of the NE. As a consequence, while I easily assimilated into the cultural norms and mores of the north Indian culture, my indigenous friends of the NE could not. For instance, I did not experience the scrutiny and practices that women from the NE in the rest of India are subjected to, including discriminatory behavior and refusal by landlords to lease houses, among others. This made me aware that I might be drawn to the stories as a co-participant rather than as an interviewee. However, shared history also made my participants recount their intimate and private interactions, which otherwise might not have been possible.

Results

The themes of *barriers due to ethnicity, barriers due to cultural and geopolitical stereotypes*, and *barriers due to professional perspectives, gender, and attitude* were arranged on the basis of open coding and are discussed below.

Barriers due to ethnicity

Most interviewees noted that their colleagues asked questions or made comments about their appearance. Indian citizens who belong to several ethnicities from the seven states of NE India have distinct facial features that are considered exotic (McDuie-Ra, 2012). Participants shared that it was common for people to draw attention to their features and, by referring to them, making the participants feel different and self-conscious. Lal (Mizoram) shared that such references to her appearance ranged from genuine to surprising to outright offensive comments. Lal talked about a time when she overheard one of her male colleagues call her a "chinki" (slang for people with slanted eyes and Mongolian features) behind her back. Lal further elaborated: "He was my boss and I heard him talking to another male colleague about me ... take the *chinki* with you ... she'll be good with the presentation ... that ass didn't have the basic decency." Similar experiences were shared by Loya (Nagaland), who found her colleagues' curiosity regarding her appearance insulting. "They stare at me like I am some weird person; once there was an office party and Revati asked me if I ever feel like having big eyes so that the kohl would look good on me." Loya found her colleague's question very inappropriate given that she was an "engineer and would have basic manners."

As well as their looks, participants' "social skills" were also commented on. Nearly all of the participants shared that most of the time their superiors and colleagues talked down to them or advised them about the importance of collegiality in the office. Monika (Manipur) shared that her supervisor often advises her on her office socializing:

> I am a private person and I've come all the way from my state to work and have a career. My supervisor keeps on telling me that if I don't mix with other people in the office it would not be good. He once said that since I am unsocial and am not outgoing, I could be picked upon. But he was only picking on me by saying those things, not to others.

Loya's quiet demeanor was misconstrued by her supervisor as lack of social skills; however, Loya added that such advice was not given to other female employees in the office. Loya's discomfort regarding social skills was echoed by Yagum (Arunachal Pradesh), who recently joined a new organization after completing her studies:

> It was my third day in the office and during lunchtime one of the female staff came to me and said that she talked to other colleagues and would have invited me to eat lunch with them but she understands that I need to be left alone. She also said that since there was no one from northeast, I wouldn't be interested in hanging out with people like them [office colleagues] who are not from northeast.

Yagum was upset that, instead of inviting her to join the office group, her colleague started making assumptions about her social habits. Both of the above examples draw attention to the assumptions and stereotypes faced by the participants that were not necessarily true.

In other instances, some participants reported that they were called upon for what they wore at the office. Participants noted both explicit and implicit messages. The participants reported that such messages were value-laden and more than individual observations, suggesting underlying broader cultural issues. Lily (Manipur) remembers that, for every client meeting, she is gently reminded to come properly attired: "'Dress properly,' my boss would tell me, 'you know how these clients are.'" Lily further shared that such benign suggestions by her boss to dress appropriately for meetings made her feel very bad about herself, especially because "my boss wouldn't tell these things to other women staff in our office and we all wear westerns in the office." That it was directed only at her was demeaning, and it disregarded Lily's professional position in the office by marking her out simply as someone who didn't know how to dress. References to dress sense was an experienced shared by Yutika (Assam), who stated:

> No matter whatever I wear, some of the office staff just stared at me. One day I wore salwar kameej [traditional Indian attire], and someone commented, how come you are wearing our dress? Later I thought why was I so upset about it? I am used to all these stupid things now.

Here, Yuthika shared her experience of wearing traditional Indian attire to the office and then being told that she was wearing Indian attire, something that is considered ordinary and mundane for the other Indian women working there. Thus, we note that the above examples highlight the prejudices exhibited in the work spaces against the participants, made salient because of their belonging to a particular place (states of the NE) and their looks, which are considered exotic and different from others in their own country. In addition, we also note their admission of these comments being something to which they are commonly subjected in the organization space.

Barriers due to cultural and geopolitical stereotypes

All of the participants interviewed noted some form of discrimination in the workplace owing to their ethnicity and prejudice against their home state. Most participants were unhappy about the everyday racial discrimination they faced in their host state. Sayonbi (Manipur), along with other participants, talks about references to unrest in their home state as issues that colleagues and supervisors display curiosity about; for example, one participant observed:

"If only these people [would] take the time to know us. I mean, how can you say [to] someone not to bomb the office if they don't like it here?" She continued:

> Even if they try to make us feel that they are joking about it, it's really insensitive when they ask us if we know how to make bombs or whether we own revolvers. They assume that if we are from this region we should either have these things or know someone who does.

Sayonbi's comments were echoed by Akokla Lucy (Nagaland) when she talked about trust and confidence:

> I see them whispering behind my back, when I come near them, they often jokingly ask me if I know the names of firearms or sometimes they ask if I know how to make a bomb? If they think they can joke about it, they have no idea what it makes us feel.

The above examples highlight the limited understanding of the situation of unrest in the region. The questions are also sometimes about drug-related stereotypes. Thoibi (Manipur) shared an experience of what happened in the office the day after she had had to be with a friend in the hospital: "Obviously my eyes were red and there was this aunty who followed me every time I was going to the bathroom." Upon probing further, Thoibi revealed:

> She suspected that I was taking drugs and asked me about it. I was so angry and I told her that I was taking care of a friend and she asked me if my friend overdosed. I cried so much that day.

Another interviewee had a similar experience; however, instead of direct references to drugs, she felt that she was being judged and scrutinized. Lalringa (Mizoram) said:

> No one ever asked me whether I was taking drugs but I knew they [office people] thought that I am into something. Only because I am not like them they could dare ask me what they asked before our annual office party.

In this statement Lalringa acknowledges that she is perceived as being different from others. She further adds, "Imagine asking me if I could get some drugs for them since I might know people who sell this stuff? Would they dare to ask any of the other women colleagues?" As understood from the interviews, the participants had an understanding that their experiences were different from those of other women in the organization.

Most often, the participants reported that colleagues' questions, interactional patterns, and knowledge exchange showed a lack of general understanding and lack of patience regarding others' norms and customs. Within the context of knowledge about their culture and customs, almost all participants noted either the complete lack of knowledge about their region or culture or indifference about the same. The participants identified examples ranging from "do you live in trees in your hometown" to "do you wear bark of trees back home?" to what they termed even more audacious and inappropriate comments. Prema (Manipur) commented that she had had to endure a lot in her former office, which ultimately led to her resignation; for example:

> Instead of my engineering knowledge, some staff would be more interested in my personal life. One day, a senior staff member called me to his office and said that I have to stop bringing beef lunches [sic] to office. He didn't believe me when I told him that I am vegetarian.

Prema further added: "He said that how can you be vegetarian? You are from north east right . . . I know you eat everything . . . It was so insulting. He is my senior but doesn't even bother to remember that I belong to Manipur." Prema noted that her superior was a senior research scientist in the organization and should not find it difficult to remember where she came from. These misconceptions about culture were also noted by Taba (Arunachal Pradesh):

> They [colleagues] don't bother knowing about us and our culture. We are not treated equally and it's not even the whole story. I have to answer more questions about who I am and why I am working in this organization and state rather than my engineering work knowledge. I am here to work but sometimes my boss and colleagues are more interested in my personal life. They treat us very badly.

Professional invisibility in the workspace, as identified by Prema and Taba, was a common strand of narrative in the interviews conducted in this study. Putoli (Arunachal Pradesh) also noted:

> When my company launched a scientific product in the market, I did all the research work but they chose another woman scientist to attend the press release. I was not even mentioned anywhere as if I am not attached to this research. Do they think I am stupid because I am from Arunachal or I got in because of my quota?

Such treatment by organizational members acted as a barrier to organization entry, as discussed by the participants. Jonaki (Assam) described her experiences in the company she is working for and talked about her limited opportunities for professional growth and development:

> You tell me, where is the inclusion? We will always be treated like outsiders. Even after working for so many projects, where is my promotion? Forget promotion, like I should be grateful for working here.

Almost all participants noted that their colleagues, bosses, and other important people in the organization raised standards and erected barriers that they were unable to navigate to achieve successful assimilation. These barriers were generally related to their region of origin, something they could do nothing to change.

Barriers due to professional perspectives, gender, and attitude

All the participants reported that they had gained their higher professional degrees from reputable educational institutes in India. In migrating from their hometown, the participants reported that they had wanted to empower themselves and their families by working in reputed organizations. However, the participants reported experiences that ranged from casual sexism to more serious forms of harassment. Participants noted that colleagues' perceptions of them were influenced more by their cultural differences than their professional competencies. As Reema (Assam) noted, "it doesn't matter if I am qualified as an engineer or doctor, I will always be a north east girl, like westerners." The notion of being a westerner was a common subtheme among the stories shared by the participants; it shaped the attitudes of their bosses, supervisors, and colleagues. Being a *Westerner* was considered a bad thing, and they were judged as such because of the clothes they wore and their lifestyles; these were deep-seated cultural stereotypes. However, Purno (Mizoram) added that,

> it's more than just a job thing; it's not easy for girls [sic] like us to survive on our own in cities. It's about how we are perceived as fast, not having Indian values, and it makes our life very difficult in these places where we work.

Participants such as Aainu (Arunachal Pradesh) summarized that women who were from the NE were considered easy prey:

> The fact that we are seen this way, *Western, Chinkis* and not as professionals so ... we are not given the same respect as other "Indian" girls. So it's considered okay to misbehave with us. I don't feel safe as any other girl but the fact that I look a certain way makes me very vulnerable to these men who constantly judge us for who we are.

Some participants noted that sexism was woven into the fabric of the organizations. For example, Mary (Mizoram) shared that her office was not a safe place for her:

> They make funny jokes when any of us girls are around, especially with me, it's another situation, and they say that girls from north east are loose. I am an engineer and it's horrible when they insult me like this in my office

Mary observed that such perceptions made some of her colleagues treat her differently from other women who were working in the organization. Others applying stereotypical perceptions was an experience also recognized by Anika (Manipur), who worked as a faculty member in a private organization. Anika said:

> We all used to sit together and this faculty member ... used to stare at me all the time. It made me very uncomfortable and unsafe. I would sometimes find him pointing at me and talking to some other men who worked in that office. I didn't like it and left my job shortly [after].

Mary complained that everyone in the office knew about this particular faculty member and his behavior towards her but no one paid any attention to it. Rani (Nagaland) had similar experiences to Mary and Anika; however, she talked about having to listen to unwanted propositions from her boss:

> He would call me in his office and talk about how he was lonely and needed company. He would tell me to do things that I don't want to talk about ... they were so bad. I confided to my friends and they wanted me to avoid him. But you tell me, how can I? He's my boss. He would ask me why am I shy? He used to say that he knows that I am not a virgin and used to these things all the time. . .

Rani's story resonated with those of most of the participants regarding their loss of control over their identities in these organizational spaces, and being vulnerable to subjective interpretations of their sexual choices based on the cultural and personal perceptions of their colleagues and bosses. Most of the accounts also discussed the policies and practices that did not support them in the organizational context. Aiko (Nagaland) recounted that, in her first job as an engineer, she was working under a supervisor who tried to get close to her:

> He always touched me on the pretext of explaining stuff. I've asked him to stay away but he said that I must like it because I am from north east. I complained about him to HR but they took no action. I resigned in disgust. It's no use going to anyone; you're the one who is going to be judged. We are not even taken seriously by the police.

Aiko, along with other participants, noted that reports of sexual harassment were largely ignored by the authorities in the organization, and most participants said that they do not bother reporting these issues. Most participants also shared that whenever someone misbehaved with them, they were likely to remain silent rather than talk about these incidents with their colleagues or superiors. The participants further shared that they would rather talk to other friends who were from the same region and try to find a solution to the problem. In some cases, participants talked about the violence they endured and the consequences of those incidents. Patricia (Meghalaya), an engineer, remembered a time when she was working for a construction company:

> The driver who took me to the worksite from [the] office took advantage of the situation where I was alone with him in the car. It was broad daylight and he thought he could do something bad with me in the deserted stretch that led to the site. I threatened to call the police and somehow escaped.

Patricia further shared that, in the company where she works, as a rule women are usually not allowed to travel alone but somehow the rule was not applied to her. She further shared that she had left the company and went through a period of feeling fearful and depressed when she started work at a new company. She refused to visit work sites because of her earlier trauma. Such incidents are not sporadic but systemic to their everyday experiences of racism and discrimination in the metropolitan Indian cities, first when they came for studies, and then when they entered organizational spaces.

Discussion and implications

Using the framework of cultural intelligence, this study addresses the experiences of female migrants from NE India in professional organizations and pays attention to the messages framing the circumstances of their cultural, social, and professional adjustments therein. The research question framing the study was about the experiences of women cultural migrants in professional organizations using the framework of cultural intelligence. First, the findings emphasize that the women from the NE face discrimination and harassment in their workplaces similar to their experiences in the broader societal context (McDuie-Ra, 2013). The participants reported that their professional degrees were from reputable and accredited institutes in India, but they were not considered professionals or given opportunities to contribute in their organizations. Their colleagues' everyday verbal and non-verbal strategies of avoidance and silence conveyed the message that their organizational presence and professional contributions were not desired; they were also not given professional responsibilities. Moreover, their professional identities and contributions were short-changed as their "other" racial identities were called upon instead. Such instances of stereotyping and stigmatizing migrants are encouraged, even for highly-educated women working in well-paid jobs and not just for migrants with low-paying jobs. Therefore, having qualifications and degrees makes no difference to the ways in which they are subjected to discrimination in organizations. Such discrimination does not allow them to access the organizational culture or to be accepted in the social space of other organizational members, no matter how qualified or socially adept the female migrants are.

This brings us to the second theme: participants feeling organizationally and socially isolated in the bounded professional spaces as a result of their racial features and ethnic identities. The participants noted that their colleagues treated them differently because they were from the NE. They noted that, given the special circumstances surrounding the political and social arrangements of NE migrants, their NE migration status/background overshadowed their professional status. Organizational spaces tagged and segregated them from other migrants working in these organizations, thus pointing to a false sense of national "unification" that bars them from participation in these organizational spaces. The study also elucidates the experiences of objectification and potential exploitation of these professional women by their seniors and colleagues in the organization. The women interviewed noted the varying levels of verbal and physical abuse that are generally sexual in nature, and talked about their helplessness in taking retaliatory action. They described the disengaged, disinterested organizational and societal members who remain alienated from these migrants and their experiences. Thus, the women noted that most of the time the perpetrators get away with it because of the attitude of the other organizational members.

Cultural vigilantism becomes operational in the bodies of these women and the spaces they occupy. The study highlights how national cultures, organizational cultures and occupational cultures intersect and interweave into everyday organizational practices which are faced by these migrant professional women amidst tensions. As seen in the study, the intersections are complex and evolving and question the individual agency and capability that is taken for granted. The study brings into focus the questions of privilege and belonging that favor certain individuals over others based on race, class, and ethnicity. Therefore, the emotional labor of adapting to organizations could be taken into consideration in future studies into cultural intelligence.

Most scholarship on cultural intelligence has tended to singularly privilege a narrative that hinges upon individual agency and adaptive abilities (Dutta & Dutta, 2013). Scholars have noted that the essence of CQ is marked by an urgency to claim and conquer organizational culture by organizational entrants and migrants. The value judgment, then, is attached to this very notion of sense-making and reclamation of space and culture, which, according to the concept of CQ, is present in varying degrees in all individuals. The study warns that the relationship between organizational members and immigrants is by no means neutral but, rather, is imbued with a specific kind of power and framed within a specific organizational context that is not narrated and is factored within a current theoretical understanding of the practice of cultural intelligence in organizations. The study attempts to counter and interrogate the framing of organizations in the context of CQ as neutral and instead posits that organizations are active sites mirroring the norms, values, and culture of the society in which they reside. Subsequently, such cultural reflections prove advantageous to some individuals and disadvantageous to others within the same organizations. Consequently, we note how female migrants from the NE struggle to adapt in professional organizational spaces in mainstream India and do not always gain equal access to the resources and capital given by organizations to their employees. We also note how individual agency is challenged and non-inclusionary practices become common in such organizational spaces, rendering them an almost non-friendly and uninviting space for the participants in the mainstream Indian professional organizations described in this study.

Earlier studies on migration and the NE have examined the notions of cosmopolitanism, racism, and occupational conundrums as they apply to those from the NE, paying attention to their everyday struggles and identifying issues in mainstream Indian cities (McDuie-Ra, 2015b, 2016). What these studies lack, and what the current study investigated, is details of the experiences and narratives of women from the NE who gain professional degrees and are employed in professional organizations. The present study focuses on the issues of gender and inclusion in professional organizations using the framework of cultural intelligence. The study also elucidates how women from the NE are not treated as professionals in these organizations, although they are trained as engineers and scientists. Rather than being valued as organizational resources and finding value in their experiences, they are short-changed because of their race and gender. In other words, organizational spaces stereotype them on the basis of who they are (gender) and where they come from (race). Most often, as noted from the narrated experiences, although they are equally qualified, these women are given "minority within minority" status. The biological markers of race and gender are used to judge them in these organizations, thus reproducing the everyday discrimination and exclusion of people from the NE in the wider societal spaces in mainstream India (see McDuie-Ra, 2012, 2016). Some women also reported facing harassment and sexual predation in the organizations in which they are employed in a professional capacity, thus drawing attention to their safety and well-being in these spaces.

However, the findings disrupt the binaries of individual abilities and organizational culture and raise important questions about what actually constitutes culture in professional spaces. For instance, the participants are not given access to organizational norms, customs, and traditions. In addition, general mistrust and stereotyping brands them as "others" by organizational vigilantes, erasing them from the common spaces that need to be managed and conquered in order to be labeled culturally intelligent. Thus, further studies need to examine and inspect the role of organizational members in granting power and agency to individuals and privileging some entrants over others in practicing cultural intelligence. Further investigation would have important theoretical and practical implications for understanding the experiences of highly-skilled migrants, especially those belonging to NE ethnic groups. In summary, this study offers potential in the field of cultural and organizational inclusionary practices and migration beyond Eurocentric constructs. Migration studies can engage more with how societal values, race, and gender intersect in Asian organizational spaces. Research can also provide traction for the role of organizational culture in Asia and its contribution to inclusionary practices, including recruitment of talented professionals irrespective of race and gender.

Limitations

Although the study makes important practical and theoretical contributions regarding the role of culture in organizations, it is not without its own limitations. The study was limited to interviewing NE migrants who work in professional organizations in metropolitan Indian cities; future studies could recruit participants from other cities and thus elicit more nuanced stories. The present study draws from the lived experiences of the participants and future studies can also examine how employers and organizational members talk about the contribution and adaptation of women migrants from the NE. Another limitation is the homogenization of all states constituting the NE without taking into consideration the unique cultural context to which each woman belonged and how those might complicate our understanding of their experiences. Future studies should address these gaps to ensure a more holistic understanding of cultural experiences in organizations.

Notes

1 North East is the collective geopolitical terrain and comprises the states Assam, Meghalaya, Manipur, Nagaland, Arunachal Pradesh, Tripura, Sikkim, and Mizoram. Connected to the rest of India by a small strip of land, the region is marked by hilly terrain and rich biodiversity. According to Cordaux, Weiss, Shah, and Stoneking (2004), most of the indigenous communities have Mon-Khmer, Tai, and Tibeto-Burman ancestry and many of these groups were protected and categorized under "Scheduled Tribes" after Independence by the Government of India. The major religious practices include Hinduism, Christianity, Buddhism and Animism, among others.

2 There has been an ongoing tension between indigenous communities of the NE and the settler Indians that came in as a part of British machinery and other migratory practices.

3 Institutional review boards (IRBs) are committees usually constituted by universities to review and advise on research ethics and uphold the practice of appropriate rules to protect the rights of human subjects, especially vulnerable populations such as children and prisoners. The purpose of the IRB is to monitor, assess, and safeguard ethical research by adhering to internationally sanctioned norms and codes.

References

Ang, S. & Van Dyne, L. (2008). Conceptualization of cultural intelligence: Definition, distinctiveness, and nomological network. In S. Ang & L. Van Dyne (Eds.), *Handbook of cultural intelligence: Theory, measurement, and applications* (pp. 3–15). Armonk, NY: M.E. Sharpe.

Ang, S. & Van Dyne, L. (2015). *Handbook of cultural intelligence*. New York: Routledge.

Baruah, S. (2003). Citizens and denizens: Ethnicity, homelands, and the crisis of displacement in northeast India. *Journal of Refugee Studies, 16*, 44–66.

Bowen, G. A. (2009). Supporting a grounded theory with an audit trail: An illustration. *International Journal of Social Research Methodology, 12*, 305–316.

Cordaux, R., Weiss, G., Shah, N., & Stoneking, M. (2004). The North East Indian Passageway: A barrier or corridor for human migrations? *Molecular Biology and Evolution, 21*, 1525–1533.

Dholabhai, N. (2007). Delhi 'profiles' to protect: police booklet for Northeast students betrays prejudices. July. *The Telegraph*. Retrieved from www.telegraphindia.com/1070710/ asp/frontpage/story_8039584.asp

Dutta, M. J. & Dutta, D. (2013). Multicultural going cultural: A postcolonial deconstruction of cultural intelligence. *Journal of International and Intercultural Communication, 6*, 241–258.

Earley, P. C. & Ang, S. (2003). *Cultural intelligence: Individual interactions across cultures*. Stanford, CA: Stanford University Press.

Eriksen, T. H. (2002). *Ethnicity and nationalism*. London: Pluto.

Fox, R. (1967). *Kinship and marriage*. Middlesex: UK: Penguin.

Harvey, D. (2003). The right to the city. *International Journal of Urban and Regional Research, 27*, 939–941.

Mahanta, B. & Nayak, P. (2013). Gender inequality in North East India. *PCC Journal of Economics and Commerce*, 7, 1–13.

McDuie-Ra, D. (2012). *Northeast migrants in Delhi: Race, refuge and retail*. Amsterdam: Amsterdam University Press.

McDuie-Ra, D. (2013). Beyond the exclusionary city: North-east migrants in neo-liberal Delhi. *Urban Studies, 50*, 1625–1640.

McDuie-Ra, D. (2015a). "Is India racist?" Murder, migration and Mary Kom. *South Asia: Journal of South Asian Studies, 38*, 304–319.

McDuie-Ra, D. (2015b). *Debating race in contemporary India*. Basingstoke, UK: Palgrave Macmillan.

McDuie-Ra, D. (2016). Adjacent identities in Northeast India. *Asian Ethnicity, 70*, 400–413.

Merelli, A. (2011). Paris, Milan, Dimapur. *Motherland, 2*(4), 14–23.
Middleton, J. (2014). *Cultural intelligence: The competitive edge for leaders crossing borders.* London: Bloomsbury.
Mumby, D. K. (Ed.). (2010). *Reframing difference in organizational communication studies: Research, pedagogy, and practice.* Thousand Oaks, CA: Sage.
Ngaihte, S. T. & Hanghal, N. (2017). The question of India's North-East identity and solidarity. *Asian Ethnicity, 18*, 38–53.
North East Support Centre and Helpline (NESCH). (2011). North East migration and challenges in national capital cities. Retrieved from http://nehelpline.net/?p=392
Ray, A. K. & Jyrwa, E. (2008). *Female emancipation: Trends and issues in North East India.* New Delhi: Om Publications.
Remesh, B. P. (2012). Strangers in their own land. *Economic & Political Weekly, 47*, 36–40.
Smith, S. H. & Gergen, M. (2015). The diaspora within: Himalayan youth, education-driven migration, and future aspirations of India. *Environment and planning D: Society and Space, 33*, 119–135.
Tracy, S. J. (2013). *Qualitative research methods.* London: Wiley-Blackwell.
Wouters, J. J. P. & Subba, T. B. (2013). The Indian face, India's Northeast, and the idea of India. *Asian Anthropology, 12*, 126–140.
Zou, D. V. & Kumar, M. S. (2011). Mapping a colonial borderland: Objectifying the geobody of India's North East. *Journal of Asian Studies, 70*, 141–170.

23

RETURN MIGRATION[1]

Re-entry acculturative experiences of Chinese returnees from Australian and New Zealand higher education institutions

Mingsheng Li & Yi Yang

This study examines foreign-educated Chinese reverse migratory experiences in China, with a focus on the graduates from higher education institutions (HEIs) in Australia and New Zealand. From 2000 to 2016, altogether 4,255,000 Chinese students had studied or were studying overseas (National Bureau of Statistics of China, 2017). Most of them studied in OECD (Organisation for Economic Co-operation and Development) countries. According to the Chinese National Bureau of Statistics of China (ibid), in 2016, 544,500 Chinese students went overseas to pursue their foreign studies and 432,500 returned to find employment in China; the return rate was 30.55 percent in 2007, but rose to 79.43 percent in 2016, an increase of 49 percent over a space of ten years. A report by the Global University China Career Union (GUCCU, 2017) stated that, by the end of 2017, the estimated number of Chinese returnees would be 660,000. Outbound migration will soon be outpaced by inbound migration.

The magnitude of reverse migration means fierce competition for employment among returnees and between returnees and the giant group of domestic graduates, 15 million, in the Chinese labor market. The GUCCU (2016) report found that, in spite of the increasing popularity of overseas education, the Chinese traditional public perception of overseas returnees as high-caliber elites has changed; these returnees are perceived with mixed feelings. There is a gap between quality and quantity. Foreign qualifications are no longer the "gold collars" they used to be. Foreign qualifications seem to have lost their glitter. Chinese parents and students have begun to question the worth of foreign qualifications. Foreign qualifications no longer guarantee higher income and better jobs when these credential holders return to China. Needham (2017) warned that, "the worsening job prospects for graduates returning to China could send a chill through Australia's third largest export market – international education – which is worth $21.8 billion annually" because what these graduates have acquired is "incompatible to domestic society" (p. 1).

In 2016, 35,415 Chinese students studied in New Zealand (Ministry of Education, 2016) and 196,315 studied in Australia (Department of Education and Training, 2016). Together, the number of Chinese returnees from these two countries amounts to 20.7 percent of total overseas Chinese returnees. There is little research on the return motivations and the prospects of job employment of these Chinese returnees, on the acculturative hardships they face, and on Chinese employers' perceptions of and attitudes towards these returnees and their foreign education. This study considers returnees' reverse migration and job-seeking experiences, cultural re-adaptation and reintegration, and career development, and seeks answers to the following three questions:

RQ1: What motivates Chinese students to return to China after graduation?
RQ2: What are the challenges facing Chinese returnees from Australia and New Zealand?
RQ3: How do Chinese employers perceive returnees' foreign education and their workplace performance in China?

Literature review

Theoretical frameworks applied to return migration

Five theoretical frameworks are presented to help explain the phenomena of international return migration. The *new economics of labor migration* (NELM) holds that return migration is a natural outcome of successful overseas experience that results from achieving goals. Return migration is enacted through a "calculated strategy" to respond to the needs of an individual and the household in relation to market uncertainty (Cassarino, 2004, p. 255). The *structural approach* argues that return migration involves not only individual experiences, but also the influence of social and institutional factors. The success or failure of reverse migration is determined by the correlation of individuals' expectations with the social, cultural, and economic realities of the origin country (Cassarino, 2004; Cerase, 1974). Other determining factors include the returnee's motivations, willingness, ability, and readiness to "readapt to the changed cultural and behavioral patterns of his community of origin and this is resocialization" (Dumon, 1986, p. 122). *Social network theory* regards returnees as bearers of different forms of capital: social, cultural, symbolic, and economic (Bourdieu, 1986). It recognizes the significance of the tangible and intangible resources they bring, as well as the multiple ties and the social and cultural networks they have formed in receiving countries (Cassarino, 2004). These resources can be secured and mobilized for the benefit of returnees and their institutions across borders (Wang & Bao, 2015). *Institutional theory* posits that return migration is influenced and constrained by institutional rules, norms, beliefs, and "rules of the game" at both individual and organizational levels (Wang & Bao, 2015). The tenet of the theory is that, in order to win, returnees should consider person-fit and institution-fit by re-adapting, accommodating, learning, and relearning the institutionalized "game rules," and understanding institutional regulatory and normative structures (Jonkers, 2010; Pan, 2016; Wang & Bao, 2015). The *push–pull model* views reverse migration as a process of decision making based on the result of weighing up the gains and losses (Castles, de Haas, & Miller, 2014). People repatriate because they are pushed by the deterrents in receiving countries, such as poor career and economic opportunities, discrimination, and lack of cultural integration, and pulled by attractions in the origin country, such as preferential policies, career opportunities, and national and cultural identity (Tharenou & Seet, 2014). These five theoretical frameworks indicate that return migration involves personal, institutional, contextual, economic, social, psychological, and cultural factors.

Literature on Chinese returnees

The literature on reverse migration highlights the push–pull effects of economic, social, and cultural problems encountered by repatriates in the host countries, and attractive government policies, career prospects, and emotional attachment to the origin countries (King & Raghuram, 2013; Sieber, 2013; Wadhwa, 2009). A number of pull and push factors influence the massive reverse migration of overseas Chinese graduates. The push factors in host countries include changes in immigration policies, the overseas "non-citizen unfriendly" job market, lack of career opportunities, discrimination, prejudice, and the glass-ceiling effects (barriers to career advancement) in organizations (GUCCU, 2017; Wang & Bao, 2015). The pull factors involve China's preferential policies, high rewards, incentives, favorable working and living environments, opportunities for career development, economic and business opportunities, family ties, advantages of multicultural and multilingual experiences, and invisible and symbolic assets such as fast promotion, and privileged class status (Wang, 2005; Wang & Bao, 2015). China has emerged as an economic giant that can provide a platform for returnees to optimize their skills, experience, and knowledge, and fulfill expectations, dreams and self-actualization (ibid).

Chinese returnees, with their human capital, talent, and wisdom, are now playing a critical role in China's "One-Belt One-Road Initiative" (Wang & Miao, 2016), which focuses on establishing links and cooperation between Eurasian countries, developing the Chinese economy, expanding the scope of internationalization, and transforming the economic, social, cultural, and geopolitical landscape of the world (Winter, 2016). Formulated by Chinese President Xi Jinping, this initiative is a very important foreign policy that provides a blueprint for Chinese economic expansion and integration by developing an infrastructural network linking China with Asia, Africa, and Europe (Li, 2017). The strategy indicates that a large number of foreign-educated graduates are sorely needed to help Chinese enterprises and multinational companies to fulfill the goals they have set for internationalization (Wang, 2016).

There is a paradox in the Chinese labor market. On the one hand, there is a severe shortage of talent in the Chinese labor market (Yao & Wang, 2014). According to a LinkedIn report, nearly 70 percent of Chinese state enterprises have difficulties recruiting talent (Chen, 2016). This means there are many opportunities for overseas returnees. There is a huge market demand for talented people (ibid). On the other hand, there are many returnees who cannot find jobs. Unemployment has caused serious concerns for parents, returnees, and local and central governments (Hao, Wen, & Welch, 2016; Hua, Jie, & Gang, 2005).

Wang and Bao (2015) observed that returnees have lost their competitive edge in relation to local peers and the situation is worsening for several reasons: returnees' foreign qualifications and skills from low-level overseas universities and dodgy certificates; a huge expansion in the number of returnees, which allows employers to choose from a much larger pool of such individuals, thus turning what had been a seller's into a buyer's market; returnees' limited knowledge of local conditions and lack of a local support network; and unrealistically high expectations with respect to salary and promotion opportunities. Hua et al. (2005) stated that returnees did not have any obvious advantage compared to locals who understood the situation in China and were equally fluent in a foreign language. Hua et al. believed that the inevitable consequence of return unemployment was associated with changes in the composition of the returnees who had been or might have been losers in the fierce competition in China, and went to study in overseas universities seen as enterprises that had been commercialized by lowering the threshold to make profits from international students. Needham

(2017) seemed to agree that educational standards in the West are increasingly declining as a result of universities tending to emphasize the research on which lecturers and professors are assessed rather than their teaching, a situation causing dissatisfaction on the part of both domestic and international students.

Method

This research was conducted in 18 cities in China from January 2010 to December 2011. We interviewed 52 returnees: 16 from Australia and 36 from New Zealand; 27 were male and 25 female. They held a range of qualifications: 4 doctorates, 14 master's, 29 bachelor's, and 5 postgraduate diplomas.[2] They had studied a variety of subjects, mostly business-related, such as business, accounting, finance, international business, management, and other subjects, such as education, IT, engineering, and digital media. The length of their stay in Australia and New Zealand ranged from 1 to 16 years and the duration of their stay in China varied from three months to nine years. The interview questions focused on their job-seeking experience, strengths and challenges in the workplace, level of satisfaction, self-evaluation of performance, and contribution to the organization (see Appendix 1). We also interviewed ten Chinese employers (CEO and senior managers) who employed returnees, who were not necessarily returning from Australia and New Zealand. The interviews asked these employers questions about their perceptions of, views on, evaluation of, and attitudes toward the returnees working in their organizations or returnees in general.

We approached some returnees who we knew personally, and asked them to introduce us to other potential participants who met our selection criteria; that is, they had studied at HEIs (excluding language training establishments) in the two countries, earned a qualification, and returned to China permanently to live and work. Of the 52 interviews, 16 were conducted face to face, and 36 through long-distance phone calls, QQ, and Wechat.[3] The interviews were digitally recorded with the participants' consent, and transcribed verbatim by a Chinese speaker. The transcripts were thematically classified, coded, and assigned meaning for data analysis based on the five theoretical frameworks mentioned in the literature review. The major themes included returnees' motivations to return, expectations, willingness to re-adapt to the new cultural reality, and social and contextual factors that facilitated and constrained returnees' return acculturation. In this chapter, for ethical reasons, all participants' and employers' names have been coded – P1, P2, P3.../E1, E2, E3... – to indicate the order of the interviews.

Results

Three recurrent major themes were identified in this study: motivation to return to China, challenges in job hunting, and employers' perceptions of returnees' foreign qualifications. These themes will be presented individually in this section.

Theme 1: motivation to return to China

The study found that, although returnees identified various reasons for their return migration, the push and pull factors were major contributors. The push factors in the receiving countries (Australia and New Zealand in this case) include immigration policy changes, difficulty finding decent employment, the glass-ceiling effect, white privilege, and discrimination. The pull factors in China include rapid economic development, career opportunities, attractive government policies, family ties, and a sense of belonging.

The push factors in receiving countries

Most participants reported that changes in immigration policies in Australia and New Zealand made it difficult for them to acquire permanent residency (PR). They were in a Catch 22 situation: without PR, it was difficult for them to gain employment as many employers required applicants to have PR status; without a job, it was difficult for them to meet the immigration requirements for PR. For example, P37, who had earned a master's degree in international business, had expected to stay in Australia. However, she had difficulty finding a job. She ended up in a Chinese-owned recycling factory, earning a very a low salary to help pay her bills. Not wanting to waste her talent, she returned to China and found a job as a lecturer at a university.

Finding employment that matches one's qualifications is tough for most Chinese students, whether they have obtained PR or not. P46 had acquired the PR status and had two master's degrees, one in banking and the other in management. He spent two years in New Zealand after graduation trying his best to gain a job relevant to his qualifications. Before he could find a suitable job, he worked as a mail sorter at New Zealand Post. Disheartened, he had to leave his parents and relatives behind in New Zealand and return to China. He was immediately appointed senior manager at Standard Chartered Bank.

For many Chinese students, unemployment, under-employment, and no prospects of career development in the receiving countries created in them a sense of low self-esteem. P38, with a master's degree in education from an Australian university, found that she was positioned at the bottom level of society, and felt a loss of human dignity and self-esteem in response to her inability to utilize her knowledge. Her observations of other Chinese graduates with doctoral and master's degrees struggling for survival chilled her heart. Other participants (e.g., P21, P32, P40, P43, P46, P47, P49, P50) expressed similar feelings. They felt that the receiving countries could not provide what they were looking for, such as respect, recognition, a sense of belonging, identity, job security, and cultural integration. It was difficult for a Chinese person to live a reasonably good life in Australia. They were disappointed to see so many Chinese people with higher degrees working as waiters, waitresses, taxi drivers, shop assistants, rubbish collectors, and kitchen hands; some living on benefits, and some marrying people they did not love.

The glass-ceiling effect on career development was mentioned by those who had secured decent jobs and had worked in receiving countries. Despite their excellent performance, they had no expectation of promotion. Promotions and leadership roles were specifically designed for white colleagues, who enjoyed white privilege in terms of skin color, the English language, accent, networks, and other hidden rules of the game. P37, an Australian university graduate with a master's degree in international business, expressed her frustration with the glass ceiling effect and white privilege. P21, a chartered accountant in New Zealand, supported this view. Having experienced the glass-ceiling effect whilst working in an organization in New Zealand, she was determined to return to China. Upon her return, she was appointed senior manager in a large state-run firm in China. She said, "I have observed in New Zealand that in all organizations, and government agencies, senior positions are taken by the white. It is very rare to see non-whites take any leadership positions."

The pull factors in China

In consensus, all returnees listed China's rapid economic development as a top factor that lured them back. The dynamic economy could potentially provide them with boundless opportunities for career advancement, realization of aspirations, and dreams; boost their self-esteem and confidence; and maximize their human capital and professional skills.

Most returnees agreed that there were many opportunities in China. There were openings in many areas, and they could seize chances to fully maximize their human and cultural capital. P5, for example, who had gained a bachelor's degree in business studies, established his own consultancy company providing services to people who wish to study overseas. His company had found the market niche in the city and his business was thriving. Like him, seven other returnees (P3, P4, P10, P11, P27, P40, and P50) had established their own companies, using the knowledge and experience they had acquired overseas to make a mark on their home cities. They had the strong support of the local government, such as the provision of start-up funds, tax exemptions, and office sites. P28 supported P27's idea, identifying that, for those who wish to achieve their big goals, China provides a battleground in which they can play a big role. Young and ambitious returnee talent could find their place and use their wisdom, intelligence, and knowledge to change and transform not only an organization but also the society in which they live.

The many incentives, preferential policies, and talent strategies geared toward returnees by the Chinese central and local governments and Chinese universities became "talent magnets," luring Chinese students back to China. P41, having spent seven years completing her master's and PhD in Australia, felt proud to return to China where she could find a feeling of "home" and hold her head high instead of struggling in a foreign land. She became a professor at a Chinese university immediately upon her return and stated that she felt she had regained her self-esteem and confidence. She had realized her dreams in China. She had also received a large research grant from the government, something her Australian supervisors could not imagine. She said, "There are many opportunities in China."

Participants 42, 48, and 51 had received their doctoral degrees in Australia and were lured back to China by prospects of employment in universities. They were each offered a professorship well before they landed in China. P42 became a senior researcher and was offered a huge grant (millions of yuan) to support her research in anthropology. P48 was appointed dean of a university college. P51 was made associate dean of a college and was also awarded millions of yuan to set up a new laboratory. According to P47, the preferential policies at all levels (university, province, and central government) facilitated the return of foreign-educated Chinese talent. Such policies also shaped positive public perceptions about returnees. Chinese universities were hungrily seeking such high-caliber talent.

Family ties is another motivating factor for returnees. Many participants were single children and it is a social expectation that families stay together. P1 returned to China because her parents wanted her to help with the family business. She said that her family business needed her professional skills and foreign experience. P36 returned to China to get married because her fiancé was in China. P48 and P50 were eager to return to China to perform their filial obligations in looking after their aging parents. Family connections are associated with the social and cultural environment. Many returnees felt very happy to live in such supportive networks, in a familiar social and cultural environment devoid of white privilege, discrimination, and glass-ceilings. P28 noted, "If I had not returned to have a taste of the flavor of comfortable life, a life under your control, in China, and a sense of belonging, I would have regretted not having done so."

Theme 2: challenges encountered by returnees

Six subthemes relating to reverse acculturative challenges were identified in this study, all contributing to the difficulties returnees experience in seeking employment, adapting to the culture, and reintegrating into society: lack of work experience, employers' suspicion of overseas qualifications, lack of competitive edge, low and inequitable salary, inflated foreign qualifications, and unsatisfactory foreign language skills.

Lack of work experience

When the quality of foreign credentials and graduate employability skills cannot be guaranteed, work experience becomes vital in the Chinese labour market. In recruiting new staff members, Chinese organizations regard work experience as a top priority. Those who had gained work experience before they went overseas to study or after their graduation could find jobs more easily than those who had not. Work experience became an indicator of the candidate's performance capability. P7 and P44, who had earned master's degrees in English education in Australia and New Zealand, respectively, were welcomed back to the universities where they had taught English. P43 had a similar experience. She used to work at the Provincial Department of Education before she went to Australia to study for a master's degree in education. Her previous work experience and her social network helped her acquire a job at a key university in the province. P6 had some work experience in marketing with Sony in New Zealand, and when he returned to China he easily found a job with Sony in his hometown. Organizations were reluctant to spend time and resources training new recruits on the job. P31 commented that work experience, local or foreign, was essential for job seekers.

However, not all returnees had work experience. Lack of work experience became a major obstacle to returnees in finding employment. P3 said, "Employers are realistic. You must have experience that can be utilized to help the company to make profits." P18, a fresh graduate from a New Zealand university, spent four months seeking employment. He sent many CVs, but never got an interview.

Employers' suspicion of overseas qualifications

Chinese employers have begun to question the value of foreign qualifications. P48 reported that, although returnees' overseas experiences were welcomed by Chinese employers, they were hesitant to recruit returnees without work experience because they were not sure of the quality of their qualifications and their actual occupational skills. P35 explained that employers took extra precautions when recruiting returnees because they were influenced by negative media reports of Chinese students studying overseas, describing them as *liuxuelaji* (rubbish from overseas). Such damaging reports shaped public perceptions about the quality of overseas Chinese students and reversed initial impressions of returnees as sought-after talent, high-end scholars and researchers. P39 agreed that there was some truth in these socially negative perceptions and therefore work experience and the ranking of universities became benchmarks.

Lack of competitive edge over locals

Unlike returnees in the 1980s and 1990s, who were considered elites, returnees after the year 2000 seem to have lost their competitive edge. P7, who had a master's degree in education from an Australian university, said Chinese employers questioned her Australian degree. When she was looking for jobs, they were more interested in her undergraduate degree from a Chinese university. The logic was clear: only good students who passed the Chinese university matriculation examination could be admitted into Chinese universities; under-achievers would pay money to study in foreign universities. Their degrees could be bought rather than earned. She stressed that such a perception was prevalent among Chinese employers and was detrimental to returnees from developed countries. P4 observed that employers preferred domestic graduates to returnees because they were trained in the Chinese educational system and they had a better understanding of the Chinese market and Chinese communication styles, manners, and etiquettes. This means that returnees were competing both among themselves and with locals.

Low and inequitable salary

Low and inequitable salaries have posed a serious challenge to returnees. Earning power reflects how a society views the qualifications and professional skills returnees bring with them; the higher their salaries, the more their qualifications and professional skills are valued. This study found that, except for those working in foreign-invested companies, almost all agreed that they had been under-paid, far below their expectations. Many returnees had paid a high price to acquire their foreign credentials and expected to get reasonable returns for this educational investment. Their expectations were not met.

Many were forced to lower their expectations and to accept low-paid jobs. P44 gained a master's degree in education in New Zealand and then returned to the university where she had taught for more than ten years. She was disappointed that her monthly salary remained almost the same, despite having gained a further qualification, at around 3,000 yuan (US$455) per month. She had to accept a job as an associate professor because she did not want to leave her hometown. P48 was lured back by the university where she had worked as a lecturer. She was the first academic with a foreign doctoral degree at this university. Upon her return, she became an associate professor and was appointed dean of a school. The university was very proud that she had returned. However, she was very disappointed with her salary – about 5,000 yuan (US$750) per month.[4] She regretted having returned to China and believed that her foreign doctoral degree and her contribution to the university were worth more than she was paid. In addition, she said, the university had made many promises none of which were kept.

Inflated foreign qualifications

Gone are the days when foreign qualifications were considered sacred in the Chinese labor market. P38 and P43 believed that Chinese employers were rational; they did not blindly believe in foreign qualifications that had been inflated or in top or non-top universities. They had to be "picky." Foreign qualifications had obviously lost their luster. Both positive and negative perceptions existed among the Chinese public. Some employers even believed Chinese qualifications were much better than foreign ones. One-year or 1.5-year master's degrees from the UK, Australia, and New Zealand were not considered as good as, or not better than, three-year master's degrees in China. Such perceptions influenced Chinese recruiting practices. P48, the dean of a faculty, indicated that her university would not consider recruiting returnees with a one-year master's degree from the UK whose academic background and professional skills appeared "dodgy." Her university preferred its own postgraduates to returnees.

Candidates' actual skills and performance capabilities are what count; qualifications are secondary. Many returnees reported that Chinese private or state-run enterprises, HEIs, and government agencies did not differentiate between Chinese and foreign qualifications in the recruitment process. P2 and P3 observed that human resource managers were interested in applicants' hands-on work experience rather than in which universities or countries they had studied. P3 realized that what employers were after were people who had adequate qualifications, domestic or foreign, who met the job requirements, had personalities that matched the organizational culture, had interpersonal communication skills, and who understood the Chinese environment. That is, employers were interested in what returnees could offer to their organizations. He reported that one of his friends had gained a master's degree from Oxford University and, nonetheless, had been trying to get a job for over a year. In a nutshell, credentials from top universities might not guarantee employment.

Returnees' unsatisfactory foreign language skills

It seems that command of a foreign language is one advantage that returnees may have over home-educated students. However, reality does not support this. P46, a bank manager, found that not all returnees had a good command of a foreign language or good communication skills. In his experience, when interviews are conducted in a foreign language, little surprise is shown when some domestic graduates perform as well as or better than some returnees. He questioned the educational quality of foreign universities. P31 explained that, during her six years of studying accountancy at both undergraduate and postgraduate levels in New Zealand, 70–80 percent of the students in the class were Chinese. In group discussions, Chinese students tended to talk in Chinese. In such a learning environment, Chinese students lacked opportunities to practice their English with native speakers. She said that her English had not improved much in her six years of study.

Theme 3: Chinese employers' perceptions of returnees

Chinese employers' perceptions of foreign-educated returnees can influence their recruiting practices. Most employers participating in this study viewed returnees holding foreign qualifications from prestigious universities in developed countries in a positive light. Some employers, however, questioned the value of foreign qualifications and the performance capabilities of returnees.

Positive perceptions

In the Chinese higher education sector, recruiting the best candidates – those who have gained qualifications in developed countries – is an important strategy. All of the senior managers in universities (E1–E4) mentioned that it was essential for Chinese universities to recruit returnees who had been trained in Western educational systems so that teaching and research in Chinese higher education could ultimately be transformed and match international standards. Returnees could act both as a bridge to connect Chinese universities with foreign universities and as agents to internationalize China's education system. They believed these returnees, armed with Western credentials, professional skills, and practical work and research experience, had contributed enormously to the high-quality teaching and research at their universities and were playing an irreplaceable role in Chinese higher education. The international educational experience, vision, and cultural and social capital returnees had acquired overseas were valuable assets to Chinese universities bent on internationalization endeavors. These returnees had changed the universities' academic culture by introducing new programs and courses, new teaching pedagogies, and new research methods.

E9 had recruited two returnees in his software development company. He believed that graduates from the world's top universities were much better performers than those from

Chinese universities. Returnees were more likely to possess strong professional skills, use critical thinking, have a flexible and effective working style, and a better work ethic than domestic graduates. He commented that the two returnees in his company took a leadership role in undertaking key projects. They made great contributions to the company's software development. They had strong professional skills and acted as exemplars to others. He was satisfied with their performance, commitment, leadership, integrity, enthusiasm, independence, willingness to learn and challenge themselves, and the profit they made for the company.

E6 explained that his government agency had recruited one returnee to enhance the agency's intercultural communication capabilities in dealings with foreign companies in the city. It was his expectation that the agency would recruit more returnees from Western top universities. He emphasized that most returnees had been well-trained in the West. Their return would benefit China's development and transformation. He argued that government agencies needed more returnees specialized in social science, media communication, organizational communication, and communication management. He commented, "In general, returnees are smarter than domestic graduates. They need a platform to make full use of their skills and talent. We must provide such a platform."

Other employers (E1, E7, E8, and E10) also mentioned the advantages of employing returnees. They all believed that their organizations had benefited from these returnees' foreign experience, their new ideas and new ways of doing things, and their professional knowledge and skills. Their participation was helping these organizations enhance their business operations, break pervasive mindsets in business, transform the company, and uplift corporate performance and branding.

Negative perceptions

Despite the positive attitudes toward recruiting returnees, most employers agreed that returnees encountered many re-entry acculturative challenges. E3 summarized these challenges in this way:

> They have difficulty re-adapting to the Chinese socio-cultural environment and cannot keep them grounded [接地气]. They have insufficient understanding and knowledge about China even though they were born and grew up in the country.

He further identified that academic returnees in his university encountered strong resistance to their Western-style teaching pedagogies and academic writing conventions, on the part of both students and other academics. Having been away from China for a long time, they had lost contact with their social networks and thus could not compete with home-educated graduates.

E1 and E2 pointed out that the overall quality of returnees has been compromised. He attributed this declining quality to a single factor – foreign universities competing with one another to enrol as many students as possible by lowering entry requirements to fill classes and coffers when budgets are shrinking. Many Chinese students who were unable to enter Chinese universities were admitted to study in Western universities. The massification of international education has changed how the Chinese perceive returnees; they are no longer viewed as the "elite" and, instead, are seen as *liuxuelaji* who have purchased rather than earned their foreign degrees.

E8, director of a construction company, had employed two returnees in his company. He had not witnessed any outstanding performance on their part or recognized that they possessed any special attributes. The company was concerned with how much profit each could make not with their qualifications, or the universities they had received them from, or the countries they had studied in.

E10, sales manager of an electrical appliances company, insisted that qualifications were not important. For him, members' loyalty to and identification with the company, personal integrity, dedication, and the professional skills needed to help the company to grow were the crucial issues. He complained that the performance of the four returnees in his company fell far short of expectations. He said, "I prefer home-educated graduates over returnees." He stressed that it was naive and unrealistic to think that returnees could directly transplant what they had learned in the West to the Chinese reality.

E7, manager of a home appliances company, held a similar view. He observed that training returnees to understand the Chinese market took longer than training domestic graduates. Lack of solid knowledge of Chinese culture, society, tradition, and business market was the biggest obstacle for returnees in their re-entry adaptation. He explained that many returnees were not familiar with interpersonal communication (*guanxi*) in the workplace, were unable to adapt quickly to the new environment and integrate themselves into the society, and were prone to disappointment when their unrealistically high expectations could not be met.

Discussion

This study highlights the key issues and challenges encountered by Chinese returnees in the process of their repatriation. These issues and challenges can be explained by the five theoretical frameworks discussed in the literature review. Chinese returnees were pushed by the deterrents in receiving countries and then pulled back to China by a range of factors. Returnees, having achieved their goal of obtaining foreign qualifications and social, cultural, and symbolic capital from overseas, were motivated to repatriate to pursue their economic interests, for career advancement, and to achieve individual goals. Their human capital, social and cultural networks, and multiple ties with Western universities and societies became valuable assets for returnees themselves, their families, organizations, communities, and the origin country. Their return migration was enacted through a very well-calculated strategy and careful planning to ensure personal and family benefits (Cassarino, 2004). Returnees vary in their expectations, motivation, resocialization, and readiness to embrace the changed cultural reality of the origin country, and therefore the outcomes (success or failure) of their acculturation, heavily influenced by structural factors, also vary from person to person (Dumon, 1986).

Institutional and structural factors facilitate and constrain returnees' reverse migration. The study shows that most Chinese employers held a positive attitude towards returnees. They sought returnees to boost organizational branding and reputation, increase production, improve services, and make a profit. Returnees also held high expectations about their return: employment, career opportunities, high remunerations, quick promotions, and an important role in the workplace. This study indicates that there was often a mismatch between the expectations of returnees and employers. The mismatch was attributed to returnees' unrealistic expectations, lack of understanding of the local reality, and poor readjustment (Tharenou & Seet, 2014).

One of the most serious mismatches concerned low salaries. Gross and Connor (2007) maintained that "market principles will dictate pay and other monetary incentives". Salaries are determined by the labor market, interaction of supply and demand for labor, competition, productivity, workers' capacity, educational qualifications, experience, prevailing salary structure of the sector, the industry, and the community. Oversupply results in the falling of earning capabilities (Boden & Nedeva, 2010). In such a labor market, it is unrealistic for some returnees to expect to recover their investment in foreign education within a short time period. Indeed, there is evidence to suggest that an overseas education still had a positive effect on the starting salary of returnees and that returnees were likely to earn more than locals (Miao, 2016). Some high-caliber returnees may be compensated for their foreign experiences, professional skills, and language advantages. However, it is unlikely that employers will create an unreasonable pay gap between returnees and locals if returnees are not able to demonstrate their outstanding performance and unique contribution.

The massification and commercialization of international education have produced a large number of graduates and have devalued the popularity of previously highly prized and competitive qualifications in the labor market (Altbach & Welch, 2011). The returns on both cultural and human capital have reduced to a disappointing level as these credentials have become less competitive than was the case a decade ago (Gribble & Blackmore, 2012). The positive image of elite Chinese returnees now seems to have altered in line with changes in the labor market and the massive influx of millions of graduates trained in China and overseas (Pan, 2016). In the already competitive labor market, returnees have to compete fiercely not only with locals but also their peers. Such a structural disequilibrium provides employers with a large pool of ready and cheap labor for any available post (Boden & Nedeva, 2010).

This study implies that there is an issue of concern for the Chinese government. Although there are hundreds of talent programs and strategies in China designed to attract top-notch scholars and researchers, policies should also exist to support returnees who may not be included in, for example, the 100-Talent Scheme. It is reasonable for the Chinese government to attract the top 1 percent of returnees, but ignoring 99 percent of them would represent a policy failure and a disastrous loss of human capital. Most of these returnees have been well-trained in the West. Their human capital is a great asset for China. They need support to readapt and to reintegrate into Chinese society. It should be understood that return migration is dynamic. Today, they repatriate to China because it suits their varied personal needs and ambitions. Tomorrow, if they are not satisfied with how they are treated, they may re-repatriate to other countries. Their human capital has become an international asset that allows them to move from one place to another on the international stage.

Conclusion

This study explored the push and pull factors that motivated returnees from Australia and New Zealand to return to China. The unfavorable socio-cultural environments in host societies pushed Chinese returnees to return to a China that is attractive for those seeking career opportunities, economic benefits, respect, self-esteem, family connections, and a sense of belonging. At re-entry, returnees had many opportunities available to them as a result of their foreign education, overseas experience, foreign language advantage, and the existing positive perceptions of returnees at a societal level. Overall, they were welcomed and highly valued by employers in China. They also encountered many challenges, such as low salaries, difficulty in finding employment due to their lack of work experience and employers' skeptical attitude toward foreign qualifications, skills acquired in foreign countries not being applicable to the local Chinese context, and strong competition in the labor market involving both locals and returnees. Foreign qualifications are no longer a guarantee of employment and a high salary.

Notes

1 This chapter was presented at the International Conference on Business and Information, Bali, Indonesia, July 7–9, 2013.
2 A postgraduate diploma is a higher-level qualification than a bachelor's degree but is shorter in duration than a master's degree. It is a one-year program in New Zealand. A master's degree program normally takes 1.5 years to complete.
3 QQ and Wechat are two social media apps in China with millions of users.
4 This interview was conducted in 2010. The first author of this chapter interviewed her in 2016. She reported that her monthly salary was around 10,000 yuan (8,000 yuan as the base salary and 2,000 yuan in bonuses).

References

Altbach, P. G. & Welch, A. (2011). The perils of commercialism: Australia's example. *International Higher Education, 62*, 21–23.

Boden, R. & Nedeva, M. (2010). Employing discourse: Universities and graduate "employability". *Journal of Education Policy, 25*, 37–54.

Bourdieu, P. (1986). The forms of capital. In J. Richardson (Ed.), *Handbook of theory and research for the sociology of education* (pp. 241–258). Westport, CT: Greenwood.

Cassarino, J.-P. (2004). Theorising return migration: The conceptual approach to return migrants revisited. *International Journal on Multicultural Societies, 6*, 253–279.

Castles, S., de Haas, H., & Miller, M. J. (2014). *The age of migration: International population movements in the modern world* (5th ed). London: Palgrave Macmillan.

Cerase, F. P. (1974). Expectations and reality: A case study of return migration from the United States to Southern Italy. *International Migration Review, 8*, 245–262.

Chen, X. (2016). Nearly 70 pc state enterprises have difficulties recruiting high-end talent. LinkedIn report. Retrieved from http://world.people.com.cn/n1/2016/1117/c1002-28875850.html

Department of Education and Training. (2016). End of year summary of international student enrolment data – Australia – 2016. Retrieved from https://internationaleducation.gov.au/research/International-Student-Data/Documents/MONTHLY%20SUMMARIES/2016/12_December_2016_FullYearAnalysis.pdf

Dumon, W. (1986). Problems faced by migrations and their family members, particularly second generation migrants, in returning to and reintegrating into their countries of origin. *International Migration Review, 24*, 113–128.

Global University China Career Union (GUCCU). (2016). Chinese overseas elites career development report 2016. Retrieved from www.guccu.org/content/pdf/CareerDevelopme.pdf

Global University China Career Union (GUCCU). (2017). *Chinese overseas elites career development report 2017*. Retrieved from www.guccu.org/content/pdf/ChineseOverseas.pdf

Gribble, C. & Blackmore, J. (2012). Re-positioning Australia's international education in global knowledge economies: Implications of shifts in skilled migration policies for universities. *Journal of Higher Education Policy and Management, 34*, 341–354.

Gross, A. & Connor, A. (2007). Managing Chinese returnees. *Mobility Magazine*. Retrieved from www.job168.com/english/resource/viewnews.jsp?info_no=38583

Hao, J., Wen, W., & Welch, A. (2016). When sojourners return: Employment opportunities and challenges facing high-skilled Chinese returnees. *Asian and Pacific Migration Journal, 25*, 22–40.

Hua, S., Jie, G., & Gang, C. (2005). Can foreign diplomas be exchanged for "Chinese opportunities"? *Chinese Education & Society, 38*, 81–86.

Jonkers, K. (2010). *Mobility, migration, and the Chinese scientific research system*. London: Routledge.

King, R. & Raghuram, P. (2013). International student migration: Mapping the field and new research agendas. *Population, Space and Place, 19*, 127–137.

Li, C. (2017). *The power of ideas: The rising influence of thinkers and think tanks in China*. London: World Scientific.

Miao, M. L. (2016). China's return migration and its impact on Chinese development. In H. Wang & Y. Liu (Eds.), *Entrepreneurship and talent management from a global perspective: Global returnees* (pp. 15–32). Northampton, MA: Edward Elgar Publishing.

Ministry of Education. (2016). *International students in New Zealand*. Retrieved from www.educationcounts.govt.nz/statistics/international-education/international-students-in-new-zealand

National Bureau of Statistics of China. (2017). *China statistical yearbook*. Beijing: China Statistics Press.

Needham, K. (2017). Chinese students question Australian education sending chills through industry. *Sydney Morning Herald*. Retrieved from www.smh.com.au/world/chinese-students-question-australian-education-sending-chills-through-industry-20170919-gykfgi.html

Pan, S. (2016). Competing for global talents. In S. Guo (Ed.), *Spotlight on China: Chinese education in the globalized world* (pp. 341–357). Rotterdam: SensePublishers.

Sieber, H. (2013). *Chinese "sea-turtles" and importing a culture of innovation: Trends in Chinese human capital migration in the 21st century*, PhD thesis, Duke University.

Tharenou, P. & Seet, P.-S. (2014). China's reverse brain drain: Regaining and retaining talent. *International Studies of Management and Organization, 44*, 55–74.

Wadhwa, V. (2009). A reverse brain drain. *Issues in Science and Technology, XXV*(3), 45–52.

Wang, C. (2016, August 12). *Making the foreign serve China, and maximize the role of haigui*. Centre for China and Globalization.

Wang, H. (2005). *The returning times*. Beijing: Central Editing and Translation Press.

Wang, H. & Bao, Y. (2015). *Reverse migration in contemporary China: Returnees, entrepreneurship and the Chinese economy*. New York: Palgrave Macmillan.

Wang, H. & Miao, L. (2016). *Annual report on the development of Chinese students studying abroad 2016 (No 5)*. Beijing: Social Sciences and Academic Press.

Winter, T. (2016, March 29). One belt, one road, one heritage: Cultural diplomacy and the silk road. *The Diplomat*. https://thediplomat.com/2016/03/one-belt-one-road-one-heritage-cultural-diplomacy-and-the-silk-road/

Yao, S. & Wang, P. (2014). *China's outward foreign direct investments and impact on the world economy*. New York: Palgrave.

Appendix 1

Interview questions for returnees

- Age: ______________
- Gender: ______________
- City in which you now reside: ____________________________
- In which country did you study?

  ☐ Australia
  ☐ New Zealand

- How long did you remain in this country? ______________
- Degree obtained: ____________________________
- Subject you majored in: ____________________________
- How long ago did you return to China? ______________

1. Are you looking for a job now or have you found a job?
2. If you have found a job, how long did it take you to find it?
3. If the job you are doing now related to your overseas qualifications? Please explain.
4. Can you apply what you learned in New Zealand or Australia to your current work? Why?
5. Do you think you have received a good return on your investment in overseas education? Why?
6. When you were/are looking for jobs, what were/are the major challenges to you? What did you do/have you done to meet such challenges? Please give examples.

7. Do you think your New Zealand/Australian university credentials have enabled you to gain a competitive edge in accessing employment? Why?
8. Compared with credentials from the US, the UK, Germany, Japan, and France, what are the advantages/disadvantages of New Zealand/Australian credentials in the Chinese labor market? How have your employers perceived your overseas qualifications?
9. Compared to China-educated graduates of a similar level, does your overseas qualification give you a competitive edge? Please explain.
10. What is your view towards the career prospects of foreign-educated returned graduates?
11. In your view, what should Australian/New Zealand universities do to promote the employability of international students so that they possess competitive advantages in the international labor market?
12. What is your future plan?

Appendix 2

Interview questions for employers

Organization (work unit): ____________________
Position: ____________________

1. Do you employ foreign-educated returnees in your company? How many of them are working in your company? Can you explain to me why they were employed?
2. What are your employment standards when you employ these returnees? What are your expectations? Do you require evidence of their domestic and overseas work and professional experiences, and do you take into account the ranking of the universities from which they graduated? Why?
3. What are the advantages of employing these returnees? Can they fully maximize their advantages in your company? Please give specific examples.
4. What are the disadvantages of employing these returnees? How can they overcome such disadvantages? What are the key challenges for them?
5. What is your opinion of the overall performance of these returnees? Are you happy with their performance? Have their performances met your expectations? Please explain.
6. What benefits have these returnees brought to your company?
7. Which of these two types of graduate do you prefer to recruit: home-grown graduates or foreign-educated graduates? Please explain.
8. When you recruit foreign-educated returnees, what aspects of the person and skills do you emphasize most?
9. Can the potential of these returnees be fully maximized in your company? Can they fully apply their professional skills in their work?
10. Does your company have preferential policies for foreign-educated returnees? If yes, what are the key points of these policies?
11. Media reports suggest that the overall quality of foreign-educated returnees has declined. What is your view? Do you support this view? Why?
12. Will your company employ more foreign-educated returnees? What is your ideal candidate?
13. What are your suggestions to those who are still studying overseas but may wish to return to work in China?

24

COMMUNICATION WITH NON-HOST-NATIONALS

The case of sojourning students from the United States and China

Yang Liu

The emergence of globalization has not only greatly boosted the transnational flow of information and commodities, but also enhanced personnel flow. As a result, more and more students decide to study abroad, and embrace different cultures. Compared to any other country in the world, the United States hosts the highest number of international students (Verbik & Lasanowski, 2007). International student enrollment at US universities in the 2015–2016 academic year amounted to 1,043,839, with a year-on-year growth rate of 7.1 percent (Institute of International Education, 2016). Of these sojourning students, 3.1 percent are originally from the People's Republic of China; 328,547 students in 2015–2016 (Institute of International Education, 2016). On the other side of the Pacific Ocean, China has steadily grown into a popular destination for students who want to accumulate intercultural experiences; 442,773 international students studied in China in 2016, an increase of 11.35 percent on 2015. The ever-increasing number of American students studying in China has made them the second-largest group of international students in China (5.4 percent in 2016), following only South Korean students (Ministry of Education of the People's Republic of China, 2017).

Owing to their sojourn in different cultures, international students will undergo changes, culturally and psychologically. Redfield, Linton, and Herskovits (1936) termed this process *acculturation*; that is, the phenomena that "result when groups of individuals have different cultures and come into first-hand contact with subsequent changes in the original pattern of either or both groups" (p. 149). At the core of intercultural communication studies, acculturation is enacted and internalized by sojourning individuals' social interaction during intercultural encounters. Specific to international students, their social interaction can be divided into three categories: inter-ethnic communication with host nationals, inter-ethnic communication with international fellows (sojourners and immigrants from other countries), and intra-ethnic communication with co-nationals. Among these three types of communication, the last two are less explored in terms of their contribution to sojourning students' acculturation in host countries. To fill this gap, this chapter will examine the impact of sojourning students' communication with their co-ethnics and with their international fellows on their acculturation in the host countries. The social circles of Chinese sojourning students in the US and American sojourning students in China will be explored as two cases to illustrate what communication with their co-nationals and international fellows mean to their acculturation in host countries.

Two perspectives on sojourning individuals' communication with non-host-nationals

Advocacy of communication with host-nationals

The idea that international students' relationship with the host culture and their home culture can impact their acculturation in host countries has been studied extensively (Liu, 2017). Some scholars argued that international students' social interaction with their co-nationals would separate them from the host culture, and thus hinder their intercultural adjustment in the long run (Citron, 1996; Kim, 1988, 2001, 2006, 2011; Kitsantas, 2004; Pitts, 2009). For instance, Citron (1996) stated that American students, who spend the majority of time with their co-nationals when studying abroad, engaged less with members of the host culture. Pitts (2009) described this phenomenon as the by-product of these American students' failure to communicate or connect with host-nationals. Kitsantas (2004) reported that the social gathering with co-nationals did not lead to sojourning students' enhanced cultural competence. The preference for inter-ethnic communication with host nationals over social interaction with sojourners' co-nationals or co-ethnics is attributed to the emphasis of intercultural communication studies on biculturalism, which places sojourning individuals' national or ethnic ties in opposition to their ties with the host culture (Liu, 2017). Consequently, the host cultural identity of sojourners and immigrants and their home cultural or ethnic identity are negotiated in a zero-sum game that is characterized by such dichotomous categories as either/or (Kramer, 2000; Liu, 2015). These negotiations encourage sojourners and immigrants to develop the host cultural identity, which is considered the optimal and ultimate goal of acculturation (Gudykunst, 1985, 1995; Kim, 1988, 1991, 2001, 2011; Ting-Toomey, 2005). Inter-ethnic communication with host nationals is thus advocated as the key to sojourning individuals' successful assimilation into the host culture. Obviously, intra-ethnic communication with co-nationals or co-ethnics is then regarded as the obstacle to the formation of the host cultural identity, especially beyond their initial phase of sojourn (Kim, 1988, 1991, 2001, 2011).

Cross-cultural adaptation theory describes the dualistic relationship between sojourners' and immigrants' host cultural identity and home cultural identity or ethnic identity (Kim, 1988, 1991, 2001, 2011, 2015). Positing that a person is an open system that coevolves with the socio-cultural environment, cross-cultural adaptation theory argues that it is "the natural human tendency to struggle to regain an internal equilibrium in the face of adversarial environmental conditions" (Kim, 2001, p. 67). Placing adaptation at the point of interaction between individuals and the environment, this theory states that a stranger who steps into a different culture will move along a uni-directional path of stress–adaptation–growth towards a universal end, which is the formation of intercultural personhood, an improvement in their psychological health, and an increase in their functional fitness in the host environment (Gudykunst & Kim, 2003; Kim, 1988, 2001, 2006, 2011, 2015). To attain successful assimilation into the host culture, sojourning individuals have to involve themselves in the interplay of acculturation and deculturation (Kim, 2015). The former, which refers to sojourning individuals' acquisition of the new cultural patterns and practices, will inevitably lead to the latter, defined as unlearning of some of their old cultural habits (Kim, 2011, 2015).

Acculturation and deculturation of sojourners and immigrants, according to cross-cultural adaptation theory, are enacted through their separation from their co-national or ethnic groups, mentally and physically (Gudykunst & Kim, 2003; Kim, 2001, 2011, 2015). By doing so, sojourners and immigrants are expected to actively conduct social engagement with the host environment at large, which is discouraged by their maintenance of home culture or ethnic culture and intra-ethnic communication (Kim, 2011). From the perspective of cross-cultural adaptation theory, sojourners' and immigrants' ties with their home cultures and co-nationals or co-ethnics are thought to function as a pulling force during their assimilation into the host culture (Kim, 1977, 2001, 2011). For the sake of better assimilation into the host culture, individuals should maximize their acculturation into the host culture through unlearning some of their original cultural habits, and staying away from their strong ethnic ties with their co-nationals or co-ethnics (Gudykunst & Kim, 2003; Kim, 1988, 1991, 2001, 2011).

Emphasis on social interaction with non-host-nationals

The dualistic understanding of host culture acquisition and home culture maintenance can be viewed in another way, whereby the role played by sojourners' and immigrants' social interaction with non-host-nationals (their co-nationals or co-ethnics and international fellows) is significant in terms of providing them with long-term social support in host countries (Emiko & Loh, 2006; Furnham & Alibhai, 1985; Ward & Kennedy, 1993; Ward & Rana-Deuba, 2000; Ward, Bochner, & Furnham, 2001). For instance, Ward and Kennedy (1993) reported that satisfaction with co-national relations strongly predicted the psychological adjustment of sojourning students in New Zealand. Ward et al. (2001) found that strong identification with the home culture was associated with international students' greater psychological well being in Nepal. Berry, Kim, Minde, and Mok (1987) revealed that Korean immigrants in Canada, who possessed close friendships with their co-nationals, experienced less stress. Emiko and Loh (2006) stated that Asian sojourning students in Australia who had more ties with their international fellows experienced better intercultural adjustment in general. Sojourners' and immigrants' tendency to establish and maintain close ties with their co-nationals and international fellows is supported by the study conducted by Furnham and Alibhai (1985), which revealed sojourning individuals' strong preference for co-national friends first, non-co-national friends second, and host nationals third. This preference pattern can be attributed to individuals' tendency to be associated with those who are similar to them, from the perspective of social categorization (Tajfel, 1981). Specific to sojourning individuals, the similarities between them rest upon their same cultural background and/or experiences of re-locating to a new cultural milieu. During intercultural encounters, sojourners and immigrants can feel a sense of empathy resulting from their shared background or experiences.

The concept of "horizon" is defined by Gadamer (1991) as "the range of vision that includes everything that can be seen from a particular vantage point" (p. 301). As socialized human beings, individuals have been endowed with certain horizons by their historically-determined situatedness that comprises their cultures and traditions. From these horizons, understandings and interpretations occur. Coming from the same culture, sojourning individuals share the same horizon with their co-nationals or co-ethnics in comparison to the horizon of host-nationals. Additionally, their re-location into a new cultural milieu will expose them to many challenges and obstacles, which are shared by other sojourners and immigrants who come from different countries. Due to the same or similar historically-determined situatedness, sojourning individuals can find common understandings and interpretations generated during their re-location to host countries. Unlike the one-way acculturation depicted by cross-cultural adaptation theory, scholars opposed to the dualistic understanding of host culture and home culture refused to place sojourning individuals' interaction with host-nationals in opposition to their communication with non-host-nationals. As cultural fusion theory states, acculturation is an additive and integrative process rather than a zero-sum closed system (Croucher & Kramer, 2016; Kramer, 2000, 2003a, 2003b). Sojourning individuals' original culture cannot be unlearned and their home cultural identity will not be abandoned during their learning of new cultures (Croucher & Kramer, 2016; Kramer, 2000, 2003a, 2003b, 2010, 2011). Unlike the assimilation-oriented approach depicted by cross-cultural adaptation theory, cultural fusion theory did not point to a universally desired result or outcome (Callahan, 2004). Acculturation was described by cultural fusion theory as a process of combining elements of two or more cultures in an unpredictable way to generate something new (Croucher & Kramer, 2016; Kramer, 2000). During this process, life was made meaningful through negotiating and celebrating the niches and differences, and moving toward, ultimately, different meanings unique to the individual (Callahan, 2004; Kramer, 2000, 2011).

Focusing on the disparity between the two perspectives elaborated above, this study will examine the meaning of sojourning students' (Chinese students in the US and American students in China) social interaction with non-host-nationals. The exploration will attend to the following questions:

- What does their social circle in the host country look like?
- How did this social circle come into being?
- What does this social circle mean to them?

Research methods

Participants

The participants in this study are 25 Chinese students who are currently studying in the US and 25 American students who are enrolled in Chinese universities. These participants were recruited through the researcher's social network in the US and China. Their age ranged from 19 to 34 years, with an average age of 26 years. They had lived in the US and China, respectively, from six months to ten years, with an average length of sojourn of three and a half years. Among these 50 participants, 21 were female and 29 male; 21 were undergraduate students, 14 were Master's students, and 15 were PhD students. All of the participants were recruited because they have already been studying in host countries for an extended period of time and their experiences of study abroad can provide rich insights into international students' social interaction embedded in their acculturation. More detailed information about these participants is shown in Table 24.1.

Data collection

All participants were interviewed about their social circles and social interaction in the host countries. The diversity of these participants' experiences informed the semi-structured interview process. On the one hand, the researcher could ask planned questions based on an interview guide; on the other, the interviewees werere allowed more freedom to provide different descriptions of their own experiences based on which the interviewer could ask unplanned questions to explore different feelings and thoughts (Fontana & Frey, 2005; Rubin & Rubin, 2011). In terms of this research, the planned interview questions were developed to explore whether sojourning individuals should avoid interaction with non-host-nationals during intercultural communication. All of these interviews were conducted in locations of the participants' choice. All participants

Table 24.1 Participant data

	*Participants**	*Nationality*	*Age*	*Gender*	*Length of sojourn (in months)*	*Degree*
1	Dong	China	25	Male	48	MA
2	Mei	China	25	Female	36	PhD
3	Yue	China	30	Male	60	MA
4	Jun	China	26	Male	24	PhD
5	Wei	China	31	Male	60	PhD
6	Cui	China	26	Female	36	PhD
7	Ying	China	25	Female	48	MA
8	Nan	China	25	Male	48	MA
9	Ru	China	23	Female	36	PhD
10	Chen	China	31	Male	60	PhD
11	Yi	China	25	Female	24	MA
12	Li	China	28	Female	48	PhD
13	Lu	China	29	Male	60	PhD
14	Yu	China	26	Female	48	PhD
15	Jie	China	30	Male	24	PhD
16	Hong	China	26	Female	48	MA
17	Jia	China	24	Female	36	MA
18	Yun	China	25	Female	48	MA
19	Xiao	China	21	Male	60	MA
20	Guo	China	25	Female	48	PhD
21	Qian	China	24	Female	48	MA
22	Cong	China	24	Female	36	MA
23	Tao	China	30	Male	48	PhD
24	Yang	China	23	Male	48	PhD
25	Xin	China	24	Male	60	PhD
26	Susan	US	22	Female	24	BA
27	Luke	US	27	Male	24	MA
28	June	US	27	Female	36	MA
29	Sarah	US	27	Female	60	MA
30	Steven	US	26	Male	60	BA
31	Mochamochi	US	23	Female	15	BA
32	Mike	US	23	Male	12	BA
33	Ryan	US	25	Male	9	BA
34	Frank	US	34	Male	54	BA
35	Sima	US	29	Male	72	BA
36	Bobby	US	25	Male	36	BA
37	Berry	US	32	Male	97	BA
38	Dylan	US	28	Male	24	BA
39	Kevin	US	27	Male	60	BA
40	Mark	US	23	Male	6	BA
41	Nick	US	20	Male	24	BA

(Continued)

Table 24.1 (Cont.)

	*Participants**	*Nationality*	*Age*	*Gender*	*Length of sojourn (in months)*	*Degree*
42	Stacy	US	22	Female	38	BA
43	Kathy	US	24	Female	15	BA
44	Jack	US	28	Male	48	PhD
45	Samuel	US	30	Male	48	BA
46	Maroon	US	31	Male	84	BA
47	Tiffany	US	19	Female	16	BA
48	Will	US	31	Male	120	BA
49	Thomas	US	28	Male	18	BA
50	Claire	US	26	Female	24	BA

*Names are pseudonyms.

signed informed consent forms prior to interview. Upon the approval of each participant, a digital audio-recording device was utilized to record each interview. The length of each interview was one to two hours, which resulted in 84 hours of interviews. In addition, notes were taken by the researcher during interviews to record participants' reactions, such as changes in volume, pauses, body language, and facial expression. Some participants did not leave the interview location immediately the interview was over and continued to talk to the researcher. Upon their consent, these descriptions were also noted.

Data analysis

Audio-taped interviews were transcribed by the researcher word by word. Guided by grounded theory, an incident was compared and contrasted with other incidents; empirical data with concept, concept with categories, and categories with categories, in order to reach higher levels of abstraction and advanced conceptualizations (Charmaz, 2006; Cho & Lee, 2014). Additionally, memos were written throughout the coding process to keep a record of research reflections at different times. By virtue of the constant comparative method, the researcher analyzed data in three steps. First, each transcript was read and re-read to locate common themes across the interviews by asking generative questions and writing analytic memos throughout the analysis period. Second, incidents provided by participants were contrasted and compared under the same theme. Through contrast and comparison, sub-themes emerged. Third, excerpts under each sub-theme were analyzed in combination with their contexts in the original transcripts.

Results

Obstacles to communication with host-nationals

Although intra-ethnic communication is considered to be helpful when an individual first enters a new cultural milieu, social interaction with non-host-nationals is still deemed destructive to the individual's successful assimilation in the long run, as the aforementioned dualistic perspective argued. To better fit into the mainstream culture in the host culture, sojourning individuals are encouraged to stay away from their co-national or co-ethnic groups and focus on communication with host-nationals (Gudykunst & Kim, 2003; Kim, 1988, 1991, 2001, 2011). However, this argument was contradicted by data collected in this study, which revealed that obstacles that hindered sojourning students' communication with host-nationals could not be simplistically ignored, as the dualistic perspective proposed. According to participants in this study, no matter how long they had already lived abroad, they found it difficult to establish close relationships with host-nationals, sometimes for the following two reasons.

One is the language barrier, which exposed sojourning students to their *otherness* in host countries. Stepping outside their own cultures, sojourners started to feel unable to fully express themselves in a second language (Suarez, 2002). As a result of limited linguistic proficiency in their second language, sojourning students were found to contribute fewer ideas and take less active roles in communication (Corder, 1983). For instance, Mochamochi, who has studied and worked in China for more than a year, stated that she had difficulty adequately expressing abstract concepts in Mandarin due to her limited vocabulary. Kathy, who first came to China as an exchange student two years ago, recalled that she did not have natural, comfortable conversations with Chinese people in Mandarin because there would always be language limitations. As long as the communication between sojourning students and host-nationals was thwarted by the former's limited linguistic proficiency, the latter's reactions, verbally and non-verbally, would separate the former from mainstream society. Wei, who has already studied in the US for six years, said that he sometimes felt uncomfortable when speaking with his American lab-mates in English:

> When you communicate with Americans, as long as you have problem in your expression, no matter how small it is, they definitely will ask you to repeat.

Reactions of these American lab-mates, from Wei's perspective, pointed out his difference from mainstream society. The highlighted difference, embodied in limited English proficiency, constantly reminded Wei that he was a linguistically incompetent *Other* in the US. Although Wei mentioned that he did a better job than his American lab-mates, his difficulty in expressing himself concisely and precisely in English made him look more stupid than these host-nationals. As a result, Wei felt that his smartness could not be recognized during his communication with Americans. Such an absence of recognition had an impact on Wei's self-esteem.

The sense of being a stupid, linguistically incompetent *Other* was sometimes further elevated when sojourning students were exposed to their difficulty in understanding the second language uttered by host-nationals. Linguistic barriers can obstruct information flow, impede knowledge-sharing and transfer, and create power and advancement (Peltokorpi & Clausen, 2011; Peltokorpi & Vaara, 2014). Given the strong influence of language on communication, sojourning students explained that they were often excluded from stepping into host-nationals' social and professional circles due to linguistic barriers. No matter how hard they studied the second language, they sometimes couldn't fully understand what host-nationals said. For instance, Susan, who has already studied Mandarin for six years, mentioned that she couldn't follow conversations with her Chinese friends because jokes were interwoven with other messages. Although she was fluent in Mandarin, Susan still expressed that it was difficult for her to catch Chinese people's culture-based jokes as a result of her lack of social understanding and the nuanced cultural contexts. Analogous to Susan, Berry also encountered the gap created by growing up outside the Chinese culture. Following his parents to China in the 1990s, he had traveled back and forth between the US and China over a period of 20 years. Even as a self-proclaimed old *Beijinger* (a local), Berry admitted that he still sometimes found it difficult to completely understand what his Chinese friends said:

> I mean as a foreigner you know without like growing up here with Chinese parents and Chinese school, you know, you don't get like the classical ... and I never studied even in English some of the classical works, I didn't like take that standard of Chinese or like for very long to get a lot of the like idioms or like cultural background for the language, so it's hard to get that ... I'm not going to stop trying to understand it but I know that I probably will never fully understand it.

The culture-based linguistic gap between sojourning American students in China and Chinese people was attributed to these sojourners' limited Chinese cultural literacy. Stepping into a new cultural system, sojourning individuals are like babies who need to navigate a new semantic field. Compared to host-nationals from the receiving countries, sojourners and immigrants lack the cultural literacy that is firmly grounded in host cultures. By the same token, sojourning Chinese students in the US reported that they found it difficult to understand the punch lines of jokes within conversations with Americans. Dong has studied in the US for four years. He described communicating with his American classmates thus:

> For most of time, I do not know why they feel a certain topic so funny. For me, I cannot tell why that topic is so funny.

Echoing Dong's feeling, Ru, who majored in mathematics, stated:

> I found Americans like to talk about sports and politics. But I have no interest in these topics. Moreover, the topic which makes them feel funny, in my eyes, is not that funny. We have the different punch lines.

As the result of the divide between sojourning students and host-nationals produced by the linguistic gap, the former felt they were excluded from the linguistic community of the host culture. These sojourners' second language distinguished them as the cultural *Other* owing to the role played by language in determining social categorization (Giles & Johnson, 1981). Functionally-speaking, sojourning students' limited linguistic proficiency in a second language separated them from host-nationals and categorized them as outsiders or members of the out-group. They were unable to fully express themselves when speaking in a second language, or to fully participate in host-nationals' conversations because they were unable to understand some cultural references and humor. These inabilities gave sojourning students a sense of losing control when interacting with host-nationals, even if some of them had resided in the host country for quite a long time. The insurmountable linguistic gap between sojourning students and host-nationals made the former believe that they would never feel a part of the host country. Ultimately, they psychologically isolated themselves from the host society by acknowledging the permanent divide between them and host-nationals caused in large part by linguistic barriers that were impossible to fully overcome.

The other obstacle to developing close relationships with host-nationals, as experienced by sojourning students, is associated with the discrepancy between their cultural values. At the core of culture, a *value* is defined as "an explicit or implicit conception, distinctive of an individual or characteristic of a group, which influences the choice and evaluation of behaviors" (Liu, Volčič, & Gallois, 2015, p. 104). In addition to linguistic barriers, cultural values function as less overt determinants of social categorization based on their impacts on social interaction (Peltokorpi & Clausen, 2011). Individuals identify their in-group members in terms of cultural value fit, and distinguish themselves from out-group members via cultural value discrepancies (Schiefer, Mollering, & Daniel, 2012). In this study, sojourning students' values, which diverged from those of host-nationals around them, were grouped on the collectivism–individualism dimension. Collectivism prefers the "we" identity to the "I" identity, and in-group interests to individual desires (Ting-Toomey, 2010). Individuals from a collectivistic culture thus value interdependence and unity (Hofstede, 1980; Markus & Kitayama, 1991; Matsumoto & Juang, 2007; Triandis, 1989, 2001). Coming from a collectivistic culture, Chinese students in the US still tended to associate friendship with a collective identity that emphasizes inter-dependence among in-group members and is enacted via friendly behaviors (Chen, 2004). However, friendship is distinguished from friendly behaviors in the individualistic American culture that values independence and autonomy (Hofstede, 1980; Markus & Kitayama, 1991; Triandis, 1995). From the perspective of individualism, the "I" identity is more important than the "we" identity, "individual rights over group interest, and individual-focused emotions over social-focused emotions" (Ting-Toomey, 2010, p. 173).

Different perceptions of friendship accounted for sojourning students' limited social interaction with host-nationals. Chinese students in the US claimed that they expected friendships with collectivistic traits. To be specific, they valued friendship that was characterized by mutual reliance and a more closely-knitted relationship. However, these traits were not embraced by Americans, who preferred self-reliance and autonomy. Anticipating what friendship should look like, Chinese students encountered expectancy violation during their interaction with the American students around them. For example, Mei once considered two of her lab-mates as friends because they took such good care of her when she first came to the US:

> They took me to a lot of places for grocery, cell phone and many other things. So I once considered them as my friends. For me, friends mean mutual help as long as you need. But for them, sometimes they do not want to help me even if they have the time and the capability. If you ask them for help but they do not want to do that, they will say No directly. For Chinese, we will help each other as long as we turn a finger to help. Maybe that is how they treat friends. I do not know. It is hard for me to make friends with them.

Likewise, Ru said she was a little bit uncomfortable about the different meaning of friendship in the US:

> For example, yesterday we chatted very happily and I thought we were friends. But the next day, when we run into each other, it seems that nothing has ever happened. The closeness I had yesterday did not exist. In China, we should behave like yesterday, so close. Maybe Chinese people more mutually rely on each other. American people prefer more freedom and independence during the friendship. I do not know. But I felt a little bit uncomfortable.

In Tao's case, he said that he had once viewed some American students in his office as friends and considered that it was his duty to actively offer suggestions before they asked for help. To Tao, this action was taken for granted by Chinese students. However, American students did not pay attention to the advice given by Tao. Under these circumstances, such different understandings of what friendship should look like drew another line between Chinese students and the Americans around them.

In similar fashion, American students in China sometimes struggled to interact with local Chinese as a result of the emphasis placed on mutual and compulsory favor exchange in

Chinese friendship. This was described by American sojourners as *guanxi*-loaded friendship; that is, as being transactional or instrumental in nature (Liu, 2017). Heavily influenced by collectivism, Chinese society operates on a structural pattern of social relationships among individuals (Chen & Starosta, 1997). By virtue of *guanxi*, Chinese people expect to move up the social hierarchy without disrupting social harmony (García, 2014). In societies that stress long-term relationships and collectivism, *guanxi* is essential to an individual's success (Hofstede, Hofstede, & Minkov, 2010) because it is interwoven with attributes of social capital, including power, social status, and resources (García, 2014; Hackley & Dong, 2001; Valentini, 2010). As a result, Chinese people are used to engaging in a friendship based on the expectation that they will benefit each other in the future. Chinese students in the US such as Mei and Ru still preferred friendship that required reciprocal exchange of favors based on mutual reliance, because they needed other people's instrumental help in navigating the new cultural environment.

However, the expectation of establishing instrumental relationships with others was rejected by American students in China. They revealed that they were approached by local Chinese people for such transactional purposes as practicing English, boosting their public image in front of other Chinese people, and bringing unique social resources to their own business. Such instrumental relationships, coated with friendship, annoyed American students in this study because they saw this *guanxi*-loaded social interaction as having nothing to do with genuine friendship. The friendly behaviors displayed by some local Chinese people transpired to be a means of accruing debt, which required that Americans offer them favors as re-payment. Coming from an individualistic culture, American sojourners indicated that they valued autonomy and viewed having social obligations imposed on them in a negative light. Therefore, these American sojourners generally felt uncomfortable about being indebted to others.

Empathy-based interaction with non-host-nationals

As mentioned above, both linguistic barriers and cultural value discrepancies made the *Otherness* of sojourning students obvious by highlighting their differences from host-nationals. To deal with the uncomfortable *Other*-identity, sojourning students paid more attention to conducting social interaction with non-host-nationals. By doing so, they could gain emotional support, actual instrumental help, and deeper understanding from their co-nationals, co-ethnics, and international fellows based on *empathy*. Empathy refers to the capability of recognizing emotions experienced by others. This recognition is based on similar or shared experience between individuals. However, it was difficult for participants in this study to find similar or shared experiences with host-nationals, especially those who had never studied abroad. In this context, sojourning students turned to their co-nationals, co-ethnics, and/or international fellows for emotional support. For example, Wei, who felt frustrated about his limited linguistic proficiency, spent a lot of time with his Turkish lab-mates:

> Therefore, I hang out a lot with other international students. The reason is quite simple. Even if my English is horrible, they still can understand what I am saying.

In Wei's opinion, he and his Turkish friends had equal English proficiency as international students. Therefore, Wei would not be seen as the incompetent *Other* by his international cohorts. On the contrary, his international fellows could protect his self-esteem through providing him with a greater sense of comfort and recognition in communication.

In a similar vein, American sojourning students in China stated that their social circles were mainly composed of other Western sojourners in China. Feeling exhausted from communicating in Mandarin, Susan preferred to hang out with other Western friends during her spare time. Although she was fluent in Mandarin, Susan still found talking in it cognitively demanding, as her second language. Therefore, Susan loved to chat with her friends in English when she wanted to relax. In addition to it being less effortful, American sojourners in China also associated speaking English, their mother tongue, with their original identity which they held dear. Sarah, who had been living in China for five years, preferred her American identity, which was associated with speaking English, to her Chinese one. When she first came to China, Sarah named herself *Xiaodan* (晓丹 in Mandarin), which denoted femininity in the Chinese culture. Working for a beer company, Sarah was often required to have dinner with or go to Karaoke bars with her Chinese clients. Her level of Mandarin at the time constrained her ability to fully express herself. She took advantage of this situation, however, by creating an impression of a pretty innocent American woman among her Chinese clients. By doing so, Sarah received invitations to various social activities as a token foreigner, and successfully promoted her company's beer during these activities. For Sarah, Xiaodan implied a kinder and simpler person, quite different from her American identity as Sarah. After leaving the beer company and ending communication with her Chinese clients, Sarah picked up her American identity by insisting on speaking English in her new company.

As well as a response to the language issue, the sojourning students in this study also paid more attention to communication with their co-nationals, co-ethnics, and/or international fellows as a means of finding cultural value congruency. For example, Mei and Ru decided to join the Chinese circle, which could provide them with a greater sense of security, constant comfort, and practical help. Coming from a department which mainly consisted of American students, Dong felt isolated by his American cohorts, who were indifferent to his struggles in the US. This unsupportive environment always made Dong leave quickly after class. In this context, Dong usually turned to other Chinese students or his Indonesian cohort for help, because they understood what international students went through in that department. These non-host-nationals frequently gave him a free ride, took him to supermarkets, or spent time with him when he was in a bad mood. For Dong, communication with other sojourners in the US provided him with emotional support and resonance, which were much scarcer during his inter-ethnic communication with Americans (Chen, 2004).

Similar to Chinese students in the US, American sojourning students in China mainly hung out with other Westerners who also valued individualism. Consequently, these American students, together with other Western sojourners, clustered into a closely-connected expatriate community in China. Within this community, American students in this study got to make friends with other sojourners who shared similar interests or experiences. Such a friendship, which had less to do with *guanxi*, provided them with strong emotional support, which helped them reduce their sense of loneliness. More importantly, as Susan mentioned, these friends were also outsiders or out-group members in China. Therefore, they could better understand her feelings of being the *Other* in this country. By connecting with these friends, Susan felt she could deal with the social isolation she felt in China. During interaction with local Chinese people, American students in this study mentioned that they had to be cautious when being approached by some host-nationals. For example, Susan insisted on paying for her meal when having dinner with her Chinese friends. When *guanxi* became inevitable, American sojourners would accommodate Chinese people to a small degree, as long as Chinese expectations were reasonable. For instance, Samuel and Maroon, who had started work in China after studying abroad, could engage in *guanxi* with their business partners for the sake of business. But when favors sounded ridiculous, they rejected repaying them.

Conclusion

Since the 1980s, the notion of biculturalism, which advocates for identification with both host and home cultures, has prevailed in intercultural communication studies (Liu, 2015). Influenced by biculturalism, researchers explore sojourning individuals' acculturation within a binary structure consisting of national or ethnic ties at one end and ties with the host culture at the other. As a result, sojourners' and immigrants' host cultural identity and home cultural identity or ethnic identity are negotiated in dichotomous categories such as either/or and us/them (ibid). Rejecting biculturalism based on a dualistic understanding of host culture and home culture, this study revealed that sojourning Chinese and American students in the US and China, respectively, still gained the long-term social support, emotional and instrumental, they needed from their communication with non-host-nationals during their acquisition of new cultures. Compared to host-nationals, these non-host-nationals, who have experienced the process of intercultural adjustment caused by their re-location to an unfamiliar cultural environment, can better help other sojourning individuals deal with the sense of loss, loneliness, disorientation, low self-esteem, and isolation in host countries (McClure, 2007; Sawir, Marginson, Deumert, Nyland, & Ramia, 2008).

That sojourning individuals instinctively make long-term ties with other non-host-nationals is also supported by social categorization theory, which argues that individuals more easily connect with those who have had the same or similar experiences (Tajfel, 1981). Similar to their co-nationals, co-ethnics, and/or international fellows, the sojourning students in this study suffered as a result of their limited linguistic competence and cultural value discrepancy with the host culture. Although these sojourning students did not avoid interacting with host-nationals, they admitted that it was easier for them to connect to other linguistically incompetent *Others* and cultural *Others* than to host-nationals, owing to the empathy created by their shared experiences of being international students in host countries. Sojourning students' tendency to engage in intra-ethnic and inter-ethnic communication with international fellows was greater when they felt frustrated, powerless, depressed, disoriented, and isolated as the *Other* in host countries. Therefore, the researcher concluded that sojourning students' communication with non-host-nationals, embedded in intercultural encounters, was based more on their mutual empathy. Compared to host-nationals, especially those who had never studied abroad, sojourning students found it easier and more natural to interact with non-host-nationals. From these interactions, they gained social support, both emotional and instrumental, increased self-confidence, a sense of recognition, a state of relaxation, and actual help in navigating the new environment, even if their sojourn in host countries had gone beyond the initial phase. Therefore, it is suggested that more international students should be recruited by schools and universities to help newly-arrived sojourning students orientate themselves to the host country's cultural milieu.

References

Berry, J. W., Kim, U., Minde, T., & Mok, D. (1987). Comparative studies of acculturative stress. *International Migration Review*, *21*, 490–511.

Callahan, C. (2004). *Theoretical description and comparative analysis of adaptation and fusion theories*. Paper presented at the International Communication Association, New Orleans, LA.

Charmaz, K. (2006). *Constructing grounded theory: A practical guide through qualitative analysis*. London: Sage.
Chen, G. & Starosta, W. (1997). Chinese conflict management and resolution: Overview and implications. *Intercultural Communication Studies, 7*, 1–13.
Chen, X. (2004). *Sojourners and "foreigners": A study on Chinese students' intercultural interpersonal relationships in the United States*. Beijing: Education and Science Press.
Cho, J. Y. & Lee, E. H. (2014). Reducing confusion about grounded theory and qualitative content analysis: Similarities and differences. *Qualitative Report, 19*, 1–20.
Citron, J. (1996). *Short-term study abroad: Integration, third culture formation, and re-entry*. Paper presented at the Association of International Educators (NAFSA) annual conference, Phoenix, AZ.
Corder, S. P. (1983). Strategies of communication. In C. Faerch & G. Kasper (Eds.), *Strategies in interlanguage communication* (pp. 15–19). London: Longman.
Croucher, S. M. & Kramer, E. (2016). Cultural fusion theory: An alternative to acculturation. *Journal of International and Intercultural Communication, 10*, 97–114.
Emiko, S. K. & Loh, E. (2006). International students' acculturation: Effects of international, conational, and local ties and need for closure. *International Journal of Intercultural Relations, 30*, 471–485.
Fontana, A. & Frey, J. H. (2005). The interview: From neutral stance to political involvement. In N. K. Denzin & Y. S. Lincoln (Eds.), *The Sage handbook of qualitative research* (3rd ed., pp. 695–727). Thousand Oaks, CA: Sage.
Furnham, A. & Alibhai, N. (1985). The friendship networks of foreign students: A replication and extension of the functional model. *International Journal of Psychology, 20*, 709–722.
Gadamer, H. G. (1991). *Truth and method* (J. Weinsheimer & D. G. Marshall, Trans.). New York: Crossroad.
García, C. (2014). Clientelism and guanxi: Southern European and Chinese public relations in comparative perspective. *Public Relations Review, 40*, 798–806.
Giles, H. & Johnson, P. (1981). The role of language in ethnic group relations. In J. C. Turner & H. Giles (Eds.), *Intergroup behavior* (pp. 199–243). Oxford: Blackwell.
Gudykunst, W. B. (1985). A model of uncertainty reduction in intercultural encounters. *Journal of Language and Social Psychology, 4*, 79–98.
Gudykunst, W. B. (1995). Anxiety/uncertainty management (AUM) theory: Current status. In R. L. Wiseman (Ed.), *Intercultural communication competence (International and Intercultural Communication Annual)* (Vol. 19, pp. 8–58). Thousand Oaks, CA: Sage.
Gudykunst, W. B. & Kim, Y. Y. (2003). *Communicating with strangers: An approach to intercultural communication*. New York: McGraw-Hill.
Hackley, C. A. & Dong, Q. (2001). American public relations networking encounters China's guanxi. *Public Relations Quarterly, 46*, 16–19.
Hofstede, G. (1980). *Culture's consequences: International differences in work-related values*. Beverly Hills, CA: Sage.
Hofstede, G., Hofstede, G. J., & Minkov, M. (2010). *Cultures and organizations: Software of the mind* (3rd ed.). New York: McGraw-Hill.
Institute of International Education. (2016). *Open doors 2016: Report on international educational exchange*. Retrieved from www.iie.org/Research-and-Insights/Open-Doors/Open-Doors-2016-Media-Information
Kim, Y. Y. (1977). *Inter-ethnic and intra-ethnic communication: A study of Korean immigrants in Chicago*, PhD dissertation, University of Chicago.
Kim, Y. Y. (1988). *Communication and cross-cultural adaptation: An integrative theory*. Clevedon: Multilingual Matters.
Kim, Y. Y. (1991). Communication and adaptation. In L. A. Samovar & R. E. Porter (Eds.), *Intercultural communication: A reader* (6th ed., pp. 383–391). Belmont, CA: Wadsworth.
Kim, Y. Y. (2001). *Becoming intercultural: An integrative theory of communication and cross-cultural adaptation*. Thousand Oaks, CA: Sage.
Kim, Y. Y. (2006). From ethnic to interethnic: The case for identity adaptation and transformation. *Journal of Language and Social Psychology, 25*, 283–300.
Kim, Y. Y. (2011). Beyond cultural categories: Communication, adaptation, and transformation. In J. Jackson (Ed.), *Handbook of language and intercultural communication* (pp. 229–243). New York: Routledge.
Kim, Y. Y. (2015). Finding a "home" beyond culture: The emergence of intercultural personhood in the globalizing world. *International Journal of Intercultural Relations, 46*, 3–12.
Kitsantas, A. (2004). Studying abroad: The role of college students' goals on the development of cross-cultural skills and global understanding. *College Student Journal, 38*, 441–453.

Kramer, E. (2000). *Cultural fusion and the defense of difference.* New York: University Press of America.
Kramer, E. (2003a). *Cosmopoly: Occidentalism and the new world order.* Westport, CT: Praeger.
Kramer, E. (2003b). *Gaiatsu and cultural judo.* Westport, CT: Praeger.
Kramer, E. (2010). Immigration. In R. L. Jackson & M. A. Hogg (Eds.), *Encyclopedia of identity* (pp. 384–389). Thousand Oaks, CA: Sage.
Kramer, E. (2011). Preface. In S. Croucher & D. Cronn-Mills (Eds.), *Religious misperceptions: The case of Muslims and Christians in France and Britain* (pp. vii–xxxii). Creskill, NJ: Hampton Press.
Liu, S. (2015). *Identity, hybridity and cultural home: Chinese migrants and diaspora in multicultural societies.* New York: Rowman & Littlefield.
Liu, S., Volčič, Z. & Gallois, C. (2015). *Introducing intercultural communication: Global cultures and contexts* (2nd ed.). London: Sage.
Liu, Y. (2017). *What does it mean to be Chinese? American sojourners' experiences of being the other in China,* Doctoral dissertation, University of Oklahoma.
Markus, H. R. & Kitayama, S. (1991). Culture and the self: Implications for cognition, emotion, and motivation. *Psychological Review, 98*, 224–253.
Matsumoto, D. & Juang, L. (2007). *Culture and psychology* (4th ed.). Boston, MA: Cengage Learning.
McClure, J. W. (2007). International graduates' cross-cultural adjustment: Experiences, coping strategies, and suggested programmatic responses. *Teaching in Higher Education, 12*, 199–217.
Ministry of Education of the People's Republic of China. (2017). *2016 statistics of international students in China.* Retrieved from www.moe.edu.cn/jyb_xwfb/xw_fbh/moe_2069/xwfbh_2017n/xwfb_170301/170301_sjtj/201703/t20170301_297677.html
Peltokorpi, V. & Clausen, L. (2011). Linguistic and cultural barriers to intercultural communication in foreign subsidiaries. *Asian Business & Management, 10*, 509–528.
Peltokorpi, V. & Vaara, E. (2014). Knowledge transfer in multinational corporations: Productive and counterproductive effects of language-sensitive recruitment. *Journal of International Business Studies, 45*, 600–622.
Pitts, M. J. (2009). Identity and the role of expectations, stress, and talk in short-term student sojourner adjustment: An application of the integrative theory of communication and cross-cultural adaptation. *International Journal of Intercultural Relations, 33*, 450–462.
Redfield, R., Linton, R., & Herskovits, M. J. (1936). Memorandum for the study of acculturation. *American Anthropologist, 38*, 149–152.
Rubin, H. J. & Rubin, I. S. (2011). *Qualitative interviewing: The art of hearing data.* Los Angeles, CA: Sage.
Sawir, E., Marginson, S., Deumert, A., Nyland, C., & Ramia, G. (2008). Loneliness and international students: An Australian study. *Journal of Studies in International Education, 12*, 148–180.
Schiefer, D., Mollering, A., & Daniel, E. (2012). Cultural value fit of immigrant and minority adolescents: The role of acculturation orientations. *International Journal of Intercultural Relations, 36*, 486–497.
Suarez, D. (2002). ESOL teacher candidates experience cultural otherness. *TESOL Journal, 11*, 19–25.
Tajfel, H. (1981). *Human groups and social categories.* Cambridge: Cambridge University Press.
Ting-Toomey, S. (2005). Identity negotiation theory: Crossing cultural boundaries. In W. B. Gudykunst (Ed.), *Theorizing about intercultural communication* (pp. 211–233). Thousand Oaks, CA: Sage.
Ting-Toomey, S. (2010). Applying dimensional values in understanding intercultural communication. *Communication Monographs*, 77, 169–180.
Triandis, H. C. (1989). Cross-cultural studies on individualism and collectivism. In J. Berman (Ed.), *Nebraska symposium on motivation* (pp. 41–133). Lincoln, NE: University of Nebraska Press.
Triandis, H. C. (1995). *Individualism and collectivism.* Boulder, CO: Westview.
Triandis, H. C. (2001). Individualism–collectivism and personality. *Journal of Personality, 69*, 907–924.
Valentini, C. (2010). Personalised networks of influence in public relations. *Journal of Communication Management, 14*, 153–166.
Verbik, L. & Lasanowski, V. (2007). *International student mobility: Patterns and trends.* London: Observatory on Borderless Higher Education. Retrieved from www.obhe.ac.uk/documents/2007/Reports/International_Student_Mobility_Patterns_and_Trends
Ward, C., Bochner, S., & Furnham, A. (2001). *The psychology of culture shock.* London: Routledge.
Ward, C. & Kennedy, A. (1993). Psychological and socio-cultural adjustment during cross-cultural transitions: A comparison of secondary students overseas and at home. *International Journal of Psychology, 28*, 129–147.
Ward, C. & Rana-Deuba, A. (2000). Home and host culture influences on sojourner adjustment. *International Journal of Intercultural Relations, 24*, 291–306.

25

INTERNAL MIGRANTS AND THEIR LEFT-BEHIND FAMILIES IN CHINA

Cheng Zeng

The Chinese economy picked up rapidly following the adoption of the open-door policy in 1978. The economic reform triggered the largest labor migration in human history, with 274 million rural residents migrating to urban cities (Li, 2016). The massive supply of cheap labor is one of the key factors contributing to the rapid urbanization and modernization of China. These migrants are mainly from less-developed areas such as western and central inlands of China and their destinations are typically the capital area, eastern coastal cities, and southern China (Zhang & Song, 2003). The huge influx of people from rural areas has a profound impact on the demographics of urban cities. For instance, migrants account for 70–80 percent of the total population in many towns in the Pearl River delta region. Most of these migrant workers, however, are not expected to stay in the destination permanently due to the restrictions set by the Chinese household registration system: *hukou*. In addition, migrants without local *hukou* are often denied access to free public education, subsidized healthcare services, and social security. Thus, migrant workers in China are commonly known as the "floating population," meaning people have no roots or security in cities.

The massive migration not only significantly shapes the receiving cities but also changes the demographics and way of life in the sending areas. The millions of migrants create millions of split families. The left-behind population is mostly made up of women, children, and the elderly. Although China has experienced rapid economic growth, the development in urban and rural areas is largely asymmetric; urban areas have been contributing to and benefiting from the growth in GDP, whereas rural areas remain largely underdeveloped. With limited support from the government and their migrant family members, the left-behind population is single-handedly facing various hardships in rural China. While previous studies on internal migration in China have predominantly focused on the economic aspects, this chapter aims to shed light on the social prices paid by rural–urban migrants and their left-behind families.

Internal migration in China

Human migration is a multifaceted event that has profound socioeconomic, cultural, and political consequences for both receiving and sending regions. There has been a significant growth in the volume, types, and complexity of migration in the twenty-first century.

Currently there are over a billion migrants in the world, 75 percent of which are internal migrants (UNOECD, 2013). In one of the earliest migration studies, Ravenstein (1885) described migration as an individual's response to the differences in regional economic development. The rural-to-urban movements represent the principal form of internal migration in developing countries. The gap in income and job opportunities is the leading force driving rural residents to urban areas. Rural residents typically move to cities with the hope of increasing the household income and gaining better access to public services. Their remittances are essential to reduce poverty and boost development in rural areas. Internal migration in China has made major contributions to alleviating poverty, accelerating economic growth and urbanization, and establishing rural–urban links (Peng & Swider, 2017).

The economy has been soaring in China over the last three decades, as has economic inequality. Informed by the communist ideology, China had been poor yet relatively equal under the Maoist regime. Economic inequality between coastal provinces and central and western provinces has been rapidly intensifying since China adopted the economic shift towards a market-oriented and liberal economy in 1978 (ibid). As a result, the rural-to-urban movements in China are often interprovincial: rural residents from western and central inlands tend to migrate to eastern and southern coastal areas. Understanding the regulations applied to interprovincial migration is vital, as the movement of people has been highly controlled in contemporary China (Chan, 2010).

The history of *hukou*

Internal migration is regulated in China through the "Household Registration System": *hukou*. Chinese citizens inherit their *hukou* status from their parents, which identifies them as either agricultural (rural) or non-agricultural (urban). *Hukou* status is not transferable between cities, and conversion from rural to urban *hukou* has been tightly controlled (Wang & Moffatt, 2008). As a major instrument of the socialist command apparatus, the *hukou* system was introduced in the 1950s along with other measures such as the collectivization of farmland to regulate population mobility and distribution in China. Traveling within China required an official permit up until the late 1980s. Only a small number of peasant workers were brought from rural areas to meet the labor needs of urban cities in the 1970s (Chan, 2009). Since the "open door" policy was adopted in 1978, China has gradually transformed into the "world's factory" and the demand for labor in manufacturing and export industries has grown rapidly. Consequently, surplus rural laborers headed to cities with the hope of encountering better income and employment opportunities. To facilitate this rural–urban movement, the *hukou* system has undergone various reforms since the early 1980s. The gradual relaxation of *hukou* first started with small towns and was later extended to medium-sized and large cities. Since 2001, migrants have been free to live in small towns where they are legally employed. Around the same time, medium-sized cities also started to remove restrictions on the number of migrants allowed in them (Chan, 2010).

Although moving to and living in urban cities became more feasible, rural-origin migrants are not treated as "locals" in the destination cities. In addition to residency control, *hukou* status also determines one's access to state-provided goods, welfare, and entitlements. In most countries, internal migrants are generally granted the right to vote and access to social welfare in the new place of residence after three or six months (Chan, 2009). However, rural–urban migrants in China are denied urban welfare benefits and their right to apply for local government jobs is restricted on the basis of their rural *hukou* status. As urban *hukou* status is closely associated with social benefits, achieving *hukou* conversion is a dream for many rural-origin workers. There are three main ways for a rural resident to obtain urban *hukou*: gaining tertiary education, joining the Chinese Communist Party or army, and utilizing connections to family members who are urban citizens (Zhang & Treiman, 2013). *Hukou* conversion is difficult and rare and those who achieve it are typically extremely rich, highly educated, or have immediate family members in the cities. Thus, the overwhelming majority of rural–urban migrants with limited education and social capital are permanently barred from the aforementioned benefits in urban cities. Typically, rural residents plan to work in cities for one or two decades and then return home with their savings. The *hukou* system has received extensive criticism for its denial of the basic rights of migrants and facilitation of the social division between locals and migrants at an institutional level (Lei & Li, 2012).

To address this widespread criticism, the Chinese government has launched many rounds of *hukou* reform to empower migrants in cities and facilitate the *hukou* conversion process. In 2009, Shanghai and Guangdong provinces were pioneers in implementing a new round of *hukou* reform to encourage migrants to become urban citizens (Zhao & Courtney, 2010). A local residential permit system was introduced and migrants who possess such a permit are entitled to many social benefits and are also eligible to apply for urban *hukou* when they have held it for seven years. The residential permit system was soon mirrored in many other urban cities and 28.9 million residency permits, altogether, were issued in 2016 (Xinhua News Agency, 2017). Despite the considerable progress made by the Chinese government, the differences between locals and migrants are not likely to diminish soon as providing healthcare, education, and social security for the millions of migrant workers in urban cities is not financially feasible. That is, for the foreseeable future, Chinese citizens will continue to be treated differently at the institutional level based on their *hukou* status.

Rural migrants in urban cities

Rural–urban migrants in China are marginalized in urban cities. For employers, migrant workers are often seen as easily replaceable and exploitable due to the large labor supply and migrants' lack of awareness of their legal rights (Li, 2002). Migrants are typically dumped in labor-intensive industries doing 3D (dirty, dangerous, and demeaning) jobs. Discrimination against migrant workers is very evident in urban cities because their low socioeconomic status is often associated with undesirable attributes, appearance, accent, and behaviors. Migrants are frequently perceived by local residents as poor, dirty, ignorant, violent, greedy, and irresponsible (Ming & Wang, 2009). Although China's economy has been growing rapidly, there has been no significant increase in migrants' income over the last three decades. Migrant workers are often paid less than the minimum wage and their average net pay is less than half of the overall salary of those in urban cities. With limited knowledge of their legal rights, migrants are exploited by their employers in various ways. For instance, delay in payment is a common strategy adopted by many factories to keep migrant workers in line and prevent them from quitting. It is very common indeed for construction workers to get paid only at the end of the year. In 2003 alone, payment disputes amounted to ¥367 billion (Wu, Kumaraswamy, & Soo, 2008). In the workplace, migrant workers commonly have to work overtime without payment, have no chance for promotion, and experience abusive management practices (Wong, Chang, & He, 2007). The internal migrants in China are at the bottom of the global supply chain and they are often the immediate victims during economic downturns. For instance, during the global financial crisis from 2008 onwards, thousands of factories in China were closed and 23 million rural migrant workers lost their jobs (Chan, 2010).

Migrant health

There has been growing scholarly interest in migrants' health. Rural–urban migrants report lower happiness and health than urban citizens and rural households. The experience of unfair treatment and discrimination is negatively correlated with self-reported health among Chinese migrant workers (Lin et al., 2011). Social stigmatization and economic pressure are key factors hindering the psychological well-being of rural–urban migrants. As rural migrants are also excluded from healthcare schemes in urban cities, migrant health has been a paramount concern for researchers and policy makers in China. Studies on migrants' physical health predominantly focus on three issues: infectious and communicable diseases; maternal and infant health; and occupational diseases and injuries. Internal migrants in China are more likely to be the victims and vectors of infectious and communicable diseases, fare worse on indicators of maternal and infant health, and are more vulnerable to occupational accidents. Furthermore, migrants are found to be more likely to ignore symptoms, delay doctor visits, and decline referral for medical treatment as the result of lack of medical knowledge and difficulty of taking time off work (Mou, Griffiths, Fong, & Dawes, 2013). Health risks among migrant women are particularly high. Unprotected sex is very common among young migrant workers. Sun (2002) surveyed 393 female migrant workers in Heilongjiang province and only 34.4 percent of them used condoms. It is also more likely for young female migrants to have induced abortions at later stages of pregnancy and to receive poorer post-abortion care. Migrant women's reproductive rights are often ignored, especially in private and small firms.

Education of migrant children in cities

The schooling of migrant children in urban cities has been a severe social problem in China. Although all school-age children in China are entitled to a free nine-year basic education, migrant children are often stuck in an education provision gap in receiving cities (Chen, 2011). In China, the education budget is allocated through local governments and thus free education in public schools is only offered to those children who are registered in the local school district. To attend public schools in cities, migrant children without local *hukou* are required to pay an annual "education endorsement fee," which can be unaffordable for migrant parents who typically have low-paying jobs. Approximately 7 percent of migrant parents have never sent their children to school (Wong et al., 2007). Attending privately-run migrant schools is an alternative approach. The emergence of migrant schools is a direct result of the difficulties faced by migrant children when trying to access public schools. Compared to local public schools, these migrant schools have no restrictions based on *hukou* status, charge much lower tuition fees, and have a simple and flexible enrolment process. On the other hand, without government support, the majority of migrant schools typically operate in poor and ghetto-like neighborhoods and have inferior infrastructure, teachers with low-level qualifications, and high safety and hygiene concerns. These unlicensed, under-funded, and under-staffed migrant schools often fail to meet official criteria and face the risk of closure. The difficulties associated with accessing high quality education means migrant children stand no chance of competing with their local counterparts in the future. Thus, many argue that this educational disparity will make future generations of the rural population more vulnerable to poverty and further widen the rural–urban social division.

The left-behind

Local communities and governments largely encourage rural–urban migration, as it is perceived as the best means to improve the regional economy. Massive rural–urban migration has resulted in numerous split families in China. In urban cities, migrants often have temporary low-paying jobs without a binding contract. Due to the low job security and high cost of living in the city, migrating with family is often considered risky. Typically, men of working age migrate to make money, while women, children, and the elderly are left behind in rural areas. It can be difficult for migrants to return home due to strict working hours, long travel distances, and considerable travel costs. Thus, migrants usually only return for key events such as serious illness, injury, and important ceremonies. In China, migrants generally travel back home only once a year, for the Chinese New Year, and usually have less than a month with their families. While the migration means that the household typically benefits significantly in financial terms, the long separation between migrants and their families also creates substantial social costs, especially for the left-behind population (Ye, Wang, Wu, He, & Liu, 2013).

Left-behind women

Although female migrants currently account for half of the global migrant population, internal migration in China remains a male-dominated phenomenon (Biao, 2007). In China, it is estimated that there are 47 million left-behind women (Zhang, 2006). They are left behind mainly because they need to deal with the agricultural work and provide care for the children and elderly at home. Women are often the principal care providers in a family, as the woman's role is to be a wife, mother, and daughter (in law), according to traditional Chinese gender norms. When the husband is away, the wife is typically held responsible for everything that happens in the household. Blame is readily placed on the left-behind women when, for example, children's school performance declines or a family member is seriously sick or injured (Wu & Ye, 2016). In addition, left-behind wives need to be extra careful when interacting with other men in the village to avoid any possible gossip. Due to the separation, left-behind women are found to be more likely to enter into extramarital relationships or experience sexual repression. Both physical and mental pressures on left-behind wives are extremely high and handling daily tasks becomes even more challenging during the busy farming season. Many studies indicate that left-behind women have poor mental health as the result of stress, pressure, loneliness, and fear (Cook & Dong, 2011; Jacka, 2012).

Left-behind children

Another group that is profoundly influenced by the growth in migration and family separation is left-behind children. The decreasing income derived from agricultural production has resulted in enduring underemployment and unemployment among the rural population. Thus, commonly all those who can migrate have already done so. The majority of these migrants choose to leave their children in the countryside. There are an estimated 58 million left-behind children in rural China, among which 47 percent have both parents working in the cities (Zhou, Murphy, & Tao, 2014). These children are often either left with temporary guardians or remain unsupervised. With insufficient familial love and care, left-behind children are found to have worrisome psychological health issues, unsatisfactory academic performance, poor self-control, and a lack of the skills and motivation necessary to communicate with others. There has been an increase in media coverage of left-behind children regarding individual cases of abuse, suicide, and accident. Public concern for left-behind children has been aroused in particular by the case of four left-behind children who committed suicide together by drinking pesticide in Bijie, Guizhou province (Phillips, 2015).

The difficulty of accessing good quality education in urban cities is often the reason migrant parents are unwilling to migrate with their children. On the other hand, many studies have also demonstrated that the school performance of left-behind children in rural areas is worrying due to the lack of parental care. Zhou et al. (2014) reported that the school performance of children whose parents have been away for more than three years is significantly lower than that of other children. Moreover, left-behind children are also more likely to drop out of school and to drop out earlier too (Gao et al., 2010).

The frequency and quality of communication between parents and children is significantly reduced when parents migrate for work. Although migrant parents are eager to maintain regular contact with children left behind, the communication between migrant parents and left-behind children is often limited. As physical reunions are often short and rare, migrant parents mostly choose to keep in touch with their children on the telephone. Phone calls are overwhelmingly initiated by migrant parents with the purpose of knowing about the health and safety of family members back home. The average length of these phone calls is less than ten minutes, and thus in-depth or emotional communication between parents and children is rare (Ye et al., 2013). Migrant parents' remittances are essential to improving children's nutrition and living conditions, as well as mitigating poverty-related stresses. However, parental absence also has severe negative effects on children's development. Children are often left with their grandparents, who may find it difficult to provide the guidance and supervision needed. Left-behind children typically have limited leisure activities as a result of helping with housework and farm work and providing care to their aged guardians when needed. More importantly, these children often feel abandoned, without parental affection and guidance, and some even start to question the meaning of their existence. Smoking, drinking, and mental problems are commonly found among left-behind adolescents (Fan, Su, Kay, & Boris, 2010). The emotional loss is likely to have long-term impacts on these children's personal development, which cannot be compensated by material possessions.

Left-behind elderly

Over the last ten years, China has experienced a significant fall in fertility and the supply of young rural labor has dropped from 18 million to 11 million (Chan, 2010). China is rapidly moving toward an aging society as the result of its 40-year-long one-child policy (Zhang & Goza, 2006). A high proportion of rural elderly are living alone as a result of the massive out-migration in China. Compared to the urban population, it is more difficult for rural elderly to receive proper care as eldercare options such as neighborhood committees and nursing homes are largely missing in the rural areas. Due to the lack of a comprehensive social pension system, three-quarters of the elderly in China depend entirely on family support (Biao, 2007). The massive outflow of young people presents an urgent threat to the current elderly support system in rural China. Although remittances from migrant children help alleviate the financial stresses, the long-term physical separation between elderly parents and adult children contributes significantly to the feelings of loss, loneliness, and abandonment experienced by the elderly. Many studies found that the elderly with migrant children tend to receive more monetary support but significantly less instrumental support (Du, Park, & Wang, 2005; Guo, Aranda, & Silverstein, 2009; He & Ye, 2013). It is likely that migrant children would return to provide daily care only if their elderly parents were in a critical situation.

Retirement is usually not an option for the left-behind elderly. One major responsibility of the left-behind elderly is to take care of the land while the migrant children are away. The majority of the elderly in rural China still need to participate in heavy agricultural work. In a survey of 400 left-behind elderly, 72 percent stated that they are frequently confronted by difficulties in agricultural production and 18 percent found farm work "unbearable" (He & Ye, 2013). Another burden placed on the left-behind elderly is child-rearing. Grandparents are often considered the best candidates to take care of the left-behind children while the parents are away. "Grandparenting" is extremely common in rural China and half of the left-behind elderly need to care for more than two children. The left-behind elderly in China are extremely vulnerable due to lack of institutional and emotional support and heavy physical work. They usually are not the direct beneficiaries of the outmigration because remittances are mostly spent on young children. He and Ye (ibid) claimed that the overall welfare of the left-behind elderly is significantly degraded by rural–urban migration in China. The traditional family-based support system faces great challenges as the principal care providers migrate for work. The need to establish a reliable and inclusive pension system in rural areas is an urgent issue in modern China.

Conclusion

The success story of "Made in China" is closely associated with massive rural–urban migration. Historically, rural residents in China have struggled with unemployment and poverty and also the restricted mobility imposed by the *hukou* system. China's economic boom has created a significant rural–urban income gap that has drawn millions from the rural population to work in the cities. The pace and scale of rural–urban migration and urbanization in China are extremely rapid and have various economic, political, and social consequences. While the economy and efficiency have been the focus of China's development strategy, little attention has been paid to the human aspect, especially migrants and their left-behind families who are paying for the social costs of this development. Peasant workers are often employed in labor-intensive industries, work in unsafe conditions with unsatisfying payment, have poorer health, face discrimination from the locals, and so forth. The *hukou* system, as the invisible wall between the rural and urban populations, is one of the root causes of migrants' marginalization in cities. It becomes ever more socioeconomically and politically imperative to extend the *hukou* reform to promote labor mobility and bridge the gap between rural and urban residents. Fan (2009) argued that the ultimate goal of *hukou* reforms is to break the link between residency status and social welfare. Under the increasing pressure of urbanization, China may need to completely abolish the *hukou* system and seek out a more sustainable and balanced growth model.

As a direct result of migration, the phenomenon of split families and its impacts on both the migrants and the left-behind family members have been little researched. Rural–urban migrants often have no choice but to leave their families behind in the rural communities. Issues such as education, health, daily care, gender roles, and agricultural production are becoming more prominent in rural China. While agricultural revenue is declining significantly in China, the majority of left-behind wives and elderly nevertheless choose to undertake grueling agricultural work to help increase the household income. The heavy workload and feeling of loneliness have great negative impacts on the physical and psychological health of the left-behind population. It is evident that the rural population mainly pays the social costs caused by migration. China's duel urban–rural economic structure leads to different growth patterns in urban and rural areas, which is causing a growing income gap between them. In spite of the rapid urban development that has occurred over the last three decades, it is nevertheless vital for the Chinese government to also invest in rural development and to empower and provide social support and care for the millions of left-behind children, women, and elderly.

References

Biao, X. (2007). How far are the left-behind left behind? A preliminary study in rural China. *Population, Space and Place, 13*, 179–191.

Chan, K. W. (2009). The Chinese hukou system at 50. *Eurasian Geography and Economics, 50*, 197–221.

Chan, K. W. (2010). A China paradox: Migrant labor shortage amidst rural labor supply abundance. *Eurasian Geography and Economics, 51*, 513–530.

Chen, M. (2011, August 26). 穷孩子遭遇问题学校——打工子弟学校的另一面. Poor kids in problematic schools—The dark side of migrant children schools. *Southern Weekly*. Retrieved from www.infzm.com/content/62514/1

Cook, S. & Dong, X. (2011). Harsh choices: Chinese women's paid work and unpaid care responsibilities under economic reform. *Development and Change, 42*, 947–965.

Du, Y., Park, A., & Wang, S. (2005). Migration and rural poverty in China. *Journal of Comparative Economics, 33*, 688–709.

Fan, F., Su, L., Kay, G. M., & Boris, B. (2010). Emotional and behavioral problems of Chinese left-behind children: A preliminary study. *Social Psychiatry & Psychiatric Epidemiology, 45*, 655–664.

Fan, M. (2009, March 19). *Shanghai hukou reform "just for show"*. China.Org.CN. Retrieved from www.china.org.cn/china/features/content_17468979.htm

Gao, Y., Li, L., Kim, J. H., Congdon, N., Lau, J., & Griffiths, S. (2010). The impact of parental migration on health status and health behaviours among left behind adolescent school children in China. *BMC Public Health, 10*, 1–10.

Guo, M., Aranda, M. P., & Silverstein, M. (2009). The impact of out-migration on the inter-generational support and psychological wellbeing of older adults in rural China. *Ageing & Society, 29*, 1085–1104.

He, C. & Ye, J. (2013). Lonely sunsets: Impacts of rural–urban migration on the left-behind elderly in rural China. *Population, Space & Place, 20*, 352–369.

Jacka, T. (2012). Migration, householding and the well-being of left-behind women in rural Ningxia. *China Journal, 67*, 1–21.

Lei, K. & Li, L. (2012). Discrimination against rural-to-urban migrants: The role of the hukou system in China. *PLOS ONE*, 7, 1–8.

Li, J. W. (2002). On protection of the labor rights of migrant workers. *Academic Exploration, 5*, 71–74.

Li, M. (2016). "Brighter the moon over my home village": Some patterned ways of speaking about home among rural–urban migrant workers in China. *Journal of International and Intercultural Communication, 9*, 35–51.

Lin, D., Li, X., Wang, B., Hong, Y., Fang, X., Qin, X., & Stanton, B. (2011). Discrimination, perceived social inequity, and mental health among rural-to-urban migrants in China. *Community Mental Health Journal, 47*, 171–180.

Man, G., Aranda, M. P., & Silverstein, M. (2009). The impact of out-migration on the inter-generational support and psychological wellbeing of older adults in rural China. *Ageing & Society, 29*, 1085–1104.

Ming, W. & Wang, G. (2009). Demographic, psychological, and social environmental factors of loneliness and satisfaction among rural-to-urban migrants in Shanghai, China. *International Journal of Comparative Sociology, 50*, 155–182.

Mou, J., Griffiths, S. M., Fong, H., & Dawes, M. G. (2013). Health of China's rural–urban migrants and their families: A review of literature from 2000 to 2012. *British Medical Bulletin, 106*, 19–43.

Peng, L. & Swider, S. (2017). Migration and regional inequality: Changing characteristics of China's economic inequality. *Eurasian Geography & Economics, 58*, 89–113.

Phillips, T. (2015, June 14). Chinese police "find suicide note" in case of "left behind" children deaths. *The Guardian*. Retrieved from www.theguardian.com/world/2015/jun/14/chinese-police-investigating-deaths-of-left-behind-children-find-suicide-note

Ravenstein, E. G. (1885). The laws of migration. *Journal of the Statistical Society of London, 48*, 167–235.

Sun, H. (2002). AIDS prevention intervention among migratory women in China–Russia border area of Heilongjiang. *Chinese Journal of STD/AIDS Prevention and Control, 6*, 348–351.

UNOECD. (2013). *World migration in figures*. Retrieved from www.oecd.org/els/mig/World-Migration-in-Figures.pdf

Wang, W. & Moffatt, P. G. (2008). Hukou and graduates' job search in China. *Asian Economic Journal, 22*, 1–23.

Wong, F. K. D., Chang, Y. L., & He, X. S. (2007). Rural migrant workers in urban China: Living a marginalized life. *International Journal of Social Welfare, 16*, 32–40.

Wu, H. & Ye, J. (2016). Hollow lives: Women left behind in rural China. *Journal of Agrarian Change, 16*, 50–69.

Wu, J., Kumaraswamy, M., & Soo, G. (2008). Payment problems and regulatory responses in the construction industry: Mainland China perspective. *Journal of Professional Issues in Engineering Education & Practice, 134*, 399–407.

Xinhua News Agency. (2017, February 11). 推行居住证制度 去年发放居住证 2890 余万张. The newly implemented residence permit system has issued more than 28.9 milllion residence permits last year. Retrieved from www.gov.cn/xinwen/2017-02/11/content_5167328.htm

Ye, J., Wang, C., Wu, H., He, C., & Liu, J. (2013). Internal migration and left-behind populations in China. *Journal of Peasant Studies, 40*, 1119–1146.

Zhang, J. (2006). Survey on the life of 50 million left-behind women. *China Economic Weekly, 40*, 14–19.

Zhang, K. H. & Song, S. F. (2003). Rural–urban migration and urbanization in China: Evidence from time-series and cross-section analysis. *China Economic Review, 14*, 386–400.

Zhang, Y. & Goza, F. W. (2006). Who will care for the elderly in China? A review of the problems caused by China's one-child policy and their potential solutions. *Journal of Aging Studies, 20*, 151–164.

Zhang, Z. & Treiman, D. J. (2013). Social origins, hukou conversion, and the wellbeing of urban residents in contemporary China. *Social Science Research, 42*, 71–89.

Zhao, L. & Courtney, F. R. (2010). *China's hukou reform: The Guangdong and Shanghai cases*. Retrieved from www.eai.nus.edu.sg/BB551.pdf

Zhou, M., Murphy, R., & Tao, R. (2014). Effects of parents' migration on the education of children left behind in rural China. *Population & Development Review, 40*, 273–292.

INDEX

Page numbers in *italics* refer to figures; page numbers in **bold** refer to tables. US spelling is used in the index

For Product Safety Concerns and Information please contact our EU
representative GPSR@taylorandfrancis.com
Taylor & Francis Verlag GmbH, Kaufingerstraße 24, 80331 München, Germany

www.ingramcontent.com/pod-product-compliance
Ingram Content Group UK Ltd.
Pitfield, Milton Keynes, MK11 3LW, UK
UKHW050755180926
475701UK00007B/1054

* 9 7 8 1 0 3 2 3 3 8 6 9 9 *